DATE DUE

GAYLORD			PRINTED IN U.S.A.

MAINE

A GUIDE 'DOWN EAST'

AMERICAN GUIDE SERIES

MAINE

A GUIDE 'DOWN EAST'

SECOND EDITION

Revision prepared by the Maine League of Historical Societies and Museums and sponsored by the 104th Maine Legislature and the State Sesquicentennial Commission.

Dorris A. Isaacson, Editor

Illustrated

COURIER-GAZETTE, INC.,   ROCKLAND, MAINE

1970

FOREWORD

ONE of the most significant and enduring contributions of the Maine Sesquicentennial Commission to the 1970 commemoration of the State's one hundred and fiftieth anniversary is its encouragement and support of the updating and revision of *MAINE: A Guide 'Down East,'* first published in 1937 as a Federal Writers Project of the Works Progress Administration.

More than a guide, the original volume quickly established itself as the most authoritative short, comprehensive narrative of Maine history, as well as the most valid and useful orientation to points of interest in historic and scenic Maine. It has been the only single volume providing an overview of the State's environment, resources, industry, and culture.

Thoroughly revised and modernized by a volunteer staff under the professional direction of Dorris Westall Isaacson, the 1937 State Director, currently president of the Maine League of Historical Societies and Museums, the new edition promises to eclipse its predecessor in popularity and serviceability. Surely in an age of universal travel and with the great surge of interest in state and local history and heritage, Maine is fortunate to have a volume of this breadth and quality as a reference work and a guide for its own citizenry and its inquiring visitors.

The Maine League of Historical Societies and Museums and the Maine Sesquicentennial Commission are to be congratulated for their cooperation in this venture.

ROBERT M. YORK, *State Historian*
Dean of Academic Affairs,
University of Maine   Portland-Gorham

"*The State of Maine*, as she is and ought to be, ample in territory rich in resources, aboundant in agricultural, commercial and manufacturing facilities; with an increasing, hardy, industrous and intelligent population; may her destiny be worthy of the Maine State in the far east."

— Mark Langdon Hill, 1839

EMBLEMS

State Seal, adopted by the legislature of 1820; 'A shield, argent, charged with a Pine Tree, a Moose Deer at the foot of it, recumbent. Supporters: on the dexter side a Husbandman, resting on a scythe; on the sinister side, a seaman, resting on an anchor. In the foreground, representing sea and land, the name of the state in large Roman Capitals. The whole surmounted by a crest, the North Star. The motto in small Roman Capitals, in a label interposed between the Shield and the Crest, viz.: Dirigo (I direct.)'
State Flower 1895): the white pine cone and tassel (pinus strobus linnaeus).
State Flag (1909): the coat of arms of the State of Maine on a blue field.
State Bird (1927): the chickadee (parus atricapillus).
State Tree (1945): the white pine (pinus strobus, Mast Pine of Colonial Days.
State Fish: landlocked salmon (salmo sebago).

PREFACE

THE cooperation and contributions of many Maine citizens have made possible the preparation and publication of this revision of *MAINE: A Guide 'Down East'* for the State's Sesquicentennial year 1970. The Maine League of Historical Societies and Museums gratefully acknowledges the generous assistance of representatives of its 102 member societies and of the many other interested persons who have participated in this effort. Special acknowledgement is made to State Department, University and college specialists for background material in their particular disciplines, and to the interested State legislators who made publication possible.

First published in 1937 as a WPA project, the book was one of 55 volumes that were cited as the first nation-wide portrait of the American people. It has been used as a reference work ever since. It is hoped that the new Guide, like the original, may be useful now and in future as a reflection of a time and place, of Maine and its people against the background of a rich historic heritage.

In updating the Guide, currently the only such comprehensive compendium of Maine, the effort has been to carry forward the original purpose in its unique format, with developments of more than a quarter of a century. The task, formidable when it was pioneered in the static depression years of the 1930s, has been equally formidable in a different way in the fast-moving 1960s.

The editor of both volumes — without a paid staff this time — notes one constant in their preparation: the spirit of the people who have been involved. In the 1930s, the book initially was one of the projects to provide money for people merely to exist — to eat, clothe and shelter themselves. It did much more, for morale. As teamwork and esprit de corps developed, there was pride in work that was felt to be worthwhile. It came to mean more than a meal ticket, vital as that was. This time, although the book was prepared under different circumstances, the warm spirit is the same among the volunteers who have generously contributed because they feel the undertaking is worthwhile.

Obviously, all of the wealth of material on Maine could not be encompassed in this book. A selected bibliography has been included for pursuit of various aspects. Notwithstanding meticulous documentation, the spectre of human error constantly shadows the aim for excellence. Critics doubtless will find sins of omission and commission according to their predilections, perspectives and frames of reference. Corrections of fact will be happily received for future editions.

The Maine League of Historical Societies and Museums hopes that the new Guide as an introduction to and source book on Maine will prove revealing to the young, remindful to the not so young and enjoyable to all interested in the State of Maine, marking another milestone of life 'down-east' on the State's 150th anniversary.

DORRIS A. ISAACSON, *President*
Maine League of Historical
Societies and Museums

CONTRIBUTORS

Dr. Robert G. Albion, Maritime Historian, Harvard College,
 President, Maine Historical Society
Charles P. Bradford, Nature Conservancy
Marian Cooper, State Department of Education
Clarence Day, University of Maine — Orono, Agriculture Department
Robert M. Elliott, State Department of Economic Development
Dr. Hilda M. Fife, University of Maine — Orono, English Department
Wendell S. Hadlock, Director, Farnsworth Museum; Archaeologist
Dr. Edward D. Ives, University of Maine — Orono, Anthropology Department
Geneva A. Kirk, President, Maine Teachers Association
Franklyn Lenthall, Producer-Director, Boothbay Playhouse
Ernest C. Marriner, Dean-emeritus, Colby College
Francis S. Merritt, Director, Haystack Mountain School of Crafts
Dr. William B. Miller, Colby College Art Department
Francis M. O'Brien, bibliopole
Elizabeth Ring, Vice-President, Maine Historical Society
Earle G. Shettleworth, Jr., B. A., Colby College
Dean R. Snow, University of Maine — Orono, Anthropology Department
David Stevens, Chairman, State Highway Commission
Dr. Robert M. York, State Historian

Mrs. David Anderson
Elliott M. Andrews
Miss Sydney Baldwin
John D. Bardwell
Mrs. Alice Beland
Mrs. Earl Betts
Miss Pauline Bill
Walter A. Birt
Mrs. Russell E. Bryant
Benjamin and Natalie Butler
Miss Mildred G. Burrage
Mrs. Helen Camp
Mrs. Ernest Chasse
Rev. Sheldon Christian
Mrs. James R. Clark
Mrs. Mary M. Cramer
Mrs. Verena N. Cunningham
Robert J. Dingley
Miss Marie A. Donahue
Sterling B. Douglas
John R. Egerton
Mrs. Edward J. Fertig
Mrs. Dorothea Flagg
Hugh B. Frey
Mrs. Lana H. Gagnon
George R. Garniss
Mrs. Edwin L. Giddings
Raymond Gross
Mrs. Frederick M. Haggett
Mrs. Persis Hall Hardy
Henry F. Hill, Jr.

Miss Mildred Holmes
Mrs. Donald D. Kimball
Mrs. Herbert B. Knowles
Mrs. Edith C. Labbie
Clark A. Libbey
Mrs. Judson P. Lord
Mrs. Lloyd Lowndes
Mrs. Mary V. McGillicuddy
Mrs. John P. Montgomery
Albert L. Pearce
Miss Mary Pike
Mrs. Clara C. Piper
Miss M. Louise Prince
Captain Albert L. Prosser
Mrs. Albert Roberts
Mrs. E. J. Rowell
Admiral William F. Royall
Ronald Sands
Mrs. Margaret M. Sawyer
Miss Elena B. Shute
Herbert T. Silsby II
Mrs. Elmer F. Staples
Miss Bhima Sturtevant
Mrs. Herman P. Sweetser
Miss Louisa M. Talbot
Dr. William Teg
Mrs. Charles G. Todd
General Clayton O. Totman
George Wagoner
Mrs. Bradford C. Wellman
Mrs. Margaret Wentworth

CONTENTS

I MAINE: THE GENERAL BACKGROUND

II. SEAPORTS AND RIVER TOWNS

(Descriptions and Local Tours)

III. HIGHWAYS AND BYWAYS

(Mainland Tours and Island Trips)

IV. RECREATION

ILLUSTRATIONS

MARITIME HERITAGE   *between* 90 *and* 91

NATURAL RESOURCES   *between* 152 and 153

Illustrations XV

Ogunquit Museum of Art, photo by Edward Hipple
P. F. Mawn
Grace Episcopal Church, Bath
Wilbur R. Ingalls Jr.
Governor Kent House doorways, Bangor
State Park and Recreation Commission
Winter vacation home
Lorimer Chapel and contemporary dormitory, Colby College
Portland's French Empire business block
Kennebec Homestead, etching by Ernest Haskell
Maine Times
United Nations Research Center, model
William Dickson Associates
Maine State Cultural Building, model
Samuel S. Silsby
Contemporary bank in Portland's Monument Square
Leonard M. Nelson

CREATIVE ARTS   *between* 364 *and* 365

Folk carving of State of Maine Seal, sculptor unknown
Macbeth at Bowdoin College
Eliot Porter's Osprey
Dahlov Ipcar book illustration
Repertory Theatre, 1970
Maine Times
Haystack Mountain School of Crafts
Francis S. Merritt
Backstage — in the dressing-room
State Commission for Arts and Humanities
Edwin Booth as King Lear, a John Rogers sculpture group at Boothbay Theatre Museum
Franklyn Lenthall
Bulman 18th century crewel embroidery at York Gaol Museum
Barbara Kimball
The BELLE MORSE, 19th century embroidery on fine silk
Bath Marine Museum
Marguerite Zorach embroidery, wool on linen, depicting the John D. Rockefeller family at Seal Harbor
Maine Art Gallery
The Country Doctor
Lady of Fashion, cigar store figure
Colby College Art Archives
York County Colonial gravestone, that of Col. John Wheelwright (d. 1745), photo by Mason Philip Smith
Gilded eagle, 1861, by Shipcarver Emery Jones of Freeport
Maine Historical Society
Shaker Crafts, cotton worsted dress, 1850; chair, baskets and loom
Clark FitzGerald, sculpture
Guy Gannett Publishing Company
Portland Symphony Orchestra, Municipal auditorium
Leonard M. Nelson

VACATIONLAND   *between* 394 *and* 395

The Swimmer, 1924, by Yasuo Kuniyoshi; Columbus, Ohio Gallery of Fine Arts
Shooting the Rapids, Saguenay River, painting by Winslow Homer
The Fox Hunt, by Winslow Homer; Pennsylvania Academy of Fine Arts
Colby College Art Archives

Illustrations

Fisherman's Family by George W. Bellows
Maine Coast by Peter Blume; semi-primitive 1926
from Maine and its Role in American Art,
Colby College Art Archives
Col. and Mrs. Thomas Cutts (Elizabeth Scammon) of Saco by John Brewster, Jr., late 18th century
York Institute Museum, Biddeford

Henry W. Longfellow portrait, Rome 1869, by Thomas Buchanan Reed
Maine Historical Society
Young Fisherman and Dory, painting by Andrew Wyeth
Farnsworth Museum

Acadian Woman, etching by Claude Picard
Madawaska Historical Society
Mark Langdon Hill, Maine Congressman 1813-1823, Frick Art Reference Library photograph of an 1818 painting by Benjamin Greenleaf
Phippsburg Historical Society
Lumberman John Ross, master river-driver of the Penobscot
Penobscot Heritage, Bangor
Statesman James G. Blaine
Maine State Museum
Lillian Nordica at Farmington
Nordica Memorial Association
Artemus Ward, pen drawing by Birch; photo by Chrispix
Sir Hiram Maxim, photo by Elmer Chickering
Rockland Courier-Gazette
John Stevens, Passamaquoddy Indian Governor
Maine Times

ON USING THE GUIDE

General Information gives practical notes on the State as a whole, with sources for detailed information, and a listing of some annual events. A specially prepared Cultural-Historic Map locating historic sites and cultural centers, with Recreation and Transportation-Industry maps on the reverse, accompanies the book.

General Background essays are designed to give a reasonably comprehensive survey of the State's natural setting, history, social, economic and cultural development. Limitations of space forbid elaborately detailed treatments of these subjects, so a classified bibiliography is included. A great many persons, places, events and so forth mentioned in the essays are treated at some length in the Tour descriptions (*see INDEX*). *MAINE: A Guide 'Down East'* is not only a practical travel book but also will serve as a valuable reference work.

Highways and Byways, the section on mainland Tours and Island Trips is designed for exploration of the diverse areas of scenic and historic Maine, and to orient the traveller in a given locale. Expressways are indicated for direct access to specific areas. Points of departure along the Maine coast are given with island descriptions. The eight principal land tours and seventeen side tours are written so that they may be taken, wholly or in part, from any point, or reversed. To facilitate individual travel arrangements, each tour description contains cross-references to other tours crossing or branching from the route described; to the cities and towns given separate treatment; and to recreational regions. Cumulative mileage from tour points of departure have been used to indicate distances generally rather than statistically. Mileage notations necessarily are relative due to changing road conditions, varying drivers' habits, and the like. The key to tour routes, easily followed on the official State Highway Map, is found in the Table of Contents.

Seaports and River Towns. For convenience, the longer descriptions of seven cities and towns with their points of interest and trips to environs, are grouped separately from the Tours. In view of changing patterns under urban renewal, model cities and similar programs, current maps should be obtained locally.

Recreation. General topical descriptions of Maine's all-season recreation and sports activities are given, with sample trips and a key to the State's Parks and their facilities.

Illustrations. Thirteen picture sections in the Guide give glimpses of the State of Maine and her people, past and present.

GENERAL INFORMATION

Information and travel bureaus, State and local agencies and institutions, Chambers of Commerce and Town Offices are the best sources for current general and specific information, literature and maps. Town histories, museum catalogs, local tour leaflets, industrial listings and the like are available in many areas. There also are numerous 'fact' booklets as well as a plethora of pamphlets and brochures publicizing the State's attractions from alewives to zephyrs. Local newspapers carry calendars of events.

INFORMATION BUREAUS

State of Maine Information Center
48 Rockefeller Plaza, New York City, N. Y. 10020

State of Maine Information Center
Laurentien Hotel, Dominion, Montreal, Canada

Maine Department of Economic Development
Augusta Plaza, Augusta, Maine 04330

Maine Publicity Bureau
78 Gateway Circle, Portland, Maine 04102

Information Building, Jct. US 1 and Maine Turnpike, Kittery

Maine Turnpike, North; Cumberland (summer)

U.S. 302, Fryeburg (summer)

Bass Park, Bangor

International Bridge, Calais (summer)

Numerous local bureaus adjacent to highways

TRANSPORTATION

Air service: commercial airports in principal cities; intra-state Executive Airlines and limited Northeast Airlines; charter service to resorts and islands. Jetports: Portland and Bangor (international).

Waterways; International ferries to Yarmouth, Nova Scotia, from Bar Harbor and Portland (vehicles carried). State ferries and commercial cruisers service islands. Summer coastal and river steamer and motorboat services, excursions, sightseeing, windjammer and steamer cruises; marinas and yacht basins; lake motorboat and air services.

Rail: summer excursions from Bangor and Belfast; fall foliage excursions from Portland.

Bus: inter-and intra- state and local; sightseeing and foliage tours from Portland; taxis and private cars available in most cities for touring.

Highways: Interstate 95, Kittery-Houlton, Portland-Bath; Maine Turnpike (toll), Kittery-Augusta; US 1 (coastal), Kittery-Fort Kent; three other US and 128 State roads, more than 200 rest areas, numerous campsites. Highway conditions posted at Turnpike entrances (15) and available at 8 Highway offices: Augusta, Bangor, Ellsworth, Portland, Presque Isle, Rockland, Rumford and Fairfield.

Drive Safely. State and local police are courteous and helpful. They are also conscientious in efforts to hold down fatalities as highway accidents mount. Motorists are expected to observe rules of good driving and the traffic regulations posted on State and local highways. *Speed limits:* rural, 45 mph; urban, 25 mph unless otherwise posted. *Turnings signals:* hand or automatic signals must be used when turning left or right or stopping. *Night driving:* lights must be turned on at sundown; headlights must be lowered within 500 ft. of on-coming traffic. *School buses:* do not pass from either direction when school bus stops for passengers. *Accidents* causing death or personal injury or damage of $100 or more ·must be reported to police at once. *Assistance:* State Police Headquarters on US 1 at Kittery, Scarborough, Thomaston, Houlton; on US 2 at Orono, Skowhegan; on State 9 at Augusta.

ACCOMMODATIONS
Year-round hotels and motels in cities and towns; hotels, motels, boatels, tourist homes, trailer parks and campsites in summer resort areas; sporting camps and campsites in wilderness areas; ski chalets and motels in winter sports areas. Advance reservations recommended in season.

CLIMATE
Variable, from infrequent extremes of the 90s in summer to below zero in winter; cool summer nights, especially along the coast. Provide seasonal clothing.

RECREATION
All seasons outdoor sports, active and spectator. Inquire locally for conditions, facilities and regulations for specific sports. Highway conditions are broadcast year-round; marine conditions in summer; snow conditions in winter.

Hunting, Fishing, Snowmobiling licenses and laws: State Department of Inland Fisheries and Game, State Office Building, Augusta, Maine 04330.

Boat registration and laws: Bureau of Watercraft Registration and Safety, Augusta, ·Maine 04330.

Vacations: Department of Economic Development, Augusta Plaza, Augusta, Maine 04330, for 30 Vacation Planners (*free folders*), and information on campsites, State Parks, Historic Sites, etc.

Cultural Affairs: Heritage and Horizons calendar of events, State Commission for the Arts and Humanities, 156 State Street, Augusta, Maine 04330.

KEEP MAINE SCENIC AND SAFE

Forest fires: This hazard in forested Maine cannot be too strongly emphasized. Almost three-fourths of the State — 15 million acres — is woodland. State law reads: 'Non-residents shall not kindle fires upon any unorganized township, while engaged in camping, fishing or hunting from May first to December first, without being in charge of a registered guide, except at (designated) public campsites maintained by the Forestry Department. No person shall kindle a fire on private property within a township without the consent of the owner. No person shall within a municipality or township set a bonfire or any kind of fire which is not enclosed with a metal or a non-inflammable material without a written consent of the fire department.

Litter: It is unlawful to dispose of trash or waste along Maine's highways. Use trash cans provided at public parks and rest areas.

Liquor: State liquor stores; 'wet' or 'dry' local option for sale of malt beverages and for serving wine and fortified spirits in hotels and Class A restaurants. Do not drink and drive. Laws and penalities grow severe in view of the mounting highway death toll.

Wild animals, poisonous plants: The only dangerous animals found in Maine are bears, bobcats, moose and occasionally lynxes, which appear only in the thickly wooded northern areas of the State; they seldom attack unless wounded or cornered. Poison ivy grows near stone walls, in pasture and woodland, and occasionally along the seashore. No poisonous snakes.

SOME ANNUAL EVENTS

January through Winter: Carnivals, Skiing Competition, Snomobile Rallies, New England Sled Dog Races

April: Maple Festival, Strong

May: White Water Canoe Race, Upper Dead River

June through Summer: Flower and Antique Shows, Garden and House Tours; Flat and Harness Horse Races, Stock Car Races

July: Beanhole Bean Festival, Norway
Clam Festival, Yarmouth
Gem and Mineral Show, Boothbay
General Knox Day, Thomaston
Homecoming Day, Machiasport
Indian Pageant, Old Town
Maine Amateur Golf Championship
Maine Broiler Festival, Belfast
Maine Potato Blossom Festival, Fort Fairfield
Maine Trap Shoot, Richmond
Old Homes Tour, Bath
Open House and Garden Day, Camden
Penobscot Indian Pageant, Old Town
Rock and Mineral Show, North Gorham
Sidewalk Arts and Crafts Show, Ocean Park
Sloop Races, Friendship
Spudland Open Golf Tournament
Tall Timber Days, Stratton
Tuna Tournaments, Bailey Island, Boothbay Harbor, Ogunquit
Windjammer Days, Boothbay Harbor
World Championship Lobster Boat Races, Jonesport

August: Antique Shows, Bath, Camden, Kennebunk
Arts and Crafts Shows, Lincolnville, Rangeley

August: Arts Festivals, Bar Harbor, Kennebunk, Portland
         Arabian Horse Association, Endurance Ride, Farmington
         Corn Festival, Skowhegan
         Falmouth-Monhegan Yacht Race
         Fishing Derby, Kennebunk
         Gem and Mineral Show, Winthrop
         Historic Week, Waldoboro
         Jordan Open Golf Tournament
         Lakewood Invitational Golf Tournament
         Lobster Festival and Races, Winter Harbor
         Lumberjack Festivals, Several Areas
         Maine Blueberry Festival, Union
         Maine Open Golf Tournament
         Maine Seafoods Festival, Rockland
         Maine State Dairy Show, Windsor
         Maine Writers Conference, Ocean Park
         National White Water Canoe Championship Races, Dead River
         Northeast Harbor Fleet Cruise
         Open-air Concerts, Camden, Rockport, Oakland
         Retired Skippers Race, Castine
         Schooner Days, Camden, Rockport, Lincolnville
         Sidewalk Arts Festival, WCSH-TV, Portland
         State All-Gauge Shooting Championship, Bowdoinham
         State of Maine Lightning Regatta, South Portland
         United Maine Craftsmen's Show, Cumberland
         Whaleback Ocean Race, Kittery
         Women's State Golf Association Championship
         Yankee Pedlar Day, Dresden

August-September: Agricultural Fairs in most counties

September: Maine State Pro Golf Championship

October: Foliage Tours

I. MAINE: THE
GENERAL BACKGROUND

THE NATION'S NORTHEAST CORNER

STATE NAME

HISTORIANS disagree on the origin of the name of Maine. Some suppose it was bestowed as a tribute to England's Queen Henrietta Marie, feudal ruler of the French provinces of Meyne or Maine. Some think the name was brought directly from France by early French colonists; others hold that it was a term used to distinguish the mainland from the coastal islands where early fishermen dried their catch. The 'mainland' theory seems especially apt since the State's serrated coastline measures some 2500 miles and there are more than 400 offshore islands ranging in area from 1100 to 16,000 acres, with a host of smaller ones. Islanders to this day speak of 'the main.' Variously spelled Main, Mayn, and Mayne, the name was in use as early as 1622. Under the jurisdiction of Massachusetts, the region was known as 'The Province of Maine.' When it was admitted to the Union in 1820, 'The State of Maine' became its official title.

NATURAL RESOURCES AND ENVIRONMENT

The State of Maine has been known long and well for its natural beauties and enviable environment. It has not escaped the consequences of violation. In an era of national concern over environmental deterioration, developments of the 1960s are germane to an account of the State's natural resources. In this decade Maine faced the critical problem of how to relate economic development with creative conservation of natural resources. The need for both was undeniable. Ecology and the total environment became of wider concern as public clamor arose over air and water pollution, waste problems, the deleterious effects of pesticides, and as big industry contemplated Maine's virtually unprotected natural resources. Protective laws had been few and toothless; agencies charged with protection had been understaffed and under-funded.

The need for long-range, over-all planning began to be recognized, as the abuse and misuse of these resources and the disturbance of ecological patterns were seen to have destructive results that could be irrevocable and economically disastrous. Industrial and human wastes were polluting the rivers and lakes; there was ill-considered development of shore and wildlands; and many other evidences of heedless, unrestrained and profligate use of the resources that mean the good life for Maine citizens and their vacationing visitors who constitute the State's second largest 'industry.' Commenting upon human depredation, Writer E. B. White of Brooklin, Maine observed that the cedar waxwing does not foul its nest.

In the 1960s as Congress debated measures to halt environmental deterioration, Maine made a start with the emergence of a coalition of conservation interests that included geologists, biologists, preservationists, historians, journalists, philanthropists and politicians. Action emanated from educational and State agencies and from such organizations as the Natural Resources Council, the Maine Fish and Game Association, the Nature Conservancy, the Garden Club Federation, the Audubon Society, the Museum of Natural History and wildlife and wild land conservationists. Phenomenal in a state long identified with industrial interests antipathetic to conservation legislation, the conservation coalition appeared to be a growing political and social force. In 1969, the 104th Maine Legislature enacted some thirty measures affecting pollution, water treatment, clean air, pesticide control, billboards, wetlands, land acquisitions and use, and mining. At a special session in 1970, bills were enacted to establish a Coastal Protection Fund to pay for cleanup of non-traceable oil spills and to regulate oil transport along Maine's coast; and empowering the Environmental Improvement Commission to regulate the selection of sites for industries that potentially endanger Maine's environment.

Although the State did not have an overall Natural Resources or Environmental Control Council in 1969, more than a dozen boards, commissions, committees and task forces were dealing with various aspects of the problems. The Water and Air Environmental Improvement Commission's pollution abatement program was scheduled for completion in 1976. With a third of the 95 planned municipal treatment plants in operation, the program stalled in 1969 for lack of matching Federal funds, approved but not allocated. The State which had received less than a sixth of the $20.9 million authorized for Maine for 1967-70, sought to pre-fund the Federal share through a $50 million bond issue subject to referendum.

A Wetlands Control Board was established for the State's marshlands, essential to the production of food since 60 percent of all marine life depends upon coastal estuaries. Scientists, pointing to their economic value, say the marshlands have been building four to five thousand years;

when they are destroyed by filling, developing or pollution, they can never be re-established. Some 6800 acres are to be held by the State and Federal governments through the Sea and Shore Fisheries, Inland Fish and Games and Parks and Recreation Departments. In 1969 only about a sixth of Maine's marshlands were under State control.

There also are Soil, Forest and Marine conservation services, centers for scientific resource studies, and wild life and wild land preserves. Among the latter is the 20,000 acre Baxter State Park, gift of the late Governor Percival P. Baxter, to be preserved in its natural state forever. The great Allagash Wilderness Waterway is under protection of the State which also maintains 22 parks. Acadia National Park at Bar Harbor is the only national park on the Atlantic coast. The U. S. Moosehorn Wildlife Refuge is in Washington County. The Maine Chapter of Nature Conservancy of which Rachel Carson was honorary chairman, organized 1956, has acquired 36 natural areas (1969) totaling 2486 acres. Of these 14 of the 25 along the coast are islands.

In this decade, environment was becoming a factor in urban renewal and industrial location. Many communities, enabled by legislation to create Conservation Commissions, were thinking twice about locating new industries that could further pollute air or water. One industry's Prestile Stream pollution had caused a Canadian 'border incident'; the Maine town of Trenton turned down a new aluminum plant. Proposals for an oil depot on a Casco Bay island and refineries at Machiasport or other downeast ports generated widespread concern. Industry was coming and it was needed. But what kind, and would Maine be prepared to cope with it?

While Governor Kenneth M. Curtis promulgated a policy of development with conservation, the measure of its success not only would be tested in legislative halls by industrial and conservation lobbies, but ultimately would be determined by the concern of the people of Maine for the quality of living worthy of their heritage.

GEOGRAPHY AND TOPOGRAPHY

The extreme northeastern State in the Union, Maine is the only one adjoined by a single sister State. Its relatively isolated position may have contributed to the reserve and renitence to change sometimes said to be characteristic of its people It is bordered by the Atlantic Ocean, by Canada and by New Hampshire. The southern boundary is the ocean; the eastern boundary follows the St. Croix River to its source, thence due north to the St. John River; the northern boundary extends roughly from the St. John Grand Falls along the river to Crown Monument; the western boundary extends from Crown Monument to the sea at the mouth of the Piscataqua River near Kittery Point. Early charters defined only northern and southern boundaries so that Maine, like other eastern colonies, once theoretically extended to the Pacific Ocean. After many bitter quarrels, the Webster-Ashburton Treaty of 1842 established the boundaries along the Canadian border where all disputed territory was granted to England in return for concessions in other matters.

Largest of the New England states, Maine's total area equals that of four of the five others combined. Approximately one tenth of its more than 33,000 square miles consists of water. Over 87 percent of the land area comprises the last great natural wilderness on the eastern seaboard, 17,425,000 acres of timberland. Another 2,590,022 acres are farmlands.

The terrain may be described as a broad plateau running from the western boundary to the northeast across the Rangeley and Moosehead Lakes regions, gradually sloping eastward toward the Penobscot River Basin and northward to the St. John. Toward the southeast, the plateau gradually inclines to sea level. Occasional mountains rise from the plateau to relatively high elevations, particularly in the central and western parts of the State. Many roads follow the course of a system of eskers or 'horsebacks' spread over the land surface. Much of the State's road material comes from these long ridges of gravel deposited by the receding glacier of the Ice Age.

Mountainous Maine has the highest elevation of any point on the Atlantic coast in North America — Cadillac Mountain with an almost sheer rise of 1532 feet. Mount Katahdin at 5267 feet is the State's highest peak, rising majestically in Baxter State Park to reign over seemingly limitless wilderness. On a clear day, it is said that more land and water can be seen from its summit than from any other known point of land in America, since no other ranges interfere. Mount Katahdin is one of four Maine spots sharing the honor of being the first on this continent to see the rising sun, depending upon the season of the year. Next highest peaks are Hamlin on Katahdin, 4751 feet; Old Spec in Grafton Township, 4250 feet; and Sugarloaf in Crockertown, 4237 feet. Five other mountains are more than 4,000 feet and 97 are more than 3,000 feet high. Most of these are more or less conical in form, their sloping sides heavily wooded and always green. Some of the best known although not necessarily the highest, are Abraham, Bigelow, Haystack, Kineo, Russell, Saddleback and Whitecap.

There are more than 2200 lakes and ponds in Maine. Moosehead Lake, about forty miles long and from two to ten miles wide, is one of the country's largest bodies of water lying wholly within the boundaries of a single state. Of Maine's more than 5100 rivers and streams, four are navigable for considerable distances into the interior and were early explored. Augusta on the Kennebec and Bangor on the Penobscot are accessible to sea-going vessels. Ten of Maine's sixteen counties are open to water traffic. North to south on the map, the longest rivers are the St. John, 211 miles from its source in St. John Pond to the point where it leaves the Maine boundary; the St. Croix, 75 miles; the Penobscot, 350 miles; the Kennebec, 150 miles; the Androscoggin, 175 miles; and the Saco, 104 miles.

The streams of Maine, marked by narrow and rapid currents and fed by springs and the melting snows of the forest regions, perhaps are the most valuable natural resource of the State. Anti-pollution measures are being taken along waterways that are no longer 'crystal clear.'

CLIMATE

Maine's healthful and invigorating climate offers a wide variety of weather for all seasons. Temperatures can be temperamental, quickly variable, but none extreme for sustained periods in any season. Paraphrasing a famous quotation, Maine weather pleases some people all the time, all of the people some of the time, but not everybody all the time.

Weather is more than a conversational gambit to farmers, foresters and fishermen who must heed the signs and portents in the interests of their livelihood. Sportsmen also have more than a passing interest in prognostications. Modern aids are the scientific forecasts especially beamed to seamen and skiers, travellers and tillers of the soil, and many other outdoorsmen.

The changeable Maine weather means large ranges of temperature both daily and annual, considerable diversity from place to place and great differences between the same seasons in different years. Maine lies in the 'prevailing westerlies,' the belt of generally eastward air movement that encircles the globe in middle latitudes. Regional climatic influences are modified by varying differences from the ocean, elevations and types of terrain, dividing the State into three parts climatologically: the Northern, Coastal and Southern Interior Divisions.

Mean annual temperature is 43-45 degrees F. in the south and 37-39 in the north. Sunny days average about 60 percent for the year; monthly averages vary little during the change of seasons although winter may have more sunny days than summer.

Warmest month is July when average temperatures range from 60 to 69 degrees, with daily maximums running as high as 80 in central sections and in the 90s during rare 'hot spells.' With rare exceptions, summer nights are comfortably cool, even a hint of frost in some areas.

Longest cold periods are near Van Buren where freezing temperature has been recorded on an average of 208 days a year in contrast with Portland's 132-day average. Freezing temperatures at night are common State-wide from October through early May.

Maine temperature records: highest, 105 degrees at Bridgton in July, 1911; lowest, — 48 degrees below zero at Van Buren in January, 1925.

The growing season ranges from 140 to 160 days in the Coastal Division, 120 to 140 days in the Southern Interior, and 100 to 120 days in most of the Northern Division, though it may be less than 100 days in the extreme north and northwest. Gardeners are alert to killing frosts from September to late May.

Precipitation is well-distributed over the State throughout the year, ranging from 40 to 46 inches annually, including average snow depth equal to 6.91 inches of rainfall. Average annual snowfall varies according to altitude from about 70 inches in northern Maine where it arrives earliest and remains longest.

In 1816, 'the year without a summer,' it snowed in July. Not quite as phenomenal but still infrequent are destructive storms, floods and droughts. Of three major floods in the last half century, the worst was in 1936 causing $25,000,000 damage. Hurricanes strike about once a decade, tornadoes rarely. The well-known 'nor'easter' with howling gale winds can lash the coast in the fall and winter. Boatmen and shoreside residents heed early storm warnings and batten down the hatches. High tides pound the mainland and create spectacular surf. Icy sleet and freezing rain may create a crystal fairyland among the trees — and glaze utility lines and highways.

Maine's large wooded areas and hills are a protective barrier against windstorms except during electrical storms and in some coastal peninsula areas. Hailstones during summer electrical storms can seriously damage gardens. Dry seasons have appeared in cycles, creating forest fire hazards, drying wells and damaging crops. Otherwise, there may be a dozen heavy rainfalls annually, and in some winters, a real old-fashioned blizzard recalling Whittier's 'Snowbound.'

Along with advances in the science of weather forecasting, the Old Farmer's Almanack and natural signs and portents still contribute to that universal serious-humorous topic, the weather. In the late 1960s the most entertaining nightly weather broadcasts were enlivened by the unlikely phenomena occurring in the mythical village of Hannibal's Crossing somewhere in the northern wilds of Maine. In reference to the diversity of Maine weather, it may be a sign of the times that 'If you don't like the weather, wait a minute' is heard more often than the old canard that there are two seasons in Maine, July and winter.

GEOLOGY

With little exception, the bedrock of Maine was formed during the Pre-Cambrian and Paleozoic Eras. The Pre-Cambrian rocks occur principally in the western and southern parts of the State, and consist mostly of sandstones, shales and limestones greatly altered by weathering and erosion. No fossils have been found in them. Where they were compacted to a crystalline rock by the intrusion of molten granite, valuable mineral deposits resulted, particularly pegmatite, coarse-grained masses of feldspar and quartz crystallized under special conditions. Where these deposits are quarried for feldspar, many gems and rare minerals are found.

The pegmatite area extends northwest across the State from Popham at the mouth of the Kennebec River to the wilderness of northern Oxford County. Well-known mineral localities in this belt are Topsham, Mount Apatite, Mount Mica, Paris, Buckfield and Newry.

In Maine, the Paleozoic rocks differ from the Pre-Cambrian; they contain fossils and are less altered by metamorphism. Covering the central and northern parts of the State, they represent most of the periods into which the Paleozoic Era is divided. The first of these, the Cambrian, is represented by beds of quartzite and slate. Cambrian fossils have been found on the east branch of the Penobscot River. Ordovician beds have not been clearly distinguished from earlier Cambrian and the later Silurian. Most sedimentary rocks in central and northern Maine are Silurian, principally shales, slates and impure limestones. Silurian fossils have been found in central Maine, along the coast at Eastport, and in Aroostook. Good exposures of these rocks are common along the State highways of central and northern Maine.

Rock of the Devonian period is represented by a belt of sandstone, the Moose River formation, extending from west of Moosehead Lake to northern Aroostook. This probably is the most fossiliferous formation in the State, including those glacial boulders containing 'clam shells' which attract attention in central and southern Maine. An earth movement in the Devonian period resulted in the intrusion of great bodies of granite called 'batholiths'; most of Maine's granite seems to have come into position at this time. Volcanoes left beds of lava and ash, erupting first in the

Silurian period. Deposits are found along the coast from Penobscot Bay to Eastport. Of these, Mount Kineo is the most famous; others are East Kennebago, Big and Little Spencers, the Coburn Hills in northeastern Aroostook, Haystack, and the Quoggy Joe Mountains near Presque Isle.

The youngest Paleozoic rocks in Maine are the quartzite slates bordering the coast from Kittery to Casco Bay. The Paleozoic Era ended in the Appalachian Revolution when mountains once more rose across New England.

The Mesozoic Era is almost without record in Maine. Studies indicate that this part of New England was then an upland undergoing erosion. The Cenozoic Era also was a time of erosion. Weaker rocks were worn away and the more resistant were left standing as mountains on a plain that extended over the State. Later uplifts of the land followed; hills and valleys were carved from the plain. The even skyline formed by the merging of the hilltops represents today the level of the old plain. Katahdin, the Blue Mountains in the western part of the State, and the Mount Desert Mountains on the coast are examples of the more resistant rock.

During the Ice Age that ended the Cenozoic Era, Maine was covered by a continental glacier similar to those of Greenland and Antarctica today. Moving southward, the glacier smoothed off the irregularities of the hills. It left large deposits of sand, gravel and clay; as these dammed the pre-glacial valleys, lakes and waterfalls were formed, rivers were thrown from their former courses to flow over bed-rock ridges and through narrow gorges, creating today's resources of water-power. During the thousands of years of the Ice Age, the weight of the glacier depressed New England below its former level. As water from the melting ice poured into the ocean, the latter's level rose to flood the coastal lowland up into the larger valleys. The receding flood left a layer of sand over the clays along the coast, creating sand plains. In some places, notably Freeport and Leeds, this sand, freed of vegetation and blown by the wind, has formed so-called 'deserts.'

Finally the land rose to about the present level and the sea retreated. The coastline has not receded to its pre-glacial position; the lower valleys still are flooded and the highlands form the projecting headlands and islands of the present Maine coast.

SOIL

All the land in Maine except low, wet, marshy areas once was covered with forest growth and most of the State still is forested. Even on farms, about half the land is woodlot and the proportion is increasing as agriculture is being concentrated on the better soils.

Of glacial origin, the soil varies greatly in texture and fertility and ranges all the way from stony loam filled with boulders through gravelly, sandy, silty, and clay loam to heavy clay. Soil surveys of large sections of the State to determine soil types and the crops best adapted to them, show that any crop suitable to this climate can be grown in Maine.

Perhaps the most fertile type is the rich Caribou loam in which are grown most of the potatoes that have made Aroostook County famous. Crop diversification is increasing in the Aroostook. The clay loams in the larger river valleys make excellent hayland. Apple trees thrive on the well-drained soils on the rolling ridges of central and western Maine. The light sandy and gravelly soils near the coast from Kittery to Calais produced the giant pines that gave Maine the name of The Pine Tree State. These soils are noted for the production of lowbush blueberries, an increasingly important crop.

Soil erosion has been a problem on numerous farms where hoed crops are raised, but in many instances it is being brought under control by modern methods of culture such as contour farming. Sodded waterways are being left in fields where needed and the steeper hillsides are being reforested or allowed to return to forest growth. Many of the poorer farms have been taken out of production and placed in the Federal Soil Bank, eventually to revert to forest. Many farmers are spreading lime to correct excess soil acidity, especially where sugar beets are planted. Agriculture continues to be an important enterprise on the better soils of Maine.

WATER

Genesis of economic development, Maine's waterways, coastal and inland, are the State's most important natural resource. Early settlements along the seaboard began the development of Maine's great maritime tradition. Expanding inland were the settlements along the State's myriad waterways that generated industrial development through water power. The coast, indented by many safe harbors, is pierced by numerous navigable rivers where tidewater sometimes reaches as far as sixty miles inland. Oceanographers and marine biologists point to the economic potential of Maine's coastal waters. Favoring water power development are natural waterfalls and other opportunities created by river sources high above sea level, and sufficient rainfall to insure a constant flow of water. Innumerable lakes and reservoirs store water for industrial and domestic use.

Although said to be less seriously affected than some states, Maine has not escaped the Twentieth century's water pollution problems that vex the nation. Maine has these problems to a degree, their causes and effects far too familiar for recapitulation here. In 1969, however, industry and government reported some progress in measures toward pollution abatement, upgrading Maine's rivers and streams, regulating industrial and municipal wastes, controlling use of harmful pesticides and arresting if not repairing the accumulated damage of generations. Community betterment programs also were attacking the problems successfully.

Excellent drinking water is the rule in Maine. Maine's pure spring water has been famous for generations, principally through the bottled Poland Spring water still sold around the world. Other plants bottle Maine water and also use it in the manufacture of soft drinks. Degrees of 'hard' and 'soft' water and mineral content vary with locality. City water is treated before reaching the consumer. Many small communities depend upon wells, the water tested by the State. Seldom seen in the days of high-speed freeways are the cool bubbling springs that invited the traveller's pause along a shady roadside. Long gone are the town pump and the huge round stone watering-troughs (for horses) that stood in the village square. Unlike Rome, few fountains grace municipal plazas, but nature more than compensates with beautiful waterfalls in many parts of the State.

Before electric refrigeration, ice harvesting on rivers, lakes and ponds was a flourishing industry, both for domestic use and in great shipments to warmer climates. Caulk-booted crews used ingenious methods by 1880 when 690,000 tons of ice were harvested on the Kennebec River. With horses, oxen and manpower, snow was removed with scrapers and shovels and the icefields were marked into huge checkerboards by grooving tools and iron sleds with verticle saw-tooth runners. Sawyers with double-handled saws then cut 200-pound blocks that were hauled to a steam elevator. Discharged onto a runway, they slid slickly into the icehouses where as much as 75,000 tons were stored under sawdust to await shipment. A familiar sight in Maine towns when 'the iceman cometh' was the horse-drawn ice cart, children clinging to the rear to retrieve chips from the household-size chunks chopped by the iceman.

Experimental and commercial scale aquacultural studies by the State Department of Sea and Shore Fisheries over a 30-year period indicate that Maine's 2500-mile concave coast with an estimated four million acres of territorial waters offers the best prospect in the United States and probably in North America to develop ecologically and economically valuable aquacultural techniques that are greatly needed. The Department has estimated that aquacultural use of ten percent of the total acreage could yield as much as the 1968 total manufacturing product value of Maine industry, $2.6 billion.

Offering conditions essential to a sound aquacultural program, with several physical characteristics not found elsewhere, Maine's coastal waters have a range of salinity, temperature, sediment and hydrographic conditions that can be controlled with a minimum of physical alteration and could be developed under a wide variety of cultural conditions. Sedimentary, igneous and metamorphic inter-tidal and subtidal rock contains a wide range of minerals and of durability. Bedrock and overburden, together with geographically variable tidal conditions provide open to closed circulation systems and fjord-type to bar-built tributary estuaries. Water depth, temperature, circulation and possible other factors contribute to a range from boreal to virginian ecological conditions.

Viable aquaculture has been handicapped historically by restrictions based on Colonial Ordinances of 1641-47, lack of funds for public research agencies, and conditions discouraging to private enterprise. Evaluation of marine aquaculture requires consideration of other uses for the Maine coast, compatible and incompatible. The Natural Resources Council says a new approach is needed in the light of controversy over oil spills and thermal pollution from nuclear and fossil-fueled electric generating plants, low income levels of many coastal residents, and the expanding number of acres of shellfish-growing areas closed because of pollution — up 75 percent from 40,000 in 1946 to more than 70,000 acres in 1968. Relatively unsophisticated management of inter-tidal growing areas has increased the average yield of several commercial molluscan species more than 100 percent. Management, however, leads to the same dead-end met by the traditional hunting techniques inherited from our Mesolithic ancestors. To meet supply requirements of marine resources, technology to permit much greater population concentration must be developed.

As the nuclear age moves toward the Twenty-first century, Maine's waters continue to be as important to the State's future as they have been since the days of the pioneers —- who never dreamed of pollution.

MINERALS

With as great a variety of minerals as any area of comparable size in the world, and with increasing national demands, Maine looks to faster development of these resources than it has known hitherto. Found here are ores of most metals — gold, silver, platinum, iridium, copper, lead, zinc. The first gold strike in this country is said to have been at Byron, Maine. The only known U. S. source of a cassiterite, important tin ore, is in Maine which also has rich deposits of bauxite, principal ore of aluminum. Among useful non-metallic minerals found here are quartz, feldspar, mica, graphite, asbestos and gem stones.

The Maine Geological Survey supports a basic research and mapping program in cooperation with industry and conservation interests, federal and private agencies and academic institutions as the need for reserves of raw materials increases. The program includes marine geological research. The Continental margin off the coast of Maine extends more than 200 miles oceanwards. Recent explorations in waters off the coast indicate the potential for hard and soft minerals from ocean waters and on the ocean floor and below. Oil and gas explorations are going on in the Gulf of Maine.

With fuel a high-cost item in a State where heat is needed much of the year, there is much interest in oil exploration off the coast. Peat bogs over the State contain large and practically untapped fuel reserves. Excavation and drying of peat for domestic horticulture, poultry litter and other uses is carried on.

The petroleum industry is expanding into the area of ore deposit exploration. Currently underway are explorations for sulphides in combination with copper, zinc, molybdenum and nickel. The occurrence of base metal sulphide ore deposits in Maine is restricted largely to two linear belts of mineralization that trend in a northeast-southwest direction across the State (*see GEOLOGY*).

Currently, mineral production is almost entirely non-metallics. Granite, feldspar and limestone are long-established industries. Structural materials, sand, gravel, crushed stone, dimension stone, cement rock, electrical slate and clay are leading products basic for highways, airports, bridges, dams and other kinds of industrial construction.

Maine granite varies greatly in color, grain and texture and has been quarried since the days of sailing vessels and galamanders; Vinalhaven and Franklin have exhibits. Many notable U. S. buildings and monuments have been built of Maine granite, most recently the John F. Kennedy Memorial.

The State has been a leader in feldspar production with modern grinding plants supplying manufacturers of porcelains and other ceramics. It is mined in central and southern Maine and there are large untapped deposits elsewhere in the State.

The limestone beds of Knox County have been mined over 125 years, with a vast reserve for various uses. Thomaston's newly enlarged cement plant, only one of this kind in New England, is based on the presence of sufficient suitable limestone to supply one of the nation's large cement manufacturers. Limestone found in other parts of the State also has an economic potential.

Beds of clay widespread over the State are used in local brickyards. The clay is adapted for use in the manufacture of linoleum, canoes, window shades and other filled products. Bauxite is found in the clay-beds of eastern Maine. Silica, obtained from bog deposits is used for insulation and filters.

Among Maine gem stones are tourmaline, beryl, amethyst, garnet and topaz. Beryllonite has been found nowhere outside Maine which also has yielded the finest emerald beryl ever found in the United States.

Some of Maine's mineral resources such as iron, lead and zinc had been discovered in the mid-Nineteenth century. The restored Katahdin Iron Works 'beehive' or kiln memorializes an industry that flourished until huge deposits were found elsewhere.

FLORA

Maine's flora falls into two classifications: Canadian in the cooler sections and Transition in the warmer. Isolated areas of one type sometimes are found well within the confines of the other.

Alpine flora occurs on the upper reaches of Mount Katahdin and other high peaks. A blue-leaf birch is known in these regions and mountain white birch and alder also are found on Katahdin. Among the more hardy plants in Alpine areas are Lapland diapensia and rose-bay, Alpine bearberry, Greenland starwort, lance-leaved painted cup, Alpine trailing azalea and holy grass, narrow-leaved Labrador tea, blue spear-grass, and fir club-moss.

The Transition flora grows below Cape Elizabeth on the coast, in all of York County, and in the southern sections of counties west of the Penob-scot River, a great wooded area of pine and oak. The Canadian flora is found along the coast north of Scarborough, and inland above an imaginary line running from Umbagog Lake in the Rangeley section to Mars Hill in lower Aroostook County.

Maine has 76 species of trees; fourteen are softwood which predominates on 60 percent of the land. The white pine, sometimes called the 'masting pine' because in Colonial times the larger trees were reserved for masts for the Royal Navy, is displayed on the State seal and gives Maine its designation as 'The Pine Tree State.' These pines are known to reach a height of 240 feet and a diameter of six feet at the butt. Once abundant in groves throughout the State, they now exist for the most part in second growth and are the major species sawed into lumber. Balsam, red spruce and hemlock also are plentiful state-wide, the first two principally used in the manufacture of paper products, the third in tanning. Balsam is grown commercially for Christmas trees and has been used in making butter tubs because the wood imparts no flavor. Spruce gum is obtained from the red spruce.

Maine's oldest and most valuable trees are the white oaks, some of them well over 500 years old. Red oaks occur in all parts of Maine except the extreme north. The burr oak is common in central Maine. Black or yellow oak is confined to the southerly coastal regions and the swamp white oak and the chestnut oak are found locally in southern Maine.

Often appearing in nearly pure stands of considerable size, the white or paper birch is found throughout all but southern Maine and is used by wood turneries. The yellow is the largest native birch though often not so tall as the white.

The white or American elm, one of Maine's largest and most graceful trees, is common throughout the State as it is through all of New England. It is said that many were planted near houses in the belief that they divert lightening. Best known is the great Lafayette elm at Kennebunk. However, several communities long known for their beautiful 'wine-glass' elms have lost them to industrial development or Dutch elm disease.

There is an abundance of sugar or rock maple. Mountain maple and the swampland red maple are seen all over; and box elder, also a maple, planted as an ornamental tree in southern sections, grows wild in Aroostook County. The silver maple grows near the coast. Tupelo or black gum is found south of Waterville. Pitch pine is the principal tree appearing on large tracts of the Brunswick district. On the shores of Bauneg Beg Lake in North Berwick there is a large stand, many of the old trees of great size. Coast white cedar is found only in York County, as is butternut, an introduced tree and the only species of walnut growing in Maine. Shagbark has been found occasionally in southern sections and as far east as Woolwich. Trees common throughout the State are tamarack, (Indian: hackmatack); white spruce which lumbermen call 'skunk' spruce because of the odor of its foliage; white cedar or arborvitae growing in dense stands on swampy ground; black willow, largest and most conspicuous American willow; the rapid-growing aspen poplar used for book-paper pulp; the large-tooth aspen, the balsam poplar and the common beech. Ironwood or hornbeam is widely distributed though not abundant. The slippery elm, so named because of it mucilaginous inner bark, and the sassafras are little known. The sycamore or buttonwood grows along streams in southern Maine. Poison sumach is found as a shrub in the Transition area. Wild cherry, found everywhere, is of little value except as cover for burned-over areas. But the wild black cherry, less prolific, provides valuable furniture wood. Also found in Maine is the beautiful mountain ash and the striped maple or moosewood. The basswood, a species of linden, is attractive for its flowers, popular with honey bees. Seen occasionally are the fragrant wild locust and the beach plum.

Trees introduced into Maine with marked success include the Norway and the Colorado or blue spruce and three poplars, the white, the Carolina or cottonwood and the Lombardy. The European and copper beeches, the English elm, the magnolia and the flowering crab are among those that have been introduced largely as ornamental trees, as has the European mountain ash or rowan tree, more brilliantly colored than the native, its bright red berries remaining well into winter. The black and honey locusts were brought into the southern part of Maine, the latter common in the vicinity of Paris. The horse chestnut, introduced from Asia by way of southern Europe, is spectacular in bloom with its large fluffy 'torcheres,' especially by moonlight. Tiny horseshoes can be discovered on the small branches of the tree whose shiny inedible brown nuts explode sharply in the autumn bonfire.

The American Forestry Association's *Social Register of Big Trees* in 1969 listed five national champion trees in Maine: an Eastern White pine (pinus strobus) at Blanchard, 18'2" circumference, 147' high, 73½' spread; and, dimensions in the same order, a Pitch Pine (pinus rigada at Poland, 11'4" by 96' by 50'; a Tamarack (larix laricina) at Jay, 9'8" by 95' by 50'; a Silver Maple at Fryeburg Harbor, 24'4½" by 90' by 110'; an Eastern Hophornbeam (ostrya virginiana) at Winthrop, 9'6" by 70' by 57'.

Among the common shrubs of Maine are the speckled alder in swamp and pasture lands; witch hazel bordering most forest areas; several nearly indistinguishable varieties of shad-bush whose white sweet-scented flowers are the first harbingers of spring and whose wood is used in making fishing rods; the hawthorn or thorn apple; the 'wine' choke-cherry, found along farm fence-rows; and the staghorn sumach. Hauntingly fragrant and nostalgic to many are the huge clumps of purple lilacs found near cellar holes and abandoned farms. Originating in Persia, they are said to have been brought to America by the Colonists.

Besides the vast commercial barrens of Washington and Hancock counties, the low-bush blueberry is found in many areas, along with bayberry in coastal regions. The leaves are a crimson sea on ledges in the fall. Mountain cranberries, abundant in the Mount Desert area, long since have given their name to the Cranberry Isles and the large bog cranberry is widely distributed in marshlands. These were called 'crane-berries' and their harvest was a small industry in some communities. A rare shrub often called Bar Harbor juniper is the prostrate savin or trailing yew, found on Monhegan and other islands east of Casco Bay.

Most flowers and shrubs of the north temperate zone are found in Maine. Many are fragrant and generally more brilliantly colored beside the sea. Among the more widely distributed species are American wood anemone, New England aster, seaside and swamp asters, wild bergamot, American bittersweet, black-eyed Susan, Quaker ladies, Queen Anne's lace, meadowcup, sweet clover, white ox-eye daisy and dandelion. Others are salt marsh and fragrant golden rods, goldthread, blue flag, blue-eyed grass, harebell, orange hawkweed, false heather, hepatica and Indian pipe.

Familiar are Jack-in-the-pulpit, Dutchman's breeches, Joe-pyeweed, seaside knotgrass, sea lavender and wild lily-of-the-valley or Canada mayflower. The most common wayside lilies are the Canada (tiger) lily and the American turk's cap. Mayflower, the trailing arbutus, ushers in Spring. Of the many orchids native to Maine, the best known are arethusa, common and yellow lady-slippers, rose pogonia and the small purple and whites.

Devil's paintbrush, spreading profusely through the fields along with buttercups and daisies, distresses the farmer and delights the passerby. Other bright flowers are the scarlet pimpernel, the sea or marsh pink, the swamp pink, pitcherplant and pokeweed. Although Maine's two rhododendrons are not common, the beautiful rhodora has been immortalized by Emerson. Best known of the wild roses are the swamp, the meadow and the sweet brier. Blossoming hedgerows of multiflora or rugosa roses are striking against old stone walls.

Also commonly found in Maine are purple and painted trilliums, yellow, purple, blue marsh and sweet white violets, the giant sunflower (escaped from gardens where it is grown for birdseed), eglantine or sweetbrier, woodbine and yellow wood sorrel.

Vying with Fall foliage tours are the Spring visits to see apple orchards and potato fields in bloom. Flower shows and garden tours are popular in Summer among garden clubs and horticulturists many of whom specialize in roses, glads, dahlias, iris, chrysanthemums and the like. There also are alpine and herb gardens remindful of the herbs and nostrums of another day. Seen seasonally in bloom around homes along the streets of towns and villages are forsythia, flowering quince, daffodils, tulips, hyacinth, heliotrope, lupin, delphinium, peonies, sweet syringa, hyderangea, mock orange, snowball and snowberry, rhododendron, azalea, clematis, morning glories, petunias, geraniums, begonias, hollyhocks and many others.

Note: Some species of wildflowers are becoming rare and should not be molested. Visitors can learn locally or from guides on nature walks of these and of harmful verdure such as poison ivy, some flowers and berries.

FAUNA

In wide areas still untouched by urban civilization, Maine today is rich in many of the species of birds, mammals and fish that attracted the early explorers. On the other hand, use of lethal insecticides take their toll and man's continual slaughter of wildlife has caused extinction of some species, and has driven the timber wolf, the panther, the wild turkey and the swan, out of the State. Northern white-tailed deer, first noticed in numbers about 1900, have increased despite the hunters' annual deerkill (*see RECREATION*). They can seriously damage orchards and frequently are victims of dog packs. Caribou have been reintroduced into Maine after an absence of more than half a century. American elk, commonly called moose from the Indian *musu*, and protected by law, are found in all northern counties and as far south as Sagadahoc. Bay lynx and bobcat have been known in every county; black or cinnamon bear along the beech ridges of northern Aroostook. But the panther and catamount are no more; and the gray wolf, once known all over Maine, was last seen in 1930 in Blue Hill. The Canada lynx, the so-called loup-cervier, is not uncommon in the Magalloway region.

Canadian beavers contribute valuable aid to firefighters with their dammed-up pools, offsetting the damage they do to streams and woods. Their dams may be seen from the air in winter flights over the wilderness and perhaps more conveniently at Moosehorn Wildlife Refuge in Washington County. Raccoons, skunks, rabbits, woodchucks and mice, Robert Burns' 'wee sleekit cowerin' timorous beastie,' wreak havoc in the produce garden, enjoying the fruits of the farmer's labor. Bounties periodically are placed on such depredators as hedgehogs (porcupines) when they become over-prolific.

The Maine weasel is the only animal to which the State has given its name, a fact of no particular significance. Other wildlife found here are muskrat, American otter and mink, fisher, marten (known as American sable), northern red and gray squirrels, the bats — brown, little brown, hoary and silver-haired, and mice — wood, field, house and deer. In the Alpine areas are the chickaree, northern flying squirrel, Canada porcupine, Labrador jumping mouse and Canadian white-footed mouse. The hare (snowshoe rabbit) and gray rabbit are common in York and Cumberland counties. The shrew and mole (short-tailed shrew) are commonly known and a rare species, sorex-thompsoni, has been found in Brunswick, Norway and Waterville. There are red foxes in all their color variations — cross, silver and black; recently these have caused epidemics of rabies among dogs.

Pickering's tree frog sounds the first note of spring in the twilight chorus from pond and bog. There are also the bullfrog, yellow-throated green frog, marsh or pickerel frog, wood frog, common or leopard frog. Turtle varieties include the snapping and mud turtles (painted terrapin), yellow-spotted and wood tortoise and the box tortoise, rare this far north. Herpetologists say there are no poisonous snakes in Maine, only the small garter snake, striped, ribbon green and water snakes and the milk adder.

Playful and easily trainable seals abound along the coast above Casco Bay. Whales have been seen and giant tuna are among saltwater game fish. Maine has a wide variety of both ocean and lake gamefish (see RECREATION). Lobster, clams, quahogs, crabs, shrimp, scallops and mussels are succulent seafoods. Some clamflats closed by pollution have been reopened to diggers for clam-cleansing plants.

Of over 300 known species of birds within the State, 26 are permanent residents. In Maine's Canadian areas are the Acadian chickadee and the eastern snow bunting, while Bicknell's thrush is known to breed on the upper reaches of the mountains. From Labrador to the Everglades, relatively few nests of northern bald-headed eagles have been discovered; two at Georgetown and one at Newcastle were occupied annually for many years. Giant eagles are known and the great golden eagle is seen infrequently. The Canada ruffed grouse, erroneously called the partridge is a highly prized game bird. Thousands of ring-necked pheasants are liberated annually along the coastal range from North Berwick to Cherryfield. Most popular game birds among the waterfowl are the common mallard and black ducks.

The more common birds of Maine's Canadian fauna are the brown creeper, American golden-eye, eastern goshawk, rusty grackle, Holboell's grebe, Canada jay (known otherwise as moosebird and whisky jay), slate-colored junco, eastern golden-crowned kinglet, common loon, red-breasted nuthatch, old squaw, the beautiful snowy owl, spruce partridge, northern raven, red poll, red-backed sandpiper, white-winged scoter, pine siskin, Acadian sharp-tailed sparrow, Lincoln's and white-throated sparrows, the olive backed and water thrushes, blackpoll, myrtle and yellow palm warblers, eastern winter wren and lesser yellow-legs.

A partial list of Maine's Transition birds includes the eastern bluebird, red-winged blackbird, bobolink, bobwhite, black-capped chickadee, American crossbill, the raucous crow, mourning dove, alder flycatcher, olive-sided flycatcher, bronzed grackle, ruffed grouse, bluejay, belted kingfisher, and meadowlark, white-breasted nuthatch, Baltimore oriole, barred or hoot owl, screech, short-eared and saw-whet owls, domestic pigeon, American robin, spotted sandpiper, Savannah and sharp-tailed sparrows, starling, bank, barn, cliff and tree swallows, scarlet tanager, brown thrasher or song thrush, hermit thrush, ruby-throated hummingbird, towhee, Philadelphia vireo, black-throated blue warbler, black and yellow or magnolia warbler, whippoorwill, northern downy, and hairy woodpeckers and house wren. Rarely seen are the least bittern, yellow-billed cuckoo, orchard oriole, field sparrow, wood thrush and pileated woodpecker.

Many species of birds may be seen at such sanctuaries as Audubon at Freeport, the Scarborough Marshes and Moosehorn Refuge and on the islands which constitute the great nursery of North Atlantic seabirds. Here are the breeding grounds of the ubiquitous herring gull, the great black-backed gulls, double-crested cormorants, the black guillemot, the northern raven and Leach's petrel. The American and red-breasted mergansers go inland in summer.

American eider ducks, largest of Maine sea ducks are frequently seen near the outer islands in January. Merrymeeting Bay is an important way station for northern seabirds including the Canada or wild goose. Also to be seen on the coast are double-crested cormorants, terns and puffins, osprey, razor-billed auks, the great blue heron and rarely, the laughing gull. While a few birds are scavengers and predators, many help the gardener with insect control — and help themselves to a share of the produce, especially small fruits, as their reward. In learning about the birds and the bees, one finds that some farmers keep bees for pollination purposes.

Note: Hunting and fishing laws and rules and regulations governing wildlife and game birds should be obtained from the Department of Economic Development, State House, Augusta, Maine 04330.

EARLIEST INHABITANTS:
PEOPLE OF THE DAWN

TEN thousand years ago, when the last of the great ice sheets was melting away and vast tracts of land in the northern parts of North America again became habitable by man, the continent was occupied by a sparse population of roving hunters. These early Indians were the descendants of immigrants from Asia that crossed over during a time when much of the world's water was locked in continental glaciers and the Bering Strait was left high and dry by the fallen sea level. These men, adjusted to the exploitation of large ice age animals that are now mostly extinct, provided the roots from which the multiplicity of American Indian languages and cultures arose. There is no convincing evidence that significant and enduring contact with the eastern hemisphere ever took place other than by way of western Alaska. For the ideas that led to the rise of great civilizations and the penetration of forbidding wilderness on two continents, the American Indian has no one to credit but himself.

Maine was one of the last areas in the United States to be relieved of its burden of ice. The great weight of the mile-thick sheet had so depressed the land that at first the rebound of the coastal areas after melting did not keep up with the rising sea level. As the melting ice fed the seas, the seawater initially drowned the present coastline and the lower portions of Maine's river systems. Eventually the land recovered and as the coastline began to assume its present shape, tundra gave way to forest, game animals and man.

By the time Maine became habitable, many of the ice age animals upon which the early Indians depended were dying out. As their main sources of food slowly disappeared, the early hunters were forced to shift to a more diversified way of life. Because of this sequence no verified examples of the early hunter's specialized tool types have been found in Maine, even though there are major finds known in both Massachusetts and Nova Scotia. The earliest known inhabitants of Maine already were diversified hunters and gatherers. Their habits were more sedentary than before, and their burial practices indicate a well developed ceremonial life.

About fifty cemeteries known in Maine can be attributed to the State's earliest inhabitants. The graves are characterized by the inclusion of large amounts of red ocher (powdered hematite), a practice found in many parts of the world where this mineral is available, and heavy stone tools not made by later Indians. Their discovery in the Nineteenth century led to creation of the 'Red Paint People.' Speculation soon took some professional archaeologists and most of the public interest well beyond the reasonable constraints of the evidence, and many popular early writings on Maine prehistory are heavily embroidered with myth. These prehistoric peoples were assumed by some to have been a now lost race of non-Indians. Others thought that they were Indians, but not linked to the modern Indians of Maine. Their assumed disappearance was accounted for in a variety of imaginary catastrophes, including one that suggested that they were wiped out by a giant wave off the Atlantic. They were even linked to the equally imaginary lost city of Norumbega, a myth that grew out of an early passing reference to a Penobscot Indian place name.

Investigations of the last thirty years have vastly increased our knowledge. There is now no reason to doubt that the 'Red Paint People' were in fact simply the ancestors of Maine's present Indian population. The elaborate burial complex has been found to stretch beyond the borders of the State as far as Newfoundland, and the cultural base upon which it was developed is found over much of the Northeast. The burial complex changed greatly over the years, but it persisted as a tradition until the coming of Europeans. In its early development, it was part of a widespread level of North American cultural development that archaeologists call the Archaic Stage. The complex never included the construction of stone tombs. The large structure at The Forks long attributed to prehistoric Indians is in fact a Nineteenth century lime kiln.

One of the oldest and best understood archaeological sites in Maine is located on a tributary of the Penobscot River in Passadumkeag. The site is a prehistoric cemetery with an adjacent camp area. Modern dating techniques have indicated that the earliest burials were deposited 5000 years ago, nearly 3000 years B.C. Typically, the burials include red ocher and heavy woodworking tools. Yellow stains in the soil and on some of the tools indicate that nodules of iron pyrite (for starting fires by the flint and steel technique) were included. The nodules themselves have long since deteriorated. Heavy stone adzes, gouges and celts indicate that these people were skilled woodworkers. The birch bark canoe was a complex craft not yet developed, but the dugout was a worthy predecessor; it is not unreasonable that the dead should need the tools to make one for their long journey.

Projectile points were also included, but they are too large to have been arrow points. The bow and arrow was not introduced to the area until much later. The most important hunting tool of 5000 years ago was the spear and the spear thrower, a powerful combined weapon used by all of the earliest American Indians. Knives, scrapers and other tools provide detailed evidence for the Indian's commitment to the hunt, but other artifacts such as plummets indicate that he was also exploiting both marine and freshwater fish. The rivers and the seacoast already were providing the inhabitants of Maine with both a means of transportation and a livelihood.

Other artifacts that characterize collections from this phase of Maine prehistory include long ground slate lance points, large tabular whetstones, and perforated 'bannerstones' or spear thrower weights that were designed to give the spear thrower greater power. Some artifacts appear to have been entirely decorative or ceremonial in character. Many of these are decorated with geometric incisions or animal effigies, but nowhere is there any evidence that the people maintained a developed form of written communication. Decorations and larger rock inscriptions such as those near Solon and Machiasport appear to have had only rudimentary symbolic significance.

Within the last 2000 years, the Indians of Maine gradually made greater use of marine resources. The earliest coastal remains indicate that they at first lived much the same way on the coast as they did in the interior. They were hunters out of their element. But gradually the potential of the dozens of shellfish species was realized and the shellheaps that dot the Maine coast began to accumulate. At first only shellfish such as the oyster, mussel and quahog were exploited, but gradually techniques for the use of the softshell clam and the scallop were developed. As the dawn of history approached, the clam was exploited almost exclusively.

On the Damariscotta estuary, however, oysters continued to be available, and the Indians of that area made heavy use of them until disease and warfare decimated the aboriginal population. The results of 2000 years of oyster collecting are the immense Damariscotta shellheaps. The largest, the Whaleback heap, was removed for commercial purposes in the last century, but its mate across the river remains under State protection. The heaps themselves contain relatively few artifacts because the Indians' settlements were located elsewhere, but they persist as monuments to the industry of Maine's aboriginal inhabitants.

With the development of the coastal economy, the way of life of prehistoric Maine took on a dual character. Indians lived on the coast in the summer and dispersed into the interior during the winter. At about the same time, pottery, the bow and arrow and dogs were introduced into the region. All of these changes profoundly altered the aboriginal traditions, but more drastic changes were to come. One of these was the introduction of maize in late prehistoric times; the other was the development of the European fur trade. Both of these allowed the Indians to become both more sedentary and more secure economically. The result was a period of cultural florescence during which the last elaborate burials were made at the cemetery in Passadumkeag and elsewhere. To be sure, the burial complex like everything else had changed considerably over the course of nearly 5000 years, and like much of the rest of Indian culture it came to an abrupt end with the encroachment of European colonists. But elements of the long tradition persist today in Maine's present Indian population.

THE WABANAKI INDIANS

The Indians of Maine, New Hampshire and the Maritimes referred to themselves as 'Wabanaki' (*Easterners or Dawnlanders*). Each local group spoke a dialect of one of four languages depending upon locale. All four belong to the Eastern Algonquian branch of the widespread Algonquian language family, and all four are complicated and expressive forms of speech. The common ancestors of the Algonquian-speaking Indians of today appear to have been responsible for the widespread culture of 5000 years ago previously described.

Many of the names by which local Wabanaki groups have been traditionally identified are in fact aboriginal place names. Misunderstandings and misspellings by European colonists have been further distorted over the years so that considerable caution must be used in the study of historically known Indians. It is sufficient to remember that an unfamiliar 'tribal' identification usually refers to a place rather than a people and that the same group might have been identified by a dozen different names. Other names such as 'Tarantine' are simply too vague and inclusive to be of use.

The Wabanaki of New Hampshire spoke a series of dialects that were closely related to those of Maine. Unfortunately, these people were either killed or dispersed as refugees during King Philip's War. The groups that inhabited western Maine and the Penobscot River drainage all spoke dialects of a second language. Most of the Indians of western Maine like those of New Hampshire before them were either killed or dispersed up to and during the French and Indian War. Many of them fled to Canada where their descendants live today. Others took refuge with the Indians of the Penobscot drainage. Several hundred of the descendants of these original western and central Maine Indians today live on the Penobscot reservation at Old Town.

The easternmost drainages of Maine were historically occupied by the Passamaquoddy. Most of their descendants still speak their native language, one that is related to the language spoken by the other Indians of Maine but nearly identical to that spoken by the Malecite of New Brunswick. Together they constitute the third Wabanaki language. The fourth is Micmac, spoken by the Wabanaki of Nova Scotia and eastern New Brunswick.

The Penobscot reservation at Old Town and two Passamaquoddy reservations in Washington County comprise all that is left of organized Indian communities in Maine. Malecite and Micmac families live scattered throughout the state, but they are not generally recognized as Maine tribes.

In the early years of their contact with European traders, the Maine tribes experienced an economic boom. Traditional trapping and hunting areas became more accurately defined, and each area was clearly identified with the family that exploited it. In this way, each family group was able to protect its interests unmolested and the fur-bearing animals, especially the beaver, were carefully conserved within each area. The family groups took on animal names as totems and both marriage practices and inheritance were probably more carefully regulated than before. The totemic names persist today alongside contemporary surnames that are derived from both French and English.

Joseph Polis, the Penobscot who served as Thoreau's guide in the Maine woods, used a drawing of a bear on his canoe as a personal emblem. The Thoreau Fellowship memorializes Polis and Henry David Thoreau in a replica of the Walden Pond cabin, on Indian Island. Thoreau who knew and respected the Indians, said of the Penobscot: 'He begins where we leave off . . . It is worth the while to detect new faculties in man, he is so much the more divine.'

The families no longer disperse annually to their traditional areas on the tributaries of the major rivers, or to favorite fishing areas on the coast but the memory of them and the customs they generated remain.

The Penobscot and Passamaquoddy Indians of Maine are the least disintegrated of the original New England Indian groups. But even they have been forced to compromise and adapt over the course of over 300 years of contact with European civilization. In order to make a living, they are now largely part of the overall Maine economy, and the Indian labor force is gradually becoming more and more dispersed. In earlier times, the pressures were less peaceful. A series of treaties, beginning in the late 1600s were made and broken with a regularity that later became customary in dealings with Indian tribes. By the middle of the 1700s the Maine tribes were caught in the conflict between French and English interests. Economically there were strong ties with the English, but their religious life was largely the product of French missionary activity. In an extension of a European war that they did not understand or care about, the Wabanaki suddenly found themselves declared the enemies of England. Large bounties were paid for Indian scalps, a single price eventually being established for men's, women's and children's scalps alike.

After the war, the tribes existed in a precarious but peaceful relationship with the English until the American Revolution during which they sided with the colonists. By that time, heavy European colonization had destroyed the balance of Indian conservation practices. As their economic base withered and warfare and disease reduced their population, the Indians found themselves under steady pressure to sell or cede their lands. Special treaties were signed with the State of Massachusetts, which controlled the Province of Maine until 1819.

By the early 1800s, nearly all of Maine was out of Indian control. In exchange for the land, Massachusetts in 1818 agreed to pay the Penobscot Indians one six-pound cannon, one swivel, fifty knives, 200 yards of calico, two drums, four rifles, one box of pipes, and 300 yards of ribbon, and in addition to supply them with 500 bushels of corn, fifteen barrels of wheat, seven barrels of clear pork, one hogshead of molasses, 100 yards of double-width broadcloth (to be red and blue on alternate years), fifty good blankets, 100 pounds of gunpowder, six boxes of chocolate, 150 pounds of tobacco and fifty dollars cash every year for as long as the tribe remained a nation. Maine assumed these obligations in 1819, but it has been a long time since these goods could be regarded as adequate compensation. Accordingly, the Maine State Department of Indian Affairs now controls services to the three reservations. Maine Indians have never been bound by treaty to the federal government.

Local leadership was originally held for life by a man of demonstrated qualities and strong personality. One of these was the Penobscot Joseph Orono for whom the town of Orono was named. The formation of the Wabanaki confederacy, created along lines similar to the League of the Iroquois, resulted in the consolidation of local Indian groups under more formalized leadership. Other member tribes of the confederacy were called upon to confirm the selection of each new chief. This practice insured the unity of a political alliance that developed primarily as a defense against colonial expansion.

In 1866 the office of chief (or governor) of the Penobscots became annually elective. Even so there was a tendency toward long tenure in office and hereditary succession. Conflicts over this tendency led to the formation of the Old Party and the New Party at Old Town, a dual division that characterized internal Penobscot politics for many years.

In the late 1800s the Wabanaki confederacy gradually disintegrated. Peace with the Colonial and Federal Government had removed the primary reason for its existence; it had become an appendage to the League of the Iroquois. One by one, the Wabanaki tribes quit in disgust. Since that time the four remaining tribes have been linked only by shared traditions. The Penobscot and Passamaquoddy maintain a somewhat closer relationship because of their mutual interests through the Maine Indian Affairs Department. Both tribes send representatives to the State legislature. As the quality of living of some of the nation's minority groups, including the American Indian, came into sharp focus in the mid-Twentieth century, Maine's Indians in 1969 demonstrated concern for their identity, status and living conditions.

Most Penobscot and Passamaquoddy Indians now live in much the same manner and with the same needs as other Maine residents. The native language is nearly extinct among the Penobscots; the Passamaquoddy cling to their language tenaciously. Traditional folklore that includes a wide range of stories, songs and dances persists in both tribes. Native crafts have been replaced by modern conveniences but both tribes continue to make sturdy ash and sweetgrass baskets in the traditional manner. Treaty rights that always seem to be remembered better by the Indians than by contemporary landowners guarantee access to ash trees in the Maine forests. Traditional foods such as 'fiddleheads' and porpoise remain popular.

Perhaps along the coast and deep in the forests of Maine, one may imagine, with an earlier writer, the days long gone when 'the Indians used to wander with the seasons, according to the location of food supplies. In the spring they went to the rivers for alewives, shad and salmon; on the banks they planted corn, squash, beans and other vegetables. In June they went to the sea for porpoise and seal in order to get oil and skins, and for the eggs and nestlings of seabirds; they dried clams and lobsters and stored them for winter use. In September they returned to the river valleys to harvest their crops, and in October they went to the big woods to hunt. Before Christmas they held their annual thanksgiving feast for not less than two weeks. Our national Thanksgiving Day is a direct imitation of the Indian festival . . . When snow came they went into the deep woods hunting for moose and setting traps. Before the ice broke up in March or April they had made their spring catch of otter and beaver. When the ice broke and the river was clear they were ready to catch muskrat; they could start out in their canoes to fish and to go to the lower valleys for the planting.'

There have been many profound changes in the landscape since the days when all of Maine was Indian land. But like that land, as the Wabanaki have changed, they have not lost their distinctive character. In the face of a dominant culture many traditions have persisted and the contributions of Maine Indians, and their Algonquian-speaking relatives, to western civilization are becoming generally recognized. Hundreds of Algonquian words that are now part of the English language are no less important than such technological contributions as the canoe and snowshoes. The Wabanaki are the oldest residents of Maine and even today they constitute a major theme in its character.

ARCHAEOLOGY

Increasing interest in Maine history in the 1960s stimulated archaeological activity, professional and amateur. Findings are steadily adding to the growing body of knowledge available to scholars and researchers and are increasing museum collections of artifacts.

The State Parks and Recreation Commission's on-going archaeological program, begun early in the decade under the direction of Wendell S. Hadlock of the Commission's Advisory Committee on Historic Sites and director of Rockland's William A. Farnsworth Museum, located the long-disputed 1607 Popham Colony Site in Phippsburg at the mouth of the Kennebec River. There are continuing examinations at Castine's Fort George and at Fort Pownall, Stockton Springs. These are among State-owned coastal forts restored and interpreted by the Department which also has restored a Katahdin Iron Works kiln and has custody of the Damariscotta oyster shell heaps, among the world's largest.

The State Museum, with an augmented professional staff, has inaugurated an archaeological program; by 1972, its comprehensive collections, catalogued and interpreted, will be on view in a new building housing State Archives, Library and Museum at the State Capitol.

The Museum of the University of Maine Department of Anthropology, noted for its Indian collections, has been enhanced through Professor Dean R. Snow's archaeological survey of the State of Maine. The Robert Abbe Museum at Bar Harbor also is known for its Indian collections and interpretations. Many area museums of the more than 100 organizations of the Maine League of Historical Societies and Museums have collections of Indian and Colonial artifacts.

One of the largest 'digs' has been at the 1617 Pemaquid Settlement under direction of Mrs. Millard Camp, archaeologist and League trustee. Maine Archaeological Society members are working in many areas, uncovering valuable material. The Arnold Trail Historical Association continues an active program along the route of the ill-fated march to Quebec in 1775.

Further information on these and many other activities in the field may be obtained from the above State departments and organizations.

DAWN OF AMERICA

INDIANS were the earliest known inhabitants of the New World discovered by explorers in the Seventeenth century. The so-called 'Red Paint' people are believed to be the prehistoric ancestors of the Indians rather than a separate race, as once thought. Although much valuable material has been lost over the centuries, continuing archaeological research reveals many links with America's native and Colonial past. Pictured here are some of the first North American coastal points known to explorers; artists' interpretations of the Indians; and examples of archaeological findings.

INDIAN GUIDES AND PARTY

ST. CROIX ISLAND, FIRST FRENCH SETTLEMENT, 1604

SAMUEL DE CHAMPLAIN

CHAMPLAIN'S ILE DE MONTS DESERT

POPHAM COLONY SITE, FIRST ENGLISH SETTLEMENT, PHIPPSBURG, 1607

ADMIRAL RALEIGH GILBERT

INDIAN PETROGLYPHS AT MACHIASPORT

REVEREND SAMSON OCCOM, INDIAN MINISTER

INDIAN CHIPPED STONE
IMPLEMENTS USED AS
KNIVES, SPEAR POINTS
AND ARROW HEADS

JOHN NEPTUNE,
A LIEUTENANT-GOVERNOR OF
THE PENOBSCOT INDIANS

ANASAGUNTICOOK INDIANS AT ANDROSCOGGIN FALLS, LEWISTON

DAMARISCOTTA OYSTER SHELL HEAPS, 2,000 YEARS OLD

MAINE INDIANS GREETED CAPT. GEORGE WAYMOUTH IN 1605

ANCIENT PEMAQUID, 1620 SETTLEMENT, AND FORT WILLIAM HENRY

EARLY AMERICAN HISTORY, MURAL

PASSAMAQUODDY INDIANS AT PLEASANT POINT

PENOBSCOT INDIANS CEREMONIAL DANCE, OLD TOWN

HISTORY

THE ancient Norse sagas tell of the voyages of Eric the Red and those of his son, Leif the Lucky, and how Eric, banished from Norway in A. D. 981, sailed westward and came to a fabulous 'green' land across the sea. Eric got no farther than Greenland, but Leif in A. D. 1000 reached the mainland, the coast of which he followed southward to a place he called Vinland, from the abundance of grapes he found there. While much has been written about the location of Vinland and the inland explorations of the Vikings on this continent, the most substantial evidence of Viking habitation thus far (1969) is found in the authenticated Viking villages and artifacts uncovered by Anthropologist Halge Instad of Norway in Newfoundland. If, as believed by some, other Norse navigators in 1003, 1006, 1007 and 1011 reached the shores of what is now New England, these early rovers would have been the first Europeans to explore that coastal region and therefore the first to sail along the Maine coast.

Nearly five hundred years passed before white men again came to the New World. In 1496, the Cabots — John and his sons, Lewis, Sebastian, and Sancius — were named in letters patent granted to them by King Henry VII of England *to discover and occupy isles or countries of the heathen or infidels before unknown to Christians, accounting to the king for a fifth part of the profit upon their return to the port of Bristol.* In 1497-99, the Cabots made a number of voyages, the reports of which, excepting the later testimony of Sebastian (which has been challenged by authorities of the period), are very meager. However, the records established beyond question that the Cabots did reach and explore the Atlantic coastline of the North American continent. One old Bristol record reads: *In the year 1497, June 24, on St. John's Day, was Newfoundland found by Bristol men, in a ship called the MATTHEW.* Again, one entry from the privy purse expenses of Henry VII reads: '*L*10 to hym that found the new isle.' A map, drawn by Sebastian Cabot, of the Atlantic coastline from 60 degrees to 40 degrees N. lat., is preserved. It is obvious, therefore, that the Cabot expeditions explored southward along the Maine coast, and if the reports of Sebastian Cabot's conversation with Butringarius, the Pope's legate, be true, he went as far as the Carolinas. At all events, it was upon the Cabot discoveries that England in the Seventeenth century based its claim to North America.

But England did not follow up the Cabot discoveries immediately, and for many years the land was left open to the subsequent exploration of the French. Giovanni da Verrazzano, an Italian navigator in the service of France, reached the Maine coast in 1524. He was followed a year later by the Spaniard, Gomez. But these two, like other early explorers, were looking for the gold and rich tropical lands of the Indies, and therefore took no interest in what they found here. About 1527, Jean Allefonsce, a French master pilot, explored and described the cape and river of Norumbega (probably the Penobscot). Thevet, a French geographer, on a return voyage from Brazil to France in 1556, followed the North American coast from Florida to Newfoundland. But perhaps the first white men actually to tread Maine soil for any distance were three English sailors, survivors in 1568 of an unsuccessful expedition to Mexico led by the freebooter, Sir John Hawkins. Put ashore from their ship in the Gulf of Mexico, they made their way north and east, eventually reaching Maine. Traveling up the coast to the St. John River, they encountered a French trading vessel on which they returned to Europe. One of these men, David Ingram, wrote a highly colored account of his adventures, in which he tells of visiting the fabled city of Norumbega. In 1602 Bartholomew Gosnold, in command of the English Vessel CONCORD reached Maine's southern shores. In 1603 Captain Martin Pring, with the vessels SPEEDWELL and DISCOVERER, entered Penobscot Bay, and thence sailed southward.

After considerable French exploration in America, Pierre du Guast, the Sieur de Monts, accompanied by Samuel de Champlain and the Baron de Poutrincourt, in 1604 established a settlement on an island at the mouth of the river that Champlain called the St. Croix. In the fall of that year, Champlain set forth to explore the coast westward, going by the great island to which he gave the name of Mount Desert (*Ile des Monts Deserts*), up the Penobscot River to the site of present-day Bangor, and then up the Kennebec the following summer. In 1606, de Monts and Champlain sailed down the coast as far as Cape Cod, looking for a more satisfactory site for colonization than the St. Croix island, (Dochet's Island, now a National Historic Site). They found nothing, however, that pleased them more than a place across the Bay of Fundy which they had ceded to de Poutrincourt and called Port Royal. De Monts accordingly moved his colony there and returned to France.

In 1605, Captain George Waymouth visited Monhegan and explored the coast. He secured valuable information about the country and assistance for future colonization by kidnaping five Indians, whom he took back to England. To this crime, much of the subsequent Indian hostility to white men on the Maine coast has been attributed. In 1606, James I granted a charter to the Plymouth Company for the lands lying between the 41st and 45th parallels; and in 1607, the Popham Colony, called St. George, was set up on Sagadahoc Peninsula at the mouth of the Kennebec, in the present town of Phippsburg. Although unsuccessful, this was the beginning of British colonization in New England. Before very long, many English settlers had established themselves along these rugged shores. The first Dutch came to Maine in 1609 when Henry Hudson, commissioned by the Netherlands to search for a northwest passage to the Indies, hove to in Casco Bay, to repair his storm-battered vessel, the HALF-MOON. The Maine Indians received him kindly but Hudson requited their hospitality by robbing them of much of their supplies. So fierce was their resentment that Hudson was forced to put from shore. He sailed southward and eventually came into New York waters, ascending the North (Hudson) River until he was sure it was not an 'arm of the sea.'

Soon the French were sending missionaries to the new world. In 1613 a Jesuit colony was established on Mount Desert Island, only to be dispersed shortly by the crew of an English vessel commanded by Captain Samuel Argall, who had come from Virginia ostensibly for a supply of fish. At the mission on Mount Desert, Fathers Biard and Masse had established the first monastery east of California in what is now the United States. In spite of active English hostility, the French continued to set up scattered settlements, notably on the Penobscot and St. Croix Rivers and at Machias. But these settlements did not prosper. Most of the immigrants of this period were unenterprising and ignorant, or they were French gentlemen in search of gold or glory and with no desire to build homes in a new world. The chief interest in America on the part of the French was always the opportunity for trade in furs with the savages.

Captain John Smith arrived at Monhegan from England in 1614. Exploring the coast from the Penobscot to Cape Cod, he made a map of the territory, which he called New England. On November 3, 1620, a new charter, known as the Great Patent,' was granted to the Plymouth, Company under a changed corporate name, 'The Council for Plymouth,' otherwise called 'The Council for New England.' It made the company 'absolute owners of a domain containing more than a million square miles,' between 40 degrees and 48 degrees N. lat., which was to be called New England. From this company the Pilgrims derived their patent to the Plymouth Colony.

The Pilgrims, arriving in America in 1620, reported a thriving fishing and trading post at Pemaquid. There were probably trading settlements at both Pemaquid and Monhegan from the beginning of the century, but Father Biard wrote that the Indians had driven the English out of Pemaquid in 1608-09. In 1622 the Council for New England gave to Sir Ferdinando Gorges and Captain John Mason the land between the

Merrimac and the Kennebec, which, the indenture stated, 'they intend to call *The Province of Maine*.' Permanent settlements were established — Monhegan in 1622, Saco in 1623, and York (as Agamenticus) about 1624. All the early settlements were easily accessible to shipping, and they grew rapidly.

In 1629 Mason and Gorges divided their province between them, with the Piscataqua River as middle boundary. Mason's land was called New Hampshire, Gorges' New Somersetshire. Mason died in London in 1635, and Gorges, who had become governor-general of all New England in the same year when the Plymouth (England) Council surrendered its patent, was in 1639 granted from King Charles I a charter to the territory between the Piscataqua and Kennebec Rivers, extending 120 miles north and south. The charter specified that the tract should 'forever be called the Province and Countie of Maine and not by any other name whatsoever.' The political status of the Province was that of a palatinate, of which Gorges was lord palatine, a vassal enjoying royal privileges. Thus Maine was for a time under purely feudal tenure. Gorges appointed a council of seven colonists to administer the Province and act as court. This body superseded the judicial court established March 28, 1636, by William Gorges, Sir Ferdinando's nephew, for a short time governor of New Somersetshire. In 1640, under Thomas Gorges, Sir Ferdinando's son sent over to Maine as his deputy, the first recorded body representative of the people in a permanent Maine settlement met at Saco, in a court having both legislative and judicial functions for the 1400 whites west of the Penobscot River.

In 1630, the Plymouth Council, among other dispensations of New England lands, granted a large tract of territory in Maine to John Beauchamp of London and Thomas Leverett, a Boston merchant. This grant, comprising about a million acres, was called the Muscongus Patent. Eighty-nine years later, Samuel Waldo was given half the grant 'for services rendered.' Eventually he bought the other half, and the grant became known as the Waldo Patent. In 1753, Waldo imported a party of immigrants from Germany, who founded a large and prosperous settlement, the present Waldoboro. The initials N.W.P., occasionally found in modern deeds and titles, signify 'North of Waldo Patent.'

French trading continued in the land east of the Penobscot, and the English trading posts at Machias and Penobscot were seized by the French in 1634 and 1635. But the region from Penobscot to Port Royal was finally subdued in 1654 by the English under Major Sedgwick; and in 1635 the whole of the Acadian province was confirmed to the English, who held it for thirteen years. Nevertheless, French missionary activities among the Indians were continued in Maine, chiefly by the Jesuits, but also by the Franciscans and Dominicans. In 1646, Father Gabriel Druillettes, accompanied by Indian converts, entered the Norridgewock territory — the first white man to travel down the Kennebec to the ocean from the north. The trail he blazed was followed by Fathers Aubry and Loyard, the Bigots, and Father Rasle, who in turn succeeded him at his post, the most important seat of missionary work in Maine.

In the meantime, the settlement originally called Agamenticus was endowed with a city charter in 1642 under the name of Gorgeana. In 1652, it was reorganized as a town, and its name changed to York. The first town in Maine was Kittery, organized in 1647. From the beginning, each settlement ordered its own affairs, local government being far more important than central. The courts were informal, deriving their authority from the general consent of the colonists.

In 1643, the four New England Colonies had formed an alliance for mutual defense, excluding therefrom the Gorges settlements. After the death of Gorges in 1647, the inhabitants of Kittery, Gorgeana (later York), Wells, Cape Porpoise (now Kennebunkport), Saco, Casco (now Portland), and Scarborough formed themselves into a body politic, experimenting with self-rule; but soon realizing the importance of a strong and settled government, they became freemen of Massachusetts in 1652 on liberal terms. They sent representatives to the Massachusetts General Court (1653), suffered no requirement of church membership or tithe, and paid only town and county taxes (the southern section of the Province of Maine became in 1658 the separate and autonomus County of York-shire). By this time the democratic form of government based on the town meeting was already assured and strong throughout New England.

Upon the restoration of Charles II to the English throne in 1660, Ferdinando Gorges, a grandson of Sir Ferdinando, claimed Maine as his property. Four years later, a royal order bade Massachusetts restore the Province to him. The investigating commissioners set up a government in the Province, but they were shortly recalled; and in 1668, Massa-chusetts assumed control. A clear title was finally secured when the Gorges rights were sold to an agent for Massachusetts, May 6, 1677.

The territory (known variously as Sagadahoc and New Castle) from Pemaquid to the St. Croix was granted to the Duke of York in 1664, together with the New Netherland. As the County of Cornwall it retained a slight connection with New York; in 1674, both Colonies were united under the rule of Sir Edmund Andros. Yet a supplementary article added to the Treaty of Breda, by which in 1667 Charles II ceded Nova Scotia to France, surrendered the whole of Acadia to France and especially mentioned 'Pentogoet' or Penobscot. On this basis, France laid claim to all of the Province of Maine east of the Penobscot. The Baron de St. Castin soon established himself in this region, and for more than thirty years protected French (and his own) interests and traded with both Indians and English. In 1673 the Dutch captured and held the French fortifications at Penobscot, the Dutch West Indies Company in 1676 appointing a governor for the conquered territory; but they were shortly driven out by the English. In 1688 Governor Andros seized Penobscot again, and sacked the house of Baron de Castin. This event marked the beginning of the rapid decline of French influence in Maine. The Governor of Canada, it is true, continued in large measure to control the Indians through the agency of the Jesuit missionaries, of whom Father Sebastian Rasle came to be the best known. The latter's interest in the temporal welfare of his Indian flock led to his death at the hands of the English in 1724, during the sack of Norridgewock, where he had taught since 1691.

After 1730 the Indians had no regular priests; and when in 1763 France finally surrendered Canada, the Catholic missions were badly hurt, for, while the English Government guaranteed religious freedom, it was taking quiet steps to rid Maine and Canada of the Jesuit influence. The last mission in Maine had disappeared by the time of the Revolutionary War. After the work of Father Cheverus and Father Romagne (1797-1818), however, the Roman Catholic Church gained strength in Maine and has not ceased to prosper since.

The French were consistently successful in their dealings with most of the eastern Indians. The Iroquois nation, always hostile to them, was an important exception, but that federation had little influence in Maine. The French sought trade rather than settlement, and unlike the English, made no attempt to dispossess the natives of their ancestral lands; while the French Catholic missionaries worked continually with great self-sacrifice and altruism in behalf of the Indians, many of whom became Christian converts. The natives naturally responded to the better treatment the French offered them.

In 1672 a new survey of the northern boundary of Massachusetts had extended the Colony beyond the Kennebec to Penobscot Bay, and after two years this region was organized as the County of Devonshire. At this time there were nearly 6000 inhabitants between the Piscataqua and the Penobscot, and at least 150 families east of the Kennebec.

In 1675 King Philip's War burst upon the startled colonists. It was seventy years from the time that Waymouth kidnaped his Indians before active warfare resulted from the almost continual aggression and treaty-breaking on the part of the whites. Yet in the following eighty-five years of sudden savage raids and skirmishes there were few inhuman barbarities aside from the custom of scalping which was practiced by both sides. Most of the Maine Indians had become Christians, and were influenced by the Church.

Saco was attacked on September 18, 1675. Two days later, Scarborough was burned and the inhabitants of Casco driven out or cut down, the survivors taking refuge on the outer islands of Casco Bay. The settlements at Arrowsic and Pemaquid were burned, and during the next summer the Indians even penetrated to Jewell Island, the farthest outpost of the bay, where the beleaguered colonists had barricaded themselves. The burning and sacking continued ruthlessly until a commission from the Massachusetts Government negotiated peace with the Indians of the Androscoggin and the Kennebec at Casco on April 12, 1678.

When peace was attained, Massachusetts provided a government for the Province, the Council in 1680 appointing Thomas Danforth 'President of Maine' to serve for one year and councilors to serve until removed; Maine towns were annually to elect a House of Deputies. After the Massachusetts charter was revoked in 1685, the Colonies were governed directly by the Crown until 1688 when New England, together with New York and New Jersey, came under the single administration of Andros. James II in 1686 appointed Joseph Dudley royal deputy; later in the same year, Dudley was superseded by Andros. In April, 1688, Andros attacked Penobscot and sacked the stronghold of Baron de Castin, thus precipitating the French and Indian conflict with the English of Maine and Massachusetts that is known as King William's War. The first outbreak occurred in August, 1688, when Indians attacked the North Yarmouth settlement. The fighting continued sporadically throughout the following winter; but the Maine colonists, aroused by the unwise measures taken by Governor Andros against the Indians and chafing under his arrogant rule, joined with the people of Massachusetts in taking independent control of the government, news having reached New England of the landing of William of Orange in England and of the flight of King James. Massachusetts appointed Simon Bradstreet as its Governor, and Maine restored Danforth as Provincial President on April 18, 1689.

The French and their Indian allies actively continued the war with the English. The garrison at Pemaquid surrendered on August 2, 1689. In 1690, Newichawannock (now Salmon Falls) was destroyed, and Fort Loyal at Falmouth (formerly Casco) was razed by Baron de Castin with five hundred French and Indians from Canada, who took many of the inhabitants, most of them women and children, back to Quebec as prisoners. Sir William Phips in 1690 carried the war to the French in Nova Scotia, captured Port Royal, and took possession of the entire coast to Penobscot. But a campaign against Quebec failed; and the capture by the French of Fort William Henry at Pemaquid, 'the most expensive and the strongest fortification that had ever been built by the English on American soil,' still further increased French prestige with the Maine Indians. By the autumn of 1691, only four towns, Wells, York, Kittery, and Appledore, remained inhabited, Falmouth and other leading settlements having been almost totally destroyed. In February 1692 the worst Indian massacre of English in Maine history occurred in a surprise attack at York. Over fifty were killed, eighty were carried into captivity, and the town was largely demolished. The fighting continued intermittently until 1697; then, under the Treaty of Ryswick, the French claimed all of eastern Sagadahoc as part of Nova Scotia.

Massachusetts' second charter, that of 1691, conferred fewer powers than had been granted by the old charter. The first royal governor was Sir William Phips, a native of Maine and perhaps the first of America's prominent self-made men. Until this time, Maine had been constantly beset by political changes and internal revolutions, owing to the succession of claimants and the zeal of the competitors for its land. The districts east of the Kennebec had suffered particularly in vicissitudes of ownership and government. With each part separated from and giving no aid to the others, the Province offered few inducements to settlers. The territory remained a sort of buffer province, subject to continual attack from Indians and French. But under the administration of Phips, the contention of royalist and republican partisans for proprietorship and government ceased. Town government in Maine now took the same form as that in the rest of New England, the county continuing to be useful as an intermediate organization for judicial purposes. Each county had a court consisting of a resident magistrate or a commissioner and four associates chosen by the freemen of the county and approved by the General Court.

During the contest over acceptance of the Massachusetts charter in 1691, there had originated the political parties of Republicans and Loyalists. Though they eventually assumed new names, their general policies continued to the Revolution, the Republicans or 'liberty men' adhering to the democratic principles in the old charter, and the Loyalists or prerogative men' professing to be more loyal subjects of the King and accordingly enjoying more of his favor.

For a long time the Province of Maine had been poor and weak, suffering greatly in the wars with the French and Indians. Obedience to the laws of Massachusetts was rendered unwillingly until the resettlement of the Colonies after King Philip's War, and the Province was early a resort for those with but small regard for creed or church. The settlers continued to aggravate the ill-will of the Indians; and the latter, greatly reduced in numbers by continual epidemics dating from the first coming of the white men, now began to see that they must fight for their very existence as well as for their lands. The colonists generally failed to discriminate between members of different tribes; an Indian was an Indian, and a good Indian was a dead one. The innocent were constantly being killed. Many were sold into slavery for the crimes of others, their women ravished, their homes destroyed. Queen Anne's War, beginning in Maine in 1703 with attacks on Casco Bay colonies and lasting to 1713, caused great damage, but it broke forever the main force of Indian strength and importance.

Although English advance into the interior of Maine was slow, since the French claimed all land east of the Penobscot, by 1722 it had made considerable headway. The British were sometimes aided by Indians of the forest lands, who joined them to fight their hereditary enemies of the coast and the east. In 1729, David Dunbar was granted royal sanction to settle and govern the 'Province of Sagadahoc.' His arbitrary acts, however, resulted in his removal from office in 1733, Massachusetts thereupon resuming jurisdiction.

In 1739 the King in council fixed the line between Maine and New Hampshire to *pass through the entrance of Piscataqua Harbor and the middle of the river to the farthermost head of Salmon Falls River, thence north 2 degrees; west, true course, 120 miles.* York and Falmouth (Portland) were now the principal towns in Maine, the former the political center, the latter the commercial center. Economic prosperity was growing; by 1743 there were 12,000 people in the Province. The Reverend George Whitefield, the famous Calvinist preacher, came to Maine with his wife in 1741 and again in 1744, where he preached at York, Wells, and Biddeford.

War between England and France broke out again in 1744, bringing the fifth Indian war to Maine, with attacks on Fort St. George and Damariscotta in the summer of 1745. A Massachusetts army aided by an English fleet won the most conspicuous success of the war, the capture of Louisburg at Cape Breton in 1745. Edward Tyng of Falmouth commanded the squadron co-operating with the English fleet, while William Pepperrell of Kittery, for years New England's most important landowner, headed the land forces. Maine, with but one-fourteenth of the total population of the Bay Colony, was providing one-third of its troops. Nearly one-third of Maine's citizen soldiers participated in the siege of Louisburg, the 'Gibraltar of the West,' the capture of which resulted in Pepperrell's being made a baronet.

Newcastle, the first of the towns in the territory of Sagadahoc and the twelfth town in Maine, was incorporated in June, 1753. In 1755, the Acadians of Nova Scotia, refusing to take the oath of allegiance to an English sovereign, were exiled and dispersed among the American Colonies. Many of them settled in Maine along the St. John River.

With the capture of Quebec by the British in 1759 and the subsequent surrender of all Canada, peace was finally secured with France and with the Indians, and Indian warfare in Maine ceased forever.

Possession of the Penobscot country was taken in July, 1759, when Fort Pownal was built and garrisoned. Peace was formally made with the remnants of the Indian tribes in the vicinity of Fort Pownal on April 29,

1760. The creation, on June 19, 1760, of two new counties — Cumberland, embracing that part of Maine between the Saco and the Androscoggin, and Lincoln, whose jurisdiction extended over that part east of the Androscoggin — was evidence that Maine was rapidly increasing in population. Pittston, the fortieth and last town established by the General Court under the royal charter, was incorporated on February 4, 1779.

The first indication of resistance in Maine to the taxes laid on the American Colonies by Parliament was the seizure of a quantity of tax stamps in Falmouth by a mob in 1765. In 1774 the people of Falmouth in town meeting declared that no power had a right to tax them without their consent or that of their representatives. Nine towns in Cumberland County sent delegates to a county convention held at Falmouth in September, 1774. The delegates advised 'a firm and persevering opposition to every design, dark or open, framed to abridge our English liberties.' Sheriff William Tyng declared his intention to obey the law of the Province, but not that of Parliament.

In the Revolution that followed, Maine suffered more than any other part of New England. Both sides enlisted services of the Indians and paid bounties for white scalps. In 1775 Falmouth was almost completely destroyed by an English fleet. In what has been called one of the most harrowing expeditions in military annals, Colonel Benedict Arnold in the fall of 1775 led his band of more than a thousand soldiers up the Kennebec River through the Dead River country to Lake Megantic and the Chaudiere on his ill-fated expedition to Quebec. After experiencing great suffering from swamped and leaking batteaux, loss of critical supplies, sickness and a hurricane in an uncharted wilderness, remnants of Arnold's band were badly defeated at Quebec December 31, 1775.

In 1779 the British occupied Castine and immediately Massachusetts sought to recapture it. But an amphibious fleet of over forty ships and 1300 soldiers and marines were routed by the British defenders of Fort George and a fleet from Halifax. Thereafter eastern Maine remained in British hands until 1783 and the area was subject to harrassing raids by enemy and 'loyalist' vessels.

The majority of the colonists were of fighting stock — pioneers, hunters and trappers, veterans of Indian wars and foreign sea battles. In the first naval engagement of the war, the citizenry of Machias, with no cannon, few small arms and little powder, attacked a British armed cutter, the MARGARETTA, and forced its surrender. Many Maine men served with Washington around Boston. Others stood 'at ready' in their home towns in anticipation of British attacks — which never came. When the fighting moved to the middle Colonies, Maine men fought at such places as Saratoga and Monmouth. More than a thousand

Maine men served with Washington at Valley Forge. Altogether, over 6000 Maine men fought for their country in the Revolution.

In 1775 the Continental Congress divided Massachusetts into three admiralty districts, of which the northerly, made up of York, Cumberland, and Lincoln Counties, was to be known as the District of Maine. At the declaration of peace in 1783, the St. Croix River became the eastern boundary of this District, and the Indian tribes became wards of the State, no longer possessing any control over the land. Immigration increased and towns were rapidly incorporated. The first town established by the new government was Bath, incorporated in 1781. In 1784 a land office was opened at the seat of government, and State lands on the navigable rivers in the District of Maine were sold to soldiers and immigrants at one dollar an acre. In 1786 more than a million acres of land between the Penobscot and the St. Croix Rivers were disposed of by lottery, the largest purchaser being William Bingham of Philadelphia.

In 1793 a new political alignment resulted from a split in the old parties over the French Revolution and basic principles of government. The Federalists opposed democracy, desiring the rule of the few and conservative rich; the Republicans (or Democrats), adhering to democracy and the town meeting method of government, consisted of the poorer and more radical elements. The District of Maine was a Federalist stronghold until 1805, when the party had become greatly diminished. The land policy of Massachusetts was highly unsatisfactory, tracts already settled by pioneers having been sold or granted to wealthy men or companies. Some owners expelled the squatters; some would neither sell nor lease; in other cases the ownership of the land remained in dispute and no one could give a clear title. Feeling that the Massachusetts Legislature favored the absentee landlords, a majority of voters in the District went Republican during a general democratic movement in 1805.

The growth of population in Maine after the Revolution was rapid — from 96,540 in 1790 to 151,719 in 1800, and 228,705 in 1810. Hancock and Washington Counties in 1789 and Kennebec in 1799 were formed from Lincoln County; Oxford was assembled from parts of York and Cumberland in 1805, and Somerset formed from Kennebec in 1809. During this period many towns were incorporated, including Portland in 1786, built on the site of Falmouth, which had been destroyed in 1775; Bangor in 1791; Augusta in 1797. Plantations were organized as governmental units for taxing groups outside the regular incorporated areas.

The Embargo Law of 1807, forbidding commercial intercourse between the United States and foreign countries, checked the rising tide of Republicanism. Various methods were used to evade the law, and Eastport became notorious as a center for goods smuggled across the Canadian line. When in 1812 the United States declared war on Great Britian, a strong anti-war sentiment existed in Maine, yet the Embargo Laws had so hurt the shipbuilding and fishing industries that there were many enlistments for military service from among Maine's unemployed.

The attempt on England's part to cripple or destroy American commerce without striking a decisive blow at Maine would have been hopeless, and British men-of-war soon appeared along the coast. But they found it no less difficult to prevent her shipyards from launching vessels and to paralyze her commerce than it had been to break the spirit of her patriots during the Revolution. Since the District of Maine, according to American interpretation of the Treaty of 1783, so separated the British provinces that there was no direct trade route between Halifax and Quebec, the English sailed down and occupied the land as far as the Penobscot, made Castine a port of entry, and proclaimed a provincial government between the Penobscot and New Brunswick. But the peace treaty of 1814 left the boundaries between the United States and Canada as they had been before the war. Ownership of the islands in Passamaquoddy Bay was settled in 1817 by a joint commission, the United States receiving Moose, Dudley, and Frederick Islands. Foreign occupation ended in 1815 when the last British troops left Maine soil. In 1817 President Monroe visited Maine and inspected her fortifications, but never since have fortifications been considered necessary on the Canadian border. It seemed too at this time that the United States had little need of warships; the United States vessel ALABAMA, of eighty-four guns, which was laid down at Kittery, was left unfinished on the stocks in 1818.

At the close of the Revolutionary War, the question of separation of Maine from Massachusetts came up repeatedly. Maine's first newspaper, *The Falmouth Gazette,* was devoted to the separation cause. The interests of Maine and Massachusetts were widely divergent; the seat of government was distant, and the expense of justice great; trade regulations were unjust to Maine; many residents in unorganized districts were denied representation in the legislature; the tax system was unbalanced; the District was separated from Massachusetts by New Hampshire; there was a different viewpoint toward national politics, and a desire on the part of Maine to avoid the burden of the State debt. But public opinion was not ready for separation; and the adoption of the United States Constitution in 1787 turned people's thoughts in another direction. Furthermore, the Massachusetts legislature quickly passed acts benefiting Maine's residents. The War of 1812, however, and the Hartford Convention stimulated anew the separation movement. Massachusetts' failure to aid in defending the District during the war had aroused great bitterness, and the State was accused of partiality in educational matters. A separate government would be cheaper. The old objection that statehood would place a heavy burden on the coastal trade was removed in

1819, when Congress passed a law permitting coasters to trade from the St. Croix to Florida without entering and clearing. Party prejudice was less active; the era of good feeling had arrived. Maine separated from Massachusetts in 1819 (at which time she possessed 236 incorporated towns), and was admitted as a State into the Union on March 15, 1820, the seat of government being placed at Portland.

In Maine's early years, the conversion of forest trees into marketable lumber and of woodlands into fields for cultivation was the chief end of labor. Wampum, corn, fish, and other products were mediums of exchange, for real money was scarce. Fishing and the fur trade were the principal early industries. As the fur trade suffered a gradual decline, commerce with the West Indies increased. Lumber was exported there in exchange for molasses, most of which was made into rum, then a popular beverage. Rum, lumber, fish, and furs were exchanged in southern Colonies and abroad for the great number of commodities which Maine did not produce. There was very little manufacturing until the embargo of 1807, when necessity proved to be the father of industry. Maine has, of course, continued to be a predominantly rural State; but even in the early Nineteenth century, farming was often combined with fishing, lumbering, boat-building, and other occupations. The Betterment Act finally ended the turmoil over land titles; since it required that the defeated litigants be reimbursed for all improvements, there were few lawsuits over property rights. Timber continued from earliest days to be Maine's most important raw material. The first sawmill in the United States was built at York in 1623; the first timberland grant of any importance was the Muscongus Grant of 1630, later known as the Waldo Patent; Brunswick, on the Androscoggin, was one of the earliest centers for the lumber business. The forest regions of the Kennebec and the Penobscot soon began to be exploited, but individual and private operations were not displaced by river driving and co-operative enterprise until after the Revolution. With the rise of lumbering, shipbuilding became an important industry. The first transatlantic trader built in the New World was launched by the Popham Colonists in 1608, and by the middle of the Eighteenth century the industry was flourishing.

In the early days, travel in Maine was accomplished by boat or on foot. Roads were only gradually developed, for horse-drawn vehicles were not numerous until the Embargo stimulated the use of stagecoaches. There was little traveling in those days; Maine's people, a sturdy middle class, stayed at home and worked. When not attending to their crops, they were shaving shingles to exchange for goods at the store, working on highways or in the woods, fishing or trapping; the boys did the chores, and the women spun and wove cloth and made the clothing. There were few.

distinctions of rank or wealth. Settlers, both French and English, wished to be allowed to live and work as they chose, to raise their large families in peace.

There was little law or respect for law. Rum was the common beverage, and spirits were consumed on all occasions; the tavern or public house and the church were among the first buildings to be erected in every community. Maine's settlers were at first wholly liberal in their viewpoint, tolerating and even welcoming newcomers of any creed. Under Gorges, the Church of England was dominant; then, with an increased population, Congregationalism and a Puritan movement spread over the land, imposing a rigorous New England code of limited suffrage (only freemen, that is, men of property, could vote), compulsory enlistment in the militia, hidebound conventional morality, prosecution of heresy (Baptists, Quakers, and Jews were to be persecuted and driven from the Colonies), prohibition of games and dancing, and strict regulations for public houses. But the people of Maine were not zealous in enforcing these laws, holding that the keys of Church and State need not necessarily be committed exclusively to the hands of ministers and magistrates. In general, a spirit of religious toleration prevailed, although the church continued always to be the principal center of intellectual and social life. Resentment against support of the church by public taxation resulted in the rise of a variety of Protestant denominations, notably the Baptist and Methodist. The State Constitution of 1820 provided that no public funds raised by taxation could be used for denominational purposes.

Common schools and orthodox ministry went hand in hand, since the Puritans considered a proper education next in importance to godliness. The Bible was the first textbook. From 1788 the State followed a policy of using land and timber wealth as a basis for school aid. Bowdoin College was chartered in 1794, and Waterville (Colby) College in 1820. Until 1820, Maine's public-school system was essentially that of Massachusetts, and since then it has developed gradually along its original lines.

With William King as its first Governor, Maine entered the Union as an anti-Federalist State in 1820. With its agricultural and seafaring population, it was naturally a democratic State. Its growth was rapid; the population increased from 228,705 in 1810 to 501,793 in 1840. The seat of government was removed from Portland to Augusta in 1832. Penobscot County had been formed in 1816. Waldo County was established in 1827, Androscoggin and Sagadahoc Counties in 1854, and Knox County in 1860.

Meanwhile, the northeastern boundary remained unsettled and in dispute. In 1831, Maine refused to accept the compromise solution offered to Great Britian and the United States by the King of the Netherlands.

Repeated minor incidents led finally to the danger of open combat at the boundary; and the State militia in 1839 marched two hundred miles through wilderness and deep snow to repel a threatened attack from New Brunswick. The mediation of General Winfield Scott prevented armed conflict, however, in this 'Aroostook War.' He arranged for a truce and joint occupation by both parties. In 1842, the Webster-Ashburton Treaty settled the fifty-nine-year-old dispute, and lost for Maine about 5500 miles of claimed territory.

Of reform movements influencing the political scene, the least important but the first to take shape was anti-masonry. A temporary triumph of this movement nearly brought about the total disappearance of freemasonry in Maine. In 1831, 1832, and 1833, anti-masonic candidates entered the elections for Governor. There was a revival of the movement in the 1840s, but the anti-slavery agitation soon took its place in the public mind.

Very few Blacks were kept as slaves in Maine even in Colonial days, most of the early Blacks being paid servants. There is no record of any slavery legislation in Maine, either as Province or as State. There had been strong, anti-slavery sentiment in some parts of the District of Maine when it was admitted to the Union as a 'free' State in 1820 under the Missouri Compromise. By 1834 a State anti-slavery society had been formed. Political fireworks were touched off as the Abolitionists and their opponents began to appeal to public opinion. Feeling against the Abolitionists was very strong in the coastal towns, much of whose prosperity depended upon the Southern trade; but in the interior of the State the anti-slavery movement, headed by the clergy, was backed by most persons. Every county had an anti-slavery society, and in 1841 an anti-slavery candidate entered the election for Governor. Since the new movement worked largely through church groups, there was violent protest from both Whigs and Democrats against its entry into politics, since they felt that the Church should keep itself above partisanship. The result was that, although the Whigs were more anti-slavery than the Democrats, anti-slavery men made up a third party, called at first the Liberty Party and later the Free-Soil Party. Between 1850 and 1855, party lines disintegrated over the prohibition and slavery questions. In 1854, the Free-Soilers and the anti-slavery Whigs united to form the Republican Party, which soon swept into power. The Kansas question in all its ramifications proved disastrous to the Democrats. Their failure to take a stand against the extension of slavery further diminished what was left of the Whigs, and the Abolitionists increased rapidly in strength. The Democrats declared that the prosperity of the State depended upon commerce which would certainly suffer if the South were alienated by a Republican triumph; they declared also that if Hannibal Hamlin, the

Republican candidate for Governor, were elected, the fishing bounties would be withdrawn. Nevertheless, the Republicans acquired the seat of power in 1856, and they held it continuously thereafter until 1879. Hamlin, after serving a year as Governor, was elected to the U. S. Senate; and in 1861, Vice-President.

Closely connected with the anti-slavery issue was the prohibition movement. At the time of separation, almost everyone drank liquor, which was sold by the most respectable citizens; but soon regulations against abuses were inaugurated. As early as 1815, a total abstinence society had been formed in Portland, and in 1834 the first convention of temperance societies was held and a State organization formed. A split occurred on whether prohibition should be brought about by legal action or moral influence, and a militant minority for legal action won. In 1846 a law was passed forbidding the sale of spirits except for medicinal and industrial purposes.

The law, however, did not prove effective, or at least it was not well enforced, for illegal traffic in liquors at once made its appearance in all parts of the State. While prohibition was not at first the goal of re-formers, under Neal Dow it was injected into the temperance move-ment and resulted in enactment of the stricter 'Maine Law' of 1851 which prohibited manufacture and sale of intoxicating liquors. The law offended many temperate citizens who felt that private rights were being invaded by the granting of warrants to search parties. A split in the Democratic party over this issue allowed a Whig governor to be elected in 1853. The Maine Law was repealed in 1858. Although attacked by Republicans as discriminatory against the poor, a limited 'sales law per-mitting liquor use as a beverage was passed. In 1862 the Office of State Liquor Commissioner was created. His first report for eight months of that year, noting sales amounting to $24,607.86, said: *It will be seen . . . that the amount of sales to cities and towns in the State falls much below what many professedly expected. This would be a gratifying fact if it warranted the opinion that the use of intoxicating drinks was actually diminishing in this State. However, this clearly is not the case at the present time, and we cannot congratulate ourselves with such a con-clusion. The appalling evils of intemperance are still prevalent among us, nor can we expect it to be otherwise, while so many dram shops are per-mitted to be open and the illegal sale of intoxicating drinks is allowed to go on with so little restraint.*

In the 1850s, the rise of the so-called American or 'Know-Nothing' Party was attended by anti-Catholic and anti-foreign agitation, directed chiefly against the Irish. In 1853 the Roman Catholic See of Maine and New Hampshire was constituted, with the Reverend Daniel Bacon as Bishop. At this time there were only eight priests in the two States. A hostile mob first desecrated and then burned the church at Bath. The Reverend John Bapst, refusing to obey the town meeting's order to leave Ellsworth, was tarred and feathered and ridden out of town on a rail. Bath in 1855 and Bangor in 1856 refused to allow construction on new Catholic church buildings; and the old Baptist church used by the Catholics in Lewiston was burned during a riot there. At Bishop Bacon's death in 1874, however, Catholics residing in Maine numbered over 80,000.

President Lincoln's first call for Civil War volunteers met with quick response in Maine; great public meetings were held, at which support of the National Government was pledged. Yet the outbreak of the war found Maine totally unprepared. The old musters had been abandoned as burdensome and useless occasions for drunkenness and dissipation. The enrolled and unarmed militia comprised about 60,000 men, and in addition there were a few volunteer companies. Nevertheless, Maine contributed thirty-two infantry regiments, three of cavalry, and one heavy artillery regiment, seven batteries of field artillery, seven sharpshooter companies, thirty other companies of infantry, seven companies of coast artillery, and six companies for coast fortifications. In all, 72,945 Maine residents served in the military and naval forces of the Union; and of these, 7322 died in the service. The State's war expenditures were about $7,000,000; while those of towns and individuals were more than $11,000,000. Many towns, feeling they would be shamed if they could not fill their quotas without a draft, bid wildly for recruits and accumulated large debts thereby. The State's commerce suffered greatly from the activities of Confederate cruisers, and companies of home guards were formed to protect the coastal districts from depredations. Two prominent generals of the Civil War were citizens of Maine — General O. O. Howard, who distinguished himself at Gettysburg, and General Joshua L. Chamberlain, later president of Bowdoin College and Governor of Maine.

After the war, the prohibition question continued to be a factor in State politics. The statutes forbidding the sale of intoxicating liquors were extended in 1871 so as to apply to wine and cider. Since the farmers were accustomed to make these lighter beverages from native fruits and berries, the Democrats hoped to use the law to turn rural districts against the Republicans. But the prohibition and total abstinence movement was continually growing, and the Democrats failed once more. It is significant, however, that the constitutional amendment passed in 1884 forbidding the manufacture of intoxicating liquors exempts cider from its list.

This amendment, virtually a re-enactment of the Maine Law of 1851, endured for fifty years. The late 1890s saw the rise of the Women's Christian Temperance Union of which a Maine native, Mrs. Lillian M. N. Stevens of Dover, was national president for sixteen years. Enforcement of the law, always difficult, was never achieved and it was repealed in 1934 after repeal· in 1933 of the Eighteenth Amendment to the Federal Constitution (Volstead Act). A three-man State Liquor Commission was created in 1934 employing the State control system. Its report in 1939 said: *Spirituous and vinous liquors have been used since the early history of the human race. Wines have always played an important part in the rituals of religious orders. Greek and Roman mythology indicate very strongly that liquors were well known and used to a considerable degree. It would appear that just so long as spirituous and vinous liquors can be manufactured, they will be consumed and that no laws which are or may be enacted are susceptible of enforcement which will prohibit their use* . . . *The principal arguments for (legalization) were first, for better control, and second to furnish the public liquors of good quality at a reasonable price. It is hard to realize that the people of this State are spending so much for spirituous beverages; however, the fact remains that during prohibition and before, large sums were spent surreptitiously for 'bootleg' and smuggled liquor.* This referred to the days of bath-tub gin and rum-running off the Maine coast. The report noted that *liquor is taxed for all the traffic it will bear* as demands for State revenue increased. In 1968 State liquor tax revenues amounted to $15,845,000 — or 6.8 percent of total operating revenues. Anti-liquor forces were represented by the Christian Civic League. A Sunday liquor sales bill was voted in 1969.

The growing tide of emigration from the State assumed sufficiently serious proportions in the late 1860s to arouse concern for Maine's future among some of her leading citizens. Determined to make a serious venture in home colonization, the State legislature commissioned the Honorable William W. Thomas, Jr., a former United States Consul in Sweden, to go to that country and bring back a party of settlers. Thomas returned from Sweden in 1870 with fifty-one persons, who immediately set about the development of a tract set aside for them by the State and given the name of New Sweden. In less than a year, the population of the district was doubled by other Swedes who came of their own accord to join the group; and by the end of three years, the original population of New Sweden had increased twelve-fold.

During the 1870s, many Maine cities and towns suffered financially from an enthusiasm for internal improvements which had been sweeping the nation since 1830. The result was a constitutional amendment severely limiting the total debit which any municipality might incur. A State organization of the national Greenback Party was formed, and nominated a candidate for Governor in 1876 and 1877. So quickly did the new party win popular favor with its stand against the resumption of specie payments and its plea for a cheap currency that the gubernatorial campaign of 1878 was fought on this issue. The Greenbackers were especially strong in the eastern counties, the majority of independent Democrats and many Republicans being drawn into the party. A great oratorical display persuaded many of the farmers that they were being abused and plundered by the moneyed interests; and with their aid the Democrats, having temporarily formed an alliance with the Greenbackers, carried the State for the first time in many years.

The next year, 1879, there was no election by popular vote. Governor Alonzo Garcelon and his council, accused of manipulating election returns so as to secure a fusion majority in the legislature, were declared in error by the State Supreme Court and the Republicans seized the legislative chambers and chose a governor from their own ranks. Although its candidate won the governorship in the next election, the fusion tide had ebbed and the State returned almost completely to the Republican fold.

Maine suffered greatly in the severe depression of the 1890s. The Spanish War drew one infantry regiment, four batteries of field artillery, and a signal corps, besides many individual enlistments in the regular army and navy, from Maine; and volunteer naval reserve associations were mustered for national service. A Republican victory in 1908 on the prohibition issue resulted in strict enforcement; but in 1910 the Democrats won for the first time in thirty-two years. Yet in 1911, a proposed amendment to repeal the prohibitory laws was defeated, though only by a very close margin. The adoption in 1911 of a direct primary law was due mainly to a new progressive movement which also placed on the statute books the initiative and referendum and a corrupt practices act; no longer were 'ring' and 'anti-ring' to struggle for party control, nominating conventions and picking political plums. In 1911 also, much valuable social welfare legislation was enacted.

Another Democratic victory came in 1914, when there was a division in the Republican Party between regulars and progressives — a phenomenon to occur again in 1932 and 1954. A consolidation of Maine's leading newspapers in 1921 left the State with virtually no Democratic press. Political contests again became largely confined to the Republican primaries.

Following the United States' entry into World War I, more than 35,000 Maine men joined the fighting services. An unknown number had already entered the war as members of Canadian units. Nearly $116 million in war loans and other contributions was raised in the State. National Guard units were recruited to full strength, the naval militia was mobilized, a Home Guard was organized. The Governor was empowered to take in the State's name any land desirable for military use. Municipalities were required to raise money to aid families of men in military service, the State providing for reimbursement of all money thus spent.

Maine's casualties in World War I were 2094; deaths from all sources numbered 1073, with 228 killed in action.

Political awareness of the importance of Maine's water-power resources dawned with the Twentieth century. Controversy began in 1909 with legislation prohibiting export of hydro-electricity on the theory that power thus held would attract industry that otherwise might settle elsewhere. An effort to strengthen this law in 1917 divided the Republican party, a split that resulted in the fight for and against the direct primary. In the 1920s, politicians constantly attacked the 'Insullization' of public utilities. Joining the fray was a Democratic newspaper published in Portland and edited by Dr. Ernest C. Gruening, later Secretary of the Department of Interior and Governor of and U. S. Senator from Alaska. By 1929 the issue subsided when by popular vote Maine decided to remain the only state in which chartered companies were forbidden to export hydro-electric power. Revived again in the 1950s during the first administration of Governor Edmund S. Muskie, the so-called Fernald law finally was repealed.

Power again became a controversial subject in the 1960s with proposals for developing public power attracting state and national attention and vigorous opposition from private power companies such as those controlling the Maine system. At issue was cheaper power for Maine whose consumers pay among the highest rates in the country. The Passamaquoddy tidal project introduced during the early days of FDR's New Deal, had sporadic support, was revived during the Kennedy administration only to be set aside again. More recently the Dickey-Lincoln proposal for the St. John-Allagash area generated support of those who believe it offers cheaper power than private utility companies can afford for both industry and rural electrification.

Maine again suffered greatly in the depression of the 1930s. During the relief period, WPA took care of some ten thousand unemployed when the total number of families without a means of livelihood was estimated at 22,000. Aid came through the Farm Credit Administration, the Agricultural Adjustment Act and other Federal programs. However, domestic goals of the Democratic party were at variance with those of the people of Maine, a factor that may have contributed to the decline of the state party during the remaining terms of Roosevelt and Truman.

Cooperating with Federal agencies during World War II, Maine made an impressive record in shipbuilding, at low ebb before the Japanese attack on Pearl Harbor. The New England Shipbuilding Corporation at South Portland turned out a total of 234 Liberty ships and seven wooden barges. The Kittery Naval complex produced 71 submarines and many torpedo testing barges. At the Bath Iron Works, 64 high-speed super-destroyers and two large cargo vessels were built, while at smaller yards on Mount Desert, in Rockland, Camden and the Boothbay-Bristol area a total of 947 smaller craft were built for auxiliary purposes, from coastal minesweepers to buoy boats. Other industries, lumber, textiles, shoes, paper, foundries, turned to, producing a flow of wartime necessities, and agricultural effort was increased to meet military demands for food. No Maine town was untouched by local draft boards for military services. An estimated 93,000 Maine men and women served in all theatres. For direct or indirect cause in all branches, Maine sacrificed 2563 lives, more than double the losses of World War I.

In 1932, Louis J. Brann became Maine's first Democratic governor in eighteen years, serving two terms. But intra-party strife soon returned State government to the Republicans who carried on during the crucial decade of the 1940s and World War II. Those years saw the rise to national prominence of Maine's U. S. Senator Margaret Chase Smith. In 1954 Republican dominance of state politics again was broken with the gubernatorial election of Edmund S. Muskie, leader of a younger Democratic group who have had notable success in reactivating the two-party system in the State. Muskie, elected to the United States Senate in 1958, also emerged as a national figure, becoming his party's vice presidential candidate in 1968. Since his governorship, voters have elected two Democratic governors, Clinton Clauson who died in office and Kenneth M. Curtis (incumbent 1969), and one Republican, John H. Reed, first to serve a full four-year term. Democrats, controlling the 102nd Legislature under a Republican governor, enacted a progressive program reflecting postwar changes. In 1966 when Democrats won the governorship and both Congressional seats, Republicans regained control of the legislature. In 1969, the 104th Legislature, faced with budgetary problems involving expanding state services, enacted Maine's first income tax.

Since World War II, Maine, never a financially wealthy state, has reflected the accelerating social and economic changes of the nuclear age. There has been progress in many fields. There are many problems to be met in the last half of the Twentieth century — even as the pioneers met theirs in earlier times. There are contrasts of poverty and affluence; of environmental deterioration and conservation; of rural decay and urban redevelopment; of housing shortages and architectural innovation; of social needs and cultural development.

Civil rights and anti-war demonstrations in Maine have not been marked so far by the riots and violence of the big city ghettoes and college campuses in other states.

Some dislocation has occurred in the textile and shoe industries, while variety and diversification is apparent in many new industries. Electronics has revolutionized communications, particularly in remote areas. A State-Federal road building program and air facilities have advanced transport.

Education has advanced and some progress has been made in better use of natural resources.

There has been an exodus of Maine youth many of whom have yet to recognize the challenges at home. At the same time, Maine always has contributed many outstanding talents to the country at large. While there are manifestations of youth's bewilderment in the mid-Twentieth century such as drug use and the like, most realize they have a contribution to make in solving today's problems for their world of tomorrow. Youth is given more voice in education and other areas. Governor Kenneth M. Curtis named a University of Maine student to the State Board of Education; other organizations are following suit. Young people are active not only in politics and the arts but also are concerned with welfare and other civic problems.

Today the State of Maine, 150 years old in 1970, is conservative but not necessarily reactionary. Her restless youth is vocal but less violent than some. A popular belief that Maine people are slow to change perhaps today is a misinterpretation of their tendency to hold to proven values. Maine people are interested in reforms — if they are not too costly. Although traditionally Republican, liberal and radical elements often have taken over the party; for example, the Greenbackers in 1879 and the Progressives in 1912. LaFollette in 1924 picked up six percent of the Presidential vote. More recently, Maine favored Eisenhower over Robert Taft. Barry Goldwater utterly failed to carry the State in 1964 and many voters favored Nelson Rockefeller over Nixon.

Situated as Maine is geographically in relation to Canada and Europe, her people have been anything but isolationist in terms of national policy. Their lands twice invaded by the British and before that, for almost a hundred years the battleground of the French and English in their struggle for power on the North American continent, Maine people have learned from history the values of international cooperation and friendship.

STATE GOVERNMENT

Maine's original Constitution of 1820 has not yet had a major revision. It grants wide powers to the Legislature, definitely curtails the Governor's power by creation of a seven man Executive Council, and limits the power of the Judiciary to seven-year terms.

The Governor is limited to two consecutive four-year terms; he is the only official elected by popular vote. While only two other states, Massachusetts and New Hampshire retain the Council, efforts to abolish it in Maine have not been successful thus far (1969). The Council is elected biennially by a joint ballot of both houses of the Legislature; its members therefore are not necessarily of the same political party as the Governor. Thus a problem may arise when the Council is asked for consent to a major appointment. Maine has no lieutenant-governor; the president of the Senate succeeds to the governorship in case of vacancy. The Legislature elects four department heads: Secretary of State, Treasurer, Auditor and Attorney General. Others are appointed by the Governor and Council.

Maine women were the first to exercise their franchise in 1920 when the 79th Maine Legislature by a 72-68 vote ratified the Nineteenth Federal Amendment. Although there had been agitation for female suffrage since the Civil War, attempts to get favorable State legislation failed repeatedly until Congress acted in 1919. At the National American Suffrage Association's final convention that year, a League of Women Voters was formed with Maud Wood Parks of Cape Elizabeth as its first national president.

Elections are held biennially on the Tuesday following the first Monday of November of even-numbered years. A plurality vote is necessary for election.

The Legislature meets biennially at the State Capitol in Augusta on the first Wednesday of January. It has been reapportioned and complies with the U. S. Supreme Court's mandate of 'one man, one vote.' The thirty-two senators are chosen by districts which in some cases cross county lines. The House has 151 members but they are not elected from single member districts. The joint standing committees of the two Houses expedite legislative hearings which are well-attended by the public. As state government has become big business with frequent necessity for special sessions, annual sessions as well as overhaul of outdated legislative machinery have been urged. A Legislative Research Committee composed of members of both houses studies matters referred to it by the Legislature.

The State's judiciary system is headed by a Supreme Court with a Chief and five Associate Justices. The Superior Courts of the sixteen counties are served by ten circuit justices. In 1961 the State created a new District Court system replacing municipal courts. The thirteen Districts are served by eighteen judges. Judges are appointed by the Governor and Council except probate judges who are elected by popular vote in each county.

The state government, according to New England tradition, exercises relatively little power over the towns and cities; home rule is jealously guarded by municipalities, though a move toward regionalism is seen in the establishment of school districts and certain other cooperative ventures as towns reach the limits of their borrowing power to meet public service demands, with the property tax reaching the saturation point. The Town in New England (known elsewhere as the township) is the important political unit. Since no minimum population requirement for the incorporation of cities exists in Maine, many towns are larger than the twenty-one cities.

The government of the towns through the medium of the town meeting, has been called the only existing type of 'pure' democracy, though challenged by some political scientists, who see its ultimate demise. Many cite dwindling interest and attendance and the dangers of corruption through minority rule. Many of Maine's cities and towns have accepted the council-manager or town manager form of government. The city or town council is the general authority, except for an independent school committee, with a specially trained executive manager or administrator.

In thinly settled, undeveloped areas, the organized plantation form exists for governing and taxing. But in large central and northern areas with insufficient population to warrant this form, the state controls these unorganized townships. The Forestry Department maintains wardens and lookout stations in these areas. A Department of Indian Affairs supervises Maine's two Indian reservations since they, unlike others, are not under Federal jurisdiction.

INDUSTRY

RAPID technological developments in the last half of the Twentieth century presage profound changes in the predominately forested and agricultural State of Maine where exploitation of water power has been a major factor in industrial development. In the 1960s diversification had become the hallmark of this development and heavy industry had become a prospect. In 1967 the value of all manufactures was estimated at $2.2 billion led by pulp and paper, food, leather, and textiles. Exports were valued at $70,000,000.

The 1968 monthly employment average was 377,780. Of these, 126,380 were in manufacturing in some 2270 establishments. Largest employment source was in wholesale and retail trades, 61,500. Second largest was Federal, State and local government, 53,100; about 56 percent are in local government and of these, 63 percent are in education. Local government employment has increased nearly three times as much as State government. The third largest employment group is services, 39,900; fourth, self-employed, 38,700 which has decreased by 6,000 since 1960 when it was the second largest source. Fifth largest source is leather, the largest source of manufacturing employment with 30,732.

In Maine as well as nationally there is more non-manufacturing than manufacturing employment. In 1968 Maine had an employment ratio of 1.6 non-manufacturing jobs for every manufacturing job. In the last decade the creative ratio has been 2.5. Economists estimate the trend toward more non-manufacturing jobs will continue.

There has been some out-migration of Maine labor to large industrial centers and some instances of labor import under certain conditions to meet special needs. Relatively few strikes have marred labor relations. One of the few women in the country to hold such office, Miss Marion E. Martin has served as Maine's Labor Commissioner for many years. Associated Industries of Maine represent management; most labor is unionized. In 1969, the 104th Legislature established a minimum wage of $1.60 per hour.

A 1969 analysis of the New England economy attributed Maine's relatively slow growth in comparison with sister states largely to extensive reliance upon slower growing employment sectors such as paper, leather and textiles, Maine being principally in the extractive activities, agriculture and forestry. Advent of so-called growth industries was expected to accelerate the State's economy, with due consideration for environmental features and natural resources that have made Maine a 'recreation' state.

WATER POWER

Although methods and facilities of early times seem simple in the nuclear age, amazing and ingenious use of falling water was made beginning in the Seventeenth century. First were the tide mills for grinding grain and sawing lumber. With the development of lumber, paper, textile and other industries, hydraulic engineers designed dams and canals with water wheels connected to long drive shafts through belts and pulleys to utilize power at industrial sites. Development of electric power made it possible to generate and transmit power wherever needed. As industry moved into the Twentieth century, hydro-electric power was emphasized. More dams were constructed for power generation and storage; watershed reforestation and flood control programs were initiated.

New techniques and improved generating equipment make for constantly changing power production conditions to meet demands that increase six to twelve percent annually, and to assure adequate reserves. In 1968 power generation from all sources was 4,324 billion kilowatts. There were 4,233,286,000 energy sales to 404,472 consumers; residential consumption was twice industrial. Steam generation (2,557 billion kW) supplied by thermal generating stations currently exceeds hydro-electric power generation (1,713 billion kW). Utilities and industries also use diesel engines and gas turbines. Maine receives a share of power from the Yankee Atomic Electric Company plant in Massachusetts, can draw from New Hampshire if necessary and will have a power link with Canada on completion of a 345,000 volt transmission line between Fredericton, N. B. and Wiscasset. The line will join the Big Eleven Loop composed of Maine Yankee and ten other utility companies to serve the northeast. The Maine Yankee Atomic nuclear steam electric generating plant of Wiscasset, largest in Maine, is expected to be in operation by 1973.

In the 1930s, Walter W. Wyman, then president of New England Power Service Company envisioned high pressure steam, high speed turbines and something very like nuclear power. One of his innovations was this country's first attempt to furnish portable power, with the conversion of a cargo vessel to a power ship. The JACONA, 396 feet, 5,238 gross tons, built in 1919, was converted into a floating power plant at a cost of a million dollars, two-thirds the cost of a land plant of similar capacity. With two 10,000 kW steam turbine generators and four high pressure water tube boilers, it had 20,000 kW capacity and began operating in November 1930 at Bucksport at the Maine Seaboard Paper Company, now the St. Regis. Portsmouth, N. H. became the first city on the Atlantic coast to receive 'floating' power when the ship was towed there in April 1931. She went on war duty in the Pacific in 1945. Whether the JACONA has survived should be of interest to industries or museums concerned with power history.

A state-wide super power system is controlled by three major private companies from whom thirteen smaller ones buy their power. There are three R. E. A. co-operatives. Revenues in 1967 were $82,124,000 from 3,818 billion energy sales to 397,059 consumers. Typical rates were $8.59 per 250 kW hours; $21.34 per 1000. Highest rates are in Alaska, $10.16 per 250 kW hours, $24.03 per 1000; New York, $9.02 and $24.16. Lowest are in Tennessee, $4.67 and $9.36; and Washington, $4.78 and $9.63.

Public power proposals such as the long-projected great Passamaquoddy development to utilize unusual tidal pools and a 20-foot average tidal fall, and more recent proposals including the Lincoln-Dickey dam project in Aroostook County had not materialized in 1969.

FISHERIES

The story of industry in Maine, antedating that of settlement by many years, begins with fishing in that vague age of adventure and exploration along the Atlantic seaboard prior to the Seventeenth century. Searchers for the wealth of the Indies also were aware of the commercial possibilities of fishing. Early settlers exploited these possibilities along with shipbuilding and lumbering, the latter continuing its dominance in the Maine economy.

Supplying some of the State's earliest and most important exports, Maine's oldest industry, the fisheries, greatly influenced later commercial development. Problems of fisheries and fishing rights have been involved in the State's international and interstate negotiations throughout its history. Captain John Smith, who carefully noted the variety of fish found here, established fisheries on Monhegan in 1614. Governor Winslow in 1622 reported thirty ships of different nationalities at Monhegan and Damariscove, most of them taking on fish cargoes. Even before the Revolution, Maine was exporting thousands of tons of fish to Europe and the West Indies. Between 1820-26, the State produced approximately one fifth of the total United States fish tonnage. With minor economic fluctuations the fisheries consistently stimulated Maine commerce throughout the Nineteenth century.

Fisheries reached a production peak of 242 million pounds in 1902. Although the industry then continued to increase in other North Atlantic states, its decline in Maine was attributed to the decline of the salted fish business, to the slow development of new handling and merchandising methods, to transportation and tariff difficulties and to periods of scarcity of certain kinds of fish. River dams and industrial pollution affected the supply of such migratory fish as salmon and alewives that seek fresh water to spawn. Clam-flats also were polluted. The supply of lobsters, scallops and clams was seriously depleted by reckless harvesting methods and natural causes.

Some recovery was seen with the advent of mechanical equipment, advances in biological research and food technology, improved transportation and diversification of seafood products. In 1968, landings of fish and shellfish in Maine ports were 218.7 million pounds valued at $25.6 million, and employing some 9,000 persons. Maine processors were operating freezing and packing plants producing a variety of seafoods, shipping nationwide and to foreign countries. These include the famous Maine lobster (Homarus americanus) which delicacy in 1969 was a costly item on Maine menus. Maine supplies the largest amount of lobsters on the Atlantic coast equalled only by the combined landings of Nova Scotia and New Brunswick. Peak landing was 24..4 million in 1957. The annual catch in 1968 was 20.5 million pounds, with a new value record of $15 million.

Trapping is the only means for inshore lobstering and only lobsters that meet the Maine size limitations may be sold in Maine. Inshore lobster decline has been attributed to overfishing, sea temperature cycles and pollution of coastal fishing areas. Experiments are being conducted to see if lobsters can be economically raised and bred in captivity.

Until the 1960s Maine's principal lobster and herring operations were in inshore waters. Now operations reach nearly 200 miles out — for lobsters, around and beyond the 100 fathom curve of the continental shelf where a big lobster could weigh thirty pounds. Biggest lobsters are found in dragging operations in the Corsair off the Georges Banks. Offshore trawling took six million pounds in 1968.

The Maine Sardine Association, one of the few such groups in the country, maintains a technical staff at Brewer for research and development. Sardine packing was producing about 120 million cans annually in the 1960s. Other commercially important fish among 38 edible varieties are alewives, cod, cusk, hake, haddock and ocean perch (in short supply), mackerel, halibut, pollock, crabs, clams, shrimp and mussels.

Shrimp landings of 14.4 million pounds valued at $1.6 million in 1968 more than doubled the previous record in 1967. The marine worm industry yielded 1.5 million pounds valued at $1.6 million. New uses for fish by-products are being added to such products as fish meal, medicinal oils, pharmaceutical chemicals, pet foods, fertilizer, industrial lubricants, glue and pearl essence. Principal fishing ports are Portland, Rockland, Eastport, Lubec, Jonesport, McKinley, Vinalhaven, Sebasco, Port Clyde and Southwest, Boothbay and New Harbors.

Adjacent to over 200,000 square acres of the world's finest fishing territory, Maine has unexcelled resources in the bounty of the sea. The fishing industry works closely with the West Boothbay laboratories of the U. S. Bureau of Commercial Fisheries established in 1947 to study the mysteries of the Gulf of Maine and to develop the best methods of sea 'farming.' A staff of 48 with four research vessels is engaged in the various aspects of marine biology and their records are used by many scientists. The Maine Department of Sea and Shore Fisheries whose film *Harvest of the Sea* won a national award, works closely with the Bureau and maintains an aquarium on the Boothbay property. Many varieties of fish and other marine life may be seen here and in picturesque villages along Maine's sea-sculptured coast when fishermen bring in their catch.

SHIPBUILDING

From the very outset, Maine shipbuilding, closely allied with fishing, lumbering and commerce, has had a distinguished history, dating from 1607 when the short-lived Popham Colony built the little pynnace VIRGINIA at the mouth of the Kennebec River. Waterways were the early roadsteads and ships were a necessity that evolved into the great maritime tradition from the days of sail to ships of steel. John Winter who established a shipyard on Richmond Island in 1642 may be called the pioneer in American shipbuilding for the export trade, for his vessels engaged in carrying lumber, fish oil and other commodities to England. Contract shipbuilding is identified with the city of Bath since it was inaugurated there in 1762 by Captain William Swanton; he and others received contracts from Spain, France and the West Indies.

By 1790 ships were being built all along the coast and up the principal rivers. Although checked by the effect of embargoes, one third of the total tonnage in the United States in 1812 was Maine-built and for half a century afterwards the State led all others in the shipbuilding industry. In the 1830s Maine built more tonnage than any other state; and from 1841 to 1857, the period when Bath became America's leading shipbuilding city, this was its most important industry. Of the 428 ships, barks and brigs built in America in 1848, Maine supplied more than half. Shipbuilding was the chief industry in some fifty coastal towns, supporting 200,000 persons.

There was good reason that Maine led the nation in volume of tonnage during most of the Nineteenth century. Wood, in one form or another, was the principal thing that Maine had to offer in exchange for what it wanted from outside. Trees not only could be fashioned into boards, planks, shingles and hogshead staves, but also, even more profitably, into vessels that could carry off such cargoes. The long jagged coastline offered innumerable opportunities for this, with oak for the hulls and pine or fir for the masts close at hand. This meant that vessels could be built about one-third cheaper than in England where timber had to be brought from a distance. The English navigation laws insisted upon English ships in many trades, but they counted vessels built on Casco Bay or the Kennebec as English as those from the Thames or the Mersey. A colonist, with almost no capital outlay except for ironware, sailcloth and cordage, could build his little vessel from his own oaks and pines, cut up more of those trees as a lumber cargo, peddle that in the West Indies and then sell island sugar along with the vessel over in England. At the outbreak of the Revolution, about one-third of all vessels in British registry had been built in America.

The Revolution ended that practice, but the long Anglo-French wars, starting in 1793, with the rich chances for Neutral trade, gave Maine shipbuilding a lively boost all along the coast. Even when things quieted down after that, there still was a fairly substantial output. Some of the vessels were little single-masted sloops, some were two-masted fore-and-aft schooners, and some were medium-sized two-masted square-rigged brigs. Some of the smaller vessels engaged in fishing but many others carried out Maine lumber cargoes to swap along the coast or in the West Indies.

Maine's real distinction, however, began around 1840 with the demand for big three-masted square-rigged ships and barks. During the next half century it produced more of them than any other state. Most of the crack Black Ballers and other transatlantic packets came from the expensive East River yards at New York, but the bulk of the general cargo carriers came from Maine yards. During the 1840s and '50s various outside causes combined to stimulate the 'golden age' of American sail. Maine ships already were carrying much of the South's cotton to Europe, but now women's styles, with the flaring skirts supplemented by a half dozen petticoats were a 'style that launched a thousand ships' with the increased demand for cotton. On top of that, the potato famine brought swarms of starving Irish to America, followed closely by large numbers of

GLIMPSES OF HISTORY

INTEREST in our forebears, the people who settled America, and how they lived, is seen in the restoration and preservation of historic sites and houses being carried on in Maine and the visitation at these sites and historical museums with their collections of memorabilia found in every county. Open to visitors are several coastal forts restored by the State Park and Recreation Commission, and many museums and houses of the more than 125 historical societies in the State. York's Old Gaol Museum is one of the oldest public buildings in the country and Montpelier, the Knox Mansion replica at Thomaston, is one of the best known State-owned historic houses.

FIRST NAVAL BATTLE OF THE REVOLUTION

FUR-TRADER TREAT'S TRUCKHOUSE, BANGOR

FORT HALIFAX AT WINSLOW, AMERICA'S OLDEST REMAINING BLOCKHOUSE

AMERICA'S FIRST WATER-POWER DEVELOPMENT, SOUTH BERWICK

FORT WESTERN AT AUGUSTA

OLD GAOL MUSEUM AT YORK

POWNALBOROUGH COURTHOUSE AT DRESDEN

MONTPELIER, KNOX MANSION REPLICA AT THOMASTON

FORT KNOX AT PROSPECT

HEMLOCK COVERED BRIDGE AT FRYEBURG

OLD KATAHDIN IRON WORKS AND KILN RESTORATION

ISLESBORO LIGHTHOUSE

MT. KINEO, FOR 5000 YEARS THE SOURCE OF
RAW MATERIALS FOR INDIAN STONE TOOLS.

BLAINE HOUSE, HOME OF MAINE GOVERNORS AT AUGUSTA

LADY PEPPERRELL HOUSE AT KITTERY POINT

KITTERY HOUSE AT ELIOT

HANNIBAL HAMLIN HOUSE AT SOUTH PARIS

BROOKSVILLE'S OLDEST HOUSE

PEABODY TAVERN AT GILEAD

BIG MOXIE
FALLS,
ARNOLD'S
MARCH
SITE, 1755

BAILEY ISLAND COB WORK BRIDGE

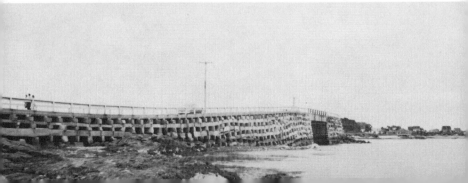

COURTHOUSE AT ALFRED

Germans. That called for many big immigrant ships, and return cargo for them came from England's repeal of her protective corn laws, permitting the importation of American grain. In 1849, moreover, England repealed her navigation laws and once again, as in Colonial times, American ships could be sold in England. Finally, there was the gold rush in California which led to the brief glamorous period of the clippers in which carrying capacity was sacrificed for speed. This was one field in which Maine lagged behind; of some 350 ships recognized as real clippers, Boston built 140, New York 53 and Maine 54, including the RED JACKET from Rockland and the PHOENIX from Cape Elizabeth, South Portland; both made distinctive speed records.

The combined impact of all those shipping demands boosted the national total of new tonnage from 118,000 in 1840 to 583,000, a figure not equalled again until 1917. Maine was in the lead with 215,000 tons in 1855. Its lead was particularly impressive in the big square-rigged vessels, with 213 of the 381 ships and barks, and 107 of the 126 brigs.

Maine's shipbuilding capacity was of tremendous value to the Northern naval effort in the Civil War, with the colossal task of blockading the entire Federal coast. The single customs district of Bath on the Kennebec in 1860 produced more tonnage than that of the whole southern coast from North Carolina around to Texas. The 1860 census showed that Maine had 1982 ship carpenters, 120 riggers, 40 rope-makers, 261 sail-makers, 56 mast-makers, 64 block-makers and 196 boat builders.

The Maine yards turned out numerous gunboats and other naval vessels. In addition to the private yards, important shipbuilding came from the Navy yard that took its name from Portsmouth, New Hampshire, though actually located in Kittery, Maine. Even before that yard had started in 1806, the locality had built two warships for the English around 1690 and also John Paul Jones' RANGER in the Revolution. The yard's most celebrated Civil War product was the cruiser, KEARSAGE, that sank the Confederate raider, ALABAMA.

American shipbuilding slumped into a long 'Dark Ages' period after the Civil War, with foreign steamships taking over much of our export and import. Maine, however, was a remarkable exception, producing two successful types of wooden sailing vessels in what has been called its 'Indian summer.' The yards at Bath and elsewhere produced a special type of big square-rigger that flourished in the 1870s and '80s. Known as 'Down Easters,' these ships were a sort of modified clipper, with greater carrying capacity than the original clippers, yet sharing much of their speed and beauty. Down Easters ranged far and wide on the distant longer sea lanes, especially in carrying grain from the West coast around Cape Horn to Europe. Outstanding in this capacity were Bath's Sewall yards that not only built a huge tonnage but also owned and operated the ships. In 1893, the last American square-rigger, the ship ARYAN, was launched at the Minott yards at Phippsburg on the Kennebec.

By that time, as the Down Easters were being phased out, Maine was developing another distinctive type, the big schooner. Whereas the square-rigger was best on the long sea routes, the schooner had two advantages in the protected coastwise trades. It could operate with less danger of being driven ashore and it required a much smaller crew. The first of the numerous four-masters was built at Bath in 1880; these vessels were useful for carrying Kennebec ice southward, bringing back southern pine timber. In 1888 came the first five-master, followed by the first six-master in 1900. During the next ten years these big vessels specialized in carrying soft coal from Hampton Roads to Boston, Portland and other New England ports.

World War I saw the last important use of sailing vessels. The British and German steamships that had handled most of our foreign commerce were no longer available; ports in Latin America, Africa, Asia and Australia needed American goods but there were no ships to transport them. Freight rates soared; old schooners were restored to service and new ones built. By 1917, with submarine sinkings causing grave alarm, the United States undertook a huge shipbuilding program which would bring the merchant marine back to the seas in force. In this emergency fleet, Maine yards built a few wooden steamships and a few steel ones, but most of the new freighters came from distant yards. Their advent marked the end for the wooden sailing vessels that had made Maine shipbuilding so distinctive. In World War II, emergency yards at South Portland and the Bath yards turned out many steel Liberty ships.

By the mid-Twentieth century Maine shipbuilding was reflecting a new era. The Bath Iron Works which for years had produced U. S. Navy destroyers, became the lead yard for the design and construction of guided missile frigates, destroyers and their escorts and was bidding on other huge government contracts. The Kittery Navy Yard (Maine always called it that), though scheduled for phase-out, had specialized in construction and repair of submarines and had built the first nuclear submarine. Rising popularity of pleasure boating brought business to scores of yards building, repairing and storing the small craft frequenting Maine waters in summer. Sail had a comeback of sorts in the racing and sailing yachts 'fair to the wind' in Maine waters.

From fishing smacks, dredges and pinkies to million dollar yachts and America's Cup winners, practically every kind of craft known along the Atlantic seaboard has been built in Maine, even to such curious vessels as the St. John wood-boats which carried wood to be burned in lime kilns. Squat and broad, with no bowsprit or overhanging stern, and having a single deckhouse and an exposed rudder, these craft used to skim into port with their decks piled so high with lumber that they often were several inches awash. Nor were all vessels built in the ordered efficiency of the shipyards. Many were constructed far inland in the midst of the lumber supply. One thirty-ton vessel, comparable in size to the VIRGINIA or Columbus' PINTA, was built in 1830 on Megunticook Mountain in Camden and had to be hauled more than six miles over the ice of Megunticook Lake and River to Penobscot Bay, there to be placed in the fishing and lime coasting trade.

Marine Museums at Bath and Searsport and collections in coastal historical society museums tell the story of Maine's maritime heritage.

LUMBERING AND ALLIED INDUSTRIES

Cornerstone of Maine's economy for 300 years, lumbering has had a varied and interesting history in three major phases in the Pine Tree State since the first sawmill was built in York County, in the Seventeenth century. Although forests have been cut back from the coast and Maine contributed a large share of the nation's lumber for decades, there still are 17,245,000 acres of forest covering 87 percent of the State's land area. Maine's forests have been called the last great wildland frontier of the East; 98.8 percent of this acreage is privately owned. Improved conservation methods and management techniques by lumber interests and the State Forestry Service seem to assure a continuing timber supply. Multiple use contributes to growth and other natural resource values of water, recreation and wildlife. With increased demand for vacation homes 'back to nature,' several companies have undertaken recreational developments on their lands.

The first phase of lumber operations, undertaken by individuals and partners, lasted until 1820; the second phase of corporation, lumbering associations and the river-drives between 1820 and 1880, was followed by the present mass-production phase, largely influenced by the growth of the paper industry, with bankers and large corporations in control.

Climate and topography, an extensive system of waterways, quantities of raw material, and cheap transportation all played their part in the development of Maine lumbering. Many of the State's industrial centers and transportation systems were established to meet the needs of this industry. Lumber and lumbering also have figured prominently in Maine's history. Resentment against the policy of reserving the best timber for the British Navy prior to the Revolution provoked ill feeling, aroused agitation and resulted in open disputes in such towns as Bath and Portland. Speculation in timberlands brought on the State's financial panic in 1835, anticipating the nationwide panic by two years, and doing much to determine Maine's subsequent land policies. The international controversy that resulted in the Aroostook War was fundamentally a dispute regarding lumbering rights along the northeastern boundary.

The early explorers were impressed by the size and extent of the Maine timberlands. Later, the Popham Colonists reported that there were 'fish in the season in great plenty all along the coast, mastidge for ships; goodly oaks, and cedars with infinite other sorts of trees.' Lumbering and sawmill operations were active at Berwick and York before 1640, and the export of timber began almost immediately. Cutting timber for shipbuilding and masts, particularly for the Royal Navy, became a distinct industry in itself. Mast ways,' or lanes carefully prepared and cleared of obstructions to prevent injury to the forest giants, were cut through the woods; and a special type of vessel capable of carrying as many as five hundred masts at a time, was constructed for their transportation. Pine, which remained king of the forests and the lumber industry until it began to be replaced in importance by spruce after the Civil War, was abundant and in great demand.

Early lumbering, like all other Colonial industries, was affected by a population rendered unstable as a result of Indian warfare. By the Eighteenth century, however, the lumber and mast trade in northern New England gradually had become centered about Portland and the Saco River basin. In Colonial times, lumber often was used as currency, and as late as 1840 shingles were used as a medium of exchange by the Aroostook settlers. The industry spread from river to river, north and northeast. Operations along the Androscoggin, which declined because of the difficulty of the 'drive' in that region, centered at Brunswick by the first quarter of the Nineteenth century. Lumbermen moved on to the Kennebec and then to the Penobscot basin, the latter becoming the State's greatest timber reservoir during the industry's heyday. Concurrently with the growth of the State, lumbering followed wherever settlements were made along the smaller rivers that had outlets to the sea. If Maine was New England's last frontier, the Maine pine lands were a special frontier in themselves. In 1846 Thoreau wrote of Maine lumbering that 'It is a war against the pines, the only real Aroostook or Penobscot war.'

In the production value of lumber, Maine ranked second in the United States during the early Nineteenth century. Her decline from this status later was accelerated by forest exploitation in the Lake States in the post-Civil War period. The actual value of timber rose consistently, however, between 1840 and 1900 when Penobscot County became pre-eminent in the industry; 1909 was a peak year in lumber production.

Although Maine lumber found extensive markets in the West Indies, abroad and on the West coast (California used five million board feet from Bangor alone in 1849), Maine imported considerable lumber in the mid-Nineteenth century from the South, New York, New Hampshire, Ohio, Michigan and Canada. At the same time, Maine lumbermen and river-drivers were following the course of the lumber empires westward, attacking the forests from the Atlantic to the Pacific, taking with them the skills, songs and legends learned on drives along the Penobscot, Kennebec and other Maine waterways.

Development of the pulp and paper and wood-using industries later in the Nineteenth century created a network of new enterprises wholly dependent upon the lumber industry. Pulp for commercial purposes first was produced in 1868 at Topsham; by 1914, Maine had assumed a national lead in this field. Pulp and paper continue to lead Maine's manufactures. Plants of nationally known companies are located at Woodland, Millinocket, Searsport, Rumford, Livermore and Madawaska. Among them are the country's largest producers of newsprint and pulp plates and containers as well as makers of fine papers and other products. The annual timber harvest in the 1960s was 2.2 million cords of pulpwood and 563 million board feet of logs and millwood products. Paper and allied products were valued at $606.4 million and lumber and wood products, $163.6 million in 1967. Some 6,000 wood-using industries annually employ 26 percent of all manufacturing wage earners in the State. In 1968 out-of-state Christmas tree shipments totalled 199,053; boughs, 122, 329 pounds; wreaths, 688,742 pounds.

Industrially important trees are white and red pine, white and red spruce, balsam fir, white and yellow birch, and red and sugar maple. Maine mills send 56 percent of their lumber out-of-state. Nearly 90 percent of the lumber used in Maine is by pulp and paper and lumber industries. Two thirds of the wood used in Maine manufacturing comes from Maine sawmills which use 70 percent spruce fir, balsam and white pine. The latter is the major species used in wood products manufacture, important in 225 communities. Wood turneries use mostly hardwoods such as white birch. About 64 percent of the quality wood used in Maine is from out-of-state because much Maine timber is ungraded.

Despite the efforts of the Maine Employment Security Commission and its programs under the Manpower and Development Training Act to interest Maine youth and adults, woods labor has been one of the largest manpower needs — 1,021 logging camp workers wanted in the spring of 1969. To help meet this need the Great Northern Paper Company was establishing a colony of Tibetans on a 73-acre potato farm in Aroostook County, and building dormitories and recreational facilities.

The large forest ownerships employ technical foresters to supervise their timber harvest programs. Many are graduates of the University of Maine School of Forestry established in 1903. In forest protection the Maine Forestry Service operates numerous fire lookout towers, the first one built on Squaw Mountain in 1905. Service foresters are available to woodlot owners for assistance in forest management techniques. Maine in 1921 was the first state to employ a forest entomologist in the interests of pest control. Maine also participates in the national American Tree Farm program with over 800 farms covering 2,541,282 acres (1969).

The story of Maine lumbering is interpreted in museums at Patten, Ashland and Orono, and by the Penobscot Heritage at Bangor. A water-powered sawmill is in operation at Vassalboro. There are guided tours at large pulp and paper plants.

DIVERSIFICATION

In the 1960s food had replaced shoes and textiles as the second largest industry after pulp and paper. Canned and frozen food production with shipments nationwide and abroad, came to the fore with agricultural diversification and new processing developments. Overall value of product in 1967 was $359.9 million. Maine is known for its fish, potato products, poultry, blueberries, corn and many other fruits and vegetables processed in some 400 plants (see AGRICULTURE).

Moccasins, boots and shoes of all kinds have been made in Maine since the first factory was established at West Auburn in 1835. Auburn became the largest of several shoe manufacturing centers now located in five counties. Total value of leather and leather products, largest source of manufacturing employment, was $359.3 million in 1967. In 1969 there was increasing concern over the effects of foreign imports.

The textile industry saw its beginnings in the pioneer mills erected in 1809-11 at Brunswick, Wilton and Gardiner. Water power and easily accessible supplies of raw materials for wool and cotton goods, once made at home or imported, attracted capital. When machinery began to replace hand labor, such centers as Augusta, Lewiston, Waterville, Biddeford-Saco and Sanford became known for their particular products — sheets, bedspreads, blankets, clothing fabric, tropical twill and the like. By 1900 there were 79 mills in Maine. But soon this number dwindled to half as cheaper southern labor, synthetics and other factors caused the textile industry to lose pre-eminence in Maine. A 1967 census showed a value of $198.3 million for textiles and allied products.

Mineral production (*see MINERAL RESOURCES*), principally in feldspar, structural materials and stone, clays, some peat and gem stones, was valued at $17,810,000 in 1968. Largest amounts were sand and gravel, 11,866,000 short tons; stone, 1,159,000 short tons; clay 42 short tons. Gem stones and peat were valued at $35,000 each. Cement production, agricultural limestone, granite, slate, peat and silica contribute to the mineral economy.

Among other principal Maine manufactures are machinery and ordnance, electric machinery, textile machinery and tools, electronics, primary and fabricated metals, transportation equipment, petroleum and coal products, rubber products and plastics, chemicals, instruments, furniture, printing, stone, clay and glass products. The country's largest producer of Christmas tree ornaments is at Lewiston which with Auburn is the approximate geographic center of the State's manufacturing population. Maine also is known for such specialties as sporting goods and canoes. Most towns have manufacturing plants, large or small. Industry is largely powered by hydro-electricity although some plants produce their own power by steam or water.

Maine industry, past and present, may be seen in historical society museums and on plant and factory tours.

COMMERCE

From sea to sky, Maine commerce has followed closely every turn in the course of the State's economic and industrial history ever since the VIRGINIA carried a cargo of Maine furs, fish and sassafras root to England in 1608. The purchase and barter of furs for export to Europe were mainly responsible for the penetration of the Maine wilderness and the establishment of trading posts and forts. The Massachusetts Bay Colony was keenly interested in the Maine fur trade and fisheries. Early commerce, necessarily by water, consisted chiefly in the export of such products as pipe staves (wood for the manufacture of oil and wine casks), clapboards, fish, fish oil and salt fish — trade that soon gave way to the more important export of masts and timber. Another commercial item, of no great note but certainly unusual, consisted of scalps. During the Indian wars from the mid-Seventeenth to mid-Eighteenth centuries, French and Indian scalps frequently brought prices from five to one hundred pounds.

Although there was a lull in commercial activity during the Revolution, ninety-nine vessels cleared from Portland alone in 1787, all but ten bound for foreign ports. Between the end of the Revolution and the War of 1812, local merchants made comfortable fortunes; this era of commercial prosperity was reflected in the number of impressive mansions built along the coast, especially during the first decade of the Nineteenth century. Circumstances were ideal for the advancement of lucrative trade; there are few coastlines with more numerous land-locked harbors suitable for the fitting out of vessels in safety. It has been noted that only the Dalmatian coast of the Adriatic and the gulfs of the Grecian peninsula are comparable.

The 1807 embargo and the War of 1812 brought commercial activity very nearly to a standstill all along the coast, although more than one Maine pocket was enriched by the proceeds from smuggling and privateering operations. As related to industry as a whole, it is noteworthy that the War of 1812 stimulated the growth of glass, woolen, cotton, metal and other manufactories all over the State, as the citizens were deprived of their maritime livelihood. The State had been predominately commercial up to this period, shipping an average of 150,000 tons annually, and had been created a separate District more than thirty years earlier for the more satisfactory administration of maritime affairs. The influx of foreign goods after the War of 1812 had a disastrous effect on home industry, the demand for agricultural produce fell off, and Maine lost 15,000 inhabitants as its farmers rushed West during the 'Ohio fever' of 1815-16.

By 1848, hundreds of vessels were engaged in foreign commerce. The West Indian trade, in which Maine merchants had been involved for decades, was flourishing, sustained principally by the rapidly growing lumber industry. Cargoes of lumber were bringing three and four hundred percent profits and over half the adult population of the coastal towns was engaged in ocean navigation. Ships whose keels had been laid in Maine shipyards from Kittery to Eastport were straining at their hawsers in ports all over the globe. Yankee shipmasters whose hands were often as accustomed to turning the pages of a Bible as to wielding a belaying pin, brought back ships whose holds were redolent with the odors of West Indian molasses, rum, spices and China tea, or with the stench of a slave cargo. Among the principal foreign and coastwise imports at this time were molasses, sugar, salt, iron, flour, corn and coal, while some of the chief exports were lumber, shooks, leather, agricultural produce and ice. Important between 1840-90, ice shipped south at negligible cost brought profitable returns. The excellent reputation of Kennebec River ice was so widespread that London companies spuriously flaunted the name 'Kennebec Ice' on their carts.

Checked temporarily by the panic of 1857 and the Civil War, Maine commerce appeared to increase steadily thereafter. In 1872, the total value of imports and exports at Portland was $45,000,000; in February that city had approximately five-sixths of the United States in-transit and trans-shipment trade. In the same year, Bangor lumber export shipments reached the record value of $4,000,000, while lime-producing Rockland was exporting more than 1,000,000 casks annually.

Yet, however imperceptibly at first, Maine maritime commerce began to decline. Contributing causes were varied — introduction of steam power in navigation, use of steel, heavy tonnage and property taxes, pilotage fees, competition of British tramp steamers, lack of demand for fishing vessels and the appearance of barges in the coastwise trade. Although the State's industrial development demanded increasing amounts of raw materials, maritime commerce continued to decline, after a World War I high point, to only 884,632 short tons during the depression of the early 1930s. Canadian, British and American tariff policies diverted elsewhere the important Canadian grain trade that reached a maximum of 43 million bushels shipped out of Portland in 1915-16. By 1930, only thirty percent of the State's manufactured products were being shipped through Maine ports. Rail and highway transport largely replaced light coastwise traffic; bulk traffic consisted largely of coal, petroleum, pulpwood, sulphur, newsprint and textile raw materials.

Industrial and agricultural developments since World War II had brought Maine a $70 million export business shipped through New York and Canadian ports to nineteen foreign countries. This included $20 million in logs and lumber transported overland by truck to Canadian ports; $10 million in food products and the rest in manufactures. An increasing percentage of Maine exports was moving by air, particularly fresh foods and manufactures, with more cargo moving out of Bangor's international jetport.

In 1968, import tonnage exclusive of fuel and sulphur at two major Maine ports was up at 359,509 over 169,885 in 1960. Portland had dropped to 49,021, from 104,370 in 1960; Searsport had risen to 310,488 from 65,515 in 1960. Of eleven commodities, china clay and wood pulp were leaders in Portland; of 16 commodities, phosphate rock was the principal import at Searsport, the only Maine port with scheduled foreign trade. Import tonnage for domestic and foreign oil in 1968 at Portland was 26,251,302, up nearly ten million since 1960; at Searsport, 962,186, up nearly two million since 1960.

Exports from the two ports had dropped from 171,785 in 1960 to 24,044 in 1968. Portland showed the greater loss from 119,439 tonnage in 1960 to 806 in 1968 when it no longer handled grain (20,973 tons in 1960), scrap iron (84,751 in 1960), wood pulp and flour. Shipping paper and potatoes, Searsport's export tonnage dropped from 52,346 in 1960 to 23,268 in 1968.

The changing face of Maine commerce involved gas and oil pipelines and revival of seaport activity if oil depots and refineries were established.

AGRICULTURE

EARLY settlers came to Maine to harvest the vast forest and the bountiful sea. To survive, they had to farm the land. They planted crops and
kept livestock and from these beginnings grew a self-sufficient way of
life that has evolved into the commercial enterprise of the Twentieth
century. In 1875 B. F. Hight wrote ' . . . labor and capital rightly applied
can make an agricultural garden of the hard soil in the hard climate of
Maine. So mote it be.' In 1967 the total cash farm income was
$212,397,000.

Through the colonial period the settlers produced what they could for
home use by most primitive methods. In 1775 came the Revolution; the
New England hive began to hum and new settlers swarmed to Maine. They
first built their towns along the coast, then pressed up the river valley
and finally out over the hills. The natural resources of forest and soil
beckoned, but until farm woodlots were depleted and forests were cut
back from the coast, lumber was king and farming was its handmaiden.

Of necessity, these pioneers became self-sufficient farmers, supplying
themselves with shelter, fuel, most of their food, much of their clothing
and even home-made furniture and crude farming tools. Corn, staple of
the Indians, was the first important crop. Water-powered grinding mills,
first of their kind in New England, were recorded in 1635 on the farms
of Captain John Mason on the Piscataqua River and in Berwick, along
with 300 head of cattle.

On the early farms sometimes there would be a small surplus for sale —
a firkin of butter, a few bushels of apples or potatoes, a little wool, a hog
or a side of beef. Demand for farm products grew with the cities;
farmers began producing more for sale; and so began the trend to commercial agriculture. Principal crops were hay, potatoes and corn, and
some oats, barley, rye, apples and garden vegetables. Flax was grown
in early times but was abandoned with the coming of cotton goods.
Livestock was mainly cattle and sheep with a few horses and hogs; hens
were kept for family use. For years before and after the Civil War, the
Kennebec Valley was famous for its beef cattle. During this period
farmers also were caring for half a million sheep. Great droves of cattle
and sheep were sent to the Brighton market near Boston.

Forerunner of the Twentieth century's many farm organizations, the
first agricultural society was formed in 1818. The Grange later became
influential in rural community life. A State Board of Agriculture was

established and in 1862 the University of Maine opened, with emphasis on agriculture and forestry whose interrelationship has remained fairly constant. The University and the State's Department of Agriculture conduct experiment stations in several localities.

During the period when western lands and eastern factories were alluring, great effort was made to keep Maine men at home. In the 1830s Major Jack Downing wrote, 'If we go to New York to mill, do we not lose our independence?' And in 1851 William A. Drew told the Cumberland County Agricultural Society, *It is no disgrace to man or woman in England to be a farmer or a farmer's wife. Would that as much could be said of Republican America. But the scrub aristocracy, male and female, of our little cities and villages, is absolutely intolerable, because misbegotten and monstrous. The truth is, God has given peculiar blessings to every region; and without following too far what he has made appropriate to other countries, the great object should be to ascertain the natural capacities and resources which Providence has placed in our way, and adapt our operations to them accordingly.*

Agriculture changed greatly between the Civil War and World War I. Growing cities created large markets and railroads gave better transportation for farm products. Horse-drawn machinery and commercial fertilizers came into general use and farmers found they needed to produce more for sale to meet their increased expenses. The trend towards commercial agriculture was accelerating.

Pressed by western competition, most farmers ceased raising beef cattle and sheep and with the greater use of farm machinery, horses replaced oxen as motive power. On the other hand, demand for dairy products increased rapidly and by 1900, dairy cattle had replaced Herefords and shorthorns in Maine pastures. Maine had become a dairy state.

The canning industry also was growing. Before 1850 Isaac Winslow of Portland had developed a method of canning sweet corn. The Civil War boom to the canning industry proved lasting and for generations Maine canned corn was considered the best on the market. By 1915 factories had long been canning blueberries, apples, beans and other products.

Blueberries were first canned about 1866 in Washington County and until recent years that county produced more canned blueberries than all the rest of the United States. At first the berries were harvested only on the 'barrens,' large tracts of land that had been burned over by forest fires. Of late, farmers have grown them in their fields where the soil is suitable and the 'blueberry belt' now extends from the St. Croix River to the Kennebec.

Another milestone towards commercial farming was reached in 1870 when the first train steamed into Houlton and the first carload of potatoes was shipped to Boston. Starch factories soon dotted the county and 'the Aroostook' was well on the way to becoming not only the 'garden of Maine' but also the 'potato empire of the East.' Three developments in the 1890s speeded the empire's expansion: completion of the Bangor and Aroostook Railroad to Caribou, the coming of special potato machinery, and the use of bordeaux mixture to control the potato's worst enemy, late blight. Before long, Aroostook was producing more potatoes than any state except one, and more barrels per acre than any other section of the country.

The first apple tree in Maine is said to have arrived ca. 1840 in a tub. For many years most apples were inferior 'natural' fruit and were used chiefly for cider which was consumed in large quantities and was exempted from the list of the 1884 Constitutional Amendment banning the manufacture of intoxicating liquor. Not until shortly before the Civil War were the better grafted varieties grown in quantity for sale. The demand was for winter fruit and for nearly a hundred years the Baldwin was the prince of Maine orchards; russets and greenings also were popular. Rare in the Twentieth century are such old favorites as Black Oxford, Blue Pearmain, Red Astrakan, Tolman Sweets, Sopsyvine and Snow apples.

Maine had four million bearing apple trees in 1900, nearly a third of them in Franklin, Kennebec and Oxford counties. Production reached its zenith in the following decades. Then came the severe winter of 1933-34 when two-thirds of the bearing trees were either killed or rendered worthless. Orcharding would recover from the terrible blow but only on a strictly commercial basis.

Outstanding among developments between World Wars I and II was the remarkable growth of the seed potato enterprise. For many years Maine had enjoyed a small but profitable seed trade with other states. Then the Maine Department of Agriculture established an inspection service and took other steps to certify the quality of Maine-grown seed. The enterprise flourished. Maine produced 128 bushels of certified seed in 1920 and 5,500,000 bushels in 1942 and led all other states in seed production.

Scientific advances in this period enabled farmers to gain better control of pests and diseases that injured their crops and livestock — the apple and blueberry fruit flies, apple scab and potato blight. Pullorum disease of poultry and tuberculosis among cattle was reduced almost to the vanishing point.

Change has been more rapid and pronounced since World War II than in any other period and is attributed in part to greater use of power on farms. Farmers are able to produce more efficiently with electricity in their buildings and with such equipment as bulk milk tanks, hay balers and potato harvesters. Another change has been the departure of horses from the rural scene, from 37,000 in 1940 to 1280 in 1964. The farmer no longer can hitch Old Dobbin to the sleigh. He has neither.

Significant development in the past twenty-five years has been the increase in the size of farms and farm operations, along with the decrease in the number of farms. Between 1940 and 1964 the so-called average farm increased in size from 109 to 201 acres and in value from $3183 to $19,979. Dairymen increased their herds from eight cattle to 22, and Aroostook potato farmers, their potato acreage from 21 to 68. Most commercial farmers in the 1960s were specializing in a single enterprise with perhaps a minor one on the side. The farmer of yesterday who grew a few acres of this and that and kept a few cows and hens belongs to those nostalgic 'good old days.'

Census figures show that there were 38,890 farms in Maine in 1940 and only 12,275 in 1964 when total acreage was 2,590,000 valued at $257 million. One might wonder what became of so many farms, for the land is still there. Thousands of them, especially the ones on the better soils, have been combined to make larger farms. Many of the poorer ones are reverting to forest. Others have in effect been rented to the government and placed in the Federal soil bank, eventually to become woodland.

The products of Maine farms in 1966 were worth approximately $250,000,000. Leading the list were poultry and eggs, $98,000,000; potatoes $80,000,000; and dairy products $34,000,000. In 1965 a 'good year,' the potato crop was valued at $125,000,000.

The small poultry flocks that supplied the housewife with pin money have vanished and large commercial flocks have taken their place. While flocks of a hundred birds were once thought large, flocks of eight or ten thousand layers now are not uncommon. Most Maine eggs are marketed in Boston and nearby cities. Poultrymen also supply eggs to the hatcheries which in turn furnish young chicks to both egg producers and broiler growers.

Swift expansion of the broiler business has been a phenomenon in Maine agriculture. Before World War II few broilers were grown; now sixty million or more are raised annually. The birds require about nine weeks to grow to broiler size, or to about four pounds in weight. Thus one producer can grow several successive broods and turn out sixty to eighty thousand broilers in a single year. Broiler houses may be several stories high, hundreds of feet long and very highly automated. Little land is involved. The establishment really is a broiler factory rather than a farm operation. The same is true of the laying houses. Broiler factories and egg factories rule the poultry roost.

Most of the stock is grown within thirty or forty miles of large processing plants located at Belfast, Waterville, Augusta, Lewiston and elsewhere. One fourth of the broilers are grown in Waldo County, another fourth in nearby Penobscot and Kennebec Counties. Kennebec, Knox and Waldo counties lead in the more widely distributed egg production.

Maine's most important crop is potatoes, most of them grown in Aroostook County where production sometimes exceeds fifty million bushels a year. The Katahdin is the leading variety, although others like the Russet, Burbank and Kennebec are popular. The markets formerly were for household use, for the certified seed trade and for starch. Now there are also large plants which take an increasing portion of the crop for the manufacture of french fries, potato chips and other prepared products.

While the number of potato farms has decreased sharply, the acreage per farm has increased threefold. More capital is involved and more efficient machinery is in use. Chemicals are employed not only to control insects and plant diseases but also to shorten the growing season and to prevent the tubers from sprouting in the storage bins. One of the newest innovations is the centralized storage and packing house. Some of these are large enough to house all the potatoes that can be grown on several hundred acres of land.

Dairying is more general throughout the State than other farm enterprises. Holsteins are the leading breed although there are excellent herds of Jerseys, Guernseys and other types. Most milk is sold wholesale to large distributors who market it in Maine towns and cities and in the Boston area. Both herds and cattle have declined in numbers but milk production has been fairly well maintained. Herds are larger, cows are giving more milk and dairymen have adopted more efficient practices. A herd of twenty milking cows once was considered large; now herds of seventy-five or a hundred are common.

Half the cows in the State are bred artificially to sires of outstanding value. Pastures are producing more and better forage, and surely no traveller has failed to note the great barns with their tall silos looming against the landscape. Milking parlors were coming into use in the 1960s. In these, the milk goes from milking machines to bulk tanks from which it is taken in tank trucks to the bottling plant. No longer do the warm creamy streams sing into the milk pail between the legs of the farmer astride his three-legged milking stool, risking the switch of bossy's tail or her foot in the pail as he rhythmically extracts her bounty. No more does the farmer's wife skim cream thick as butter from the broad milk pans in the "butt'ry' to coddle sweet wild strawberries.

Maine's small but thriving orchard enterprise annually produces between one and two million bushels of apples, principally MacIntosh, known for their crispness and flavor. Leading orchard counties are Cumberland, Oxford, York, Androscoggin and Kennebec. Maine apples are shipped as far west as California and there is a small foreign trade, chiefly with the United Kingdom. Apple crops in 1967 were valued at $3,567,000, over half the total fruit income of $6,618,000. Growers experiment with new strains but the demand is for Macs, Cortlands and Delicious. At the State Agricultural Experiment Station at Monmouth, a new mouseguard to protect treebark has been developed. A mechanical picker is being developed which would replace local and migrant workers who now pick by hand.

Orchardists use efficient culture and storage methods. Innovations are the use of special fertilizers, including liquids, and controlled pesticides that also have nutritional value. Immense storage sheds are moisture and temperature controlled; fall fruit can be kept in perfect condition until spring. Appleblossom time in spring and harvest time in autumn are good seasons to visit the orchards.

Raspberries and strawberries are grown in Maine but blueberries are the aristocrats of the berry field. Although the price fluctuates, the crop usually is worth between two and three million dollars annually. More than half the berries are grown in Washington County; Hancock and Knox rank next. Much of the crop is frozen and many new blueberry products are on the market such as muffin mix, pie filling, syrup, jams and jellies.

The canning industry has seen adjustments in the mid-Twentieth century. Many corn factories have closed but more peas are being grown. Beans, berries and apples are raised for canning. Other minor farm products include oats, dry beans, and cucumbers for pickles; market gardening is carried on near the cities. An experimental crop in the 1960s was sugar beets with a large processing plant at Easton. While most of the crop is grown in Aroostook, it has been introduced into other sections of the State.

While very few farmers now keep hogs, there are excellent flocks of sheep in most parts of the State. The number of beef cattle has increased slowly, the largest gains being in Kennebec, Knox, Waldo and Hancock counties.

What of the future? Farming as the old-timers knew it is well on the way out in the 1960s and a vigorous commercial agriculture is taking its place. It would appear that as time goes on there will be fewer and larger farms located on the better soils, fewer and larger herds of higher producing cows, fewer and larger flocks of birds that lay more eggs, and fewer and larger potato farms. Farmers will be highly skilled and will be successful businessmen as well as agriculturists.

Soon to be gone from living memory is the Maine farm life of yesteryear as sung by Poets Whittier, Coffin and others. Today's 'barefoot boy with cheeks of tan' is likely to know more about motorcycles than manure. Beyond the recollection of most are snow-bound winters and the sleigh ride to grandma's house; the woodshed, the barn chores before dawn; the long walk to the one-room school; the Saturday night bath in the kitchen washtub; the creak of wagon wheels on a dusty country road; 'treading' the sweet new-mown hay as it was pitched into the hayrack by the hot and thirsty farmer who cooled himself from time to time with a swig from the jug of ginger and water 'switchell'; pie for breakfast, and in hard times, a diet of potatoes, salt fish and pork scraps. Maine cookbooks abound with 'down-East' recipes but there are TV dinners in the freezer; few public eating places serve genuine old-time Maine dishes. However, the Old Farmer's Almanack, published since 1792, still prognosticates the weather, science notwithstanding.

Different points of view have been expressed at various periods on the Maine characteristic of resourcefulness — the 'Yankee ingenuity' that grew out of the necessity for survival. In the 1930s, Maine Writer Gladys Hasty Carroll said of the New England farmer: 'These people not only live their lives and think their own thoughts, but make their own jokes of the type suited to their group personality. It may be this ability to produce among themselves whatever they need which has saved them so long from encroachments of a leveling civilization.' In the 1960s some scholars aver that the reactionary aspects of Maine's agricultural history do much to delineate the Maine character and attitude.

An authentically restored Eighteenth century farmhouse, the Old Conway House, may be seen at Camden. A Farm Museum at Union has cooper's and cobbler's shops. There is a gristmill museum at Dexter, a blacksmith shop at Dover-Foxcroft and country stores at Newburgh and Bass Harbor. Fine Shaker furniture and tools are shown at the Shaker Museum at Sabbathday Lake, Poland Spring.

TRANSPORT AND
COMMUNICATION

INDIAN trails and canoes, totems and tomtoms, sign language and smoke signals — these Seventeenth century means of transportation and communication seem remote indeed from the rockets and satellites that put men on the moon in 1969. In the Twentieth century, technology has developed instant news, nuclear ships, super tankers, super jets and super highways. The communications satellite at Andover, Maine played an important role in the first moon landing. The world's most powerful radio transmitters are at Cutler, Maine. Establishment of oil depots and refineries on the Maine coast would mean that downeast deepwater harbors, once the home of masted schooners and square-riggers, will see super tankers like the MANHATTAN that made history through the Northwest Passage. Maine builds guided missile frigates at Bath and nuclear submarines at Kittery; engineers a vast highway system; moves freight by air from its international jet ports as well as overland by truck and rail. Yet, every link in the history of American transportation, except perhaps the stagecoach, still is in use in Maine.

The geographic and climatic factors of great distance, rigorous northern winters and intermittent coastal fogs always condition Maine transportation as travel facilities and equipment improve. Areas of the great northern wilderness can be reached only by walking or canoe as they have been for centuries, or by plane; snow removal equipment and the snowmobile keep open many areas formerly inaccessible in winter; shortwave radio is a boon in emergencies. Horse-drawn vehicles and trains still are in use, although largely supplanted by motorized vehicles. Water-borne traffic, once the chief means of transportation for early settlers, travellers, traders and merchants, has become important in the vacation industry. Commercial airlines are supplemented by feeder and charter service; bad weather means land transport.

The earliest recorded transportation system in Maine was that used by the Indians, an unusually comprehensive network of routes requiring no maintenance — the waterways. By rivers and streams, alternating with 'carries' or portages from lake to lake or to other rivers, the Maine tribes could thread their way over most of the State. The waterways were particularly important in autumn when inland tribes sought the more clement living conditions along the coast, as their primitive ancestors doubtless had done before them. Today's hunters and sportsmen use many of the old Indian highways.

One of the longest trails (meaning by 'trail' a combination of waterways and 'carries') was that between what is now Quebec and the mouth of the Kennebec River. The journey was made from Quebec, up the Chaudiere to Lake Megantic, the Chain of Ponds, Dead River, to the Kennebec and down to the sea. Benedict Arnold reversed this route on his ill-fated march in 1775. Another trail followed the same route to The Forks of the Kennebec, then turned eastward along the Kennebec by various ponds, Moosehead and Chesuncook Lakes, and so on down to the Penobscot River and Bay. Another series of waterways linked the Penobscot and Kennebec, starting from the Sebasticook River at Winslow.

Three well-defined trails led from Rockland Harbor to Mill Stream, the Wessaweskeag, and St. George's River. Indians from the Penobscot also came down the St. George's to New Harbor where they turned off over a 'carry' to the Sheepscot waters. A main trail went up the Sheepscot to Eastern River, the Kennebec and Androscoggin, and Merrymeeting Bay where, near Brunswick, a three-mile 'carry' gave access to Casco Bay. Again, a route lay between Gardiner and the Sandy River district by way of Cobbosseecontee Stream, Lake Maranacook and several ponds, into the Little Norridgewock. Among other well-known Indian trails were the Abnaki or Saco from Saco to Fryeburg; the Pequawket from Portland to Fryeburg; the Ossipee into the White Mountains; the long Mohawk Trail originating in Massachusetts, crossing the New Hampshire line into Maine and passing through Naples, Farmington, Skowhegan, Bangor and thence to Eastport and Calais. Parts of many of these early Indian routes now are motor highways.

Maine's social and economic history is closely tied to its major waterways which saw the development of industrially prominent river towns, the lumber industry, and settlement of the rich Aroostook region. Early white settlers and those who came later availed themselves of the same means of transportation used by the Indians. These trails and paths gradually were supplemented by woods roads and 'mast ways' for transporting timber to be converted into ship masts. There were mast ways between High Pine and Kittery, between South Sanford and Berwick, at Bath and elsewhere.

Land transportation in Colonial Maine was not a thing to be undertaken lightly. During the Seventeenth and Eighteenth centuries Maine towns often were rebuked and fined for their failure to maintain roads. In 1653 the Massachusetts commissioners could get no farther than Wells for want of roads; they ordered the inhabitants of Wells, Saco and Cape Porpoise to *make sufficient roads within their towns from house to house, and clear and fit them for foot and cart travel, before the next county court under penalty of 10 pounds for every town's defect in this particular* and to *lay out a sufficient highway for horse and foot between towns within that time.*

First named public highway following Indian trails in the 1600s was the King's Highway with markers from Boston to Machias for mail couriers and horse-drawn vehicles as settlements grew along the coast. Some segments of US 1 follow this course and may be noted in several communities, but few Eighteenth century taverns and stagecoach inns survive. In the State's current highway system, there are sixteen named highways, some bearing the names of the Indian trails they have incorporated, such as Ossipee, Pequawket and Sokokis. Well-known are the Arnold and Mt. Katahdin Trails and the Acadia and Aroostook Scenic highways.

As roads were laid out, bridges were needed to cross Maine's numerous waterways. Oldest still in use is Sewall's Bridge (1797) at York. Ten covered bridges survive among the State's several thousand bridges. Unusual is the wire suspension bridge (1842) at New Portland. Built in 1931, one of the handsomest Twentieth century bridges is the Waldo-Hancock suspension bridge 137 feet over the Penobscot River at Verona.

Stagecoach lines of any extent did not come into existence until after the Revolution. The first stagecoach began operating in 1787 between Portland and Portsmouth, a three days' journey; today the ninety miles over the Maine Turnpike takes a little over an hour. The first advertisement stated: *Those ladies and gentlemen who choose the expeditious, cheap and commodious way of stage travelling will please to lodge their names with Mr. Motley. Price for one person, passage the whole way, 20 shillings.* Five years later, an enterprising citizen made the first attempt to carry passengers between Portland and Hallowell by way of Wiscasset, making two trips weekly by sleigh in winter and one trip by coach in summer. Prior to the stagecoach, horseback and the ox-cart were modes of travel. Two-wheeled gigs appeared in Portland in 1760 but these were rare and expensive. The first four-wheeled vehicle in the State is said to have appeared in Augusta in 1800.

In eastern Maine, transportation was much slower in developing. For a long time there were no roads, and until 1800 no land communication with interior towns was possible except by foot. It was easy to get lost going from Belfast to Bangor and even in 1804, no one would attempt to bring a load of goods across country from Augusta.

An early transportation concern of the Maine inhabitants was the postal service. Mail was entrusted to ships, or to men journeying through the woods on foot or horseback. A post route between Portland and Boston was established in 1775 but the weekly service was very irregular. In 1790 the only post road in Maine ran along the coast southwest of

Wiscasset and connected with the post road to Boston. There was no post service east of Wiscasset until some years later. An arrangement in 1788 brought the mails from Boston to Portland three times a week. The first express service between these points was a tri-weekly schedule by water in 1839. Maine's first postoffice (1775) was at Portland (then Falmouth). Oldest postoffice in continuing use (1811) is at Castine.

As the population increased, land transportation began to expand. Stagecoaches, minus the comfort, speed and fumes of Twentieth century busses, operated between Boston and New York and Bangor in relays by 1816. About this time and a little later more than fifteen stage lines were operating out of Hallowell alone. Lines increased along the coast and up the major river valleys and travel conditions improved. Portland was connected with almost daily service to all important points in the State. By 1823, stages made the trip between Portland and Bangor, now a two-hour drive, in thirty-six hours, fare $7.50. Two years later the route to Conway and the White Mountains was established. It should be borne in mind that throughout the stagecoach period and even after the coming of the railroad, the most important means of transportation for freight and passengers was by water.

The most romantic of the stage routes was the so-called Airline between Bangor and Calais — 93 miles of day and night travel, 18 hours through wild unsettled territory, with a change of horses at six stops, and tales of wolves and robbers (see TOUR 5).

Local transportation began with so-called omnibuses, first appearing in the streets of Portland in 1850. They proved unpopular and were succeeded by horsecars in 1862. These became extensive systems in Lewiston, Biddeford, Waterville, Norway and Fryeburg. The early Twentieth century saw the arrival of the electric trolley, now gone the way of the horsecar and superseded by city buses. Trolleys were named for streets or areas they traversed; such as the Figure 8, the course of whose rails formed that figure in Lewiston and Auburn.

There were open and closed trolleys; interurban lines between Portland and Lewiston had plush 'parlor cars.' Colorful and popular were the trolley parks — Lake Grove at Auburn, Riverton and Cape Cottage at Portland, Island Park at Winthrop, Riverside at Hampden, New Meadows near Bath — where amusements and refreshments were enjoyed on family outings. The Seashore Trolley Museum at Kennebunk has a large collection of vintage trolleys from all over the world.

Land transport now is served by a 21,000 mile road network. In 1913 the State Highway Commission was created and shortly thereafter a system of 'main' roads was laid out. Of these, most important were Route 1 from Kittery to Fort Kent via Rockland, Belfast, Machias,

Calais and Houlton, (see TOUR 1) and Route 2, Houlton to Gorham, N. H., via Lincoln, Bangor, Skowhegan, Farmington and Bethel (see TOUR 4). Until after World War II, many rural roads were nearly impassable or closed in winter, but now most parts of the State are accessible year-round. The first super highway in Maine, the Maine Turnpike was opened between Kittery and Portland soon after World War II and subsequently was extended to Augusta, a total of 106 miles. At Augusta it connects with Interstate 95 NE to Houlton. While most major highways cross Maine north and south, studies are being made for a major east-west route. State Highway funds disbursed in 1966 amounted to $84 million, in addition to Federal funds.

Beginning in the 1920s many short-line bus companies sprang up. Gradually those of western, central and coastal Maine were combined and controlled by the Maine Central Transportation Company, a Railroad subsidiary. Similarly in northern Maine the Bangor and Aroostook Railroad acquired control of bus transportation. In the mid-1950s the Maine Central sold its holdings to Greyhound Corporation which in 1969, with the Bangor and Aroostook, provide the bulk of Maine bus service. Vermont Transit operates between Portland and Burlington, Vermont; Continental Trailways provide interstate service between Portland, Boston and New York.

Increasingly, highways have become the avenue of freight transportation. Well over fifty percent of the movement of goods is now by road rather than rail. The railroads still carry large quantities of paper, pulp, cement, potatoes and heavy goods, but companies like Cole's Express, St. Johnsbury and Merrill Transportation send their trucks to all corners of the State. There are also pipe lines carrying oil from Portland to Montreal and from Searsport to Limestone.

In 1965 there were 1711 trucking companies operating 18,847 vehicles in the State. Of these, 685 were Maine-based, operating 3,071 vehicles. In 1966, drivers' licenses totalled 474,000. In 1968, motor vehicle registrations totalled 379,601. Of these, 88,739 were trailers; 43,660, long-term trailers; 9,546 snowmobiles; 6,374 motorcycles.

RIDING THE RAILS

Maine's first railroad, one of the earliest in New England, began operating for lumber transport between Bangor and Old Town in 1836. The Maine Legislature granted the first railroad charter in 1832 for a line to run three quarters of a mile between Calais and Milltown but this was not completed immediately. The third Maine railroad, the Portland, Saco and Portsmouth, began operating in 1842. Another early road ran from Whitneyville to Machiasport; of its primitive locomotives, THE LION was given to the Crosby Laboratory at University of Maine. The Moosehead Lake Railway, a two-mile narrow-gauge road at Northeast Carry, remained the crudest in the State until it was destroyed by the fires of blueberry pickers in 1862. Hardly highballing through the wilderness, locomotion was provided by draft animals; the tracks originally were fifty and sixty-foot pine logs, and the first wheels were wooden disks of pine.

Within the next half-century there were thirty-one railroads, including branch lines in the State. The Atlantic and St. Lawrence Division of the Grand Trunk Railway between Portland and Montreal was opened to travel in 1853. Portland wrested from Boston the position as Atlantic terminus for this road in one of the most curious episodes in Maine's railroad history. The Boston and Maine Railroad in Maine was completed in 1873 and the majority of the roads within the State began operating in the quarter-century between 1850 and 1875.

The Consolidated Maine Central Railroad in 1881 comprised the Portland and Kennebec Railroad between Portland, Brunswick, Augusta, and Bath; the Somerset and Kennebec Railroad between Augusta and Skowhegan; the Androscoggin and Kennebec Railroad between Danville and Waterville, and the extension between Danville and Cumberland; the Penobscot and Kennebec Railroad between Waterville and Bangor; the Androscoggin Railroad between Brunswick and Leeds Junction and Lewiston; and the Leeds and Farmington Railroad between Leeds Junction and Farmington. Leased roads at the time were the Belfast and Moosehead Lake Line between Belfast and Burnham, and the Dexter and Newport Railroad.

Ultimately the Maine Central dominated Maine railroading through purchase or lease of new lines such as the Knox and Lincoln between Bath and Rockland, the Maine Shore Line between Bangor, Ellsworth and Hancock Point with steamers to Bar Harbor, the Washington County Railroad between Ellsworth and Calais, the European and North American Railroad between Bangor and Vanceboro, and Portland and Ogdensburg, N. Y., Portland and Rumford Falls, and Rumford Falls and Rangeley Lakes.

The most significant construction in the last decade of the Nineteenth century was the Bangor and Aroostook line that ultimately reached Fort Kent on the Canadian boundary. This made possible the rapid development of the Aroostook County potato empire and contributed directly to the development of Millinocket and East Millinocket as centers of the rapidly growing paper industry.

By the end of World War I, Maine had over 2000 miles of standard gauge railroads. Schedules made it possible for passengers to travel to most parts of the State conveniently and in relative comfort. There were also five narrow-gauge railroads: Sandy River and Rangeley Lakes; Bridgton and Saco Valley; Waterville, Wiscasset and Farmington; Kennebec Central, Randolph and Togus; and the Monson Railroad. The Sandy River Line, over 100 miles in Franklin County, even boasted a Pullman parlor car.

Shortly after World War I, increasing use of the automobile began to cut into passenger revenues. The depression beginning in the late 1920s further reduced rail travel. Leased lines were cut loose, branch lines were abandoned and even main line schedules were significantly curtailed. In an effort to retain passengers, the Boston and Maine and Maine Central Railroads in the mid-1930s inaugurated the first East Coast streamline service with the Flying Yankee on the Boston-Bangor run. It was highly successful but other service continued to decline. There was a brief respite during World War II. Shortly thereafter, the two major railroads acquired a new fleet of modern coaches and locomotives and for a few years, name trains such as the Bar Harbor Express, the Kennebec, the Gull and the Pine Tree Limited afforded riders some of the finest equipment in the land. However, more and more travellers were turning to automobiles, bus and plane services. In the fall of 1960 the Maine Central dropped all remaining passenger service. The Boston and Maine continued an abbreviated service between Portland and Boston until 1965 when it removed its remaining self-propelled service. Portland's large Union Station with its familiar clock tower succumbed to the wrecking ball and was replaced by a shopping center. The Canadian National similarly curtailed its service between Portland and Montreal, retaining a weekend service through the summer of 1968. In 1969 the only passenger service in Maine was that of the Canadian Pacific passing through via Brownville Junction and Vanceboro between St. John and Montreal.

Railway freight tonnage in 1965 was over fifteen million, up nearly two million over 1950. In 1967, seven railroads were operating 1757 miles of track, 135 miles less than in 1950. They were the Canadian National, Canadian Pacific, Boston and Maine, Maine Central, Bangor and Aroostook, Aroostook Valley and Belfast and Moosehead. In 1969 Maine Central was considering abandoning or curtailing five of its unprofitable branch lines.

The Portland Railroad Club has fall foliage tours by rail; an organization of railroad buffs arranges summer excursions offered by two companies and there is a Railway Museum with rides at Boothbay Harbor.

THE BOUNDING MAIN

Steamboat transportation antedated the railroad by more than a decade, the steamboat KENNEBEC making the trip between Portland and North Yarmouth in 1822. Two years later, the PATENT, 'strong, commodious and elegantly fitted up for passengers,' began the run between Portland and Boston. As steamboat lines became numerous, steamers soon were touching at nearly all important coastal and river towns, even steaming up the Kennebec as far as Waterville. During the keen competition, the fare between that city and Boston was only one dollar.

One of the earliest iron steamships in America, the BANGOR, was built in 1845 to run between Bangor and Boston. Transatlantic transportation by steam first affected Maine when boats began plying between Liverpool and Portland in 1853. Water transportation to the latter port reached its height in the 1850s, with 246 sailing vessels and twelve steamships calling at Portland regularly. Among the larger steamship lines, the Portland Steam Packet Company, the Maine Steamship Company, the International Steamship Company, the Kennebec Steam Navigation Company, the Bath-Boothbay Steamship Company, and the Boston-Bangor Steamship Company eventually became associated as the Eastern Steamship Lines. Previous to World War I, the Allan, Leyland, and White Star Transatlantic Steamship Lines operated out of Portland.

With increasing motorized land transport, war and depression, water transportation went into decline. When the Eastern Steamship Lines ended their service in 1936, that was the end of passenger traffic except for a few local lines. Freight cargoes dwindled to a fraction of the tens of millions of tons carried annually in the past (see COMMERCE). The Canadian National Railroad abandoned its great grain elevators. The Portland waterfront continued to decline, tankers being the most frequent visitors. While repeated efforts to revive the decadent shipping industry and to emphasize the State's advantages in harbors and navigable rivers, have yet to meet with marked success, there were indications in the 1960s that Maine water transport might regain historic significance through exploitation of Alaskan oil reserves, the Northwest Passage and supertankers that can be accommodated in the State's deep-water harbors. Current studies of oil exports and imports with large-scale facilities in Machiasport, Eastport and Casco Bay could eventuate vast industrial changes affecting shipping along the Maine coast.

In the 1960s, revival of excursion steamers and pleasure craft was gaining momentum in the vacation industry (*see ISLAND TRIPS*). The State has several ferry services. Several private companies run daily schedules to the islands and coastal points. The Canadian National Railroad's popular BLUENOSE ferry between Bar Harbor and Yarmouth, Nova Scotia would have competition in 1970 when a Swedish Company inaugurated its service between Portland and Nova Scotia. There was even talk of Caribbean cruise ships coming to Maine islands and ports in summer.

ON THE AIRWAVES

In the early 1930s the Boston and Maine and other railroads inaugurated air transport, linking the major cities — Portland, Lewiston, Augusta, Bangor, Rockland and Presque Isle with other states. Ultimately the railroad companies were forced to divest themselves of control of a competing form of transportation and Northeast Airlines took over. In 1970, Executive Airline, with increased service, superseded Northeast.

By the late 1960s, Portland, Bangor and Presque Isle were served by jets. Many of the smaller airports, some of them constructed with WPA funds in the 1930s cannot accommodate the newest planes, so local companies provide feeder services. There also are charter services for island and wilderness areas. The Bangor jetport, formerly the Dow Air Force Base, and the Portland jetport have international designation, the former handling overseas passenger traffic and moving increasing amounts of freight. Portland won a State award in 1968 for the excellence of its new terminal. By legislative act in 1969, Maine's three-man Aeronautics Commission was replaced by one man.

Communications in Maine have developed along lines similar to those elsewhere since the days when the Morse code was tapped out at the railroad depot. There are seven commercial television stations, a State-supported Educational television network on four non-commercial channels; one or more radio stations in twenty-seven communities; seven commercial FM stations; forestry, marine and police shortwave and radar.

Maine, whose first newspaper, *The Falmouth Gazette*, was published in 1785, has nine daily newspapers with a combined circulation of 80,000 in five area editions. Only Sunday paper is the *Maine Telegram* published in Portland. The weekly *Maine Times* established in 1968, with state-wide circulation has received State awards for its cultural and conservation coverage. There are some forty weekly newspapers serving their own areas and numerous periodicals covering special fields. These include

Down East Magazine whose 55,000 circulation is 67 percent out of state; *Architecture and Construction; Maine Digest, Maine Life;* historic, farm, fishing, labor, industrial and business publications.

From Indian trails to airways, transportation and communication have developed along lines similar to those of other states. In today's mobile society, while the State has not felt the problem of traffic congestion as seriously as more heavily populated areas have, there is seasonal heavy traffic with the influx of vacationists. As the Indian once travelled to his campgrounds in the wilderness, so the white man, responding in great numbers to the call of the wild, takes to the highways and byways with his camping trailer and other paraphernalia to get back to nature — with all the comforts of home and waves of debris in his wake. It costs the State many thousands of dollars for waste removal on the Maine Turnpike alone, notwithstanding 'Keep Maine Scenic' and 'Tidy Coon' campaigns.

MAINE AMERICANS

IN the State of Maine's Sesquicentennial year, the 1970 census was expected to show a population increase to over one million in the last decade over the 1960 figure of 969,265 persons. In the mobile society of the mid-Twentieth century, social and industrial changes, out-migration of youth and other factors have varied ethnic patterns to some degree. However, the basic population stock remains predominately of English-Scotch-Irish ancestry with a generous proportion of French, some German, and other nationalities in lesser numbers.

At the beginning of the Nineteenth century, Maine's population was representative of English, French, Scotch-Irish, Welsh, Irish, Dutch, German and Acadian French stock. Men from western England began group settlement of the province as early as 1623 at Kittery, though there had been scattered settlers in the territory before that year. This stock combined with that of the Scotch-Irish, who followed soon after, to produce that shrewd, dry, somewhat dour type known as the Yankee — an appelation that later came to be applied to all New Englanders of this same general ancestry. These people weathered the protracted Indian wars and their settlements grew slowly but steadily along the coast. By 1662 there had begun as well a gradual infiltration of Quaker settlers whose frugal and peace-loving ways helped to mold the Maine character.

In 1740, General Samuel Waldo imported forty families from Brunswick and Saxony to settle in Waldoboro, supplementing a Moravian colony established there a year earlier. Succeeding years brought more Germans to this section of Maine; many of them later migrating elsewhere. Dresden was settled by German Lutherans, accompanied by French and Dutch immigrants of the same faith.

Irish settlers were especially plentiful in York, Lincoln and Cumberland counties; it was they who gave Limerick its name, after the city in the old country. In 1808, Irish Catholics were numerous enough in the vicinity of Damariscotta to build a place of worship, now the oldest Roman Catholic church building in New England.

From their early but unsuccessful settlement in 1604, the French held control of the land east of the Penobscot River until 1759, when they relinquished all their claims in what is now Maine. At one time this territory had been controlled by the New Amsterdam Dutch who were driven out only when the French returned in stronger force. Although the French were not active colonists, many of the Huguenot settlers early gained prominence in Maine. Descendants of the old French Protestant families still live in some coastal towns. They are not to be confused with the Canadian French, nor the latter with the Acadians originating in Brittany and Normandy who, refusing to swear allegiance to England or Canada, settled along the St. John River when they were exiled from their homes in Nova Scotia. Many of these people preserve intact their language, religion and customs.

From 1869 for over half a century there was a continual influx of workmen from Scotland and England and from the French-speaking sections of Canada for specialized labor in the State's factories and mills which then had no training programs. In recent years the State has established vocational institutions and industries have set up training programs.

In 1870 a Swedish Colony was established in Aroostook County in efforts to offset out-migration in the mid-Nineteenth century. Northern European peoples, particularly Finns joined the Canadian French in the lumbering industry; Norwegians, Swedes and Icelanders engaged in fishing, shipping and quarrying in the coastal regions. Russians, Lithuanians and Poles, like the Finns, settled most thickly in Knox County. Growth of the cities brought large numbers of Italians, Greeks, Jews and Syrians who migrated chiefly from Russia, Lithuania and Poland; and a scattering of other southern European nationalities, Albanians, Turks and Orientals. By the 1960s there were small contingents of Chinese, Japanese and Filipinos and there was a broadening of cultural experience in student foreign exchange programs and increased travel. In 1969 a Tibetan colony was being established in northern Maine.

Of the minority groups drawing national attention in the 1960s, Maine has small populations of Blacks and of its first inhabitants, the Indians. In Maine which was admitted to the Union as a 'free' state, descendants of the paid servants of wealthy landowners and shipping families formed the nucleus of the Black population, now over 3000, chiefly resident in Portland and Bangor. Their achievements have been notably in education and religion. In early times there were instances of intermarriage with Indians and with whites in remote coastal areas. Most are members of the NAACP and strong supporters of Civil Rights. In 1970, Bowdoin College was the first Maine institution of higher learning to establish a center for Afro-American studies — in a building once used to aid in the escape of slaves.

Less than 2000 Indians were living on the Penobscot and Passamaquoddy reservations in 1970. Their tribes had dwindled over the centuries and there had been intermarriage with the French. The Federal government enfranchised Indians in 1934, Maine, whose Indians are not under Federal jurisdiction, was the last to do so, in 1954. In 1965 Maine was the first State to establish a department of Indian Affairs. In 1970 as Indians pressed for improvements in their living conditions and sought to preserve their culture, the Federal government named the Maine reservations as redevelopment areas to allow Maine Indians 'to create self-help projects needed to improve their economy.' Off-reservation Indians, living in Aroostook County, chiefly Malecites and Micmacs, formed the Association of Aroostook Indians, a non-profit corporation, to sponsor a housing program and to establish an Indian center for research and education; a first program was held at Ricker College, Houlton.

FOLKLORE

OUT of the mists of time have come the songs, stories and legends, the beliefs, customs and proverbs handed down by generations of mankind, the folklore that reveals universal human qualities colored by race and region. As in all regions, many influences have contributed to the special character of Maine folklore which intrinsically is part of the Euro-American genre engendered by pioneers from western Europe who settled on America's eastern seaboard and gradually moved westward. Maine's special blend comes from forest, farm and sea, with strong French-Canadian influences as the Nation's northeasternmost state thrusts into the Maritime provinces.

While a ballad, story, proverb or belief found in Maine will have numerous counterparts elsewhere in Europe and America, an overview of the oral traditions of Maine shows the particular pattern or origin, influences and relationships that make for a body of folklore with a very strong regional quality.

The cultural picture may be divided roughly by an imaginary line from Mt. Washington to Eastport. In coastal regions and counties south of the line, there is the feeling of old New England; north of it, the ties with Canada are felt everywhere. For example, Bangor has as much in common with Moncton or Charlottetown, P.E.I., as it does with Portland. And if geography is a clue, the great Nineteenth century development of the lumber industry is an explanation of the cultural similarity of northern Maine and the Maritime provinces.

If the forests have contributed greatly to whatever unique qualities Maine folklore can claim, so has the sea, identified with Maine life since the arrival of the first settlers. Maine has over two thousand miles of shoreline and a young Maine boy likely went to sea or into the Maine woods, if he didn't do both by turns. Sailing and fishing have been important to Maine folklore. And underlying the traditions of the woods and the sea, of course are those of the small farm and the rural life of the tillers of the soil; such farms, of fifty to a hundred acres now are diminishing in numbers with the trend toward large agricultural operation as seen in the Aroostook potato country. From the folklorist's standpoint, then, Maine's culture is basically that of the small farm with strong coloration from the woods and the sea. A Maine farm usually has at least one lumberman's peavey in its kit of tools, and nearer the coast, the farm loft or shed often reveals an old pair of sea boots.

The impress of French culture, both Acadian and Quebecois, also has

MARITIME HERITAGE

DATING from the dawn of America, Maine's great maritime tradition has inspired poets and painters as well as historians. Since the days of sail, Maine ships and Maine seamen, many of them famous in maritime history, have been known in ports around the world. From the Maine Downeasters and the great six masted schooners such as the WYOMING, the shipbuilding tradition is carried on, not only in Bath-built guided missile carriers and the nuclear submarines of the Kittery-Portsmouth Navy Yard, but also in Friendship sloops and many other kinds of small craft built in yards along the coast, from fishing vessels to fibre-glass racers. Maritime aficionados find much of interest at the yards and launchings as well as at the Bath and Penobscot (Searsport) Marine Museums which have outstanding collections, and at the Maine Maritime Academy at Castine.

FRENCHMAN BAY

MASTS FOR THE KING'S NAVY, ENGRAVING

AT THE PENOBSCOT
MARINE MUSEUM, SEARSPORT

THE **VIRGINIA**, FIRST AMERICAN TRANSATLANTIC TRADER, 1608;
AND MARITIME MEMORABILIA

BATH MARINE MUSEUM

RIGGING OF THE **ARYAN** OF PHIPPSBURG, LAST FULL-RIGGED WOODEN VESSEL
BUILT IN AMERICA

THE **WYOMING**,
AMERICA'S
LARGEST
SIX-MASTED
SCHOONER

THE **RED JACKET**, ROCKLAND CLIPPER WHOSE TRANSATLANTIC SPEED RECORD
WAS NEVER SURPASSED

THE **RANGER,** AMERICA'S CUP
WINNER (1937), BATH-BUILT
J-CLASS SLOOP

THE **STATE OF MAINE**, MARITIME ACADEMY SHIP BASED AT CASTINE

THE **USS DEWEY**, FIRST U. S. NAVY MISSILE DESTROYER, BUILT AT BATH

THE PENOBSCOT, PROPOSED CONTAINER SHIP, BATH IRON WORKS

THE **USS SWORDFISH**, FIRST U. S. NUCLEAR SUBMARINE, BUILT AT KITTERY

FASCINATION
AT THE MARINE
MUSEUM

BUOY STATION, SOUTH PORTLAND

had an important effect on the regional quality of Maine folklore. While most of the present French-speaking population is concentrated in the larger manufacturing towns such as Lewiston and Biddeford, or in the upper St. John Valley, there are many more people of French ancestry scattered over the state, including descendants of French Protestants along the coast. Although the influence of French-Canadian folklore often is difficult to assess, it unquestionably has contributed much to Maine tradition.

Folksongs are the best collected of all traditional genres of Maine folklore. As might be expected, the basic repertoire is British. The older ballads like *Barbara Allan* and *Lord Randal* probably were as well known in Maine as in the southern Appalachian mountains. But the most popular ballads were the later broadsides, often called 'come-all-ye's' from their characteristic first line: 'Come all you people great and small and listen unto me,' or some variation of it. The murder ballad, *The Wexford Lass,* the pirate ballad, *The Flying Cloud,* and love ballads like *The Dark-Eyed Sailor* were prime favorites. Native American ballads in the broadside pattern were popular, too: Civil War pieces like *The Cumberland Crew* or *The Last Fierce Charge*; or sea songs like *Fifteen Ships on George's Banks,* telling of a fishing tragedy in the 1862 gale; or that New Brunswick import that told of the great fire of 1825, *The Miramichi Fire.* Songs of death in the woods and on the river-drives were common; *The Jam on Gerry's Rock* probably was the best-known ballad in the State. Many of these lumber-woods songs were locally composed, like the one about 'Guy Reed' killed on the Androscoggin, or 'John Roberts' killed on the Union River. Recent research has brought to light the names of many of the authors of Maine songs: Larry Gorman, Joe Scott, James O'Hara, John Mitchell, all lumber-woods poets, and the little-known Amos Hanson of Orland, a fisherman and sailor.

These songs were not sung to guitar accompaniment or to any accompaniment at all. They were sung simply with a rather hard voice in a tense but undramatic manner. Often the last word or even the entire last line was spoken to indicate that the song was over. Although we today find the tunes hauntingly beautiful, the important thing to traditional singers and their audiences was always the words. The highest praise that could be given to a lumbercamp singer was that he knew his songs all the way through and got his words out good and clear.

If the old songs (that is the name they go by in Maine, not 'folksongs') are fast disappearing, the sea chanties, once well-known to Maine men, have all but entirely gone. Traditional songs burgeon only when there are abundant occasions for the singing of them. The chanties were work songs that flourished when hand labor by small gangs of men kept the big sailing ships going. They were never sung for fun; therefore when the need for

them died, the songs died too. On the other hand, the old ballads were sung
as a form of entertainment in leisure hours. As other forms came in — the
phonograph, radio, television, as well as better light for reading — the
old songs no longer served an important function. But some of the older
residents who recall them with pride and pleasure, still sing them well in
the 1970s. Westport is one of the communities having regular 'sings.'

Less specific information is available on the folk tale than on the song
traditions of Maine. While there are many literary re-workings of pur-
portedly traditional tales, there are very few well-documented, carefully
recorded stories taken directly from oral tradition. From these, a few
generalities may be hazarded. Apparently the long *Marchen* or wonder
tale of kings, princesses, dragons, giants, magic rings and the like was not a
popular form in Maine, although there is some evidence that it was better
known in French-speaking groups than elsewhere. It is the short, funny
story — the joke and the tall tale — that has survived best in Maine as
it has elsewhere in North America. Such stories, especially the tall tales,
often have formed local cycles as the exploits of this or that person who
was known for telling them. There is a splendid cycle of tales about Ed
Grant of Rangeley, and others less well-known about Robert Townsend the
salve peddler from Sumner, Jones Tracy of Mount Desert Island, and
Hiram Wright of Houlton. However moribund traditional songs may be in
Maine, jokes and anecdotes about local characters still are very much alive,
and once one knows the proper character to ask about, any number of
good stories are forthcoming.

While most such cycles of tales are humorous — anecdotes of some local
character's antic doings or the tales told by or associated with some
egregiously splendid liar who used to live thereabouts, — there are what
may be called 'serious' cycles. There are those that accumulate around
some man of enormous strength, like Barney Beal of Jonesport who once
killed a horse by hitting it between the eyes with his fist. There are cycles
about famous hunters like John Ellis, or George Magoon of Crawford and
his life-long standoff with the game wardens. One of the most interesting
concerns the mysterious doings of a George Knox in the Mars Hill-Blaine
area. This 'wizard' could draw whiskey out of a tree, and make woodchips
turn into money and back again.

Maine shares most of its supernatural legends with the rest of the
United States and Canada. Stories of appearances of the Devil are common enough especially in areas of strong French-Canadian influence.
Perhaps the best known legend in the State is that of the Witch's Curse to
which is attributed the outline of a leg that appears on Colonel Buck's
monument at Bucksport, a story that owes at least as much to literary
tradition and the tourist trade as it does to folklore. Maine has haunted
houses and ghosts that haunt particular stretches of road, neither more

nor less numerous than anywhere else. But the story of the man who pulled all the feathers off a gorby (Canada jay) and awoke next morning to find he had lost all his hair has been popular in Maine and neighboring New Brunswick, though almost unknown elsewhere in America.

Fascinating facets of folklore of course also include popular beliefs and superstitions, folk architecture and medicine, proverbs, children's games and rhymes, taunts, nicknaming, cookery, weather and many others. For bibliography and specific information on Maine folklore, interested readers may write or visit the Northeast Folklore Archives, Stevens Hall, University of Maine, Orono.

EDUCATION AND
RELIGION

FROM forest missions in the wilderness to Twentieth century cathedrals and college campuses, generations of Maine people have followed paths of learning and of prayer. As settlements grew, community life centered for many years around the meetinghouse or church and the 'little red schoolhouse.'

EDUCATION

Since Maine was a part of Massachusetts until 1820, the early history of education in Maine is relatively that of the Commonwealth. However, the more widely scattered settlers of Maine, primarily traders and fishermen of primitive interests and little wealth, and long harassed by Indian wars, were slower to achieve and develop educational advantages. When school taxes became a burden to the communities — as they are once again in the Twentieth century — 'moving schools' were organized, travelling from town to town for a few weeks in each. The situation greatly improved after 1789 under the Massachusetts law requiring liberal instruction for all children and college or university education for schoolmasters. After gaining statehood in 1820, Maine modeled her own school laws upon those of Massachusetts.

The first real school in Maine probably was the mission established on the Kennebec in 1696 by Father Sebastian Rasle, whose valuable work among the Indians suffered greatly from, and was finally ended by the depredations of the English colonists. Other early Jesuit teachers were Father Romagne at Passamaquoddy and Father Bapst at Indian Island. The missions established by the Jesuits provided schooling for the Indians they sought to convert.

The first teacher to be hired by a town was at York in 1701 and the first building to be constructed as a schoolhouse was at Berwick in 1719. Nearly all Maine schools before the Revolution were elementary schools. In a few instances there was the semblance of a Latin grammar school (secondary) to help prepare Maine boys for Harvard College and the

Congregational clergy. In 1794 the Massachusetts General Court granted a charter to Bowdoin College.

Academies which for 150 years provided Maine youth its finest educational advantages, date from those established at Hallowell and Berwick in 1791. By 1821 there were twenty-five academies. From this beginning, higher education in Maine has progressed slowly but steadily. The free high school law of 1873 brought some 150 high schools that operated on a single community basis until 1957. In 1853, normal schools were established at Farmington and Castine. In 1878, the Western Maine Normal School was founded at Gorham and the Madawaska Training School at Fort Kent was opened expressly for the preparation of teachers to instruct the French settlers, exiled Acadians from Nova Scotia, in the St. John Valley. Subsequently the Twentieth century normal schools were established at Machias and Presque Isle. During the depression of the 1930s, the training school at Castine was closed permanently; in 1941 it became the home of the Maine Maritime Academy which prepares officers for the U. S. Merchant Marine. In 1945 the Normal schools became Teachers Colleges when they established four-year programs. In 1965 they became State Colleges and in 1968 by legislative act were joined with the existing campuses of the University of Maine (Orono, Portland and Augusta) to form a new University of Maine.

In the second half of the Twentieth century, the most significant development in public school education has been the formation of School Administrative Districts under provisions of the 1957 Sinclair Act. This legislation, permitting communities to cross town lines for operation of schools, has gone far toward the elimination of small high schools and the advancement of elementary and secondary schools, upgrading instruction in all areas. For the first time, modern laboratories, adequate libraries and specialists are provided for thousands of Maine boys and girls in rural as well as city areas. There are fewer, larger and better equipped high schools than in 1957 when there were more than 125 with under a hundred students. About fifty-one percent of 1968 high school graduates went on to further training. Centrally located secondary schools enrolling 33 to 2000 pupils are replacing obsolete facilities and the two- or three-teacher schools with small enrollments and limited programs. Extensive curricula geared to all youth and not limited to preparation of the college-bound are taught by well-qualified certified teachers. By 1968 more than seventy-five percent of Maine boys and girls were attending school in cities or school administrative districts. With 7500 new employes in public education since 1960, student-teacher ratio was estimated at 20.8 for 1968.

While the Little Red Schoolhouse looms large in the history of Maine, recalling the days when a single small community boasted of six or seven 'district' or one-room schools, this is a thing of the past. One village after another has consolidated its elementary schools until adequate one-grade-to-a-teacher schools with gymnasiums, lunchrooms and other ancillary service areas are available for the majority of Maine youngsters. In 1945 at the close of World War II, there were some 1200 one-room rural schools with one teacher coping with eight grades. Twenty-three years later only 48 remained. Usually in isolated areas, only twelve house all eight grades. The others serve as neighborhood schools for beginners, with the children in upper grades transported to central facilities.

A 1937 report indicated that a smaller proportion of the State income then was spent on its schools than was spent a century ago and that more than 200 schools were operating on an annual budget of less than 360 dollars. In 1969, the largest item in the annual budgets of Maine cities and towns, based on the property tax, was the support of schools. Local communities pay the greater part of the cost of public education; State subsidies provide 28 percent and Federal funds provide some supplemental assistance. Total expenditures for public elementary and secondary school education in 1966-67 were $105,188,918. Teachers salaries had risen as the result of legislative action on minimum salaries and the vigorous agitation of local school associations and the Maine Teachers Association. The level of local and State support for public education had become a critical financial and political problem for Maine citizens.

A State Board of Education sets educational policy and its Commissioner directs the State Department of Education. Specialists are available in curriculum, school construction, transportation, finance and teacher education. Teacher certification assures qualified instructors; a placement bureau brings together prospective teachers and employers.

Five vocational-technical institutes at Calais, Presque Isle, Bangor, Auburn and South Portland, offering two-year post-high school courses in numerous fields are the Board's responsibility. In operation are twelve vocational-technical regional centers. There are three schools of practical nurse education at Presque Isle, Waterville and Portland. The Division of Vocational Rehabilitation works with handicapped adults.

One of the country's five Outward Bound programs is carried on at Hurricane Island near Vinalhaven. A cultural supplement in elementary school has been Operation Treasure Hunt.

Education for exceptional children with physical or mental handicaps is available in nearly all communities through special classes or home instruction. There is also some experimentation in Maine with ungraded schools and adult behavioral studies.

Since World War II the impact of the great increase generally in attendance at public institutions of higher learning has been felt in Maine where such institutions also have increased in number. Programs have been broadened in the arts and sciences, including such disciplines as law, oceanography, ecology and the newer sciences. The Orono campus of the University of Maine is the largest unit of higher education in Maine, with colleges of arts and sciences, agriculture and life sciences, education, engineering, business administration and a school of forestry. Besides undergraduate programs, it offers many master's programs and a selected number of doctoral programs. Its student body exceeds 8000. The University which has a Continuing Education Division and operates a faculty extension service largely in rural areas, was founded as an agricultural school at Orono in 1865, became co-educational in 1872 and was named the University of Maine in 1897.

Among sixteen private colleges that have become cultural centers and well-represented in the arts are three with traditions deep in Maine's early history. With the University, they have graduated statesmen, diplomats, theologians, teachers, writers, engineers and others who have received world-wide recognition. Bowdoin, incorporated at Brunswick in 1794, is one of the outstanding small liberal arts colleges in the East, recently began admitting women students. Colby at Waterville was chartered in 1813 as the Maine Literary and Theological Institute. From 1831 to 1842, as Waterville College, it was one of the first institutions in the country to experiment with manual training. It became co-educational in 1871 and acquired its present name in 1899. By 1952 Colby had forty buildings including an Art Museum on a sightly new 700-acre campus on Mayflower Hill. Bates at Lewiston, a non-sectarian college renowned for its debaters, is an outgrowth of the Maine State Seminary, founded in 1855 by Free Baptists; co-education began in 1864. A broad expansion program was undertaken in 1970.

Other collegiate institutions are St. Joseph's at North Windham, St. Francis at Biddeford, Nasson at Springvale, Ricker at Houlton, Husson at Bangor and Thomas at Waterville. Identified as colleges by the 1967 Legislature and currently working toward degree-granting status are Bliss at Lewiston, Beals at Bangor, Unity at Unity and Kennedy at Fort Kent; and more recently the College of the Atlantic at the former Oblate Seminary at Bar Harbor.

There are several institutions of special study such as the Bangor Theological Seminary which has trained young men for the ministry since 1814, the Northern Conservatory of Music also at Bangor, and the Westbrook Junior College for Women (1831) at Portland, the only two-year terminal college for women in the State; early degrees were for Ladies of Liberal Learning. There are also business schools and professional schools in the arts (see THE ARTS).

Oak Grove Seminary, founded in 1849 as a Friends School for Girls, was merging with Coburn Classical Institute of Waterville in 1970. Other private preparatory schools and academies include Protestant, Jewish and Catholic institutions. Changing conditions in the mid-Twentieth century had caused the closing of several parochial schools by 1969.

RELIGION

With the rise of ecumenism in the mid-Twentieth century, Maine generally reflects the ebb and flow of religious feeling and practise in historically conservative New England. Religion has been practised more fervently in some periods than in others over the years. There have been 'revivals' and new 'movements', on the whole indicating the reserved temper of the people, as contrasted with more perfervid expression in other parts of the country.

The first Christian missionary to Maine was the Jesuit priest, Nicholas Audbry or d'Aubri, who preached to the Indians at Dochet's Island in 1604. The first Protestant clergyman was the Reverend Richard Seymour, minister at the unsuccessful Popham Colony of 1607. Early Jesuit churches and schools were built in the wilderness by Gabriel Druillettes (1646) and Father Rasle (1696). Most of the Wabanaki were converted to Christianity by these scholarly and progressive men, and Father Rasle wielded tremendous influence over the Indians. Partly from fear of his power and partly from bigotry, he was persecuted and eventually killed by the English. But between him and his Protestant contemporary, John Eliot, there developed a mutal tolerance and esteem akin to Twentieth century ecumenism. Eliot's Indian converts at that time were spread widely through southern Maine. Today's Indians however, retain a heritage of Jesuit teaching.

Bearing in mind that colonization was motivated by the desire for expansion of empire rather than for religious freedom, it is not remarkable that the first settlers were more concerned with temporal rather than spiritual matters. However, since the English settled most of colonial Maine, it was to be expected that their religious heritage could be perpetuated here. And indeed it was. Until Massachusetts gained control of Maine in the 1650s, Anglicanism was favored. The most celebrated preacher of the day was the Reverend Robert Jordan of Cape Elizabeth. When he was driven out by the Indians in the 1670s, Anglicanism virtually disappeared in Maine for a hundred years. Under Massachusetts the Congregational Church was favored, even an established church, and usually was referred to as The First Parish Church. The Congregationalists (presently United Church of Christ) dominated the Maine scene until well into the Nineteenth century. There were no Roman Catholic churches in Maine before the Revolution, no Methodist and very few Baptist churches.

In the 1790s the first Methodist churches were established and soon they and the Baptists (both Calvinistic and Free Will) were growing rapidly with their camp meetings and revivalistic fervor. They made serious inroads into Congregational strength. And the Congregationalists lost some of their own largest and most influential churches to the Unitarians. The Universalists also flourished. The Quakers who had gained a foothold in Kittery, Portland and Windham before the Revolution, spread and grew strong in such towns as Durham, Vassalboro, China, Unity and Temple. The Episcopalians began to burgeon in such places as Portland, Lewiston, Bangor and Damariscotta. More and more, Maine took on the pattern of the rest of the country.

Among the first religious colonies to be established in Maine were those of the Shakers (United Society of True Believers) who settled in Alfred, Gorham and New Gloucester around 1793. Only the latter survives in 1969, with few to perpetuate a way of life that has contributed much to American culture.

In the middle years of the Nineteenth century, Irish immigrants brought their Catholicism to the State as they settled around Damariscotta and Whitefield, Portland and Bangor. The Irish got jobs as coachmen, railroad workers, canal builders, dock workers, and soon St. Patrick's in Damariscotta, St. Dominic's in Portland, St. John's in Bangor and St. Denis' in Whitefield were flourishing parishes.

When the Irish were joined by the wave of Catholic French Canadians who came after the Civil War to work in the mills of Biddeford, Lewiston, Old Town, Augusta, Waterville and Sanford, Roman Catholicism quickly became the largest denomination in Maine. The Diocese of Portland was created just before the Civil War to direct ecclesiastical affairs, build parishes and provide priests and nuns.

Meantime other Protestant denominations took root — the Adventists, the Reorganized Church of Jesus Christ of Latter Day Saints, Lutheran, Christian, Evangelical, Greek Orthodox, Church of God, Pentecostal, Church of the Nazarene and Christian Science. There was also a Jewish migration to several Maine cities and synagogues were built in Portland, Lewiston and Bangor.

There were even some 'splinter' groups that blossomed briefly — the Bullockites of Porter, the Higginsites of Carmel, the Cochranites of York County, the Palestine Emigration Association of Jonesport and environs. The latter group, 156 strong, set out in 1866 under the leadership of George Jones Adams to prepare the Holy Land for the Second Coming of Christ. Later came the Shiloh experiment (Holy Ghost and Us Society) of the Reverend Frank W. Sandford who in 1897 established 'The Kingdom' at Durham where at one time over 1000 followers lived in elaborate buildings. Dissension set in and the community disintegrated after unfavorable publicity attending Sandford's efforts to evangelize the whole world through a cruise that ended disastrously in Portland in 1911, with Sandford sentenced to the Atlanta penitentiary. However, The Kingdom survived and in 1969 some 2000 followers continued religious work based on literal belief in the Bible. The Kingdom's headquarters and Bible school were moved to Durham, N. H., but a hundred followers attend Sunday services at the Shiloh Chapel, all that remains of the original buildings. The Buchmanites appeared briefly in Maine in the 1930s.

In 1970, the Roman Catholics, United Church of Christ, Baptists, Methodists and Episcopalians are the largest denominations. Increasingly active are the fundamentalist denominations, Nazarene, Church of God and Pentecostal, with numerous lay preachers.

Maine was the first State to have a radio parish. Founded in 1926 by the Reverend Howard O. Hough, it was designed especially for shut-ins and continues interdenominational in character. The world-wide Christian Endeavor Society for young people was founded in 1881 in Portland's Williston Church by the Reverend Francis E. Clark. The Seacoast Mission, an independent philanthropic enterprise, has headquarters at Bar Harbor. Its boat *Sunbeam* brings religious, educational, hospital and recreational facilities to the islands and lonely outposts on the Maine coast.

Notable in the 1960s was the accord among Catholics, Protestants and Jews, if not a marked increase in church attendance. Growing unity among Christians was significant. Not only were local churches federating and denominations uniting, but also a new ecumenism was diminishing the old antagonisms between Christians as new ways were sought to meet spiritual needs in a troubled materialistic world.

Early churches of architectural and historical interest as well as some in contemporary style may be seen in many Maine communities (see TOURS). Among educational institutions, contemporary architecture mingles compatibly with traditional on college campuses. America's oldest frame schoolhouse (1791) is still in use at Berwick Academy.

ARCHITECTURE

EVOLVING in the northeastern environment of New England since the Seventeenth century, Maine architecture has its own indigenous quality. Eminently suited to its time and place, it has expressed a people and a way of life belonging to a particular background and landscape. Developments from period to period have reflected the reserved and substantial characteristics of Maine people. The best examples from the Eighteenth and early Nineteenth centuries are notable for their aesthetic and practical qualities in humanized relation to the environment. Many of these architectural traditions have been upheld in the Twentieth century which has seen the introduction of contemporary forms that in the best examples not only suit the environment but also are compatible with earlier forms.

Presumably the earliest Maine dwellings were the turf and thatch huts such as the first English settlers had known in their homeland. The log house or cabin was then unknown in England, was not native to Maine or New England and probably was introduced to America in mid-Seventeenth century. Wood, of superior quality and in great abundance in forested Maine, was the basis of construction until early in the Nineteenth century. A rare exception was the Old Stone Gaol (1653) (NHL), at York, now a museum and believed to be the oldest stone building still in use in the United States.

Early Maine architecture admirably met the standards of structural beauty and practicality. A definite indigenous quality characterized the designs derived and adapted from existing forms. As elsewhere in New England, native architecture, particularly that between 1760 and 1820, influenced later architecture throughout the country, although it had little effect on any other than domestic design. Architectural types prevailing in the State until well into the Nineteenth century fall into several divisions: defensive garrisons, farm houses, manor houses, meeting-houses, public buildings, schools and jails. Considering the long period of intermittent French and Indian warfare from 1675 to 1763, it is remarkable that there are any existing buildings that were erected prior to 1765. Few early stagecoach inns survive and fewer taverns such as Burnham Tavern (1770) at Machias, Jed Prouty Tavern (1804) at Bucksport and Jefferd's Tavern at York.

The need for protection produced such defensive buildings as the McIntire Garrison House (1640-45) (NHL) at York and Fort Halifax (1754) (NHL) at Winslow, America's oldest blockhouse. Simplicity, strength of design and defensive requirements were stressed. The Maine garrison or blockhouse was, in effect, an adaptation of English and medieval fortifications, as evidenced by such a feature as the overhang which made it possible to protect the walls beneath by firing upon the enemy from the projection of the second story. Of all the architectural types in Maine, this was the slowest to change; little or no alteration in form occurred in defensive buildings between the McIntire Garrison House and Fort Edgecomb (1808). The United States government constructed a series of fortifications in Maine ranging from the wooden Fort Kent blockhouse (1839) to the large granite Fort Knox (1844) at Prospect used during the Civil War. Ten of these have been restored as State Memorials.

Because of the rarity of existing buildings erected before 1730, it is difficult to trace early architectural development in Maine, although it doubtless corresponded to that of Massachusetts and Connecticut. The ordinary farmhouse remained unchanged in design during the last three quarters of the Eighteenth century, whereas the meeting-house underwent clearly defined changes between 1760 and 1820. The plan of the typical Maine house was patterned after that farther south, the type which prevailed throughout the State during most of the Eighteenth century having been evolved from an earlier design that consisted of one, two, or three rooms with a central chimney, and a half-story in the roof above. The characteristic Eighteenth century house was a rectangular structure with a central entrance hall, a huge central chimney usually seven or eight feet square built behind the stairs, two spacious rooms on either side of the hall, a central kitchen at the rear of the chimney, and two small rooms filling out the rear corners of the rectangle. On the second floor there usually were two large rooms at the front of the house, called 'chambers,' and two small corner 'bedrooms' at the rear. A rough lean-to often was added afterward at the rear of the house. No exact architectural balance was sought and it was customary for nearly all houses to be built with the front facing the southern, or warmer and more protected side. When waterways were the roadsteads, many houses faced the water.

The framework of the early Maine house consisted of sills, plates, girts and 'summers' or girders, and was constructed with the utmost care. Timbers were hewn, while all pieces of the framework were broad-axed or adzed until nearly as smooth as if they had been planed. Boards, studs and light joints were sawed; joints between braces, girts and posts were mortised and tenoned. Roofs were commonly gabled, with the ridge parallel to the road. Roof boarding covered the roof framework and at an early date before the use of shingles, roofs were occasionally thatched with river sedge. Ridgepoles were a later development, a ridge purlin or horizontal member being used on the early buildings to support the common rafters. With the exception of those on defensive buildings, there is no very early example in Maine of the overhang.

The exteriors of Eighteenth-century houses were covered with clapboards, with or without sheathing. No outside cornices existed in the earlier architecture, although subsequently there were cornices of moderate projection with a bed mold. These gradually became elaborate, bed molds becoming profusely ornamented; and in the early Nineteenth century, cornices were used across gabled ends, and the rake molds became as heavy as horizontal cornices. Early small and narrow casement windows were replaced by double-hung windows, three lights (panes) wide by five or six high, and later by still wider twelve-light windows. Much of the glass used was imported. Shutters were built either in one leaf, covering the entire window with a track on the window stool, or in two parts. Entrances were merely frontispieces built without a projecting hood or canopy over the door and were of three types: flat entablature (the horizontal member over the entrance), pediment and broken pediment (the triangular ornamental space over the doorway), and scrolled pediment. Sidelights are usually associated with Nineteenth century construction; while the use of the broken frieze above fluted pilasters is an odd departure from classic precedent. Circular heads of doorways were common, while elliptical heads occurred after 1800. Front doors were broad and low, and simple molded entablatures with pilasters formed the usual design.

The interior woodwork of front rooms in the Eighteenth and early Nineteenth century houses centered about the fireplace whose wall usually was paneled. Two broad panels appeared over the fireplace itself and an elaborate bolection molding surrounded the fireplace opening. In more formal houses, the moldings and horizontal panels were flanked by narrow fluted pilasters. The remaining parts of the fireplace wall were completed with vertical panels to the doorway, and a small horizontal panel above it. Wood cornices gave height and scale to the low-studded rooms and nearly always there were dadoes the height of the window sills. Staircase newels were approximately three inches square, and skirt moldings were cut to elaborate and interesting forms. Handrail moldings often were mitered to form the top of newels and the handrails themselves were small and delicately wrought. The bead and bevel molding was most frequently used, serving as panel mold for interior and outside doors, shutters, wainscot, dadoes, paneling and cupboards. A dominant ceiling molding was a form of cyma recta, a molding of reverse curve at the top of the cornice; while a large cove or concave molding was characteristic of outside window caps.

Cellars, if any, in early Maine buildings were usually under only one part of the house and used chiefly for food storage. Their walls either were unfinished or finished with poor quality mortar. Chimneys were of underburned brick laid in puddled clay, great care being taken in the construction of brickwork. The woodwork of many extant old houses is in much better condition than the masonry because of the inferior brick and mortar that had to be used. Fireplaces were large, their hearths finished with tiles seven or eight inches square. Bricks were not uniform in size and in all Colonial work were handmade, as in the McLellan House (1770-74) at Gorham. Flemish bond was the common design for good brickwork, being used especially in the construction of important facades.

In the Colonial period and later, iron was scarce and in great demand in Maine. Hardware was hand-wrought and frequently showed much delicacy and refinement of design and a fine sense of scale. Hand-wrought nails were of two types: a thin pointed nail for finishing work, and a larger, stronger nail for heavier construction. The first paint used on exteriors was dark Indian red, composed of red ocher and fish oil. Although one or two rooms might be painted, only the well-to-do could afford this practise until well into the Eighteenth century. Records indicate the use of hangings and tapestries in the homes of the wealthy. Imported wallpapers and stencilling appeared in the Eighteenth and Nineteenth centuries.

Manor houses were larger and more elaborate than the typical Maine house of the period. The earliest recorded example in Maine is the William Pepperrell House (1682) at Kittery Point. Others are the Lady Pepperrell House (1760) and the Cutts House (1783) at Kittery Point and the Sarah Orne Jewett House (1774) at South Berwick. Many of these manor houses represented precisely what the term implies: they were the 'big houses' in the English sense, the centers of prosperity and culture. Indeed, several of the pre-Revolutionary landowners such as Dr. Sylvester Gardiner of Gardiner were to all intents and purposes 'lords of the manor,' operating their estates under a feudal system of tenancy.

The mansions of the late Eighteenth and early Nineteenth centuries are characterized by larger scale, higher ceilings and more elaborate detail. Maine carpenters and carvers brought their own skill and originality to the designs they derived from English pattern books, for moldings, cornices, entablatures, portals and facades. Adapting English Georgian architecture to their own ends, the architects used their materials intelligently, retaining a delicacy and refinement of treatment even after the style became ornate and heavy in England. Simplicity without crudeness was sought; architectural charm was the result.

Cornices on the more elaborate early Nineteenth century houses show far more detail, windows are larger and have more complex moldings, and the entrance motives of the larger homes are outstanding features. Although the work usually was executed by local artisans, the designs were far richer than those of more modest buildings and the influence of the Renaissance in England is obvious. Exceptionally fine interior work is found in the mansions built between 1790 and 1820. The elliptical arch for door heads and recesses was adopted, the Palladian window appeared, as did sidelights in connection with entrance doorways, as well as porches and free columns. More generous lighting, space and circulation was provided. Architectural restraint is a salient feature of the best of these designs.

As the Eighteenth century ended, the Federal style based on the work of the English Adams brothers gained wide popularity through the builders' manuals of William Paine and Asher Benjamin. Elongated proportion and delicate ornament are its common features. Scale often is larger and brick is used more frequently than in the Colonial period.

The first decade of the Nineteenth century was an important period in residential building in all eastern American cities. By 1800, Maine's maritime economy was flourishing and shipmasters and merchants were transforming some of their increasing wealth into fine homes. In that year the three-story brick Hugh and Stephen McLellan Mansions rose in Portland, each costing about twenty thousand dollars. Others soon were built in the town including two surviving examples by Alexander Parris: the Ingraham House (1801) and the Hunnewell House (1805). The scale is matched by Wiscasset's Nickells-Sortwell House built in 1807 when the town was at the height of its prosperity and its houses represented the 'apogee of the Georgian style as the culmination of colonial and early national architecture.' Another distinguished Wiscasset home is the Wood-Carlton House (1804-05) by Nicholas Codd, designer of the Kavanagh Mansion at Damariscotta Mills and the Cortrell House at Damariscotta, both dating from 1803. These three dwellings are two stories and reflect in more elegant form how a large number of Federal period Maine houses appeared.

From the Embargo of 1807 to the close of the War of 1812, building activity was suspended, but the coming of peace saw almost two more decades of the Federal style. A handsome example of the post-war home is the Ruggles House (1819) at Columbia Falls, erected from plans of Aaron Sherman of Machias. Its wealth of Adamesque detail is in contrast to the simpler Robinson House in Thomaston designed by William R. Keith in the 1820s.

The Alna Meeting-house (1719) is a satisfactory example of another architectural type found in Maine. Simply but sturdily constructed, with windows on all four sides, the building rests securely on a dry foundation of large squared slabs of granite over a rubble wall. As on most of the old meeting houses, the outside finish is plain; rake molds are flat and windows are finished with simple architraves. Galleries run around three sides of the interior which is dominated by a splendid two-story pulpit. Great skill of design and beauty of workmanship went into the old pulpits which often resembled the Alna pulpit in height, and had a canopy and a high, elaborate enclosure for the preacher. The box pews in the Alna galleries are set at varying levels, several seats being hinged so that worshippers might more comfortably stand to sing.

Fine Federal ecclesiastical architecture is found in Kennebunkport's Second Congregational Church (1824) while the Lincoln County Courthouse of the same date in Wiscasset exemplifies a good civic building of the period. The oldest courthouse in continuous use in the United States, it is a fine example of brickwork, its entrance an elliptical niche with half ellipsoidal dome, a unique exhibit of brick-laying.

Old stone buildings in Maine are rare. Some originally were used for schoolhouses such as one now a private home at Phippsburg (1853). During the 1820s the use of granite began to be popular. It appears in the Paris Hill Jail (1822), now a Library, in Portland's First Parish Church (1825) and Mariners' Church facade (1828). While the first structure is utilitarian in design, the other two are Federal. In 1829 two granite buildings mark the start of a new style in Maine. Charles Bulfinch's State House at Augusta is of mostly Roman inspiration but has the classical dignity and discipline of the coming Greek Revival. Directly influenced by it is the nearby Kennebec County Courthouse, like the capitol building in general form but with more pronounced Greek Revival treatment.

Favoring large, simple forms, the Greek Revival lasted in Maine from about 1830 to 1860, an important period before the Civil War in which much growth occurred. Thus, throughout the State, a wide variety of examples can be found, including homes, churches, schools, business buildings, warehouses, mills and at least one bank, a firehouse and a hotel. Many of these structures reflect a dependence on the books of Asher Benjamin, Minard Lafever and Edward Shaw, with always a degree of originality. They were created in wood, brick and granite and range from the work of an architect to the vernacular expression of a housewright. Therefore, within the same style can exist an 1833 columned brick mansion by Portland's gentleman designer, Charles Q. Clapp, and modest mid-Nineteenth century farmhouses by Fairfield Center's carpenter-builder, Charles D. Lawrence.

In this Hellenic movement, not only were features of Greek architecture adopted but also Maine towns were given Greek names such as Troy and Athens. Variations on the Greek temple home appeared although Colonial traditions were carried through. Houses were built with end rather than side facing the street; Greek colonnades, columns, entablatures, bold and heavy moldings and extensive variations on Doric, Ionic and Corinthian designs were used.

With the arrival of the Greek Revival duplex house, Portland and Bangor took on an urbane appearance between 1830 and 1860. Portland saw the building of such fine examples as the Ward Houses (1933) and the Neal Houses (1836), and Bangor saw the erection of the Governor Kent Houses and some on Broadway about 1835. Portland went a step further in 1836 with its Park Street Block, a complex of twenty houses and a park. Bangor could boast of the new Bangor House built in 1835 from designs by Isaiah Rogers and now the only survivor of the earliest American luxury hotels.

Although the Greek Revival dominated the pre-Civil War Maine scene, it was by no means the only style in evidence. As early as 1819 the Gothic Revival appeared in Christ Church, Gardiner, by the Rev. Samuel F. Jarvis of New York. Beginning in the early 1820s, simple Gothic details found their way into the designs of otherwise Federal or Greek Revival churches. The next churches completely in the style were built about 1833 at Machias and East Machias, probably from plans by Edward Shaw of Boston. From that city three years later came Richard Upjohn to create his first important building, St. John's Church at Bangor, a handsome Gothic structure that is no more.

As work on the Bangor church progressed, it was ending at 'Oaklands,' the Upjohn-designed home of the Gardiner family. Maine's first Gothic Revival dwelling, the battlemented mansion at Gardiner stood alone in style until the next decade when architects and builders began to draw upon the new romantic ideas supplied in such books as A. J. Downing's *Cottage Residences*. This popular volume has plates from which probably were derived Portland's J. J. Brown House by Henry Rowe and other Gothic cottages in the State.

In 1845, Richard Upjohn did two Gothic Revival churches in Brunswick, the First Parish with intricate timber roofing inside and the more modest St. Paul's, both of board and batten on the exterior. Somewhat in the manner of the latter, he published a plan for a rural church in 1852 which was imitated in Hallowell and Thomaston where fine examples of other Maine architectural styles also may be found.

From professional designs grew a widespread carpenter Gothic vernacular, an often incorrect or partial rendering of the original style which nevertheless possesses a vitality and delight of its own. Maine's prime illustration is the Wedding Cake House in Kennebunk. A less flamboyant example is the Jackson House at Winslow.

Georgian and Gothic were frequently combined, as in the beautiful First Congregational Church at Kennebunkport.

Although not as popular in the 1840s and '50s as the Greek and Gothic Revivals, the Italianate Style with its bracketing, rustication and square towers did have an impact on Maine, especially in the domestic architecture of Portland and Bangor. Its great monument is the brownstone Morse-Libby House built in Portland in 1859 from designs by Henry Austin of New Haven. A country cousin to this is the wooden Lord Funeral Home in Norridgewock. Italianate features appear on the customs houses that Treasury Department Architect Ammi B. Young planned for Belfast, Wiscasset and other coastal towns in the 1850s. The style is also recognizable in three large buildings of the same decade by Gridley J. F. Bryant of Boston: the Androscoggin County Courthouse and Jail at Auburn, the Kennebec County Jail at Augusta, and Hathorn Hall, Bates College, Lewiston.

The Civil War ended the Greek Revival and transformed other revivals into a less definable, more eclectic Victorian Style. A taste for French forms became particularly apparent in the erection of streets of mansard-roofed homes and business blocks in Portland after the Great Fire of 1866, and was reflected on a smaller scale in other parts of the State. However, through the late 1860s and the 1870s, the distinctive French roof was forced to play a secondary role to a conglomeration of forms. One Maine architect who managed to follow a definite design program at this time was Francis H. Fassett of Portland. During the 1870s he applied a modified Gothic in brick, stone and ironwork to most of his designs, from a large building at Gorham State College to his own home.

With the growth of cities after the Civil War, the wealthy and middle classes began to spend their summers at nearby beaches and lakes or to travel by train and steamboat to resort areas. Maine was popular and each year drew Philadelphians, New Yorkers and Bostonians to Bar Harbor, Mt. Kineo and other regions. Large hotels arose at the resorts, the outstanding survivor being the Poland Spring House used in the 1960s as a rehabilitation center.

Especially along the coast, the more affluent built 'cottages' the size of large homes. Architects designed these somewhat informally to complement the landscape. Thus, on Mt. Desert in the late 1870s and early 1880s, Boston Architect William R. Emerson employed large simple shapes, wooden shingles, native stone and spacious floor plans. His work in the Shingle Style had great impact on John Calvin Stevens, then Francis H. Fassett's junior partner. Beginning with his own Portland house in 1883, Stevens applied Emerson's lessons in a more organized fashion. From 1885 to 1891 he maintained a partnership with Albert Winslow Cobb and began a practice of high quality that reached across the State and made him the dean of Maine architects in his time. Although Stevens used a Shingle Style formula for cottages into the Twentieth century, he started to adapt academic Colonial Revival details after 1886. These came to dominate his designs and turned him away from the important work of creating a simpler more unified domestic dwelling.

A prime example of the late Nineteenth century academic movement is Bowdoin's Walker Art Museum (1894) designed in Italian Renaissance manner by McKim, Mead and White. Like Stevens, the famed New York trio had worked earlier in the Shingle Style but was now making careful interpretations of the past.

Another aspect of the State's Nineteenth century architecture is a forward-looking expression of functionalism. A variety of forms is used to fulfill specific needs, and popular styles have little or no influence on their designs. The most dynamic of the utilitarian structures are the huge brick mills in Lewiston, Brunswick, Waterville, Lisbon Falls and other manufacturing communities. Their large scale and rows of like windows give them a Twentieth century appearance. This feeling also is found in smaller mills like the wooden Cascade Woolen Mill at Oakland. In some cases such as in Westbrook and Waterville, rows of identical low-cost homes were built for mill workers, a forerunner of modern housing developments. Another form of massive building was the warehouse, erected of brick and granite mostly in Portland and Bangor. Railroads built stations throughout the State, most of them quite plain except in some cities and towns. Many have been demolished or converted to other uses. The Bucksport depot is now an historical museum.

Based on theories expounded in Orson Squire Fowler's *Home for All,* a few octagon houses were built. Brick ones at Wiscasset and Farmington, wooden ones at Oakland and Gardiner, and others. These were supposed to cost less and provide more space than the conventional dwelling. Unadorned barns were an integral part of the rural scene and there were elaborate carriage houses such as the one attributed to Alexander Parris that formerly stood on the University of Maine's Portland campus.

The Nineteenth century in Maine was a period rich in architectural diversity and creativity, but following the decline of the Greek Revival, there is little to distinguish it from that of the rest of the country, although the soundness and simplicity of the Georgian and Greek Revival traditions were not altogether abandoned. Following general architectural trends in the Twentieth century, Maine saw readaptation of classical forms and increased use of iron, steel and stone in construction, and later, concrete and more glass. Mid-century developments brought new styles and materials to meet new needs. Notable examples of good contemporary architecture compatible with its surroundings are seen on Bowdoin and

Colby campuses, and in new homes, churches and other public buildings in some communities. But in an era of rapid change, mass production, housing shortages and the inflation of the 1960s, housing 'developments' and many public buildings have not achieved distinction.

Variations of the 'ranch' style have rivalled the 'Cape Cod' which may turn up with the ubiquitous 'picture' window whatever the vista; mobile homes often replace low-cost building. As year-round recreation became Maine's second largest industry, A-frames and streamlined summer cottages and cabins appeared in numbers. Motels and boatels, some garish, some pseudo-Colonial, competed with turn-of-the-century hostelries in resort areas. With the decline of small farming, the buying and restoration of old farmhouses became popular as more people sought vacation homes in Maine.

In 1969 the 104th Legislature created a State Housing Authority to help meet what the State's Department of Economic Development called a billion dollar problem. A 1968 housing survey described forty percent of Maine homes as 'sub-standard,' many rural area housing units as 'structurally unsound,' lacking in proper plumbing, wiring and heating. Needed by 1975 would be some 25,000 housing units. To upgrade existing housing by that time would mean improvements on more than 20,000 per year.

Unfortunately, fire such as the conflagrations of 1775 and 1866 in Portland, and 1911 in Bangor, and the Twentieth century wrecking ball, have destroyed many examples of Maine's finest architecture; some survivors have been marred by remodeling and alterations; others have been allowed to deteriorate. However, the genuine regard for Maine's architectural heritage and traditions still can be seen in many private homes and restorations, and in the work of many historical and preservation groups who maintain surviving examples of distinguished old homes and buildings throughout the State.

An inventory of these may be found in the Colby College Architectural Archives and many are open to visitors (see TOURS) including Montpelier, replica of the General Knox Mansion at Thomaston, maintained by the State which in 1969 had undertaken an overall survey for the National Registry of Historic Landmarks.

THE ARTS

WHEN the arts fuse with the imperatives of life to form the culture of a people, they preserve the past, embrace the present and search the future. As a generic part of the community, the arts express the spirit of a region — life and art illuminate one another. First land in the northeastern United States to know white settlers early in the Seventeenth century, the State of Maine in its pristine beauty and its elemental life of the sea and the forests has ignited many talents to illuminate American life. Over the years Maine has produced or drawn unto itself writers, painters, sculptors, camera and graphic artists, musicians, craftsmen and members of the performing arts. Maine has given inspiration to men and women who have had something to say about the human condition. Maine thus has contributed to the American mainstream a tradition that reflects the spirit of its region, a spirit of value in our time. And the arts are livelier than ever in Maine today.

Man's age-old struggle with his environment always has found expression in the arts since the time of cave paintings. Perhaps Maine's heritage, to which the Indians early contributed, derives from the harsh struggle for existence of the first settlers who had no time for self-portrayal, although their tombstones reveal some of the earliest artistic expression in America. As they gained a foothold in the New World, creation of the necessities of life took on a simple artistry, along with the customs, ballads and folkways of their homelands. With the wealthy landowners, shipmasters and lumber barons came imported decorative arts and other aspects of more gracious living. It was late in the Nineteenth century when nature was being threatened by man-made destruction that Winslow Homer's genius bloomed to portray with artistic integrity the story of life on the Maine coast where the strength of body and spirit still battled against the elements — a world in which 'the soul was not measured by gain, but was tested by its capacity merely to exist.'

By the mid-Twentieth century, creative energy and diversity could be seen in the whole spectrum of the arts. Like other states, Maine had a State Commission for the Arts and Humanities, created by the 103rd Legislature in 1966 to 'encourage and stimulate public interest and participation in the cultural heritage and programs of our State, to expand the State's cultural resources and to encourage and assist freedom of artistic expression essential for the well-being of the arts.' By 1970 its impact was felt in every county, its annual calendar *Heritage and Horizons* reflected a wide range of activities and State awards were being given for excellence in specific cultural fields.

Maine's institutions of higher learning had become broad-based cultural centers in their communities with programs valuable to human ecology in art, music, the performing arts and related activities, involving many nationally renowned figures. Notable was the Bixler Arts Center on the new Mayflower Hill campus of Waterville's Colby College which in the 1960s brought recognition to Maine's important artistic tradition that includes many of the finest painters and sculptors in American art. In two of many distinguished exhibitions, Bowdoin College, noted for its literary lights and for its Walker Art Museum whose collections include famous Colonial and Federal portraits, had graphically warned of despoliation of Maine's natural resources, and had won international recognition for its portrayal of the Negro in American art. Known for its ecological studies, its anthropological and folklore archives, its Art Museum and its theatre, the University of Maine, now a complex of three campuses and five additional State colleges, had initiated travelling art shows. Bates College was honoring Lewiston's native son, Artist Marsden Hartley, and was concerning itself with a new Arts Council in Lewiston-Auburn, central Maine's industrial community. Other colleges and pre-paratory schools were giving increased attention to the disciplines of the aesthetics.

Not confined to the campus, burgeoning activity in the arts was recognizing and expressing a public need. Art in many forms was reaching formerly isolated areas. Maine had legitimate, musical, experimental and community theatre, happenings, ballet, modern dance, Indian ceremonials, crafts, avant garde and traditional art and music. It had music centers not only on college campuses but also at Camden, Blue Hill and Hancock and at summer music camps, as well as the Bangor and Portland Symphonies, numerous bands and choral groups. For several seasons, Music-in-Maine performers travelled State-wide to bring music to school children. The Maine Art Van was bringing paintings to many communities. Local arts councils were bringing to their communities concerts, cinema and other events in the performing arts for school children and adults and there were reciprocal programs with Canada. There were art centers at Ogunquit, Boothbay Harbor and inland; art schools at Skowhegan, Deer Isle and Portland. In 1969, the Maine Chapter of the American Institute of Archi-tects sponsored a program to stimulate integration of art in schools, en-couraging incorporation of original works of art into the school environment.

Photography as an art medium was receiving recognition in exhibitions of the work of Eliot Porter, John McKee, Kosti Ruohomaa and others, and in experimental films. Handcrafts as art were appearing in more and more studios and shops.

Besides the museums at educational institutions there were the Portland Museum of Art, the architecturally delightful Museum of Art of Ogunquit, and the William A. Farnsworth Library and Museum at Rockland known for its Wyeth collection. Not the least of graphic arts were handsome exhibition catalogues. There were innumerable galleries, studios, shows and festivals, a sidewalk festival at Portland drawing thousands. Art was appearing in banks and other public buildings and was interpreting historic sites. The State's new cultural building housing Archives, Library and Historical Museum was scheduled to open in 1971.

Over a hundred historical societies were active in the State's sixteen counties, interpreting local history including art and crafts in their museums, publications and restorations. Maine's great maritime heritage was being interpreted in museums at Bath and Searsport; lumbering by the Penobscot Heritage at Bangor and museums at Patten, Ashland and Orono. There were Indian dioramas at Bar Harbor's Robert Abbe Museum; the nationally known Shaker collection at Poland Spring; *Montpelier*, replica of the General Knox Mansion at Thomaston, to mention a few. In 1969 the State Museum was inaugurating programs for its new quarters and the State Parks and Recreation Commission had restored for public visitation coastal forts and other sites with interpretations. There were also continuing archaeological programs.

In the literary field, Maine (and its people) continued to be a popular subject as well as a haven for writers on other matters. There were novels, poetry, local histories, reprints of rare books, photography and art books, not to mention special studies, periodicals and the like. There was an abundance of publications on area cultural activities and the communications media had begun to give serious attention to the arts.

In honor of Maine's 150th anniversary of statehood, the State Sesquicentennial Commission in 1970 emphasized the cultural aspects of Maine's historic heritage, sponsoring a History-mobile prepared by the State Museum, to tour the State.

A history of the development of the arts in Maine would note increasing momentum since World War II. While the Federal Arts programs of the depression years in the 1930s were primarily sociological rather than artistic, they perhaps generated the beginning of a greater public awareness of the relationship of life and art, once the provenance of the few. The brief outline of the arts in Maine in this volume necessarily must be limited to general trends and to the mention of only a few of those whose creativity contributes to the State's artistic heritage.

PAINTING AND SCULPTURE

First assayed by Colby College in the 1960s, Maine's art tradition embodying the influence of nature upon the artist gained world recognition through the 1963-64 exhibitions at Colby when Robert E. L. Strider was president. Among those responsible for this valuable contribution to the history of American art were James M. Carpenter, chairman of the Art Department, William B. Miller, director of the Archives of Maine Art, Christopher Huntington, curator of the Colby Art Museum and Mrs. Ellerton M. Jette, chairman of the Advisory Council of the Friends of Art at Colby.

The development of the arts in Maine relates to the styles and preferences, the changes and contrasts in the larger picture of American art. The first Colonial settlers preferred portraiture which flourished while Maine was a Province of Massachusetts. The sitters were well-to-do landowners prominent in the military who patronized the best New England artists, usually in Boston. The suggestion is persuasive that the earliest Eighteenth century art associated with Maine is the work of an unrecorded artist who came to Kittery in the early 1700s to paint the portraits of the Pepperrell family. The portrait presumed to be *Jane Pepperrell* (Lady Pepperrell House, Kittery Point) shows a young girl holding a flower in one hand, the half-length figure framed in an oval. Its characteristics reveal a composition and manner fashionable in England more than a generation earlier.

About mid-century, Jane's brother, William, commander-in-chief of the victorious expedition against the French fortress at Louisburg, had his portrait painted full length by John Smibert (1688-1751) who had brought to the colonies and to Boston where he had settled the 'latest London manner.' But after twenty years of provincial isolation, Smibert achieved less than an heroic quality in the portrait of *Sir William Pepperrell* (Essex Institute, Salem, Massachusetts). Robert Feke (active 1741-1750), the colonial-born and younger contemporary of Smibert in Boston, reworked and to a degree revitalized the sagging style of Smibert. Feke's portrait of *Brigadier Samuel Waldo* (Bowdoin College Museum of Art, Brunswick), also a hero of the Louisburg expedition, has a pretension based on an effective handling of artistic means more linear than plastic. Colors tend to be flat tones and areas are crisply defined by sharp edges. The illusion of a flesh and blood person in a three-dimensional world has been translated into the terms of a decorative surface. This is the method of the 'primitive' artist found flourishing well into the Nineteenth century.

Samuel Waldo who owned half a million acres of land in the Penobscot region, died near the site of Bangor in 1759.

Feke also painted likenesses of the Bowdoin family for whom the Brunswick college is named, among them the Museum's portrait of *James Bowdoin, II*. Joseph Blackburn (active 1752-1763) painted with stylish charm the double portrait of *James Bowdoin, III and his sister* as children in a landscape setting, in the Museum's collection. Joseph Badger (1708-1765) painted Colonel William Lithgow (Colby College Art Museum) in three-quarter length about 1760. Lithgow once commanded the Fort Halifax garrison at Winslow, where the blockhouse, oldest in America, still stands. Soon the brush of John Singleton Copley (1737-1815) began to record the gentry of Maine. The portrait of *Mrs. Samuel Waldo* (Museum of Fine Arts, Boston) is an example of Copley's mature style. The Waldos lived in Falmouth until 1770.

Gilbert Stuart became established in Boston after the Revolution and the same sort of patronage continued. In the Bowdoin College collection is the matching pair of Stuart portraits of *James Bowdoin, III* and his wife *Sarah Bowdoin*. Stuart also portrayed *William King* (State House, Augusta), soon to become the first governor of the State.

In the second phase of Maine and national art history, portraiture was joined by other subject matter. The itinerant limner brought portraiture, miniatures, silhouettes and other phases of pictorial art to rural communities from Saco to Hampden. These artists were largely self-taught and contact with prevailing fashionable art was minimal and by way of prints and engravings.

In the early Nineteenth century idyllic landscapes appear on over-mantel boards and in wall decoration. Townscapes and individual residences provided other subjects. The limner ordinarily included the frame in the price for his work.

One of the first itinerants in Maine was John Brewster, Jr., (1766-1854). Arriving in Buxton in 1795, he itinerated in Maine for the next quarter century, being recorded in Windham, Portland, Stroudwater, Kennebunk, Denmark, Bangor and Thomaston. Brewster's portraits of children are particularly appealing, such as *Elizabeth Abagail Wallingford*, age two, (Brick Store Museum, Kennebunk). His modest accomplishments are the more impressive since he was a deaf mute.

Benjamin Greenleaf (1786-1864) as a young man travelled in Maine. Portraits by him are related to Phippsburg and Bath. He painted in reverse on glass — difficult to do in the first place, but once framed, impervious to dust and loss of color. Other itinerants coming to Maine briefly include Susan Paine of Rhode Island and Joseph Davis, the left-handed painter from New Hampshire. This situation is reversed in the career of William Matthew Prior (1806-1873) who began painting in

Bath, progressed to Portland by the 1830s, and finally left the State. Prior and his relatives, the Hamblens, developed a virtual manufactory production of portraits, extending to two distinct styles. One was in a more quickly done flat manner, the other more expensive with shades and shadows.

Stencil art enjoyed a patronage in rural Maine. The repeating pattern would be applied to walls, floors and other surfaces. Rufus Porter (1782-1884) as a young man did many stencils and some freehand work. The State Museum, Augusta, has an example of his wall decoration.

Of quite a different turn was Jonathan Fisher (1768-1847) who began in 1796 a long tenure as pastor of the Blue Hill Congregational Church. Mary Ellen Chase has written a book about this extraordinary man whose curiosity propelled him along many avenues of science and art. He made woodcuts to illustrate a book he wrote and printed; he made careful studies from nature in watercolor; two versions exist of his *Self Portrait* (Bangor Theological Seminary). His *Morning View of Blue Hill Village, September 1824* (Farnsworth Library and Art Museum, Rockland) ranks as a very early topographic view of a particular place in Maine.

As Portland was becoming the largest city in Maine, a few artists were attracted to permanent residence. One of the first of these was Charles Codman (1800-1842) whose career proceeded from ornamental to landscape painting, from clock faces, signs and banners, to the decoration of the Elm Tavern in 1826 with landscape murals. John Neal, the local promoter of good works, encouraged the young artist with commissions for landscape paintings. Codman exhibited in Boston and New York. He was commissioned by Governor Dunlap to paint the *State House* as it appeared in 1836 (Maine State Library, Augusta).

Charles O. Cole (1817-1858) came to Portland in 1833 from Massachusetts where his father had instructed him and his brother John Greenleaf Cole (1806-1858) in portrait painting. At twenty-one Charles won a prize at the Maine Charitable Mechanic Association fair for his portrait of Mayor Cutter of Portland and in 1842 he painted the likeness of *Henry Wadsworth Longfellow* which is preserved in the Wadsworth-Longfellow House in Portland. In the 1840s Cole arranged two large exhibitions in Portland. Appropriately his tombstone is engraved with a painter's palette.

In Bangor the resident artist was Jeremiah Pearson Hardy (1800-1888) who had some apprentice experience as an engraver in Boston and later studied briefly with Samuel F. B. Morse in New York. Hardy's best work is portraiture, especially his sympathetic rendering of older people. He experimented modestly along lines suggested by the mid-century Luminists and gave instructions in painting in Bangor. Hardy's talents and paints were called upon for a variety of things. His account book reveals such items as 'painting the figure of a moose, lettering a tavern sign, bronzing an eagle, gilding ornaments upon a fan-light, framing a print, making india ink drawing of a machine.' Through his connection with Morse who introduced the daguerreotype to the United States in 1840, Hardy learned the new process and made use of these photographic images in his portrait work. His son, Francis W. Hardy, operated a photographic gallery in Bangor. His daughter, Annie Eliza Hardy (1839-1934), painted quiet and composed still lifes well into the Twentieth century. Paintings by the Hardys may be seen in the Bangor Public Library.

The romantic naturalism of the Hudson River School of landscape painting dominated American art in the 1840s and 1850s and of course the artists of the movement travelled beyond the Hudson River Valley in search of landscape themes and motifs. Canvases from Thomas Cole, Alvin Fisher, Thomas Doughty and Thomas Birch first record the 'rock-bound coast of Maine' and this conjunction of rock, water and sky in Maine has attracted artists of virtually every recognized and labelled movement in the subsequent history of American painting from the Luminists and Impressionists to the Abstractionists. Thomas Doughty's (1793-1856) *Desert Rock Lighthouse, Mount Desert*, 1847 (Newark Museum), which was engraved for publication is typical of the work of these professional artists who visited Maine in the summers of more than a hundred years ago.

Seeking to heighten the illusions of atmosphere, the younger men of the Hudson River School were labelled Luminists. Frederic E. Church (1826-1900) produced several notable works with Maine motifs. He may well be the first artist to have assayed to capture the monumental splendor of *Mount Katahdin* (Colby College Art Museum, Waterville). Fitzhugh Lane spent five summers in Castine before 1855, painting in the Penobscot Bay region where he found majestic ships and quiet mornings to record, as seen in his view of *Castine Harbor* (Witherle Memorial Library, Castine).

The local carving of Colonial gravestones was the forerunner of the art of sculpture in Maine. The Old Cemetery Association seeks to preserve such stones now fast disappearing from the southern counties. Sir William Pepperrell's tombstone in Kittery is one of the very few of the Colonial era imported from England. The Mason Philip Smith photographic record of Maine's Colonial gravestones, *Images in Stone* is at the Maine Historical Society, Portland, and includes the second oldest portrait stone in New England, that of John Wheelwright of Wells (d. 1745).

The innumerable 'family' cemeteries in Maine communities dating from the days when burials were near the family homestead, have provided material for gravestone rubbings and the verses for many anthologies. While the carvings often are macabre, the verses sometimes reveal human traits of piety and wit. A familiar one, found frequently, with variations:

> Come look at me as you pass by
> As you are now so once was I
> As I am now so you will be
> Prepare for death and follow me.

The first markers were simple fieldstones; later, Maine slate and granite were hand-carved and elaborate iron work and fences came into use. Still later came the rococo sarcophagi and mausoleums such as that of Opera Singer Emma Eames in Bath cemetery.

For the most part, sculpture in the Eighteenth and Nineteenth centuries was an adjunct to the house and shipbuilding that saw the development of decorative woodcarving (see HANDICRAFTS). The short career of Paul Akers (1825-1861) of Westbrook demonstrated that talent from the State of Maine could compete in larger fields. Clearly the ambition to become a sculptor of high art prompted Akers to seek artistic fulfillment abroad. Three times he travelled to Italy where in the 1850s his important works were done. Nathaniel Hawthorne, sojourning in Rome, found Akers an engaging young man. For the Marble Faun Hawthorne 'borrowed' two works from Akers. The Pearl Diver belongs to the Portland Museum of Art and the ideal bust of John Milton is in the Colby College Library. Akers worked in the prevailing Neo-Classic idiom of the first half of the Nineteenth century.

Edward Augustus Brackett (1819-1908) from Vassalboro preceded slightly the fame of Akers. His best known work is a bust of Washington Allston. Franklin Simmons (1839-1913) born in Webster, produced his mature work in the latter part of the century. He received commissions for public memorials in Portland (the Longfellow statue) and Lewiston where he spent part of his boyhood. Maine's first war memorial, his Civil War soldier, stands in Lewiston City Park. In portraiture he is represented in Statuary Hall of the National Capitol with figures of Roger Williams of Rhode Island and William King of Maine.

In the Groce and Wallace Dictionary of Artists in America to 1860 some fifty names of artists are associated with Maine. During the second half of the Nineteenth century, the number of ornamental painters, photographic artists, teachers of art, amateur and professional artists increased considerably. More than four hundred names can be found in the Business Directories. Increasingly few were locally taught and by the end of the century, the young men and women who had been drawn to the arts had migrated to urban centers for training and patronage. At the same time, marine and landscape artists painted in Maine in summer, and exhibited in Boston and New York. This continues to be the prevailing pattern, drawing the comment that art seems to be extracted from Maine rather than exported.

Returning to mid-Nineteenth century Portland, a trio of native sons produced the best work and promoted art interests in the area. John Bradley Hudson, Jr., (1832-1903) studied with the portraitist, C. O. Cole, in Portland but preferred landscape as his subject matter. Harrison B. Brown (1831-1915) began as an ornamental and decorative painter, later built his reputation on marine views. He interpreted White Head Cliff in Casco Bay many times on his small delicately painted canvases. One of his paintings was included in the Maine pavilion at the 1893 Columbian Exposition in Chicago. Charles F. Kimball (1831-1903) also studied with Cole. A landscape artist, he married the daughter of Portraitist John Greenleaf Cloudman and with Hudson, Brown and others, was active in an informal sketching group called 'The Brushians.' Kimball was one of the founders of the Portland Society of Art whose permanent collection includes works by all three of these men.

Eastman Johnson (1824-1906) lived as a boy in Augusta, pursued his art education to an extended stay in Europe and practiced professionally in New York. He returned to Maine to find genre subjects in the maple sugar-making camps of Fryeburg and in the barns and fields near his sister's home in Kennebunkport. To this list of professionals may be added the names of J. Foxcroft Cole (1837-1892), landscape painter and Frederic Porter Vinton (1845-1911), portraitist. Charles Lewis Fox (1854-1927), known for his allegorical murals, became famous for his exquisite mushroom studies, now at the Columbia School of Biology. He was among the earliest to record the American Indian in expressive character studies. Among the lesser renowned may be cited D. D. Coombs (1850-1938) of Lewiston who painted country scenes and Percy Sanborn (1849-1929) of Belfast who painted ships. Alfred Thompson Bricher (1837-1908) interpreted the sea and rocky coast; Franklin Stanwood (1856-1888) explored the mood of the sea in marine paintings and one engaging amateur recently has come to light in the watercolors painted around Castine by Alice McLaughlin (1869-1906). More eclectic was the work of Harry Hayman Cochrane of Monmouth. On the walls of the banquet hall of the Kora Temple Shrine building, an architecturally interesting structure in Lewiston, are his murals *Pilgrimage to Mecca* painted after study at Harvard and travel to the middle East. In 1934 he published a book with reproductions of the paintings and Arabic fanes, forerunner of today's large 'coffee table' art books. His work also decorates Cumston Hall at Monmouth. A spontaneous American art form rarely seen today are the Nineteenth century spirit paintings by the Shakers in the Shaker Museum at Poland Spring.

The French Impressionists of the 1870s and 80s delighted in painting views of the countryside and especially favored motifs that included river or ocean. Americans who later began to paint in this idiom found Impressionist subject matter ready at hand in Maine. The results can be seen in the works by Emil Carlsen (1859-1932); Willard L. Metcalf (1858-1935); and Frederick J. Waugh (1861-1940). John Singer Sargent (1856-1925), more famous as a portrait painter, found informal subjects for his watercolor brushes in summer. Among artists born in Maine who worked in this manner were Ben Foster (1852-1926) who came to Anson in spring to paint apple trees in bloom. Charles Hovey Pepper (1864-1950) explored the Impressionists' interested in Japanese art. Born in Portland was Walter Griffin (1861-1935) whose effects on canvas were obtained with palette knife and fingers as well as brush.

By the early 1880s Winslow Homer (1839-1910) was familiar with Maine. His mother came from Bucksport. In 1884 he converted a small building at Prout's Neck into a studio, now a National Historic Landmark. As a painter of pleasant genre subjects, Homer had a national reputation. However, it was during his last twenty-five years based in Maine that he reached his full artistic maturity. Homer's greater reputation rests upon his vigorous seascapes that make previous marine painting look old-fashioned. In the large oil paintings the viewer confronts nature's elements in vital action, and he is invited to ponder the role of man in this world of natural immensity, power and beauty. Although Homer never taught classes, many younger artists admired his broad handling of paint, his compositions which bring the viewer 'right into the battlefront between sea and shore.' Homer's career parallels and at times his art is seen as consonant with French Impressionism; American painting, particularly seascapes, in the early Twentieth century partakes of influence from Homer and Impressionism. His reputation has never sagged. Homer's oils and watercolors are seen in and are still sought by America's largest museums. Bowdoin College Museum of Art possesses etchings, watercolors and oils by Homer and received a legacy of the major portion of the material that had been in Homer's studio at Prout's Neck.

TWENTIETH CENTURY ARTISTS

At the turn of the century when marine painting had unlimited stature and as Realism began to challenge Impressionism, noted artists continued to find inspiration in Maine. Childe Hassam was at Isles of Shoals, Charles Ebert at Monhegan, and at North Haven, Frank W. Benson became famous for his ladies in white. The greatest concentration of artistic activity early in the Twentieth century was at Monhegan, beginning with Realists Robert Henri, Rockwell Kent, George Bellows and their contemporaries. At Ogunquit there were Charles Woodbury, Ogunquit's first significant painter, Hamilton Easter Field whose inspiration accounts for one of the richest chapters in the State's art tradition, Bernard Karfiol, Edward Hopper, Sculptor Robert Laurent, Maurice Prendergast; Leon Kroll who worked with Bellows at Monhegan (1913); Walt Kuhn who produced exciting and personal fauve-like pictures that sing of brisk Maine days.

After World War I more impressive 'perennials' were drawn to Ogunquit — Ernest Fiene, Abraham Walkowitz, Steiglitz, Georgia O'Keeffe, Kuniyoshi, Niles Spencer, Maurice Sterne, William Von Schlegel and Stefan Hirsch whose *Alfred, Maine* expresses the simple beauty and dignity of the Maine village. With Field's school on one side of the cove and Woodbury's on the other, Ogunquit became an energetic lively art colony. Many of the artists were influenced by the new modern painting from abroad where a number had studied, and the variety of their styles applied to Maine subjects brought interesting results.

Although the mainstreams of American art movements are evident in the work of artists in Maine, they appear as points of stylistic departure for the artists who are moved by nature itself. Artists were compelled to observe in a different way than elsewhere and their work was colored by an unlimited respect for the land and sea. Wherever the artists came from or whatever their backgrounds, Maine made an impact upon them that was expressed in their art.

John Marin who found his spiritual home at Small Point in 1914 was one of the first to apply abstract ideas to the art of the region, to communicate the secrets of nature. Also in the Phippsburg area, at West Point, Ernest W. Haskell, one of the world's great etchers, was finding subjects for his talents.

Marguerite and William Zorach were painting at Stonington before 1920, later settling at Robinhood not far from Sculptor Gaston Lachaise. Both the Zorachs' work sprang from and harmonizes with the environment they loved. At Robinhood began the sculpture that was to bring world renown to Zorach who like Laurent adapted both material and forms natural to the locale for his sculpture. His fountain, *Spirit of the Sea,* enhances Bath City Park. Early attachment of Lachaise, Laurent and Zorach to the region gave Maine a rich sculptural heritage.

Edmond Marsden Hartley of Lewiston who began painting in 1900, achieved recognition as a true spokesman for Maine, his strongly conceived landscapes capturing the big forms of nature. In the early Twenties Carl Sprinchorn at Monson painted the first significant pictures of the world of inland Maine since Hartley's work a decade before. N. C. Wyeth, a great American illustrator of his day, brought his family to settle at Port Clyde. His son Andrew, then three years old, was to become the most popular of living American painters.

The tradition of sea-painting was carried on in the Twenties by the old-timers and by some younger men — but American taste was changing. Alexander Bower, for many years director of the Portland Museum of Art, was active during that period. In 1921 William Hekking came to Monhegan and Jay Connoway to Jonesport. Waldo Peirce, son of a Bangor lumber family, came home from worldwide escapades in 1928 to paint the happy side of Maine with more exuberance than a dozen artists. His pictures were exhibited around the world in the late Thirties. Stephen Etnier and Henry Strater who is identified with Ogunquit's Museum of Art became two of Maine's most popular painters in the Twenties and Thirties. About 1936 Andrew Winter, one of the best of the later Monhegan Realists, made his home on the island.

In 1938 toward the end of the depression, Maine was flowering artistically. Marin was painting at Cape Sprit. Hartley had rediscovered his home State, first painting in the Georgetown area such works as *Fox Island* that embody the essence of Maine. In the late Thirties Sprinchorn began his long romance with Shin Pond and the lumber region of the Penobscot's East Branch northeast of Katahdin, living alone or with other lumberjacks for fifteen years. Hartley wrote in 1942: *Sprinchorn has had the luck to go with the lumber crews right to the centers of action, and this by the kindness of the lumber crews themselves, into the deep woods and down the river drives and knows this kind of man and his labours thoroughly. I congratulate him on this alone, as if he had done me a personal service and as you look at these pictures you can smell the pungent wet autumn leaves, you can smell the odour of burning wood and food in frying pans and all that. As I am the first serious artist to get to the foot of Mt. Katahdin and to paint it, Sprinchorn is the first to come out with his complementary documentation, and so together we have given a reasonable account of the qualities of Maine, along with Homer and Marin.*

John Heliker came to Stonington in the late Thirties to paint the environment as a distillation of the 'bigness' that had preoccupied the earlier painters. He and William Kienbusch who came in 1940 found at Cranberry Isles the particular Maine most compatible to their seeing. Their work, communicating the sounds, movements, colors and textures of nature has established them as two of our finest painters. Also finding inspiration at Cranberry Isles are Carl Nelson and Robert La Hotan.

Sculptor William Muir came to Stonington in the Forties and Ivan Albright, and his brother and father were painting at Corea and New Harbor; while young Andrew Wyeth was painting the marshes and back coves of Cushing and Port Clyde and mastering the techniques that have made him perhaps the most admired of living American painters.

After World War II more and more artists fled from the thrust of mechanization and materialism, seeking solitude in the tiny villages of the Maine coast. A self-taught painter who settled at Port Clyde after Navy service, William Thon expresses his feeling for Maine in the fine and delicate work that has won him international recognition. Vincent Hartgen who came to the University of Maine after the war, sees Maine in a way akin to Thon; his dynamic personality is communicated through his explosive water colors of forests and crashing surf. About this time, George Curtis came to Owl's Head in 1946, became known for his fish sculpture. Another resident sculptor is Clark FitzGerald of Castine who is deeply concerned wih sources. His *Continuity of Community* commissioned for the City of Bangor was unveiled in 1969. Maine-born Bernard Langlais lives at Cushing, brings to the medium of wood construction (popularized by Maine-born Louise Nevelson) a humor resembling that found in primitive art. His gigantic sixty-foot Maine Indian stands in Skowhegan.

Some of the more modern artists became interested in Monhegan in the early Forties. These were more interested in expressing their inner reactions to life rather than interpreting outer forms. Jean Liberte and Joseph De Martini brought their mysterious style reminiscent of Alfred Ryder. Morris Kantor came to paint decorative impressions. Reuben Tam's painting is highly personal and inspired by his environment; where Kent saw Monhegan from without, Tam sees it from within. Other painters who became regular visitors in the late Forties and Fifties were Lamar Dodd, Mike Loew, Henry and Herbert Kallam, Ernest Fiene, Morris Shulman. Living on the island are Hans Moller who paints bold impressions and Alan Gussow who paints with a modern touch the same churning seas Bellows did fifty years ago.

Richard Lahey has carried on the Ogunquit art tradition since the Thirties. Ogunquit Artist John Laurent is one of the few whose work continues the brooding spiritual quality of Maine found in Hartley, Marin and Kent. The wood sculpture and construction of Ogunquit's David Schlegell has a New England clarity and precision that has evolved through realistic and abstract approaches.

Tom Cavanaugh for many years has headed a small art center at Boothbay Harbor where Laurence Sisson also makes his home. Long-time residents of Maine are artists Dahlov Ipcar, daughter of the Zorachs and well known for her paintings of animals; Denny Winters of Rockport and Jeana Dale Bearce of Brunswick. Fairfield Porter captures mood and atmosphere found nowhere but in Maine. Like Porter, Alex Katz paints the summer world of rich green trees and relaxed people. Joseph Fiore's landscapes show the not often painted Maine farmland. Leonard Baskin works in Maine although not interpreting the Maine scene. Anne Arnold creates highly sophisticated wood sculptures embodying a rich sense of New England primitive art. James Elliott, long associated with the Portland Art School, does seascapes in water color. Eliot O'Hara another water colorist, taught for many years until his school at Goose Rocks was destroyed by fire. Portraitist Willard Cummings is a founder of the nationally known Skowhegan School of Painting and Sculpture.

Contemporary artists working in Maine reflect the inward tensions of a world in which the future of man is uncertain. They differ from the relaxed calm of the Impressionists and the early Realists' literal combat with the elements. Yet through the land and sea that they love and respect, they continue an art tradition indigenous to the region. While it is impossible to mention all of the artists working in Maine — more and more each year — it may be noted that the names of contemporary painters are far more numerous than those of earlier painters. Only the passage of time will afford a perspective of those whose importance will endure.

HANDICRAFTS

Evolving from the making of household necessities, crafts were the earliest expression of art in Maine, developing a character of their own. Often the discipline of necessity made for beauty in the articles made with needle, loom and hook and the few metal and woodworking tools. Many of the simple, sturdy, practical articles showed the characteristics of their creators. The outside influences on Maine craftsmanship, though slight, included English, greatly simplified; French through Canada, in floral motifs for rugs and embroidery; and Oriental from objects brought home by ships in the China trade. Early stenciling often shows designs with oriental figures surrounded by New England flower and leaf motifs. By the Nineteenth century, woodcarving was flourishing, particularly house and ship carving. Of special interest was the artisanship of the Shakers who had early settled in Maine.

Rug hooking originated in Maine and Nova Scotia and the earliest and best rugs represent true native craftsmanship. The designs were original, inspired by familiar objects; the material was of wool from home-raised sheep, carded and spun at home and dyed with home-made colors. The most beautiful were floral and wreath patterns, free and intricate in design, the finest revealing as much esthetic sense and mastery of craft as a piece of glazed terra cotta or a stained glass window. Though not so fine, pictorial and geometric patterns also were common. Designs were sketched freehand on the background material, first on hand-loomed linen, later on burlap or sacking. Much of the beauty of design disappeared when stamped patterns became available in the Nineteenth century. Bits of calico and cotton and other woven material were used with wool yarns in many of the early hooked rugs. Characteristic of Maine and Nova Scotia was the practice of creating an effect of relief either by hooking parts of the design higher than the rest or by contrasting clipped and unclipped areas.

Colors for rugs, clothing and embroidery were ingeniously concocted. Extract for black and indigo for blue could be purchased; browns and dull greens came from white maple, butternut, sumac, hemlock bark and sweet fern; yellow, from onion peelings and urine. Until housewives could buy vermillion, reds were extremely difficult to create. Beet root and berries made rich magenta but was not permanent. All colors were set with copperas and lye, the latter made by pouring boiling water over wood ashes. Revival of the art of rug-hooking which nearly disappeared in the Nineteenth century, lacked the sincerity of creative craftsmanship in efforts to copy the old patterns, until artisans began once again to create original designs.

The earlier hand-made braided rugs are not particularly native to Maine, although still made here. The Williamsburg, Virginia Restoration used rugs made by the Old Sparhawk Mills of South Portland; local artisans designed the rugs, dyed the materials and sewed them in the original manner.

Weaving in the early days was a universal craft, scarcely less important than cooking. Cottons, linens, woolens and other fabrics such as 'linsey-woolsey' or 'luster,' a glazed linen and wool material, were made by every housewife. There is some decorative hand-weaving today and materials for apparel and household use may be found in Ogunquit and Damariscotta.

Many of the best quilts used on the featherbeds of Maine were not of patchwork, but derived their beauty from intricate quilting and lovely materials. One such was made of indigo blue linsey-woolsey backed with a light-weight yellow homespun blanket and quilted in a pattern of pineapple, feather and shell motifs.

Maine crewel embroideries of the Seventeenth and Eighteenth century show much originality and inventiveness in the use of bird, animal, monogram, basket and ribbon motifs, the materials prepared the same as for hooked rugs. The finest crewel embroideries in Maine are the bedspread and hangings made between 1745-50 by Mrs. Mary Bulman of York where they may be seen at the Old Gaol Museum. A fine spread of the same period is at Waterville's Redington Museum.

Innumerable lesser related crafts practiced in early Maine included the making of dolls, embroidered pictures, plain and mourning samplers, needlepoint and the like.

In the Nineteenth century woodcarving became notable in Maine particularly as it related to shipbuilding, one of the State's first great industries. Of earlier work, the cockerel weathervane, carved in wood in 1788 for the Cumberland County courthouse survives today on a Portland bank. William Deering (1741-1813) supplied carved ornaments for ships built at Kittery and Portsmouth. His work for the U. S. frigate *Congress* was cited favorably in the local press in 1798.

Although carving for decoration of ships had been done in Europe for centuries, the figureheads, trail boards, mast sheaths and the like carved in Maine, New Hampshire and Massachusetts represent an artistic development as genuine, native and inventive as any craft at any time. In Maine, many carvers established shops near the shipyards — Charles A. L. Sampson and Woodbury Potter of Bath, William Southworth and Harvey Counce of Thomaston, Edward S. Griffin of Portland, Thomas Seavey of Bangor, John Haley Bellamy of Kittery Point, and their apprentices. Of course the work of these men sailed away from Maine on the ships they adorned and today very few authenticated carvings are found in the State. A ship's figurehead called *Minerva,* attributed to Seavey, is preserved in the Bangor Historical Society Museum and varieties of carving may be found in the Penobscot Marine Museum at Searsport and in the Bath Marine Museum. Southworth carved more than five hundred figureheads, taking about eighteen days to a figure and receiving up to four hundred dollars for each. Made of pumpkin pine, brightly painted, the subjects usually were life-sized females, although Indians, military figures, birds and animals were fairly common. Sampson's famous *Bell of Bath, Belle of Oregon* and *Western Belle* were gleaming gold and white. Although many of the figures seem generous in porportion, they have extraordinary realism and grace. Sampson frequently portrayed his figures in stylish dress blown swirling backward in the wind, with head erect and one arm extended, creating on the whole an effect of life, strength and beauty.

Although the figureheads were the most spectacular, many smaller decorative pieces were carved to adorn the ships. Nearly always, the stern bore a carving in relief partially or entirely surrounding the name of the vessel; these commonly depicted cornucopiae of fruit, eagles with spread wings, crossed flags, portrait heads and sometimes landscapes embellished with gold or white scroll-leaf forms. Many a pilot house was topped with an eagle or rooster. Billet-heads of curling acanthus leaves, lovely in design, were sometimes used instead of figureheads. In all of these pieces the carving is bold and direct. The tools used were few and simple; the size and curve of the chisels can be judged from the long even grooves in leaves and drapery. The use of tools and material to best advantage with no attempt to camouflage either is evidence of the sincere craftsmanship that went into their making.

The use of carved decoration spread beyond the adornment of ships and crept into the houses and public buildings of coastal towns. Weathervanes, architectural details, insignia for public buildings, chests and other furniture reveal the hand of the ship carver. Edbury Hatch who completed apprenticeship with Southworth in 1870, adorned his house in Newcastle with carved floral and animal motifs and the Maine seal. Examples of scrimshaw, the sailors' art, may be seen in Maine's marine museums.

Also important in the Nineteenth century was the making of ship models. Revealing much delicate and patient craftsmanship, ship models from one inch to four feet in length, fully rigged, have been made ever since ships were built, often by the builders or sailors of the ships thus reproduced. So-called half models, beautifully finished and mounted on a flat background were made for every new vessel and are now frequently used for decorative purposes. Those from the Sewall yards may be seen in the Bath Marine Museum.

Most of Maine's great houses were built in the Nineteenth century and much beautiful woodwork, though often derivative, may be seen in Maine's old houses (*see ARCHITECTURE*). Their furnishings, objects of taste and beauty, commonly were brought from other countries by seafaring members of the families.

Early Maine cabinet work, generally similar to that in the rest of New England, was cruder and more provincial. Much of the furniture was adorned with stenciled leaf, fruit and flower motifs, sometimes a landscape, often against a black background. Bronze powders of various shades were applied. Intricacy of cutting, delicacy of shading, and the gradual building up of a pattern from a number of stencils characterize the best work. Trays and boxes also were stenciled in bronzes, and floors and walls sometimes were stenciled with colored paint.

In the late Eighteenth and early Nineteenth centuries, Stevens Plains, now a part of Portland was the center of activity for a number of metal workers. Zachariah Stevens (1778-1856) one of the first to introduce gold and silver leaf ornamentation, founded a tin industry employing some forty men in the early 1880s. This early tinware consists of charming little chest-like boxes, trays of various shapes, tea caddies and so forth. It is painted, most frequently in black, sometimes in yellow or white, in Japan colors with small leaves and bright red, green and yellow flowers. Tinsmiths travelled through the countryside selling their wares, at the same time buying up at a low price much old pewter to melt for tin.

Pewterers also were working in this region at this time. Allen and

Freeman Porter established the trade; they were succeeded by Rufus Dunham who until 1882 employed some thirty artisans in his shop. Britannia ware became popular soon after 1845 and much fine old pewter undoubtedly was melted to go into the new and inferior metal.

Until recent years, work of Maine artisans in ceramics, stone, glass and metals has been rather primitive. There were only two recorded silver-working establishments in the State before 1830 and no glass works of any importance until after 1863 when the famous Portland glass began to be made. The Maine Historical Society, Portland, has an outstanding collection of this; the Phillips Historical Society, another.

In the Shaker Museum at Sabbathday Lake, Poland Spring, are examples of the unsurpassed artisanship and renowned inventions of the Shakers — hardware and tools of beautiful workmanship, textiles and fine handwork, and the furniture that is now eagerly sought by collectors and is described in an 1870 handbook. The Museum is in a meetinghouse (1794) in the style of a Dutch home.

Craft becomes art at Haystack Mountain School where for fifteen summers the finest craftsmen from this country and abroad have gathered to make Haystack one of the best art school influences in America. Eminent personalities of the faculty over the years are those who have shaped trends in design and crafts in America for some time to come. Calling attention to the spirit at Haystack, August Heckscher has said that the work there speaks in its own way and 'tells a story of significance about our civilization and some of its best hopes.' The *Wall Street Journal* has called the school 'a place of eminence in crafts.' In 1959, Haystack received an award citation by *Progressive Architecture Magazine* — 24 roofs, same pitch, shelter the Arts and Crafts Camp, a summer community of 60 students and faculty who work and live on a lichen-covered granite slope looking southward to the sea.

Haystack Mountain School was founded in 1950 by a group of working craftsmen in the Belfast area. Its first sponsor was Mary B. Bishop of Flint, Michigan, who underwrote the first facility at Liberty, Maine, and continued to contribute substantially as the school grew and established a new enlarged facility at its present Deer Isle site in 1960-61. The school is an independent organization controlled by its own board of trustees and managed (1969) by Executive Director Francis S. Merritt, member of the State Commission for the Arts and Humanities. Credit and non-credit students pursue a self-directed routine of research and study in courses that include ceramics, glass, graphics, jewelry, painting and weaving. Teachers and students from colleges and universities throughout the country have been awarded scholarships for study at Haystack which occupies an isolated point of fir forest bounded by half a mile of rocky shoreline at the easternmost extension of Deer Isle in a locality called Sunshine, halfway up the Maine coast. Its Maine Gallery, Centennial Hall has been the exhibition center and sales outlet for professional craftsmen representing the highest standards in contemporary crafts in the State.

Qualified professionals among Maine craftsmen include: pottery, Richard Miller, Yarmouth; Frank Stoke and Denis Vibert, West Sullivan; pottery and sculpture, Robert and Susan Dunlap, Town Hill; ceramics and sculpture, Lionel Marcous, Cumberland Center; silver smithing, James M. Hamlin, North Bridgton; jewelry, Madeleine Burrage, Wiscasset; silk screen prints and jewelry, Fred and Kate Pearce, Deer Isle; printed fabrics, Stell and Shevis, Camden; weaving, Janet Ten Broeck, Bar Harbor and Ebba Kossick, Deer Isle. The Maine Coast Craftsmen's brochure *Handcraft Trails in Maine* lists 45 communities where craft work from hooked rugs to driftwood and slate work may be found. In 1969 a State-wide crafts organization was formed with plans for a 1970 exhibit.

LITERATURE

Although the term *Maine literature* may include many writers by virtue of their having been born or having lived in the State — such as Rufus Jones (Quaker philosopher), Dorothy Clarke Wilson (novelist), Louise Bogan (poet) — the use of it here will be limited to works about Maine, regardless of the birthplace or residence of the writers. Thus Harriet Beecher Stowe may be considered a Maine writer because of *The Pearl of Orr's Island*, not because of *Uncle Tom's Cabin*, even though that famous book of the Nineteenth century was written in the town of Brunswick.

Maine literature is a part of American literature. Especially after the Civil War, Americans began to be conscious of their heritage. It was then that genealogy became an indoor sport for hundreds of people and that both slim and voluminous accounts of family lines began to appear in print. It was then that people began to form historical societies and to celebrate anniversaries of founding fathers and of early historical events. It was then that writers began to make greater use of American customs, American people, and American ideas as sources for their poetry and novels — instead of borrowing from and imitating European literature. Thus arose what is called the 'local color' school of writing — Bret Harte's stories of the West, Joel Chandler Harris' tales of the South, Mark Twain's narratives of the Mississippi area, Sarah Orne Jewett's quiet, sensitive sketches of life in Maine towns along the coast. These are regional writers, but they have more than just local color to offer — their works have *universality*, a quality of faithfulness to the laws of physical nature and of human nature that makes them appeal to readers everywhere, transcending time and place. So a study of Maine literature is no mere boasting; it is part of our heritage as Americans, with particular emphasis on people, places, customs, and ideas of that part of our country known as the State of Maine. Until 1820, Maine was a part of Massachusetts — the Province of Maine, it was called; hence when it did become an independent state, its inhabitants, with understandable pride, spoke and wrote of it as the STATE OF MAINE.

In the Seventeenth century the settlers' energies were devoted to establishing their homes and settlements and to defending them from the Indians and the French. During the Eighteenth century, however, some of the Harvard or Yale educated clergymen such as Banjamin Stevens of Kittery Point, Samuel Moody and Isaac Lyman of York, Jonathan Fisher of Blue Hill, and Jacob Bailey of Pownalborough, by precept and example awakened in the more leisured inhabitants an interest in books. In their homes, as in similar ones in England, on the shelves stood rows of leather-bound books, not only the classics, theology, and philosophy, but also the works of poets, essayists, and novelists of the period. And some of the colonists began to try their hands at poetry and novels.

Sentimental and didactic, these attempts followed the patterns of the popular works of the English writers. Characters and settings were European, not American. *Julia and the Illuminated Baron*, by Sally Sayward Barrell Keating Wood of York, was published in 1800. It has been described as 'a mixture of the Gothic romance, the seductive story, and the moral tale.' With a good moral, one gathers, anything goes — kidnaping, seduction, rape, murder, even incest. In her own words: *an aversion to introducing living characters, or those recently dead, rendered Europe a safer, though not a more agreeable theatre.* In her later works, however, Madam Wood tried writing of places and people she knew — Maine and New Hampshire in Revolutionary times and in the first quarter of the Nineteenth century. Although not a familiar writer — her novels because of their scarcity are now found only in collections of rare Americana — she is the first Maine novelist in point of subject matter as well as in respect to time. She also left some letters of reminiscences that have served as less-than-reliable, but very interesting, documents of Maine life.

During the first half of the Nineteenth century, several other novelists in Maine wrote of pioneer and colonial life, among them John Neal, Sara Parton (Fanny Fern), and Ann Sophia Stephens. Nathaniel Hawthorne wrote an early novel, *Fanshawe,* which, however, because of his dissatisfaction with it, he tried to destroy soon after it was published. It is Harriet Beecher Stowe's *The Pearl of Orr's Island*, 1862, that is usually named as first of the local color narratives in Maine.

Inspired by *The Pearl of Orr's Island*, Sarah Orne Jewett of South Berwick began writing the perceptive stories and sketches of simple country people in coastal villages and on inland farms of Maine that culminated in *The Country of the Pointed Firs* in 1896. And acknowledging the influence of this American classic, Mary Ellen Chase of Blue Hill and Gladys Hasty Carroll of South Berwick have continued the pattern, as have many others during the Twentieth century. Since the hundredth anniversary of Miss Jewett's birth (1849), there has been a noticeable revival of interest in her works. Her delicate humor, her mastery of Maine patterns of speech, and the universality of her quiet Maine characters appeal increasingly to students of literature, to the literary critic, and to the understanding reader. F. O. Matthiessen in 1929 named her with Emily Dickinson as 'the two principal women writers that America has had,' and her *Country of the Pointed Firs* was listed by Willa Cather with *Scarlet Letter* and *Huckleberry Finn* as 'three American books which have the possibility of a long, long life.'

The list of Twentieth-century Maine writers of novels and short stories is a long one. Among others, it includes Kenneth Roberts and Ben Ames Williams. Both these writers did meticulous research for the historical and geographical backgrounds of their books, making them not only interesting and popular best-sellers but also more accurate in detail and atmosphere than some histories. As a person reads *Arundel* and *Rabble in Arms*, he lives in the Revolutionary period. In *Boon Island*, he suffers hunger and pain and discouragement along with the castaways on the bare, rocky island. Williams in *Fraternity Village* shares with us the tales and troubles and jokes of his neighbors in a small town in Waldo County, and in his *Strange Woman* Bangor lives again in its exciting, competitive days as the center of the lumber industry. A ballet based on the *Strange Woman* was performed in Bangor in 1969.

Robert Peter Tristram Coffin is another who has given to his readers not only some of his own boisterous joy in the tales, experiences, personalities and achievements of his seagoing, farming ancestors in the Brunswick area, but also the loveliness of the sea, of the shore, of the rivers, of the hills, in all seasons. He can make a reader smell and taste and feel and hear as well as see what he so aptly called 'the State of Grace that is Maine.' He was awarded a Pulitzer Prize for his poetry, but his prose is no less a work of art and worship. He can tell a story, he can make history live. Often exaggerated, yes — but exaggeration is an accepted technique of the teller of tales and of the lover. And Robert Coffin was in love with Maine all the sixty-two years of his life. Mary Ellen Chase, a contemporary of Coffin's, is another writer who brings to the reader stories and reminiscent essays of seafaring, farming ancestry and of scenes of the Maine coast and the small town. Patriotic but not chauvinistic, both these writers present appreciatively the contributions to Maine made by various groups — Indians, French Canadians, Americans, Yankees, and others.

It is impossible to list the many other writers of novels, tales, essays, and reminiscences of Maine life, for such a roll becomes incomplete as soon as it is made. From 1800, the year of Madam Wood's first novel, to the day that this is being read the catalogue continues — and next week or next month will appear or be reviewed another book on Maine. Not all are about the coast or about the past. Potato fields of Aroostook, experiences in the Allagash region, sagas of the sportsman, conflicts between youth and age and between natives and those 'from away,' and between conservation and 'progress,' struggles of all kinds, whatever shows life difficult, exciting, depressing, hopeful, romantic, real — of all these is the 'matter of Maine.'

Of poets in Maine there is indeed 'God's plenty.' One of the earliest was Enoch Lincoln, later a governor of the state, whose book *The Village* was published in 1816. At that time a lad in Portland was absorbing experiences that would later make him the best known American poet of his generation, Henry Wadsworth Longfellow. Less well known to the general reader, Edwin Arlington Robinson of Gardiner, 'doomed,' as he wrote, 'to be a poet,' struggled against economic, social, and personal handicaps to become in the Twentieth century one of the really great poets in American literature. Recipient of the Pulitzer Prize for poetry three times, he achieved popular success with his poetic tale *Tristram* when it was recommended by the Book-of-the-Month Club. Another poet well known beyond the borders of the state is the gay-fearful, young-mature, flip-serious Edna St. Vincent Millay, also awarded a Pulitzer Prize. She brings to the reader the flowers and the weeds, the birds and the deer, the sea and the hills of coastal Maine, along with the love of life and the fear of death that is a part of us all. Both Robinson and Millay were masters of poetic technique as well as creators of the Maine scenes, the people, the memories, and the mysteries that somehow we see as something new and yet recognize as what we have always known.

As with the novelists, there is no covering the subject of Maine poets thoroughly. In 1888 an eight-hundred-page book, *Poets of Maine*, was published, including poems by over four hundred writers. A list of those known outside the State ranges from the early hymn writers, including Samuel Francis Smith, author of 'America,' and Henry W. Longfellow, to the romanticists (Celia Thaxter) to the rhythmical robustness and humor of Holman Day to the delicately humorous, sensitive, observant sonnets of Florence Burrill Jacobs. The Poetry Fellowship of Maine encourages not only its members but also, by contests in the schools and elsewhere, those who are just beginning the art.

Maine has been prolific in its writers of books for children. Jacob Abbott of *Little Rollo* and *Marco Paul* fame and popularity was followed by Elijah Kellogg with his *Elm Island* and *Whispering Pine* series. Noah Brooks of Castine and C. A. Stephens of Norway carried the pattern into the Twentieth century, to be succeeded by James Otis Kaler's and Gilbert Patten's books for boys. Rebecca Clarke of Norridgewock and Kate Douglas Wiggin wrote stories of more interest to girls. Laura E. Richards' poems and stories, composed for her own youngsters, spilled over into print and became classics for children elsewhere. Several among the writers primarily for adults have written also for young people, among them Sarah Orne Jewett, Mary Ellen Chase, Rachel Field, Ruth Moore, Elizabeth Ogilvie, Gladys Hasty Carroll, Henry Beston, Elizabeth Coatsworth, and E. B. White, whose *Charlotte's Web* became a classic. For over a century the *Youth's Companion*, established by a Maine editor, Nathaniel Willis, served as an outlet for many local writers and instructed and delighted children and families all over the country. Since the establishment of the Newbery (1922) and the Caldecott (1938) awards for children's books, eleven permanent or summer residents of Maine have been winners or runners-up, some of them more than once. Among the most popular is Robert McCloskey, who has written and illustrated books for several ages, following the ages of his own children and sometimes using them as his models. *Blueberries for Sal, One Day in Maine* and *Time of Wonder* appeal not only to children but also to adults. Once more, lack of space forbids even the bare listing of those who have used Maine material in their stories and poems. A reference book, *Maine Writers of Fiction for Juveniles*, prepared by the Maine Writers Research Club, lists over a hundred Maine writers of children's literature in the past century and a half.

Although a number of summer theatres flourish in Maine, besides college and civic theatres during the year, the state has not as yet produced many playwrights. Only a few plays with Maine setting and characters can be listed. James Herne's *Shore Acres* was popular at the turn of the century. Golden's *Old Jed Prouty* and Owen Davis' *Ice Bound* were Broadway successes in the first quarter of the century. Kate Douglas Wiggin wrote *The Old Peabody Pew* in 1904 for production in the Tory Hill Meeting House in Buxton, where it is still given every August. Gladys Hasty Carroll's popular novel, *As the Earth Turns*, was dramatized for local and for Hollywood production. *Captain January* by Laura E. Richards and *Northwest Passage* by Kenneth Roberts also became popular films, as did several other Maine novels including Ruth Moore's *Spoonhandle*.

A growing interest in folklore is making available the `pre-literature` that passed by song or word of mouth from person to person, from generation to generation, from lumber camp or shore to town. Writers have found this a rich mine of material for their more sophisticated works. Under the direction of Dr. Edward C. Ives of the University of Maine, songs, tales, and accounts of customs and traditions are being recorded, taped, and sometimes printed just as they are told or sung — oral history in the making.

Humor has been part and parcel of Maine literature, and it appears in one way or another in the works of most of the writers. Sometimes it is a friendly laughing with the victim, sometimes a less kindly laughing at him. Sometimes its appeal is to the eye (the unconventional spelling of Artemus Ward, the drawings that illustrate the tongue-in-cheek histories of Bill Nye, the Victorian engravings that accompany the advice in John Gould's *Pre-Natal Care for Fathers,* and the photographs that give focus as well as beauty to the comments in Keith Jennison's *The Maine Idea*). And sometimes the appeal is largely to the ear — Maine ways of saying things. Sarah Orne Jewett, Ben Ames Williams, and E. B. White are especially observant and skillful in the handling of Maine speech. The humor is sometimes ornamental and sometimes the very heart of the matter. From run-of-the-mill corn here and there to the subtle, unexpected parallelisms and surprise sentence endings in E. B. White's account of life on a salt-water farm, *One Man's Meat,* the humor crops up, lightening and illuminating even the most serious writing.

Writers of Maine, like painters of Maine, whether born in `this neck of the woods` or elsewhere, have contributed greatly to the reputation of the State. To those `from away` they give a touch, a view, a fragrance, a taste, a note, an idea of what Maine has been like, is like. And to those who have lived and worked in the State for many years, even for generations, they reveal the beauty and the truth that lie in the commonplace and in the familiar.

Finally, literature about Maine is not a phenomenon of the past, completed and done; it is being conceived and written and published today, in stories, reminiscences, poetry, essays, biographies, plays, in weekly papers, in monthly and quarterly magazines, in student and faculty publications at the colleges, and in books. The end is not yet.

MUSIC

Great music, opera, symphony and the like, have not been made part of the life of all the people in America, as it has in many European countries.

Not until the 1960s did the Government begin to foster the arts among the people when national and state councils and commissions were established. But music in some form perhaps has been the most familiar cultural expression in Maine from the time of the early settlers. Scholars today are tapping a rich vein of balladry and folk songs (*see FOLKLORE*) stemming from the sea chanteys, woodsmen's ballads and the songs of English, Scottish and Irish origin that were the beginnings of music in Maine. And the mid-Twentieth century has brought music in its highest form to Maine and opened many doors of opportunity for students.

As Maine's frontier communities grew, singing in the homes and meetinghouses was part of social life. Instrumental music and the higher forms of the art were for the wealthy few. Church music became important and gradually 'music education' was introduced into the schools, and there were private music teachers. With the growth of population, musical activitity increased in the larger communities. Serious and talented · students who could went to metropolitan centers to further their musical education. Maine has produced a number of great musical artists including Lillian Nordica, Emma Eames and Anna Louise Cary. John Knowles Paine, one of America's earliest composers, was a Maine man. In the Twentieth century Maine's most celebrated composer has been Walter Piston, born in Rockland, three times a Pulitzer winner, and former head of Harvard's Music Department, whose works are played by famous orchestras around the globe.

Among composers of note working in Maine is Peter Re, chairman of the Colby College Music Department and conductor of the Bangor Symphony. His *Maine Profiles* has become part of Maine's musical literature. The work was dedicated for the State Sesquicentennial, to be performed by community and school choral groups following a Bangor Symphony premier. Other modern composers are Morton Gold at Nasson College, Jerry Bowden at University of Maine, Gorham, and Elliott Schwartz of the Bowdoin College Music Department who is known for his contemporary music.

In the Nineteenth century, soon after the Civil War, choral societies, quartets and bands sprang up in profusion. Nearly every community had one or more; even the island plantation of Monhegan had its band. One of the first was the Damariscotta Band of 1871. Bandstands were erected in parks and on commons where whole communities turned out for the frequent band concerts that became a colorful part of Maine social life. Maine's Nineteenth century March King was Robert Browne Hall (1858-1907) of Richmond who wrote some 62 marches, one of which was played by the U. S. Navy Band at the John F. Kennedy funeral. Besides composing, Browne conducted several municipal bands in his lifetime. Out of fashion for a time, band music has seen a revival, not only in the competitive school bands that participate in national events. The Shriners' Band is well known and of the dozen or so municipal bands, the Bath Band is one of the most active, reviving the music of March King Hall.

In Hall's Waterville Military Band was Arthur Flagg Roundy of Fairfield who was to be called the Kennebec Valley Master of Music Education. Also a composer and band leader, he taught music in Maine schools after study in the 1920s in Boston. One of the last survivors of Hall's Waterville Military Band, Mr. Roundy in Waterville in 1953 conducted the U. S. Navy Band in one of his own compositions.

Frederick Chapman of Damariscotta began the Maine Music Festivals of which William R. Chapman later was the motivating force in the first third of the Twentieth century. The world's great artists were brought here and Maine's own chorus of carefully chosen singers was trained for the occasion. The concerts began in Portland, travelled to other cities and were an important event for music lovers. During this period, most communities had one or more music clubs such as Portland's Rossini Club, now one of Maine's oldest.

Since World War II music has become a strong cultural force in Maine, particularly in the last decade, at popular as well as at academic levels. Bringing world-renowned artists and teachers to the State, Maine's institutions of higher learning and summer music centers have flourished, affording music lovers and students increased opportunities for great music. At the college level, the accent has been on developing chamber musicians. There is the Hungarian Quartet School at Colby College; the Aeolian Chamber Players at Bowdoin's Summer School of Music. High level students from all over the country come to the University of Maine's String Music School at Orono, a cultural entity now known from coast to coast.

There also are many college choral groups such as Bowdoin's Meddybempsters. Well known are the New England summer music camps at Sydney.

Madame Pierre Monteux has revived the educative impulse of the famed Domaine School for conductors at Hancock with sight reading classes for symphony orchestra players, the only such classes in the northeast. The School was founded by Pierre Monteux, known worldwide for his consummate musicianship and musical dedication. The Monteux Forest Studio orchestra continues to bring celebrated artists and conductors to Maine. There also are the Bay Chamber series at Camden, known as the summer harp center for the school of the great Salzedo. The Franz Kneisel concerts at Kneisel Hall, Blue Hill, long have been famous. There are concert groups at Northeast Harbor and other areas and a summer festival at Bar Harbor where Walter Damrosch once conducted summer concerts.

Portland's metropolitan Symphony Orchestra, Paul Vermel, conductor

(1969), plays its winter season in the handsomely renovated City Hall auditorium, has many guest stars. It has travelled to other cities in Maine and Canada and has provided ensembles for the Music-in-Maine program that brought fine music to Maine schools and remote areas. There is a Portland Junior Symphony. The auditorium's Kotzchmar organ provides frequent recitals and other outstanding musical events take place here including appearances of such artists as Van Cliburn and Benny Goodman.

Bangor, in close proximity to University of Maine, Orono, is an area of much musical activity. Besides conducting the Bangor Symphony's winter season, Peter Re also has conducted outdoor summer concerts and with Glen Hedsell, project director for Music-in-Maine, has assisted seniors of the Central Maine Youth String orchestra in expanding to a full orchestra. In 1969 the Symphony participated in an original ballet for the city's bicentennial.

Community concert associations, choral groups and church choirs are active in many communities. Old-fashioned community 'sings' have seen a revival with a modern touch, such as the weekly 'sings' at Westport Town Hall where old and young gather to take part in folk, historical, country and western, rock, protest and traditional music. And the barbershop quartet survives. Jazz has its place in indoor and outdoor programs.

THEATRE

There were neither theatres nor theatrical performances of any kind in Maine prior to the Revolution. The Playhouse was thought to be a direct road to perdition. This is not surprising because Maine was part of Massachusetts where a law of 1750 prohibited the performance of stage plays. It seems a performance by professionals and amateurs in a Boston coffee house had resulted in a riot, thus provoking the Puritans to pass a law to rid New England of the 'house of the devil' for all time. The reason given: *They have a pernicious influence on the minds of young people and greatly endanger their morals by giving them a taste for intrigue, amusement and pleasure.* The remnants of Puritan influence may account for the fact that some aspects of modern theatre had not yet appeared in Maine in 1969.

That the cultural climate of Maine was not exactly conducive to theatre was evident in 1767 when two Portland men and their wives were indicted for dancing. Stimulated by a growing literary movement, travelling troupes of players from New York, despite still hostile authorities began presenting performances under the guise of Moral Lectures in

New England, though not immediately venturing into Maine. Lovers of theatre knew what they were about when they purchased tickets for the Lectures; they were insuring themselves seats for favorite plays; such as *The Gamesters*, billed as *The Vice of Gambling, The School For Scandal* billed as *The Pernicious Vice of Scandal,* and *She Stoops to Conquer* billed as *The Disadvantage of Improper Education.*

As early as 1792, however, Portland's newspaper, the *Eastern Herald,* reported an active interest in the efforts of certain respected citizens of Massachusetts to bring about repeal of the Drama Law. John Gardiner of Pownalborough (now Wiscasset) and a representative to the Court, editorialized: *The bright sun of reason is rising fast upon us; the thick fog of superstition must, necessarily, be dispelled and vanish before the ascending luminary, and the dark gloomy bigot must soon go off the stage of life; when a new set of actors will appear, of more liberal ideas, and of a more refined taste, formed to enjoy the polished refinements of social life, and to delight in the rational entertainments of a chaste and well regulated theatre. The old things are rapidly going away; — already (within the last twenty years) the face of the political and of the moral world is changed — and greatly for the better; for, metaphorically speaking, there are now new heavens and a new earth — novus hascitur ordo.*

Dr. Gardiner came by his opinion honestly; he was the son of another theatre advocate, the Rev. J. S. J. Gardiner of Boston. Church leaders and many influential citizens were opposed to the repeal of the law and their objections were reflected in the comments of a Mr. Martin of North Yarmouth who said, among other things: 'A theatre for the exhibition of stage plays would be a great evil!' His sentiments were decidedly against licensing any house for theatrical entertainment; for instead of promoting piety, morality and religion as the gentleman from Pownalborough (Dr. Gardiner) conceived it, they would operate the very reverse.' However, after a long debate in the House of Representatives and by the small margin of ten votes, a Theatre Bill was passed March 29 1793, permitting the town of Boston to erect a theatre where stage plays could be performed under certain regulations and restrictions. In less than two years, professional theatre came to Maine.

In an assembly room in Portland's King Street (now India) on October 7, 1794, the English actor, Charles Stuart Powell, presented a group of players in two plays: *The Lyar* by Samuel Foote and *The Modern Antiques* which was often billed as *The Merry Mourners.* Mr. Powell of London's Covent Garden Theatre Royal had arrived in Boston in 1792 'to give public entertainments.' The King Street theatre, advertised as The New Theatre, soon became known as the Temple of Drama. Previously in this same location a 'knowing dog' and a Waxworks had been exhibited.

It appears that a drama critic was created on the spot by the *Eastern Herald* and after sitting on the rough benches before a crudely built stage, he had this to say: *The theatre in this town during the past week was crowded. The performances were well chosen, judiciously cast, and supported to admiration . . . In The Lyar, Mr. Powell told some 'Unconscionables' and with as good a face as if he had been used to it. In a word, we do not recollect ever to have heard greater lies, or lies better told . . . Mr. Jones in the character of Marquis was excellent. He bowed and shrugged like a Marquis; he grinned and made mouths like a Marquis; and when Mr. P. told a plumper, he would sometimes swear to it like a Marquis . . . The agreeable impressions of Tuesday evening were heightened and confirmed on those of Thursday and Friday.* And to convert those who still might be viewing the whole theatre project and especially the actors themselves with jaundiced eye, our reviewer goes on to say: *It is a circumstance peculiarly fortunate to the temporary introduction of a theatre into this town that with respect to the foregoing characters their theatrical talents are only to be equalled by their domestic virtues.*

Records indicate that Maine's first theatre season was for a period of five weeks. There were no performances in 1795, but in 1796 Portlanders were privileged to see Mr. and Mrs. Tubbs, also of London's Theatre Royal; in the same company was Mrs. Tubbs' daughter, Elizabeth Arnold, of charming voice and acting ability, who was to become the mother of Edgar Allen Poe. Their first performance was recorded as a dismal failure. Their second, Garrick's *Miss in Her Teens or a Medley of Lovers*, brought a blast of censure — 'the Ladies perhaps ought not to attend till it is known whether ears are again to be offended with expressions of obscenity and profanity.' The Powell Company returned to Portland in 1799, presenting *Romeo and Juliet*, the first Shakespearian play performed in Maine.

Until the passage of the Licensing Act in 1806, it may be assumed that in this initial period of its theatrical history, Portland saw as much theatre as any city of its size in America. The Licensing Act made it illegal to build, remodel or rent any building for the purpose of 'acting or carrying on, any stage play, interlude or other theatrical entertainment in any country within this Commonwealth (Massachusetts), without the license of the Court of the General Sessions.' Quite obviously the Licensing Act would be supported by such men as Everett Howard who kept a diary from November 1807 to August 1908. He was a teacher and portrait painter and referring to a visit in Wiscasset, made this entry in his daily journal: *Stayed at Dow's Tavern, met a young Sam Ellis who had just been suspended from Bowdoin, went to Squire Woods to see some brushed portrait likenesses. Much interested in shipping but shocked by card playing and a Frenchman's puppet show at the tavern.*

Not until Maine achieved statehood in 1820 were theatrical performances sanctioned by law. The first theatre was erected in Portland in 1829.

From that time, theatre in Maine developed along lines similar to those of other New England states. By 1870 Portland's interest in the theatre included opera. After the great fire of 1866, City Hall was rebuilt and Brignoli's Italian Opera Company presented *Il Trovatore, Martha* and *Ernani.* The city became surfeited with performances of Gilbert and Sullivan. John Neal wrote ' . . . such is the rage for theatricals that we have not only amateur clubs, dramatic associations and itinerant companies, but not less than two theatrical companies with two regular organized theatres.' But the companies were not financially successful. To sell seats, one manager in the late 1870s announced special 'perfumed matinees' when patrons were sprinkled with fragrant water as they entered the theatre. Companies continued to perform however, in town, at Peaks Island where Bartley McCallum pioneered summer stock, at the Cape, and at Riverton, reaching a peak of excellence with the opening of the Jefferson Theatre in 1897.

But its wide popularity among the people was declining by the early 1930s with the advent of new forms of entertainment. During the peak of theatrical activity, every city and town of size had a theatre where visiting companies could present the latest successes of Boston and New York. Actress Florence Mack records in her diary that from 1893 until 1907 she appeared with four different companies touring northeastern Maine, her many engagements including stops in Calais, Castine, Stonington, Islesboro, Belfast, Rockland, Boothbay Harbor, Bangor, Waterville, Augusta, Lewiston and Portland. Some cities established their own stock companies such as the Jefferson Players in Portland and the Carroll Players in Lewiston where French language companies also played. Leaders of the large French-Canadian population in the textile city were active in musical, literary and other cultural pursuits; preceding the era of community theatres, operettas and dramas were presented by talented local citizens to full houses.

Between the first performance in 1794 and the last performance at the Jefferson Theatre in Portland in 1932, a period of 138 years, all of the great actors played in Maine, from the Booths to the Barrymores. One of the Shakespearian companies playing in Maine early in the Twentieth century was that of Richard Mansfield. Except for the occasional professional company that comes to Maine briefly in the winter months, the final curtain at the Jefferson marked the passing of the 'legitimate' stage as a continuing cultural influence in the State; its revival was being sought in the late 1960s.

Summer theatre has been popular in Maine since the opening in 1902 of the Lakewood Theatre at Madison, now the State's oldest playhouse. Lakewood and the Ogunquit Playhouse which for a time had a training school, offers package plays and musicals featuring one or more stars on the 'straw-hat' Circuit. The Brunswick Music Theatre on the Bowdoin College campus has offered a season of musicals for a decade, was to be housed elsewhere after 1970. The Boothbay Playhouse is the only professional resident company in Maine, presenting a season of drama. Its unique Theatre Museum has the Franklyn Lenthall collection of rare theatrical memorabilia.

As late as the 1920s, 'theatre' was a not quite respectable profession, academically or otherwise. It was difficult for the young and talented to make it a career. There were few schools of drama such as Mansfield's in Connecticut. On college campuses, speech and debate were taught; plays were extracurricular. Herschel Bricker of the University of Maine was among the handful of teachers who pioneered drama in American universities. As Bricker and his students moved from the more traditionally academic approach to plays and theatre, toward creative participation in the art form, he published a textbook, *Our Theatre Today* in 1936. In the early 1940s, University of Maine was the first school to offer degrees in the theatre.

Influential nationally in professional associations, Bricker who directed the first uncut *Hamlet* in educational theatre, founded the Camden Hills Summer Theatre (1947-56). Drawing audiences from all over the East, productions were staged at Camden Opera House, the season ending with a Shakespearean Festival at the Garden Theatre which was featured in National Geographic and Holiday magazines. For two years *Macbeth* was played at Fort Knox in Prospect. Many can remember driving up to the great granite fort and seeing Elizabethan guards patrolling the battlements with their armor and banners.

Bricker was a member of the National Theatre Conference that administered Rockefeller Foundation funds for young theatre aspirants and was president of the American Educational Theatre Association (1943-45) when the Children's Theatre Association became part of AETA. He has been a member of the State Commission for the Arts and Humanities, was director of the International Theatre Celebration (1956-62) and his Maine Masquers have travelled around the world. In 1962-62 on a good will mission for the State Department, Bricker took the Masquers to India and Pakistan on a four months' tour. For seven summers, children of the Orono area participated in his Children's Theatre programs. Many of his students over a period of 41 years have gone on to become prominent in the theatre and related professions. In 1969, Bricker directed the Maine Masque production of *Noah* by Andre Obey. In the title role was one of his former students, now with credits from the Lincoln Center Repertory, the New York Shakespeare Festival Company and off-Broadway productions.

In the late 1960s a new trend of experiment and change in summer theatre was discernible among new and talented groups endeavoring to establish themselves. There were the Downeast Players at Ram Island Farm, Cape Elizabeth, who also were re-opening the Kennebunkport Playhouse, with challenging plays and new techniques. With the assistance of the Arts and Humanities Commission, they brought African and Carribean dance companies to Maine. The Cape Players were providing a training ground for young Maine talent. The Thomas Players of South Casco were presenting musicals. There was Deertrees at Harrison and a music theatre had opened at York Harbor. New at Orono in 1969 was the Red Barn Theatre which was also to have a day school for plays and films. The Treteau Company of Paris had played in Lewiston. A classic repertory company was scheduled to open in 1970 at Monmouth's Cumston Hall where a company had played Gilbert and Sullivan for several seasons. The Camden Opera House planned weekend musicals. In academic circles there was a new Art theatre at University of Maine, Portland; and the Bates College Theatre was taking on new dimensions under a new director who had inaugurated a Summer Drama Institute for high school students.

Recognition of films as an art medium has seen experimental work by film clubs such as one at Gardiner. There are art films, natural history, documentary and educational films being made and studies of early and foreign films.

Theatre interest during the winter months is stimulated by community and college theatre productions. The Arts and Humanities Commission has assisted a State Touring Theatre Foundation which with the Boothbay Playhouse as its first producing agent, brought drama to Maine audiences from York at the bottom of the State to Madawaska at the top. For Bangor's Bicentennial observance in 1969, the Maine State Ballet and the Bangor Symphony presented an original work based on *The Strange Woman*, a Ben Ames Williams novel of Bangor's early lumbering days.

The dance as an art form developed even more slowly in Maine. There had been ballroom dancing in the Eighteenth century but the lingering Puritan idea of its frivolity did not begin to give way until around the turn of the century when it could be seen to have some value in the deportment training of reluctant little ladies and gentlemen. In Lewiston a dancing master over half a century ago would admonish his wayward charges with `Chris -tian chil-dren!' His recitals at City Hall featured a whist game, the children costumed as playing cards, the Dancing Master calling the plays.

Adults, too, learned the amenities of the 'ballroom' along with the waltz and schottische, later to be enlivened when Irene and Vernon Castle, swingers of their era, appeared on the national scene. Square dancing, widely popular in the 1960s, was always performed at country dances, but there was little folk dancing. Dancing was an expression of social mores rather than aesthetics.

By the 1920s, the dance as an art form began to be recognized. Community dancing schools offered ballet and 'classical' dancing. Notable among these was the Denishawn School of the Dance established in Lewiston by Marian Murphy, a pupil of Ruth St. Denis and Ted Shawn. Isadora Duncan's free style was emulated on college campuses, although the dance remained for many years an appendage to women's physical education courses. As Hollywood musicals came in, tap and acrobatic dancing became the vogue.

While few of the world's great dancers had appeared in Maine, the dance as an art form was receiving more attention by the 1960s at institutions of higher learning and such schools as the Albertine at Hull's Cove, Bar Harbor, and at the Polly Thomas School in Portland which directs the Maine State Ballet in performances with the Portland and Bangor Symphonies. In 1970, the Murray Lewis Dancers of New York drew large audiences for a series of programs in Maine. And in New York, a Maine native, Jacques Damboise of Lewiston, had become a premier American ballet dancer. In an unprecedented appearance before the Maine Legislature, Agnes deMille, noted dancer and choreographer, pleaded for more support for the performing arts.

CULTURAL CENTERS

While all cultural activities cannot be listed here, principal art museums and galleries, music centers and theatres are given for quick reference. National Registry historic sites, houses and historical society museums are listed preceding the Index. For detail see city and tour descriptions. An annual booklet on cultural events is available from the State Commission for Arts and Humanities, 156 State Street, Augusta, Maine 04330. Check locally for seasons, dates and hours.

ART

Bar Harbor, Collier Gallery
Belfast, Red Barn Gallery
Biddeford, York Institute
Blue Hill, Paint Box
Boothbay Region Gallery
Bristol, Pemaquid Gallery
Brunswick, Bowdoin College Museum
Camden, The Gallery
Cape Neddick, Norton Hall
Deer Isle, Haystack Gallery
Freeport, Frost Gallery
Gorham, College Gallery
Hallowell, Harlow Gallery

Kennebunk, Brick Store Museum
Lewiston, Bates College Gallery
Norway, Art Center
Ogunquit, Museum of Art;
   Barn and Ogunquit Galleries
Orono, University of Maine
Portland, Museum of Art
Rockland, Farnsworth Museum
Rockport, Maine Coast Artists
Waldoboro, Gallery Association
Waterville, Colby College
   Museum, Jette Gallery
Wiscasset, Maine Art Gallery

MUSIC

Bangor Symphony Orchestra
Bar Harbor, Festivals
Blue Hill, Kneisel Hall
Brunswick, Bowdoin College
Camden, Bay Chamber Concerts
Hancock, Pierre Monteux Concerts
Northeast Harbor, Chamber Music

Oakland, New England Music Camp
Orono, University of Maine
Portland Symphony Orchestra
Raymond, Amherst Music Center
Vinalhaven, Fox Islands
Waterville, Colby College

THEATRE

Boothbay Playhouse
Brunswick Music Theatre
Camden, Maine Music Theatre
Cape Elizabeth, Downeast Players
Harrison, Deertrees Theatre
Kennebunkport Playhouse

Monmouth, Classic Repertory
Ogunquit Theatre
Orono, Skitikuk Red Barn Playhouse
Skowhegan, Lakewood Theatre
South Casco, Thomas Players

Winter: Portland Players and Children's Theatre; University and
College Campus Players; Community Little Theatres.

II. SEAPORTS AND RIVER TOWNS

AUGUSTA

Alt. 120, pop. 21,680. sett. 1754, incorp. town 1797, Kennebec County seat 1799, State Capital 1832, city 1849.

Access: N and S, Maine Turnpike and I-95; US 201; State 27. E and W, US 202; E, State 3-9-17.

Information: Chamber of Commerce, Memorial Circle; State Department of Economic Development, Augusta Plaza, Western Avenue.

Accommodations: two hotels, five motels.

Transportation: airport; bus, inter-city, local.

Parks: State Park, opp. Capitol; Nature Park, Malta Hill; six playgrounds.

Recreation: environs, swimming, boating, Lake Cobbosseecontee, Togus and Three Corner Ponds; golf, country club, Manchester.

Cultural, historic sites: see POINTS OF INTEREST.

AUGUSTA, State capital and Kennebec County seat, rises in a series of terraces and sharp inclines east and west of the bisecting Kennebec River. The city is at the head of river navigation, 45 miles from open sea, with an approximate tide range of four feet. Augusta is the State's population center and as the seat of State government, is the hub of central Maine — 30 m. to Lewiston, 60 to Portland, 72 to Bangor and 175 to Boston, all minutes by air. Although lying on both sides of the river, it has not developed into twin municipalities; most of its industrial and business establishments and an extensive residential area are on the west side. However, like most cities in the past decade, Augusta has felt urban congestion, and is stretching outward on both sides of the river. Expansion of State government, faster than new building to house it, has resulted in unplanned growth of the area dominated by the Capitol Complex and in continued need for departmental space; many departments occupy old houses away from the Complex.

The capital city is distinguished by its handsome century-old elms, its parks and the Capitol with its Bulfinch facade. There are seventeen churches, eleven public and two parochial schools. University of Maine - Augusta, established in 1965, will occupy a campus on the east side of the Kennebec northwest of the city. Also on the east side is the Augusta Nature Education Center and the Maine Veterans Cemetery. Six municipal playgrounds (*summer weekdays, 9-4*) in various parts of the city have full-time supervisors and extensive programs and equipment. There are three libraries, a daily newspaper and two radio stations. A State-wide art exhibition is held in summer and community theatre is among other cultural events sponsored by local organizations.

The social groups common to an industrial city of its size are augmented in Augusta by a wide variety of county, State and Federal employes.

Predominating racial groups are of English and French-Canadian descent, the latter concentrated in the northwestern section and making up approximately fifteen percent of the city's population. There are a few tenement areas, no slums. As elsewhere in 1969, more housing was needed.

Since 1959, the city has had a council-manager form of government. The city manager is the administrative head and purchasing agent for the city and with advice and consent of the council, controls appointments of all department heads. The mayor presides at council meetings and carries out other official duties imposed by the council.

With its business center on Water Street and three shopping plazas on Western Avenue, Augusta is the trading center for more than 135,000 city and suburban residents. Many conventions are held here. Some 24 industries employ nearly 4000 people exclusive of the hundreds in government and commercial employ. The city has a high level water supply from ponds and wells and the first primary treatment (sewage) plant on the Kennebec River.

The Kennebec having its source at Moosehead Lake, has flowed through all Augusta history and shaped the course of its development. To the Indian, *Manitou Kennebec* (river-god) was not only a highway and a source of food; at times it was an angry god that crushed canoes and swallowed its victims or swept away entire villages when in flood. To the early traders the river gave ingress to the treasures of the Kennebec Valley, furs and fish; later it carried wealth for the men of Augusta in the form of lumber, brought prosperity in trade through river traffic, turned the city's mills and provided a lucrative harvest in ice in winter. Today, long after the Indians and traders, the ships and the ice harvest have departed, the river continues to supply the city with wealth in another form — water power. And still, too, it strikes out at man's bridges, dams and buildings when in flood.

The Indians called Augusta *Cushnoc*; it also has been known variously as Cushena, Cushanna, Cusinock, Koussinock and Harrington. *Cushnoc* has been given several interpretations: one that the site was so-called because 'the tide runs no farther up the Kennebec'; another that it meant 'the consecrated place,' since the Indians held annual meetings there and seemed to consider it in a sense hallowed.

Sacred or not, Cushnoc was of value to the Plymouth Colony of Massachusetts. Trade on the Kennebec was begun immediately after the grant of the Kennebec Patent in 1628-29. In 1628 the Plymouth men established a trading post on the approximate site of Fort Western, 'ye most convenient place for trade.' John Howland, the 'lustie yonge man' who was washed overboard during the MAYFLOWER crossing and nearly lost, was the first agent in command of the Cushnoc post. In 1634 he shared this office with John Alden, immortalized in Longfellow's *The*

Courtship of Miles Standish. Alden was falsely accused of murder because of two deaths in that year arising from a dispute with a rival company over the trading rights at Cushnoc. Miles Standish made frequent trips to the post and Governor William Bradford is said to have visited it. Captain Thomas Willett, later Governor of New York, was a successor of Howland and Alden and another notable commander of the post (1647-53) was John Winslow, brother of Governor Edward Winslow of Massachusetts. Winslow was an intimate friend of Father Druillettes, the Jesuit missionary, frequently making him welcome at the post.

Fur trading was so highly profitable to the Pilgrims that it is said their debts to the Merchant Adventurers of London for the expenses of the MAYFLOWER expedition were paid with furs brought from the Kennebec. After more than 32 years of trading, amicable relations with the Indians were severed by the Indians wars, and English occupation at Cushnoc was abandoned for more than three quarters of a century. However, industry and the white man's civilization had gained their first foothold at Cushnoc, and the Plymouth Patent was the foundation of future land titles.

During the middle of the Eighteenth century, the Proprietors of the Kennebec Purchase sought to bring settlers into the region. In 1754 Fort Western was erected on the east bank of the river. Named for Thomas Western of Sussex, England, a friend of Governor William Shirley, the fort was one of three built on the Kennebec that year: northernmost was Fort Halifax about 65 miles from the mouth of the river, near the present town of Winslow; Fort Western, and Fort Shirley, on the site of the present town of Dresden. Captain James Howard, the first and only commander of Fort Western, was Augusta's first permanent settler and a strong influence in the early development of the city.

The defeat of Montcalm at Quebec in 1759 made the Kennebec safe for the pioneers and the fort was dismantled except the garrison building, the only one extant in Maine built prior to the Revolution, without ever having been attacked. The Benedict Arnold expedition gathered here for a week in September, 1775 on its way to Quebec.

A few miles south of the Fort a settlement called Hallowell had been made in 1762. At the time of its incorporation as a town in 1771, Fort Western was included. The two settlements became known as the Fort and the Hook, the latter name taken from Bombahook Stream at Hallowell. At this time, the western side of the Fort settlement began to outstrip the eastern, aided by the industrial advantage of a sawmill at Bond Brook. Lumber was an important source of wealth and in many instances pine boards took the place of currency. In 1780 the town voted to pay each of its Continental soldiers 2500 feet of pine boards plus the other bounty granted.

On the whole, however, the settlement at the Hook advanced more rapidly in wealth and population than the Fort, and rivalry gradually arose. In 1796 the Hook's leadership was threatened by Fort inhabitants who sought construction of a bridge to replace the ferry that ran from the foot of Winthrop Street to the Fort landing. To the chagrin of the Hook people, the first bridge over the Kennebec was completed at Augusta that same year. The resultant jealousy between the settlements necessitated a division. Hallowell retained its present name and the Fort became Harrington, after Lord Harrington when it was incorporated as a separate town in February 20, 1797. The name, however, was not agreeable, probably because the Hallowell wits corrupted it to 'Herringtown' and on June 9 of the same year it was changed to Augusta. Accounts of the origin of the name differ, but one interpretation is that the town was called Augusta in honor of Pamela Augusta Dearborn, a daughter of General Henry Dearborn, the prominent Revolutionary soldier who was elected Representative to the Continental Congress from the Kennebec District in 1783. Two years after its incorporation Augusta became shire town of Kennebec County.

After the turn of the century, Augusta entered upon a new era of development, although Hallowell was the social and commercial metropolis of the region. The settlers' struggle for possession of the land against the claims of the Proprietors came to a sharp focus in Augusta. In 1809 Paul Chadwick, one of a party of surveyors sent out to establish a land claim in Malta (Windsor), was murdered by squatters disguised, in Boston Tea-Party style, as Indians. Seven of the squatters were put in the Augusta jail. Shortly after, about 70 men descended upon the town in an attempt to release the Malta prisoners, and the community was thrown into great turmoil. Several companies of soldiers were called out from nearby towns to guard the courthouse, jail, and the homes of some of the land proprietors, and a cannon was placed on the west side in a position to sweep the bridge. With continual rioting, it was deemed necessary to keep the guards for six weeks until after the prisoners' trial. Fortunately for the general peace, they were found not guilty. 'The Malta War' as it was called, was one of the most serious disputes between settlers and landowners in Maine; it cost the Commonwealth of Massachusetts over $11,000 for supplies and military services.

River traffic on the Kennebec already had entered upon an era that was to see a whole fleet of schooners plying weekly between Augusta and Boston by 1840. Freight from deep-water vessels often was transferred to longboats at Augusta and thence towed up-river through the rapids by oxen that were driven through the shoals when there was not enough room to permit their passage along shore. Augusta had its share of the more than 500 vessels built between Winslow and Gardiner; thousands of tons of shipping were owned in the city and neighboring communities; and it was not rare to see a score or so of vessels berthed at Augusta wharves.

Although the arrival of the first train in Augusta in 1851, announced by 'wild screams such as locomotives are rarely permitted to utter,' predestined the decline of the river trade, schooners and tug-drawn barges conducted a profitable export business into the Twentieth century, exchanging cargoes of ice or lumber for produce and coal. Steamboat travel to Bath and Boston was inaugurated in 1826, and six years later a line ran upriver to Waterville.

The establishment of a United States Arsenal at Augusta in 1828 and the founding of the State Hospital eleven years later, two events contributing to the town's prestige, supplemented the even more important occasion of 1832 when Augusta became the State capital.

By 1849 the population of the town had increased (8225 in 1850) so that the town was authorized to adopt a city form of government. At no period had wealth been so great or indications of prosperity more marked. A cotton factory and sawmills at the dam, constructed in 1837, were in full operation, while the tonnage of ocean and river traffic was increasing. However, various checks such as the gold rush of '49 and the Civil War, interfered with the city's development. Steamboat traffic like that of the sailing vessels fell off in time because of railroad competition and the lack of patronage. In 1865 a devastating fire razed nearly all of the business district.

Various distinguished men visited the city during its mid-Nineteenth century period of growth. General Winfield Scott made Augusta his headquarters for three weeks in 1839 while negotiating the settlement of the northeastern boundary dispute at the conclusion of the 'Aroostook War.' General U. S. Grant stopped in the city on several occasions, and in 1867 General Phil Sheridan visited Augusta as a guest of the State. A local account of the visit runs: *General Phil Sheridan rides into Augusta. School children sing 'Sheridan's Ride' from elevated steps . . . Phil rides off in closed carriage after singing, and wasn't seen again . . . Mothers check up on their daughters to see if they had gone for a ride with Sheridan, but none were missing. This was known as Sheridan's Second Ride, but no poem was ever written about it that we know of today.*

Six Augusta citizens have become Governors of Maine. A native son, Melville W. Fuller (1833-1910) became Chief Justice of the U. S. Supreme Court, writing 829 decisions during his 22 years of office (1888-1910).

Maine's most conspicuous statesman in the latter half of the Nineteenth century perhaps was the brilliant and articulate James Gillespie Blaine (1830-93) of Augusta, editor of the *Kennebec Journal*, a founder of the Republican party in Maine, Speaker of the U. S. House of Representatives for three terms, Secretary of State under two presidents, and instrumental in the development of the Pan-American Congress. The 'Man

from Maine' whose influence and personal magnetism earned him the
sobriquet 'The Plumed Knight,' was at the turbulent center of national
politics for thirty years. Some of his vicissitudes have a contemporary
ring — he faced a Congressional inquiry into his use of official position
to further private business. A sparkling orator, he was one of those dominant party figures like the earlier Henry Clay and Daniel Webster who
seemed inevitably destined for the presidency but somehow never made it.
In 1884 the Republican convention nominated Blaine by acclamation.
Following what has been called one of the most vituperative campaigns
in American politics, Grover Cleveland won the presidency. Contributing
to Blaine's defeat were said to have been his association with the so-
called 'money kings' and his alleged application of the alliterative 'rum,
romanism and rebellion' to the Democratic party, a remark that was in
fact made by a minister, the Rev. Mr. Burchard. Blaine's association
with such men as John J. Astor, William Vanderbilt, Jay Gould and
Andrew Carnegie was satirized in a biting cartoon in Joseph Pulitzer's
New York World.

Blaine married Harriet Stanwood of Augusta. Three of their seven children and three of their grandchildren were born in Blaine House, now the
home of Maine's governors. Mrs. Blaine's letters reveal a lively warm-
hearted family living at Blaine House in a whirl of arriving and departing
visitors, political entertaining and family parties. Their daughter Margaret
became the wife of Walter Damrosch. Ill health caused Blaine's retirement as Secretary of State under President Benjamin Harrison and he
died in 1893.

Lumber and the paper industry, textile mills, shoe manufactories and
publishing and printing houses figure largely in the history of Augusta's
economic development. The presence of State and county departments
has had much to do with this development; otherwise Augusta might
have remained a small industrial town. As the capital of the State of
Maine it has the characteristics of a modern political-industrial metropolis.

POINTS OF INTEREST

Fort Western (summer, weekdays, 9-5; Sunday 1-5), Bowman Street and the
land it occupies are replete with historic associations. On the site of the Plymouth trading post established a few years after the landing of the Pilgrims in
America, a fort was erected in 1794 as protection against Indians. There
were two blockhouses, a building for storerooms, barracks, officers' quarters
and parade grounds, all enclosed by a palisade. The original garrison house
has been restored and furnished with antiques, and reproductions of the original
blockhouses and palisades were built by William Howard Gannett, a descendant
of the fort's first commander. One room is furnished with material from Switzerland brought by Mr. Gannett. Another, chiefly devoted to collections from the
Southwest, is dedicated to W. Herbert Dunton, Augusta artist and illustrator.

A *Boulder* in fenced enclosure south of Fort Western commemorates Benedict Arnold's ill-fated expedition to Quebec in the fall of 1775. About 1100

NATURAL RESOURCES

ENDOWED with abundant natural resources in ocean and forest, rivers, mountains and fertile fields, Maine in the last quarter of the Twentieth century is looking to their protection, seeking to harness progress with conservation. Power of course has been the genesis of industry since the early settlers began moving up the rivers and building grist and sawmills. Maine's forests, 'last great wilderness of the northeast,' supply the leading pulp and paper industries whose huge plants are dotted over the state. Fishing is Maine's oldest industry, modernized with advances in marine biology. Manufacturing of some kind, from textiles and shoes, machinery and electronics, to Christmas tree ornaments, is carried on in most towns. Many plants are open to visitors.

MOUNT
KATAHDIN

THE WAVE

ANDROSCOGGIN FALLS AT LEWISTON

MODEL OF YANKEE ATOMIC ENERGY PLANT AT WISCASSET

SPRING LOG DRIVE AND PEAVEYS

THE RIVER DRIVERS, BANGOR

GREAT NORTHERN
PAPER COMPANY
CHEMICAL CONVERTER,
MILLINOCKET

GREAT NORTHERN AT NIGHT

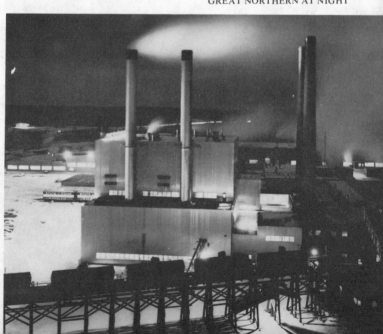

OLD-TIME LOG-HAULING

DE-ICING THE FISHING BOAT — SOME ICE-BOX!

MONHEGAN
LOBSTER TRAP
WINTER

SARDINE BOATS AT THE DOCK

THE TOW, EARLY FISHING BOATS AT EASTPORT

THE HERRING NET

ROCKPORT LIME KILNS

NEW ENGLAND'S LARGEST CEMENT PLANT, THOMASTON

VINALHAVEN GRANITE QUARRIES WITH GALAMANDER

NORTHERN CHEMICAL COMPANY PLANT, SEARSPORT

BATH IRON WORKS EXPANSION MODEL

POLARIS MISSILE
SILOS, KITTERY
NAVY YARD

SPRAGUE ENERGY CORPORATION OIL TANKER

KITTERY PORTSMOUTH NAVY YARD

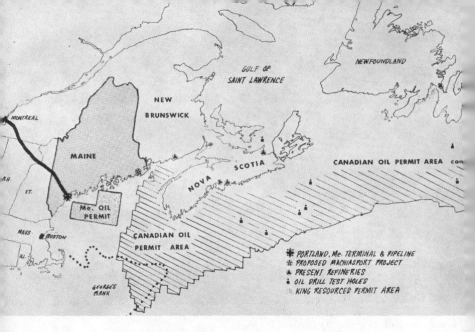

NORTHEAST OIL AREA MAP

MARINE BIOLOGY LABORATORY, BOOTHBAY HARBOR

men rendezvoused at the Fort, landing from a fleet of 200 bateaux that had been built at Agry Point, two miles below the village of Randolph. A bronze tablet, missing since 1958, carried these words:

> An Expedition under Colonel Benedict Arnold for the capture of Quebec marched from this point in September 1775.

> To Record and Honor the service of its members who took part in this effort toward American independence this tablet was placed August 19, 1912 by the Second Company of the Governor's Foot Guards of New Haven, Connecticut.

Augusta Water District, 12 Wiliam Street. The city's main sources of water supply are Carleton Pond in Readfield and Winthrop and three deep wells in the Bond Brook drainage, with Lake Cobbosseecontee as standby. The Kennebec River as a source of supply was abandoned in 1906. Construction in East Winthrop in 1968 allowed for water use of nine million gallons per day, with future provision for 16 million gallons.

Augusta State Hospital, S. end of Arsenal Street, established in 1834 as the Maine Insane Hospital, occupies the stone buildings of a former United States Arsenal. The cornerstone of the first Arsenal building 'for the safe-keeping of arms and munitions of the United States for the northern and eastern frontier' was laid June 14, 1818. The next year Congress made an appropriation for construction of fifteen buildings, ten of them of blocks of unhammered concrete to be laid in a most permanent manner. In 1834 the Arsenal was under command of Lt. Robert Anderson who afterwards as major was in command of Fort Sumter during its defense under Confederate attack April 12, 1861. During the Civil War the Arsenal was a depot of valuable military stores. In 1905 President Theodore Roosevelt signed a bill introduced by Congressman Edwin C. Burleigh authorizing the Secretary of War to transfer the property to the State of Maine and it has since been used by the State Hospital. The entire tract covering some 40 acres was enclosed by a massive iron fence, seven feet high, set in solid masonry, some of which remains (1968). Reuel Williams of Augusta and Benjamin Brown of Vassalboro matched State funds of $20,000 to purchase a 400-acre farm south of the Arsenal grounds. A large building of unhammered granite was constructed to house 120 patients; the first was admitted in October, 1840. By legislative act in 1913, the institution's name was changed to its present one.

Cony High School, cor. Stone and Cony Streets, had its origin in the Cony Female Academy, founded in 1818 to provide 'instruction gratis . . . to a number of orphans or other females under 16 years of age.' The High School, built in 1880, was enlarged in 1930, again in 1965.

Augusta Nature Education Center (summer tours 1:30 from Hodgkins School), between South Belfast Avenue and Cony Street Ext. The Augusta Nature and Rotary Clubs and the city have preserved 97 acres of natural environment with programs for children to get to know the land so they will care what happens to it. The basic work-study program is a summer day camp in four two-week sessions week days from 9:30 to 3, with emphasis on field work. Fourth through eighth grade pupils are eligible and the staff includes a director and four qualified college students. Center facilities are used by Bates College of Lewiston for a botany course and by high, elementary and grammar school classes for biology and botany studies.

City Hall, E end of old Kennebec Bridge not far from Fort Western, was dedicated July 4, 1896. The building, owned by the city since 1934, houses all city departments except Public Works. A second floor hall has a seating capacity of 2000.

Cushnoc, a small island about a quarter mile N of the bridge, is visible only at low water. Navigation past Old Coon, as the early settlers called it, was difficult and dangerous, and many boats were sunk attempting the passage. About 1820 an effort was made to drag the island from its bed. Mill chains were fastened around the island and linked to a hundred yoke of oxen which headed upstream along the river bank. The first terrific pull succeeded only in throwing the hindmost yoke of oxen into the river. Subsequent attempts during the day effected no more than broken chains and crescendos of curses that rivaled the combined ox-power in volume. The island is still there.

Kennebec Dam, just N of the bridge, was first built in 1837. Partially destroyed four times, the structure was entirely rebuilt in 1870. Drainage waters from an area of more than 5000 square miles pour over the 22-foot face of the dam, supplying the city with 7150 horsepower.

Memorial Bridge, downstream, a high level span connecting the East and West Side Circles, was completed in 1949 and named for those who served in World War II. A walk across the bridge gives a fine view of the city and the Kennebec River.

Bates Manufacturing Company, Inc. Mill, Edwards Division (*visitors' permits at office*), cor. Canal and Water Streets, is Augusta's largest industry, employing about 1200 workers and producing cotton cloth. Established in 1845 by the Kennebec Lock and Canal Company, the mill today is a modern plant with well-kept grounds.

Augusta House, State Street at Western Avenue, West Side Circle, landmark hostelry associated with State government, was opened in 1831 to accommode legislators who were expected to hold their first session in Augusta the following winter. It originally had a mansard roof with dormer windows but was remodelled to a six-story building in 1910 to meet threats of insufficient accommodations raised by proponents of a change of State government to Portland. The Augusta House has been the home away from home of legislators ever since.

Blaine House (NHL, Classical Revival 1830) (*Mon. through Fri. 2-4*), Capitol and State Streets, residence of Maine's governors since 1921, was occupied by Statesman James G. Blaine and his family during his political career. The original square structure with cupola and ell was built by James Hall, a sea captain, on land that was part of Lot No. 5 on the 1770 survey for the Proprietors of the Kennebec Purchase. Blaine who was born the year the house was built, bought it in 1862 and made a large addition to the ell. During World War I the house was used by Maine's Committee of Public Safety. Harriet Blaine Beale, Blaine's youngest daughter, gave the house to the State of Maine in memory of her son Walker who was killed at St. Mihiel in 1918. Remodeled under the direction of Architect John Calvin Stevens, the old house was restored to its original dignity and charm. The long drawing room has the original marble fireplaces and white pilasters. Kept much as he used it is Blaine's study with its black marble fireplace; here he received President Grant and other dignitaries, and at his old Congressional desk, wrote *Twenty Years of Congress*. In the State dining room are pieces from the silver service the State had presented to the Battleship MAINE, sunk in Havana Harbor in 1898. The ornate silver pieces, with pine needles and cones in high relief, were returned to the State of Maine when the vessel was raised in 1912. The house is furnished with period pieces and reproductions, with some original possessions of the Blaines. Shown in Blaine House are works of art belonging to the State of Maine or on loan from Maine museums.

State House (Mon. through Fri. 8-6, Sat.-Sun. 9-6; guided tours in summer).
The State Capitol rises on a knoll at Capitol and State Streets overlooking
the State Park. Its colonnaded front is a prime example of the work of the
great American architect, Charles Bulfinch. Augusta was named Maine's
capital city February 24, 1827 in a bill signed by Governor Enoch Lincoln.
The cornerstone was laid in Masonic ceremonies July 4, 1829 and the building
of Hallowell granite was completed three years later at a cost of $140,000,
a sizeable sum at the time. The Legislature first met at Augusta in 1832. The
original Bulfinch building was 150 feet long and included a central section
with north and south wings, a rotunda with columns and a rounded vault
described as a 'cupola.' The interior was remodeled in 1852 and again in
1860. In 1890-91 another wing was added and the cupola was replaced
by the present dome which is visible for miles around. It is 185 feet high,
surmounted by a gold-plated copper figure of the Goddess of Wisdom
designed by Sculptor W. Clark Noble of Gardiner. After agitation had subsided for the removal of the seat of government to Portland where the
Legislature had met prior to 1832, the building in 1910-11 was greatly
enlarged according to designs of G. Henri Desmond. Although most of the
old building was demolished, the original Bulfinch front was retained.
The four-storied building has a 300-foot front with colonnaded portico and
granite steps in the center section and two 75-foot wings facing east. In the
dignified Rotunda with its eight Doric columns are displayed Maine battle
flags and portraits of distinguished Maine public figures. The Executive
offices and Senate chambers are in the south wing. The House of
Representatives occupies the third and fourth stories of the north wing.
Also in the building are a Law Library of some 75,000 volumes and various
State departments. A tunnel leads to the State Office Building (1955)
housing other State departments and a cafeteria.

State Cultural Building. To be completed in 1971, this new building was
authorized in 1967 when Maine citizens approved a $4,800,000 bond issue.
It will house the State Archives, Library and History Museum, all now
located in the Capitol building. The ground-breaking ceremony took place
July 16, 1968 at the building site south of the State House. The State
Library's 300,000 volumes include a large collection of Maineiana; its
eight bookmobiles, a service established in 1953, travel to communities having
no library facilities. Maine had no State Archives until 1965; Samuel S.
Silby was named first State Archivist. The State Museum which hitherto has
emphasized natural history, plans broader interpretation of Maine history
through its collections and programs for the public.

State Park, a 20-acre tract between Capitol and Union Streets, stretching from
State Street before the Capitol to the banks of the Kennebec River, offers
pleasant vistas and walks over more than a mile of paths. Historically the
Park is of interest because of its Civil War associations. Maine regiments
were encamped here during the war and the soldiers endured the rigors of at
least two winters before setting out into the heat of southern campaigns. At
the end of a long lane of trees is a marble shaft marking the grave of Enoch
Lincoln, Maine's sixth governor. His 2000-line poem, *The Village,* having its
setting in Fryeburg and written while he was a lawyer there, was the first
book of poetry published in Maine.

Augusta Sanitary District Plant (guided tours) in an attractive setting on
Britt Road began operating in 1963, the first primary treatment plant on the
Kennbec.

Kennebec County Jail, SE. corner of State and Court Streets, with Italianate
architectural features, was the most modern of its kind when it was erected
in 1858-59. Its workhouse now houses the Kennebec County District Court.

Kennebec County Courthouse, N side of Court Street cor. State and Winthrop Streets, across from the jail, shows the architectural influence of the State House. It is of stone, built in 1829-30, with enlargements in 1851 and 1907, and first occupied in June, 1830 when the Supreme Court session began.

Augusta Y.M.C.A., N side of Winthrop Street across from the Courthouse, is on the site of the original *Kennebec County Gaol,* and was erected in 1914, the gift of the Governor John F. Hill family. The original Gaol, a not very secure wooden building constructed in 1793, was replaced by a stone jail in 1808. It was from this stone jail that Joseph L. Sager of Gardiner was led to the scaffold and hanged on a wintry day, January 2, 1835. He had been convicted of murdering his wife by arsenic. The gallows was erected on Winthrop Street near the southeast corner of the jail and the attending minister read a manuscript 'partly by narrative and partly by exhortation' that the murderer had prepared. A crowd estimated in the thousands thronged the streets radiating from the jail, awaiting the hanging. There was much jeering and throwing of stones, and 'liquor flowed freely and was disposed of by the barrel.' It was said that after Sager was pronounced dead, his body was carried to Hallowell and that attempts were made to restore his life by galvanism. The trap door of the gallows presently (1968) is in one of the blockhouses at Fort Western. Capital punishment was not finally abolished in Maine until 1887.

Lithgow Library and Reading Room (Mon. through Thurs. 10-6; Fri. 10-9; Sat. 9-12) W of the Y.M.C.A.; is of Maine granite in Romanesque-Renaissance style after designs by Joseph Neal and Alfred Hopkins and was opened January 27, 1896. It is on the site of a famous old tavern, the Cushnoc House. In its book room six stained glass windows designed by Charles Willoughby of Augusta, later a curator at the Peabody Museum of Archaeology and Ethnology, treat historic subjects important in the annals of the city. In addition to nearly 31,000 volumes (1968), the Library houses the collection of the Kennebec Historical Society, mostly classified and indexed and containing scores of items pertinent to Augusta and New England history.

South Congregational Church, 59 State Street, is Augusta's oldest church, although the present Gothic granite structure was not built until 1866. The tower and spire rising 178 feet were rebuilt in the early 1950s. The present building replaced the original meetinghouse of 1806 which burned in 1865. The parish dates to 1771, its first building being completed in Market Square on Water Street eleven years later. A Roman Catholic church established in 1836 on the east side of the river was sold in 1845; another, now gone was erected on State Street. Erected in 1915, *St. Augustine's Catholic Church* is an impressive structure dominating the northern section of the city on the west side. The growth of the French population with increased lumbering and mill employment assumed such proportions that a second Catholic Church, *St. Mary's* on Western Avenue, was built in 1927. This stately granite edifice of modified Norman-Gothic design is considered the most beautiful of Augusta's churches.

Winthrop Street is an eight-rod rangeway between Lots 7 and 8 as shown on Nathan Winslow's plan of 1761 for the Proprietors of the Kennebec Purchase. In May 1853, the citizens residing on Winthrop Street, inspired by a commendable public spirit, united and set out elms and other ornamental trees on each side of the street. They were set forty feet apart and sixteen feet in from the lines of the street, leaving a wide avenue of a hundred feet between the rows. Most of those trees still exist (1968). In this street at the corner of Granite Street is buried the body of Capt. James Purrinton who settled in Augusta in 1805. On July 9, 1806 this man attacked his family with an axe, killing and mangling in a manner too shocking to relate, his wife and six children, wounding two others. With a razor he then cut his own throat. The mother and children were buried in the northeast corner of the burying ground, but Purrinton's body was buried without ceremony in the street.

Grave of General Henry Sewall, Revolutionary war hero, marked by a stone in an iron fence enclosure near two Bunker Hill-shaped monuments, is in the old *Burnt Hill Burying-ground* off Granite Street, where the town powder house once stood.

Augusta State Airport is on the site of Camp Keyes, formerly a State muster field where the 43rd Division of the National Guard encamped periodically. The State Adjutant General's Department occupies buildings at left on Blaine Avenue and Winthrop Street; E of Green Street is the training school for Maine State Police recruits. This hilltop affords fine views of the city and valley. Augusta State Airport's new terminal building was completed in 1969.

The James G. Blaine Memorial, cor. Green Street occupies a State Park on the east side of Blaine Avenue, overlooking the city. Visitors are asked to walk in around the roadway.

Kennebec Journal Building, 274 Western Avenue at Storey St., houses Augusta's daily newspaper established in 1825 and one of the few in the country with a record of more than a hundred years of continuous publication. It has been said that the 'KJ' was the first of the American press to advocate Abraham Lincoln for the presidency.

Hallowell Shoe Company, on Whitten Road off Western Avenue (*visitors*), one of Augusta's three shoe factories, moved to this location in 1966. It employs 250 workers, with production of 2800 pairs of shoes daily.

Maine Veterans Cemetery, all wars, W. of Old Belgrade Road bordering I-95.

University of Maine — Augusta Campus (1970), Townsend Road near I-95.

Augusta is the birthplace of Author Holman F. Day (1865-1935) and Sculptor Granville W. Carter (1920-   ).

ENVIRONS

Several arteries radiate from Augusta for short tours that may be extended to connect with principal points on major road tours (*see HIGHWAYS and BYWAYS*).
Tour 1 — S on US 201 to *Gardiner, 6 m.* (route continues via Richmond and Bowdoinham to Brunswick (*see BRUNSWICK*), 32.3 *m.*

At 2.2 *m.* HALLOWELL (alt. 110, pop. 3380), an interesting old city in a natural amphitheatre formed by hills facing a bend in the Kennebec River. It must have been a handsome sight in the era when giant Ox-heart cherry trees lined the streets and shaded the homes. Phenomenal in Maine, the Hallowell cherry trees, unlike today's 20-ft. trees seen elsewhere, were large as maples and drew visitors from miles around when they bloomed in late spring. The huge oval juicy dark red cherries were harvested and marketed by the bushel — and were free to all who could reach them on the public streets.

Hallowell provides an interesting study in riverport architecture both downtown and on the hillside. Pease and Peter Clark were the first settlers in 1792 and Hallowell, called the Hook, developed in industry, commerce and agriculture to rival the Fort settlement at Augusta until the mid-1800s. A shipbuilding and printing center for many years, the community advanced culturally through the presence of men of intellect, wealth and influence. Old Hallowell families include the Vaughns, Dummers, Sewalls, Moodys, Otises, Pages, Merricks and Hubbards. Maine Governors Hubbard and Bodwell resided in Hallowell and their homes, as well as many others belonging to men attached to the sea, gain interest when interpreted through local and State history.

Earliest remaining architectural examples begin in the 1790s. Homes of the Federal, Greek Revival and Victorian periods predominate in Hallowell and there are many interesting groupings of workers' dwellings and early boarding houses, and buildings reflecting the city's industrial, civic and religious history including a rare wooden row house, a large brick factory, the early town hall (now the fire station), the well-known Worster House, a Federal church and a granite Victorian church. Collections in the unusual granite Library include an illustrated architectural study of Hallowell's old buildings. The oldest church still standing is the *Cox Memorial Methodist Church* (1826). One stained glass window depicts the Rev. Melville B. Cox, a missionary, among the natives of Africa. Many Hallowell homes and churches are open to visitors during the annual summer Open House and Garden Tour.

Water Street is lined with Federal period brick business blocks with numerous antique shops, called the 'antique center of Maine.' The riverfront Park borders the historic Kennebec where Benedict Arnold led his expedition to Quebec and where in later years an ice-harvesting industry flourished. A granite Marker at the intersection of Water and Central Streets indicates the height of heavy floods that have ravaged the city.

Second Street parallel to Water Street has many of the oldest homes and buildings in the city. Another old thoroughfare is *Winthrop Street*, part of what was once known as the Coos Trail from Hallowell to New Hampshire. Much agricultural traffic went along this trail to the interior and later it was the main road to the now abandoned granite quarries. Stone from here was hauled by ox team down to Middle Street where it was stored and carved by skilled Italian immigrants, then shipped all over the country for use in public buildings and monuments.

Stevens Training School (1875), High and Winthrop Streets, is a State rehabilitation center for women.

The old brick *Powder House* and *Cannon* on High Street are monuments of the War of 1812. The charm of Hallowell's location along the river is apparent from this lookout.

GARDINER (alt. 90, pop. 6897), 6 *m*. Because they are now so closely populated, a stranger might think that Gardiner, Hallowell and Augusta are part of one large city — a dream of early days — but the settlements developed independently. Dr. Sylvester Gardiner (1708-86) came into possession of 100,000 acres of Kennebec land in 1754 and zealously applied himself to its settlement and development as a feudal manor to be controlled by his descendants. Came the Revolution . . .

In 1803, Dr. Gardiner's son Robert devoted himself to the prosperity of the area. For the next 50 years activity on the river grew rapidly. Large wharfs were built as well as saw, grist and lumber mills; later came the paper mills, and finally the shoe factories and electric power. In the mid-1800s large shipments of fish went to Boston. The river was the spawning ground for deep-sea fish and weirs lined the river banks; shad were netted with seine nets and even 6-8 ft. sturgeon were caught.

In winter there were schools of sea smelts caught by handline through holes in the ice. Kennebec River ice was cut and shipped around the world. In other seasonal activity, the river was the scene of great log drives, booms and cables guiding the long supply to the mills. The influx of shipping brought boats of all sizes from Boston, Portland and Bath.

In 1896 a great flood swept out to sea the Gardiner-Randolph bridge and for some time people were shuttled back and forth in rowboats.

The area developed culturally, contributing substantially to the world of letters. A *Granite Monument* memorializes the poet Edwin Arlington Robinson (1869-1935) who was born at Head Tide (*see TOUR 1 sec. b*). His family soon moved to Gardiner which became the poet's 'Tilbury Town.' A psychological poet in a special sense, with a mysterious, unfathomable personality, Robinson is the poet of secret lives. He wrote of the interactions of human beings, daring to tell what he knew of the constants of human behavior. He wrote simply about reality and a review of his work reveals Maine at the turn of the century.

Gardiner at the end of the Nineteenth century was a city of the Maine aristocracy of which the Robinsons were not members. In his book on Robinson, Louis D. Coxe, Bowdoin College playwright and poet, describes the death of Robinson's mother: 'She had never really cared much about her husband's death, but her going was of a kind almost Jacobean in its horror. She had black diphtheria and noone — doctor, pastor, undertaker — would enter the house. Her sons ministered to her, the parson said a prayer through the window, the undertaker left a coffin on the porch and the three brothers buried their mother where Edwin lay and where three years later Dean would go.' An outstanding collection of Robinson memorabilia may be seen at Colby College Library, Waterville.

Among Gardiner authors was Mrs. Laura E. Richards whose *Captain January* was the best known of her works that included novels, biographies, short stories and poems. Kate Vannah, prominent in literary and musical circles and Sculptor W. Clark Noble were Gardiner residents.

At West Gardiner an Indian village is said to have occupied a site on Cobbosseecontee Stream where 'the mighty Manitou hewed a channel called The Hazards out of solid rock.'

Dedicated in Balboa in 1962 was a park in memory of 'John F. Stevens, Master builder of the Panama Canal 1853-1943' who was born in West Gardiner. He attended Western Maine Normal School in Farmington and taught in Westport and Manchester. He studied engineering in Lewiston before moving west to Minnesota. During the period of railroad expansion he nearly lost his life in the treacherous weather conditions of Montana where he located and engineered a pass across the Rockies. A bronze statue of him stands at the pass location. Stevens, known as 'Big Smoke' overcame many vicissitudes to complete preparatory work on the Panama Canal for which he was given complete credit when Army Engineers took over. He held many posts in railroading and was honored with numerous medals and awards in his lifetime.

Tour 2 — SE on State 17 to *Rockland (see TOUR 1 sec. b)*, 42.8 *m.*, scenic route through farming country of gently rolling hills and numerous lakes and ponds, arriving at the port city with handsome views of the Camden Hills.

At 4.6 *m.* the *Veterans Administration Center*, (1866) was the first of the

National homes for disabled veterans. Built for Civil War veterans it is now open to men of all wars. On 1752 acres of land at Togus (Ind.: Worromontogus), the center has several barracks, a large modern hospital, administration building, workshops, chapel, library, theatre, clubhouse, store and officers' homes in landscaped grounds. There is a staff of 800 and emphasis is on rehabilitation. There are 849 hospital beds and a new 60-bed Nursing Home Care unit. The chapel serves all denominations; services are conducted by Protestant, Catholic and Jewish clergymen.

SOUTH WINDSOR (alt. 300, Windsor Town, pop. 878), 10.6 *m.* was the scene of the 'Malta War' land squabbles among early settlers. Windsor furnished masts and spars for the frigate USS Constitution (1797). Red Cross founder Clara Barton (1821-1912) summered here.

At 14 *m.*, junction with State 218 R to NORTH WHITEFIELD (alt. 205, Whitefield Town, pop. 1063), 3.1 *m.*, where the annual Game Supper in the fall features such esoteric items as squirrel and rabbit pie, venison, coon and bear. The town was settled in 1770, principally by Irish Catholics.

R from North Whitefield on State 126 is *St. Denis Church*, 1.5 *m.*, brick with Gothic tower (1822); in 1818 Rev. Denis Ryan, first Catholic priest ordained in New England, was named pastor of the parish. The bricks of the church and of the Knights of Columbus building opposite, formerly a convent, were handmade in the churchyard.

L from North Whitefield on State 126 to *Pleasant Pond*, 2.7 *m.* An unusual *Cemetery* here is laid out on 12 terraces at 4-ft. intervals connected by granite steps. From the hilltop is a fine view of the Pond and surrounding farms. At 5.7 *m.*, the circular *Jefferson Cattle Pound* is 30 ft. in diameter with 8-ft. fieldstone walls. At 6 *m.*, the north end of Damariscotta Lake is called Great Bay. At 7 *m.*, a white First Baptist Church (1808) and nearby a Baptismal Beach. JEFFERSON (alt. 110, Jefferson Town, pop. 1048), 8.5 *m.*, is a community of comfortably rambling farmhouses, A mile on is *Crescent Beach (boating, fishing, picnicking)* with views of Haskell Mt. 493 ft.

Continuing on State 17 to UNION (alt. 105, Union Town, pop. 1100), 30 *m.* Settled in 1774 and once called Taylor, Union is known for the annual Knox County Fair in August and for the *Matthews Farm Museum (Tues. through Sun., 12-5)* which has a large collection of early farm implements and utensils. It was at Union that the 'one-hoss shay' was originated; an example is in the Smithsonian Institution.

Soon may be seen where the St. Georges River Canal system (*see TOUR 1 sec. b*) crosses the route.

At 35.6 *m.*, is South Hope, between Grassy and Fish Ponds. At 38.4 *m.* *Mirror Lake* at the foot of Ragged Mt. (1300 ft.) is a frequent subject for artists. *Chickawaukie Pond* recreational area is just outside Rockland, 42.8 *m.*

Tour 3 — NE on State 3 to *Belfast (see TOUR 1 sec. c)*, 43 *m.*

At 11.5 *m.*, SOUTH CHINA (alt. 209, China Town), a resort village at the S end of China Lake. Born here was Leroy S. Starrett, inventor of a washing machine, a meat chopper, a butter worker and numerous hand tools and precision instruments.

Lake St. George State Park (see RECREATION), 27.2 *m.* Road R to LIBERTY (alt. 377, Liberty Town, pop. 458) on St. George Stream. Early settlers of the township, originally granted under the Waldo Patent, sought to maintain their rights to land titles by appropriating the land agent's papers; they seized the agent and threatened to drop him through a hole in the ice of St. George Lake unless he gave up the papers. This he promised to do, but later his intimidators were arrested and tried in Wiscasset Courthouse.

Around 1843, a religious group, convinced that the end of the world was at hand, turned loose their pigs and cattle and foregathered on nearby Haystack Mt. to await the cataclysm. Added to their disappointment in due course was the task of collecting their scattered livestock.

Liberty too had its pirate tales. On the shore opposite the village, one Timothy Barrett lived in a cave and raised his vegetables on a floating garden of logs. He was thought to have been a buccaneer, for after his death, kettles of French coins were dug up near his home and the hollow rail of a fence yielded $100 in gold coins.

N of Liberty on State 220 is FREEDOM on Sandy Pond, 12 m. Between Liberty and Freedom is photographer's country — sharply rising mountains (Frye Mt. R 1140 ft.), long views of valleys and fields, forests, old homesteads, a New England church. In the Halldale section of Montville, the remains of Civil War soldier Martin Hannan's scythe is embedded in a tree, a maple sapling when he hung it there as he left for the war in 1860.

NORTH SEARSMONT (alt. 235, Searsmont Town, pop. 628), 32 m. is the 'Fraternity' of the stories of Ben Ames Williams who had a summer home here.

BELMONT (alt. 160, Belmont Town, pop. 295) 36.4 m., was Green Plantation, home of the 'Green Indians.' These were squatters who resorted to subterfuge to avoid eviction. Alerted to the impending arrival of visitors, the squatters quickly donned feathers, paint and moccasins. When law officers arrived they found an apparently deserted settlement except for a few loitering 'Indians' who greeted the baffled visitors with stolid indifference.

State 3 continues into Belfast at 43 m.

Tour 4 — N on State 27 to *Belgrade Lakes,* 18 m., well-known resort region in a chain of lakes connected by streams (*fishing, boating, canoeing*). This is a pleasant drive, length optional, through the lake district dotted with villages and vacation homes.

Tour 5 — W on US 202 to *Winthrop* 10.8 m., (route may be continued to Lewiston (*see LEWISTON-AUBURN*) at 30.6 m.).

MANCHESTER (alt. 205, Manchester Town, pop. 1068), 4.2 m. was known as The Forks, an overnight stop for settlers from surrounding communities travelling to the river port of Hallowell, 4 m. E for trading. It took most of a day on the return journey, horses hauling their purchases up the two-mile hills to Manchester.

R from Manchester on State 17, *Monk's Hill Cemetery,* 2.6 m. overlooking Lake Cobbosseecontee. Early Baptists of the town of Readfield are buried here. There is a monument to Elder Isaac Case, a Baptist preacher who gathered the first church at Thomaston in 1784 and 8 years later came to Readfield where he officiated until 1800.

Carleton Pond, 3.2 m., is Augusta's city water supply.

The *Methodist Meetinghouse*, 3.9 *m*., was the first of that denomination in Maine. The plain white church with spire overlooking Lake Maranacook was dedicated in 1795 by the handsome and courtly Methodist clergyman, the Rev. Jesse Lee (1758-1816) who traveled about on horseback. Said he, 'We had to beat through the woods between Winthrop and Readfield which are as bad as the Allegheny Mountains and the shades of death.' Lee, known as the Apostle of Methodism, was chaplain of Congress 1809-15. The New England Conference of Methodists with an attendance of 1500 was held in this sparsely settled community August 29, 1798.

Lake Maranacook, 7 m. (boating, fishing).

READFIELD (alt. 260, Readfield Town, pop. 1029), 7.6 *m*., hilltop settlement, was the birthplace of two Maine governors, Jonathan G. Hunton (1781-1851) and Dr. John Hubbard (1794-1869). In 1851, Governor Hubbard signed Maine's first law prohibiting sale and manufacture of intoxicating liquors. The Kennebec Agricultural Society (1787), compiled the first agricultural statistics in the State, on the production of cider. Its Kennebec County Fair has been held annually since 1856.

KENT'S HILL (alt. 545, Readfield Town), 9.7 *m*. overlooks Torsey Pond and the hills of Mt. Vernon. *Kent's Hill Seminary* in a sightly location was founded as Maine Wesleyan Seminary in 1824. R on State 4 is MOUNT VERNON (alt. 335, Mount Vernon Town, pop. 596), 16.9 *m*., a lovely spot among hills and lakes. Here is the late Elizabeth Arden's *Maine Chance*, luxurious beauty spa for women, retreat for many celebrities. Elizabeth Marbury (1856-1933), play broker and prominent in the world of theatre and charities of her time, restored the 68-acre Higgins-Slocum farm here in 1925. Miss Marbury was decorated by the Belgian, French and Italian governments for her services during World War I.

At 4.9 *m*., *Augusta Country Club (golf)*.

At 5.6 *m*., *Theatre Island* (L), once a trolley park, on Lake Cobbosseecontee (Ind.: place of salmon or abundant sturgeon). The 9-mile lake, popular summer and winter playground, has several small islands including Lady's Delight with small lighthouse.

At 8.8 *m*., road L leads to BAILEYVILLE 1.2 *m*. where Quakers settled in 1780. Ezekiel Bailey, a Quaker, began the manufacture of oilcloth by hand here around 1830. The business expanded into several factories that flourished until they burned in 1921. The Baileys contributed much to Quaker churches and schools in the state, notably Oak Grove Seminary at Vassalboro. Nearby is a *Y.M.C.A. Camp* where leadership conferences are held annually in June.

WINTHROP (alt. 200, Winthrop Town, pop. 4000), 10.2 *m*., settled in 1764, was called Pondtown Plantation for the 12 bodies of water in the area. The lakes and streams of the Cobbosseecontee drainage area, like all others in early days were highly valued for their direct water power. Twenty bodies of water drain into Cobbosseecontee Stream, outlet for a chain of lakes extending from Mt. Vernon to Gardiner. Its natural fall between Great Cobbosseecontee Lake and the Kennebec River is about 150 ft. In 1716 Ephraim Ballard ascended the chain of ponds between Litchfield and Richmond to stake out a claim for the Kennebec Proprietors who paid him 7 *L* 19 shillings for his work. Another chain of ponds is known as Tacoma Lakes (*summer resort area*). In the drainage, other lakes have romantic but practical Indian names: Annabessacook (good place for fishing); Maranacook (where water fowl rear their young) and where the drone of motor boats has replaced the whistle of the lake steamer; Cochnewagen (place of bears, also translated as the place of praying Indians or place of battle), described lyrically by an early writer 'as clear as an angel's tear and sparkling like a gem in the bosom of a fairy queen.' In the 1960s, however, gardens of algae on some lakes had created problems less poetical, prompting official clean-up action to redeem a heritage. The white man must learn from the Indian to live with nature, not on her.

In Winthrop, several early homes are still standing in the Metcalf neighborhood where a Plaque indicates that Talleyrand stayed overnight at the home of Col. Nathaniel Fairbanks. A nearby cemetery has one of the largest hornbeam trees in the U. S. Shoes were made by hand here in the first half of the Nineteenth century and in 1820 Daniel Noyes opened one of the state's first temperance hotels.

Winthrop is the trading center for surrounding towns and lakeside cottagers and campers. It has inter-state bus service and float-equipped planes land within walking distance of the business district. It is the center of the Maine apple industry and has a woolen mill and chemical manufactory.

R from Winthrop on State 133 at 6.7 *m.* in WAYNE (alt. 300, Wayne Town, pop. 498) is the *Birthplace of Annie Louise Cary* (1842-1921), opera star. Sharp L a road leads to *Morrison Heights* (alt. 680), at 8.5 *m.*, a conical hill with a spectacular view of the surrounding countryside (*picnic grounds*).

At 16.2 *m.*, road L leads to *Monmouth Academy* (1803), and MONMOUTH (alt. 285, Monmouth Town, pop. 1884), residential and commercial settlement on the E shore of Cochnewagen Lake. *Cumston Hall*, an ornate cream and white building with minarets and other middle eastern architectural features, was designed by Harry H. Cochrane, muralist and writer who decorated many churches and other public buildings in Maine. His murals decorate the interior. Gilbert and Sullivan operettas were presented here for several seasons and in 1970 a Classical Repertory Company planned to open.

Lorettus S. Metcalf (1837-1920), founder and editor of *Forum*, and Benjamin Shaw, inventor of a hosiery knitting machine were born here.

Cochnewagen Lake is said to have been the scene of a sanguinary battle between the Mohawk and Wabanaki Indians.

Leaving Winthrop, with Mt. Pisgah (809 ft.) (r), US 202 continues SW to Lewiston, 30.6 *m.*

BANGOR

Alt. 100, pop. 38,912, sett. 1769, incorp. town 1791, city 1834.

Access: N and SW, Interstate 95 and US 2; E, State 9; SE, State 1A; S, US 1A and State 15.

Information: Chamber of Commerce, 23 Franklin St.; Maine Publicity Bureau, 519 Main St.

Accommodations: one hotel, 8 motels.

Transportation: International jetport; busline, 152 Main St.

Parks: Seven.

Recreation: golf, Penobscot Valley Country Club, Bangor Municipal Golf course; summer-winter sports, environs.

Cultural, historic sites: see POINTS OF INTEREST.

BANGOR, on the hills along the west bank of the Penobscot River that determined its destiny, is Maine's third largest city and the most northerly cultural and trading center below 'the Aroostook.' Thousands of historic and resort acres along Penobscot Bay and eastward lie south of the city which is head of tidewater 23 miles from deep anchorage. From the north, Kenduskeag Stream runs through the central business district from which the hills rise sharply to residential Bangor. There are several parks and outlying recreational areas.

With its international jetport, Bangor once more is becoming as well known as it was as a lumber capital. Its trading area of 390,000 people is approximately 40 percent of the State's population and in the 1960s the city was growing rapidly. In 1967 there were 393 retail establishments and 2250 industrial workers, principally in shoes and electronics. Bangor has two television and four radio stations; its morning newspaper's daily circulation is the largest in the State.

Along with its identification with the lumber industry, Bangor, in close proximity to the State University, has strong cultural traditions. For many years it was the only Maine city to have its own Symphony Orchestra. Now the second oldest in the country, Bangor Symphony gave its first concert November 2, 1896. From 1897 to 1926, the annual Music Festival directed by William R. Chapman brought such stars as Alda, Alma Gluck, Nordica, Galli-Curci, Leginska, Gogorza, Farrar and Schumann-Heinck. In 1969 music by the Symphony accompanied the Maine State Ballet's presentation based on a novel of Bangor's lusty lumbering days. The city also has active theatre and art groups. Artists identified with Bangor are Waldo Peirce and the earlier Jeremiah Pearson Hardy and his daughter Annie Eliza. The work of Sculptor Charles E. Tefft of neighboring Brewer is seen in several of the city's memorials.

Bangor's historical heritage is interpreted at the Museum of the hundred-year-old Historical Society and by the Penobscot Heritage which provides changing public exhibits, each with a carefully developed theme, coordinating with educational needs. Its first at City Hall in 1969 comprehensively covered fur trapping and trade in Maine from early days.

One of the State's most distinguished citizens, Vice-President Hannibal

Hamlin, once lived in Bangor. Before he was first elected to Congress in 1843, he was active in State politics and served three terms as Speaker of the Maine House of Representatives. Hamlin did much to advance the economy of the State of Maine. He succeeded in having Bangor declared a port of entry into the United States and pushed the development of Maine railroads. Hamlin was primarily responsible for defeating a move to make the new Maine State Agricultural College an adjunct of a private college and succeeded in having it established as an independent institution on a tract of land in Orono, eight miles away. He became the first president of the board of trustees of the college that became the University of Maine.

Despite the city's public disasters over the years, civic improvements were continuous. Many of the 28 churches and numerous early residences are of architectural significance. Charles Bulfinch surveyed a 100-acre lot about 1830 and laid out the streets south of State Street. While mindful of its traditions, the city's attitude is contemporary. It interprets its history and builds for the future. Unveiled during Bangor's Bicentennial observance in 1969, an outdoor sculpture by Clark Fitz Gerald called *Continuity in Community* expresses the progressive outlook that has brought the city through many vicissitudes to its present place as one of Maine's most important urban centers.

One of the State's major rivers, the Penobscot, in prehistoric times wound clear and sparkling through a vast forested wilderness to the sea. The Tarratines and other Wabanaki Indian tribes camped along its shores, traveled its circuitous routes, fished its tributaries and gave to its beautiful valley the name *Penobscot,* 'place of rocks.' Many explorers sought here the fabled *Norumbega,* the golden city of Milton's *Paradise Lost* and the river was first called *Norumbegue.* Ancient Norumbega, according to some old charts, extended from Pemaquid to St. Croix, comprising Mount Desert and the territory of the Penobscot. Old French maps also show that the bounds of Acadia commenced in Bangor.

Exploring in 1604 out of St. Croix in his 16-ton vessel, Samuel de Champlain that September became the first chronicler to sail up the Penobscot. Anchoring in the vicinity of Kenduskeag Stream because of Treat's waterfall, the explorer went ashore and on the east bank of the Kenduskeag found a peaceful Indian village he called Kadesquit. His tact and courtesy in conference with the Etchimin Chief Bessabez laid the foundation for the amicable French-Indian relations that lasted as long as the French controlled Acadia. Captain John Smith explored the Penobscot in 1614 and in the next decade Miles Standish, John Alden and others from the Plymouth Colony visited to trade in furs with the Indians.

Both France and England claimed the whole region as a result of such explorations. The King of England claimed the 'County of Mayne' as 'North Virginia' and to the King of France, it was his 'Acadia.' Because

of these rival claims, no Englishman or Frenchman dared attempt permanent settlement on the river until Quebec fell to the English in 1759.
Then Governor Thomas Pownall of the Province of Massachusetts Bay,
with General Samuel Waldo and a force of men, selected the site of
Fort Pownall and sailed up the Penobscot. Near Eddington they planted
a lead plate and claimed all of what is now eastern Maine as part of the
Province of Massachusetts Bay. A treaty between England and America in
1783 recognized this act and the northeast boundary of the United States
was fixed at the St. Croix River.

Kadesquit, where Indian trails met, was an important link in the French-
Indian river trade that flourished from Castine to Quebec for well over
a century before the first white settler, Jacob Buswell, arrived in 1769.
Buswell was a squatter who chose to squat with his wife and nine children
on the high land east of the Kenduskeag near the present intersection of
Bangor's York and Boyd Streets. Others soon followed and with the
erection of a sawmill in 1772 at the mouth of the Perjajawock Stream,
Kenduskeag Plantation began its precarious growth.

Often omitted from history books was the unfortunate affair known as the
'Penobscot Expedition' of 1779 when Massachusetts sent a fleet of 23
vessels under Commander Richard Saltonstall and about 1000 men under
General Solomon Lovell to disperse the British who had taken possession
of Castine and were building a fort there. General Wadsworth, Poet
Longfellow's grandfather, was second in command of Revolutionary forces
and Lt. Col. Paul Revere was in charge of artillery. The British fleet
of four ships commanded by Sir George Collier routed the expedition and
without firing a single shot, the American ships were destroyed by their
own crews. Some 20 vessels escaped up the Penobscot. Ten of them
reached Kenduskeag Stream where they were blown up. And Paul Revere
was arrested for cowardice and court martialed when he returned to
Boston.

In 1791, Kenduskeag Plantation having acquired 576 inhabitants, the
village elders decided to petition the Legislature of Massachusetts for an
act of incorporation and to that purpose dispatched the Rev. Seth Noble,
described as a 'hard-drinking frontier Calvinist,' to the General Court in
Boston with instructions to change the name of Kenduskeag Plantation
to Sunbury. Stories of what happened in Boston are varied and unreliable.
Whether by accident or design, the word communicated by the Rev. Noble
to the Clerk at the crucial moment of incorporation was *Bangor*, the title
of a rather lugubrious hymn the intemperate parson was known to sing
with special fervor. No one seemed to mind the change of names and
Bangor, suggesting to some the sound of trumpets, seemed an apt banner
for the town that was destined to battle for survival against recurring
disaster.

Bangor entered upon the Nineteenth century with a small population but

with the first Bangor-built ship sailing the high seas and a growing reputation as an import-export center for lumber and fish. Until the turn of the
century no settler had a legal title to his land. In 1801 the General Court
of Massachusetts passed a resolve giving deeds of land to bona fide
settlers on most liberal terms. This act, plus the lure of expanding industry, brought scores of settlers and it was not long before two taverns,
those bellwethers of prosperity, were in full swing.

But embargoes, and the War of 1812, with British ships lying offshore and
threatening the Penobscot settlement, made financial gain possible only
by privateering or the running of contraband. A sorry sequence of events
led to British occupation of the town in 1814. The militia chose the
better part of valor and the British sacked the undefended port with
impunity, plundering and pillaging despite the town's pleas that life and
property be spared. Eight merchant vessels were taken or burned at
the wharves; stores, offices and deserted dwellings were vandalized. This
blow to the struggling community was followed by a decade of feverish
activity that presaged an era of fabulous growth and prosperity.

In 1815, Peter Edes founded Bangor's first newspaper *The Bangor Weekly
Register* which soon raised an influential voice in behalf of the movement of separation of Maine from Massachusetts that succeeded in 1820.
In 1834 Bangor became an incorporated city with a form of government
much like the present, replacing the cumbersome though highly entertaining town meetings. In 1835 Maine's first railroad, second in the
nation, the *Veazie* began running between Bangor and Old Town.
Bangor's population swelled to nearly 8000 between 1830-34. Land
speculation was rife and timberland speculation ran wild. Fortunes were
made and often lost overnight; township lots were sold over and over
again, sight unseen. A courier line from the Bangor brokers' offices
ran to Boston. The city overflowed with speculators, swindlers, gamblers
and the easy money flotsam and jetsam. One company held a land
auction at which 'champagne from the original bottles (was poured)
into huge washtubs from which each man helped himself at his own sweet
will.' And then the bubble burst.

The mid-Nineteenth century saw Bangor's lumber boom. The forests were
cut back from the Penobscot up-river to the East and West Branches —
the great woods country that produced men and legends as integrally a
part of Maine as its pine trees. During the 'pine period' between 1820
and 1860, real lumbermen scorned the lowly spruce that came into its
own as a forest product after the Civil War when pine became depleted.
Spruce continues to be the principal cut. Although the last of the great
lumber drives are going out of existence, millions of logs once tumbled
down the Penobscot from its network of tributaries to be converted to
lumber in Bangor mills. In the 1850s Bangor was the world's leading
lumber port and in the next two decades was second only to Chicago.

Nearly 250 million board feet valued at $3,233,958.53 were handled at Bangor in 1872.

It was a gilded gaudy age. The lumber barons built their great mansions, lived in style, traveled to Europe, encouraged the arts and made Bangor the cultural center of Maine. Loggers and sailors, however, gave Bangor a considerably different and more widespread reputation. Their stamping ground, comparable to San Francisco's Barbary Coast, was the section of town in the vicinity of Washington, Hancock and Exchange Streets still known as the Devil's Half Acre, celebrated in Ben Ames Williams' novel, *A Strange Woman*. It was here in spring that hundreds of lusty lumber-jacks, fresh from the log drives, with a winter's thirsts — and a winter's wages — and ready for pleasure, thronged to sample the fleshpots of Bangor. No trace remains of the taverns and grogshops, lodging houses and brothels that catered to the teeming life of the busy seaport; gone are the salt-water shellbacks and tall-timber men who swapped tales, drinks and blows in a colorful era.

The boom lasted as long as the tall timber. Henry David Thoreau had written in 1846: *The mission of men there (Bangor) seems to be, like so many busy demons, to drive the forest all out of the country as soon as possible.* The statement was prophetic. By 1880 the once mighty forests were largely denuded of readily accessible timber, the loggers were heading West and the heyday of Bangor's famous port was over. Pulp operations replaced sawmills along the river; the ice business flourished for half a century and 1889 saw Maine's first trolleys on the streets of Bangor.

Essential to the lumber industry were the ships, many of them Bangor built and owned, that sailed with pine boards and brought back molasses, sugar and rum from the West Indies. A brisk trade developed with Europe and western Atlantic coastal ports. From April until late November the harbor was crowded with vessels of all rigs and sizes, from bay coasters to full-rigged ships. Records show that as many as 700 vessels from 400 to 4000 tons were anchored in the harbor at one time. First ship construction was the RED BRIDGE in 1791. The THINKS I TO MY-SELF was one of the Bangor vessels captured by the British during the War of 1812; she was later reported as a privateer under British colors. The GOLD HUNTER was the first to carry a band of adventurers around the Horn to California in the gold rush of '49. The age of steam navigation was inaugurated at Bangor with the arrival of the steamboat BANGOR in 1824. This wooden side-wheeler later was engaged in conveying pilgrims from Alexandria to Mecca — after its coat of white, the Mohammedans' mourning color, was changed to black. Still later, the Sultan of Turkey used the BANGOR as a private yacht. Another ship of the same name, one of the first American steamboats with an iron propeller, was built in 1845 to run between Bangor and Boston.

Disaster struck the city again when a $3 million fire destroyed more than fifty acres of business and residential areas in 1911. Once more Bangor rebuilt, this time to a different economy, gradually becoming largely the trading and transportation center for northern and eastern Maine as it is today. From lumbering operations to shoe manufacturing, Bangor's industrial base shifts once again to include electronics. The Eastern Maine Vocational Technical Institute produces machinists and electronic technicians. The University of Maine has a two-year Engineering Technology program qualifying graduates to meet local industrial needs. Bangor also has two business colleges, Husson and Beals.

The Penobscot River still flows, no longer clear and sparkling, to the sea. Pollution takes its toll. The once famous Bangor salmon pool boasts no more of the first salmon of the season, sent traditionally to the President of the United States. As railroads replaced ships in the city's economic growth, so today the airplane is the symbol of Bangor's place in history.

POINTS OF INTEREST

Norumbega Parkway, crossing Kenduskeag Stream to Central Street, a garden spot in the midst of the city, was created in 1933 through a bequest from Luther H. Peirce. Its name, once applied to Penobscot Bay and vicinity, is the old Spanish word meaning country of the Norwegians or Northmen and is also interpreted as the Penobscot Indian word signifying 'still-water between-falls.' The Park's high vine-covered walls overlook pleasant landscaped walks. Centered in the Mall is a memorial to the martyred dead of all wars. Designed by Charles E. Tefft, the figure of a woman, palm fronds in one hand and a lambent light in the other, rests on a bronze pedestal.

Kenduskeag Mall, a continuation of the Parkway, lies between Central and State Streets. The name, also Condeskeat and Kadesquit signifying 'eel-catching place,' was applied to Bangor until its incorporation in 1791. A bronze Plaque and boulder here commemorate the landing of Samuel de Champlain. Near the boulder are two cannon, one a relic of the Spanish-American War, the other a piece recovered from one of the American ships sunk off Bangor during the Saltonstall retreat in 1779. Charles Tefft also executed the bronze *Statue of Hannibal Hamlin*, Lincoln's vice-president, rising in the center of the Mall.

Joseph D. Garland House, 117 Court Street, now the Pentacostal Temple. Built in 1830 of red brick after designs accredited to Richard Upjohn, it bears out the better features of traditional Greek Revival architecture. Standing on high ground amid giant elms, its pillared porticoes, front and rear, command prospects up and down the Kenduskeag Valley.

Bangor Theological Seminary (*visitors*), NW cor. Union and Hammond Streets, the oldest institution in Bangor and the only one of its kind in northern New England, was incorporated as the Maine Charity School in 1804. In the rigorous days of its past when the students got their water from a campus well and used stoves and oil lamps, they could save ten cents a week on board by not drinking tea or coffee.

Hannibal Hamlin House (*visitors by permission*), NE cor. Fifth Street, built between 1848-51, was acquired in 1851 by Vice-President Hamlin. It is of Colonial style with deep eaves and Doric porch columns. Mr. Hamlin converted the original flat roof to a mansard type, adding a third story. Features of the gracious interior include two black marble fireplaces, a gracefully curved white staircase, ceiling to floor drawing room windows with paneled shutters, and beautifully paneled and grooved doors with prism-like glass knobs. The Hamlin House became the official residence of presidents of the Theological Seminary when Hannibal E. Hamlin of Ellsworth, son of the vice-president, gave the house and its furnishings to the Seminary in 1933.

Symphony House (*visitors*), 166 Union Street, modified English Renaissance, was designed by Richard Upjohn and built in 1833 by Isaac Farrar, pioneer Maine lumberman. The red brick for its construction was brought from England, each brick individually wrapped for shipment. The slate for the roof was imported from Bangor, Wales, and a circular room is finished throughout with solid mahogany from San Domingo. The house has been occupied at various times by Playwright Owen Davis and Gene Sawyer, author of the Nick Carter series. When University of Maine bought it in 1911 it became a law school until 1919. On the initiative of then Symphony Conductor A. W. Sprague, the house became a music center in 1929 and is headquarters for all Bangor musical organizations, and the home of the Northern Conservatory of Music.

Bangor House, SE cor. Main and Union Streets, a survivor of stagecoach, schooner and steamboat days, probably has as colorful a history as any hostelry in the country. The original hotel is retained in the present building's annex. Financed by wealthy lumbermen, the Bangor House opened in 1834 — only a stone's throw from the Penobscot River teeming with ships, and the wild and wooly Devil's Half Acre where red lights blinked and rum flowed deep, and many a head was broken in brawls between giants from the woods and giants from the sea.

A grand New Year's Ball celebrated the opening. The American Magazine described the hotel which boasted a 'bathing room' as being surpassed in elegance only by the Tremont in Boston. One of the hotel's first function's was a dinner for Daniel Webster, then New England's favorite son as Presidential candidate. President Ulysses S. Grant stayed at the Bangor House when he came to Maine to officially open the European North American Railroad. Among other notable guests have been Presidents Arthur, Harrison and Theodore Roosevelt; Stephen A. Douglas, Oscar Wilde and John L. Sullivan, world heavyweight champion.

Meats and fowl were spitted over the open blaze of the huge kitchen fireplace. The cuisine was famous — chicken and steak for breakfast, Penobscot River salmon and venison and moose meat in season. All these delectables were included in the American plan rate of $3.00 per day with fine room and private bath. Originally the rooms were heated by fireplaces and lighted by lamps or candles.

In those days of prohibition in Maine, hotels and restaurants operated under the 'Bangor Plan': the bar operator paid a standard fine in court twice a year and was politely ignored by police the rest of the time. John G. Chapman is the fourth generation of Chapmans to manage the Bangor House. Captain Horace Crockett Chapman was the first, taking over in 1888. It was during his stewardship that the hatchet-wielding prohibitionist, Carrie Nation, created a memorable scene in the dining room but had no chance to use her weapon. The bar was nowhere to be found. Capt. Chapman ejected her screaming from the room — in her memoirs she wrote that he was 'the worst rum-seller in the country.' The bar went out during National prohibition; liquor wasn't served again until repeal of the Maine law. Early in the Twentieth century, guests crowded the Bangor House for such events as the Music Festival, fairs and circuses and included hunters and fishermen heading for the north woods. Arriving by train and steamer, they were driven to the hotel in horse-drawn carriages or hacks.

Davenport Park, NW cor. Main and Cedar Streets. The *Remember the Maine Memorial* here, a granite wedge-shaped monument surmounted by a bronze shaft bearing an American eagle, was erected in 1922. On the monument are the original shield and scroll recovered from the Battleship MAINE, blown up in Havana Harbor in 1898. The base of the monument, triangular in shape to resemble a ship's prow, was designed by Edwin S. Kent and was dedicated in memory of soldiers and sailors of the Spanish-American War.

Boutelle House (private), 157 Broadway, was designed by Charles Bulfinch and built in 1834. The four Doric columns of the front support an entablature consisting of an ornamental architrave frieze, with carved wreaths and a cornice. A balustrade surrounds the porch roof. Doric pilasters form the framework of the recessed doorway as well as that of the leaded sidelights, and support a carved entablature in place of the conventional leaded glass fan. During the stirring political campaigns of the last century, distinguished speakers such as James G. Blaine and William McKinley reviewed torchlight parades from the balcony.

Peirce Memorial, Harlow Street, a gift to the city from the late Luther H. Peirce, memorializes Maine's colorful river-drivers in a bronze statue executed by Charles Tefft. A group of three drivers are depicted prying the key log out of a jam. They are shown with axe, cantdog and peavey engaged in the hazardous task of freeing the logs for the journey downstream. The base, approach and pedestal are the work of Crowell and Lancaster, Bangor architects.

Bangor Public Library, 145 Harlow Street, founded in 1883, is outstanding among small city libraries, with an endowment of $5 million. Its book collection of more than 415,000 volumes is larger than that of many cities of 100,000 population. Its Reference Department is a State-wide resource and is called upon by many other states here and abroad.

Bangor Library is noted for its special tradition of service, its historical collections and Hardy paintings and for its Music Branch at Symphony House. The Library has provided books for all of the city's schools, public and parochial, and supplies book services for over 180 agencies in the city and for doctors' hospital libraries; the Extension Department serves hospitalized patients. The Library prepares teaching units for school use and in its Lecture Room arranges exhibits of historical materials, travelling exhibits and shows by local artists.

Strickland Gallery, (daily except Mon., 1-4), 144 Broadway, shows works by local artists.

Bangor Historical Society Museum (weekday afternoons 2-4 and by appointment) cor. High and Union Streets, in Grand Army Memorial Home, a distinguished structure built in 1834 by Thomas A. Hill, pioneer lumberman, has a collection of more than 20,000 items. One of the four owners of the house since it was built was Samuel E. Dale, mayor of Bangor during the Civil War years, whose famous hospitality brought many noted visitors. The Daniel Chaplin Camp, Sons of Union Veterans share the house with the Historical Society; both groups were founded in the 1860s. When Ulysses S. Grant, III visited the Museum, he was greatly impressed with the vast collection of Grand Army material and the many mementos of his grandfather's visit when he, as the first president of the United States to come to Bangor, was entertained in this house in 1871. Also on display are Indian artifacts, memorabilia of early Bangor and Far Eastern art objects.

Grotto Cascade Park, State Street at Summit Avenue. A 45-foot cascade terminates in a pool and fountain bordered by rocks and flowers. Illusion lumiere, effecting sunlight, moonlight and other simulations, is created by colored lights submerged in the fountain.

Bangor International Airport, from Hammond Street downtown, W 2 *m.* In 1923 General Billy Mitchell and the entire United States Air Force of 26 planes landed at Bangor. In 1940 the U. S. Government began construction of Dow Air Force Base which with its population of 5000 and its 2200 acres became an integral part of the community. The Base was de-activated in 1968, is now owned by the City of Bangor. Besides the International Airport with a runway two miles long and 300 feet wide, and the U. S. Customs Service, several other properties are located in the area. Increasing amounts of air freight are handled here as well as international passenger traffic as congestion increases at metropolitan airports. In the area are the South Campus of University of Maine, Beals Business College, Trans-East Air International Pilots Training School, Restaurant Associates and seven other private business firms.

Environs: University of Maine — Orono, 8 *m.*(*TOUR 4*): Indian Reservation, Old Town, 13.2 *m.*, *TOUR 4*): Acadia National Park, Cadillac Mountain, Mount Desert, Bar Harbor, 26 *m.*(*TOUR 2*): Dorothea Dix Memorial Park which honors the Hampden, Maine woman who gained world-wide recognition in the Nineteenth century for her achievements in reforms of jails, almshouses and insane asylums. The Park is on the site of Isaac Hopkins' farm where she was born in 1802.

BRUNSWICK

Alt. 65, pop. 18,000, sett. 1628, incorp. town 1738 O.S., 1739 N.S.

Access: N — US 201; NE and SW, US 1 and I-95; NW, State 196.

Information: Chamber of Commerce, 59 Pleasant St.

Accommodations: numerous motels.

Transportation: Air, bus; Brunswick Tour & Travel Service, 222 Maine St., Stowe Travel Agency, 9 Pleasant St., World Travel Service, 51 Pleasant St.

Parks: The Mall

Recreation: golf, Brunswick Country Club; swimming, boating fishing, Coffin Pond, Thomas Point, Mere Point, Harpswell-Bailey Island area (*see Tour 1C*).

Cultural, historic sites: see POINTS OF INTEREST.

BRUNSWICK, seat of Bowdoin College and site of a major U. S. Naval Air Station, commingles industry, commerce, education and national defense with a cosmopolitan air to become the cultural and trading center of a wide area of inland, coastal and resort communities. The tree-shaded town with its broad main street has grown out fan-wise from the early industrial development around a Falls of the Androscoggin River. Lying on a broad coastal plain once favored by Indians, the township extends

44 square miles, from the river and Merrymeeting Bay on the north to the waters of Casco Bay on the south. From the Falls the land rises toward a hill and Bowdoin College, beyond which stretch the Plains, former resort of blueberry pickers and fowlers now occupied by the Naval Air Station. Modern shopping centers form the hub of a wheel whose spokes reach out to Topsham, Bowdoinham, Richmond, Durham and Freeport, to Bath, and to Harpswell and her islands.

Brunswick's tree-lined streets have been well-planned and laid out since the town was organized in 1717. Zoning laws preserve the character of residential areas. Maine Street, so named when Maine achieved statehood in 1820, was first known as Twelve Rod Road and is the widest in the State — 198 feet. It was voted in 1717 as a measure to discourage lurking Indians and was intended to reach four miles from a fortification near the Falls to the head of Maquoit Bay. Above Pleasant Street it is divided by the *Mall,* a pleasant oasis that was a beaver swamp. The Mall has seen many public gatherings from band concerts, political rallies, evangelistic speeches and Fourth of July observances, to art shows, youth congregations and protest meetings.

The town, with a selectmen-manager form of government since 1949, has a property valuation of $40 million, an exemplary school system, 14 churches, a hospital, a daily newspaper, a radio station, civic and recreational activities including summer theatre and a lively interest in community affairs. A State-wide weekly paper, the *Maine Times,* emphasizing culture and conservation began publication in 1968 across the river in Topsham.

Early Indian inhabitants of this region which was called Pejepscot were the Pejepscots, the Canibas and the Anasagunticooks. They called the area around the Falls *Ahmelahcogneturcook* — they didn't have to spell it. This 'place of much fish, fowl and beasts' in the 1620s attracted Thomas Purchase, a trader who raised corn and engaged in extensive fishing operations. One of his fishhouses is thought to have been near 10 Water Street, a site known as Fishhouse Hill. Another Purchase post was at Merrymeeting Bay where Indian trails converged. Famous today among sportsmen, Merrymeeting is a rendezvous for migrating ducks and Canada geese in the Atlantic flyway. The Bay was formed by a junction of six rivers, the Pejepscot (later incorporated into the Androscoggin), the Kennebec, the Muddy, the Cathance, the Abagadusset and the Eastern.

As white settlements pushed the Indians from their ancestral lands, a century and a half of French and Indian conflict with the English began. In 1675 the small settlement at Brunswick was abandoned after Indians raided Purchase's place on Fishhouse Hill, and King Philip's War then erupted throughout New England. Purchase retreated to the comparative safety of Lynn, Massachusetts, later to England where he died. Richard

Wharton, a Boston merchant, bought Purchase's holdings and came to Brunswick in 1684 to make peace with the Indians. Death three years later halted his ambitious plans. In 1688 Governor Andros had a fort built near the Falls, one of several to protect new settlers in efforts to hold the Eastern frontiers against the Indians. Within two years, the Indians destroyed the fort and the settlement. When peace came in 1699 a Boston syndicate, called the Pejepscot Proprietors, bought the entire region and in 1714-15 laid out twin towns, naming them Brunswick and Topsham; they built a new and larger fort nearer the Falls and called it Fort George. These names reflected current history, for King George I, the German prince of the Duchy of Brunswick had ascended the British throne in 1715 and the settlers around Pejepscot Falls were among his most loyal subjects.

During Lovewell's War, Indians destroyed the town for the last time (1722). After the destruction of Norridgewock, within fifteen years their power was broken, and Brunswick was resettled. Up to this time the settlers could take no important action without the approval of the Proprietors. Their application to the Massachusetts General Court for incorporation was granted in 1738 (Old Style), 1739 (New Style).

The Falls have been important in Brunswick's industrial development, its water power today converted by a Central Maine Power Company plant and used by Pejepscot Paper Company. During the Eighteenth and Nineteenth centuries water was the sole source of power for the mills that grew up around the Falls. Early in its history the town was a lumbering center. The first boom above the Falls was built in 1789; several more came into operation as Brunswick became known as a sawmill town. In 1820 there were 25 saws on both sides of the river, and in the next decades Brunswick led the State in lumber export. A college pastime was watching the great logs tumble over the Falls, destined for the sawmills. An attempt at cheap transportation had to be abandoned when it was found that logs couldn't be floated to Humphrey's sawmill in a canal dug between Merrymeeting Bay and the New Meadows River. The water level at both ends of the canal was the same; there was no movement to carry the logs. Maine's first cotton mill opened at the Falls in 1809.

Early Brunswickians were seafarers as well as farmers and lumbermen. It was common to see vessels taking shape on stocks in timber-littered yards around the coves of the Androscoggin River, along Middle Bay and the shores of Harpswell peninsula and her islands. The area was called 'a complete nursery of seamen.' The last vessel built on the river was the brig PERPETUA in 1864. The lower railroad bridge had been built after construction of the vessel had begun; a channel had to be dug to let the PERPETUA pass under the bridge at low tide. The bridge was rebuilt after being swept away in a 1936 flood.

Among arrivals early in the Nineteenth century was Aaron Dennison who learned watchmaking here and later founded the Boston Watch Company that became the famous Waltham Watch Company. In the 1840s he set up in Brunswick a factory that turned out some five million jewelry boxes annually.

From 1880 for half a century the growth of pulp and textile industries in Brunswick brought a French-Canadian increment that gave largely of its character to the town. On the closing of the textile mill in the 1930s as northern mills moved south, the town's complexion began to change with the arrival of new industries, development of the college and the influx of men and women of varied origins in the military and civilian service at the Naval Air Station and the Air Force SAGE installation at Topsham. A sign of the times in the Sixties: Maine's oldest institution of higher learning, Bowdoin College, all-male for 150 years, became co-educational in 1969.

Brunswick has been the birthplace or residence of many persons of notable achievement. Among them:

Matthew Thornton (1714-1803), last signer of the Declaration of Independence, was as a child carried to safety by his parents who fled their home at Maquoit when Indians sacked Brunswick in 1722. He became an outstanding New Hampshire physician, was responsible for 500 men during Col. William Pepperrell's assault on Cape Breton, and was one of the patriot trumpets who called their fellowmen to Revolution. Having survived the rigors of the Maine frontier, Dr. Thornton in his 80th year died of whooping cough.

Brig. Gen. Samuel Thompson (1735-97) who helped make certain the Bill of Rights, led 'Thompson's War' for the capture of Capt. Henry Mowatt of the British man-of-war, CANCEAU, lying in Portland Harbor. Mowatt later avenged himself by laying Falmouth in ashes. *(see PORTLAND)* A man of informal education, Thompson prophecied the chartering of Bowdoin College, gave land for it and was a member of the first Board of Overseers.

Capt. John Dunlap (1737-1824) was credited in 1803 with being the wealthiest man in Maine, lived in Brunswick's Gilman Mansion. Noting his father's pain upon the death of the family's only cow, Dunlap resolved not to remain poor and after some soldiering, became a trapper and later a mill owner and ship operator.

Benjamin Titcomb, Jr. (1761-1848), became Maine's first printer, striking off with his own hands the first sheet of the *Falmouth Weekly Gazette*, the first newspaper printed in Maine January 5, 1785. Around 1798 he became a minister, serving 40 years in Brunswick. At the invitation of General William King, the Rev. Mr. Titcomb opened with prayer the Constitutional Convention that convened in Portland in 1820. He was an original trustee of Waterville College, now Colby.

Samuel Melcher, III (1775-1862), an untrained carpenter—builder, became an architectural artist who built several Federal style mansions in Brunswick and Topsham, the first chapel and other buildings at Bowdoin College, the 1806 First Parish Church at Brunswick, the Congregational Church at Topsham and a Congregational Church at

Wiscasset.

George Skolfield (1780-1866), 'Master George' of Harpswell, built 60 first class vessels in his lifetime, moved his yard a slight distance north into Brunswick's jurisdiction when Harpswell selectmen taxed an unfinished vessel on the stocks.

Robert Pinckney Dunlap (1794-1859), son of Capt. John, became Governor of Maine in 1834, served four one-year terms. An illustrious Mason, he was the first in Maine to receive the Rose Croix degree. A bust of his likeness by Franklin Simmons surmounts a pedestal over his grave in Pine Grove Cemetery.

John S. C. Abbott (1805-1877), historian, was the author of 25 volumes. His history of Napoleon won him the friendship of the Little Corporal. Abraham Lincoln said of Abbott's histories: 'To them I am indebted for about all the historical knowledge I have.'

Harriet Beecher Stowe (1811-1896) came to Brunswick in 1850 when her husband Calvin Ellis Stowe became professor of Natural and Revealed Religion at Bowdoin. During their residence at 63 Federal Street, Mrs. Stowe wrote most of the novel that appeared first in *The National Era*, later to electrify the world as *Uncle Tom's Cabin*. She later wrote *The Pearl of Orr's Island*.

George Palmer Putnam (1814-1872), a poor Brunswick boy, became the founder of G. P. Putnam & Sons, publishers.

Gen. Joshua L. Chamberlain (1828-1914), a Bowdoin professor, became Lt. Col. of the 20th Maine Volunteers in the War between the States, received the Congressional Medal of Honor for his leadership in defense of Little Round Top at Gettysburg, a turning point in the war. Participating in 24 engagements, he was wounded six times and breveted Maj. Gen. on the field by Gen. Grant. After Lee's surrender, he received the Confederate Infantry's arms and colors at Appomatox. It might be said then that the Civil War was triggered by the righteous cry for humanity of a Brunswick woman, wife of a Bowdoin professor, and terminated under the compassionate surveillance of a Brunswick man, another Bowdoin professor. Chamberlain was elected Governor of Maine (1867-70) and was president of Bowdoin College (1871-83). In 1878 when a coalition of Democrats and Greenbackers sought to gain control of the State Legislature and were opposed by Republicans who seized the legislative chambers and chose their own governor, Chamberlain as head of the State Militia, declared martial law until the State Supreme Court rendered a decision. The Court found the coalition in error.

Henry Wadsworth Longfellow began his career as Bowdoin's first professor of Modern Languages in 1829. He, Historian Abbott, Franklin Pierce, 14th President of the United States and Novelist Nathaniel Hawthorne who as a student roomed at 76 Federal Street, were members of Bowdoin's illustrious class of 1825. Longfellow's poem *Morituri Salutamus* written for the 50th anniversary of his class was delivered at Commencement 1875 in the First Parish Church.

John McKeen, son of Rev. Joseph McKeen, Bowdoin's first president, was an historian whose *Lectures* are a valuable source of knowledge on early Brunswick and environs.

Robert Peter Tristram Coffin (1892-1955), Pulitzer prize-winning poet, was born at 26 College Street, the son of a humble saltwater farmer. He became a Rhodes scholar, Bowdoin professor and writer of romantic prose.

Marie Peary Stafford Kuhne of Brunswick, daughter of Rear Admiral Robert E. Peary, was the white person born farthest north during one of the Peary expeditions and was internationally petted as *Ahnighto* — snow baby to the Eskimos.

Since its founding in 1794, Bowdoin College has significantly influenced the intellectual and literary life of the State and has made Brunswick an important cultural center. Its scholars always have been highly knowledgeable in their fields of human endeavor and its faculty members have enjoyed international reputation. Besides those mentioned above, graduates who have attained eminence include William Pitt Fessenden, Secretary of the Treasury under Lincoln; Thomas Brackett Reed, Speaker of the U. S. House of Representatives; Senator William P. Frye; Rear Admiral Robert E. Peary, first to reach the North Pole, and Commander Donald B. MacMillan, Arctic explorer whose Schooner BOWDOIN now is a museum at Camden. In recent years, modern architecture of Bowdoin's new buildings has added a new dimension to the traditional campus.

Governor James Bowdoin of Massachusetts and his family, wealthy and sympathetic to education and the arts, were patrons of the college. At the Governor's death, start of the college was delayed for a time by his successor and political enemy, Governor John Hancock, until he too died and Governor Samuel Adams in 1794 signed the bill granting the college official status.

Governor Bowdoin's son, James Bowdoin, III fulfilled the hopes of the founders by giving generously of land and money. The college opened in 1802 with eight students. Today the student body is multiplied a hundred fold and its weekly paper the *Orient* is the oldest college paper in continuous publication in the country. In the Walker Art Building is the collection of 70 Dutch and Italian masters that James Bowdoin III had gathered while he was U. S. Minister to Spain and France. He bequeathed the collection to the college in 1811, the first private collection of European art to be made by an American and brought to this country. It reveals the discriminating taste of the owner who was one of the first of a series of New England 'gentlemen of culture' who combined the life of refinement with a commercial and political success.

Governor Bowdoin who was the first president of the American Academy of Arts and Sciences, a friend of Washington and Franklin and politically prominent during the Revolution, was the grandson of Pierre Baudoin, a Huguenot refugee who landed at Casco Bay in 1687 and migrated to Boston. The Baudoins anglicized the name, prospered in trade, became wealthy and enjoyed a relatively aristocratic relationship toward the artisans of Boston and the many local institutions and enterprises — the

Down East college among them — seeking to benefit by the prestige gained by consociation with a distinguished name that has never lost its lustre.

POINTS OF INTEREST

Bowdoin College Campus (guided tours Admissions Office, Longfellow Hall), College and Upper Main Streets. Among buildings to be seen:

Massachusetts Hall (1802) NHL, housing faculty offices, was the first building on the campus. President Joseph McKeen and his family, his faculty of two and the first class of eight boys lived here.

Pickard Theatre was Memorial Hall built in 1868 in memory of Bowdoin men in the Civil War. The interior was rebuilt in 1954-55 to create adequate drama facilities. Victoria Crandall's summer musical theatre played here in the 1960s.

Walker Museum of Art (ded. 1894), of brick, limestone and granite in a style derivative of Romanesque, designed by Charles F. McKim, is one of the first and finest of its kind. Modeled on two Florentine masterpieces, the Loggia dei Lanzi and Brunelleschi's beautiful little Piazzi Chapel, the building with great lions at the entrance, is surrounded on three sides by a paved terrace with supporting walls and parapets of granite. Granite and bronze sculptures adorn the front. Inside, in four tympana under the arches of the central dome, each 26 feet wide, are murals executed by John LaFarge, Elihu Vedder, Abbott Thayer and Kenyon Cox, symbolizing the artistic achievements of Athens, Rome, Florence and Venice, respectively. Among the treasures of the Museum are the James Bowdoin collection of paintings and drawings which includes sketches by Rembrandt, Breughel and Tintoretto, and American Colonial portraits by Badger, Feke, Stuart and Copley (*see THE ARTS*). Here is the original Stuart portrait of Jefferson that the artist is said to have journeyed to Maine four times to copy; the Copley portrait of General Knox, the Feke portrait of General Waldo. These and the James Bowdoin bequest constitute an historical collection of portraits remarkable for the distinction of the subjects as well as the artists. The Museum has a valuable Winslow Homer collection; the Warren Collection of Classical Antiquities contains many rare objects. Also to be seen are Chinese ceramics, primitive art from Oceania, Latin America and the Pacific Northwest and massive carved Assyrian tablets. Besides numerous special and minor collections, a guest exhibition is usually current.

Gibson Hall of Music (ded. 1954), another McKim design, has a common room paneled in carved walnut from a music salon designed in 1724 by Jean Lassurance for the Hotel de Sens in Paris.

Hawthorne-Longfellow Library and Hall, (1964-65), a modern functional design by Steinmann and Cain of New York, is compatible with traditional Bowdoin architecture. The Library and facilities are housed in the eastern end of the building. The Robert P. T. Coffin Reading Room is in the northern bay of the first floor. College administrative offices are in the Hall at the western end of the building.

Hubbard Hall (1902-03) from designs by Henry Vaughn was the college library for 60 years, now houses the Geology Department, and offices. A Computing Center in the basement has an IBM 1620 Central Processing Unit with appurtenant equipment. The Rare Book Room on the second floor is an art treasure in itself. Designed by C. Grant LaFarge, it was the library in a sumptuous New York mansion. It has an antique ceiling from a Neapolitan palace, a Sixteenth century Istrian stone mantelpiece, Italian Renaissance tables, and contemporary paintings of religious and allegorical subjects in the wax-rubbed French walnut woodwork. The Peary-MacMillan Arctic Museum is on the first floor of Hubbard Hall which was a gift of General Thomas H. Hubbard, a chief supporter of Peary's expeditions.

Senior Center, (1964) designed by Hugh Stebbins and Associates, is a striking modern complex of three buildings. Most conspicuous is the 16-story tower with living and study quarters for seniors. Wentworth Hall, a two-story building contiguous to the tower, has a handsome lounge for special events, a dining room and other facilities. *Chamberlain Hall* adjacent to the tower contains apartments and a banquet room.

The Chapel (1845-55) whose familiar 120-foot twin towers rise above the treetops, is Romanesque, designed by Richard Upjohn and built of undressed granite from a Brunswick quarry. While the New England house of worship usually was built with attention to the laws of acoustics, Bowdoin Historian George T. Little said the college chapel was built according to the law of optics. Designed on the plan of English college chapels, its broad center aisle is faced with tiers of pews. In panels on the walls behind them are twelve large paintings of Biblical subjects. Brunswick people were models for the third panel on the south side, a copy of Raphael's *Moses Giving the Law to the Children of Israel.* Samuel Melcher, III, then advanced in years, supervised installation of the mahogany woodwork. The Chapel's organ was a gift of Cyrus H. K. Curtis in 1927. A set of eleven chimes is in the southwest tower. Flags in the Chapel represent each of the Thirteen Colonies and the State of Maine.

Seth Adams Hall (1860-61), once housed classrooms of the Maine School of Medicine (1821-1921). Harpswell Street formerly passed in front of Adams Hall, forming a triangular field known to many generations as *The Delta. Winthrop Hall* (1822) has a white marble tablet outside Room 27, once occupied by Longfellow. *Sills Hall,* a memorial to Bowdoin's eighth president, Kenneth C. M. Sills, familiarly known as 'Casey,' has the Peneucian Room (1951) paneled with lumber from Bowdoin Pines. Over the fireplace is carved the motto of the Peneucian Society: *Pinos loquentes semper habemus.*

Gymnasium (1964-65), a 50,000-foot square building seating 2500, adjoins Sargent Gymnasium (1912). On the terrace in front of the building is William Zorach's sculpture, *The Linesman.* An Observatory stands in the SE corner of 75-acre Pickard Athletic Field.

Dudley Coe Memorial Infirmary was licensed by the State in 1962 as a private general hospital.

Moulton Union, another McKim design was built in 1927-28 as a recreation, social and service center. A two-story extension was added in 1965. Housed here are an art gallery, the College bookstore and radio broadcasting center.

President's House, (private), 86 Federal Street, is in the style often called modified Mediterranean, which apparently meant substantial and status-making, much as a good Yankee captain would like his home to be, four-square to ride out a gale, exterior walls of siding to keep out wind, wave and weather. It has the original ornamental cast iron fence and gate with anchors. Granite steps lead to the imposing entrance, flanked by columns, topped by fan and portico with ornamental side-lights. The cupola and widow's walk mark it as a sea captain's do-main — built in 1860 for Captain Francis G. Jordan. Two living rooms combine to make a classic formal drawing room with Italian furnishings. In 1926 during the Sills presidency, a ballroom was added, modeled after the Gadsby Tavern at Arlington, Virginia. Grays, green and gold are featured here and in the drawing room.

First Parish Church (1846), Victorian Gothic, from designs by Richard Upjohn, while not a part of the college, has been the College Church for generations. Baccalaureate ceremonies are held here. A com-memorative Plaque marks the pew where Harriet Beecher Stowe was sitting when she had her inspiration for Uncle Tom's Cabin. Long-fellow in 1875 delivered from the pulpit his famous poem, 'We Who Are About to Die, Greet You.' For nearly half a century an Inn stood across from the Church (no road between then). Hawthorne in his first novel, *Fanshawe*, describes some of the 'blows' at Moorhead's Tavern as the Inn was called. Prof. Nehemiah Cleaveland wrote, in a somewhat patronizing and pious tone, that Hawthorne liked to be present at these 'blows' but never offered any ribald songs and stories — 'his voice was never heard in any shout or merriment; but the silent beaming smile would testify to his keen appreciation of the scene and to his enjoyment of the wit.'

Thorndike Oak (1802) and *Elijah Kellogg Pine* are campus landmarks. The college *Sailing Basin* is on *New Meadows River* and *Little Pond Wildlife Sanctuary* is at Bethel Point, East Harpswell.

Bowdoin Pines on US 1 have long been popular as a picnic area, inspiring such poetic lines as 'Bowdoin pines are fair to see.'

Paradise Spring, on US 1 a mile from the college, 'rose in an alcove of dense ferns and evergreens surrounded on three sides by steep banks and approached by a winding path.' It was an early trysting place and was celebrated in Kirkwood's *Brunswick's Golden Age*. The spring's waters are commercially bottled.

Pejepscot Falls, best seen from the Brunswick-Topsham Bridge, has a descent of 40 feet down three levels over a distance of approximately 200 feet.

Swinging Bridge, between Brunswick and Topsham, one of two in the State, is used daily by a thousand people.

Bronze Tablet, marking the sites of Fort George (1715-37) and Fort Andros (1688-90), is near the Brunswick-Topsham bridge at the end of the former Cabot Mill yard, site of Maine's first cotton mill (1809).

Verney House (private), 10 Water Street, a Samuel Melcher structure, is near the site of early settler Thomas Purchase's Fishhouse Hill post.

Gilman Mansion (1799) *(private)* NE corner Oak Street, now hemmed in by other buildings, once was Brunswick's Great House, built for Capt. Dunlap, 'richest man in Maine.' The 24-room white Federal mansion sur-rounded by wide lawns and flower gardens, rose imposingly among the fountain elms of its own small park with an unobstructed view of the river.

White paneling of the principal rooms was cut from Brunswick pine. Twin rooms opened to make a 50-foot drawing room with gilded wallpaper and French crystal chandeliers. A circular baluster rose from the first to third floors and there were many fireplaces. When Nancy McKeen, daughter of Bowdoin's first president, married David Dunlap, son of the Captain, and a representative of the District of Maine in the Massachusetts Legislature (1810-1817), family mementoes were united and the house saw many important visitors in an era of gracious living. When Charles J. Gilman married Alice McKeen Dunlap, it became known as the Gilman House and was the scene of lavish entertaining.

Granite Obelisk, NW cor. Maine and Lincoln Streets, marks the town's incorporation, 1738. A portion of the house at 3½ Lincoln Street is the oldest in the village (1772). While it was a public house, Talleyrand stopped here enroute from Castine to Boston.

Federal Street, laid out in 1819, its elms set out in 1824, for many years was Brunswick's chief residential street. Its beautiful old dwellings are still there but all have suffered alterations.

Leonard Woods, Jr., House, 7 Federal Street, retains the original door and fanlight. In Europe following his retirement from the Bowdoin presidency, he discovered Hakluyt's long-lost *Discourse on Western Planting.* The college chapel is his memorial.

Muncipal Building, Federal Street. Set in the upper lefthand corner are two dolls' heads which had been similarly set in an earlier Town Hall. A Youth and Recreation Center also is on Federal Street.

Emmons House (1814) (*private*), 25 Federal Street, has been greatly altered since Longfellow and his wife lived here (1831-35).

Harriet Beecher Stowe House (1806) NHL, 63 Federal Street, was built by Samuel Melcher, III for the Rev. Benjamin Titcomb, Maine's first printer. The room Longfellow occupied when he was a Bowdoin sophomore has been 'restored.' A quarter century later Harriet Beecher Stowe was writing Uncle Tom's Cabin here. The house is now a motor hotel.

Haskell House (c. 1820) (*private*), 72 Federal Street, was Maine's first 'hospital.' It was the home of Dr. Nathan Smith who established the Maine Medical School at Bowdoin College. In private practice his patients came from a wide area and when surgery was indicated, it was performed in his home. Dr. Alaric W. Haskell, a later owner of the house, often quipped that Dr. Smith must have been a good doctor, for no skeletons were ever found. The house is now the residence of the Dean of the college.

Parker Cleaveland House (1806) (*private*), 75 Federal Street is architecturally the most distinguished of the Melcher-designed homes, with its balustrades, columned porch, numerous chimneys and line of carriage houses with arched entrances.

Gen. Joshua Chamberlain House (*private*), 226 Main Street, was first a story and a half cottage built in a field on Potter Street and occupied for a time by Longfellow and his bride (1831). Chamberlain bought it in 1861, later moved it to its present location, raised it and built a first story under it — a poet's cottage became a general's 20-room mansion. William M. Wallace, Chamberlain's biographer, says that probably few houses in Maine have seen more of the nation's great as guests — such military men as General Grant who received an honorary degree from Bowdoin in 1865, and Generals

Sherman, Sheridan, McLellan, and political leaders, Fessenden, Blaine, Sumner and Hale.

First Parish Cemetery, off South Maine Street. In this area was the first meetinghouse, cattle pound, town stocks and whipping post, Spear's Inn and garrison house. Among early settlers buried here was Thomas Means and his son Robert killed in an Indian massacre at Flying Point in 1757. The memorial stone of Andrew Dunning (1664-1736) relates that his life spanned the reigns of six English monarchs and 'London Burnt (1666)'.

St John's Church, 37 Pleasant Street, is a Twentieth century interpretation of ecclesiastical Gothic architecture in native stone.

Pejepscot Historical Society Museum (summer, weekday afternoons), 12 School Street, was an 1825 church acquired by the Society in 1891, and houses regional Americana.

Bungamuc Schoolhouse, Pleasant Hill Road. Elijah Kellogg and Thomas Brackett Reed taught here.

ENVIRONS

Brunswick Naval Air Station (annual open house; visitors by permit), largest aggregation of patrol aircraft on the east coast with some 3000 Navy and civilian personnel, occupies 3298 acres on the Brunswick Plains and engages in a complex of operations. Part of the installation is on land that once was the Town Common that consisted of 1000 acres when the Pejepscot Proprietors set it aside in 1719 'to Ly in General and perpetual Comonage to the Said Town of Brunswick Forever.' But squatters built; other encroachments diminished the tract. Bowdoin was given 200 acres. The site had been used as a civilian flying field prior to 1943 when it was chosen for a Naval Air Station. The purpose then was training of Royal Canadian Air Force pilots and anti-submarine warfare. Deactivated in 1946, the Station's land and buildings were leased to University of Maine and Bowdoin College. In 1951 it was reactivated as a Naval Air Facility with anti-submarine warfare its primary mission, and a master jet base was projected. Squadrons based at Brunswick deploy to northern portions of the globe and the Mediterranean. New facilities have replaced temporary World War II buildings. The Air Force Control and Warning Facility, now the 654th Radar Squadron, was part of continental circumferential radar screen. In 1954 an Operations and Maintenance School was established; in 1956, an Arctic Survival Training School was inaugurated. In 1959, the Station became part of the Advanced Underwater Weapons Complex in the National Defense System. From 1961, Navy Brunswick with its 100-foot tower was part of the coastal network of radar stations detecting and tracking hurricanes until taken over by the U. S. Weather Bureau in 1969.

East Brunswick has an early cemetery and cattle pound. *Thomas Point Beach (public facilities)* is off US 1 and *Simpson's Animal Park* is on US 1A, Old Bethel Road.

Merrymeeting Bay (see RECREATION). Near this bird sanctuary and hunters' resort was Merrymeeting Park, one of the turn-of-the-century family resorts developed by the trolley companies. In July 1898, the thousand-acre fenced Park opened with a three-story Casino, an open-air amphitheatre, a zoological garden boasting buffalo, moose, bears, elk, deer, foxes and monkeys. Two white horses engaged in a high-diving act. There were hills, woods, meadows, rustic bridges, ponds, a dance floor and concessions. Mount Washington

FARMING

MAINE has been known as an agricultural state, famous for its Aroostook potatoes, fine apples, blueberries, dairy and other products. Farming, too, is changing with the times. The small old-time farms are disappearing. There are fewer, but larger farms with highly mechanized operations, so farming becomes more of an industry — such as raising several thousand broilers instead of the flock of hens in the barnyard. The Old Conway House at Camden is an authentically restored Eighteenth century farmhouse. Many early implements may be seen at the Matthews Farm Museum (Union), the Dexter Gristmill Museum and the Dover-Foxcroft Blacksmith Museum. And of course farms large and small, orchards, potato fields and market gardens are seen throughout the countryside.

'HE THAT TILLETH HIS LAND SHALL BE SATISFIED'

TREADING HAY

DRINKING HARD CIDER

SUGARING OFF

MONTPELIER KITCHEN

'DOTH THE PLOUGHMAN PLOUGH ALL DAY TO SOW?'

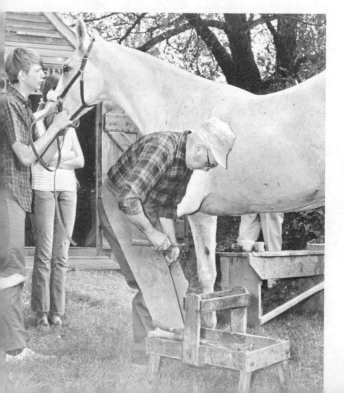

ONCE THERE WAS A
VILLAGE BLACKSMITH . .

LUNCH TIME —ON THE HOOF

JEFFERSON CATTLEPOUND

APPLE BLOSSOM TIME

READYING FOR THE BROILER FESTIVAL

HARVESTING BLUEBERRIES

POTATO BLOSSOMS IN THE AROOSTOOK

FARM AT BERWICK

MAINE FARMHOUSE

could be seen on a clear day from the Casino, famous for its shore dinners the likes of which are unknown today according to some who partook. I-95 now curves through the hillside where a thousand persons sat to view performances in the amphitheatre. The real showpiece was the trolley car, *Merrymeeting,* equipped with plush drapes, velvet carpets, easy chairs and tables, and observation platforms at both ends. The automobile put an end to these simple pleasures.

Mere Point, S on Maine Street, a mile-wide strip of land nine miles long divides the waters of Maquoit and Middle Bays which merge into larger Casco Bay. From its tip overlooking a splendid view of wooded islands and hazy shores, the Portland Observatory 18 miles distant can be seen. The Point's name is spelled 'Mair' in documents relating to Brunswick's organization in 1717 and was pronounced 'mair' or 'mare.' This may have been a corruption of the French word 'mer' meaning sea; 'mair' also is the way Scotch-Irish settlers pronounced the word 'more.' Indians councilled here and large beds of shells, stone tools, and skeletons buried erect with ornaments and weapons have been found. In mid-winter of 1677, Majors Waldron and Frost landed at Mair Point and parleyed with Chief Mugg and others. It was said this was the only occasion when the Indians lost the war but won the argument.

The Point was the scene of what Historian Williamson called the Treaty of Mare-point. It was the implementation of the Treaty of Ryswick, news of which was received in December 1697, bringing to a conclusion the ten-year war between England and France, and that meant between the French-inspired Indians and the English settlers of Massachusetts and Maine. Some 450 English had fallen; 250 had been carried into captivity. In 1699, Col. Phillips and Maj. Converse as peace commissioners, left Boston in the *PROVINCE GALLEY* and met with the Maine chiefs at Mair Point to Ratify this treaty. The famous Chief Bomaseen was taken aboard the *GALLEY* with two others and held as hostages until the English captives were delivered as promised.

Robert Given (pronounced Giveen) and the Pennell family built ships at Middle Bay in the era of wooden vessels. Local oak and pine were used, with Carolina pitch pine for planking below the water line to repel worms.

Simpson's Point. From 1842 for thirty years the Brunswick Wharf Company's New Wharf provided berths here for shipbuilders. With the passing of shipbuilding after the advent of railroads, General Joshua Chamberlain bought the five-acre promontory, planning to establish an art colony. He named the place Domhegan for one of the Indian chiefs who had deeded land to white men 200 years ago. The General rehabilitated the decaying area and brought his charger, Charlemagne, there to rusticate. But his plans for an art colony never materialized. The Simpson homestead burned down; Charlemagne died and was buried with honors in the field now overlooked by a modern ranch house.

HOULTON

Alt. 340, pop. 8289, sett. 1807, incorp. town 1831.
Access: N and S, US 1; SW, I-95 and US 2 and 2A.

Information: Chamber of Commerce, 109 Main St.

Accommodations: 2 hotels, 4 motels, 17 guest houses, motor courts.

Transportation: bus station, Market Sq.; airport, International Port of Entry, U. S. and Canadian Customs, Immigration Station, 2 *m.* E on US 2.

Parks: four, 14 acres.

Recreation: hunting and fishing; swimming, Nickerson, Drew's and Grand Lakes, Pleasant Pond; golf club, Nickerson Lake; ski slope, skating rink.

Cultural, historic sites: see POINTS OF INTEREST.

HOULTON combines the qualities of the old-fashioned country town with those of a modern city in its attractive community. The seat of Aroostook County, one of the richest potato-raising regions in the United States and focal point of the northern third of Maine, has become a large commercial center. Yet in spite of its heavy traffic through Market Square, spacious heart of the business district, Houlton still is a lovely little town with quiet residential sections of fine old homes and modern new ones on both sides of the Meduxnekeag River (Ind.: where people go out). A delicacy on local tables are the fiddleheads gathered along the river banks in May. Proud of its beautiful elms, the town is spending thousands of dollars to save them from Dutch elm disease.

Houlton is a gateway to hunting and fishing territory (*see RECREA-TION*) — big game deer and bear, small furred and feathered game; salmon, trout and togue in the lakes and streams that ring the town.

This single township of 36 square miles adopted in 1939 the council-manager form of government, retaining its lively town meeting. Residents are mostly of English-Scotch-Irish descent with a small percentage of French-Canadian ancestry and about a dozen Indian families. The presence of Ricker College drawing students and faculty from many states and foreign countries lends a cosmopolitan air to Houlton whose convivial people are cultural and sports minded. The town has an Arts and Historic Museum, a Recreation Center, riding, flying, bowling, fish and game clubs, summer and winter sports and a Community Park with race track, swimming pool and tennis courts. A Potato Feast is an annual event in July.

The area surrounding Houlton has gently rolling topography between wooded ridges, with an average elevation of 500 to 800 feet above sea level. The town lies at the southern end of the Aroostook Valley. To the east along the Canadian border the terrain rises to a higher elevation; to the west at Ludlow and Smyrna it rises high enough to be considered a plateau. At the west end of town the fertile land is traversed in a general north-south direction by a great esker system, probably the largest in the world.

The economy of the area centers around agriculture, particularly potatoes, the number one crop. The recent addition of sugar beets as a second major cash crop has served to strengthen the economy as have the diversified industries brought by Houlton's Regional Development Corporation. Houlton industry reflects the natural resources of its fertile farmlands and vast timber areas. Located here are the country's most modern potato starch factory, a fertilizer plant, a grain mill and several woodworking industries, as well as a shoe factory and one that manufactures firearms parts. Houlton, the retail and service center for some 34 communities within a 40-mile radius, has 13 churches, two hospitals, a newspaper and radio station.

Lumbering operations began in Houlton in a small way. The first settlers made a business of turning out limited quantities of shingles and boards, which they rafted to Woodstock and Fredericton. A sawmill was erected in 1810 by Aaron Putnam when Houlton's first dam was built across a small creek. Early lumber drives were worked under severe handicaps, the greatest of which was the necessity of trucking the rafts around Jackson Falls. Since potato farms quickly supplanted the wooded districts, the lumber industry soon ceased to be of primary importance.

When the citizens of New Salem, Massachusetts, in 1799 petitioned the legislature of the Commonwealth for money to found an academy, they were granted, as was customary, a piece of land in the wilderness of Maine to sell if and as they could. This grant is now the southern half of Houlton; the northern part is a section of the Williams College grant, presented a little later to the Williamstown, Massachusetts institution. A group of New Salem men purchased the academy land. Of the original thirteen, however, only three — Joseph Houlton, for whom the town is named, and Aaron and Joseph Putnam — ever actually saw the land. These men established their settlement in 1807. They found that ingress to their new home was not only arduous but dangerous, for beyond Old Town, the District of Maine was largely unexplored forest, dense and trackless. The journey to the site of Houlton had to be accomplished by way of a complicated system of waterways and carries from the Penobscot, or up the St. John River to Woodstock and thence through the woods. Development of the land was slow. The newcomers had to struggle for their existence as if on a distant frontier, for supplies were brought in to them only after infinite labor, and the growing season was very short. A cow was a luxury, and every piece of mill machinery was worth its weight in gold.

In 1822, William H. Cary of New Salem came to Houlton, where he built a spacious house just below Garrison Hill. With his son, Shepard, he founded Cary's Mills, a combination of foundry, carding, and grist mills, thus establishing the town's first industry of importance. Shepard Cary was largely instrumental in opening much of the Aroostook timberland, since he actively engaged in developing large-scale operations on the Allagash and St. John Rivers. Besides conducting numerous local business enterprises, he was highly influential in county and state affairs, serving several terms in the Maine House and Senate, and as Congressman in 1844. The Houlton library is named in his honor.

In 1828, Brevet Major Newman S. Clarke and four companies of U. S. Infantry came up over the Baskahegan Trail, a rough corduroy road connecting Houlton with Danforth. They constructed Hancock Barracks, named for the Revolutionary War patriot, and laid out a parade ground on 25 acres of land purchased by the Federal government. The presence of the post served to defend the boundary between Canada and the United States and to stimulate local trade as well. These soldiers, in 1832, completed the construction of the Military Road, now US 2A, from Macwahoc to Hancock Barracks.

With the outbreak of the Bloodless Aroostook War (1839) that climaxed the old border controversy, Houlton jumped into national prominence. Clarke and his men had been replaced by Major R. M. Kirby and three companies of the 1st Artillery Regiment, and after twelve companies of Maine militia were sent into Aroostook, Major Kirby was concerned with preventing these hotheaded militiamen from starting a shooting war. The boundary dispute was finally settled by the Webster-Ashburton Treaty in 1842. Five years later the post was abandoned.

Houlton then entered upon an economic slump from which it began to recover in 1862 when the New Brunswick Railway (now the Canadian Pacific) was built from St. Andrews, New Brunswick, to a point on the Woodstock turnpike only five miles from town. By 1870 the branch had been extended into the town so that communication with the seaboard by way of New Brunswick was opened. The following year the European and North American Railway (now the Maine Central) was completed from Bangor to Vanceboro, thereby giving Houlton rail connections by a circuitous route with the cities to the south. In 1894 the Bangor and Aroostook Railroad reached Houlton; within a few years, through the perseverance and the financial support of Albert Burleigh, it had extended its line through the northern territory as far as Fort Kent. By this linking of Houlton and the surrounding country with the great national markets, a new prosperity was brought to the people of Aroostook; they expanded their farming operations, the population began to increase rapidly, and Houlton was prominent in the development of the county.

Although railroads are still of great importance to the economic success of this region, since the days of the Houlton Air Base in World War II, use of highway transportation has rapidly increased until now almost as many potatoes are shipped by truck as by rail. Huge snow removal equipment is in operation on a 24-hour basis and trucking moves daily throughout the winter on modern highways, including the interstate system.

One hundred years ago John Carpenter, a surveyor, traveled in one day by stage to Mattawamkeag Point and the next day took a boat down river to Old Town, then on to Bangor by rail. Today Bangor is an easy two-hour drive from Houlton, northern terminus of I-95. Businessmen fly by chartered plane from Houlton International Airport to Boston and return the same day.

POINTS OF INTEREST

Aroostook Historical and Art Museum (Tues, Sat. 1-5), 109 Main Street, was established in 1938 by Ransford W. Shaw and is housed in the *White Memorial Building* given to the town by Mr. and Mrs. S. L. White. The stately mansion was restored by Mrs. Marian Woodbury MacIntyre after a fire in 1902. The Museum has historical collections and seasonal art exhibits.

Gentle Memorial Building (open during school year), Main Street, a modern recreation and community center, was built in 1951 through a bequest of Edna B. Gentle. A strong recreation program for youth and adults that includes athletics, dancing and arts and crafts classes is under direction of the Houlton Parks and Recreation Department. Community gatherings are held in the auditorium, gymnasium and lounges.

Garrison Hill (picnic facilities), a 583 foot elevation 1 *m*. E of town on Military Street, is the site of Hancock Barracks (1828-1847) where U. S. troops were stationed to guard the border during the so-called Aroostook War, or Northeast Boundary Controversy. The stockade and buildings around the parade ground are being reconstructed. A diorama presenting the story of the Aroostook War is being prepared for the Administration Building, a replica of the old Sutler's Store inside the gate. The panoramic view from Garrison Hill includes on the east the U. S. and Canadian Customs buildings and the industrial parks at the airport; below on the west lies the town.

Old Soldiers' Graveyard (1830), on land deeded to the town by Joseph Houlton was the family burying ground until 1907 and for U. S. soldiers and their families. Few stones remain, the best preserved being that of Benjamin Ames of Bath, acting Governor of Maine in 1821, who died at Hancock Barracks during a visit to his sister in 1835. The Graveyard was restored by the DAR in 1941.

Ricker College (guides furnished at Administration Building), Military and High Streets, a rapidly expanding fully accredited liberal arts college, is an outgrowth of the former Ricker Classical Institute established in 1847. It is non-sectarian and coeducational, with an enrollment of 625 in 1968. Town and gown cooperate in programs of art, music and drama.

Aroostook County Courthouse, Court Street, built in 1850 has had additions in 1885, 1928 and 1958. A 'New County Jail and Jailer's Residence' was erected in 1889 of Houlton brick, with additions in 1931 and 1960. Harmonizing with the County Buildings are the Northland Hotel, Post Office and Telephone Buildings on the opposite corners.

Cary Free Library (Mon., Fri. 9-5, 7-9; Sat. 9-5) was built in 1903 of Maine granite with the aid of a Carnegie grant and its large new addition was built in 1968.

Black Hawk Tavern (1813) *(visitors by appointment)*, 22 North Street, was erected by Samuel Wormwood for Aaron Putnam, one of the first settlers, and is the second oldest house in Houlton. Constructed of wood cut and sawed on the site of the building, the house was walled up with brick on the outside in an attempt to make it bulletproof. In the course of alterations, the original roof was replaced by one of much steeper pitch and all but one of the stone fireplaces that were formerly used to heat each room are closed up. The first county court was held in the northeast room of the second floor; the corner that was occupied by the judge's bench is still marked by a four-foot wainscoting. The first county jail was a dungeon in the basement of the building.

Pearce Homestead (visitors by appointment), 98 Court Street, built by Amos Pearce about 1826, is the oldest Houlton residence; its original exterior remains unchanged. A feature that distinguishes it from its neighbors is the absence of eaves. In its front hall under the narrow, winding stair, a smoke-house, complete with hooks, stepladder, and other meat-curing equipment, is intact. The town's original post office occupied the room to the right of the hall. Many of the original fireplaces are retained, and the rooms are furnished with antique furniture, old dishes, candlesticks, etc., belonging to descendants of the Pearce family.

Morningstar Products (visitors by appointment), 2½ *m*. W of Houlton at Cary's Mills, is the most modern potato starch plant in the East, a division of the A. E. Staley Company. Morningstar processes a complete line of starch products to serve the food, paper and textile industries and besides potato starch, uses tapioca starch imported from S. E. Asia, principally Thailand. The total output of chemically treated or modified starch products is 30,000,000 lbs. a year.

L E W I S T O N - A U B U R N

LEWISTON, alt. 196, pop. 42,436, sett. 1770, town charter 1795, inc. city 1861.

AUBURN, alt. 210, pop. 25,000, sett. 1786, inc. shire town 1854, city 1869.

Access: NE and S, Turnpike and US 202; SE, State 196-136; NW, State 4; W, State 121.

Information: Chamber of Commerce, 95 Park St., Lewiston; Development Corporation, 45 Spring St., Auburn.

Accommodations: 13 motels.

Transportation: airport, Hotel Rd., Auburn; bus lines, 216 Main St., 255 Lisbon St., Lewiston; 240 Court St., Auburn.

Parks: Kennedy Park, Lewiston.

Recreation: golf, Apple Valley, Lewiston, Martindale Country Club, Auburn; swimming, boating, Sabattus Pond, Lewiston, Taylor Pond, Auburn; fishing, Lake Auburn; skiing, Lost Valley, Auburn.

Cultural, historic sites: see **POINTS OF INTEREST**.

LEWISTON and AUBURN lying on either side of the Androscoggin River at Lewiston Falls are twin cities forming the industrial and trading center of south central Maine, second largest metropolitan center in the State, 32 miles from Portland (S) and Augusta (N).

On the east side of the river, Lewiston, second largest city and seat of Bates College, has been identified with the textile industry since 1819 and the majority of its population is of Canadian-French descent. On the west side, Auburn, county seat and fourth largest city has been a major shoe manufacturing center since 1835. Many residents of one city work in the other, daily congesting South Bridge, connecting New Auburn and Lewiston's 'Little Canada,' and North Bridge between the cities' principal business districts. In 1969 plans were underway for a third bridge. From north and south on the Maine Turnpike which has relieved the bridges of through traffic, the cities are reached from Exits 12 and 13. Coastal and mountain areas lie to the southeast and west, respectively.

Best views of the spectacular 'Twenty-mile' Falls roaring over massive ledges are at freshet time from the North Bridge or from West Pitch, an Auburn promontory. Otherwise most of the time, the main water flow is diverted into the Lewiston canal to power the textile mills, the great Nineteenth century brick structures that are hallmarks of the city's industrial growth.

The Falls have figured largely in the history of Lewiston and Auburn since earliest times. In the days when the Androscoggin River teemed with salmon and great forests lined the shores, Indians frequented the locality and called the Falls 'Amitigonpontook.' They camped on a point where the Little Androscoggin joins the mother river. One legend is that when the Indian tribe at Canton Point above the Falls planned to destroy the white settlement at Brunswick below the Falls, they were so certain of success that the entire tribe, infants and elderly as well as warriors, set out in their canoes. At dusk, guides went ahead to set signal fires for the night's encampment. Two white hunters captured the guides, learned of their errand and built the signal fires so near the Falls that the currents caught the light canoes and pulled them into the grinding maw of the rapids. Realizing their fate, the Indians went to their doom chanting their death song. Bodies were recovered as far downstream as Brunswick.

On Laurel Hill in Auburn, not far from Beth Jacob Synagogue, is the site of an Anasagunticook Village, wiped out when Major Benjamin Church led an expedition in reprisal for a coastal raid. Recovery of many Indian artifacts and skeletons indicates the area was a great Indian gathering place with burying grounds where ceremonials were held.

In the mid-Twentieth century when the Androscoggin River had become an odiferous liability from sewage and industrial wastes, public pressure brought action. A River Master and a team of biologists keep the pollution level under control. Valley communities are working on a long-range program to upgrade the waters so they once again may be suitable for recreation purposes.

While the Falls were destined to become a water power asset, they made river navigation impractical as compared with the Kennebec and Penobscot Rivers; consequently, although the region at the mouth of the river was settled about 1630, settlements farther upstream came later than similar spots on the other two great rivers. Growth of the Lewiston-Auburn area also was doubtless retarded by the tangled skein of land claims and counterclaims, with endless disputes among the Pejepscot Proprietors, settlers and original owners. A prominent Indian chieftain active in land treaties was Warumbee, a man of exceptional discernment and ability.

The original patentees of the present site of Lewiston and Auburn received what became Bakerstown Township in New Hampshire in 1730, but not until 1768 were agents of the Proprietors granted a tract of land along the Androscoggin. The original movers for the founding of Lewiston were Jonathan Bagley and Moses Little, Boston merchants and members of the Pejepscot Company, who obtained the grant for about five square miles on the north side of the river around the Falls. Terms of the grant were that fifty families in as many houses should settle upon the claim before 1774, 'the houses to be 16' x 20' with a seven foot stud and the name of the town, Lewistown.' First settler, Paul Hildreth, with his wife and child arrived in 1770 and built his cabin near the present site of the Continental mill building. That same year Lawrence J. Harris and eight workmen began constructing a mill at the Falls. He received large land grants and 100 acres each for his five sons. Other settlers arrived and Amos Davis, carpenter and shoemaker, who surveyed the area in 1773 and laid out 50 lots of 100 acres each, became a leader in community affairs. He built the first meetinghouse and schoolhouse and advanced the interests of the Society of Friends. The Plantation of Lewiston and Gore (gore being a triangular piece of land left when surveyors' calculations do not result in an even division into townships) was incorporated in 1795.

Among influential leaders in early days was John Herrick who founded the first tavern, served in the Massachusetts legislature and participated in drawing up the Maine Constitution in 1820. His son Ebenezer, elected to Congress, became one of the State's great legislators. Daniel Reed was Lewiston's first school teacher and first postmaster, appointed by President Washington in 1795.

Primitive operational methods had made small mill sites more practical, so the first industrial growth was along smaller streams. Col. Moses Little's combination saw, grist, fulling and carding mill, erected at the Falls in 1809 was the greatest industrial achievement early in the Nineteenth century — it burned five years later. Many townsmen were involved in the War of 1812 but the community's religious and educational interests continued advancing. By 1830 a large woolen mill had been erected to replace the first one built in 1819 which had burned.

The Androscoggin Falls Dam Locks and Canal Company, acquired in 1857 by the Franklin Company, was the first to harness the mighty power of the river in 1836. Thomas B. Harding was the first man to manufacture cotton, setting up two looms in 1844. The Canal Company built the massive granite locks at the Falls and a great canal 62 feet wide and three fourths of a mile long. The Lincoln Mill, one of the first large mills to be built, began cotton manufacture in 1846, with 21,744 spindles, producing 3,500,000 yards of sheeting annually. The first mill erected on the Canal was the Bates No. 1 which started cotton manufacture in 1852. Three other divisions followed for a total at the end of the century of 63,672 spindles, annual cotton consumption 5,184,000 pounds, annual production of cotton goods 10,400,000 yards. Soon after came the Hill, Androscoggin and Continental mills, then the Lewiston Bleachery and the Avon, Cowan and Cumberland mills. Northern mills began moving south in the 1930s and while some mills ceased operation and others consolidated during the depression, cotton mills have operated in Lewiston from the era of tent cloth to the Twentieth century when quality Bates bedspreads and disciplined fabrics are nationally known.

With burgeoning industry other affairs prospered. Churches were built, a high school was opened in 1850, the Maine Seminary (Bates College) in 1856 and the *Daily Journal* began publishing in 1861, the year the city was incorporated. Jacob B. Ham took office as the first mayor in 1863. The city contributed large sums during the Civil War and lost 112 of its 1150 enlistees.

Auburn grew even more slowly although Abel Davis had cleared land in the Danville-New Gloucester area known as Little's Gore in 1763. Settlement was delayed because grants of the Massachusetts Legislature in 1736 conflicted with claims of the Pejepscot Proprietors and some of the same land was sold or given away several times. Auburn village, nucleus of future growth, was first settled by Joseph Welch who built his log hut at Goff's Corner (near the west end of the North Bridge) in 1791. Mr. Dobelmeyer put up the next house, a framed one, and ran a gristmill. Another village station was near the present Library building, others on the Little Androscoggin and around Lake Auburn where mills were built.

Although rarer in Maine than in Massachusetts, Auburn appears to have had its stories of witchcraft in mild form. In early days Aunt Molly Merrill is said to have hexed her husband and neighbors whenever they failed to carry out her wishes. Apparently she disapproved Mr. Merrill's sale of a yoke of oxen to a neighbor; the oxen were found dead on their backs in the neighbor's barn next day.

Col. Moses Little was as prominent and influential in founding Auburn as he was in Lewiston. He was agent for the settlers and owning much property himself, arduously endeavored in the interests of their rights and titles. His son Edward led in establishing the First Congregational Church and the Lewiston Falls Academy in 1835, which latter became the high school named in his honor.

Not until 1822 did the first trader, Jacob Read, open the first store and a hotel at Goff Corner. A bridge connecting Lewiston and Auburn was built the following year. By 1842 Auburn had become a town and continued to expand despite a fire in 1855 that razed some 25 buildings. The County buildings were completed in 1857 and in 1869 Auburn became a city with Thomas Littlefield as the first mayor.

Auburn's shoe industry originated in the little hamlet now known as West Auburn, then a part of Minot. In 1835, Martin and Moses Crafts established the Minot Shoe Company. A Turner man invented the first copper-toed shoes manufactured at North Auburn. Early shoe manufacturing was crudely conducted and the products were coarse and heavy. Work was cut out by the manufacturer himself with perhaps a cutter or two, in a small shop, then sent to the neighbors for finishing at home. All work was done by hand until about 1850 when the first labor-saving machine was introduced. By this time shoe manufacturing had moved to Auburn and in fifteen years was a million dollar industry. During World War I an Auburn factory made 75 percent of the world's canvas shoes. All kinds of footwear currently are made in the area.

While high union demands and low tariffs have dealt heavy blows to textile and shoe industries as foreign goods flood the markets, the twin cities have developed a widespread diversified economy. Manufactories turn out products ranging from Christmas tree ornaments and plastics to machinery and electronics. There are several industrial parks and branches of national concerns located in the area. Urban renewal here as elsewhere is changing the face of both cities.

With the formation of an Arts Council in 1969, there were signs of a change in the cultural image of the area which through ethnic and academic insularity had fragmented over the years. The French love of music, art and drama had mainly influenced the French sector. Bates College as a cultural center had had little rapport with the municipalities. Public cultural events had dwindled and there had been a long hiatus from the time when there was a local stock company, a Denishawn School of the Dance and French drama and operetta. The Arts Council brought the Portland Symphony and concerts for school children. The success of its first week-long arts festival with events in both cities involving the college, Canadians and other groups, appeared the harbinger of a more communcative approach to the arts in this industrial milieu which has an active Community Theatre, art groups, community concerts and school bands. Bates College is welcoming townspeople to its enlivened theatre and art museum as well as lectures and the Jewish Community Center's art show has become an annual event. Also in 1969 Auburn had observed its Centenary with numerous events and publication of its history and Lewiston had appointed a History Commission.

From Lewiston have come world famous Artist Marsden Hartley and such less renowned painters as Scott Leighton, a painter of horses, whose works were used by Currier and Ives, and his pupil, D. D. Coombs, who specialized in cows. Ignored for many years, Coombs' work, once familiar on the walls of the Poland Spring House, was being sought by collectors in the 1960s. Henry Sprince formed one of the first jazz bands of the Twenties at Bowdoin College and later directed several Lewiston musical productions. Another Lewiston native that became a national figure in the 1960s in the world of the dance is Jacques d'Amboise, top performer in the New York ballet. An able art critic writing for several publications is Phillip W. Isaacson, Lewiston attorney.

Ecclesiastical and institutional architecture as seen in the numerous churches and public buildings is perhaps more notable than the residential in Lewiston and Auburn although some distinctive contemporary homes have been built. Auburn was formerly regarded as the more 'residential' city and still gives that appearance since new industries are locating in the environs. Lewiston's environs are developing new residential areas.

In 1917 Auburn was the first city in Maine and the second in New England to adopt the council-manager form of government. In 1960 the city manager was elected president of the International City Managers Association. In the 1960s Auburn was named an All American City by the National Municipal League and *Look* magazine as the result of a successful program that attracted new industry and created new facilities after a decade of apathy. Conservatively leaning to Republicanism, Auburn is less colorful politically than Lewiston, a Democratic stronghold that has been a potent factor in the resurgence of the party in a long traditionally Republican state. Lewiston's Council sessions are — lively.

Louis Jefferson Brann, Lewiston lawyer, heading the State Democratic ticket in 1932, was elected Governor, serving two terms. Brann, a brilliant and colorful trial lawyer whose cases drew large audiences at the Androscoggin County Courthouse, also was mayor of Lewiston. In the 1936 presidential election when Maine was one of two states in the nation to vote Republican, Brann was defeated for the United States Senate by incumbent Wallace H. White, Auburn Republican who held the post many years. A quarter of a century later, young Democratic leaders, spearheaded by Edmund S. Muskie, a Bates graduate, now U. S. Senator and his party's 1968 vice presidential candidate, brought the party to power again in Maine; in 1970 he was emerging as a likely presidential candidate.

Some facilities and services in the twin cities are used interchangeably.

Each city has a business college, a large high school, numerous elementary and parochial schools, public library, parks, playgrounds and recreation areas. Two large hospitals are located in Lewiston, a vocational school in Auburn where a riverside esplanade was under construction in 1969.

Lewiston has three radio stations and a morning and an afternoon paper with Saturday magazine. The city has a long newspaper tradition since the founding of the weekly *Lewiston Journal* in 1847 by Alonzo J. Garcelon and his brother-in-law, W. H. Waldron, and the French language paper *Le Messager* by J. B. Couture who was an influential figure in Lewiston politics and French culture. Garcelon was one of the first doctors in the area and served as surgeon in the Civil War. He was the first Democratic mayor of Lewiston and became Governor of Maine. Nelson Dingley, Jr., who with his brother Frank bought the *Journal* and who authored the Dingley Tariff Bill, also was a Maine governor and succeeded U. S. Senator William P. Frye of Lewiston in Congress. Frye was chairman of the Commission that negotiated the 1898 treaty with Spain.

Among distinguished journalists who staffed the afternoon daily *Journal* were Holman Day (1870-1935) and Arthur Gray Staples (1862-1940). Day captured the Maine vernacular in his poetry and was the first author to feature the drama of the Maine lumberman and lumber baron. Several of his 25 novels were filmed. His Victorian home, now a private residence in Auburn, is at the corner of Court and Goff Streets. Staples, affectionately known as 'A.G.S.' was a noted editor and columnist of diminutive stature and salty wit who traveled and lectured throughout the country. His perceptive columns, *Just Talks*, published in book form were reprinted in 1969 in the Journal Magazine. His home, a private residence, is a brick house at the junction of Court and Lake Streets. Staples' granddaughter, Anne Sexton, won the 1967 Pulitzer Prize for her third book of poems, *Live or Die*.

Another former Journal staffer is Erwin D. Canham of Auburn, editor of the *Christian Science Monitor*, a Bates graduate who has been president of the U. S. Chamber of Commerce, a New England Man of the Year (1967) and has received honorary degrees from 21 colleges and universities. His father, Vincent W. Canham, was agricultural editor of the *Lewiston Sun*, now part of the same company as the *Evening Journal*.

Area citizens also have been inventive. Freeman and Freelon Stanley of Auburn invented the Stanley Steamer, improving upon the first steam automobile put together by Clarence Rand in Lewiston at the turn of the century. The Stanley brothers, born in Kingfield (*see Tour 4F*), also developed the dry plate photographic process. One of the brothers was an artist-photographer, maintaining his studio in the Sands building on Lisbon Street in Lewiston where the dry-plate factory occupied three floors. An

1889 publication by Boston's Mercantile Publishing Company describing Lisbon Street stores, emphasizes the integrity of the merchants and the high quality of their goods.

Spiritual expression was not lacking during the industrial development of the Lewiston-Auburn area, as attested in the remarkable number of churches erected. Several of the earlier churches have survived among the newer ones built as consolidations took place among Protestant denominations, and the Roman Catholic parishes expanded. Architectural styles range from Gothic to contemporary, ornate to simple, in wood, brick, granite, concrete. Religious practices have seen many changes since baptism by immersion in the Androscoggin River ceased in 1868, but spiritual faith remains strong in the area's 40 churches. First in Maine to implement the ecumenical movement of the 1960s were St. Patrick's Catholic Church in Lewiston and the Elm St. Universalist Church in Auburn.

Early religious groups organized and held meetings in various places before they were able to build their houses of worship, often with great effort and sacrifice. The first organized religious group in the area was the Society of Friends in the Eighteenth century. Amos Davis, who arrived in 1773 and had given land for a burying ground (Davis Cemetery) where he built a small meetinghouse and school, was the first elder. Trinity Presbyterian Church (1959) occupies the meetinghouse at 93 College Street, built by the Friends in 1875 and later occupied by Christian Scientists.

The *Clough Meetinghouse* (Baptist), Old Lisbon Road, Lewiston, and the *West Auburn Congregational Church* (both 1846) are the oldest churches still standing in the area.

Baptist missionaries had arrived by 1783 and over the years, several Baptist churches were built. Prior to forming a parish in 1853, some Baptists met in the porticoed building at 95 Park Street occupied (1969) by the Chamber of Commerce. Others met at Rechabite Hall over a grog shop in Auburn, Rechabite being the Biblical term for an abstainer from strong drink. The *United Baptist Church*, Main Street, Lewiston, is the result of a Baptist merger in 1917-22. The brick and granite *Court Street Baptist Church* (1870), next to the County Courthouse in Auburn, has murals by D. D. Coombs on either side of the altar. Other Baptist churches are at East Auburn (c.1869) and two, more than a century old, at South Auburn, one with interesting wall stencils.

Supreme Court Justice Donald W. Webber of Auburn in 1961 was moderator for the national conclave of delegates that resulted in the merger of Congregationalists with Evangelical and Reformed churches. United Church of Christ is now the name of Auburn's *High Street Congregational Church* (1858), New Auburn's *Sixth Street Congregational* and the early

West Auburn church. The *First Universalist-Unitarian Church* (1876),
Elm Street, Auburn, has been refurbished since 1963. Night lighting
enhances the 100-foot bell tower and steeple and the rose window by
Harry H. Cochrane who also created murals over the chancel. The
Church has a sound-proof crying room. The *First United Church of
Christ*, (1903) is the former Universalist Church on a triangle at Sab-
batus, College and Bartlett Streets.

Methodism arrived in Lewiston-Auburn with 'Campmeeting' John Allen in
1848. Lewiston Methodists attend *Calvary Methodist Church* (1876),
on Hammond Street, Auburn Methodists built a new Church in contemporary design on Park Avenue in 1963. The *New Auburn Methodist
Church* (1858) has a unique bell tower.

Arrivals from Lancashire England in the mid-Nineteenth century, at-
tracted by the textile industry, built *Trinity Episcopal Church* (1882) of
Maine granite at Spruce and Bates Streets. Settling in an area around
Bartlett Street that became known as English Hill, they brought their
custom of Christmas carolling in the streets of their neighborhood. Auburn's
Episcopal Church is *St. Michael's* (1890) on Pleasant Street.

Irish and French Catholics also began arriving in the mid-Nineteenth
century to work in the mills and suffered considerable persecution at
the hands of the 'Know-Nothings.' Parochial schools, staffed by various
religious orders, were built along with churches. The changing economy of
the 1960s was forcing some of these schools to close. Irish Catholics
began worshipping in St. John's Chapel, a small wooden building between
the Androscoggin River and the Canal. *St. Joseph's Church* (1867), Main
Street, Lewiston, was the first Roman Catholic Church to be built in the
area. The parish's Sisters of Mercy Convent at 364 Main Street was built
in 1894. St. Peter's parish church (1873) was on the site of the present
SS. Peter & Paul Church (see POINTS OF INTEREST). *St.
Patrick's Church* (1890) overlooks the City Park, has a Cochrane mural
in its Marian Chapel and its thirteen stained glass windows are from
Munich. The largest of two spires on the brick and granite structure
extends 220 feet, tallest in the community and a familiar landmark. The
parish's Notre Dame Convent is on Walnut and Blake Streets. *St. Louis
Church* (1918) is in New Auburn and *St. Mary's* (c.1930) on Cedar
Street, Lewiston, a handsome granite edifice which is now hemmed in by
other buildings. Three new parishes established in 1923 have these
churches: Sacred Heart (1938), Auburn; Holy Cross (1948) and Holy
Family (1959), Lewiston. In 1970, St. Phillips was being constructed in
Auburn.

Other churches are: Lewiston, *Holy Trinity Greek Orthodox* (1920) at
39 Lincoln Street, visited in 1932 by Athenagoras, now Patriarch of Con-
stantinople; the fieldstone Grace Evangelical Lutheran (1927), at 336

Main Street; Beth Jacob Synagogue (1928), Shawmut Street; Salvation Army Citadel (1960) at 67 Park Street; Assembly of God (1954) at 19 High Street. In Auburn, Advent Christian Church (1892), Turner Street; Beth Abraham Synagogue (1934), Laurel Hill; Church of the Nazarene (1945), Summer Street; Seventh Day Adventists (1951), granite semi-Gothic, Minot Avenue; Stevens Mills Interdenominational (1952), Manley Road; Church of God in Christ (1954), black congregation, Dennison Street; Christian Science (1961), contemporary, Lake Street; Church of Pentecostal Assembly (1961), Broadview Avenue; Jehovah's Witnesses, Kingdom Hall (1964), Old Hotel Road.

POINTS OF INTEREST

LEWISTON

Hulett Square at Main and Lisbon Streets, was Union Square until it was named for a World War I veteran. In early days it was *Haymarket Square* where farmers tethered their wagons of hay, wood and garden produce and sold fat oxen. The Square has seen many military parades since the departure of soldiers for Lake Champlain during the War of 1812.

Lewiston Canal (c.1850) Imported Irish labor removed tons of rock and placed the granite blocks forming the banks of the Canal which was financed by Massachusetts money to tame the waters of the Androscoggin River. *Markers* on a grassy plot beside the Canal describe an old mill wheel and turbine on display.

Bates Manufacturing Company (*visitors, permit at Office*), Canal Street, whose acres of machinery turn out fine fabrics, has a retail store (*open week-days*). Other industries offering plant tours include *Paragon Glass Works*, Westminster Street, the country's largest manufacturer of Christmas tree ornaments, and *Geiger Brothers*, Mt. Hope Avenue, printers of the *Old Farmers Almanac*.

City Park (1861) was named Kennedy Park after the President's visit to the city. In the NE corner is the city's first military monument, the statue of a Civil War soldier, created by Sculptor Franklin Simmons who was born in nearby Webster. Names of the 112 Lewiston officers and men who fell during the War are inscribed. The city's U. S. Senator William P. Frye delivered the dedicatory address in 1868.

City Building, Pine and Park Streets, across from City Park, has a portion of a more elaborate structure dedicated in 1872 and costing $200,000. The larger original building which later burned also fronted on Lisbon Street and contained 'a large and admirably selected and arranged library, bearing ample evidence to the intelligence and strength of intellectual things in Lewiston,' according to an 1889 review which described the finely decorated hall seating 2500 people as 'one of the finest in New England,' where 'numerous dramatic, operatic, orchestral and other first-class entertainments are furnished, to the delight and instruction of the citizens.' Rock and roll dances were the vogue here in the mid-Twentieth century.

Public Library, in the granite building across from City Hall, in 1969 was planning its much-needed new building elsewhere in the city. Public programs will be expanded in the larger quarters. The Library's art collection includes a painting by native son Marsden Hartley. Opposite the Library on the other corner facing the Park once stood the DeWitt Hotel, host for generations of social affairs and visiting notables. Next to this lot, now occupied by a bank, is the plant of the *Lewiston-Sun-Journal Company*.

Central Maine Youth Center, Birch Street, has an indoor arena and winter and summer sports.

SS. Peter and Paul Church (1936), NW cor. Ash and Bartlett Streets, modified French Gothic in Maine granite, dominates the city from its eminence, its two pinnacled towers with eight spires lighted at holiday time. The massive 168-foot structure, second largest church in New England, was 30 years a-building at a cost of nearly a million dollars. Supervised by the Dominican Order which had an adjoining monastery, the church with transept gallery seats 2100, has oak woodwork, traceried panels in the sanctuary and rectory, and choir gallery and organ over the narthex. Its principal facade suggests the Thirteenth century ecclesiastical architecture of Provence.

Davis Cemetery, Sabbattus Street, oldest in the city contains graves of early settlers, among them Amos Davis and his son David for whom David's Mt. is named.

Central and *Campus Avenue Area*. Here are St. Mary's General Hospital, the Marcotte Nursing Home, Lewiston High School and the Memorial Armory. Militia bivouacked at the Armory during the 1937 shoe strike that tested the National Labor Relations Act. Cultural, social and athletic events are held in the building. An Agricultural Trades show is an annual event.

Bates College (1856) (*guided tours, Dean of Admissions, Lane Hall*), off Campus Avenue, a co-ed liberal arts college that grew out of a Baptist Seminary, has over 30 buildings spread over some 75 acres, with David's Mt. and Andrews Pond in a setting of lawns, gardens, maples and elms. Holiday bonfires once lighted the mountain which gives a panoramic view of Androscoggin Valley and the White Mts., in the distance. Bates has been acclaimed for the international debating activities it initiated and many of its graduates have achieved prominence in public life. More recently it has assumed leadership in cultural activities. Its first president was the Rev. Oren B. Cheney and in the 1880s the Nichols Latin School was its preparatory department.

Among college buildings of note are the English Gothic *Chapel* (1918) designed by Jefferson Randolph Coolidge of Boston; *Hathorne Hall* (1856), a fine example of Georgian architecture; and *Carnegie Science Building* (1908) which houses the *Stanton Museum* bequeathed by Jonathan Young Stanton, patriarchal professor of Latin and Greek. The valuable ornithological collection is one of the finest outside Harvard and the Museum has a rare Audubon Folio. The classic columns of *Coram Library* whose voluminous collections include the Isaac L. Rice French Library, formed an appropriate setting for the classic Greek drama formerly presented outdoors during Commencement. Among the newer buildings is the *Lane Building* housing Admission offices and the Ham Room furnished in period style. Bates has an exceptionally fine theatre and the *Treat Art Gallery* has a major collection of the works of Marsden Hartley.

Jewish Community Center, College Street, has an annual art show and other cultural events.

Riverside Cemetery is in a beautiful setting beside the Androscoggin River.

Civil War soldiers lie in the old G.A.R. burial section.

Hospital Square was called Lowell's Corner and once was centered with a picturesque stone watering trough. In this area are several churches, the *Central Maine General Hospital* and the *Kora Temple Shrine Building*. In Saracen style architecture the Temple's verdigris domes are seen from various parts of the city. *Journey to Mecca* murals by Harry H. Cochrane in the banquet hall may be seen by permission and during annual open house day. Cochrane, a Monmouth artist whose work is in several other area buildings and at Cumston Hall, Monmouth, studied at Harvard and journeyed to the ancient cities of the Middle East in preparation for creating the murals which have been reproduced in a special volume with text.

Environs: Brann Hill, Thornton Heights Bird Sanctuary; Sabbattus Pond, 5 *m.*

NE from Lewiston on US 202 about 2.5 *m.* to road (L) to *Gulf Island Dam* 2 *m.*, built in 1927 to harness the Androscoggin River for hydro-electric power. It is named for an island that once divided the river into two channels and is now part of the dam's mid-section. US 202 continues to *Highmoor Farm (visitors)*, 12.4 *m.*, a University of Maine Agricultural Experiment Station, its white buildings set on a hill in a 305-acre tract of apple orchards and vegetable fields. At 13.9 *m.*, road L to *Lilac Gardens*. Some 500 varieties delight visitors during spring blooming period. US 202 continues to *Winthrop (see Augusta Tour 5)*, 20.7 *m.*

AUBURN

Androscoggin County Courthouse (1857) houses the *David Wagg Museum* of the Androscoggin County Historical Society (*third floor, by appointment*). A Harry H. Cochrane mural, *Law the Defender of Civilization*, is in the courtroom. The Museum's extensive collections include microfilmed Shaker history, early newspapers, shoe-making and Indian artifacts, a research library and well-documented archives.

Knight House (1796), first framed house constructed in central Auburn, was being restored in 1969 to be used as a civic and information center.

Lost Valley is an attractive ski and recreation area off the Hotel Road.

Perkins Ridge, a quarter of a mile beyond Lost Valley, affords a scenic drive spring and fall through apple orchards, with fresh cider available in season. To the east, Lake Auburn lies in a wooded setting.

Lake Shore Drive, winding through scenic and residential areas around Lake Auburn which supplies city water, may be taken out Turner Street from the Courthouse. At 2.5 *m.* the *Central Maine Technical Vocational Institute* has a 150-acre campus. The Institute serves 300 local and resident students, offering 30 subject areas. At East Auburn, 3 *m.* was *Lake Grove*, a trolley park where family parties enjoyed outdoor theatre, shore dinners, dancing, a menagerie and steamer trips. There was an inn, and hotels and cottages across the lake. Bobbin Mill Brook, the Lake outlet, once provided power for a furniture factory, cider and gristmills. Right on State 4 is wooded *Mt. Gile* (L) or White Oak Hill where in Lake Grove's heyday, stage teams brought patrons to a five-story observatory, croquet grounds, bowling alley, restaurant and stables.

Continuing around the Lake there are picnic and recreation areas before reaching North Auburn where the Little Wilson Pond outlet is a favorite fishing spot for prize togue. the road (R) from the Grange Hall curves around an ancient cemetery with slate stones marking graves of early settlers, and offers a fine view of Lake Auburn from Dillingham Hill before descending to return to the city. Alternatively, the Drive passes through the West Auburn residential suburb.

North River Road, R from Turner Street, along the Androscoggin, affords views of Boxer's Island, site of a new inter-city bridge, and the Androscoggin Valley.

South River Road or Riverside Drive leaves New Auburn on State 136, following the Androscoggin to Southwest Bend in the village of Durham, home of Shiloh and the Holy Ghost and Us Society (*see Tour 1 sec. a)*. L on State 9 to a bridge spanning the Androscoggin just below another falls that provide power for more textile mills at Lisbon. The Lisbon Weaving Corp. (*permit at Office*) is the former century-old Worumbo woolen mill, named for an Indian chief. The Austin Mills at Lisbon, employing 250, occupy the former Farnsworth Mill.

Environs: Lake Tripp 14 *m.*; Taylor Pond Yacht Club 3 *m.*; Mt. Apatite feldspar mines; Auburn Maine School of Commerce, Hardscrabble Road.

N from Auburn on State 4 to LIVERMORE FALLS, 29.8 *m.* Skirting Lake Auburn, the route reaches TURNER (alt. 290, Turner Town, pop. 1890) 12.5 *m.*, an agricultural town known for *Leavitt Institute*, antiques and as a former rug-making center. The village is R on State 117. At 18.9 *m.*, junction with State 219 R to Howe's Corner, 2.1 *m.* and the *Devil's Den*, a four-level cave penetrating deep into a hillside around a central passage that extends upward 100 ft. to emerge onto a great ledge. From here, Androscoggin River 2 *m.* E can be seen. L from junction on State 219, is Bear Pond Park (*recreation*), 1.5 *m.* and Bear Mt. (1207 ft.).

LIVERMORE (alt. 540, Livermore Town, pop. 1363), 21.8 *m.*, is the corporate center of a town composed of several small villages in a fertile belt of orcharding and dairying. At 22.8 *m.*, a road R leads to the *Norlands (Wed. afternoon and by appointment)*, which has portraits and mementoes in the Library of the family of Israel Washburn whose 7 sons became nationally prominent:

Israel, Representative from Maine (1851-61), Governor of Maine (1861-61); William D., manufacturer, railroad builder, Representative from Minnesota (1879-85), Senator from Minnesota (1889-85); Samuel, captain of a Union ship during the Civil War; Charles, U. S. Minister to Paraguay, and author of a history of that country; Cadwallader, banker, lumber and flour manufacturer, Representative from Wisconsin (1855-61; 1867-71), major general in the Union Army during the Civil War, Governor of Wisconsin (1872-74); Elihu, Representative from Illinois (1853-69), Secretary of State in Grant's Cabinet, U.S. Minister to France (1869-77); and Algernon, a merchant and banker of note.

At Livermore, State 108 goes 21 *m.* NW to *Rumford (see Tour 4)*.

LIVERMORE FALLS (alt. 390, Livermore Falls Town, pop. 3500). Here and at nearby Chisholm are *International Paper Company Mills (visitors by permit)*, which in 1969 installed the world's largest paper making drum. The new Androscoggin mill at Livermore Falls turns out 520 tons of magazine and printing papers per day. The Otis mill at Chisholm runs some 300 tons per day of wallpapers and specialty coated papers for printing. Livermore Falls has a shopping mall and other industries include shoes and lumber.

State 4 continues 17 *m.* to *Farmington (see Tour 4)*.

PORTLAND

Alt. 20, pop. 72,566. sett. 1633, incorp. town 1786, State Capital 1820-31, city 1832.

Access: N, Turnpike and US 202; NW, State 26 and US 302; W, State 25; SW, State 4; S, Turnpike and US 1; NE, Interstate-95 and US 1.

Information: Chamber of Commerce, 142 Free St.; Maine Publicity Bureau, cor. St. John and Danforth Sts.

Accommodations: Eight hotels.

Transportation: Jetport, 986 Westbrook St.; bus stations, 108 Spring St., 579 Congress St., 117 St. John St.; ferry service, 24 Custom House Wharf.

Parks: Deering Oaks, Baxter's Woods sanctuary, Western and Eastern Promenades, Payson, Fessenden, Lincoln and numerous neighborhood parks.

Recreation: golf, Portland and Purpoodock Country Clubs, Riverside Municipal Course; swimming, environs. Consult information bureaus and local newspapers for sightseeing and island tours, cultural and sports events and facilities.

Cultural, historic sites: see **POINTS OF INTEREST**

PORTLAND, Maine's largest city and Cumberland County seat, holds the economic key to a vast territory extending north and east to the Canadian boundaries. In the jet age, the city is a major center of commerce and culture as it has been through the great days of sail and rail. At its feet lies Casco Bay with its many picturesque and beautiful islands, a miniature New England Aegean. Called Machigonne (great knee) by the Indians, Portland itself is almost an island; access to the city without passing over water is possible only from the northwest. The concentrated business area, extended on a saddle-shaped arm of land, is almost surrounded by the waters of Casco Bay, Back Cove and Fore River. Lying between two elevations crowned at either end of the city by Eastern and Western Promenades affording magnificent views, the central section stretches along a sagging ridge in a general east-west direction.

Although the Maine Turnpike and I-95 bypass the city, it is the hub for a great resort region during the height of the tourist season when vacationists pour in by air and highway to make their way over a dozen divergent routes to summer homes and playgrounds to the north and east. Cited for excellence of design, Portland's new jetport was completed in 1968. Turnpike Exits 8, 9 and 10 lead into the city.

Oil currently is the principal harbor tonnage as seen in the huge waterfront storage tanks and great tankers in the Bay. Portland also is the distributing center for chain units throughout the State and has numerous industrial parks and shopping centers. As the State's largest city, Portland is a center for the lively arts, with a Symphony orchestra of metropolitan

status, an art museum and two art schools, three theatrical groups, and a
school of dance. The city's Arts Council stimulates cultural activities.
A television station sponsors an annual sidewalk art show that draws thousands each summer. The several cultural sectors, such prestigious organizations as the Maine Historical Society, the Society of Art, and the like, together with University of Maine colleges and Westbrook Junior College
carry on worthwhile cultural programs and bring nationally known artists
to Maine.

Tall elms and other trees line the streets and shade the city's 400 acres
of parks. Some 25,000 street and shade trees and gardens of flowers and
shrubs ornamenting the city are tended by the Park Department. As its
model city plans developed in the 1960s, Portland was taking advantage
of its natural assets and architectural wealth in enhancing its environment.
The Greater Portland Landmarks, Inc., established criteria for preservation
of historic sites and buildings of which the city has many notwithstanding
three devastating incidents that scarred its history. Early on, Indians
destroyed it; as a prelude to the Revolution, the British burned it; and in
1866 a great fire, that destroyer of many Nineteenth century communities,
left Portland virtually a city of embers. And like so many early settlements in Maine, its first years were marked by the conflict for North
America between England and France.

The first recorded settler on the site of Portland was Christopher Levett,
'the King's Woodward of the County of Somersetshire in New England.'
Levett built a stone house on Hog Island or House Island (historians do
not agree on the site) where he and his company spent the winter of
1623-24. In the spring he returned to England apparently with the intention of arousing interest in forming the city of York at a place he called
Quack, near Casco, presumably where Portland now stands. He left his
house garrisoned with ten men. There is no indication that he ever
returned and no one can say what happened to the company left occupying
the stone house.

Next reported settler was an unscrupulous trader named Walter Bagnall,
of such size he was called 'Great Walt.' As early as 1628 Bagnall was
living on the Spurwink River, not far from Richmond Island, in a hut with
a solitary companion known only as John P. Walt exchanged firewater
and worthless trinkets with the Indians for valuable furs, netting considerable profit before he was killed in 1631 by the Indian Chief Squidraset
and other dissatisfied customers chafing under such 'beneficent.' trading
practices.

Some time later George Cleeve and Richard Tucker established themselves on the land now occupied by the city proper which was known
successively thereafter as Machigonne, Indigreat, Elbow, the Neck, Casco
and Falmouth. The name Portland, of English origin, was first given to
Portland Head on Cape Elizabeth and to the sound between the Head

and Cushing's Island. Cleeve, an ambitious knave, ingratiated himself with Sir Ferdinando Gorges, Proprietor of Maine (then New Somersetshire), and served for awhile as Deputy Governor. When he was ousted, he found a new English patron who purchased the 'patent of the Plough' (so named for the ship of a religious group to whom the patent had been granted in 1630), and put Cleeve in charge as Deputy President, calling the estate the Province of Lygonia. A tedious quarrel ensued between Gorges' agents and Cleeve over proprietorship of the Colonies of the Casco Bay region. The Maine Colonies submitted to Massachusetts government in 1658 and Cleeve died in poverty, ruined by his protracted litigations.

By 1675, Falmouth, as it was then called, had attained some stability. There was a meetinghouse on the Neck and more than four hundred settled inhabitants were within a short radius. But in that year Indian wars broke out, and in 1676 several attacks were made on the town itself. In a final ruthless assault that summer the Indians advanced on The Neck, killing and burning as they came, as far as the easterly foot of what is now High Street, where the colonists made their stand. Many of the inhabitants finally took to their boats, some of them escaping to Salem, Massachusetts, where they were admitted as citizens. Others retreated to Jewell Island far out in the bay, and there threw up bulwarks against attack. An early historian wrote: 'The doom of Falmouth was pronounced at once . . . it was crushed by a single blow.'

No permanent settlement was effected after this until 1716, when Samuel Moody received permission from the Massachusetts Government to take up land at Falmouth. At his own expense he built a fort and persuaded others to join him there. Three garrisons were established in the township, but Falmouth was never again molested by the Indians or by the French. The town entered upon a harmonious development that continued unchecked for more than fifty years. It acquired outstanding commercial importance, exporting lumber, fish and furs in exchange for sugar and molasses from English, French and Spanish ports of the West Indies and the Caribbean. Shipbuilding grew apace with commerce, and the export of masts for the British navy and merchant marine was a lucrative business. It was reported in 1765 that 'the ships loading here are a wonderful benefit; they take off vast quantities of timber; masts, car-raters, boards, etc . . .' By 1770 Falmouth was as prosperous as many of the Colonial cities; her citizens were sturdy, independent, and comparatively well-to-do.

Forebodings of the impending war were felt as strongly here as anywhere: strong resentment of the Stamp Act was manifest; and when Boston was closed by the Port Bill, Falmouth sent liberal supplies to the Massachusetts city. In May, 1775, Thomas Coulson, a Tory sea captain, attempting to outfit a vessel for shipping masts, was restrained by a local committee which asserted that masts for the British Navy were in the nature of military supplies and therefore could not legally be exported. The captain appealed to Captain Henry Mowatt of the British sloop-of-war, CANCEAU, which shortly thereafter dropped anchor in Falmouth Harbor. Falmouth, strongly Whig, became the scene of anti-British demonstrations; revolutionary sentiments were expressed everywhere. Companies of Militiamen, responding to the call from the Continental Congress, were assembled about town. In the midst of the excitement, Captain Mowatt, who was strolling about Munjoy Hill with his surgeon, was seized by a company of Colonials who maintained that he was spying on their activities. The British officer was released on parole, after giving his word to return when requested.

He did return, though not upon request. October 16, 1775, four British naval vessels and a store ship hove to off Portland. Mowatt, in command of his small fleet, sent word to the people of Falmouth 'to remove all human specie from the town' within two hours. Frantic parleys and efforts to arrive at terms of surrender were of no avail. It must be said for Mowatt, however, that he would have spared the city had the inhabitants agreed to surrender all large and small arms in their possession. But this ignominy the people courageously spurned. Accordingly, at 9:30 on the morning of October 18, Mowatt's ships opened fire on Falmouth. Discharge after discharge of bombs, grapeshot, and cannon balls rained upon the defenseless town. Since most of the buildings were upon the level land between India and Center Streets, they were within easy range. The bombardment continued throughout the day, and at night parties were landed to apply torches to whatever structures had escaped the shots. Some 414 buildings, including a new courthouse, the town house, and the customs house, with many barns and warehouses, went up in the general conflagration. Nearly two thousand persons were left homeless, although none were killed and only one was wounded. Some members of the British landing parties were believed to have been shot down by the citizenry.

One building that escaped the flames was the Widow Alice Greele's tavern in the heart of the city. The doughty widow refused to leave her house; whenever flames burst forth around it, she kept dousing them with pails of water. Court sessions were held in one of the tavern rooms after the fire until 1787 when a new courthouse was built. The Widow's tavern which had been one of the few pleasure spots in a somber era, was a Portland landmark for many years.

A month after the Mowatt bombardment, a visitor reported 'no lodging, eating, or housekeeping in Falmouth.' The British came and went, but they found little about the ruined wharves and buildings to make occupation desirable. The town, though, was never abandoned because it was still a central point for the assembling of military recruits, and in 1777 there were upwards of seven hundred people living here under conditions of extreme hardship.

Cheerless predictions as to Falmouth's future after bombardment, the Revolution, and the period of post-war stagnation proved groundless. The town, which took the name of Portland on July 4, 1786, was once more the scene of great commercial activity. Business began to expand in volume and variety, forts were constructed, bridges were built connecting the city with the surrounding country, Maine's first banking house, the Portland Bank, was established with a capital of $100,000, and Maine's first newspaper appeared. Commerce with England, even more profitable than before, was restored, and the French Revolution gave new impetus to American shipping. In 1800, Portland's population was 3704, an unusually large number when it is considered that 97 percent of the Nation's total population at this time was rural. When, in 1803, Commodore Edward Preble subdued the Barbary Coast pirates, making shipping safe in the Mediterranean, Portland, the commodore's home, basked in the acclaim that the world accorded him. The rise of Napoleon in France and the subsequent European conflicts furnished valuable markets for Yankee enterprise, and Portland especially profited in the subsequent shipbuilding boom.

The new-found prosperity experienced sudden decline in 1807 with the two-year Jeffersonian Embargo. The Portland waterfront was deserted; ships literally rotted at their moorings; hundreds of citizens lined up each day in Market Square to be fed from public soup kettles. From 1807 to 1809, the city experienced a depression more profound than any during its subsequent history.

Recovery came quickly. The War of 1812 provided new stimuli for commerce and industry, and shipyards again hummed with activity. Fortunes were made in privateering. The whole town assumed a new aspect of enterprise. During the War, trade by land had increased. Land grants made to the military in areas neighbor to Portland brought added prosperity to a town that was fast becoming a trading center. By shrewdly purchasing some of these claims from soldiers who were ready to sell, some Portland men profited greatly. Among them was General Peleg Wadsworth who acquired holdings in neighboring Hiram.

As agitation grew for separation from Massachusetts, it was expected that Portland would become the capital of the new State of Maine. And so it did until 1832 when more centrally located Augusta replaced it.

Through the Nineteenth century, Portland's progress was rapid. Chartered as a city in 1832, it continued to expand as steam-powered transportation was developed both by water and by rail. In 1828 the opening of the Cumberland and Oxford canal brought great increase in trade to the Casco Bay area and to Portland in particular. In the two decades preceding the Civil War, rail transportation was also accelerated. In 1842 rail connection was made with Portsmouth and Boston. Two years later the tireless promotor of railroad schemes, John A. Poor, arrived in Portland and until the Civil War and to his death in 1871, he was back of every move to expand rail connections — first with Montreal in the Atlantic and St. Lawrence Railroad, which eventually became the Grand Trunk Railroad, and then with Halifax, the European and North American Railroad, which was to become the Maine Central line. Many failures occurred, but by the time the Civil War broke out, Portland had established impressive rail connections which in part compensated for the absence of a river offering the advantages enjoyed by Bangor and Bath on the Penobscot and Kennebec Rivers, respectively. Shipyards were busy, too, and during this period Portland did not relinquish her position as a maritime city. In 1853 the SARAH SANDS made a safe crossing from Liverpool to be the first transatlantic steamer to dock in port. Only thirty years before, the first steamboat to ply Casco Bay, the KENNEBEC, nicknamed the GROUNDHOG, had established connection with neighboring Boston and the Kennebec River.

To the Civil War, Portland contributed one-fifth of its total population, then 25,000. During the war a young Confederate naval officer conceived a plan for entering Portland Harbor, his goal the destruction of two gunboats lying there and the capture of a steamer in which to continue his already extensive depredations on the sea. Disguising his men as fishermen, he had no trouble bringing his small vessel past the forts and anchoring it near the wharves. That night he boarded and took the revenue cutter, CALEB CUSHING, and sailed her out of the harbor. The following morning the Collector of Customs and the Mayor with a crew of volunteers manned the Boston steamer, FOREST CITY; another crew took the New York boat, CHESAPEAKE, and this 'fleet', set out in pursuit, eventually overtaking the CUSHING. The Southerners aboard her, failing to find any ammunition, set her afire and were taken as prisoners from the lifeboats.

The war over, Portland resumed its accustomed activity. Then, on the afternoon of July 4, 1866, there occurred what was probably the greatest of Portland's series of catastrophes. A great fire almost wiped out the city. Starting in a boatshop on Commercial Street near the foot of High Street, and fanned by a strong southerly wind, it swept diagonally across the Neck to Back Cove and up Munjoy Hill. Except for a line of buildings on Commercial Street and another on Oxford Street, the whole lower and most densely settled area of Portland was brought to the ground during the fifteen hours the fire raged. Only by blowing up buildings in the path of the flames, and by the most strenuous efforts on the part of fire fighters was the rest of the city saved. Longfellow, viewing the city some weeks after the conflagration, wrote to a friend: 'I have been in Portland since the fire. Desolation, desolation, desolation! It reminds me of Pompeii . . .'

Most of the public buildings, all the banks, half the city's churches and manufacturing establishments, and hundreds of dwellings were razed by the flames. The financial loss amounted to millions. Yet, despite the extent of the disaster, not a life was lost. Colonies of tents sprang up to shelter the homeless, and contributions of money, provisions, clothing and building materials poured in from all parts of the country. Thieving and extortion were more than balanced by countless deeds of heroism and acts of generosity.

Rebuilding commenced immediately, with many improvements. Narrow streets were widened and crooked ones straightened; much of the congestion caused by poor planning was changed. Once more Portland bound up its wounds and settled down to serious business, and shipping and industry were soon vying with each other in the renewed commercial expansion. Unlike that of some cities that have grown around one industrial enterprise, Portland's business complexion has changed with the times. It reflected the rise and fall of such major industries as lumbering and wooden shipbuilding; it was marked by the changes in the industrial life of the United States as a whole and so continues in the latter half of the Twentieth century.

Portland's population increased without benefit of industry and big business. In a fifty year period, from 1860 to 1910, the city's population doubled. This was helped appreciably by the annexation of Deering in 1899, yet other explanations are necessary. More and more upstate Maine was on the move and more and more rail and water connections in Portland served as the artery to move products to and from the upstate area. During and shortly after World War I, the city experienced great prosperity. Millions of dollars came to the city annually from Canada, symbolized by two immense grain elevators erected in the railroad yards of the Grand Trunk. Nearly all Canadian grain was exported through this port which had facilities for handling large export and import cargoes. During these years there was no lack of employment on the waterfront. Real estate was in demand and much of suburban Portland, as it is today, was built.

Portland shipping which was of first importance during its entire history declined after World War I but grew immensely during World War II. Business caught in the Depression of the 1930s, was pulled out of the doldrums by the activity in the yards of the newly established New England Shipbuilding Company in South Portland. From December 1941 to July 1945, 266 Liberty Ships were built in the East and West Yards. Population in the Greater Portland area all but doubled during the War. Naval activity was everywhere. Government installations were built on Long Island and Portland was a port of call for the regular fleet.

During the 1950s the city settled down to its routine, but it was never to be the same again. New industries were introduced in the yards formerly producing ships. Terminus for the Portland Pipeline, enormous cargoes of oil were brought in to be pumped to Montreal. Tanks sprang up as the Bay area became an important distributing center for gasoline. In

1968 it was estimated that 26 million tons of petroleum products came into Portland by tanker. While spillage that year amounted to less than one millionth of one percent, concern grows as increased expansion of the oil industry appears in the offing. Other tonnage entering the harbor is of minor importance compared to oil. In 1970, environmentalists strongly opposed King Associates' planned expansion of its Long Island oil operations. The Associates also have acquired, for oceanographic study and research, 190 acres and 125 buildings of Fort McKinley on Great Diamond Island, owned by the General Services Administration until 1961.

Both Portland and South Portland have well-developed industrial parks; the latter with its greater space has been particularly successful in introducing new industry. Shopping centers have drawn from the hard core of the city, with the result that the City Council, in conjunction with the Greater Portland Chamber of Commerce, in 1965 hired the Victor Gruen Associates to make a study of the local problem. The result has been a face-lifting master plan already partially achieved. Demolition of slum areas, automated traffic at rush hours, an improved modern fire protection system, and renovated Portland City Hospital have resulted. New housing projects for both high and low income families are already completed. A model city program, one of the first begun under the Federal program, is well along. Perhaps the greatest change will result with the completion of a spur from State-295, which now bypasses the city. This will improve the traffic problem at rush hours and bring more business to the city. In 1970, Portland became the Maine terminal for a new ferry to Nova Scotia.

As Portland achieved commercial stability, its citizens turned to cultural and intellectual pursuits. First in the arts was the work of early artisans, the tinsmiths, pewterers and furniture makers. Books and other reading matter were the luxuries of the wealthy few in the Colonial settlements. The first public library was established in 1766. Although frowned upon by the Puritans, public interest in theatre and music was evident in the 1790s and by the end of the century a simple but genuine culture had developed. A vital force in this development was Maine's first newspaper, the Falmouth *Gazette* established in 1785 by Benjamin Titcomb, Jr., and Thomas B. Wait — the same Mr. Wait who with his wife and another couple, was indicted for dancing. The paper's support of the theatre was the first time a newspaper had fought for a civic movement.

The Nineteenth century saw the flowering of culture in Portland, in art, literature, music and theatre (*see THE ARTS*). Portland had a reputation as a theatrical town, with its own stock companies and visiting stage luminaries of the period. Its heyday was during the era of the Jefferson Theatre which opened in 1897 and flourished until the Depression of the 1930s. In recent years a community little theatre and two drama groups are reviving interest in live theatre. Portland always has been a music center. Concerts, musical clubs and visiting artists are recorded from earliest days of hymn-singing and sacred music. Portland's composers are numerous, among the most famous being John Knowles Paine, Francis Crouch, Herman Kotzschmar, William McFarlane and Latham True. Paine (1839-1906) was the first American composer to have his music played in Europe and the first to hold a chair of music in an American university (Harvard 1875). Minnie Plummer, an organist, won acclaim in opera circles in Italy where she was known as Madame Scala. Singing groups always have been popular; among the earliest was the Handel and Haydn Society. The still active Rossini Club is said to be one of the oldest women's musical clubs in the country. Portland was the seat of the Maine Music Festival organized and conducted by William R. Chapman from 1897 to 1926.

In 1912, the Kotzschmar Municipal Organ, gift of Cyrus H. K. Curtis, was installed at City Hall auditorium, handsomely redecorated in 1968, where free concerts are given and where the Portland Symphony performs, currently under the baton of Paul Vermel. Seven concerts a season are given and the Orchestra travels to other Maine communities and Canada. It has eminent soloists and has premiered the works of such composers as Walter Piston. The Symphony grew out of the Portland Municipal Orchestra founded in 1926 and preceded by numerous orchestral groups.

Many well-known artists have been associated with Portland, among them Charles O. Cole, Charles F. Kimball, Charles L. Fox, Harrison B. Brown, Walter Griffin, Alexander Bower and the architect, John Calvin Stevens. Early sculptors were Benjamin Paul Akers and Franklin Simmons who executed the Longfellow and Monument Square memorials.

Literature also bloomed in the Nineteenth century. Madame Wood, one of America's first novelists, had moved to Portland from York in 1811. A contemporary was John Neal (1793-1876), one of American literature's most versatile and startling figures. Nathaniel Deering (1791-1881), was the town's 'wit and gentleman poet.' Seba Smith (1792-1868), famous humorist and satirist, was on the staff of the Portland *Eastern Argus* 1818-37. There were Nathaniel Willis, Jr., who founded the Youth's Companion in Boston and Fanny Fern (Sarah Payson Willis) of whom it was said, *She is well posted in politics — thinketh as Pa does, and sticketh to it through thunder and lightening . . . She is as prim as a bolster, as stiff as a ram-rod, as frigid as an icicle, and not even matrimony with a New Yorker could thaw her.* And of course there were Henry Wadsworth Longfellow and a host of lesser luminaries.

In more than 175 years of publishing in Portland, Thomas Bird Mosher (1852-1923), whose Bibelot series of reprints became world famous, was perhaps the most distinguished among printers and publishers. Designing his own styles and formats, he reprinted many well-known books. His various editions on pure vellum and on Italian handmade, Van Gelder Dutch and English papers gave a unique format to some of the choice works of English and American authors. The Mosher Press was the first in America to adopt the dolphin and anchor colophon which originated with Aldus Manutius, a Venetian printer in the Fifteenth century.

From 1936 to 1969, the Athoensen Press was noted for its quality printing of high artistic merit. Fred W. Athoensen (1882-1969) applied the principles of the best typography of the classical period of printing to the volumes he produced during his first 20 years of limited edition printing. In 1936 he acquired the Southworth Press of which he had been manager since the early 1920s. He studied the most famous examples of craftsmanship in England and his reproductions of noted works were usually among the annual selections of the 'Fifty Books of the Year.' The great museums called upon his services and his book, *Types and Bookmaking* (1943), is an interesting account of his career. University of Maine-Portland has the Fred W. Athoensen Memorial Collection of 1360 volumes of his work.

Since John Neal's *Yankee*, a literary magazine of 1828, attempts to launch such publications have not been successful; *Sun-Up*, copyrighted in 1926 collapsed within a few years. Currently there is some private printing, particularly in the historical field and creative literary efforts on college campuses are receiving recognition. While in the past there have been as many as fifteen simultaneous news publications, communications in the 1960s are served by the Gannett Publishing Company with morning, afternoon and Sunday paper and television and radio station; two other television networks and five radio outlets.

With the lusty life of the waterfront in its past, the fashions in manners and morals in the 1960s had no surprises for Portland which in the 1920s had its 'free love' colony and other avant-garde manifestations. For a time in 1929, Erskine Caldwell operated a bookshop in Portland where 'Villagers' foregathered, much in the manner of today's coffee houses. Youth concerts were inaugurated at Deering Oaks in 1969 and 'mod' shops catered to latter-day bohemians.

Portland's population is predominately Anglo-Saxon, with minority strains of Jewish, Irish, Italian, Greek and Scandinavian and a few Blacks. Portland has more than 65 churches and religious meeting places accommodating a wide variety of denominations. The first radio parish of America was introduced over a Portland station in 1924 by the Rev. Howard O. Hough. Private educational institutions include a Hebrew school, a junior college for women, a girls' preparatory school, a Roman Catholic Academy for girls, several business colleges and the University of Maine Portland-Gorham.

The social, economic and political pulse of the State is felt in metropolitan Portland which remains predominately commercial. Today's business and yesterday's history, new enterprise and old romance, are combined in this city which recalls Longfellow and his well remembered line describing the city wistfully as 'the beautiful town that is seated by the sea.'

The following selected points of interest are located generally from the principal Squares, Monument Square NE. and Eastern Promenade and Longfellow Square SW. and Western Promenade, and include waterfront and outlying areas. In view of changing traffic patterns, current city maps and the brochure, 'A Walking Tour of Portland,' available at the Chamber of Commerce are recommended.

POINTS OF INTEREST

MONUMENT SQUARE, busy junction of Congress, Middle, Federal, Elm, Center and Preble Streets, was for generations Portland's forum, the center of the city's commercial, social and political activity. In 1746 a blockhouse was garrisoned here for defense against Indians.

A few years later a jail and jail-keeper's house were built adjoining the blockhouse. Since the jailer received only £15 annually for his services, he kept a tavern, called the Freemason's Arms. A loyalist sea capatin, captured in 1780 while recovering iron from the wreck of Saltonstall's fleet (*see BANGOR*) wrote of the Falmouth Jail that he 'had neither bed, blankets, or anything to lay on but the oak plank floor, with the heads of spikes an inch high and so thick together that I could not lay down clear of them.' Small wonder that he broke jail and escaped after his first few weeks of imprisonment. The blockhouse jail was removed in 1797.

Up to the Twentieth century, Market Square, as it was then called, was the scene of all popular gatherings in the city, surrounded as it was by stores, hotels, public halls, and places of amusement. The central building, Military Hall (1825-88), was both 'town house' and market place. Military companies had their armories in the building and town meetings were held there. More than one riot took place in the square before the hall — one of them in 1856 when, during the mayoralty of the prohibitionist, Neal Dow, a man was shot during the attempt of an anti-liquor-law mob to seize the city-owned liquors stored in the building. On holidays the square was always the focus of the city's life, and in the evenings crowds gathered about the peddlers and showmen who displayed their wares by the light of flaming torches.

The *Monument* (1891), by Franklin Simmons is a memorial to Portland's Civil War soldiers. The Casco Bank is on the site of the United States Hotel of stagecoach days, Portland's premier hostelry until the Civil War.

Wadsworth-Longfellow House (1785) (*June 1 - Sept. 15, weekdays 9:30-4:30*), 487 Congress Street, was the childhood home of the poet, Henry Wadsworth Longfellow. The dignified old house, built by Longfellow's grandfather, General Peleg Wadsworth (*see Tour 7*), was the first brick house in Portland. In 1815, after fire destroyed the gable roof of the original two-story structure, the present third story and hip roof were added. Set back from the street behind its high iron fence, rectangular, solid and simple, it is almost severe in its plainness, its only ornamentation being the Doric portico forming the front entrance. The 16 rooms open to the public are filled with documents, manuscripts, portraits, costumes, household utensils, and furnishings used by the Wadsworth and Longfellow families, items pertaining to early Portland history, and numerous personal belongings and souvenirs of the poet himself. A pleasant shaded garden with quiet walks lying behind the house has been restored and cared for by the Longfellow Garden Club. Although the view of Back Bay that added much to its charm in olden times is shut off by buildings, the garden today is much the same as it was when the poet walked there.

Henry Wadsworth Longfellow, born on Fore Street, lived in the Congress Street house until he was 14. The poet's formal education began at the age of three, when, still in dresses and accompanied by a Black servant, he went to a school on Spring Street. Longfellow entered Bowdoin College in 1821, when he was only 14, and a few years after his graduation he became a professor at the college. Later he was made a member of the faculty of Harvard University, and from that time his home was at Cambridge, Massachusetts, where he died March 24, 1882. After his death, a memorial bust of the poet — the first American to be so honored — was placed in the poet's corner of Westminster Abbey. A replica of the bust is on exhibition at the Museum of the Maine Historical Society.

Maine Historical Society (1822) (*weekdays 9:30-5; Sat. 9:30-12*), occupies the building at the rear of the Wadsworth-Longfellow House. Its valuable historical and genealogical library is widely known (*library privileges on request*). Its collections include the Pejepscot, Kennebec Purchase, King, Knox, Baxter and Northeastern Boundary Papers and the John W. Penny Collection of Indian Relics and other articles that belonged to Father Sebastian Rasle (*see Tour 4*). There are occasional exhibits pertaining to Maine and local history and archaeology.

Natural History Museum (Mon. through Fri., 9-4:30), 24 Elm Street, has exhibits of Indian relics, mounted North American fauna, shells, minerals, plant life, wood and paper samples, clothing and household utensils. Here the Natural History Society maintains a library of 5000 volumes dealing with natural history, geographical surveys, scientific treatises and the like, and works with the Audubon Society.

First Parish (Unitarian) Church (1825), 425 Congress Street, is second successor to the original Falmouth meetinghouse that stood at the corner of Middle and India Streets, and served the Community from 1718 to 1746 as a place of worship, and for a time as courthouse. Parson Thomas Smith, first regularly ordained minister in Maine east of Wells, recorded in 1747: 'I prayed with the Court in the afternoon. Justice came drunk.' Smith, succeeding a series of itinerant ministers of whom one was the Rev. George Burroughs, who preached here in the 1670s and was hanged for witchcraft in Salem in 1692, attended to the theological, and also the medical, needs of his parishioners for 70 years. The church became Unitarian in 1809 and attained its greatest prominence under the Rev. Ichabod Nichols, who was called to the parish at that time. 'Old Jerusalem,' the second structure, occupied the present site from 1746 to 1825, when it was replaced by the stone church as it now stands. The former church was for years a Portland landmark, and the young Longfellow wrote a poem protesting its destruction. 'Old Jerusalem' withstood the Mowatt bombardment, although a cannonball, now embedded in the ceiling of the present church, with a chandelier suspended from it, penetrated one of its sides.

It was in 'Old Jerusalem,' a model of which is displayed in the present church lobby, that the Constitution of Maine was drafted in 1819, a fact noted on a plaque attached to one of the church doors. In March of 1970, Maine's Sesquicentennial year, the Portland Players re-enacted this historic event in the

GETTING AROUND

ALTHOUGH time telescopes with Telstar, and the age is faster than the speed of sound, some of the earlier modes of travel are still around. Past and present meet in the wilderness, accessible only by plane or canoe. Maine does have jetports, a communications satellite and the world's largest radio transmitters. Still, horses and oxen are seen at work and there are rides to be had at Boothbay's Railway Museum and the Seashore Trolley Museum at Kennebunk. There are windjammer trips out of Camden, not to mention hayrides and sleighrides. The famous 'one-hoss shay' now at the Smithsonian Institution was built first at Union and it was Maine's Stanley twins who built the first steam-driven motor car, long before air-pollution. The Veazie railroad was one of the country's earliest. Getting around now and then is pictured here.

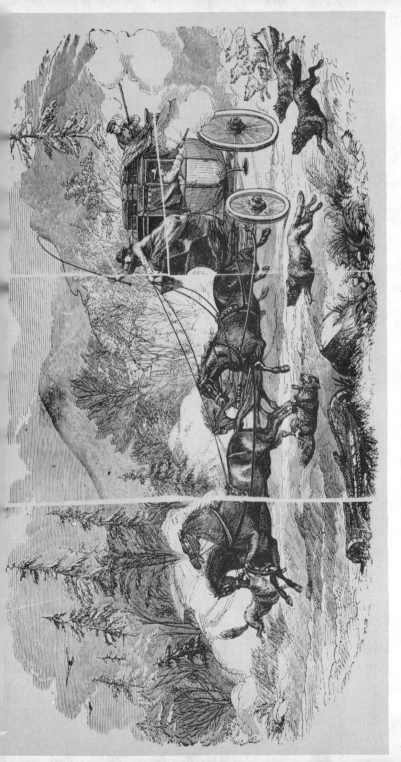

AIRLINE STAGE. BANGOR-CALAIS "WOLF ROUTE." 1860

FURBISH'S DASH TO MONTREAL, C. 1845

PORTLAND'S JETPORT

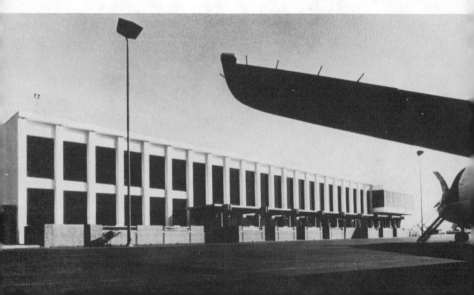

ICE-CUTTING ON THE KENNEBEC RIVER FOR WORLD TRADE

OXEN HAUL LUMBER AT BETHEL IN 1970

DORY, WATERCOLOR BY WINSLOW HOMER

FIRST ELECTRIC
CAR, 1847

**THE STANLEY TWINS ABOARD THEIR FIRST STEAM
HORSELESS CARRIAGE, 1897**

ENGINE 470 AT COLBY COLLEGE

THE STEAMER **BANGOR**

TUGBOAT SEQUIN, 1884

FISHING SCHOONER MUSEUM, BOOTHBAY

INTERNATIONAL BRIDGE AT LUBEC

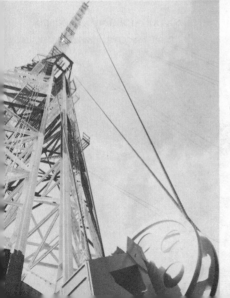

COMMUNICATIONS SATELLITE AT ANDOVER,
ABOVE, AND WORLD'S LARGEST RADIO
TRANSMITTERS AT CUTLER

church, in *The Birth of a State*, a presentation written by Playwright Louis Coxe of Bowdoin College. In dramatizing and making pertinent to modern concerns certain issues of the Constitutional Convention, Playwright Coxe realistically suggested the drama of conflict and resolution that took place in 1819 and showed that 'men can sometimes rise above self-interest, if only briefly, when their imaginations are fired by a good and noble aim.'

Portland City Hall and *Municipal Auditorium*, 380 Congress Street, occupies a plot of ground associated with city, county, and State government for more than 175 years. The first structure on this site was a two-story frame courthouse (1782-1816) whose cupola was surmounted by the carved weathercock now adorning the Maine National Bank Building. Gallows, stocks, and pillory had a prominent place in the first floor hall of the courthouse, and the whipping post stood outside its door. The first capital conviction in the United States Courts after the adoption of the Constitution (Article I, sec. 8: 'The congress shall have power . . . to define and punish piracies and felonies committed on the high seas . . .') occurred here in 1790, when one Thomas Bird was sentenced to be hanged for piracy and murder. Bird's petition for pardon was refused by President Washington, and he was promptly executed on Bramhall Hill. A jail (1797-1859) and a jail-keeper's house were built in the rear of the courthouse, the former having a dungeon with chains, shackles, and ringbolts. The debtor's rooms in the attic 'were not so replusive, yet those who were then confined in them — did not appear as if they were happy.' A new brick courthouse was erected in 1818 and, four years later when Maine became a state, it was used by the legislature. Until 1822, spirituous liquors were sold on the premises, a practice which was discontinued in that year 'during the sitting of the Court of Legislature.' Another building adjoining the courthouse had been erected in 1820 to accommodate the Senate and State offices, and was in use until the State capitol was removed to Augusta in 1831. At the time of Lafayette's visit to Portland in June, 1825, an awning was spread from the front of the statehouse to the elm trees lining the street before it, and the General held his public reception on a platform built from the entrance.

Two other city and county buildings on the site of the old courthouse, jail, and statehouse were built and burned before the construction (1909-12) of the present city hall, designed by Carrere and Hastings of New York and Stevens and Stevens of Portland. The *Municipal Auditorium*, elegantly decorated, seats some 3000 for performances of the Portland Symphony and other outstanding events including summer organ concerts. The organ, one of the world's largest, is really eight instruments in one; it has 177 speaking stops and couplers, over 6500 pipes and a carillon. The organ is a memorial to Hermann Kotzschmar (1829-1908), composer, teacher and for 47 years, organist of the First Parish Church.

Cumberland County Courthouse (1907) (*weekdays*), NE cor. Federal and Pearl Streets, an impressive neo-classic structure of Maine granite designed by George Burnham, houses county governmental and judiciary offices and archives. The similarly impressive granite building directly across SE is the *Federal Court Building*.

Lincoln Park, bounded by Congress, Franklin, Federal, and Pearl Streets, occupies the heart of the city. Formerly a heavily congested residential area, it was set aside after the fire of 1866 by the city fathers as a 'protection against the spread of fire and to promote the public health.' The land was purchased for a public square and market place, designed accordingly in 1867, and named Phoenix Square. At the protest of the common council, the name was shortly changed to Lincoln Park. With the judicious planting of trees and the installation of a fountain in 1870 the spot soon became a welcome and restful breathing space in a section of the city which in the course of time has grown somewhat drab. There is an open-air market here Wednesday and Saturday mornings when farmers bring in their fresh vegetables and poultry in season.

Franklin Towers, opp. the Park, low-cost housing unit, was Maine's largest and tallest apartment building in 1969.

Cathedral of the Immaculate Conception, 307 Congress Street, its main entrance facing Cumberland Avenue, is the seat of the bishopric and the mother church for the entire· Catholic diocese of Maine. Completed and dedicated in 1869 in spite of repeated setbacks in its building during the Civil War and the great fire of 1866, after which the bishop was obliged to celebrate mass in the shed of the Grand Trunk Depot for want of a church, it has been remodeled once, in 1930. Apparently an agglomeration of several structures, the Cathedral is designed in a modified French Gothic style. The main building's lofty interior, resembling somewhat those of the cathedrals of Europe, is embellished with walls of Carrara, Brescia, Pavonazzo, Porta Santa, and Numidian red marble and adorned with delicately tinted ornament. The Stations of the Cross are executed in mosaic and the 18 stained-glass windows are of Munich glass.

Eastern Cemetery, extending below Mountfort Street, from Congress to Federal Streets, has been in use for more than 250 years, and for more than two centuries of that period was the only graveyard within the city limits. The six acres of this crowded burial place, almost in the heart of the city, contain the graves of many of Portland's early and most prominent families. The oldest legible stone is dated 1717. Here, side by side, lie the bodies of the two gallant young commanders of one of the decisive naval battles of the War of 1812, Lieutenant William Burrows, commander of the victorious U. S. brig, ENTERPRISE, and Captain Samuel Blyth, commander of the British brig, BOXER, who were killed in action between Seguin and Monhegan September 5, 1813. Two days after the sea fight the ENTERPRISE arrived in Portland Harbor with the defeated British vessel. Then, to the accompaniment of booming guns and followed by nearly all the boats in the harbor, the officers' bodies were brought to shore in ten-oared barges rowed by ships' masters. Congress subsequently had a commemorative medal struck in honor of Lieutenant Burrows.

Near the graves of the commanders of the ENTERPRISE and the BOXER is a memorial to Lieutenant Henry Wadsworth, the uncle for whom Henry Wadsworth Longfellow was named. In September, 1804, this 20-year-old officer was killed off Tripoli when the fireship, INTREPID, dispatched to destroy the Tripolitan navy, was blown up to save it from capture. A monument commemorating this event stands at the western front of the Capitol in Washington.

An impressive marble tomb marks the grave of one of Portland's famous citizens, Commodore Edward Preble (1761-1807). In 1803, President Jefferson chose Preble to command the forces sent to conquer the Barbary pirates. Sailing for Tripoli with the celebrated CONSTITUTION for his flagship, Preble conducted so effective a campaign that the Barbary powers sued for peace at any terms. Pope Pius VII said of him that 'he had done more for Christianity in a short space of time than the most powerful nations have done in ages.'

Fore Street is as integrally a part of Portland as the far busier main thoroughfare, Congress Street. Its crooked course, lined with rows of weathered often ramshackle, brick and frame buildings, indicates the contours of the original Portland waterfront. Fore and contiguous streets which once were lanes bearing such names as Love, Fiddle, Fish, Lime, Turkey, and Moose Alley were long the commercial and residential centers of the city, and comprise the district which suffered most from the fire of 1866. Longfellow recalled the Fore Street of his youth, with its 'black wharves and the slips . . . and the Spanish sailors with bearded lips,' when the fashionable residential section still lay east of Congress Street. Here on Fore Street were the counting-houses, chandleries, slopshops, saloons, lodging-houses, and the warehouses crammed with West Indian goods. Wharves and piers were piled high with barrels of Jamaica rum, hogsheads of Puerto Rico molasses, and the thousands of feet of lumber that were hauled in from the surrounding country by ox teams, a practice which occasioned a bit of popular verse, which with many variations, was repeated all over the globe:

> 'From Saccarap' to Portland Pier
> I've hauled boards for many a year;
> Since this hard work, with much abuse,
> I'm salted down for sailor's use.'

Later on in its history certain sections of Fore Street acquired an unsavory reputation. With the laying out of Commercial Street in the middle of the 19th century, Fore was relegated to a position of secondary importance, but suffered only slight diminution of activity. By the close of the Civil War, however, the center of the city's business had moved away, and while Fore Street today is by no means devoid of traffic, the turbulent bustle of its heyday is long past. Many of its buildings are the tombs of a former prosperity and, whereas midnight was once but another hour to the scores of brawling and carousing sailors who frequented the street, its silence is now broken only by an occasional, perhaps furtive, footfall or the caterwauling of the stray cats that live in the deserted lofts and cellars. In the 1960s art shops were becoming the vogue in the area.

Henry Wadsworth Longfellow Birthplace Site, cor. Fore and Hancock Streets, is marked by a *Plaque* mounted on a boulder that came from his Grandfather Wadsworth's farm in Hiram. Born here in his aunt's house February 27, 1807, he was taken a few months later to the Congress Street house, now something of a shrine to his memory.

The great parliamentarian, *Thomas Brackett Reed* (1839-1902) born at 15 Hancock Street, grew up in this humble neighborhood. Serving in the Maine House and Senate and as Attorney General, Reed went to Congress in 1876 and was three times Speaker of the House. He was the author of *Reed's Rules.* His Portland home during adult life was at Deering and State Streets.

Grand Trunk Station Site, NE cor. Fore and India Streets is worthy of citation for its prominence in Portland history. Razed when passenger service declined, the station, a granite building with clock tower, was built in 1903 on the site of its predecessor, depot of the Atlantic and St. Lawrence Railway (1846). When grain became a principal cargo, two huge elevators rose east of the station, the company's three wharves with berthing space for nine vessels, alongside. The elevators had a capacity of two and a half million bushels. Unloading from freight cars to the elevators averaged 40 cars per ten-hour day. The grain was delivered from the bins to four steamers at a time at the rate of 10,000 bushels per hour per steamer. In earlier days, a rude steam-powered elevator on a scow operated like a mill hopper, delivering about 500 bushels an hour into a vessel's hatches.

It was here in 1680 that a stockade was built, later to become Fort Loyal.

In the year of the fort's erection, Thomas Danforth of Boston was appointed 'President of Maine,' and, invested with governmental authority, came to Falmouth Neck, where he held formal court within the fort's enclosure and established municipal government, the first ordered rule since Indians had destroyed the settlement in 1676. Grants of land were made, most of them in the India Street section, and a village was built along defensive lines. Ten years later the fort was enlarged into a strong fortification with four blockhouses and eight cannon. On May 17, 1690, nearly all the houses of the new community were destroyed by a force of 500 French and Indians, the inhabitants fleeing to the fort. After a three-day seige, during which the attackers had begun to undermine the defenses, the fort surrendered. The French commanders assured the defenders quarter and liberty to march south, but as soon as the gates were opened, the English were abandoned to the Indians. The survivors, many of them women and children, were taken captive and forced to make the arduous 24-day journey northward to Quebec. Fort Loyal was fallen and deserted. Two years later a party under Sir William Phips (*see Tour 1, sec. b*) and Captain Church stopped to bury the bleaching bones of those who had perished within and around the fort.

Until the laying-out of Commercial Street and the filling-in of the land, the tidewaters of Clay Cove approached to within a short distance of the fort plot. In 1826 this location became the site of a marine railway, a horse-drawn cradle affair, which was the first approach to a modern drydock in this region. Much of the land later occupied by the station and railroad yards was for some time given over to the clean wood-and-tar atmosphere of a shipyard. Vessels of small tonnage for the West Indian trade were launched here, but not before the Cove had been filled with floating logs which, piling up before the sterns, lessened the momentum of the vessels so that they did not run aground on the flats.

In 1853 the old fort site assumed a new and international importance. In that year the Atlantic and St. Lawrence Ry., subsequently leased to the Grand Trunk Ry., Co. of Canada, was completed between the port of Portland and Montreal. Dispute between Boston and Portland as to which city should be the American terminus for the railroad was settled in unique fashion. A boat leaving Liverpool bore two special mailbags for Montreal one to be left at Portland and one at Boston, the city from which the mail arrived first naturally becoming the choice for the terminus. A tug sent out from Portland intercepted the steamer, and in February, 1845, the Montreal-bound mail left Portland. Relays of horses, changed every seven miles, drew a sleigh northward through the snows of a severe New England winter. Three miles from Montreal a team of spirited horses and a stylish sleigh were given the driver, one Grosvenor Waterhouse. Bearing his immense figure erect, the American flag streaming out beside him from the whipsocket, Waterhouse urged his horses to a final tremendous burst of speed. The 255-mile drive was completed in the unparalleled time of 18 hours and 6 minutes, several hours ahead of the Boston mail. Thus Maine had demonstrated that Portland was the logical terminus for the projected railroad.

Commercial Street, with the waterfront, is vitally important in the city's commercial life. In 1850 increased trade and the projected railway to Canada seemed to demand better and more ample transportation and terminal facilities than were possible on Fore Street, which at that time bordered the water. Accordingly, in that year, Commercial Street, 100 feet broad, more than a mile long, with a 26-foot space in its center reserved for the railroad, was laid out across tidewater, running over the heads of the wharves. The area between Commercial and Fore Streets was later filled in;

the drop between the levels of the two streets is noticeable today. Thus, leaving Fore Street stranded, Commercial Street became the focus of maritime activity and trade.

Portland Waterfront, lying adjacent to Commercial Street, perhaps best gives the essential flavor of old Portland, its history and its dependence upon its position as a seaport. Portland is in transition here as it is uptown where a new look is apparent. The boom days of 1812 when, according to Kenneth Roberts' novel *Lively Lady,* there was free rum for the workers and free food on the waterfront, and those busy days of World Wars I and II are long gone. In 1937 there were more than a score of wharves, chief of which was the $1,500,000 Maine State Pier which today dominates the shoreline. A thousand feet long, the Pier provides two ocean berths with a 35-foot depth at mean low tide on the east side and three berths with lesser depth on the west side. With modern transit sheds and ample equipment for rapid handling of cargoes, the Pier has direct rail connections with tracks on Commercial Street and is the only public terminal directly served by railroads entering the city. In the 1960s, a few fishing schooners and freighters could be seen discharging their cargoes. Only the Casco Bay Lines serve island residents and summer tourists. With the disappearance of the Grand Trunk wharves and grain elevators, comes a new great terminal and development for the Portland-Yarmouth ferry that began operations in 1970. Of the old wharves that remain, their ends are now more than a quarter of a mile away from the original shoreline.

Portland Harbor presents a decrease-increase paradox. With some 26,260,000 tons of crude oil brought in to pipeline terminals in 1969, Portland is second in this category only to Philadelphia on the East coast. At the same time dry cargo tonnage dropped from 244,914 tons in 1961 to 50,000 in 1968; there were no exports. Although oil terminals get busier, Portland is a poorer port than it was in 1916 when only a seventh of today's tonnage passed through it. A ton of oil adds only about $2 to the waterfront economy, against the figure of $23 a ton for dry cargo. The Port of Portland's decline in the past half century has been attributed to regional economic changes.

Fort Allen Park, junction Fore Street and Eastern Promenade, affords an exceptional and unobstructed view of Casco Bay and its islands. Fort Allen, named for Commander William Henry Allen of the sloop-of-war, ARGUS, who was killed in action in 1813, was hastily built on the site of previous fortifications in 1814 when it was rumored that a British fleet was approaching Portland. The fort mounted five guns and was manned by regular soldiers and volunteers. In September, 1815, between 5000 and 6000 of the Cumberland and Oxford County Militia were encamped in the vicinity of these fortifications on Munjoy Hill. It was doubtless to these that Longfellow referred in his poem, *My Lost Youth*:

> 'I remember the bulwarks by the shore,
>   And the fort upon the hill;
> The sunrise gun, with its hollow roar,
>   The drum-beat repeated o'er and o'er,
> And the bugle wild and shrill.'

Fort Allen Park is landscaped with evergreens and other trees, shrubbery, and flower beds. Benches line the cement walks, and a large summer-house where band concerts are often held during the summer fronts the harbor mouth. Two large Civil War cannon face seaward, and an eroded cannon recovered from the MAINE is mounted in cement on a rough ledge. Recently added to the Park have been the main mast and the navigation bridge shield of the USS PORTLAND, a ship that served creditably in World War II.

A *Plaque* commemorates local boys who lost their lives in naval action during this war.

Eastern Promenade, more than a mile long, begins at Fore Street and extends to Washington Avenue. The scenic parkway, laid out in 1836, has a circular drive affording a panoramic view of the outer Harbor and Casco Bay. Extensive recreational facilities have been added. The *First Civic Monument* of Portland (1882), a granite shaft at E end of Congress Street on the Promenade, commemorates George Cleeve and Richard Tucker, the founders of Portland.

Fort Sumner Park, 60-80 North Street, is the site of fortifications built in 1794 when Congress made an appropriation for coast defense. Named in honor of Governor Increase Sumner of Massachusetts, the fort had little to recommend its site except its elevation; during the War of 1812 it was found necessary to erect new fortifications near the waterfront. In the spring of 1808 a company of 'sea fencibles' was organized here to 'do military duty at Fort Sumner': sentinels were stationed to watch for fires, and the firing of a cannon was to be the signal for the fire bells' ringing.

Portland Observatory (mid-June to Labor Day, weekdays 10-8; Sun. 1-7) opposite the junction of North and Congress Streets, rises 82 feet above Munjoy Hill, only remaining Nineteenth century signal tower on the Atlantic coast. A heavy-timbered octagonal structure resembling a windmill, with 10-by-14 inch corner posts 63 feet long, it was erected by Captain Lemuel Moody, a Revolutionary water boy, in 1807 and for 116 years did active service in informing the townspeople of approaching ships and noting cases of distress on land and sea. The top of the tower is estimated to be 223 feet above sea level; the builders weighted the cribbing above the sill with 122 tons of stone to hold it secure against Atlantic gales. From the lantern deck of the tower there is an extensive view of the coast from Wood Island, off the mouth of the Saco River, to Seguin, off the mouth of the Kennebec, while inland the Presidential Range of the White Mountains and peaks farther south are visible. A lookout was once on duty from sunrise to sunset, and flags were flown from the observatory to announce homecoming vessels. President James Monroe inspected the tower during his two days' visit to Portland in 1817.

CONGRESS SQUARE is the conjunction of Congress, High and Free Streets. Most of Portland's old homes spared in the 1866 conflagration are to be seen on High, Spring, Park, Danforth and State Streets, off Congress and Monument Squares, within a small radius. They signify the worldly success and the dignified and cosmopolitan culture of the seafaring and trading class of Portland's earlier days.

Public Library (1889), 621 Congress Street, is a Romanesque structure of red brick with facade of Ohio sandstone and Connecticut brown freestone, designed by Francis H. Fassett. First president was Portland historian William Willis. Collections include many of Thomas Bird Mosher's famous reprints and paintings by early Portland artists.

Cumberland Club House (1800) (*private*), 116 High Street, a well-preserved Georgian house designed from sketches by Alexander Parris.

L.D.M. Sweat Museum (1908) (*weekdays except Mon. 10-4;30; Sun. 2-4;30*), 103 High Street, a gallery of ivy-covered yellow brick, was designed by John Calvin Stevens and attached to the rear of the Sweat Mansion (*see below*). It houses such famous works as Gilbert Stuart's portrait of General Wingate, Douglas Volk's portrait of Abraham Lincoln, and paintings by John Singer Sargent, Winslow Homer, Chester Harding; a collection of paintings chiefly representative of Nineteenth century artists, outstanding among which are those of Maine's Harry W. Watrous; the Perry collection of Sixteenth-century Belgian tapestries; collection of Mexican and Indian potteries; all the work left by Franklin Simmons, famous Maine sculptor of the Nineteenth century; and Paul Akers's marble figure, the 'Dead Pearl Diver,' known to readers of Hawthorne's 'The Marble Faun' (*see THE ARTS*). The museum holds monthly exhibitions of contemporary paintings, water colors, and prints, an annual photographic salon which is internationally known, and an annual exhibition of the work of local artists. The Portland Society of Art, owner of the museum, conducts in an adjacent building the Portland School of Fine and Applied Arts. The school building, Greek Revival, was built in 1833 by Charles Q. Clapp.

Sweat Mansion (1800) (*hours as above*), cor. Spring and High Streets, is reached from the entrance hall of the Sweat Museum. It is a fine post-Colonial structure with a semicircular porch. It was erected by Hugh McLellan according to plans by Alexander Parris, a distinguished Boston architect who designed several of Portland's lovely houses of this period and at one time was the home of General Joshua Wingate, whose wife was a daughter of General Henry Dearborn, Secretary of War in the Cabinet of Thomas Jefferson.

On Spring Street, opposite the School of Fine Arts, is the *John J. Brown House* (1845) (*private*), Gothic Revival, and at No. 78, the *Nathan Cummings House* (1828), home of the Women's Literary Union.

On Pleasant Street are the *Thomas Delano House* (1800) at No. 127, an early Federal house now architects' offices, and the *Park Street Church* (1828) at No. 133, a Federal building owned by the Greek Orthodox Church.

The *Park Street Block* (1835) (*private*), W side of Park Street is an impressive Greek Revival row of city apartments. At 79 Park, the Greek Revival *J. B. Carroll Mansion* (1851) (*private)* was an elegant home of its era.

Victoria Mansion (1859) (*summer weekdays except Mon., 10:30-4:30*), cor. Danforth and Park Streets, home of the Victoria Society of Maine, was the Ruggles Sylvester Morse Libby Mansion. It has a flying staircase, carved woodwork and ornate furniture.

LONGFELLOW SQUARE is the confluence of Congress, State and Pine Streets. State Street resembles Boston's Beacon Street in the impressive old mansions built by wealthy merchants and shipping men during the wave of prosperity at the turn of the Nineteenth century and the boom following the Embargo depression. Although the stately interiors that saw the elaborate social functions of another era are not open to the public, the graceful porticoes and fine architectural lines retain an enduring charm. Some have the original landscaped gardens and grounds. Many of the city's finest churches are in this area.
Longfellow Statue (1888), a seven-foot bronze executed by Franklin Simmons, centers the square, a faithful and highly prized portrait of the poet. Money for the statue which cost $8500 was raised by penny donations from school children.

Neal Dow Homestead (1824) at 714 Congress Street is owned by the Maine W. C. T. U. which plans to open it to the public. The sedate gray-painted brick house was built by the ardent prohibitionist and author of the old Maine prohibition law, opposite his birthplace, 717 Congress Street. Many of the rooms are kept much as they were during the great agitator's occupancy. Neal Dow (1804-97), through his ceaseless activity, aroused statesmen and citizens all over the world to the social ramifications of prohibition; he inaugurated legislation that in many sections still is the subject of political controversy.

Deering Oaks, N downhill on State Street, the city's largest park lies between Deering and Forest Avenues. It was part of the historic estate of Nathaniel Deering, a shipbuilder who came from Kittery in 1761. His mansion stood back of the Park on property now part of the University of Maine's Portland campus. Longfellow found that 'Deering's Woods are fresh and fair' and so they have remained to this day, enhanced by flower beds, a pond with swans and fountain; tennis and bowling on the green in summer and skating in winter. In 1689, the wooded area was the scene of a long and bloody battle when Major Benjamin Church and his men succeeded in defending the town and routing a large force of Indians. Nearby on Park Avenue are the Park Department's greenhouses and the Maine Institute for the Blind.

S on State Street from Longfellow Square are the *John Neal Houses* (1836) (*private*), at Nos. 173-175, of granite blocks in Greek Revival style. John Neal (1793-1876), prominent Portland lawyer, athlete, and poet and a prolific writer, built these houses and settled here after a diversified career during which, at one time, he was self-appointed apostle of American letters in London, having gone there for the purpose of proving that there really existed an American culture. During his later life in Portland he greatly influenced many artistically gifted young people, such as Paul Akers.

Mellen-Fessenden House (1807), now the Monastery of the Precious Blood (*public chapel*), 166 State Street, its former post-Colonial charm considerably altered, was built by Prentiss Mellen (1764-1840), statesman, U. S. Senator, and Chief Justice of Maine. In 1848, the house came into the possession of the Hon. William Pitt Fessenden (1806-69), lawyer, politician, and financier, godson of Daniel Webster and son of General Samuel Fessenden, leader in the anti-slavery movement. He served in the House of Representatives and Senate, and in 1864, was appointed Secretary of the Treasury by President Lincoln who called him 'a radical without the petulant and vicious fretfulness of most radicals.' In 1934 the house was made the cloister of the Catholic Monastery of the Precious Blood, and seven Sister Adorers entered the building at the time, not to emerge until death.

Shepley House (1805), now the Portland Club, 162 State Street, the best preserved of the State Street houses. Designed from sketches by Alexander Parris for Richard Hunnewell, this three-story post-Colonial mansion was built of brick with frame walls in front and rear. The front doorway that replaced the original one is especially beautiful, with its leaded fan-light and side-lights. Over the door is an interesting Palladian window. The interior of the house has elaborate ceilings, fine paneling, and delicate mantelpieces. Many of the windows retain the original Belgian glass lights, marked with bubbles and other imperfections. On one window on the second floor someone has scratched with a diamond the names 'Lucy,' 'Annie,' 'Nellie,' and 'General George Shepley,' with the date July 19, 1816.

Saint Luke's Cathedral (1835), 137 State Street, is architecturally one of Portland's finest churches, the work of Henry Vaughan, distinguished English architect. The cathedral, of early English Gothic design, is constructed of soft blue Cape Elizabeth ledge stone. Buttresses and copings, door and window sills, are of Nova Scotia freestone, alternating in red and gray. One of the outstanding features is the rose window in the Sanctuary. The reredos, an unusually beautiful native piece of woodcarving, was done by Kirschmeyer, considered the finest woodcarver in the world at the time (1925), under the direction of the noted church architect, Ralph Adams Cram. In the Codman Memorial Chapel (1899) is a Madonna and Child, painted by John LaFarge.

Milliken House (1802) (*private*), 148 State Street, much changed from its original appearance, was built by Neal Shaw, a rope-maker. Until rope-making machinery came into use, the strands of hemp, in process of twisting, had to be pulled taut to their required length. The reaches of ground over which the rope was stretched were called ropewalks. Winter Street, parallel with State, originated as a ropewalk.

Ward Houses (1833) (*private*), 97-99 State Street were occupied at one time by James Rangeley whose name is borne by Maine's famous Rangeley Lakes, and by U. S. Senator Frederick Hale. No. 97 houses the American Red Cross.

Dole or *Churchill House* (1801) (*private*), 51 State Street, was designed by Alexander Parris for Joseph Ingraham, one of the town's wealthiest and most enterprising citizens. Now an apartment house, its classic lines, with applied pilasters and ornamental cornice, are worthy of attention. In this mansion for many years lived one of Portland's famous citizens, William Pitt Preble (1783-1857), jurist, diplomat, and railway president. Under President Jackson he was U. S. Minister to the Netherlands; upon his retirement from Government service in later life he became president of the new Atlantic & St. Lawrence Ry., and was instrumental in making Portland the terminus of the line.

Western Promenade, reached from Longfellow Square via Pine and West Streets, extends along a high ridge from Danforth to Arsenal Street and is the counterpart of the Eastern Promenade, planned at the same time. Here is a fine panoramic view of the Presidential range and other peaks, South Portland and Fore River. Along the Parkway are many fine homes. Sitting as a citadel on the north end of the Promenade is the *Maine Medical Center* whose four-story central section completed in 1874 from designs by Francis H. Fassett, has had many additions. A *Statue of Thomas B. Reed*, executed in bronze by Burr C. Miller, stands midway of the Promenade. In natural posture, 'Czar' Reed dominates the scene here as he often did when ruling the U. S. House of Representatives.

Williston Congregational Church (1878), modified English Gothic, 32-38 Thomas Street, is the birthplace of the Society of Christian Endeavor. Here in 1881 Rev. Francis E. Clark conceived the idea of organizing the young people of the world into one body for greater Christian growth. Twenty years later the society had become International.

Western Cemetery, Promenade, Danforth and Vaughn Streets, occupies ten acres on Bramhall Hill. Its memorial gateway of random rubble stone from Trundy's Island was erected in 1914.

Rotary Traffic Circle, (1939), St. John and Danforth Streets, was the first in Maine. The three-ton *Anchor* was the gift of the Propeller Club.

WOODFORDS, NE of Deering Oaks, is a part of Portland once known as Stevens Plains where a flourishing settlement of tinsmiths sprang up after the Revolution. It is now a residential area with several parks, churches and a shopping center.

Baxter Boulevard, 2.25 *m.* covering 30 acres, skirts Back Cove, haven of aquatic birds in migration. The Baxter Memorial near Woodford Street honors James Phinney Baxter, (1831-1921), Portland mayor who proposed the parkway. *Payson Park*, 47.75 acres between the Boulevard and Ocean Avenue, is a recreation area with playgrounds.

Baxter's Woods, between Forest and Stevens Avenues, is a 30-acre woodland and bird sanctuary maintained by the Longfellow Garden Club, with trails and two ponds. It was the gift in 1933 of Percival P. Baxter, Maine Governor 1921-25, whose generosity to the State and its people includes 3,000-acre Baxter State Park near Mt. Katahdin. Adjoining the Park is *St. Joseph's Convent and Academy for Girls,* 605 Stevens Avenue, opened by the Sisters of Mercy in 1881.

Westbrook Junior College, 716 Stevens Avenue, was incorporated in 1831 as a Seminary, the only co-ed boarding school in America at the time. Early degrees for women were LLL — Ladies of Liberal Learning. The Junior College for Women began in 1933 and many new buildings have been added.

STROUDWATER, reached from Congress Street on Waldo Street, 2 *m.* on direct route to Portland Airport, has some of the oldest homes in the city. Settled as early as 1680, the old Colonial village lying at the confluence of Stroudwater Stream and Fore River has been continuously populated since 1727, as a mill site and then as the terminus of the Cumberland and Oxford Canal which connected Casco Bay with the upper edges of Long Lake in Harrison, 18 miles distant (*see Tour 6*). Completed in 1830, the Canal required 27 locks. One account of the period says, 'The locktenders were generally characters, the boatmen as a rule wore red shirts and nobody, including the tow-horse grazing on the tow-path bank, was in any particular hurry. Sometimes if things didn't go right, there was some unScriptural language, and if boats were held up by breaks in the canal banks, so much the better. The combined crews would adjourn to the nearest public, where they would indulge in wrestling, boxing, story-telling, not omitting spiritual (sic) refreshment and the consolation of tobacco.'

While the area has undergone changes as elsewhere, the heart of Stroudwater as a closely built architectural unit has miraculously survived so that in its homes it is possible to trace its growth and decline. Nearby, the remains of the mill on the falls, the tidal mill and the canal excavations are reminders of man's ingenuity before the age of mechanization even as jet planes zoom from nearby airport runways.

In the center of the old village is *Tate House* (1775) (*Tues.-Sat., 11-5*), with its unusual wood paneling brought from England. Overlooking the old mastyard where its owner George Tate, mast agent, saw to the pines marked with the broad arrow of the King's surveyor, the house was authentically restored by the Maine Society of Colonial Dames.

Also in the area are the following private homes: *Captain James Means House* (1797), 2 Waldo Street, where General Lafayette was entertained in 1825. Capt. Means met the General when the captain was a member of Washington's Life Guard. *David Patrick House* (1743), cor. Congress Street, is the oldest in the group. *Tristram and Samuel Steven House* (1805), at 1282 Westbrook Street, was built by two ship carpenters and was once the home of Mrs. Lillian M. N. Stevens, a national president of the W.C.T.U. *Martin Hawes House* (1835), at 1266 Westbrook Street, is a charming stone house that replaced a wooden frame house of 1793. *Oakes Sampson House* (1802) at 1246 Westbrook Street, was later the studio home of Artist Walter Griffin of international reputation. *Francis Waldo House* (c.1765), also known as the Captain Daniel Doel House, 1365 Westbrook Street, had a huge fireplace in the attic and a stout door behind which the captain's slaves were locked each night.

RIVERTON once had a paper mill on the Presumpscot River which still furnishes power for Westbrook and Cumberland Mills. Mt. Sinai, Portland's only Jewish Cemetery is located here and a Friends Meetinghouse and Cemetery (1851) where Indian Chief Medoc, a Friends minister, lies buried. At the turn of the century Riverton had a popular trolley park for family outings.

WATERVILLE

Alt. 95, pop. 19,000, sett. c. 1754, incorp. town 1802, city 1883,

Access: NE and S, Interstate-95; NW and S, US 201; E, State 139; W, State 137-225.

Information: Chamber of Commerce, 82 Elm St.

Accommodations: Seven motels.

Transportation: Airport; buslines.

Parks: Monument Park.

Recreation: North St grounds, swimming pool; summer, winter sports, environs.

Cultural, historic sites: See **POINTS OF INTEREST**

WATERVILLE, known as the Elm City for its graceful wineglass trees, lies on a broad terraced plain along the west bank of the Kennebec River at Ticonic Falls. Historically important in the industrial development of the Kennebec Valley, it has become also a commercial, medical and cultural center crowned by Colby College on Mayflower Hill. The community's metamorphosis in recent years from a drab mill town to a pleasant small city, northernmost on the river, has been brought about through urban renewal, 'town and gown' rapport and the enterprise of its citizens. The city has become nationally known for its manufactures and in the fields of education and culture.

In the heart of the summer vacation and winter sports area, with the Belgrade Lakes chain to the west and China Lake and Weber Pond to the east, Waterville is a trading center for an outlying population of some 70,000. Special attraction is the Concourse, a spacious and agreeable shopping center created by urban renewal. Shopping areas, motels and other facilities also have grown up around exits of I-95, a four-lane divided through-way mid-State, at Kennedy Memorial Drive (S) and Upper Main St. (N). I-95, cited for scenic beauty in this area, reduces highway travel time to Boston to less than four hours. LaFleur Airport, 2 *m.* from the city, currently is served by Executive Airlines.

Waterville has two colleges, three hospitals, library, daily newspaper and radio station. Representing all branches of medicine, the hospitals form central Maine's medical center.

While the falls of the Kennebec power Waterville's mills, the drainage basins in the vicinity, those of the Kennebec, Messalonskee Stream west of the city and the Sebasticook River at Winslow, are equally important in the agricultural life of the region. Numerous farms in the suburbs suppiy dairy and farm produce for large city markets as well as local garden crops. Major industries are paper and molded products, worsteds, shirts, roofing and lumber. Two renowned products that originated in Waterville are Hathaway shirts, first made by C. F. Hathaway in 1847 and made famous in the Twentieth century by 'the man with the eye-patch,' and the Lombard Log Hauler, forerunner of the war tank and all other caterpillar treads.

Cultural life has burgeoned in Waterville, emanating from Colby's Mayflower Hill campus, particularly its Bixler Art and Music Center (*see THE ARTS*) which attracts a wide segment of the public interested in aesthetic and civic affairs. National figures lecture here and many Statewide seminars are held, as well as concerts and other presentations of the performing arts. Colby is known for its Art Museum and Jette Gallery and its Music Department whose current director, Peter Re, also is director of the Bangor Symphony.

The shores of the Kennebec in the Waterville area have seen much history — centuries ago the daily life of a large Indian village across the river and the solemnities of Indian burial ceremonies in what is now Waterville; the coming of the white man and the struggles of discontented soldiery at Fort Halifax in the winter of 1755, they 'being in a manner naked' and waiting miserably for shoes, clothing and supplies to be dragged upriver from Fort Western at Augusta; the shrill echoes from the snorting, puffing river steamers that churned their way to the city more than a century ago; and the thundering logs plunging over Ticonic Falls after their sweep through the Five Mile Rips above the city in the great days of the river-drivers.

The Canabas tribe of Indians, maintaining a large village along the banks of the Kennebec and Sebasticook Rivers opposite Waterville long before the coming of the English, held the central territory of the Wabanakis and were surrounded by sub-tribes of allied blood. The Jesuits already had begun their successful missionary work among the Indians but a few miles farther north at Norridgewock, penetrating the State from Canada, when the first English trading post was established in 1653 at Teconnet, as the Indians called the Waterville-Winslow region. Successful trading relations were sustained until the outbreak of Indian wars in 1675, and for seventy-five years thereafter the Indians are reputed to have used the first trading post and two successive ones as forts. In 1724 the Massachusetts expedition to subdue the Norridgewock Indians rendezvoused at

Ticonic Falls before going upriver to wipe out the settlement at Old Point and kill Father Rasle.

The construction of Fort Halifax at the confluence of the Kennebec and Sebasticook Rivers, forming the frontier and northernmost line of defense on the river, was begun in 1754 to prevent further Indian raids and to put an end to the war councils of the Penobscots and Kennebecs. Before the fortification was completed, Captain William Lithgow wrote Governor Shirley of Massachusetts concerning the state of affairs at Fort Halifax in January 1755, reporting that 'the men in general seem very low in spirits, which I impute to their wading so much in ye water, in ye summer and fall, which I believe has very much hurt ye circulation of their blood and filled it full of gross humors . . .' Like the Indian village before it, the fort was so strategically placed that the Penobscot Indians were cut off from their travel route by way of the Sebasticook and connecting waterways to the Kennebec, and the war council meeting grounds at Teconnet.

The fort also commanded the vital Indian route northward to Quebec by way of the Kennebec and the Chaudiere River. However, despite the hardships and 'gross humors' of the Halifax garrison, the fort was never attacked by French or Indians; it was dismantled with the exception of one blockhouse (now a National Historic Landmark), in 1763. During the decade of military occupation, contact was maintained between Teconnet and the settlements to the south by a military (carriage width) road cut through the wilderness to Augusta, and by whaleboat express to Portland. The scattered settlements of the upper Kennebec were too young and unorganized to give much aid during the Revolution, yet the men of Teconnet did assist Benedict Arnold and his force in 1775 when they made their one-third mile portage around Ticonic Falls on their disastrous march to Quebec. Waterville's pioneer physician, Surveyor John McKechnie, ministered to the sick among Arnold's soldiers.

When the town of Winslow was incorporated in 1771, its territory included land on both sides of the river. The first settlements had been made under the protection of the fort on the east side. It soon became apparent however, that the Messalonskee Stream on the west side of the Kennebec offered advantages for the small mills of the period. In its four-mile course the Messalonskee, emptying the seven Belgrade Lakes into the Kennebec, had four falls capable of producing power. When a dam was built across the Kennebec in 1792, its sluices were placed on the west side, facilitating erection of several mills there.

As the settlements grew on both sides of the Kennebec, government became increasingly difficult. The first meeting house, used both for religious services and town meetings, was built on the east side and still stands, the oldest church edifice north of Merrymeeting Bay. Soon after, another meeting house was erected on the west side near where Waterville City

Hall now stands. For several years, as worship and town affairs were conducted alternately on both sides of the river, citizens complained whenever an assigned meeting compelled one group or the other to cross the unbridged stream; not until 1825 was a toll bridge built across this place. Dissension also was caused by a double set of officials including two tax collectors. By 1802, the west side community, then called Ticonic Village, with a population of 800 had grown so fast that the Massachusetts legislature granted its petition to become a separate town, to be known as Waterville.

The new town grew rapidly; its early growth may be attributed largely to its geographical location and the development of facilities during the eras of water and rail transport. Passenger and freight service on the river was inaugurated in 1832 by the steamship, TICONIC, and competition in river traffic soon became so keen that the fare from Waterville to Boston was only one dollar. Despite the low steamship rate, building of the Androscoggin and Kennebec Railroad in 1849 and the completion of the railroad to Portland and Bangor six years later presaged the doom of water-borne commerce up and down the Kennebec. Through alliance with the ubiquitous railroad promoter, John Poor, the incorporators of the Androscoggin & Kennebec made connections with Poor's Atlantic & St. Lawrence (later the Grand Trunk), at Danville Junction near Lewiston, thus bringing the iron horse to Waterville several years before it reached the capital city of Augusta. When the Brunswick-Augusta line was extended through Waterville to Skowhegan, Waterville became the most important rail junction between Portland and Bangor. After the several lines were consolidated into the Maine Central System, establishment of the Maine Central railroad shops at Waterville assured the city's industrial and commercial prominence. With the decline of rail travel, passenger service was eliminated but the Shops were retained and Waterville remained an important freight junction in 1969.

Until transfer was completed in 1952 to Mayflower Hill, Colby College campus for more than a century occupied a once scenic riverbank site on College Avenue that grew progressively more dingy and depressing amid the railroad tracks. In 1970, the smoke-stained old college buildings and Maine Central station are gone and Engine 470, last steam locomotive operated by the Maine Central (June 13, 1954) were an historic landmark on the old Colby campus.

Colby College originated in 1813 when, upon petition of prominent Baptists in the State, a charter was granted to the Maine Literary and Theological Institution. Five years later the Rev. Jeremiah Chaplin with his family and seven students from Danvers, Mass. ventured up the Kennebec, traveling by sloop to Augusta and thence by longboats to Waterville, and began the theological department of the institution. In 1820 the Legislature granted power to bestow degrees and the following year the name was changed to Waterville College. The theological department was discontinued after 1825 and in 1867 the institution became Colby College, in honor of the benefactions of Gardner Colby, a Boston merchant. Colby became co-educational in 1871 and has become a progressive liberal arts college attracting students from all over the United States and a dozen foreign countries. In 1968 Colby had 1540 students and a distinguished faculty of 133. Its 40 buildings adorning Mayflower Hill include contemporary as well as traditional architecture, new dormitories in 1968 winning a national award.

The roster of illustrious Colby graduates includes many who have distinguished themselves in education, law, and politics. One of the two members in Colby's first graduating class in 1822 was George Dana Boardman (1801-31), pioneer missionary to Burma. Elijah Parish Lovejoy (1802-37), an 1825 graduate, was a strong anti-slavery newspaper editor who fought for freedom of the press. In Missouri and Illinois Lovejoy expressed his convictions in the face of threats and mob violence. Shot by a mob of pro-slavery rioters in Alton, Illinois, twenty-four years before the outbreak of the Civil War, Lovejoy became one of the earliest martyrs in the cause of freedom for slaves. An annual award is named in his honor. Benjamin Butler, Civil War general, governor of Massachusetts and a figure in national politics, was graduated with the Colby class of 1838.

POINTS OF INTEREST

Colby College, Mayflower Hill, 2 *m*. W. of city center, or from N and S Exits I-95 (*guided tours by advance arrangement, Eustis Administration Building; summer tours leave frequently from the Admissions Office*).

The *Bixler Art and Music Center*. The notable collections and changing exhibits of the Art Museum and the Jette Gallery are open to the public. The Center also includes Given Auditorium where lectures and concerts are held, and modern facilities for art and music instruction.

Of special interest in the *Miller Library* are the Edwin Arlington Robinson Memorial Room with its several thousand rare books and manuscripts, the James Augustine Healy Collection of modern Irish Literature, the model of Memorial Hall, last building to stand on the old campus, Milmore's famous copy of the Lion of Luzern commemorating Colby men who fell in the Civil War.

In *Lorimer Chapel* is a tablet recognizing Colby's long list of missionaries to all parts of the world, plaques honoring Elijah Parish Lovejoy, Samuel Francis Smith and other distinguished Americans with Colby associations; and the Walker organ constructed from specifications drawn by Albert Schweitzer.

The college has a recently completed physical education and athletic complex and dormitories designed by Benjamin Thompson.

Thomas College, formerly a proprietary business school, has been since 1956 a non-profit trustee-managed college granting degrees in Business Administration and Education and secretarial studies. Although professionally oriented, the curriculum is based on a solid foundation of liberal arts. The Silver Street campus was moving in 1970 to a spacious expandable site on Sydney Road with a $3 million plant.

Coburn Classical Institute, founded in 1829 as Waterville Academy, took its present name when its major building and an impressive endowment were given by Maine's Governor Abner Coburn. After the main building was destroyed by fire in 1955, it became a country day school. It too has a new site away from the city center, near the north exit of I-95. In 1970 it merged with Oak Grove Seminary, Quaker school for girls at Vassalboro.

Redington Museum (May 1 - Nov. 1, Tues., Sat., 2-6), 64 Silver Street, is one of Waterville's oldest residences where Colonial and early Nineteenth century artifacts are exhibited. Built in 1814 by pioneer settler, Asa Redington, it was given by a descendant to the Waterville Historical Society in 1905. The Society's collections of artifacts, pictures, costumes, books and documents have become so voluminous that an addition to the building is planned.

Monument Park, Elm Street, with its Civil War monument, is the site of the first municipal cemetery, becoming a park when graves were removed to the larger Pine Tree Cemetery on the city's outskirts. Its neighbor is the *First Baptist Church,* oldest denominational meetinghouse in Waterville. The sanctuary is on the original foundation of 1825. Across from the Church is the *Carnegie Library* with more than 50,000 volumes and special services for all ages.

Indian Burials. Along the river bank adjoining Front Street, from Temple Street to Lockwood Square, is the site of an ancient Indian burying ground where modern excavations frequently reveal bones and artifacts of the red men of long ago.

Footbridge. Crossing the river at the foot of Temple Street is the only remaining toll footbridge in the country, it is said.

Ticonic Falls may be seen from the bridge between Waterville and Winslow. Since the first bridge was thrown across the Kennebec at this point in 1824, reconstruction has been necessary six times due to flood damage.

ENVIRONS

Fort Halifax Blockhouse in Winslow, 1.4 *m.,* is the last one of this period extant in the U. S. Like others of its time, this structure was designed like the old English forts. A stockade formed a square enclosure and blockhouses stood in the SW and NE corners; a row of barracks extended along the E side and a sentry box stood at the SE corner. Officers' quarters, storehouse and armory were housed in a two-story building. Two small blockhouses enclosed by stockades stood on the hill at the rear of the Fort, one overlooking Ticonic Falls on the Kennebec. The remaining weather-beaten blockhouse, built of hand-hewn timbers fastened with wooden dowels, is typical of such structures used during the Indian wars. The upper story, with musket and look-out holes, overhangs the lower one, enabling the defenders to fire through the holes before the enemy could reach the door to force it or get close enough to set the blockhouse on fire.

WINSLOW (alt. 100, Winslow Town, pop. 5891) at the confluence of the Kennebec and Sebasticook Rivers is within the boundaries of a former large Indian village. Many artifacts were unearthed in the vicinity before the land was inundated in the building of a dam. Capt. William Lithgow, first commander at Fort Halifax, built a home in Winslow. *Ticonic Falls* is seen from the bridge.

In *Fort Hill Cemetery*, dating from 1772, the epitaph on early settler Richard Thomas' gravestone reads:

'A Whig of seventy-six
By occupation a cooper
Now food for worms like
An old rum puncheon
Marked, numbered, and shooked
He will be raised again
And finished by his creator.'

Buildings on the river bank are the *Hollingsworth Whitney Company Mills* (*permit at office*), pulp and paper manufacturers.

N from Waterville on State 11 to *Good Will Farm (visitors)* 10 *m.*, an endowed institution founded in 1889 by the Rev. George W. Hinckley, for boys and girls. Its Museum contains collections of minerals, flora and fauna, Indian artifacts, early farm implements and Colonial furniture.

En route, State 11 passes through FAIRFIELD (alt. 115, Fairfield Town, pop. 5829), home of the Keyes Fibre Company and other manufactories. Half a mile N of the business section, on the river bank, a *Granite Seat* marks another stopping place on Arnold's march to Quebec. In Fairfield, Martin L. Keyes, founder of the fibre company, built an elaborate turreted and crenalated structure as his home in 1905.

From Waterville W on State 11 (S) or State 137 (N) through the *Belgrade Lakes* chain of resort areas, via Oakland, home of the New England Music Camps.

E on State 137 to CHINA (alt. 222, China Town, pop. 1561), 8 *m.*, resort town at NE end of China Lake, a clear blue body of water lying below highway level in a long hollow between the hills. In 1818, when the town was incorporated, the name was changed from Harlem to China. There was considerable controversy over boundaries and Postmaster J. C. Washburn wrote: 'My house was in Winslow, my store across the road in Albion, and my potash works 40 rods S were in Harlem.'

Quaker and Baptist churches (ca. 1835) are located here and the Albert Church Brown Library, over 130 years old, has collections of area memorabilia. Rufus M. Jones, Quaker minister and long a president of Haverford College, summered here. He authored many books on ethics and Quaker history.

NE from China 2 *m.* on State 9 is *Lovejoy Pond* on whose S shore stood the birthplace of Elijah Parish Lovejoy (1802-1937), anti-slavery leader and pioneer in defense of freedom of the press. Graduating with honors from Colby College which has established an award in his honor, he went to St. Louis, Missouri, where he preached and fought against slavery. In 1833 he began editing the *St. Louis Observer*, a religious paper in which his anti-slavery views were expressed. Strong opposition in the slave state forced him to move across the river to Alton, Illinois. Mobs attacked him and his presses were frequently destroyed. He procured new ones and demanded protection as an American citizen to carry on his work. He was killed while defending his press against a mob. On a 93-ft. granite shaft topped with a bronze statue of Victory, erected to his memory in Alton, Ill., are these words: 'As long as I am an American citizen, and as long as American blood runs in these veins, I shall hold myself at liberty to speak, to write, and to publish whatever I please on any subject, being amenable to the laws of my country for the same.'

Another 1.3 *m.*, near Albion, *Rum and Water Elms* were planted during the temperance agitation of 1845. Members of the village Washingtonian Society, a temperance group, and the anti-prohibitionists agreed to plant rows of elm trees on either side of the road; the group whose elms made the finer showing was to be considered the one favored by Providence. The Washingtonians planted on the S side, the anti-prohibitionists on the north. The 'rum' elms grew larger and gave better shade than the 'water' elms.

III. HIGHWAYS AND BY WAYS

MAINLAND TOURS

A road network of some 21,000 miles with numerous parks and picturesque rest areas invites exploration of many-splendored Maine in all directions and the discovery of her infinite variety in all seasons. Coastal and inland tours along these highways and byways are designed to give a wide spectrum of the Maine scene for visitors and residents, sportsmen and armchair travellers.

Here is Maine and her people, the past illuminating the present. Here is the Nation's northeast corner, first to see the morning sun, her rocky ramparts ever embracing the ceaseless assault of the sea. Here is the historic land of pine and pioneer, of ship and sail, of forts and lighthouses and Atlantic isles; of farm and forest, mountain, lake and stream; of potato field and parkland; of landscape and seascape unsurpassed; of fisherman and factoryman, lumberman and logger, poet and painter — and an enviable way of life, generated in a rich historical heritage since the Seventeenth century. This euphoria is not to be confused with utopia. In the changing world of the Twentieth century, Maine too has her problems, economic and environmental. Nor is poverty and want unknown. Ways are sought to harness economic development with conservation, to preserve and enhance the exceptional environment and the priceless and economically basic natural resources whose delights are among the discoveries 'on tour,' to be enjoyed with thought for those who come after.

While each season has its special attractions, summer and autumn of course are the touring seasons in the northeast (*see GENERAL INFORMATION*). Tours are arranged for their interest enroute rather than for rapid transit. They may be taken in reverse or in selected segments. Recommended for direct access to specific areas and for connections with Guide tours are the Maine Turnpike (toll) and Interstate 95 bisecting the State from Kittery to Houlton with exits to principal population centers and resort areas (*see Guide and State Highway maps*). Mileages are approximate due to road and driving variables.

TOUR 1: *From* NEW HAMPSHIRE LINE (*Portsmouth*) *to* CANADIAN LINE (*Clair, N. B.*), 551.8 *m.*, US 1.

Via (*sec. a*) York Corner, Wells, Kennebunk, Biddeford, Saco, Portland, Falmouth Foreside, Yarmouth, Brunswick; (*sec. b*) Bath, Wiscasset, Thomaston, Rockland; (*sec. c*) Camden, Belfast, Searsport, Stockton Springs, Bucksport, Orland, Ellsworth; (*sec. d*) Cherryfield, Machias, Robbinston, Calais; (*sec. e*) Woodland, Princeton, Danforth, Houlton, Littleton, Mars Hill, Presque Isle, Van Buren, St. David, Madawaska, Fort Kent.

For side tours see TOURS 1A to 1K and ISLAND TRIPS.

US 1 from one end of the State to the other follows the east coast, then swings north along the St. Croix River and the Canadian boundary, finally doubling back west along the St. John River. It connects the two ends of Maine's 3500 mile tidal coastline, equal to half the entire Atlantic seaboard but only 225 air miles. With side roads from seven to 25 miles long fingering the shoreline to the sea, US 1 unfolds a vast historic and scenic panorama from Kittery to Eastport and Calais, neighboring with Canada before reaching the St. John Valley. Sandy beaches and resort areas of the southern section give way to rugged bluffs and granite headlands eternally pounded by the sea as the route winds through marsh and meadow, rolling farmlands, rocky pastures, fishing villages and residential towns, primitive woodlands, blueberry and potato acres, over high hills and along broad river banks.

Industries as well as summer pleasures are identified with towns and villages all along the coast where three centuries ago the early settlers first fought to colonize a new land, wresting their livelihood from the wilderness and raising their families, dwellings and houses of worship. Here they built the ships that became famous around the world, and the sawmills, forerunners of the great industry that made Maine the lumber capital of a young nation. Human continuity is sensed as the story of this past evolving into the present unfolds in the old forts, homes, meeting houses and museums and the current customs and life styles of these colorful coastal communities.

While fishing, Maine's oldest industry, shipbuilding and shipping continue along the coast, pleasure craft share these waters in summer — sailing, speedboating, excursion steamers to the islands, and the like. Swimming, snorkeling, surfing, sports fishing and shoreside activities, golf, theatre, concerts, art shows, festivals, are highlights in the resort areas. Accommodations along the coast range from inns, hotels and motels with swimming pools to more modest quarters, as well as boatels and campsites. Advance reservations are recommended. Dress is informal; wraps are needed most evenings. Seafood, especially Maine's famous lobsters are featured on most menus, with occasionally superlative 'down-east' dishes and European cuisine.

Snow-covered headlands and icy seas have special charm for the winter visitor whether or not he is headed for nearby ski and winter sports centers. In fair weather unreal saffron suffuses the gray dawning light; briefly at midday the skies are blue as Persian tiles; under the streaming green and rose of late afternoon, the snow becomes pale heliotrope with purple shadows. Not so charming may be the snowstorm that created this lovely picture — the blustering nor'easter with its 'wolf-winds howling from their Norways' even as they did in the days of the rugged pioneers.

To reach its terminus, US 1 moves from the coast inland north and west through the vast forests and farmlands of the 'Aroostook'; from men of the sea to men of the land. This is big country, another world, a land of mountains, lakes and streams, great woodlands and broad, fertile plains. Diversified large-scale agriculture and industry go hand in hand with the pursuits of the outdoorsman — hunting, fishing, hiking, canoeing, winter sports (*see RECREATION*). Hotels and motels provide accommodations in cities and towns; there are sporting camps for hunters and fishermen, camping and tenting sites for nature lovers, and visits to neighboring Canada for foreign flavor. The State of Maine provides a number of campsites and rest areas, is strict about fire in the woods and likes visitors to 'keep Maine scenic.'

Sec. a NEW HAMPSHIRE LINE (Portsmouth) to BRUNSWICK, 76 m.
Two interstate bridges span the Piscataqua River, southern boundary between the State of Maine and New Hampshire, at Kittery in York County, significant historic area settled early in the Seventeenth century. A third high-level bridge (1972) will connect directly at York Corner 5 *m.* with the Maine Turnpike (toll) and I-95, inland and express routes for principal cities and resort areas. The Maine Information Center (*maps, literature, exhibits, rest rooms*) is located to serve all motorists coming into Maine.

US 1, once part of the King's Highway from Boston to Machias, crosses the New Hampshire line in the center of Memorial Bridge. Bearing R never far from the sea, this section of US 1 and side tours pass through historic coastal towns and resort areas, touching Portland, Maine's largest city. On the southern half of the route, efforts are being made to improve shabby and congested commercial areas marred by unsightly signs that have burgeoned over the years of unplanned development.

From Memorial Bridge, 0 *m.*, US 1 crosses Badger's Island where the

RANGER, first ship to fly the American flag, was built in 1777. At end of bridge in *John Paul Jones Park* State Memorial are three monuments with bronze plaques. The granite rock near the flagpole bears this inscription:

> THE PROVINCE OF MAINE originally extending from the Merrimac to the Kennebec Rivers was granted Aug. 10, 1622 to Sir Ferdinando Gorges and Captain John Mason by the Council for New England established at Plymouth by King James I in 1620. This territory was divided between them in 1629 and confirmed by the Council in 1635, when Gorges received the eastern portion, extending from the Piscataqua to the Kennebec, which thereafter retained the original name of the Province of Maine.

The plaque on the tall granite rectangle reads:

> In memory of the continental sloop of war *RANGER* launched from this island May 10, 1777. Sailed for France November 1, 1777, JOHN PAUL JONES, CAPTAIN, with dispatches of Burgoyne's surrender. Received February 14, 1778, The first salute to the Stars and Stripes, from the French fleet. Captured the British sloop of war *DRAKE* April 14, 1778.

The maternal figure by Sculptor Bashka Paeff honors Maine's World War I sailors and soldiers with Kipling's words: 'Lord God of Hosts, Be with us Yet, Lest We Forget, Lest We Forget.'

At traffic light, junction with State 103 (*see Tour 1A*).

> Left on State 103, once an Indian trail and said to be Maine's oldest road in constant use, to ELIOT (alt. 50, pop. 3500), 15 *m.*, formerly a farming, fishing and lumbering community now predominately residential, with an inn, picnic grounds and marina where once brick and shipyards lined the six-mile Piscataqua River shoreline.

> Inscribed bronze plaques identify 13 of Eliot's noteworthy landmarks. Among them: *Site of William Everett's Tavern* where Maine's submission to Massachusetts was signed Nov. 16, 1652; *Grave of Rev. John Rogers* (1714-68), direct descendant of the martyr and Eliot's first minister whose 52-year pastorate is one of the longest of record. Greenacre Bahai School occupies the river-bank site of the Hanscom Shipyard (1846-55) that built the clipper *NIGHTINGALE* in 1851 for the Swedish singer, Jenny Lind.

> In Eliot also are the sites of Maine's first Normal School and the first Quaker Meetinghouse (1776). A *Marker* opposite post office proclaims: 'Here lived Moses Gerrish Farmer, the electrical pioneer. Born Feb. 9, 1820, died May 25, 1893. He invented the fire alarm telegraph, the duplex telegraph and was the discoverer of the self-exciting power of the dynamo.' One of the many historic homes is that of Noah Emery (1699-1761), first King's Council for the Province of Maine.

US 1 veers R, soon crosses York River over Rice's Bridge, 1702 ferry site.

At 7.6 *m.*, junction with State 91.

> Left on State 91 to *Grave of Handkerchief Moody 1.9 m.* (L). The Rev. Moody whose guilt feelings prompted him always to wear a handkerchief

over his face, was the subject of Hawthorne's story, 'The Minister's Veil.'

At 2.6 *m.*, *McIntire Garrison* (L) (NHL) (*private*), one of the oldest still standing in Maine. Built before 1692 by Alexander Maxwell it has been in the McIntire family since 1707. The building is constructed of heavy timbers interlocking at the corners, and sheathed on the outside with weather-beaten shingles. As was customary in early garrisons, the second story overhangs the first so that beleaguered defenders could pour hot pitch and grease upon the enemy below.

Maud Muller Spring, 4.5 *m.* (R) where a maiden raking hay inspired Whittier's familiar poem.

YORK CORNER (alt. 60, York Town, pop. 5660), 7.8 *m.* Maine Information Center, Turnpike Tollhouse. Junctions with Chase's Pond Road and State 1A.

Right on State 1A for the Yorks and Shore route to Ogunquit (*see Tour 1A*).

Left on Chase's Pond Road is *Snowshoe Rock* 1.4 *m.* (L) where Indians planned the 1692 Candlemas Massacre.

Mt. Agamenticus (alt. 692) 7 *m.*, center of Big A ski resort and summer playground and highest of a three-pronged hill, has been a navigation point since the days of square-riggers. A huge cairn of stones is a landmark on the summit where a fire tower affords a spectacular view encompassing the White Mountains W and the Atlantic Ocean E.

The great Indian sachem, 'Saint' Aspinquid, is said to be buried on the mountain. He was born in May 1588, a Pawtucket of the Algonquians, then the largest and most powerful Indian family in America. At 43, after John Eliot had converted him to Christianity, Aspinquid traversed the forests from coast to coast, telling of a sure way to the Happy Hunting Grounds. As age grew upon him, he was greatly venerated by all Indians. When he died in 1692, aged 94, his funeral was conducted with great pomp and ceremony. A huge collection of animals, numbering 6723 accounts say, was sacrificed to the departed spirit. One antiquarian believes Aspinquid and Passaconaway to be the same person because of the similarity of age and reputation in accounts of the two, theorizing that Passaconaway returned to Agamenticus during King Philip's War, received the name of Aspinquid from the Wabanakis, and died there. Traces of the burial cave are sought to this day.

CAPE NEDDICK (alt. 50, York Town), 11.7 *m.* On the River Road are *Cape Neddick Park (woodland trails, picnic and play areas)* and *Kuhn House (art exhibits).* Junction with State 1A.

Right on State 1A to Shore Road for Ogunquit N and York S (*see Tour 1B*) At 14 *m. Pinetree Design Galleries* (L), and beyond, *Ogunquit Summer Playhouse* (R). Soon, junction with Mountain Road (L) to Big A recreation area, 6.7 *m.*

OGUNQUIT (alt. 50, Wells Town) 14.8 *m.* Indian scholar, Fannie Eckstrom, interpreted the Wabanaki word 'Obumkegg' (sandbar) as Ogunquit which also is said to derive from 'O'dawonkak,' appearing in

Abenakis (1884) by Chief Sozap Tolo (Joseph Larent). Colonial records indicate the Maine Wabanakis camped along the Ogunquit River in summer, gathering seafood and planting and harvesting crops. Their shell heaps, often several feet deep, on the seaward edge of the fields have yielded many artifacts.

Mingling past and present, Ogunquit in its verdant setting by the sea has become known for its special charm as an art center (*see THE ARTS*) and summer resort. Artists and actors, vacationists and innkeepers, fishermen and fishing smacks, pleasure craft and excursion boats, lobster pounds and continental cuisine, studios and boutiques along village lanes color the summer scene, at once lively and leisurely. A street from the village square leads to dockside and the three-mile sandy beach and its rolling sand dunes.

Ogunquit's reputation as an art center had its beginning at the turn of the century when Charles H. Woodbury arrived in 1890 and called it Artists Paradise. Sharing with him were Elihu Vedder, Walt Kuhn, Harrison Easter Field, Yasuo Kuniyoshi and later artists who have become widely known in many styles of painting. The Ogunquit Art Association was born in Woodbury's Studio in 1928. Among those helping to form the colony was Rudoph Dirks, post-Impressionist, who created Hans and Fritz, the Katzenjammer Kids whose antics in a syndicated comic strip continued through two world wars and several revolutions in public taste. Each summer, 50 professional Association members exhibit in the *Barn Gallery* on Shore Road, which also is the home of the Field Art Foundation collection and the J. Scott Smart Sculpture Court (*weekdays 10-5; eves. 8-10; Sun. 2-5*).

In its 38th year (1970), John Kane's Summer Playhouse on US 1 presents nationally known stars in a variety of plays and musicals.

Museum of Art of Ogunquit (summer weekdays 10:30-5; Sun. 1:30-5), architectural gem on Shore Road overlooking Narrow Cove, shows work of American artists and sculptors. Henry Strater built the Museum and presented it to the village. Glass wall vistas to the sea are a breathtaking setting, particularly for the sculpture.

Memorial Library (1897), also on Shore Road, gift of Mrs. George Conarroe of Philadelphia, is built of matching fieldstones, the interior having the dark oak beams and high windows familiar in old England.

Ogunquit Art Center (annual exhibits), Hoyt Lane, was created from the studio of Nunzio and Dorothy Vanya who came to Ogunquit half a century ago. *Maxwell House* in the Lane was a stagecoach Inn in 1742.

Pinetree Design Gallery (Mon.-Sat. 9-5) (special exhibits), S on US 1, is one of the larger galleries. Scattered through the area are many small galleries, studios and workshops. Art classes have been held here for many years.

Most scenic is *Marginal Way*, a mile-long footpath winding above the edge of the sea, serene and unspoiled, with endless long views and close-ups of plants, minerals, tide pools, birds and marine life. A gift of Josiah Chase of York in 1925, the path was dedicated in 1947 by his daughters, with a bronze marker on Onzio Hill where the Way begins, to follow the shore to *Perkins Cove*, a focal point for visitors with its shops, restaurants and boating.

Crossing Josiah's River at the Cove is New England's only *Foot Drawbridge*, an unusual sight in operation. It is raised to allow boats to go in and out, lowered for pedestrians to cross the Cove. Ogunquit's oldest house is now the Whistling Oyster, restaurant and gift shop, at the Cove. Poor Richard's Inn here was once a stagecoach tavern.

Folklore tells of an island once about a mile offshore where villagers often took their swine for the summer, and annually went to gather beach plums and blueberries. They called it Plum Island — until one day they looked and no island was there. It had disappeared overnight. When fishermen went to investigate they found a shadow indicating a reef at the site. Here is said to be Sunken Island where fishermen now set their lobster traps.

WELLS (alt. 50, Wells Town, pop. 4750), 20 *m*. Settled by the English, Wells was named by Sir Ferdinando Gorges for the English city of that name. Edmund Littlefield came in 1641 and built the first mill on the Webhannet River. Shipbuilding and trading were followed by produce farming. Wells-built brigs and barks sailed to the West Indies, Turk's Island, the Leewards and Venezuela bearing lumber and dried fish to trade for rum, molasses and salt.

Near Wells Corner is the *First Congregational Church* (L), home of the Wells-Ogunquit Historical Society. The first church in Wells, built on this site in 1643 by Rev. John Wheelwright, was burned by Indians in 1692. The Rev. Wheelwright who shared the beliefs of Anne Hutchinson, the non-conformist, was exiled from Massachusetts and New Hampshire, found refuge in the Province of Maine and later made his peace with Massachusetts. While he was a student at Oxford, a classmate was Oliver Cromwell who later in life said that he had never felt so much fear before any enemy as before Wheelwright in competitive sports. Rev. Wheelwright's grandson, Col. John Wheelwright (d. 1745), is among early settlers buried in *Ocean View Cemetery* at Wells, his likeness carved on a stone marker, the second oldest in New England, recorded in the Maine Historical Society's photographic Archives of Colonial Gravestones.

On a short distance is *Storers Garrison* (R), a two and a half story building with granite foundation. A *Marker* tells of a three-day siege by French and Indians in June 1692. Wells, the only town not conquered, suffered many attacks during the Indian Wars between 1650 and 1730. In August 1703, Indians captured Esther Wheelwright, great-granddaughter of the minister and daughter of the colonel. She was taken to Canada and sold to Father Bogot who brought her to the Governor. She lived with his family and went to the Ursuline Convent, the only English girl ever to become Mother Superior of the Ursulines. She is said to have nursed Montcalm and participated in his burial after the seige of Quebec.

From the days of witchcraft trials, the story is told of one George Burrows who preached in Wells and proved a brave man during many Indian raids. But no one dared to come to his aid when Salem men carried him off under arrest for witchcraft. Enroute to Salem, it is said, a black, witch-like form swooped from the woods to follow the team and horses which were now swept up and borne through the air amid horrendous thunder and lightening. To this day, the place is known as Witch's Trot. Burrows? He was tried and hanged for a witch, on testimony of a young girl who accused him of practising witchcraft on her in Salem while he was living in Wells.

Of the many taverns and ordinaries that stood in Wells which was on the King's Highway and two other stagecoach routes, only two remain: the *Lindsay Tavern* (1799) *(public)* and the Lydia *Littlefield Tavern (private)*.

At Wells, three roads (R), one opposite Moody's post office, lead to the beaches (*marina, bathing, fishing, sailing, shops, restaurants*). Junction with State 9 (*see Tour 1B*).

KENNEBUNK (alt. 20, Kennebunk Town, pop. 6,500), 25 *m.*, is notable for its fine Nineteenth century architecture and great elms, among them the huge Lafayette Elm named for the French Marquis. Settled c. 1650, Kennebunk like other early communities was threatened by Indians for nearly a century. By 1730, shipbuilding had begun along the Mousam and Kennebunk Rivers. This industry and lively West Indian trade gave the town importance until the Revolution. After the War, industry resumed in small mills along the Mousam. Today Kennebunk manufactures surveying instruments, drafting machines, electronic devices and plastic products. It has one of the few municipally owned power plants in the State.

The *Brick Store Museum (Tues.-Sat., 10-4:30),* is a complex of six units restored to resemble their Colonial past. There are historical exhibits and collections, art galleries, monthly programs May through August; art exhibits July-August; workshop classes.

The *Storer House* (1758) *(private)*, first house (R) on Storer St., birthplace of Kenneth Roberts, was the home of Revolutionary General Joseph Storer who entertained his friend General Lafayette here in 1825 during Lafayette's American tour. The large yet simple structure is representative of the excellent taste in home building of the pre-Revolutionary period. Nearby, the spreading *Lafayette Elm* has grown so large that several of its massive limbs have had to be supported.

The *Bourne Mansion* (1812) *(private)*, second house (L) on Bourne St., is a square three-story structure with four chimneys, one at each corner. Interior features are the fine-paneled fireplaces and the spiral staircase of three flights with an arch-embellished niche for a tall clock between the second and third floors.

The *Nathaniel Frost House* (1799) *((private)*, (R) on Main St. is another of the splendid homes built by prosperous merchants and shipowners, in the town's affluent period.

The *First Parish Unitarian Church* (1774) (L) at the north entrance to the village, was remodeled in 1803 and in 1838. The steeple surmounts a three-story tower with front windows; over the open belfry is a three-faced clock beneath an octagonal lantern cupola with elliptical windows. In the tower hangs a Paul Revere bell (1804).

Right from Kennebunk on State 35 is the *Robert Lord House* (1801) *(private)*, similar in formality and dignity to Coventry Hall at York (*see Tour 1A*).

The massive two-story rectangular structure with low hip roof and parapet rail is a fine Federal addition to the 1760 house that forms a rear wing. The symmetrical facade is finished with carefully matched siding simulating stone, and is broken by the lines of slender Doric pilasters, by a slightly projecting central pavilion with crowning gable pediment and by a narrow belt course at the second level. The entrance doorway's elliptical fanlight and dark louvered shutters are repeated in a large sentinel window in the pediment. Paneled pilasters separate sections of a triple rectangular window in the second story. Unusually fine trim frames the wall openings. The parapet rail's design is notable for its delicately turned balusters.

The *Taylor House* (c. 1803) (*private*), adjoining the Lord House, has three exterior entrances of similar proportions and detail, designed with flanking pilasters, semi-circular fanlights and crowning pediments. Putty stucco ornament, a medium used during the period to simulate carved decoration on flat surfaces, decorates the interior.

Right from State 35 on Sea Road to Ocean View Road, 1 *m.* Right here to a field where a bronze plaque on a granite monument marking the *Site of Larrabee Garrison* and the first permanent settlement of Kennebunk (1714-24), depicts the Garrison that contained five houses.

At 1.2 *m.* on State 35 is the much photographed *Wedding Cake House* (*private*), one of the most extraordinary relics of the scroll-saw period extant. The house, built 20 years before the decorations were added, is square, two-storied and of good proportions, with a graceful Palladian window above its central doorway. Photographs show the elaborate ornamentation remindful of a lacy old-fashioned valentine. Some of this has been removed. At the corners a series of ornamented wooden pinnacles rose several feet above the low roof and were duplicated on each side of the entrance and in miniature in front of a trellised canopy over the entrance steps. Elaborate tracery suspended between the pinnacles at the tops of the first and second stories rose to Gothic peaks over the entrance and the Palladian window. A long barn, touching the rear of the house on the right, also had pinnacles and small high windows outlined by large wooden arches. A romantic though unverified story has it that a sea captain had the decorations added for his bride who was deprived of her wedding cake when he was ordered precipitately to sea during their marriage festivities.

At Kennebunk, left on Fletcher St. to Maine Turnpike. Right on State 1A to Kennebunkport (*see Tour 1B*).

From Kennebunk, US 1 follows the post road of the early mail carriers.

At 27.9 *m.*, junction with Log Cabin Road.

Right on this road to *Seashore Trolley Museum (summer, daily, 10-6; off-season, Sat.-Sun., 12-5)* (New England Electric Railway Historical Society), said to be the first and largest of its kind in the country. There are about 100 vintage trolleys dating from 1873 and a mile-long track for visitors' rides. The antique cars from all over the United States and many foreign countries are restored by New England trolley car buffs in many hours of painstaking work to preserve this bit of Americana that played an important role in the development of cities. Some of the thousands of visitors have nostalgic memories of the turn-of-the-century 'Now' generation as they read such signs as these on Car 724: CASH ONLY, in big white letters over the motorman's cubicle; and in antique lettering, 'Passengers are forbidden to ring the bell to start the car . . . All persons are warned not to enter or leave this car while it is in motion or by the front platform . . . No disorderly or otherwise obnoxious person, whether or not under the influence of liquor, will be allowed to ride upon this car . . . Persons riding on the platform do so at their own risk . . .' The 1873 model originally was drawn by horses.

BIDDEFORD (alt. 80, pop. 19,255), 33.6 *m*. The twin cities of Biddeford and Saco (*see below*), on opposite banks of the Saco River, are united historically, industrially and socially. The largely Franco-American population is employed in textile, shoe, electronics, and wood products manufactories, also at the Portsmouth Naval Shipyard and in Portland industries and provides much of the civic leadership.

The *West Point Pepperell Manufacturing Company Plant (visitors by permit)* 170 Main St., an industry established in 1845, occupies 56 acres and manufactures nationally advertised cotton products.

SACO (*Saw' ko)* (alt. 60, pop. 10,515), 34.5 *m*.

As far as is known, Richard Vines was in charge of the first company of Englishmen to explore the site of Saco. He had been sent out from England in 1616 by the enthusiastic Gorges who had interested others in the enterprise. In 1629, Saco was granted to Thomas Lewis and Richard Boynton and a permanent settlement was made shortly thereafter.

It is said that in 1675 some drunken sailors rowing in the river saw an Indian woman and her infant in a canoe nearby and decided to test the truth of a prevalent rumor that Indian offspring swam from birth by instinct. They overturned the canoe; the woman reached the shore safely, but the child died a few days later as a result of the experience. Unfortunately for the settlers, the child was the son of Squando, an Indian leader who wreaked terrible vengeance upon the whites.

The *Cyrus King House*, 271 Main St., now the rectory of Holy Trinity Roman Catholic Church was built in 1807 by a member of the Scarborough family that produced the first Governor of Maine. A later occupant of the house was Horace Woodman, the inventor who in 1854 devised the self-stripping cotton card and many other textile manufacturing appliances.

First Congregational Church, Beach and Main Sts. Harriet Beecher Stowe's son was minister here and his son Lyman Beecher Stowe was born in Saco.

York Institute (1926) (*Tues.-Sat. 1-3*), 375 Main St., has collections of Colonial costumes and furniture, paintings, statuary, minerals, Indian relics and historical documents. A new wing was added in 1969 for permanent and travelling exhibits.

Thornton Academy (1811), 438 Main St., a co-educational general preparatory school.

At Saco, junction with State 9, alternate shore loop 9.5 *m*. rejoining US 1 at Dunstan (*see below*).

Right on State 9 about a mile to road (R) leading to mouth of Saco River 4 *m.*, views of Biddeford Pool and Wood Island Light.

At 1.6 *m.*, Biddeford-Saco *Country Club* (*visitors*).

At 2.2 *m.*, road (R) leads to *Ocean Park Community* (1881) where the Maine Writers Conference takes place every summer. Many religious conferences also have been held in this area.

OLD ORCHARD BEACH (alt. 40, pop. 4580), 4 *m.* Carnival atmosphere on one of the largest and best-known beaches on the coast, popular for over a century, with many Canadian visitors. Hotels and cottages crowd closely along the streets branching from the compact village where restaurants, concessions and fun houses are centered. The old *Pier*, noted for its promenade and dance hall with big-name bands, has been mostly demolished. The *Old Orchard Historical Society* holds exhibits in various localities. The post office has a mural honoring letter carriers.
The resort section continues to PINE POINT (alt. 15, Scarborough Town). 6.5 *m.* (*seafood*). Across the Point (R) is Prout's Neck (*see below*).

Continuing left, State 9 crosses *Scarborough Marshes*, a State-protected wild bird refuge. Large crops of salt marsh hay formerly were gathered on hundreds of acres of marshland. To keep the hayrack horses from sinking into the marsh, 7"x10" oak slabs were fastened to their hooves.

At 9.2 *m.*, a millstone indicates the Site of *Birthplace of William King*, Maine's first governor (1820).

At 9.6 *m.*, rejoin US 1.

DUNSTAN (alt. 50, Scarborough Town), 40.2 *m.* The *Scarborough Historical Society Museum* (*visitors*), St. Louis School for Boys and many shore dinner inns. US 1 crosses Scarborough Marshes over the former post road.

At 41.7 *m.*, left on Scottow's Hill Road, former stagecoach route, to *Beech Ridge* stock car raceway, 2.5 *m.*

At 42.2 *m.*, *Scarborough Downs*, the State's only flat horse racetrack.

OAK HILL (alt. 100, Scarborough Town), 43.2 *m.* Junction with State 207.

Right on State 207 to SCARBOROUGH VILLAGE, 1.2 *m.* John Libby, progenitor of the Libby family in America settled here c. 1636. The white *First Parish Congregational Church* (R), on the site of one built in 1728, has a fan window, belfry and spire.

At 1.7 *m.* in *Black Point Cemetery* (L), dark gray slate stones date from 1739.

At 3 *m.*, left on State 77 to *Higgins Beach* resort area.

PROUT'S NECK (alt. 40, Scarborough Town), 5.5 *m.* In the vicinity of this colony, several points of interest include Artist *Winslow Homer's Studio* (NHL) (*visitors*), and a Marker on the *Site of Blockhouse Fort* where in 1703 Capt. John Larrabee and seven others withstood a seige by 500 French and

TOWN AND COUNTRY

JONATHAN FISHER'S BLUE HILL

CHURCH AND
COURTHOUSE IN
OLD WISCASSET

LIVERMORE FALLS SHOPPING CENTER

SNOW FALLS AT WEST PARIS

WINTER ROAD TO A FARM HOME

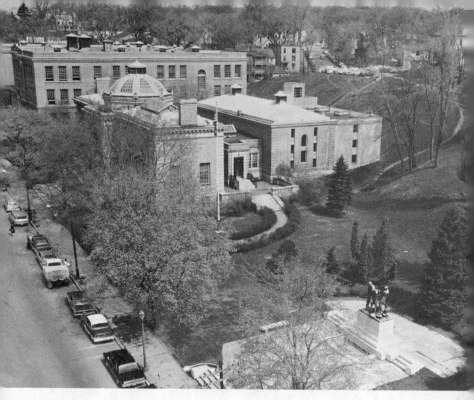

ONE OF NEW ENGLAND'S OUTSTANDING LIBRARIES, BANGOR

ROOSEVELT SUMMER HOME, CAMPOBELLO INTERNATIONAL PARK

THE MAINE
HISTORICAL
SOCIETY AND
LIBRARY,
PORTLAND

YACHTS IN PORTLAND HARBOR

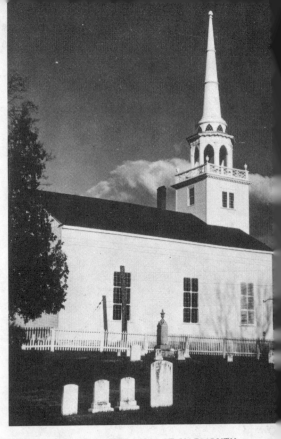

MEETINGHOUSE-ON-THE-HILL AT YARMOUTH

KENNEBUNK CHAPEL

SARAH ORNE
JEWETT MEMORIAL
PORTICO,
SOUTH BERWICK

WADSWORTH-LONGFELLOW HOUSE, PORTLAND

IRIS BY THE BROOK

WINTER AT DEERING OAKS PARK, PORTLAND

Indians. There are also a Yacht Club and a Bird Sanctuary. At Garrison Cove, at the site of Jocelyn Fort, defense headquarters in the first Indian War, a *Marker* denotes the spot where Chief Mogg Heigon, subject of Whittier's poem 'Mogg Megone,' was slain in 1677.

Opposite Massacre Pond on the edge of Prout's Neck golf course fairway (*private*), a *Marker* commemorates the slaughter in 1703 of Indian Fighter Richard Hunniwell and 18 men surprised by an Indian attack. All were buried together under a mound called the Great Grave. Also on the course is a *Marker* on the site of the first Anglican Church in Maine (c. 1658).

The *Nonesuch River* 44.9 *m.*, so named for its crooked course to the sea, figured prominently in the affairs of Scarborough settlers and is mentioned in many histories. Because sizeable boats could not navigate this sharply winding tidal river, a canal was constructed to follow its general course. Instead of digging the canal by hand, workers made a narrow ditch along the proposed course. Tidal action carried away the loose soil, finally completing a project that otherwise would have required much backbreaking toil.

THORNTON HEIGHTS (alt. 80, South Portland), 46.1 *m.* US 1 crosses Fore River, S boundary of Portland, on Veterans Bridge, spectacular approach to the city. Huge oil and gas tanks line the highway on both sides of the river which separates Portland from South Portland.

At Brackett St., R across Million Dollar Bridge to South Portland's Knightsville, with Portland waterfront (L).

SOUTH PORTLAND (alt. 60, pop. 25,000) 1 *m.*, at the mouth of Fore River, was a part of Cape Elizabeth until 1895. Its original charter (1898) was revised in 1963. Phenomenal growth of the city followed the building of the East and West Yards of the New England Shipbuilding Corp., in 1940-41. Formerly a 'bedroom' community for Portland, it was reborn with the charter revision. Expansion of industry and a resurgence of civic pride resulted in its designation in 1964 as an All American City in a national competition. Since 1957 two industrial parks and the Maine Mall have been developed and 35 new industries have been introduced.

Southern Maine Vocational-Technical School (*visitors*) occupies the former Fort Preble (1808-11), named for Commodore Edward Preble. It commands a splendid view of Portland Harbor with Peaks Island and Fort Gorges in the distance, and the breakwater jutting into the ocean. Fort Gorges (1858), only toponymical recognition of Sir Ferdinando in America, is a granite-blocked garrison honeycombed with passageways, on Hog Island Ledge in Casco Bay. Built but not used as a Civil War garrison, it was a storage area for underwater mines in two world wars. One cannon here is the lonely sentinel to the historic defense of Portland.

Following the Shore Road winding past many estates, to CAPE COTTAGE 4.7 *m. Portland Headlight* (1791), (oldest on the Atlantic coast) (*visitors*) is within the former Fort Williams enclave, its white conical tower 101 feet above high water. From the hurricane deck many of Casco Bay's islands may be seen. The U. S. Fifth Infantry (1808), one of the oldest regular Army regiments formerly was stationed at Fort Williams (deactivated). Its motto,

'I'll try, Sir,' were words spoken by Col. James Miller in the battle of Lundy's Lane (1814).

CAPE ELIZABETH has two State Parks, *Crescent Beach* (*swimming*) and *Two Lights* (*picnicking, no camping*), named for two light towers (1829). A Coast Guard Station here (1887) has served from the Kennebec River to Biddeford Pool. Storms bring a magnificent display of surf on ledges at this extended point.

PORTLAND, 49.2 *m.*, at Longfellow Square. (*see PORTLAND*). Here are junctions with State 26 (*see Tour 6*), with State 25 (*see Tour 7*), and with State 25-4 (*see Tour 8*).

East of Portland from Baxter Boulevard, Interstate 95, express route to Brunswick, parallels and merges with US 1 at intervals. Exits on I-95 for Falmouth, Yarmouth, Freeport (*see below*).

At 54.8 *m.* on US 1, Entrance to Portland Country Club (*visitors*).

Junction with State 88.

Right .3 *m.* on State 88 to a Marker near pine grove (L) indicating the *Site of Fort New Casco* (1698), also a trading post. The Indians who at first had been friendly with the English, became hostile and vengeful after they repeatedly had been abused and mistreated. The French then won and exploited the Indians' friendship in their efforts to drive the English from American shores. Maine, part of the territory the French claimed longest, was particularly subject to attack. A conference with Indians at Fort New Casco in 1703 failed to bring safer times and the fort was the center of defense for Casco Bay settlements.

The attractive castellated stone edifice (R) is the Episcopal *Church of St. Mary the Virgin.*

FALMOUTH FORESIDE (alt. 100, Falmouth Town), 2.3 *m.* a residential section overlooking panoramic views of Casco Bay. The English explorer George Waymouth wrote in his journal of being allowed to fill his casks at a spring here where Indians maintained a permanent settlement in the early 1600s.

At 6.6 *m.* a *Burial Ground* dating from 1732.

At 7.5 *m.*, YARMOUTH (*see below*).

At 59.3 *m.* on US 1, Tuttle Road.

At end of Tuttle Road ramp, L on King's Highway to an original *Milestone* .2 *m.*, it's 'B 136' meaning 136 miles from Boston on the King's Highway, laid out in 1760 from Boston to Machias by the Massachusetts Court of General Sessions when Cumberland was part of Ancient North Yarmouth. United Craftsmen of Maine Fair here 1970.

Right from the end of ramp to CUMBERLAND CENTER (alt. 190, Cumberland Town, pop. 3500), 3.5 *m.* The Congregational Church here was established in 1794 and the present building was erected in 1831.

CHEBEAGUE ISLAND (Cumberland Town, pop. 250) *(ferry from Portland)*, 10 *m.* off Portland, 5 *m.* from Cumberland mainland, has many summer residents. Settled in the 1760s, it became in the late 1800s the center of granite transportation, being home port for over 50 'stone' sloops.

At 61.3 *m.* US 1 joins Interstate 95. First exit (R) .5 *m.* to YARMOUTH (alt. 80, Yarmouth Town, pop. 4000). Historical Society exhibits from collections of some 5,000 objects and several *Markers* in the area enliven appreciation of this seaport town settled in 1638 and well known in the Nineteenth century for its shipbuilding and seamen.

William Royall of England for whom the River is named, arrived in 1636, settling in the Wolf's Point area. The early plantation was called Westcustogo (Ind.: clear tidal river) until in 1680 it became the Plantation of North Yarmouth, then including Yarmouth and Cumberland, by grant of the Massachusetts General Court. Following a disastrous period during the French, Indian and King William's wars, population increased and the settlers became prosperous.

By the early 1800s there was traffic in lumber, hay and produce for export. By 1820 there were grist, saw, carding, fulling and paper mills; jewelry, clock, cabinet, saddle and wagon establishments; three blacksmith shops, two tanneries, a brick yard, two taverns and a stage line. In 1849, Yarmouth and North Yarmouth became separate communities.

Shipbuilding which Dana Pratt began in 1818 with the *CORDELIA* (1826), reached its peak in 1874. In that year the Forest Paper Co. was the first in New England to manufacture soda pulp. The Royal River Manufacturing Co. (1857) was producing 400,000 pounds of goods including yarns and grain bags by 1871.

Fishing, crabmeat packing and lobstering are today's industries, with some small craft building. Yarmouth has a marina and pony racetrack.

Lewis Hall, Merrill Memorial Library *(Apr., Jan.; Wed.-Sat. 2-4)* historical exhibits.

Site of First Meetinghouse (Congregational, 1730), in a lane between Gilman St. and State 88. As the center of religious and civic activities, it saw the first town meeting in 1733. The engraved Marker is the original doorstep.

In Pioneer Cemetery, Gilman St., *Tombstone of Indian Scout Joseph Weare* (1737-74) who swore to kill an Indian for every drop of blood they drew from the veins of his brother-in-law. A carved scroll borders each side of the stone, with a winged death's head at the top. Since there were no sculptors in Colonial times, local cabinetmakers usually adapted their decorative furniture scrolls to the stones. The Death Head found on many pre-Revolutionary graves reverts to European artistic tradition of the Middle Ages when death was frequent and familiar during the miseries of the Black Plague and squalid living conditions. The Death figure persisted in European art even during the Renaissance, often appearing among Eighteenth century rococo cherubs. The traditional themes of the cemetery seem the last to be relinquished. In their survival as folk art, they are infused with a certain optimism and humor — interpreting the greatest joke of all.

A *Monument* at the foot of Lafayette St. hill is in memory of Capt. Walter Gendall, killed Sept. 19, 1688 by Indians while attempting to defend his men at Callen Point at the beginning of King William's war. The plaque quotes Cotton Mather: 'Thus was the vein of New England opened that afterwards bled ten years together.'

The *Old Meeting House on the Hill* (Baptist, 1796) (*visitors*) stands out on Brimstone Hill. When Dr. Thomas Green was chosen as first pastor, it was stated that he 'would be received as pastor as long as it may appear for the glory of God, and the mutual happiness of the church and Brother Green.'

On Main St., *North Yarmouth Academy* (1814), preparatory school.

At 66.8 *m.* the route divides, I-95 continuing (L) to Brunswick, US 1 bearing R to Freeport and Brunswick.

On US 1, first road L to *Desert of Maine*, 2 *m.*

A not unusual coastal phenomenon, this one began late in the Nineteenth century and spread to become a prime visitors' attraction. A glint of mica in the fine-textured sand leads some geologists to believe the spot covers the bed of an ancient lake formed by glacial deposits.

FREEPORT (alt. 140, Freeport Town. pop. 4055), 68 *m.*

When Freeport was incorporated in 1789 it is said to have been named for Sir Andrew Freeport, the character representing the London merchant class in Addison's *Spectator Papers*. The town's early Indian attacks included the well-known Means Massacre of 1756 at Flying Point. Since the decline of wooden shipbuilding, industries are shoemaking, crabbing and crabmeat packing. L. L. Bean, nationally known sporting goods emporium, is open 24 hours a day.

Directional signs to *Bradbury Mt. State Park (games, hiking, picnicking)*.

SOUTH FREEPORT, 2.7 *m.* (R) from Freeport is at the mouth of Harraseeket River on Freeport Harbor, navigable year-round. A fishing center since earliest times, its heyday was between 1825-30 when as many as 12,000 barrels of mackerel were packed and shipped annually. In the 1800s numerous shipyards lined the river banks and Freeport ships and captains were known around the world. At Porter's landing, the privateer *DASH* was built for service in the War of 1812. In 1815 she became a legendary ghost ship when she was lost at sea with all hands, her fate never fully determined.

Mark Twain made famous the ordeal of Freeport Capt. Josiah A. Mitchell in 1866 in a tragic sea fire, one of the most feared disasters in the days of wooden sailing vessels. Capt. Mitchell was in command of the clipper *HORNET*, carrying 45 barrels and 2,000 cases of oil and 6,000 boxes of candles, when she burned off the Pacific coast of South America. Against regulations, a sailor had carried an open lantern into the booby hatch where it ignited fumes from a cask of varnish. When the ship could not be saved, the crew took to the longboat and two lifeboats with provisions for 10 days, and a live rooster they voted not to eat because his cocky crowing cheered the men. From his charts the Captain, commanding the longboat, estimated they were about 1,000 miles from nearest land, east of the Galapagos Islands, south of the Revillagigedos chain and southeast of Acapulco, Mexico.

After 43 terrible days of hardship, covering 4,000 miles of treacherous waters and loss of two of the lifeboats, the survivors arrived at Lapahoehoe, Hawaii. The story of the tragic *HORNET* which Mark Twain who was staying nearby in Honolulu, sent by steamer to San Francisco newspapers, brought fame to him and to Capt. Mitchell of Freeport.

Casco Castle Tower (1902), 80 feet high with walls three feet thick, is a well-known landmark for navigators. It is all that remains of a picturesque summer hotel modeled after a medieval stronghold. The *Audubon Wildlife Sanctuary* on Lower Mast Landing Road invites a leisurely visit.

At 68.9 *m.* a road (L) to *Shiloh*, 10 *m.*

High on a windswept hill in the town of Durham, this is The Kingdom, headquarters of an evangelical sect that maintains housing for the elderly, conducts Bible services and other activities. With branches in New Hampshire and the West, the sect evolved after the decline of one that flourished more flamboyantly earlier in the Twentieth century. New buildings replace some of the original colony's more unusual ones whose gilded tower was visible for miles around.

The Rev. Frank W. Sandford, an Elijah of the early 1900s, founded the Holy Ghost and Us Society whose converts from many parts of the world poured their money into a common fund. Elaborate buildings were erected and various crafts practiced for a time. But when the world did not end as he predicted, the Rev. Sandford, on what he said was Divine call, purchased the 150-ton sailing vessel *CORONET* to go forth on the high seas and convert the heathen. With flowing beard, purple robe, sailor hat and Bible under arm, he was a colorful figure as he set sail from Portland.

Results of several voyages in various ships were unremarkable except for the *CORONET's* last voyage in 1912 when eight members of the party were said to have died of scurvy. This created some difficulties with authorities when the ship hove to in Portland Harbor. Returning to Shiloh in 1914, Rev. Sandford found his power gone, his flock scattered. He dropped from sight, his fate to remain a mystery unless it is revealed in a forthcoming history of the sect.

BRUNSWICK, 76.9 *m.* at business center (*see BRUNSWICK*). Junction here with State 24 and 123 (*see Tour 1C*).

L on State 24 to RICHMOND (pop. 2185) and *Swan Island State Game Preserve (visitors' permits, camping reservations: State Dept. of Inland Fish and Game)*, 15 *m.* A permanent deer herd of about 300 live on this 1300-acre reservation, part of the Merrymeeting Bay Wildlife Sanctuary. Visitors are ferried to the island from Richmond in a large flat-bottom boat and then are taken on a bus tour of the island. Some of the deer are quite tame and other small game to be seen are squirrels, woodchucks and rabbits. Except the coastal cottontails, most Maine rabbits are snowshoe hares (so-called because of their hind feet); witches were believed to have taken this form in the Twelfth century. There are thousands of ducks and geese during the spring and fall migratory seasons. The once prolific bald-headed eagle is seen less frequently since pesticides have been so greatly misused; the last known eggs several years ago turned to jelly. On Little Swan Island is the second largest eagle's nest known in the U. S., 20 ft. vertical, 6 ft. horizontal.

Wabanaki Indians once councilled on Swan Island. Later, a dozen families made a tiny agricultural community. Fields and orchards and old cellar holes remain. Two houses have been restored, one said to have sheltered Benedict Arnold, the other a fine example of the salt-box style.

Sec. b. BRUNSWICK to ROCKLAND, 48.r m.

Leaving Brunswick on I-95 at 0 *m.*, the route travels along the Androscoggin River to Bath where it rejoins US 1 to cross the Kennebec River bridge, gradually moving northeast to follow the western edge of Penobscot Bay. Subtle changes in coastal scenery mark this section of US 1 and its side tours passing through fairly open countryside, tree-shaded towns with their handsome Eighteenth century homes and boating centers before reaching beautiful Camden Hills. Forts, historic sites, State Parks, museums, island trips, beaches, roadside inns and art and antique shops offer diversion.

BATH (Alt. 50, pop. 11,000), 7 *m.* Junction (R) with State 209 (*see Tour 1D*)

> *Municipal Pier*: temporary boat docking free. *Boat trips*: old stern-wheeler river boat, twice daily to Boothbay Harbor and islands.
> *Bus Service*: local and inter-city; daily (*summer*) to Popham and Reid State Parks.
> *Concerts*: Municipal Band, City Park, Wed. eve., (*summer*).
> *Guided tours*: Bath Marine Museum; Bath Iron Works.

World-renowned shipbuilding city that once was a part of old Georgetown on the Kennebec River 12 miles from open sea, Bath was the first town incorporated in the District of Maine under the Massachusetts Constitution of 1780. It was named for Bath in Somersetshire, England, the famous watering place founded by the Romans in the first century B. C. Alexander Thwaitt and the Rev. Robert Gutch obtained land titles in 1660 from the Indian Sagamore Robinhood. It is believed the Rev. Mr. Gutch, 'a preacher to the fishermen' built his cabin on the Kennebec shore near where the present city building now stands.

A large portion of land purchased from Indians by Thomas Stevens became in 1753 the parish of Georgetown which included present-day Bath, West Bath, Phippsburg, Georgetown and Arrowsic. Preceding the shipbuilding era, early settlers built small boats as their means of transportation.

The first transatlantic trader was the 30-ton pynnace *VIRGINIA* built in nearby Phippsburg by Popham Colonists in 1607 (*see Tour 1D*). The first full-rigged ship launched in Bath was Capt. William Swanton's *EARL OF BUTE* in 1762. Since then, nearly 5,000 vessels have gone down the ways in the Old Georgetown area, including almost half of the sailing vessels built in America between 1862 and 1902.

By the mid-1800s Bath had become America's fifth largest seaport. The Patten fleet was the largest privately owned commercial fleet in the world, and 'Bath-built' had become synonymous with excellence in ships. In the great days of wooden ships, more than 200 concerns flourished on Long Reach, a four-mile stretch of level shore beside deep water along the Kennebec at Bath. The mile at the north end of Front Street is believed to have launched more oceangoing vessels than any area of comparable size in the world.

Bath's long list of significant contributions to maritime history include such vessels as the *HENRY B. HYDE,* classic example of the 'Down Easter,' a clipper; the six-masted schooner *WYOMING,* largest commercial wooden sailing vessel ever to fly the American flag; the only fleet of American-built four-masted steel barques, beginning with the *DIRIGO* in 1894; the *KAUILANI* (1899), now the last surviving American square-rigged merchant vessel (being restored by the National Maritime Historical Society); the sloop *RANGER* that successfully defended the America's Cup; and a wide range of U. S. Naval vessels built by the Bath Iron Works, long dominant area industry (*see INDUSTRY*).

Once the hub of surrounding resort areas, Bath in the late 1960s was endeavoring to recover the prominence it had lost to outlying cultural and shopping centers. Its Memorial Hospital is an outstanding small institution. Its educational institutions include remedial, vocational and apprentice schools. Handsome Eighteenth century homes in the residential area have given the title 'Street of Shipbuilders' to Washington Street. Notables whose homes were in Bath: opera, star, Emma Eames; William King, Maine's first governor; Harold M. Sewall, first ambassador to the new republic of Hawaii; and Sumner Sewall, governor in the 1940s.

Davenport Memorial Building, Front St., housing municipal offices and a Paul Revere bell (1805) in its tower, is the city's focal point. The building, with curved facade, is named for a local philanthropist.

In a pool beneath graceful willows in the City Park on Washington St., stands *The Spirit of the Sea,* bronze fountain given to the city by Sculptor William Zorach who summered at Robinhood in Georgetown. The *Cannon* in the Park is from the British man-of-war, *SOMERSET,* that anchored in Boston Harbor when Paul Revere made his historic ride. In the background is the *Patten Free Library (Mon. through Fri. 12-8; Sat. 12-6; art exhibits).*

Beyond the Park among stately old homes is the Bath Marine Museum (R) (*summer, daily 10-5; year-round by appointment*). The century-old 28-room two-story Georgian mansion formerly owned by Ambassador and Mrs. Sewall, houses an outstanding maritime collection. Over 5,000 artifacts include full rigged ship models, half models, paintings, photographs, carvings, tools, special equipment and ship fittings evoking Maine's great maritime heritage. There are also many fine antiques and examples of period furniture and decor. Of particular interest are rooms devoted to histories of Bath's shipbuilding families; the Gov. William King Room; the Ship's Lore Room devoted to the arts of the builder, rigger, sailmaker, navigator and blacksmith; and the Children Only Room where everything is marked 'Please touch.' The definitive *Maritime History of Bath* by William Avery Baker was commissioned by the Marine Research Society of Bath which operates the Museum.

Retrace Washington St. past junction with Center St. to *Bath Iron Works Offices* (L) (*shipyard guided tours 4 p. m. Tues. and Thurs., mid-June to mid-Sept.; scheduled launchings open to public*). One of the nation's largest producers of U. S. Navy guided missile frigates, BIW has built naval, merchant marine and private vessels since 1889. Its history begins in 1826 with William and Oliver Moses' small iron foundry that made mostly stove castings. When Gen. Thomas W. Hyde returned from the Civil War in 1865, he bought the foundry and soon began to manufacture equipment for the wooden ships being built in Bath. Organized as the Bath Iron Works Ltd., the concern began to build ships in 1889. The steel gunboats *MACHIAS* and *CASTINE* were the first in a long line of vessels built for the U. S. Navy. Among 30 vessels built between 1890-1900 were the *APHRODITE*, then the largest and fastest steam yacht ever built; the *WINIFRED*, first ocean-going tramp steamer; and the *DAHLGREN* and *CRAVEN*, then the Navy's fastest torpedo boats. Between 1900-10, the company built the battleship *U.S.S. GEORGIA* (1906), the steamers *CAMDEN* and *BELFAST*, second and third passenger ships propelled by steam turbines, and the cruiser *CHESTER* (1908), first major Navy warship successfully propelled by turbines. The destroyer *WADSWORTH* (1915) was the Navy's first geared turbine vessel. BIW designed and built many of the famous 'four-stack' destroyers in World War I.

Following the 1922 disarmament conference, there were no new Navy contracts. In 1927 a new company was incorporated and the plant gradually was rehabilitated, building steel yachts, fishing trawlers, Coast Guard patrol boats and tugs. The 343-foot turbine electric yacht *CORSAIR IV* was delivered to J. P. Morgan, II in May 1930. In 1937, the company built the last and best of the J-Class sloops, the America's Cup defender *RANGER* for Harold S. Vanderbilt which defeated the British challenger *ENDEAVOR II* in four straight races. By 1940 the company had built 16 Navy destroyers and became one of the country's principal destroyer-building yards prior to World War II. The plant covered 48 acres, and had 12,000 workers during the war when the company delivered 21 destroyers per year, a quarter of all U. S. wartime destroyers — 67 between the 1941 Pearl Harbor attack and 1945. Among destroyers of the Forrest Sherman Class was the *U.S.S. JOHN PAUL JONES.* From 1941-45, together with the Todd Shipyard Corp. of South Portland, now defunct, BIW engaged in merchant shipbuilding. Thirty 10,000 ton cargo ships were built for Great Britain and 244 Liberty ships for the U. S. government. In a diversification program, manufacture of Pennsylvania crushers began in 1947. By 1965 BIW had acquired other manufactories and also was building commercial cargo vessels.

The company has served as a lead yard for the design and construction of guided missile frigates, destroyers and their escorts. It built the *U.S.S. DEWEY*, first Naval missile ship (1962) and the *U.S.S. LEAHY*, first frigate to carry guided missiles fore and aft. It also built the 125-foot MIT bow for the mammoth experimental tanker *MANHATTAN* that in 1969 opened the Northwest Passage to Alaska.

Farther along Washington St., the old wooden Percy & Small Shipyard plant (L), one of the few remaining, is a reminder of the building of the great *WYOMING*.

The sightly white building (L) on a knoll overlooking the meadows and the river near the southern end of Washington St. is the *Old Folks Home.*

In the city's out-lying areas are several landmarks. *Stonehouse Farm* (c. 1805) (*private*) on Whiskeag Road was Gov. King's hunting lodge, distinguished by its cathedral windows and doors. *Thorne's Head* on Upper High St. affords a view of Council Point, Indian meeting place, and the confluence of seven rivers funneling through *Merrymeeting Bay*, wild fowl preserve open at certain seasons to duck hunters (see *RECREATION*). On the Head is Murderer's Cave, temporary hideout for an English sailor who was convicted of murdering a Bath night patrolman in 1883 and became the last person to be hanged legally in Maine (1885). The ornately carved *Emma Eames Mausoleum* is in the Old Bath Road Cemetery. Tombstones in the Dummer Sewall Cemetery, corner of Dummer and Beacon Streets, date from the early 1700s.

Left from Front St. near the Post Office, US 1 crosses *Carleton Bridge* (1927), a drawbridge high over the Kennebec, commanding a sweeping view of the shipyards and waterfront, the Woolwich shores opposite, and up and down the river, roadstead of watercraft for many generations, from Indian canoes to guided missile carriers.

The Kennebec is one of the historic rivers of America. A principal waterway flowing 150 miles from its source at Moosehead Lake into the Atlantic at Phippsburg, with usable water storage of 50.24 billion cubic feet, it was one of the earliest to be explored on the North American coast. The main means of travel and communication for the early settlers, it became the roadstead of commerce and industry as cities grew.

Adventurers had made fragmentary reports on the Kennebec before 1600 and Champlain had explored it to some extent before 1606. It was named as one of the boundaries of various large land grants during rivalry of the French and British for control of the continent. In 1607, George Popham and Raleigh Gilbert, commanding the expedition promoted by Sir Ferdinando Gorges and Sir John Popham, are said to have sailed up the river past the place now spanned by the bridge, seeking a site for their Colony (*see Tour ID*) that was to send fur, sassafras and other commodities back to England to make fortunes for the London investors. Two decades later, there was a steady stream of traffic to and from the Cushnoc trading settlement at the present capital city of Augusta for the 'Undertakers' of Plymouth. Rich cargoes of this traffic saved the Massachusetts settlement from extinction.

Military annals recount the grim saga of the ill-fated attempt to capture Quebec in 1775 which began with the rendezvous of Benedict Arnold's fleet of 11 ships at the mouth of the Kennebec. Plagued by fall storms, the long and torturous trek along the river through the Maine wilderness with many portages of the batteaux ended in disaster at Dead River. Despite heroic endurance of untold hardships, many of the sick, half-frozen men perished, defeated by the elements. Interpretations of this harrowing expedition may be seen at scenic spots along the *Arnold Trail* northwesterly across Maine to the Canadian border.

But the Kennebec did not escape the consequences of profligate use of this natural resource as an open sewer. The wastes of increasing population and industrial development along its banks brought water pollution, closing clam-flats and decimating fish. Gone in the mid-Twentieth century was the Kennebec's fame for Atlantic salmon which the Indians had found teeming in these waters and which in 1820 sold for a penny apiece. In the late 1960s, however, as anti-pollution and clean-up efforts slowly were getting underway, scientific methods were undertaken to induce the fish to return to their spawning grounds.

The Kennebec has seen continuous activity of log drives, ship launchings, commercial travel, power and industrial development. Today's traffic consists of pleasure craft, fishing boats, tugs, barges and oil tankers, and Bath-built ships.

WOOLWICH (alt. 30, Woolwich Town, pop. 1417), 8.2 *m.* Farming supplanted shipbuilding and shad and sturgeon fishing in this community opposite Bath that saw the Preble Massacre in the mid-Sixteenth century.

Junction with State 127 (R) (*see Tour 1E*).

Left on State 127 to Day's Ferry 3 *m.*, eastern terminal of the *HOCKAMOCK* that ferried passengers and cars across the Kennebec until the Carleton Bridge was built. The ice cream man was a popular feature of the short trip.

Portions of the *Harnden-Hinckley House* (R) (*private*), formerly known as the Appleton Day House, on the site of the Samuel Harnden Blockhouse, date to 1747. An underground passage was said to have extended to the river for use during Indian attacks. Other early homes in the vicinity include the Fullerton House (1765) and the Reed-Coffin House (1768).

Nequasset Meeting House (1757), 11 *m.* (R), oldest Congregational meeting house east of the Kennebec, has the simple style and good proportions of such buildings of the period. Its first pastor, Josiah Winship, was ordained in 1765 when there were but 20 families and two frame dwellings in the settlement. Sixteenth century gravestones are in the adjoining cemetery. Across the road in the Harnden family cemetery, the *Preble Monument* is a reminder of the Massacre when Mrs. Preble, daughter of Samuel Harnden, was killed and her children carried to Canada.

At 12.7 *m.*, junction with Montsweag Road.

Right on this road at 4.4 *m.*, a view of Hockamock Bay and islands. At Phipps's Point, 4.8 *m.* (R) in a private estate is the *Homesite of Sir William Phips,* first Royal Governor of Massachusetts, a colorful, arrogant figure who was one of America's first self-made men. Born here in 1651 of poor parents, he worked as a shepherd and ship's carpenter until he went to sea at 25. In sophisticated Boston, where he was scorned for his homespun appearance and lack of education, he learned to read and write and decided to make his fortune by treasure hunting. In 1683, through a commission from the British Crown, he recovered Spanish treasure near Turk's Island off the Bahamas, for which he was rewarded with 16,000 pounds and a knighthood, one of the two bestowed upon Americans.

He next commanded an expedition that captured Port Royal without difficulty, but his second Canadian expedition failed. Through Cotton Mather's influence, Phips was appointed Royal Governor of Massachusetts. He did much for his native Maine in stabilizing the troubled settlements and establishing the town form of government. Lack of tact and education, however, made him unable to cope with all his problems. He became involved in difficulties that resulted in his recall to England where he died in 1695 during an investigation of the charges against him. The town of Phippsburg (*see Tour 1D*) is named for Sir William, having been a part of Old Georgetown which included his birthplace.

WISCASSET (alt. 50, Wiscasset Town, pop. 2000), 17.3 *m*. Although bisected by the through coastal route 'down-east', Lincoln County's shire town, long known as one of the most beautiful on the coast, maintains its Nineteenth century serenity and charm chiefly through the attitude and effort of its citizens. Its many fine homes built during the prosperous days of a seafaring economy, have been preserved along the tree-lined streets. Art and history play an important role in the community through the Lincoln County Cultural and Historical Association. Writers and artists have come to dwell in the Sheepscot area, among them the late Rachel Carson for whom the Nature Conservancy has preserved acreage as a memorial. While its early prosperity ended when the 1807 Embargo Act closed the port, Wiscasset (Ind.: place where three waters meet) retained its stability and has seen industrial revival in the second half of the Twentieth century.

First visitor to the site was Samuel de Champlain who met with a group of 'savages' July 5, 1605 and 'gave them some cakes and peas with which they were greatly pleased.' The English began settling 40 years later, but fled during King Philip's War. After 1730, the seaport grew and life became 'monstrous fine,' a visitor commented. In 1791 there were 35 square riggers owned here and often a man could walk across the harbor on decks of ships lying at anchor. A handsome town was built during this era; some of the houses of those days are still in use. Oceangoing vessels still call occasionally, sailing 12 miles up the Sheepscot into the protected deepwater harbor that made Wiscasset soon after the Revolution the busiest port east of Boston.

In the late Eighteenth century the salt and spar trade was brisk. Masts and spars of local pine were carried to Europe in Wiscasset ships in exchange for cargoes of salt, not yet produced in the new country. West Indiamen left Wiscasset wharves, too, with dried fish, ice and lumber, returning with rum, cotton and molasses from the West Indies. Shipyards flourished early, thanks to active foreign trade, vast supplies of native lumber and 'the great depth and comparative stillness of the water in the Sheepscot.'

The ship *STIRLING*, launched three miles up river, sailed from Wiscasset on New Year's Day 1806, bound for London and St. Petersburg. One of her foremast hands later that year was a boy named James Fenimore Cooper. Another was Ned Myers, 13, who long after became a hero in Cooper's *Tales of the Sea*.

Another Wiscasset ship, the whaler *WISCASSET*, made her first visit to the South Pacific whaling grounds in 1833, returning after 40 months with 2800 barrels of sperm oil and 80 barrels of whale oil, 'all bills paid.' When she sailed in 1848 out of Glasgow for home, among her passengers was Andrew Carnegie, then a boy of 11. The Town Hall weathervane, a scale model of the *WISCASSET*, was hand-forged locally from a scrimshaw likeness carved on a huge whale's tusk.

In the summer of 1777, the *GRUEL*, a captured British transport fitted out to carry masts to France, was loading at a mast dock near Wiscasset when His

Majesty's frigate *RAINBOW* entered the harbor and seized her and a brig. When the Lincoln County Regiment Commander Col. William Jones demanded their release, the British commander refused; but fearing the Colonel would mount a gun battery on Doggett's Castle Heights and block their departure, the British withdrew without their prizes.

Forest and river carried Wiscasset through the days of sail despite the disastrous effects of the Embargo Act, the War of 1812 and a spotted fever (spinal meningitis) epidemic. Thousand-ton clippers were launched here shortly before the Civil War. The advancing machine age ended the opulent shipbuilding era and fires in 1866 and 1870 destroyed wharves and homes along the waterfront. The population shrank and Wiscasset became 'very quiet — so dead that the dogs don't even wake up when the train goes by,' remarked a conductor. The last two four-masted schooners, the *LUTHER LITTLE* (1917) and the *HESPER* (1918) became picturesque 'derelicts' in the harbor.

Now new industry has come to town and there is an airport and a yacht club. The Central Maine Power Company has a large generating plant on Birch Point where in 1875 the schooner *FANNIE TUCKER* was launched and set off on her maiden voyage to Calcutta with a cargo of ice. Farther down the river, the Yankee Atomic Corporation has constructed the largest nuclear conversion plant in New England. Worm-digging has become a new means of livelihood. Bloodworms and sandworms which sports fishermen use as bait are shipped live daily by truck and air all over the country. In all weathers, Wiscasset wormers can be seen stooped over the flats in the six hours between mean low and half-flood tides, making up to $30 in the short but rugged workday.

The facade of the *Lincoln County Courthouse* (1824), oldest in continuous use, (R) on the Common, is much admired. Although a new wing has been added, the original building and courtroom that once resounded to the rolling periods of Daniel Webster are little changed. Complete court records here are in excellent condition. Between 1760-89, the County extended from the Kennebec to the Canadian border and many records of the period relate to parts of Maine not now in Lincoln County. Next to the Courthouse, the *First Congregational Church* (1773).

Right on High St. to *Wiscasset Public Library* (*Mon. through Sat. 3-5:30; Thurs. eve. 6:30-9*). Its 13,000 volumes include a definitive reference work, *Wiscasset in Pownalborough* by Fannie S. Chase.

Opposite the Library, the *Lee-Payson-Smith House* (1792) was built for Judge Silas Lee. The square two-story frame house of subtle proportions and refined detail illustrates the skill of the carpenter-architects of the day and their sensitive appreciation of classic detail executed in wood. It has singular grace and delicacy. Notable are the fine modillioned and dentiled cornices of the exterior. A Chippendale pattern is suggested in the open railing on the captain's walk.

Farther along, the *Abiel House* (1824) is another fine example of the Federal period.

Castle Tucker (1807) at High and Lee Streets, still owned by descendants of Tucker shipowners and sea captains, is said to be copied from a castle in Dunbar, Scotland.

Musical Wonder House (summer, daily; weekly candlelight concerts), large collection of early mechanical musical instruments played on guided tour, in a restored Georgian house (1852).

Returning to US 1 and Federal Street.

On the corner, the *Nickels-Sortwell House* (1812) *(summer; Society for Preservation of New England Antiquities)*. Five years in the building for retired shipmaster Capt. William Nickels, the large mansion was begun in 1807. The front hall carving reportedly took one man two years to complete and it was a full winter's work for another to keep the open fires supplied with wood. Circular stairs rise to the third story; woodwork and furnishings are distinguished. The main portal with its elliptical fanlight and elaborate mullioned side-lights is particularly notable for the slender Corinthian pilasters with herringbone carving, and the delicately carved transom rail and architrave. Above the long Palladian window over the entrance portico is a semi-circular window interpolated between two square ones in the third story, a characteristic motif in the facades of such houses along the Maine coast. Capt. Nickels did not long enjoy his house. He lost his wife and only child the year it was finished and died soon afterward himself. The *Sunken Garden*, across the street, is an inviting public park, laid out in the foundations of an old tavern.

Off Federal on Warren St. is the *Maine Art Gallery (Old Academy 1808), (weekdays 10-5; Sun. 12-5)*. July and August exhibitions of paintings, sculpture, prints and drawings by artists who work in Maine, many of national renown.

On Federal St., the *Fire Museum (summer, 10-5 week days; Sun. 12-5)*. Fire-fighting equipment dating from 1803; ancient stage coach and hearse.

Farther along, the *Lincoln County Museum and Old Jail, (weekdays 10-5; Sun. 12-5)*. The Museum's outstanding collection of Maine arts and skills of the past 200 years, including fine contemporary crafts, is in the red brick jailer's house (1837).

In the early 1800s, a great lumber industry had developed and port towns were crowded with shipping. The influx of seamen and woodsmen introduced a new element of disorder. The jail, of Edgecomb granite with walls 41 inches thick at the foundation, was completed in 1811 and in use until 1953 when it was acquired by the Lincoln County Cultural and Historical Association. Forty prisoners could be held in its dungeons and cells. It was Maine's principal penitentiary for safekeeping of felons until the State's prison was built at Thomaston in 1824. Prior to this fort-like stone structure, Wiscasset had two wooden jails for short-term confinement. If a fine or bond did not fit the crime, there was hanging for several offenses or stripes on the bare back at the whipping post. And there was punishment by public humiliation in the stocks or standing at the gallows with the hangman's noose around the neck.

At Wiscasset, junctions with State 27 and State 218.

N on State 27 to DRESDEN MILLS (alt. 70, Dresden Town, pop. 766), 8.1 *m.*, a tree-shaded village on the S bank of the Eastern River. The town was first settled as Frankfort in 1752 by German and French Huguenot immigrants introduced by the Proprietors of the Kennebec Purchase, owners of a huge tract of land along the Kennebec. In 1760 a new township named Pownalborough replaced Frankfort; it was much larger, extending to the Sheepscot River and including present day Dresden and Wiscasset. Dresden took its name when incorporated as a separate town in 1794.

At 9.7 *m.*, L on State 128 to *Pownalborough Courthouse* (1761) (*summer, daily 10-5*), 2.6 *m.* This is Maine's oldest court building and the only one built prior to the Revolution. The large three-story white building is owned and operated by the Lincoln County Cultural and Historical Association and appears much as it was when first built on the site of Fort Shirley. It reveals old paneling and beamed ceilings, great timbers and details of construction. On display are looms, spinning wheels and examples of hand weaving as well as copies of old documents and maps telling the history of the house and the Kennebec Purchase which saw years of litigation with other claimants who held grants and Indian deeds. The exact bounds intended by the Patent of 1630 are not known to this day. Another exhibit illustrates the ice industry on the Kennebec; ice was shipped all over the world in sailing vessels from the 1880s to the early 1900s and the largest icehouses on the river were located near the Courthouse which was built by housewright Gersham Flagg who had built Fort Western in 1754; the first court was held before it was completed. Major Samuel Goodwin, a Proprietor and Commander of Fort Shirley, as well as agent and attorney for the Plymouth Company, was the first occupant with his family. His descendants continued to occupy the building which has also been used as a meetinghouse, a tavern and a post office, until 1930.

A half-mile S stands the *Jonathan Bowman House* (*private*), a fine two-story house contemporary with the Courthouse. Bowman was Lincoln County's first Registrar of Deeds.

A short distance from the Courthouse, a *Tablet* marks the site of the church and parsonage. The first Episcopal Church in the Province of Maine was established in Pownalborough in 1760 by the Rev. Jacob Bailey, a colorful figure and a Loyalist, who was forced to depart for Nova Scotia during the Revolution. He was a Harvard classmate of John Adams, second President of the U. S., who as a young lawyer appeared in court at Pownalborough.

William and Charles Cushing came to Pownalborough in 1760. William, a Harvard graduate, was Pownalborough's first person to be educated in the law and was Lincoln County's first Judge of Probate. He soon returned to Massachusetts, however, where he served as Chief Justice of the Supreme Court. In 1789 he was appointed a Justice of the U. S. Supreme Court and administered the oath of office to President Washington at his second inauguration in 1793. Charles Cushing was a Harvard classmate of Bailey and Bowman. He was Lincoln County's first sheriff, serving for 20 years. He was a Brigadier General during the Revolution and responsible for defences east of the Kennebec. In 1780 he was abducted from his house in Pownalborough by Loyalists and carried as a prisoner to Castine where the British were in occupation. He was later released in an exchange of prisoners.

At 15.1 *m.*, on State 27, a side road (L) leads a short distance to the Major *Reuben Colburn House* (1765) (*private*). It was built by four Colburn brothers who came here from Massachusetts with their four sisters in 1761, and is identified by a tablet on a boulder by the roadside. Col. Benedict Arnold and his officers were entertained by Major Colburn Sept. 21-23, 1775, in this house while the soldiers bivouacked nearby during the transfer of the army of 1100 men to the 220 batteaux Major Colburn had built for the expedition to Quebec.

NE on State 218 to SHEEPSCOT (R) 2.5 *m*., a lovely historic old village at the head of the Sheepscot River. Known as Sheepscott Farms for its former principal industry, it was settled in 1634. When a commission organized a county (called Cornwall) under the jurisdiction of the Duke of York in 1665, the Sheepscott settlement became the shire town and was called New Dartmouth. In his book *The Life of Sir William Phips*, Cotton Mather reports on the building of a ship at Sheepscott in 1676:

'Within a little while after his (Phip's) Marriage, he indented with several Persons in *Boston*, to Build them a Ship at *Sheeps-coat* River, Two or Three Leagues Eastward of *Kennebeck*; where having Lanched the Ship, he also provided a *Lading* of Lumber to bring with him, which would have been to the Advantage of all Concern'd. But just as the ship was hardly finished, the Barbarous *Indians* on that River, broke forth into an Open and Cruel War upon the *English*; and the miserable People, surprised by so sudden a storm of Blood, had no Refuge from the Infidels, but the *Ship* now finishing in the Harbour. Whereupon he left his intended Lading behind him, and instead thereof, carried with him his old Neighbours and their Families, free of all Charges, to *Boston*; so the *first Action* that he did, after he was his own Man, was to *save his Father's House*, with the rest of the Neighbourhood, from Ruin; but the Disappointment which befel him from the Loss of his other *Lading,* plunged his Affairs into greater Embarasments with such as had employ'd him.'

Old Alna Meetinghouse (1789) (L) 5 *m*., well-preserved example of early meetinghouse architecture. Original clapboards were ship-lapped on the NE corner against storms. Curiously designed hand-wrought foot scrapers grace the sides of the doorstep. Inside, the box pews with carved spindles seated nearly 500 people. The raised hour-glass pulpit with a winding flight of steps and finely molded handrail is paneled in contrasting dark and light wood; behind, an octagonal bell-shaped canopy and sounding board above the pulpit is a long arched window flanked by fluted pilasters. The pulpit, arranged to accommodate ministers of varying heights, has been used by men of diverse oratorical talents since the first minister, Parson Wood, preached of fire and brimstone and vainly fought against the introduction of instrumental music.

At Head Tide, 10 *m*., is the *Birthplace of Poet Edward Arlington Robinson.*

Enroute on State 218 is the 'World's Smallest Church' (1966), four by eight feet, always open.

US 1 crosses the Wiscasset Bridge over the Sheepscot into the town of EDGECOMB (alt. 50, pop. 453). At the E end of bridge, road (R) leads to *Fort Edgecomb* 1.6 *m*. and junction with State 27 for the Boothbay Region (*see Tour 1F*).

At 23.6 *m*., spur (R) to Newcastle-Damariscotta.

NEWCASTLE (alt. 60, Newcastle Town, pop. 1101) .5 *m*., on W bank of the Damariscotta River is the home of the Lincoln County orchestra and Lincoln Academy regional high school.

Left on a local road is the village of DAMARISCOTTA MILLS, 2.5 *m*. On a hill (R) is the *Kavanaugh Mansion* (1803) (*private*), home of Edward Kavanaugh, acting governor of Maine (1843). The two-story building has an octagonal cupola, balustraded roof and fine doorway with fanlight and side-lights under a semi-circular portico.

Farther on the right is *St. Patrick's Church* (1803-08), Maine's oldest Catholic church, dedicated by Father Jean de Cheverus (1768-1838), who became the first Roman Catholic bishop of New England in 1808. Father Cheverus came from France in 1796 to work among the Indians on the Maine coast. In the final year of his life, after he had returned to France, he was made a cardinal. The thick-walled church has a 250-year-old painting from France over the altar. Another painting was brought from a Mexican convent during the Mexican War. The sarcophagus-style altar is unusual in the United States.

DAMARISCOTTA (alt. 30, Damariscotta Town, pop. 1093) across the bridge on the E bank of the river, is another formerly prosperous shipbuilding center that has become the focal point for a large vacation region including lakes to the east. Its fine shops — apparel, gifts, books, art, gourmet foods — draw many visitors. Salt Water Farms ships lobsters and other seafood all over the country and its riverside restaurant facilities include wharf-side dining aboard the *LOIS M. CANDAGE*, 1880 coastal schooner. The County Fair, Cheechako and other outlying inns offer appetizing menus. The weekly *Lincoln County News* is published here.

Damariscotta (Ind.: river of many fishes) is within the boundaries of the first deed given in the present territory of the State July 15, 1625 by the Indian Chief Samoset to John Brown. Until it became a town in 1847, it was part of Bristol (Walpole district) and Nobleboro. In 1730 the Jones, Huston and Lermond families came from Boston in their own vessel and settled grants along the Damariscotta River in the Walpole section. Locations of these families and Thomas Hutchins in Nobleboro appear on North's 1751 map for the Kennebec Proprietors. As other settlers came, there was steady development from 1754 in lumber, agriculture and shipping. Damariscotta was known for its brick-making and its fast clippers and shipping merchants. Many of the Main St. brick business buildings in use today were constructed after a fire in 1845.

Chapman-Hall House (1754), Main St. (*summer, daily except Mon. 1-5*), is a restored house museum with period furnishings, shipbuilding and other historical exhibits and an herb garden.

Cortrell-Stetson House (1800) (*private*) nearby has an ell dated 1790.

Skidompha Library (1902) (*daily*) got its name from the initials of its founders.

On Main St. hill, an attractive Information Center. Junction (R) with State 129 (*see Tour 1G*).

Prehistoric Oyster Shell Heaps E of village in a State-owned three-acre tract, are among the world's largest Indian 'kitchen middens.' Past excavations exposing the strata have shown deposits to contain more than a million cubic feet of shells in three main layers, often 30 feet deep. Huge individual oyster shells ranging from a foot to 20 inches long have been found. Although oysters have not grown in quantity in the Salt Bay on the river for nearly 350 years, archaeologists estimate that their growth conditions were favorable for about 2000 years. There is a layer of soil between the bottom layer and the second; in this second layer, approximately six feet thick, the shells are mixed with the bones of animals. The top layer containing smaller shells, is covered with earth holding good-sized trees. Artifacts, stone fireplaces and human skeletons have been unearthed, indicating that the site was used by successive tribes of prehistoric people. The top deposit was made by Wabanaki Indians who came to the region in summer to catch fish and smoke them for winter use. Similar heaps on the Newcastle side of the river are privately owned.

Rejoin US 1 at 26.8 *m*. Road (L) to NOBLEBORO (alt. 170, Nobleboro Town, pop. 599), 3 *m*., part of the Pemaquid Patent, and named when incorporated in 1788 for an heir of the proprietor.

At 32.9 *m*., junction with State 220.

Right on State 220, WALDOBORO (alt. 120, Waldoboro Town, pop. 2882) .7 *m*. at the head of Medomak River navigation, is named for Gen. Samuel Waldo, proprietor of the Waldo Patent. In the *Old German Cemetery*, W side of river, a grave marker bears this inscription: 'This town was settled in 1748 by Germans who immigrated to this place with the promise and expectation of finding a prosperous city, instead of which they found nothing but wilderness.' Nearby is the *German Meetinghouse* (1770-72); its gallery overlooks a hand-made communion table and contribution boxes, straight unpainted pews and a cabinet containing a collection of German books and mementoes.

When the town engaged in shipbuilding, the first five-masted schooner, the *GOVERNOR AMES* was built here. Sonar buoy testing, canning and electric and plastic manufactories are current industries. An old *Cattle Pound* may be seen here and a Paul Revere bell from an early church now rings at the high school. Waldoboro Day is observed annually in July. Gov. Frederick G. Payne (1949) who also served in the U. S. Senate, made Waldoboro his home town.

FRIENDSHIP (alt. 90, Friendship Town, pop. 806) 10 *m*. is famous for the sloops that bear its name and has a history of boat-building since 1753. The Friendship Sloop Society has held annual homecoming week and sloop races each July since 1961; new entries for 1970 were of fiberglass. The Historical Society's museum has marine exhibits in a former one-room schoolhouse (1851) (*summer weekdays 10-5; Sun. 2-5*).

At 38.7 *m*., junction with State 90A.

Left on State 90A is WARREN (alt. 70, Warren Town, pop. 1678), 1.3 *m*., on the banks of the St. Georges River. Part of the Waldo Patent, it was set-tled in 1736, incorporated in 1776. A bronze plaque identifies Warren Academy (1877) now housing the Town offices. Shoe and woolen manufacturing have been supplanted by the manufacture and repair of trawler nets. Alewives and smelts running in the St. Georges are fished in season. *Meadow Mountain* (*visitors*) a 282-acre wooded tract with Quiggle Brook trout stream, is preserved in its natural state by the Nature Conservancy.

The uncovering of the *Powder Mill Locks* of the General Henry Knox Canal system has generated interest in the preservation of extant remains and restora-tion of some portions as an Historic Site and Park area. The Warren Develop-ment Corporation uncovered the locks, foundations and drains at Upper Falls above the town during a river beautification project begun in 1966. Canal banks are intact and rockwork of the locks — the upper lock wall is nine feet high — may be seen from a path between the gates. The canal system dates from 1793 when it connected tidewater at Warren and 'its headwaters, St. George Lake at Liberty. First affording passage for rafts and gundalows, the waterway later opened up the rich timberlands bordering the Georges River and its tributaries. Lumber and lime were moved over the route in narrow barges. The locks fell into decay after the death of Gen. Henry Knox (*see Thomaston*), first to build lock canals in New England. In 1848, the Georges Canal Company, through shareholders at a cost of $80,000, opened navigation of the Georges River to its sources. The steamer *MOLLIE* was used for excursions and as a tugboat to haul barges and alewives. The Warren Powder Manufacturing Company moved to the site in 1865, their mills consisting of seven separate buildings for the various processes. The firm's bankruptcy in 1873 followed a series of explosions. The German-American Powder Company then began operations, manufacturing gunpowder, blasting and mining powder. Again, explosions rocked the area, arousing the ire of the populace. The climax came on Sept. 5, 1876 when over 130 kegs of unfinished powder blew, shattering windows for miles around, including those of the two churches and the Academy, with losses estimated at $15,000. The company rebuilt and resumed production, but adverse public feeling was so strong the mill was forced to close in 1877.

Warren was the home of Cyrus Eaton whose *The Annals of Warren* (pub. 1877), has been reissued by the Warren Historical Society.

The founder of Christian Science spent some time here in 1864. Then Mrs. Patterson, she gave several lectures which she reported in a series of charming letters. Publicly advertised title of one of her lectures was 'P. P. Quimby's Spiritual Science Healing Disease — as opposed to Deism or Rochester-Rapping-Spiritualism.'

Warren Day is observed annually on the third Saturday in July.

THOMASTON (alt. 100, Thomaston Town, pop. 2780), 44.2 *m.* Handsome homes with notable doorways along its tree-shaded main street distinguish Thomaston, lying at the head of a long inlet that drains the St. Georges River. High on a hill at the E end of town, once part of the Waldo Patent, the imposing white Montpelier Mansion overlooks the countryside. At the W end is the State's Prison.

The foot of Knox St. is the site of a trading post established in 1630 and continuously occupied despite frequent Indian raids. Settlement started in 1783 and real development began after the Revolution. Thomaston prospered and in the 1800s was an important port and shipbuilding center. Around 1840, of the seven millionaires recorded in the United States, two were sea captains living in Thomaston.

Noted citizen was Daniel Rose (1771-1833), physician, engineer, magistrate, land agent and temporary governor of Maine (Jan. 1822), who was the State Prison's first warden. He is commemorated in the memorial volume *Maine Physicians of 1820.* His daughter Olive, a leader in the Women's Rights party, was among the first women to hold public office when she was elected Registrar of Deeds in Lincoln County in 1853.

Montpelier, replica of the General Knox Mansion (1795) (State Memorial) (*summer daily 10-5*) stands at the junction of US 1 and State 131 (*see Tour 1H*). The large two-story structure with basement, built through the generosity of Mrs. Efrem Zimbalist, has a low roof surrounded by a balustrade and surmounted by a monitor that rises between the four chimneys. The central third of the facade is elliptical and ornamented by four engaged columns. The pedimented doorway is reached by a stairway to the wide roofless piazza. Elegant Montpelier's 19 rooms, furnished with many valuable pieces from the original mansion, attracted robbers as well as sightseers in 1969. There are many of the General's mementoes and a portrait of him by Gilbert Stuart.

Major General Henry Knox who made a name for himself during the Revolutionary War, became a trusted advisor of George Washington and was Secretary of War under the Confederation and during President Washington's first term. At the close of his Cabinet career, he came to live in Thomaston which had been incorporated in 1777. Gen. Knox had married proper Bostonian Lucy Flucker, granddaughter of Gen. Samuel Waldo, proprietor of the Waldo Patent, a King's grant of more than 300,000 acres. Through purchase and marriage, Gen. Knox acquired much of the Patent and made many plans for the development of his holdings — shipbuilding, brick-making, lime-burning, farming, lumbering and other enterprises. In 1713, on the site of the trading post, Gen. Knox built and furnished a fine mansion where he and his wife entertained lavishly. The mansion was razed in 1871 to accommodate the railroads. Of the many buildings of the original estate, one remains, identified by a marker nearby.

At 25 Main St. is the *Cilley House, (private)* home of Jonathan Cilley, Congressional Representative from Maine when he was killed in a duel in February 1838 on the Bladensburg Dueling Grounds in Maryland. In Congress, Cilley had denounced a New York newspaper article that charged another Congressman with immorality. When he blamed the article on a Virginian, Rep. William Graves of Kentucky challenged him to a duel. Cilley fell at the third shot. Next door is the *Ruggles House, (private)*, built by U. S. Senator John Ruggles who established the U. S. Patent Office and held the first patent to be issued.

In 1824, Gov. William King sold to the State of Maine the site of the *Maine State Prison (visitors; 9-11 a. m.; 1-3 p. m., daily)*. A salesroom on Main Street offers furniture and other articles made by the prisoners. The first and perhaps the only military execution in Maine took place on Limestone Hill, the Prison site, when Jeremiah Braun was hanged for having guided a British raiding party that in 1780 captured Gen. Peleg Wadsworth, grandfather of Henry W. Longfellow. Capital punishment was abolished in Maine in 1876, then re-established in 1883, and again abolished in 1887 at the request of Gov. Joseph R. Bodwell who said it had not deterred crime.

The route soon passes the Dragon Cement Company (*visitors by appointment only*), one of the largest of its kind in New England. Limestone quarries are on both sides of the road.

ROCKLAND (alt. 40, pop. 8769), 48.5 *m.*

State Ferry Terminal, service to North Haven, Vinalhaven, Lincolnville, Islesboro, Bass Harbor, Swan's and Matinicus Islands (see ISLAND TRIPS). Seafoods Festival, August.

The world's fastest clipper ship, the *RED JACKET*; the poet of the Twenties, Edna St. Vincent Millay; and the William A. Farnsworth Art Museum identify with Rockland, the state's largest fishing port and midcoast retail center. The city is also the birthplace of Composer Walter Piston and Actress Maxine Elliott. Its deep-water harbor, railhead, airport and highway system have made Rockland a trading and shipping center for over a century. Knox County seat, settled in 1769, set off from Thomaston as East Thomaston in 1848, the city was chartered in 1854. Rockland is noted for lime, steel fabricating, and food stabilizers made from sea moss.

In the 1960s an extensive waterfront beautification program, new industrial development and recreational programs enhanced the city's environment.

Services include a modern general hospital, radio station, Maine's largest weekly newspaper, the *Courier-Gazette*, and Coast Guard Station with museum. Community-minded Rockland has been cited nationally in civic betterment programs. Annually in summer lobster is King at the Maine Seafoods Festival that draws thousands of visitors. Beaches, Penobscot Bay sailing and fishing, an art colony, arts and crafts workshops are attractions.

Catawamkeag (great landing place) was the Indian name for Rockland's beautiful harbor seen from most parts of the city. More than two miles long and a mile deep, it is protected by a *Breakwater* extending seven-eighths of a mile from Jameson's Point. Reached from Waldo Avenue, the Breakwater with lighthouse at the end, is a vantage point for surveying the city and environs. Harbor anchorages are over 40 feet deep and there are dock and service facilities for pleasure, fishing and freight vessels.

At 200 Broadway is the *Birthplace of Edna St. Vincent Millay*, (1892-1950) whose 'Conversations at Midnight' spoke for another young generation.

The *William A. Farnsworth Museum (Tues. through Sat. 10-5; Sun. 1-5; closed legal holidays and Mon. except July-August)*, and the adjoining *Farnsworth Homestead (June-Sept., same hours)* are on Elm St. Lucy C. Farnsworth, last of her line, was an astute business woman with wide real estate holdings who lived in frugal seclusion in the Farnsworth House until she died at 96 in 1935. To the surprise of her fellow citizens, she bequeathed her $1.3 million estate to the city for the establishment and endowment of a library and art museum and the maintenance of the Homestead.

The well-preserved Victorian house (c. 1840) with its original furnishings, the best of the period, is evocative. The formal parlor has its original wallpaper, draperies and cornices, satin-upholstered love seats and matching chairs. marble-topped tables and handsome mantel over an imported marble fireplace facing. A large oil painting of Miss Lucy and her brother James hangs on one wall. In the sitting room, a combination piano and organ, is one of few in existence. China and silver of unique design enhance the dining room. In the kitchen an early style cook stove has two fireboxes and two ovens. It is said these were to accommodate Miss Lucy and her mother who for some years were not on the best of terms. Upstairs the bedrooms are furnished in black walnut. In Miss Lucy's room is the worn old black handbag she always carried, and the sleigh bed in which she was found dead.

In 1948, the Farnsworth Museum opened, a fine building of modified Greek design by Architects Wadsworth, Boston and Tuttle of Portland and advisor Robert Bellows, then head of Boston's Art Commission and an architectural adviser for Colonial Williamsburg. The $600,000 building has three exhibition galleries, a library, craft shop, studios and classrooms. Under direction of Wendell S. Hadlock, the Farnsworth is identified with the work of Artist Andrew Wyeth, and its collections of representational paintings, drawings, prints and sculpture, mostly by American artists of the Nineteenth and Twentieth centuries. The Farnsworth collection shows paintings of the clipper *RED*

JACKET whose sheer grace and beauty have inspired many maritime painters. The giant clipper, swiftest of them all, was named for the Seneca Chief (1758-1830) of the Wolf Clan who often wore a red jacket. In 1792, President Washington presented the Chief with a medal for scout work during the Revolutionary War. Designed by Samuel A. Pook of Boston and built at the George Taylor yards in Rockland, the big ship was destined for a glamorous career — and an inglorious end. She was 260 feet long with a 44 foot beam and was advertised at 4000 tons burthen. Her figurehead, carvings and taffrail scrolls were all Maine-inspired, though she was coppered and decorated in Liverpool as was then customary. Launched in Rockland in 1853, the RED JACKET was purchased by the White Star Line for the Liverpool-Melbourne run. Carrying immigrants to Australia and gold coming back, she shattered records between those and other ports. Her most famous record-breaking run and all-time high among sailing ships was her maiden voyage, Capt. Asa Etheridge in command. Her time from New York to Liverpool, dock to dock, 13 days, one hour and 25 minutes, was never surpassed. For 30 years she was a proud and peerless ocean beauty.

In 1854, on a Great Circle course for running down the easting, Liverpool to Melbourne, the *RED JACKET*, Capt. Samuel Reid in command, established another unbeaten passage record: — under sail for 67 days 13 hours, she covered 13,880 miles. In Basil Lubbock's *Sail* Vol. 1, a passenger recounts the harrowing return voyage through field ice and towering icebergs. In 1870 she was sold into the Canadian timber trade, battling the North Atlantic until 1882 when she was sent to the Cape Verde Islands, there to expire ignominiously as a coal hulk in some forgotten cove. But the *RED JACKET* lives on in the annals of maritime history, in paintings by Grant Gordon, Montagues Dawson and Frank Vining Smith, in Currier and Ives lithographs and in tales of her beauty, grace and speed.

At Rockland, junction with State 17 (*see AUGUSTA*).

Right from Rockland on Main St.; at 2 *m.*, L on a tarred road; at 2.1 *m.*, L to large triangular *Range Beacons*, 3.7 *m.* U. S. Navy vessels use these open structures in sighting their positions on the measured trial course marked by six buoys off Rockland. New and reconditioned vessels test there for speed and engine efficiency.

OWL'S HEAD (alt. 40, Owl's Head Town, pop. 994), 4.6 *m.*, a summer resort on the far end of a tree-sheltered cape, was called Bedabedec Point (Ind.: cape of waters) when Champlain visited in 1605. A bloody encounter occurred here in 1755 when Indian fighter Capt. Carlyle killed and scalped nine braves, receiving a bounty of 200 pounds each. British and American privateers were active in nearby waters during the Revolution and the War of 1812.

Left from Owl's Head to the *U. S. Lighthouse Reservation,* 5.3 *m.*, (*visitors, 9-11:30 a. m., year-round July-August, 1-5 p. m.*). Built in 1826 during President John Quincy Adams' administration, the white tower light, although only 26 feet high, can be seen 16 miles at sea because of its elevation. Three strokes of a bell welcome cruising yachts.

At road's end, a short walk to the shore reveals the red and yellow quartz-streaked face of the headland rearing nearly 100 feet above sea level. Tall spruce, their roots clinging tenaciously to the soil, crown the summit.

Sec. c. ROCKLAND TO ELLSWORTH, 66 m.

This section of US 1 affords some of the finest scenery along the Maine coast, magnificent views for the most part unhampered by pleasantly located inns and shops that do not obtrude. North of Belfast it continues along the West bank of the Penobscot River over the route located by Richard Stinson in 1764 to Sandy Point, and over a bridge to the East bank before reaching Bucksport where it crosses a peninsula through old farmlands and wooded hills to Ellsworth.

US 1 leaves ROCKLAND (*see Tour 1, sec. b*), 0 *m.*

At 9.4 *m.*, junction road (R).

This road leads quickly into ROCKPORT (alt. 100, Rockport Town, pop. 2,000). Artists, architects, musicians, and horticulturalists have made Rockport and its villages an area of unusual charm, its harbor a summer haven for sailing and power boats. The entire town is planted with flowers and shrubbery by the Rockport Garden Club. Noteworthy estates with large gardens may be seen during the Camden Garden Club's annual July Open House Day. Goose River forms the V-shaped waterfront landscaped through the generosity of Mrs. Mary Louise Curtis Bok Zimbalist. There are two parks and the town maintains a recreation area beautifying the head of the harbor with its restaurant, marine services and shipyard. The Rockport Boat Club was formed in 1948. Picturesque feature of the landscape is the Chatfield herd of belted Galloways, hardy beef cattle from Scotland.

In 1891, a bitter dispute over construction of a new bridge over Goose River caused the separation of Rockport from Camden when the latter refused to pay her share of the costs. From the bridge at the south end of the village, an exceptional view encompasses the harbor dominated by the Indian Island lighthouse separated by a narrow passage from Beauchamp Point on the mainland. On summer Friday nights, Windjammer Cruise boats anchor in the harbor. In the river banks beneath the bridge, three old lime kilns are all that remain of Rockport's important Nineteenth century industry that included a narrow gauge railway. When the industry flourished it produced lime for use as mortar and plaster in this country and abroad. Some 300 casks of lime were shipped to Washington in 1817 and used in building the Capitol. A recreation area is being developed around the kilns.

A serene and inviting spot is Mrs. Helene Bok's *Vesper Hill Chapel* where many marriages take place, and its Biblical herb garden, flowers and shrubs amid the native tamarack, pine and spruce.

The Maine Coast Artists hold exhibits in the old Fire Station.

Efforts of Mr. and Mrs. Ambrose C. Cramer and a group of Rockport citizens in 1948 resulted in donation of land for the town's *Walker Park*, a beach and recreation area on the harbor's west side. Its programs have become models for other towns. *Mary-Lea Park* was created in 1966 as a memorial to Mme. Lea Luboshutz, violinist, and also honors her friend Mrs. Zimbalist. Rockport long has been a center for musicians, including Mme. Luboshutz' brother Pierre and his wife Genia (duo pianists Luboshutz and Nemenoff), and the Walter Wolfs and their sons Thomas and Andrew who initiated the Bay Chamber Concerts in Camden.

Perhaps best known among the estates is *Spite House*, massive structure moved by barge to Deadman's Point in 1925 from Phippsburg, 85 miles away. The story of this house is closely associated with the James McCobb House (1794) at Phippsburg Center (*see Tour 1D*). James married, and built for his second wife the home in Phippsburg now known as the Minott House. Some time after his third marriage, he died while his son Thomas was at sea. His widow, who also had been previously married, arranged a marriage between a son by her first husband and the sister of Thomas McCobb, thereby obtaining practical control of one of the largest estates in the area. When Thomas McCobb returned and learned of this, he became incensed and declared he would build himself a mansion of sufficient grandeur to overshadow the residence occupied by his step-mother. In 1806 he built the beautiful dwelling that ever after was to be known as Spite House. Outstanding in the surrounding gardens are the alpine plantings and boxwood. A collection of 5,000 lilies of 60 varieties, and many rare plants are skillfully handled.

Not to be missed is the performance of Tree Surgeon Harry Goodridge's trained seals at Rockport's Town Landing. 'Luigi' who will deliver lines from shore to boat and retrieve many objects, is receiving advanced training at the New England Aquarium to aid scientists in oceanographic studies.

The *Old Conway House* (*see below*) is on the Camden-Rockport line.

CAMDEN (alt. 100, Camden Town, pop. 3988), 11 *m.*, one of Maine's loveliest towns in a year-round resort area, lies 'under the high mountains of the Penobscot, against whose feet the sea doth beat,' as Capt. John Smith described the site. Champlain who visited in 1605, named the Camden Hills the 'mountains of Bedabedec' on his map. So steeply do they rise from the blue waters of Penobscot Bay that the numerous yachts at anchor seem to ride in the heart of the business district. A splendid fleet of windjammers that draw cruise-minded tourists from many parts of the globe has its home port in Camden where the first six-master *GEORGE WELLS* was built. Camden's attractiveness is enhanced by the Camden Garden Club's flower boxes on its street lamps and store fronts.

Besides golf, fishing, sailing and other water sports in summer, the community-owned Snow Bowl with trails, ski-lift and lodge is a popular winter sports center.

Behind the Public Library on Main St., the *Bok Amphitheatre* seating 1500 and landscaped with native flora, is across the street from the Civil War Monument overlooking the harbor. The old *Camden Opera House* at Elm and Washington Sts., is now a modern elaborately decorated auditorium where town meetings as well as theatrical productions take place. Mrs. Efrem Zimbalist, wife of the violinist and daughter of Cyrus H. K. Curtis initiated many municipal improvements. In the succession of world-famous musicians who have made Camden their summer home have been Josef Hofmann, pianist; Zaltko Balokovic, violinist; and the harpist, Salzedo, whose summer school continues under the direction of Alice Chalifoux. A summer series of Bay Chamber concerts carry on the tradition of fine music and a growing number of contemporary artists also live in the vicinity.

At Bay View wharf the 88-foot schooner *BOWDOIN* (1921) (*visitors*), custom-built for Rear Admiral Donald B. MacMillan's arctic expeditions, is part of a developing historical complex including a dockside museum preserving the heritage of wooden shipbuilding. On April 6, 1969, the 60th anniversary

of the Peary Expedition to the North Pole, Admiral MacMillan, aged 94, last
survivor of that 1909 expedition, received congratulations from President
Nixon and the Apollo X astronauts. The Schooner Bowdoin Association which
maintains the vessel, presented the veteran polar explorer with a half-round
model of the *BOWDOIN*, built by George Hodgdon of Boothbay whose
family launched the original vessel in 1921. Admiral Robert E. Peary invited
MacMillan to join the North Pole Expedition in 1908. He led one of the supporting parties that sledged over the Arctic Ocean with supplies for Peary's final
dash to the top of the world. Later MacMillan with a crew of college youths
conducted expeditions to Greenland and Labrador every summer for 40 years.
Both Peary and MacMillan were graduates of Bowdoin College where an
arctic museum on the campus houses many of their collections (*see BRUNSWICK*).

Left from Camden on Mountain St. which enters State 52 at 1 *m.*, a trail leads
to the summit of *Mount Battie* (800 ft.) which is reached by car from the
State Park (*see below*). From this height, occupied by cannon during the
War of 1812, are fine views of Penobscot Bay, the surrounding hills and
countryside that inspired the poem 'Renascence' by Edna St. Vincent Millay
who spent her girlhood in Camden. On the summit are a commemorative
plaque honoring the poet and a stone tower in memory of Camden World
War I veterans.

Lake Megunticook (fishing, boating, water sports), 2 *m.*

At Conway Road is the *Old Conway House (summer, daily except Mon. 1-5)*,
an Eighteenth century farmhouse that was the home of Robert Thorndike, Jr.,
son of the area's first settler in 1768. Restored by the Camden-Rockport
Historical Society, the house has authentic furnishings, with original four-light
transom over the front door and an unusual curved entrance hall with 'parson's
cupboard.' The kitchen bake oven is built with the early small bricks. Roof
timbers are fastened with trunnels (treenails) and ceilings are of hand-split hemlock, beams and heavy sills hand-hewn with broadaxe and adze, and rose-head
nails used in some of the fastenings. Many cellar beams retain their bark
covering. Other features include wide floorboards, a double brick hearth, L
and H hinges, bean latches and one butterfly hinge.

In the old barn, one of the best known examples of the heavy timbered type
of the period, are early carriages and farm implements. There is also a Blacksmith Shop and a 76-year-old Camden steam fire engine, the 'Molyneaux.'

At 12.8 *m.*, *Camden Hills State Park (camping and picnic grounds, foot
trails)* looks upon Penobscot Bay. A paved road leads up Mount Battie,

LINCOLNVILLE BEACH, 17.2 *m.* has a lobster pound, restaurants,
motels and year-round ferry service to Islesboro (*see ISLAND TRIPS*).

At 18.2 *m.* where a stream enters Penobscot Bay, DUCK TRAP is known
for good hunting and fishing.

At 22.2, a road (R) leads to NORTHPORT near Saturday Cove, an arm
of Penobscot Bay.

At 28.5 *m.*, bear right to Belfast City Park.

BELFAST (alt. 160, pop. 6,140). Named for the Irish city by Scotch-

Irish settlers in 1770 and observing its 200th anniversary in 1970, Belfast was first known as the Settlement of Passagassawakeg, its river still bearing this name. Now a center for poultry and allied industries, it is the shire town of Waldo County, part of the once great landholdings of Brig. Gen. Samuel Waldo, wealthy Boston merchant known for his fondness for fine raiment, who distinguished himself in King George's War 1740-48. Richard Stinson, pioneer settler of Belfast and Searsport, located lots and boundaries for Gen. Waldo's heirs in 1768-69 and was paid with 100 acres of land of his choice. After building a log house in his clearing, he hunted and trapped the abundant game, selling his furs at Fort Pownall and Bagaduce (Castine), and meat to Belfast settlers. Came the Revolution, a British Army occupied Bagaduce and the Belfast settlers fled. Stinson remained, however, and aided in the apprehension of a notorious plunderer of the deserted homes. After the war, settlers returned, were joined by others and development of the area began. By the mid-Nineteenth century Belfast had become a thriving shipbuilding community.

Parallel streets follow the rolling terrain that rises in a majestic sweep from the river banks to overlook the W side of island-sprinkled Penobscot Bay. Travelling in the area in 1795 with Gen. Henry Knox, the Duke de la Rochefoucauld-Liancourt commented, 'The view of the bay of Penobscot is one of the most agreeable prospects the eye can enjoy. The bay is very extensive and is interspersed with numberless islets of various magnitudes . . .'

After shipbuilding declined, reviving only briefly in World War II, the poultry industry grew to become the economic mainstay of Waldo County which before the industry became widespread, produced more broilers than any other place in the world. The annual July Broiler Festival and exhibits in Belfast Park draw hundreds of visitors. The birds are cooked in huge open pits and basted with a 'secret' sauce. Other industries include shoe and clothing manufacture, woodworking and sardine-packing, soy bean and peanut oil being first used here for this purpose.

Railroad buffs from all over the world come every summer to ride in the open gondola cars of the Belfast & Moosehead Railroad's 'Bull Moose,' the world's only city-owned and operated railroad that once carried passengers and freight over 33 miles of road through the towns of Waldo, Brooks, Knox, Thorndike, Unity and Burnham where the Maine Central Railroad covered the main line. When the main lines discontinued passenger service, so did the now diesel-engined 'Bull Moose' except for the special runs for railroad buffs.

Seagull Special Excursion (late July; barbecue, swimming, photo stops), Belfast to Burnham Junction, 33.7 *m.* The round trip in gondola cars is through lush green woods and open fields with many rivers and streams and sometimes wildlife to be seen. The train is turned on the wyes at Burnham Junction for the return trip. The Railroad provides a history of the line and a mile-by-mile roster of points of interest which include the huge hatcheries, processing plants and feed mills of the Maplewood and Penobscot Poultry Companies, two of Maine's largest, processing about 150,000 chickens per day, a half of the State's daily production. Also to be seen are tugs of the Eastern Maine Towage Co. that dock at nearby Searsport. The 80-pound rail between Waldo Station and Burnham Junction is unique in that all rail joints are opposite one another rather than being staggered. The Brooks station agent is Linwood Moody, famous authority on shortline railroads, author of *Maine Two-Footers.* Shortly after leaving 25-Mile Stream Bridge, rail weight of 80 pounds per yard with opposite joints changes to rail weight of 90 pounds to the yard with alternate joints. The 'clack-clack' changes to 'clackety-clack.'

The Maine Central and Bangor & Aroostook Railroads cooperate in arrangements, the latter also running a similar excursion to Northern Maine Junction, providing a unique experience for many in the jet age. Ellis, Wilson & Hogan of Canada laid the first track, of 50-pound Welsh iron, June 16, 1870. The engine 'Windsor' with two platform cars bearing some 20 citizens of Brooks and Unity arrived in Belfast in September and the road was formally opened in December. During the first year of operation, passengers furnished 22 percent of the road's total revenue. During the last year of passenger operation, 1959, passengers furnished only one half of one percent of total revenue.

Many handsome Federal and Greek Revival homes were built in Belfast and the community was a center of cultural activity until into the Twentieth century. The Arts and Crafts Association and the Belfast Historical Society are reviving these interests. Much of the city's historical environment, however, has succumbed to construction needs. Gone are the Woolpullers Stream and mill site, the Robert P. Chase House (1807) and Clay House (1825), and the home of Gov. William G. Crosby, along with some 40 native and imported trees and the great elms in the square. Whig Governor Crosby (1850-52), became a Democrat at the inception of that party in 1856. A member of the Maine Historical Society from 1846 until his death in 1881, he was the author of *Crosby's Annals.*

The *Birthplace of William Veazie Pratt* (1869-1957; is next (S) to the Peirce School. A distinguished orientalist and Annapolis graduate who served in the Far East, Admiral Pratt became president of the U. S. Naval War College and Chief of Naval Operations (1930-33). When President FDR wished to continue Admiral Pratt as CNO, Congress refused — 'we didn't do it for Dewey.' Until his death he was a *News Week* contributing editor and maintained extensive rose gardens at his home on Primrose Hill.

The brick house, NW corner Church and Market Sts., was the *Home of Hugh Johnston Anderson,* Congressman 1837-41; three-term governor beginning 1843; U. S. Post Office Department treasury auditor.

Other distinguished Belfast citizens: *John Cochran* (1749-1839), last of the 32 Penobscot proprietors whose monument in Grove Cemetery indicates he was a member of the Boston Tea Party on Dec. 16, 1773. *Hugh Dean McLellan* (1876-1952), a Boston Federal judge known nationwide for his courtroom wit. Congressman *Nathan Read* (1760-1849), Harvard valedictorian (1781) and inventor, who served as Chief Justice of the Court of Common Pleas. Of him Historian Williamson wrote: 'It is claimed that about this time (1788-89) he invented the necessary machinery to adapt Watt's steam engine to boat and land carriages . . .'

Two artists associated with Belfast: *Hartwell Leon Woodcock,* built Belfast's first telephone (acoustic, 1878); after study in Paris, he maintained a winter studio in Nassau and became known for his water colors. *Percy A. Sanborn* (1849-1929), expert in heraldry and graphics and painter of ships and animals also was a violinist and composed a symphony.

At Belfast, junction with State 3 (*see AUGUSTA*).

Belfast Memorial Bridge and the city's waterfront are seen from the high bridge over Passagassawakeg River as the route rejoins US 1.

At 32.8 *m.*, *Moose Point State Park* (R) on Penobscot Bay (*picnic sites, facilities; no camping or swimming.*)

SEARSPORT (alt. 50, Searsport Town, pop. 1888), 34.7 *m.* (*parks, wharf, landing ramp*). The State's second largest deep-water port, Searsport has contributed much to Maine's great maritime tradition. Busy today with export and import cargoes, the port had 17 shipyards and built 200 ships of different rigs in the Nineteenth century. From this community then came a tenth of the Merchant Marine's deep-water captains. Searsport ships were built and mastered by Searsport men who 'rounded the Horn' and sailed the southern seas to India and China. A lad once asked an old-time windjammer skipper 'What is the most important thing to learn?' He replied with a twinkle in his eye, 'It's very simple, son. Just always remember to spit to leeward.'

Captains' wives sometimes went along on the long voyages that could last three years and were a far cry from the Twentieth century pleasure cruise. Family life aboard those sailing vessels has been vividly recalled by two Searsport women born at sea, Marietta Pendleton, b. 1868 on the bark *THOMAS FLETCHER* near Cardiff, Wales, and Ethel M. Atwood, b. 1882 aboard the bark *ARLETTA* off Cadiz, Spain. The latter's first land 'shelter' was Mme. Tussaud's Waxworks in London. At home, the masters built fine houses and furnished them with foreign treasures.

Observing its 125th anniversary in 1970, Searsport was settled first in 1670-80. Massachusetts militiamen who built Fort Pownall, and seafaring families from southern New England came to put down roots in the wilderness where Indians had roamed so freely. A hundred years later, a treaty in 1786 fixed boundaries for Penobscot Indian hunting grounds; the Commonwealth of Massachusetts 'conveyed' certain portions to the Penobscots 'to hold and enjoy in fee,' together with '350 blankets, 200 pounds of powder with a proportion of shot and flint' in consideration for which the Penobscots relinquished certain other portions — 'we do for ourselves and on behalf of said Tribe, remise, release and forever quit our claim . . . so that we nor our heirs shall have any right to the same or any part thereof . . . and . . . shall be utterly excluded and debarred forever.'

In 1747 Searsport narrowly escaped becoming the capital of Massachusetts when fire destroyed Province House of Boston and a lengthy controversy ensued over changing the location of the seat of government. Samuel Waldo fought vigorously but unsuccessfully to this end, for the advancement of his holdings.

Mail delivery began in 1793 when George Russell travelled fortnightly between Wiscasset and Castine carrying letters tied in a handkerchief. Later the mail courier on horseback made his lonely journey through the woods, a 'twanging horn' announcing his arrival in the scattered settlements.

Besides shipbuilding, early industries included an iron foundry, cooper shops and brickyards. Today the port handles paper, potatoes and other Maine exports, and import cargoes of coal, salt and fuel oil. The pipeline to Limestone Airbase (*see Tour 1 sec. e*) begins here at the U. S. Military petroleum facility. Chemical, grain, oil and transport companies have plants, warehouses and terminals here.

Tow and steamboat service began in 1847. Until 1920, the old side-wheelers of the Eastern Steamship Lines carrying passengers and freight were a familiar sight. In 1891, the 'fleet' included the *PENOBSCOT, LEWISTON, KATAHDIN, MT. DESERT* and *ROCKLAND*. Round-trip fare between Boston-Searsport: $5.70. Of later fame was the *CITY OF BANGOR*.

Penobscot Marine Museum (summer, daily), a complex of four buildings at Main and Church Sts., has an outstanding maritime collection, including paintings and figureheads. The brick Old Town House was the Museum's first home in 1936. When Searsport was named for his forbears, David Sears, a wealthy Boston China merchant, gave $1,000 toward construction of this building as a meeting house. Other buildings in the complex are the Captain's House (1813), the Yellow and True Houses.

Searsport Historical Society (1964), cor. Main and Leach Sts., has collections of town memorabilia, documents and photos.

Carver Memorial Library (1910) is built of fieldstone from the 170-acre Carver Farm that included the Moose Point area given for the State Park.

A natural causeway at low water tide connects *Penobscot Park* with Sears, formerly Brigadier Island. A popular picnic area at the end of Sears Island Road, the Park was a recreation center developed by the Bangor & Aroostook RR. for its excursion passengers from Bangor and points north. In the 1960s, the B & A has operated special excursions in gondola cars from Searsport to Northern Maine Junction at Hermon, through the hilly country at Prospect, Frankfort and Winterport.

At *Mosman Memorial Park* an inscribed Rock, in memory of World War I veterans.

The *Penobscot*, Maine's second oldest hand-tub, displayed by Fire Department (1854).

The white *Harbor Church* (1819, Congregational), first church in the area, has a Christopher Wren steeple and Tiffany stained glass windows. The Rev. Jonathan Fisher (*see Tour 3*) was the moderator of the Ecclesiastical Council that recognized the parish organization in 1815. After the congregation moved to a larger meeting house in 1834, the church was used as a schoolhouse where Elijah Kellogg (*see Tour 1C*), preacher and author, was schoolmaster for a time.

In 1855 the Harbor Church again became a house of worship when a Second Congregational Church was organized. The old Church record makes this unusual statement: 'This movement for a Second Church has been made with the cordial consent of the First Church and with kind and fraternal feelings of all parties.' The Tiffany windows were installed in 1904 when Eugene Carver underwrote extensive repairs and improvements planned by his father, Capt. Nathan Carver. It was recorded that Mr. Carver 'has a strong affection for his native town and holds in high esteem the early settlers and the institutions which they toiled bravely to establish.'

At 34.9 *m.*, the *Home* of *Lincoln Colcord,* writer of sea stories, was for several generations the snug haven to which his forebears retired at the end of their voyages. More erudite if less well-known was Joanna Colcord, author of *Sea Chanties* and other works, who was born at sea two years before her brother Lincoln, and is buried at Searsport. She became head of the Russell Sage Foundation and in her seventies married a retired minister.

Artist Waldo Peirce also is associated with Searsport.

STOCKTON SPRINGS (alt. 150, Stockton Springs Town, pop. 1189), 38.4 *m.*

Road (R) through village to *Fort Pownall* (1759) State Memorial and Old Fort Lighthouse 3.5 *m.* (*interpretive displays, current archaeological program*). The British twice fired the fort, 1775-1779, to prevent it from falling into enemy hands.

At 39.1 *m.*, junction (L) with US 1A to Bangor (*see BANGOR*).

State 1A passes Mt. Waldo (1062 ft.) (*snowmobiling*) and several lesser peaks and a granite works site near Frankfort where a recreation development of 125 acres to be called 'Mohamed's Mountain' was projected in 1969.

SANDY POINT (alt. 110, Stockton Springs Town), 39.6 *m.* In the center of this village of green-shuttered white frame houses, the graceful facade of its white church faces Penobscot Bay. In the small burial ground opposite the church, many stones are marked 'Lost' or 'Died at Sea.' In memory of Capt. Albert Partridge, a polished granite globe bears the names of the many distant ports he visited.

At 45.2 *m.* entrance (L) to *Fort Knox State Park* .3 *m.* (*interpretive displays, nature trails, picnic facilities*).

This formidable Penobscot bastion built of Mt. Waldo granite by master craftsmen was named for the first U. S. Secretary of War, (*see Tour 1 sec. b*). Notable are the huge brick arches, circular stairs and underground passages. The site was selected in 1844 as a defense in the Aroostook War. In the Twentieth century the fort was an effective setting for several seasons of such Shakespearian drama as *MACBETH* directed by University of Maine's Herschel Bricker.

The Waldo-Hancock Bridge (137 ft.) takes US 1 across the Penobscot River. Completed in 1931, this suspension bridge was cited as the most beautiful of its time.

VERONA (alt. 80, Verona Town, pop. 378) 45.8 *m.*, (*picnic area*), is an island in the Penobscot River and a former shipbuilding village. The last vessel built here was the *ROOSEVELT* (1905) which carried Commander Robert E. Peary on his final Arctic expedition to the North Pole.

US 1 crosses Verona Bridge to

BUCKSPORT (alt. 80, Bucksport Town, pop. 3501) 46.7 *m.* The main street follows the E bank of the Penobscot. High on the opposite shore, the gray ramparts of Fort Knox look like a medieval castle.

Principal industry of the area, settled in 1762, is the internationally known St. Regis Paper Company which produces high quality papers. The mill (1930) with its huge piles of pulpwood occupies the northern part of town, along with a group of Colonial-style company houses with landscaped grounds. Bucksport also has large tank farms where oil is brought in by barge.

Merchants' and shipmasters' houses of an earlier day line Franklin St. Crowning a hilltop N are the buildings of *St. Joseph Seminary* (1930) on the site of the Eastern Maine Conference Seminary (Methodist-Episcopal 1851). From the campus, Verona is an emerald isle and the Waldo-Hancock Bridge, a shining ribbon of steel flung across the blue Penobscot.
The old railroad depot here is now the Historical Society's Museum.
Birthplace of William and Dustin Farnum, stage and screen stars, S side of Franklin St.

Doctor Moulton House (1799), cor. Federal and Franklin Sts., was occupied by British raiders during the War of 1812.

Jed Prouty Tavern (1804), Main and Federal Sts., a fine inn, was the setting of a popular comedy 'Old Jed Prouty.' The white, three-story hostelry was a well-known stop on the stage route between Bangor and Castine in summer. Travellers rested beneath a great blackheart cherry tree among white rosebushes by the fence and watched the busy river traffic while they waited for supper. On the pages of the old register are 'Martin Van Buren, The White House,' written in bold letters; 'Gen'l Jackson — Hermitage'; the name of William Henry Harrison; and 'John Tyler, Washington,' after whose name some wag had written 'And the Old Nick is after him.'

Seen from the highway near the Verona bridge entrance is a *Granite Obelisk* in Buck Cemetery, marking the resting place of Col. Jonathan Buck for whom Bucksport was named. Legend has it that while living in Haverhill, Mass., before coming to Maine, Col. Buck was called upon officially to execute a

CHURCH AND SCHOOL

IN education and religion are seen both continuity and change since the early days of the travelling schoolmaster and the itinerant preacher. Central schools have long since replaced the 'little red schoolhouse' which survives only occasionally as an historical museum. New architectural forms as well as curricula are seen in secondary schools and on spreading college campuses as seats of learning more and more become cultural centers. While new forms also are seen in houses of worship, fine examples of early meetinghouses and churches are found in many Maine communities where they have been preserved and restored.

OLD STONE SCHOOL AT ROUND POND

MT. BLUE HIGH SCHOOL, FARMINGTON

FOGG MEMORIAL BUILDING AT BERWICK ACADEMY

SOUTHERN MAINE VOCATIONAL-TECHNICAL INSTITUTE
AT SOUTH PORTLAND

BATES COLLEGE CHAPEL AT LEWISTON

HAWTHORNE-LONGFELLOW LIBRARY, BOWDOIN COLLEGE, AT BRUNSWICK

COUNTRY CHURCH

INDIAN TEACHER,
WASHINGTON COUNTY

HARRINGTON MEETINGHOUSE AT PEMAQUID

OLD GERMAN
MEETINGHOUSE
AT WALDOBORO

CHURCH AND MONUMENT AT NOBLEBORO

SS. PETER AND PAUL
CHURCH AT LEWISTON

ZOOLOGICAL BUILDING,
UNIVERSITY OF MAINE, ORONO

ST. FRANCIS COLLEGE AT BIDDEFORD

woman condemned as a witch. It was said the woman placed a curse on him; after his death the likeness of a leg and foot appeared on the side of his granite monument. The mark, undoubtedly a defect in the stone, reappears after every effort to efface it and is called the Witch's Curse.

At ORLAND (alt. 180, Orland Town, pop. 1,206), 48.5 *m.*, junction with State 175 (R), to Castine 15 *m.* (*see Tour 3*).

At .3 *m.* on State 175, Orland Village with neat homes and churches lies on the banks of the Narramissic River. Edwin Ginn, Boston publisher, was born here in 1838.

EAST ORLAND, 52.6 *m.*, a crossroads.

A road (L) leads to *Craig Brook National Fish Hatchery (visitors)*, 1.3 *m.*, at Alamoosook Lake where salmon and trout are propagated. The road completely circles the lake shores where *Five Prehistoric Indian Cemeteries*, together with Indian relics and workshops have been unearthed during extensive excavations.

Right from the Hatchery on a trail 2 *m.* along the course of Craig Brook to Craig Pond, then N to Great Mountain (alt. 1,037). A deep *Cave* on the slope burrows over 60 feet into the heart of the mountain. Wall and ceiling formations give its several rooms an eerie air.

At 63.5 *m.*, a *Picnic Area* (R).

ELLSWORTH, (alt. 100, pop. 4,444), 66 *m.*, county seat and business center, is the gateway to world-famous Acadia National Park and the Mt. Desert region (*see Tour 2*).

Settled in 1763, the community has seen extensive lumbering operations, a period of shipbuilding and an industrial era with development of its water power. The business district, rebuilt after a disastrous fire in 1933, now is a happy mingling of old and new as seen in the Scandinavian-style City Hall in juxtaposition with the old white Congregational Church (1812) dominating the east side of State St. hill. The Church has a portico with delicate fluted columns and a slender spire.

A 60-foot *Falls* is seen from the bridge (R) over Union River flowing through the city's center. There are also Indian cemeteries and shell heaps in Ellsworth.

The *Black Mansion* (c. 1802) (*June-Oct. daily*), W. Main St., is widely known as an excellent example of modified Georgian architecture, an elegant structure in the then tiny frontier settlement. It was the home of Col. John Black, land agent for William Bingham (*see Tour 4E*), who owned two million acres east of the Penobscot. Col. Black's predecessor in the agency was his father-in-law, Col. David Cobb, an aide-de-camp of General Washington. The two-story house with one-story wings has no front entrance: four triple-hung shuttered windows open out on a low porch with five Ionic columns. Running the length of the main building, the porch is surmounted by a balustrade. An ornamental cornice and balustrade surround the low roof. Inside, a gracefully curving

staircase rising from a spacious hall divides the house and parallels its front.
Many possessions of Col. Black and his wife remain just as they left them.
Among valued relics are a miniature of Washington by one of the Peales and
a rare volume of the Colonial laws of Massachusetts.

Public Library, State St., once the Tisdale House (c. 1820) retains such
architectural features as arched doorways and fireplaces.

At Ellsworth are junctions with State 3 (*see Tour 2*); *State 172*, (*see
Tour 3*), and US 1A to Bangor (*see BANGOR*).

Sec. d. ELLSWORTH to CALAIS, 121.4 m.

Seekers of untrammeled natural beauty are discovering 'Way Down East,'
the magnificent lands of Washington County that once were the territory
and hunting grounds of the People of the Dawn, the Passamaquoddy tribe
of Wabanaki Indians. Accessible by land, sea and air, its 2,628 square
miles of woodland, lakes and mountains lure Twentieth century white
hunters and fishermen; others find the rugged Atlantic coastal scenery
exhilarating and the colorful fishing villages enchanting. There is a 22,665-
acre National Wildlife Refuge and such natural phenomena as reversing
falls, record tides and the world's second largest whirlpool, as well as
fascinating specimens for the amateur geologist and botanist and endless
inspiration for artists of the palette and the lens. The Nation's first president made his only recorded visit to Maine, then a District of Massachusetts, when Washington County was named for him in 1789.

Glacial boulders mark the colorful and fragrant blueberry barrens whose
thousands of acres produce 90 percent of the Nation's crop. Fishing, shipbuilding and lumbering have been important in the history of the region
which has seen the last of the great spring log drives east of the Mississippi.
Vacation areas are developing and some of the Nation's largest paper industries have plants in Washington County, sometimes called the 'Sunrise
County' since it is the most easterly point in the United States. Friendly
international relations are exemplary in the border towns of Maine and
New Brunswick, Canada, along the St. Croix River, international boundary,
and in the Campobello-Roosevelt International Memorial Park.

With many side roads inviting exploration, US 1 proceeds along the heads
of numerous bays in Hancock and Washington Counties and then along
the St. Croix River before branching inland to the big lake country and
southern Aroostook County. Washington County's coastline wanders
around 700 miles of coves and estuaries between Steuben and the New
Brunswick, N. S. line.

US 1 leaves ELLSWORTH (*see Tour 1, sec. c*) 0 *m.*

At 1.9 *m.*, junction (R) with State 184 to *Lamoine State Park (picnic and
campsites, boating facilities)*, 8 *m.*, on Mt. Desert Narrows in Frenchman

Bay.

At 2.4 *m.* (L), *White Birches Golf Course and School*, boys' camp.

At FRANKLIN ROADS (alt. 40, Hancock Town) at the head of Skillings River inlet is the Ellsworth-Hancock Tannery (L), principal area industry.

Here is a junction (L) with State 182, a much-travelled short-cut (23.2 *m.*) through a range of mountains separating Hancock and Washington Counties and following the shores of several lakes and ponds to rejoin US 1 at Cherryfield (*see below*).

> Left on State 182 at 2.2 *m*, Egypt Stream, Hancock-Franklin boundary. At 4.1 *m.* (R) is the Franklin Historical Society's *Memorial Park*, two acres of gardens and granite exhibits, a blacksmith shop and a galamander, once used to carry large granite blocks.

> FRANKLIN (alt. 20, Franklin Town, pop. 729), 6.2 *m.* Blueberry processing has supplanted earlier lumbering, shipbuilding and quarrying operations in this quiet town at the head of Frenchman Bay. A modern plant processes some 4 million pounds of frozen blueberries annually. Tree-farm production of Christmas trees is another sizeable industry. Also a vacation area with several ponds and lakes, Franklin attracts city folk who acquire and restore old farms and homes for retirement.

> Moses Butler was the first settler in 1764 at Butler's Point, an Indian settlement where many artifacts have been found. The Point jutting into the Bay overlooks all water approaches which was important to the settlers on guard against surprise Indian attacks. As lumbering began, great mast ships were built; first exports were ship masts and knees. Later, Franklin produced more railroad ties than any other town in the Country. Granite quarrying began around 1840, to flourish nearly a century. Schooners were built to carry the white granite to all principal cities of the eastern seaboard where cutting and styling was done. It was used principally for cemetery stones, paving and curbing. A limited amount of extremely hard black or emerald green granite was quarried, some of it used in balustrades in the White House.

> At 13 *m.* the road winds north along Fox Pond shore then ascends *Catherine Mountain* (942 ft.). At the bottom of the descent, it passes between Spring River Lake (L) and Tunk Lake (R) through a beautiful area called Black's Woods.

> At 23.3 *m.* State 182 rejoins US 1 at Cherryfield.

HANCOCK (alt. 40, Hancock Town, pop. 919), 8.9 *m.*, settled in 1794, was named for John Hancock, first signer of the Declaration of Independence. Hancock Point Road (R) leads to a summer colony with a spectacular view of Mount Desert Island across Frenchman Bay.

From an elevation (R) at 11.5 *m.* is a view said by Henry Van Dyke to be one of the most beautiful in the world, across Frenchman Bay to Cadillac Mountain.

SULLIVAN (alt. 60, Sullivan Town, pop. 676), 12 *m.*, a summer resort, was another granite center; its paving blocks laid the dust of many streets in America's cities. The *Granite Store* (R) (*closed*), built to store salt, is a reminder of the granite and fishing industries.

At 13.1 *m.*, State 185 (R) leads to Sorrento, summer resort (*golf, scenic views.*

At 18 *m.*, junction with State 186.

> R on State 186 for a scenic peninsula loop drive to Winter Harbor, Schoodic Point, a section of Acadia National Park, Prospect and Birch Harbors. Pointed spruce crown windswept ledges along the jagged coast of this exclusive resort area. The route over winding rolling terrain follows the west shores of Frenchman Bay through the small villages of West and South Gouldsboro which overlooks Stave and Jordan Islands and across to the hills of Mt. Desert.
>
> At 3.8 *m.* a local road (R) leads about 2.5 *m.* to WINTER HARBOR (alt. 50, Winter Harbor Town, pop. 1188), so named because its waters never freeze and sailing vessels could be moored here safely. The town is now a harmonious combination of Navy personnel, wealthy summer residents and fishermen. The Navy has a large housing development, and at Grindstone Neck (*golf course*) and Sargent's Point are many outstanding modern summer homes.
>
> At 7 *m.* a local road (R) goes to Schoodic Point in a section of Acadia National Park (*picnic area, landing wharf*), and to the U. S. Navy Security Group Activity, a large radio communications station. The road winds through the Park following the shore of the Point between walls of spruce trees, opening from time to time to unparalleled views of Mt. Desert and numerous small islands. In the foreground is the ancient but discontinued Mark Island Light. Within the Park the road ascends a mile to the summit of Schoodic Head (alt. 437) where the entrance to the Bay of Fundy can be seen NE.
>
> The road leaves the Park at Wonsqueak, a small fishing village whose curious name is said to have derived from an Indian legend. A brave became jealous of his squaw, took her out in his canoe and threw her overboard. Before the waters closed over her head, she gave one squeak. A road (R) leads to the Navy Station and to Schoodic Point parking area for fine views of surf, ocean and Cadillac Mt.
>
> After leaving the Park and passing through Bunkers Harbor, the road rejoins State 186 to continue to BIRCH HARBOR (alt. 50, Gouldsboro Town), a fishing village with a summer colony and fine seascapes. At 10 *m.*, PROSPECT HARBOR (alt. 30, Gouldsboro Town), called Watering Cove in early days of settlement. The Stinson Canning Company here is Maine's newest and largest sardine factory (1969). Many women are employed in packing the herring taken in weirs and seining boats all along the coast, for round the world shipment.
>
> At 10.9 *m.* State 195 (R) goes to COREA, 3 *m.*, a fishing and recreation village where wind-swept sand dunes contrast with the otherwise rugged coastal scenery. This village with its lobster boats and lobster pounds and fishermen's cottages has been much photographed.
>
> On the outskirts of Gouldsboro State 186 rejoins US 1 at 15.9 *m.*

GOULDSBORO (alt. 80, Gouldsboro Town, pop. 1,344), 21.6 *m.*, has many separate fishing and summer colony villages. Gen. David Cobb who served as President of the Massachusetts Senate, lived here (1796-1820) while he was agent for the Bingham Estate (*see Tour 4E*). He had expected Gouldsboro would be the principal town in Hancock County, not anticipating the growth of the lumber industry centering in Ellsworth.

STEUBEN (alt. 40, Steuben Town, pop. 561), 25.7 *m.*, (pronounced Stu-BEN), a fishing and summer residential village reached from roads (R) was incorporated 1795 and named for Baron Von Steuben, Inspector General of the Continental Army. Joel and Rebecca Moore settled here in the Bingham Tract in 1795. Their descendants, Cousins Henry and John Moore became influential American business leaders in railroading and other enterprises in the 1800s. John successfully fought the first income tax law in 1886; there was none thereafter until 1913. Henry gave the *Parish House* here as a community center and library.

MILBRIDGE (alt. 20, Milbridge Town, pop. 1001), 31.3 *m.*, area shopping center, lies at the mouth of the Narraguagus, its main street paralleling the river, with views of off-shore islands. Nearby is *McLellan Park* on a bluff overlooking the bay (*service building, trails, tenting and picnicking*). Century-old Jasper Wyman & Sons, one of the largest growers and processors of blueberries, produces the largest single crop in the world, 29 million pounds in 1967, raking 4,000 bushels a day on 36,000 acres south of Cherryfield. These are the blueberry barrens of the glacial plain where modern methods have improved the fruit over the days when the only 'cultivation' was periodic burning over the barrens. Hollis Wyman's 2,000 acres of blueberries are pollinated in June by 80 million bees trucked in from New York in 1600 double hives.

At 36.2 *m.* (L), junction with State 182, the short-cut from Franklin Roads rejoining US 1 at

CHERRYFIELD (alt. 50, Cherryfield Town, pop. 733), 36.4 *m.*, lying on both sides of the Narraguagus River, fishermen's favorite for taking Atlantic salmon. In honor of this piscatorial prize, the road between here and Milbridge is designated the Narraguagus Highway. Built in this former shipbuilding community was the full-rigged bark *BELGRADE* that carried 56 local men around Cape Horn to California in the days of the gold rush. Blueberry packing is the local industry.

Here is a *Picnic Area* and junction with State 193 (*see Tour 5*).

At 40.7 *m.* (L), Narraguagus High School, serving several surrounding towns, is distinguished by its circular and domed gymnasium.

HARRINGTON, (alt. 4, Harrington Town, pop. 670), 42.3 *m.*, settled c. 1765. Like other villages between Ellsworth and Calais whose populations have dwindled with the decline of shipbuilding and fishing, Harrington retains its charm in neat, well-kept homes and a compact orderliness.

At 45.2 *m.*, junction with the Jeff Davis Trail, cut in 1858 for the U. S. Coast Survey to transport supplies and heavy instruments to the top of Humpback Mountain. Jefferson Davis, close friend of Alexander Bache, superintendent of the survey, visited the camp.

Left on the Trail road is COLUMBIA (alt. 60, Columbia Town, pop. 151), 1.5 *m.*, settled soon after the Revolution. The road continues NW on a 200-square-mile plateau through blueberry country. Small brooks meander through acres of low bushes covered in mid-June with inverted bell blossoms. Later there is the memorable fragrance of ripening berries and the woods under the hot sun. Blueberry packing begins in August and lasts through September. Workers labor from dawn to dusk raking, winnowing and boxing the berries to be trucked to canning factories and freezing plants. The blueberry industry grew in the wake of lumbering; plants quickly cover the thin sandy soil after trees are cut. Spruce in this area was removed early in the Nineteenth century to provide masts and spars for nearby shipyards. Blueberry plains or barrens are privately owned and protected by the State.

COLUMBIA FALLS (alt. 60, Columbia Falls Town, pop. 432), 46.3 *m.*, roads (R) leading to the village whose fine old homes recall prosperous lumbering and shipbuilding days. Atlantic salmon leap in the rips and pools of Pleasant River.

The *Ruggles House* (c. 1818) (*summer weekdays 8:30-4:30; Sun. 10-4*), constructed after a design by Aaron Sherman of Duxbury, Mass., who planned several homes in Washington County, was built for Judge Thomas Ruggles, wealthy lumber dealer. The house is notable for the delicate detail of its exterior trim. The interior woodwork, executed by an unknown English artisan, is unusually fine. In the drawing-room are rope beadings on the fireplace cornices, done with great skill; exquisite carvings on the molding and delicate indentures on the chair rail of the wainscoting and on the frames and sills of the wide-shuttered windows. When the house was restored, workmen uncovered rich mahogany-inlaid panels. The house was the setting for Arthur Train's short story, 'The House that Tutt Built.'

The *Maude Bucknam House* (c. 1820), opp. post office, a Cape Cod style dwelling with wing, also is notable for its woodwork.

The *Lippincott House*, opposite, is square, with hip roof and such interesting interior details as rope moldings and many fireplaces.

At 48.3 *m.*, junction with State 187.

Right on State 187, through the deep stillness of the woods and along the western shore of Englishman Bay, with many attractive scenes, to JONESPORT (alt. 40, Jonesport Town, pop. 1,430), 12 *m.* Across a bridge is BEALS (alt. 40, Beal's Island, pop. 635). These are colorful fishing communities where sardine factories, boat-building shops and peat digging operations may be visited. Island views, camp sites, fishing and beaches are its resort attractions.

In 1865, G. J. Adams, a disgruntled Mormon elder from Philadelphia, succeeded despite local opposition in recruiting followers here. Prevailing upon many to sell their worldly goods, he organized the Palestine Emigration Association, issuing a religious publication, 'The Sword of Truth and the Harbinger of

Peace.' After arrangements with the Turkish government through the American consul, 175 members left on a 52-day voyage to Palestine in the barkentine *NELLIE CHAPIN*, and settled near Jaffa. Beset by internal dissension, misunderstanding with the natives, and disease caused by poor sanitary conditions, the colony was disbanded within a year and survivors returned to the United States.

Barney's Point on the island was named for Barney Beal, a son of Manwaring Beal, the first settler. Colorful island legends are woven around the bold exploits and feats of strength of 'Tall Barney,' who always wore a butcher's coat and whose six feet seven inches of brawn earned him fame as cock of the walk from Quoddy Head to Cape Elizabeth. It was said when he sat in a chair his hands touched the floor. Once, while he was fishing off Black's Island, armed sailors, objecting to his proximity to English territory, boarded his sloop, intent on capture at gun point. Barney relieved the sailors of their guns which he promptly broke over his knee and tossed back into the British boat. When the Canadian guards persisted, Barney twisted the arm of one until he broke the bone. In Rockland, Barney was said to have felled a horse with his fist. In a Portland saloon without argument or assistance, he proved to 15 men the folly of deriding a 'down-easter.'

Perio's Point near the Freeman West Beal wharf, was named for Perio Checkers, an Indian who is the only man known to have scaled the perpendicular side of the steep cliff here that still challenges climbers.

In the past when shipwrecks were frequent, companies were formed on the mainland to salvage boats and cargoes.

The *Gravestone of Aunt Peggy Beal* in the cemetery near the public square, recalls the days of witchcraft when Aunt Peggy is said to have exorcised the powers of a witch in the person of a Mrs. Thomas Hicks who had the habit of borrowing from Aunt Peggy. If she didn't get what she wanted, it either died or disappeared. The last item Aunt Peggy refused to loan was a sheep which died the following day. Whereupon a Salem sailor who claimed to know all about handling witches, told Aunt Peggy to build a hot fire and scorch the sheep. This was done. 'Now,' he said, 'a boat will come over for something three times and you must refuse each time.' It all came about as the sailor predicted, so the story goes, and the day following the third refusal, Mrs. Hicks was dead.

Separated from its larger but much less populous neighbor, Great Wass Island, by the Flying Place, a narrow strait where there is a spectacular display of surf on stormy days, Beals Island affords views of surrounding islands and curious sea-wrought formations.
State 187 may be continued 11 *m.* along Chandler's Bay to rejoin US 1 near Jonesboro.

US 1 continues through blueberry lands and at 51.4 *m.* (R) is the University of Maine's Blueberry Hill Experimental Farm; just beyond (L) a *Picnic Area.*

JONESBORO (alt. 60, Jonesboro Town, pop. 514), 55.5 *m.*, a small farming community on the Chandler River, had a Revolutionary War heroine in the person of Hannah Weston, a descendant of Hannah Dustin, famous in the Haverhill, Mass. Indian Massacre in 1697. With a younger sister, Hannah Weston carried 50 pounds of lead and powder through the woods from Jonesboro to Machias for use during the *MARGARETTA* episode (*see below*) in June, 1775. Her grave is near the highway at the northern end of the village.

At 57.2 *m.*, junction with US 1A.

Left on US 1A is WHITNEYVILLE (alt. 70, Whitneyville Town, pop. 200), 4 *m.* This small lumbering community on the banks of the Machias River has been the terminus of the annual spring log drive, one of the last of the long lumber drives east of the Mississippi. A *Marker* near the river indicates the spot where the *MARGARETTA*, after being towed up the river following her capture, was beached and concealed from the British with foliage. US 1A runs through blueberry country 4.5 *m.* more to rejoin US 1 at Machias.

MACHIAS (Ind.: bad little falls) (alt. 80, Machias Town, pop. 2,328), (*fishing, boating*), 62.9 *m.*, Washington County seat, lies along the Machias River. The gristmill in the center of the bridge across the river looks down on roaring waters of a narrow gorge. From the bridge are seen the buildings of University of Maine's *Washington State College* on a hill overlooking the town. Fishing and boating are available at Machias.

The river has been important in the town's development as a lumber and shipbuilding center. One of the few remaining 'long lumber' drives takes place on the Machias in spring. Logs are hauled over the snow to the landings and when the ice goes out, they are shoved into the fast-moving water to hurtle downstream. When one of the numerous log-jams occurs, a daring river-driver walks out on it to pry loose the key logs with his peavey; if this does not free them, the jam is blasted.

Washington County's industrial and economic potential in the 1960s was evident at Machias. Land values were rising as out-of-state buyers sought shore properties. Among industries operating in the area: Deering-Milliken subsidiary, St. Regis Paper Company, Machiasport Canning, Cedar Mill Fences and Passamaquoddy Lumber of the Dead River Company which was rapidly diversifying and developing the Paul Bunyan Shores at Corea, Duck Cove, Sorrento and Treasure Island on Frenchman Bay, and Cow Point on Englishman Bay, with similar plans for Lubec. In 1969 Machias made national news as major oil companies fought Maine's effort to establish a free port and subsequently a refinery that would mean cheaper fuel for New England.

Early trading post. After the French destroyed the Plymouth Colony trading post at Pentagoet (Castine), the English in 1633 established another post under command of Richard Vines here in a' spot much closer to the French head-quarters. La Tour, French Governor of Acadia, wiped it out almost at once. In 1675 the pirate Rhodes used the site as a base for repairs and supplies. A few decades later another pirate, Samuel Bellamy, came for the same purpose and liked the place so well he determined to establish a permanent strong-hold. Piracy was rampant along the Atlantic seaboard at this time, partly be-cause of English and Spanish trade restrictions designed to force colonists to buy from the mother country alone; this created a good market for stolen goods in the Colonies. Privateering provided good training for piracy, as Cotton Mather warned in 1704 in one of his 'hanging' sermons, and many men who started out to prey on shipping for their governments soon decided to keep the booty for themselves. Bellamy, from all reports, developed a Robin Hood philosophy on the matter; when he had captured a ship he would harangue its crew, invite them to join him, arguing that the men had as much right to rob as had the ship-owners who were merely powerful bandits who had had laws made to protect their operations.

Bellamy erected breastworks and a crude fort before leaving for another expedition with three objectives — recruits, loot and women. He had left the river and was plundering along the Nova Scotian banks when by mistake, he attacked a French naval vessel. His vessel, the *WHIDAW,* narrowly evaded capture before he escaped. Sailing south, he had further bad luck when he captured a New Bedford whaler whose captain pretended to join him and agreed to act as navigator through the dangerous reefs and shoals, which he did for a time. Then he deliberately ran his ship aground on a sandbar near Eastham, Mass. The pirate ship, following the whaler, went on the rocks and Bellamy and most of his crew drowned. In 1763, settlers from Scarborough in southern Maine established the first permanent English colony.

Burnham Tavern (1770) (*June-Oct.; Sat. p. m.*), High and Free Sts., is a plain two-story gambrel-roofed structure with the lower section of the roof broken back to a vertical wall with five windows. Beneath each of the four corner-stones, owner Joe Burnham placed a box containing a slip of paper inscribed with the words 'hospitality,' 'cheer,' 'hope," and 'courage.' Over the door the original sign reads: 'Drink for the thirsty, food for the hungry, lodging for the weary, and good keeping for horses.' Townspeople gathered here to plan their movements against the British and discuss events of the day. Here Jeremiah O'Brien and his comrades planned the capture of the British schooner *MARGARETTA* whose captain died in the Tavern. Nearby in the O'Brien Cemetery is the *Grave of Captain O'Brien* and just beyond (L) is a *Marker* indicating the site of his home.

The small stream at Elm St. is called *Foster's Rubicon.* Machias men met on its banks in June 1775 to discuss demands that they furnish lumber to be shipped to Boston for barracks for British troops. The debate was long; some townsmen advocated compliance, others, resistance. Benjamin Foster, a church leader as well as a rebel, sprang across the stream, inviting those who shared his views to follow him. The rebels went first, then those who had been wavering, and finally the compliants. The settlement as a whole thus was committed to the Revolution.

Roque Bluffs, 7 *m.* S of Machias was named for a Hessian soldier who, angered when the British failed to pay him for his services, came over to the American side in the Revolution and was granted this land at war's end. The State has acquired a 275-acre scenic coastal area here for future use.

Junction here with State 92.

Right on State 92 to MACHIASPORT (alt. 80, Machiasport Town, pop. 1,368), 4 *m.,* and *Fort O'Brien* (1775) State Memorial, 5 *m., (interpretive displays).*

When news of the battle of Lexington reached this part of Maine in early May 1775, Ichabod Jones who had left Massachusetts because of the increasing disturbance to business caused in part by the Boston Port bill, hastily left for Boston to secure his personal property. The Boston Port commander, however, permitted Jones to take his boat from the harbor only if he returned to Maine for lumber for the British barracks. The armed schooner *MARGARETTA* was sent along as a convoy to enforce the order. Meanwhile, public opinion

in Machias had been inflamed and Capt. Moore of the *MARGARETTA* found
a Liberty Pole in the little frontier coast town and citizens incensed at the idea
of providing supplies for armies to be used against them. Led by Benjamin
Foster and the fiery Irishman Jeremiah O'Brien, the local citizens commandeered
two boats, one of which became stranded, and on June 12, 1775, closed in on
the *MARGARETTA*. In the fight that followed, the British officer was mortally wounded and his boat captured. The following month the Machias men
captured a British schooner from Nova Scotia. The British sent Sir George
Collier with the *RANGER* and three other vessels to punish the rebels; Collier
routed the local forces from the breastworks they had hastily thrown up along
the river and burned several buildings before his fleet moved on. The capture
of the *MARGARETTA* has been called the first naval battle of the Revolution;
the battle itself was not important, but it provided the Revolutionary leaders in
Philadelphia with a talking point in urging the establishment of a navy.

After the Collier raid, Washington ordered a regiment of militia recruited and
sent to protect the settlement. In 1781, Fort Machias (O'Brien) was made
part of the national defense. The British did not return to the little town until
1814 when they took the fort and burned the barracks.

Machiasport was the terminus of the narrow-gauge Machias-Whitneyville
railroad built in 1841 to carry lumber from Whitneyville to Machiasport for
shipping. One of the locomotives used on the railroad is at the Crosby Laboratory, University of Maine, Orono.

The *Gates House* is the Machiasport Historical Society Museum (*visitors*).

From *Wright's Lookout*, a bold rock on Corn Hill, is a splendid view of the
Machias headlands and the western end of the Bay of Fundy.

At Clark's Point, 7 *m.* (L), are the so-called *Picture Rocks*, figures somewhat
resembling men, animals and landscapes on a slanting ledge below the high-
water mark. They have been identified as Indian petroglyphs.

At *Great Jasper Beach* in Buck's Harbor, fine specimens of jasper may be found.

At Machias, junction (L) with State 192 to *MARSHFIELD* 6 *m.*, (*ramp,
fishing, shelters*).

EAST MACHIAS (alt. 60, East Machias Town, pop. 971), 67.1 *m.*, is
divided by the East Machias River, the residential and business sections
being on opposite sides of the river.

On a hill across the river (R) is *Washington Academy* (1823), established
through a petition granted by the Massachusetts General Court in 1791.
Nearby is the *Congregational Church* designed by Edward Shaw and
called by Talbot Hamlin 'a charmingly original type Carpenter Gothic.'
The design appears in Shaw's *Rural Architecture*.

In the *Library* (R), a brick building with two millstones from an early
gristmill set strikingly in the front wall, one on either side of the entrance,
is a canvas showing a panorama of the community in its prosperous lumbering and shipbuilding days.

At East Machias, junction with State 191.

Left on State 191, inland lake route to Calais, 67.2 *m.*

Right on State 191 to CUTLER, 10 *m.* where the U. S. Navy operates the world's most powerful radio transmitting station. Some of the 26 towers are 990 feet high and visible for miles around.

WHITING (alt. 60, Whiting Town, pop. 339), 79.7 *m.* formerly was called Orangetown for the nearby lake and the river so-named that flows into one of the long arms of Cobscook Bay (Ind.: boiling tide). West and north are one and a half million acres of forest lands and over 100,000 acres of lakes and ponds. US 1 along here is part of the Heritage Trail. The *Grave of Col. John Crane*, first white settler, is among those near the small white church (L). He was one of the pioneers holding this area against the British during the Revolution. Many were veterans of the Massachusetts fighting at Bunker Hill, Lexington and the Boston Tea Party who came to take up land and help build a new nation.

Here is a junction with State 189 for Lubec, Campobello 11 *m. (see Tour 1J).*

US 1 soon enters *Cobscook State Park (June-Oct.; camping, picnicking, fishing, launching ramp, fire lookout)* in Moosehorn National Wildlife Refuge. Much of the 864 acres of the forested Park is surrounded by waters of Cobscook Bay. Campsites are wellspaced and secluded, some at water's edge in the coves and capes, and some as high as 80 feet above sea level.

The Moosehorn Refuge, 22,665 acres, was established in 1937 for the protection, study, and management of regional wildlife species, particularly waterfowl, migratory birds and deer. It is in the principal breeding range of American woodcock and in the Atlantic waterfowl flyway. Species recorded include 200 birds, 39 mammals. The many miles of trails and old woodroads from the boom days of lumbering offer many possibilities to observe in their native habitat such wildlife as Canada geese, ducks, deer, moose, bear, bobcat, fox, mink and other fur-bearers. Sometimes beaver may be seen at work in the evening on the Refuge flowages. The harbor seal is found along the shore waters. Besides the State Park recreation area, there is a Refuge Visitors' Center at Baring (*see below*). Detailed information on Moosehorn may be obtained from the Refuge Manager, Moosehorn N. W. Refuge, Calais, Maine 04619.

DENNYSVILLE (alt. 30, Dennysville Town, pop. 303), 89 *m.* Old elms arch over the main street of Dennysville, named for an Indian chief. Atlantic salmon taken from the river here are famous. In fact, side roads between Whiting and Dennysville lead north into the outdoorsman's world of lakes, streams, mountains and woodlands, beautiful in all seasons and inviting hunting, fishing and canoe trips (*see RECREATION*). In spring, schools of alewives buck their way up-river to spawn.

Artisan James Chubbuck built the first frame house, the *Lincoln Homestead* (1787) (*private*) N of the village center facing the Dennysville River, for

Theodore Lincoln, son of Gen. Benjamin Lincoln of Hingham, Mass., to whom the township land was granted in 1786. A survivor of Yorktown, Gen. Lincoln directed the laying down of British arms. Dr. Arthur Lincoln, last direct descendant, was married to Opera Singer Anna Maxwell Brown.

WEST PEMBROKE (alt. 80, Pembroke Town) 94.2 *m.* and Pembroke Village originally were part of Dennysville. In the village is the *Birthplace of Dr. Charles H. Best (visitors)*, co-discoverer of insulin. Maintained by the American Diabetes Association, the white frame house has the medical office and furnishings of Dr. Best's father, a general practitioner in the days of the 'country doctor.'

Directional signs to *Reversing Falls* at Mahar's Point on Leighton's Neck, 2 *m.* (*140-acre park, trails, picnicking*). Tidal current between the Point and Falls Island alternately fills and empties Dennys and Whiting Bays. The swift water flowing at 25 knots strikes rocky projections to create the falls. This pleasant spot also can be reached by boat from Eastport or Lubec (*see below*).

Here is a junction (L) with State 214 to *Meddybemps Lake*, 10 *m.* (*fishing*).

Also a hunting region, this area once saw the illegal practice of 'deerjacking.' At night, a bright light was used to mesmerize the animal, making him a standing target for the 'sportsman's' bullet. When shot, the deer seldom drops immediately, but runs, sometimes for hours, the hunter in hot pursuit. This phase, known as 'deer-running,' developed fleet runners, particularly in deer-jacking expeditions when the law pursued the hunters as swiftly as the hunters pursued the deer.

There is one story of a Washington County stripling, who, left unwarned on sentry duty at Cedar Creek, Va., when a retreat was ordered, found himself alone facing the advancing enemy. He made his solitary retreat from Cedar Creek with the speed he had acquired in Meddybemps deer-running and is said to have reported at Harper's Ferry, 19 miles from his post, ahead of the dispatch bearer on horseback.

PEMBROKE (alt. 80, Pembroke Town, pop. 871), 95.2 *m.* is the birthplace of a noted Maine wit of the early Twentieth century, Chief Justice William R. Pattangall (1865-1942).

Known to intimates as 'Pat,' he was born of a seafaring family, graduated from University of Maine in 1884 and studied law while earning his living at various occupations. He became a leading trial lawyer and one of Maine's outstanding figures — jurist, politician, editor, bank president and author of political satires so scathing that the unfortunate subjects pilloried bought up and destroyed as many editions as they could. These were the 'Meddybemps Letters' and 'Maine's Hall of Fame,' a series of biographies of the State's leading political figures.

The major thrust of Pattangall's barbed wit was to point out the graft and conflict of interest amid the leading Republicans of the day. It was said the Letters 'made an entire State laugh. They began to undermine the very foundations of Republican Party domination. For the first time, the sacred careers of the great were dissected by simple humor.'

Aside from his writings, anecdotes of his spirited behavior were legion. Typical is an episode in Farmington where as a young lawyer he was to try a case. No rooms being available, the lawyer was allowed to bed down in the hotel's livery stable. Next morning, Pat appeared at the office to pay his bill. 'Here is the key to my room,' said he, tossing a well-used manure shovel on the desk.

From the highway bridge opposite *Pennamaquan Park* can be seen the remains of an old stone Iron Works (1828) where skilled English and Welsh immigrants were employed. Ore came from bogs in the vicinity.

In the tall grass on Liberty Hill still may be found some of the metal lawn ornaments that graced an ornate home once maintained by Dr. Pomeroy, a faith healer, whose trances and teapots of steeped herbs were part of his practise. He is said to have received a medal from Queen Victoria for effecting a cure for a member of the Royal family.

PERRY (alt. 40, Perry Town, pop. 564) 101 *m*. John Frost, the first settler, established his trading post on the St. Croix River in 1758. Subsequently many family fortunes were made and lost in development of the forests and fisheries. The people along this frontier from Machias eastward were patriotic Americans during the struggle for independence. Named for Naval hero Commodore Oliver H. Perry, the town was incorporated Feb. 12, 1818 while Eastport, six miles away, still was held by the British who had seized Fort Sullivan in 1814 and renamed it Sherbrooke. Four months after Perry's incorporation, the British returned the fort to the Americans.

This area is popular with hunters, fishermen, camera fans, amateur botanists and geologists who find many fascinating specimens along the shores and in the fields. Glaciation left its mark here in the deep scourings found in bedrock and the giant boulders strewn about. Also exposed are frozen red and gray lava flows from ancient volcanoes.

There is a Picnic Site at a red granite *Marker* (L) indicating the 45th Parallel of Latitude halfway between the Equator and the North Pole which crosses southern France, Turkey, Mongolia, China and Canada.

The River Road paralleling US 1 affords a panoramic view of majestic Passamaquoddy Bay, Canadian islands, Chamcook Mountains and Bocabec Hills.

South Meadow Road leads to Boyden Lake camps.

At Perry, junction with State 190 to Eastport (*see Tour 1K*).

ROBBINSTON (alt. 60, Robbinston Town, pop. 476), 107 *m*. The Ridge Road here is part of the first road to the St. Croix River from the 'west.' It began in Cherryfield, following an Indian trail by lakesides to the river.

Robbinston has provided access roads and boat landing ramps at Boyden and Western Lakes.

Here as at Perry, red volcanic sand is much in evidence. In the village, the 150-year-old Methodist Church has its original altar Bible and service.

The ladies' church suppers are renowned. Sardine and tuna factories give area employment in this former shipbuilding center where many vessels were launched during the Civil War.

The *Granite Markers* along US 1 from here to Calais were pacing markers for James S. Pike's race horses in the Civil War era. To place the three-foot markers, he first measured the diameter of his wagon wheel and then tied a red flag on it. A farmer perched on the back of the wagon counted the number of times the rag whirled around, so Pike knew when a mile had passed. Accuracy of the 12 milestones (L) can be checked with a car speedometer.

RED BEACH (alt. 90, Ward 9, City of Calais), 110.5 *m.* takes its name from the color of the granite outcrop along the shore. The village lies along the main highway with views of the St. Croix River.

Opposite Red Beach, in the St. Croix River is *Dochet's Island*, National Historic Site (*visitors, restoration, beaches*). In 1603, Pierre du Guast, the Sieur de Monts, received the trading concession for Acadia, defined as a territory extending from Cape Breton Island to a point well below the present New York City. The following spring, he set sail with his lieutenant, Samuel de Champlain, and fourscore colonists including a Huguenot minister and a Catholic priest, landing June 26, 1604 on Dochet's Island which he called St. Croix, where he expected to establish a trading post and settlement. So sketchy was knowledge of the New World at the time that the settlers brought with them timber for their buildings. Before winter, the island held a storehouse, dining-hall, kitchen, barracks and blacksmith shop, and carefully laid out gardens. An unusually severe winter and scurvy wrought such discouragement that in the spring of 1605 de Monts and Champlain sailed off south seeking a more suitable place for the colony; in August, however, they decided to move it to what is now Annapolis Royal in Nova Scotia. Dochet's Island was not entirely abandoned for the French used it as a garrison at intervals for some years.

This early settlement played an important part in the adjustment of the boundary question at the end of the Revolutionary War. Both the United States and Great Britian acknowledged the River St. Croix as the point of departure in drawing the line, but did not agree on what river bore this name. Discovery of Champlain's map and the subsequent examination of the ruins of the early settlement decided the matter. Had the British won their point, eastern Maine probably now would be Canadian territory.

CALAIS (alt. 82, pop. 4,223), 121.4 *m.* (pronounced CAL-lus). Maine's only border city, a port of entry, is truly international, widely known for neighborliness with its Canadian counterpart, St. Stephen across the St. Croix River. At the opening of a new international bridge connecting the communities, the first U. S. flag to have 50 stars was flown for the first time. Commercial and professional services cater to thousands of Canadian and American tourists. On the Canadian side, highways lead to Chamcook Mts. and Bocabec Hills. From US 1 on the American side, State 9, now frequented by sportsmen, is the old Airline or smugglers' route through the wilderness (*see Tour 5*). Calais also is the starting point for hunting and fishing trips (*see RECREATION*).

Nestled in the St. Croix valley and protected by ridges on all sides, the city spreads along the River's W bank with St. Croix Country Club at its southern end. Encircling the business district are quiet streets with fine old houses surrounded by trees, broad lawns and trim shrubbery. Arching elms lining the streets give vistas reminiscent of the allee or pleasance of France.

Wood products and Hathaway Shirts are the major industries. With the river's great tide variations, the pier on Steamboat St., with its floating dock and stairway is the only one on the river accessible at all tides. On Hog Alley near the waterfront is Calais' 29-year-old weekly newspaper.

Noah Smith, Jr., (1800-68) who lived here is said to have been one of the last persons having official business with President Lincoln before his assassination. He received the President's signature to a pardon granted a young Calais soldier who had been convicted of treason. Smith was the paternal grandfather of Kate Douglas Wiggin.

First settlers arrived c. 1770 in this forested territory where fertile soil invited farming, and fish and game resources made for good living. The launching in 1801 of the *LIBERTY* marked the beginning of a thriving industry that lasted until the end of the 'era of tall ships.' In 1809, the Massachusetts Legislature named the settlement for the French port of Calais because of French aid to the struggling Colonies during the Revolution. By 1850, the town had become an important lumbering center and was incorporated as a city. In 1935 when the *NORMANDIE* made its maiden trip to America, the French city of Calais (CalLAY) sent to the American Calais (CALlus) a hand-carved mahogany chest containing soil from its ancient cemeteries, four volumes of Calais history and a dozen pieces of lace which are in the St. Croix Historical Society collections, Main St. The next year, the American city shipped to France a tablet of red granite taken from Dochet's Island.

Sec. e. CALAIS to FORT KENT (CANADIAN LINE), 205.8 m.

Leaving the coast at Calais, US 1 winds northward through the sparsely settled forest and lake region of northern Washington County before reaching 'the Aroostook,' Maine's vast forest and farm lands that are attracting more and more industrialists and vacationists. Recreational development and modern science in forestry, agriculture and transportation brought steady economic growth in the 1960s to this largest county, a 6,353 square mile area like no other in the State. Lively optimism and open-handed hospitality characterize the civic-minded citizenry who make a sizeable contribution to the State's economy and are progressive in education, health and environmental matters.

With a million acres under cultivation and nearly four million acres of commercial forest land, the Aroostook is 'big country,' settled in the 1800s by English, Scotch, and Irish from southern Maine moving north with

lumber operations, and by the Acadians from Nova Scotia. Something to
see are the miles of potato fields in bloom — some 150,000 acres — an
undulating sea of green topped by white and purple-tinged blossoms.
Crops valued at $80½ million are grown in the east and north, shipped
centrally. Aroostook with six processing plants is the Country's major
producer of seed potatoes, a highly specialized and strictly regulated
business. The ubiquitous potato, known to the Incas centuries ago and
brought to America in 1719 by the Irish, began to be grown in the
Aroostook after the Civil War. By 1880 the County was producing a
fourth of the Country's needs. In the 1960s production reached 38,500,000
cwt. Although innovations were slowly accepted, diversification crops of
oats, peas and sugar beets now are worth several millions.

Wildlands of Aroostook have been called the last frontier of the east.
Here are the forestry harvest, reforestation and multiple use of millions of
acres, the famous Allagash region, Adirondacks range mountains, lakes
and streams of the great hunting and fishing country. (*Fire wardens,
lookout stations, warning systems*). Guides are recommended for sportsmen unfamiliar with wildland terrain. Seven large paper companies and
48 primary and wood-using mills including an automated lumber mill
are located in Aroostook. Freight transport is over 540 miles of Bangor &
Aroostook RR track, and by truck and air. Tourists find fascinating the
'on site' story of lumbering and farming in Aroostook.

The County's eastern strip is the most densely populated. Along the
northern border in the St. John's Valley live the descendants of the Acadians
who fled Nova Scotia and were made famous in Longfellow's poem,
'Evangeline.' Theirs is still the soft-spoken cadence of their forebears.
Whether predominantly French or English, border towns enjoy friendly
relations with their Canadian neighbors. The County itself was involved
in an international dispute over 125 years ago. This was the long
boundary controversy between Britian and the United States finally settled
by the Webster-Ashburton Treaty of 1842. Of the border clashes preceding
the Treaty, best-known was the 'Aroostook War' of 1839-40 when Maine
men went north to rout Canadian lumbermen believed to be cutting in
U. S. Territory.

Development of the county settled by these defenders was much hampered
by lack of transportation facilities until completion of the Bangor & Aroostook railroad in 1894, after which potato production began to gain national
importance. The line was extended to Fort Kent in 1902.

CALAIS, 0 *m. (see Tour 1, sec. d).*

MILLTOWN (alt. 85, Ward 1, Calais), 1.5 *m.* The beauty of the swift
St. Croix River rapids and Magurrewock Mountain rising precipitously
near the road are notable here.

Soon (L) is Charlotte Road to Moosehorn National Wildlife Refuge (*Visitor Center, exhibits, displays, auditorium; May-Sept.*).

BARING (alt. 100, Baring Town), 4.6 *m.*, was named for Alexander Baring, Lord Ashburton, England's representative in the Webster-Ashburton Treaty negotiations and the son-in-law of William Bingham (*see Tour 4E*).

Junction with State 191, (L) inland lake route to East Machias (*see Tour 1, sec. d*).

Just beyond, junction with State 9 (L) (*see Tour 5*). Picnic Area.

WOODLAND (alt. 130, Baileyville Town), 10 *m.* Georgia Pacific Corporation's St. Croix Paper Company mill here is Washington County's largest industry. (*guided tours Mon. through Fri., June-Sept.*) Latest methods of newsprint production from river logs to finished rolls may be seen. Over 400 tons daily are manufactured for U. S. and export customers. The company's subsidiary, St. Croix Pulpwood Company, owns immense tracts of land in northern Washington County and across the border in New Brunswick, open to the public for recreation. Certain working sections may be closed in the fall hunting season to protect woodsmen and horses.

PRINCETON (alt. 210, Princeton Town, pop. 829), 19.5 *m.*, a small, elm-shaded village centering a lake and mountain region (*guides, hunting and fishing equipment; canoe trip terminus*) (*see RECREATION*).

A. U. S. Forestry Camp is located in this area. US 1 now crosses a bridge to enter the Unorganized Township of Indiantown, inhabited in part by Passamaquoddy Indians (*see EARLIEST INHABITANTS*). This area, their favorite hunting ground, granted to them by treaty in 1796 saw many fierce engagements between the Passamaquoddies and roving bands of Mohawks. In the vicinity, roads (R) lead to Leweys Lake and Grand Falls Flowage, and (L) to Pocomoonshine, to Grand Lake Stream (*State Fish Hatchery*) and to an *Indian Reservation* at Peter Dana Point on Big Lake (*basketry, seasonal ceremonials*).

WAITE (alt. 330, Waite Town, pop. 78), 28.9 *m.* A local road (L) to West Musquash Lake 6 *m.* (*camping*); half a mile farther, road (R) to Tomah Stream named for an Indian chief who aided Machias settlers during the Revolution.

TOPSFIELD (alt. 495, Topsfield Town, pop. 201), 35 *m.* Fire lookout on Musquash Mountain (L). An agricultural village in fine hunting country, Topsfield is a fire ranger headquarters.

Junction here with State 6.

> L on State 6 about 4 *m.* to East Musquash Lake (*fishing, picnicking*) and Musquash Mt. (1238 ft.) (*Forest Lookout*). The road continues W through Carroll, Springfield and Lee to Lincoln at 21 *m.* (*see Tour 4*).
>
> R on State 6, past Tomah Mt. (1034 ft.); picnic area near Tomah Stream, 9 *m.* At 16 *m.*, Lambert Lake and Pirate Hill (*Forest Lookout*).
>
> VANCEBORO, port of entry on Canadian border, 21 *m.*

BROOKTON (alt. 420, Brookton Town), 43.3 *m.*, a four-corners near Jackson Brook Lake.

> Right on local road to FOREST CITY, 12 *m.*, sporting camps on East Grand Lake shore.
>
> Left on local road to Baskahegan Lake, 1.5 *m.*, one of the largest bodies of water in this section (*deep woods, fishing*).

EATON (alt. 407, Danforth Town), 49.7 *m.*, woods hamlet near Crooked Brook Lake.

DANFORTH (alt. 387, Danforth Town, pop. 821), 55.1 *m.*, lumbering community in the Baskahegan Valley. Aroostook County begins here.

WESTON (alt. 720, Weston Town, pop. 63), (*picnic area*) 60 *m.* lies in a setting of great natural beauty. From every point on the highway running along a hillside then climbing abruptly to the summit, the view of East Grand Lake is magnificent. Apple orchards, pasturelands, woodlots and hay fields slope from the homes that face the road, to the wood-fringed shores of the lake. In the distance a chain of smaller lakes makes an intricate design in the dense forests that stretch to the green-clad Canadian hills. Peekaboo Mt. (1085 ft.) (L) (*Fire Lookout, picnicking*).

ORIENT (alt. 720, Orient Town, pop. 124), 66.2 *m.* Right on a local road to *Sunset Park* 3 *m.* on East Grand Lake (*boats, bathing*).

NORTH AMITY (alt. 580, Amity Town, pop. 206), 74.2 *m.*, along a high ridge, presents a fine view of Mount Katahdin.

CARY (alt. 435, Cary Plantation, pop. 208), 78 *m.* is surrounded by dense woods.

HODGDON (alt. 470, Hodgdon Town, pop. 926), 82.5 *m.* is at the foot of *Westford Hill* (R), a tree-crowned elevation within easy walking distance of the highway. Here the checkered pattern of Aroostook farmland greets the eye, the farmsteads showing as on a picture map, with Mt. Katahdin's bold peak on the skyline (L).

HOULTON (alt. 340, pop. 6,805) (*see HOULTON*), 88.1 *m*. Junction with US 2 (*see Tour 4*).

At 89 *m*., junction with Interstate 95 to its eastern terminus at Canadian border, 2 *m*. S on I-95 to Bangor, 125 *m*.

At 93.9 *m*. shopping center. Junction with Carson Road (R) to the *Watson Settlement Bridge* (1911), 2.5 *m*., only covered bridge in the county.

LITTLETON (alt. 440, Littleton Town, pop. 982), 94.4 *m*., lies on a plain, with rows of potato sheds along its railroad tracks. In 1800, when the territory still was part of the Commonwealth of Massachusetts, the southern half of the then unsettled town was granted to Williams College; in 1801 the great forest-covered northern half was given to Framingham (Mass.) Academy.

Settlements were founded shortly after these dates, but the town was not incorporated until 1856. Visible from the highway (L) is a group of eskers, or 'horsebacks' whose long ridges are remnants of the vast sheets of ice that covered this part of Maine during the glacial period.
The State Fish and Game Department has a fish hatchery here.

MONTICELLO (alt. 415, Monticello Town, pop. 1109), 100.6 *m*., formerly Wellington Township, settled by the owner, Gen. Joel Wellington, in 1830, was incorporated in 1846. The north branch of Meduxnekeag River divides the one-street village which spreads over two hilltops. (*Conroy Lake, fishing; surrounding woods, hunting.*)

BRIDGEWATER (alt. 415, Bridgewater Town, pop. 1000), 108.5 *m*., with its neat homes along the main highway, is the principal settlement of a heavily-wooded township which was granted to Bridgewater (Mass.) Academy and to Portland Academy. (*Portland Lake, swimming and camping. Whitney Brook, trout fishing*).

BLAINE (alt. 410, Blaine Town, pop. 945), 114.1 *m*., is a small farming village having a continuous main street with Mars Hill. First called Alva, when incorporated in 1874, this half township was named for Gov. James G. Blaine. The settlement of Robinson in the southern part grew up around William Robinson's mill (1859). Blaine now has two modern potato processing plants.

MARS HILL (alt. 710, Mars Hill Town, pop. 2062), 114.8 *m*., takes its name from nearby Mars Hill (alt. 1660), a notable eminence in the low rolling country here. The Hill entered into the hotly contested boundary dispute when Great Britain contended that this peak was 'the highlands which divide those rivers that empty themselves into the river St. Lawrence, from those that fall into the Atlantic Ocean,' named in the Treaty of 1782; the United States maintained that the highlands were much farther north and nearer the St. Lawrence River. The Hill also has entered into a more recent controversy as one of the claimants to being the first land the sun touches in eastern United States. Validity of these claims depends upon the season of the year. The township was originally lotted in 200-acre blocks to Massachusetts veterans of the American Revolution. Mars Hill, long a potato shipping center, has a large potato packing plant. *Aroostook Health Center* (1960), is a modern extended care facility.

Right from the village 2 *m.* to *Mars Hill Skiway,* largest skiing area in Northern Maine, with a Poma lift of 2,450 ft.

Right from Mars Hill on US 1A to Easton Center, 9 *m.*; (L) on State 10 to EASTON (alt. 580, Easton Town, pop. 1500), 2 *m.*, a small village in pleasant farm country where Vahlsing, Inc. potato processing plant (1961) and the multi-million dollar sugar beet processing plant of Maine Sugar Industries, Inc., partly owned by Vahlsing, are located. Industrial pollution of Prestile Stream here caused a border incident in 1967 when Canadians dammed the stream to emphasize the mounting protest of citizens of both countries who continued strong pressures for relief. The road continues to wind through rolling farm land 7 *m.* to Presque Isle. (*see below*)

At 125.2 *m.*, (L) to 600-acre *Aroostook State Park* on Echo Lake, 2 *m.* (*camping, fishing, water skiing, boating, picnicking, swimming, nature walks; mountain trails on Quoggy Joe, 1213 ft.*).

At 126 *m.*, *Aroostook Farm* (L) (*visitors*), a 275-acre experiment station where the U. S. Department of Agriculture, in cooperation with the University of Maine and the Aroostook County Farm Bureau, conducts farm research work. Experiments in plant foods, soils, plant diseases, growing methods, and crop control, particularly for potatoes, sugar beets and grains, are carried on both in the field and in a modern, well-equipped laboratory. A field day and barbecue is held in August. Seen on the left skyline from Aroostook Farm is Haystack Mt. (1341 ft.), the cone of an extinct volcano.

At 127 *m. Aroostook State College* (L).

PRESQUE ISLE (alt. 450, pop. 12,886), 129 *m.*, is said to have been so named because Presque Isle Stream and the Aroostook River make it 'almost an island.' In 1816, Jonathan Parks and Ferdinand Armstrong made their way from New Brunswick and the headwaters of the Aroostook River to the mouth of Presque Isle Stream and there built their campfire. Four years later, the year Maine became a State, Armstrong returned with his bride and built a cabin on Bradley's Island at the mouth of the Stream. Other pioneers followed and in 1828 Dennis Fairbanks made a clearing and built a mill around which a little settlement sprang up.

Presque Isle was not connected with 'outside' until 1839 when the State built a road from Monticello. The first mail was brought on horseback in 1842. A hundred years later, Presque Isle became a city.

During World War II a vital air transport installation here was the ferry base for Britain-bound planes. When it was phased out in 1961, enterprising citizens turned potential economic disaster into prosperity by acquiring most of the base and transforming it into an exemplary industrial park whose 29 tenants now have a $2.7 million payroll. These endeavors, still continuing, won Presque Isle a National award as the 1966 All America City. Potato Service, Inc., one of Aroostook's largest processors, is the city's principal employer, and there are many potato marketing organizations.

Freight transport is handled by the Bangor & Aroostook, Canadian Pacific and Aroostook Valley railroads and four interstate truck companies. Passenger service: bus and airline.

Also located here are an International Paper Co. plant, a University of Maine Agricultural Experiment Station, Northeastern Maine Vocational Technical Institute, University of Maine's Aroostook State College, the Maine School of Practical Nursing and the Aroostook Convalescent Center.

Presque Isle Historical Society (Wed. 2-4), City Hall, regional articles and records.

Turner Library (1966), art exhibits. There is a community art club, which sponsors regional art contests for school children, and active drama groups.

Besides hunting and fishing in the environs, there is Country Club golf, parimutuel harness racing *(July-August)* and the annual Northern Maine Fair *(August)*.

At the first Cattle Show and Fair in 1851, Jabez Trask took honors in Winter wheat with 22 bushels per acre. The first fairs lasted two days and families tented out on the fairgrounds. Today's huge Fair covers several exhibition halls and show rings with week-long offerings of general exhibits, horse shows, horse pulling, dairy and beef cattle shows, 4-H baby beef auction, family entertainment and harness racing, a prime favorite of Aroostook folk. Fort Fairfield, Caribou and Houlton used to band together and buy a racehorse for the competition. Special interest is in pacing and trotting. Light sulkies are used and drivers often are native sons skilled in the complicated 'racing start.' Of verdant memory is *John R. Braden,* called the greatest pacer of them all, so fondly regarded he was led into the banquet hall and toasted. A *Granite Monument* memorializing the pacer stands opposite the grandstand, and in 1947 a theatre was named for him.

Some other notable dates in Presque Isle's chronology: 1858, first excursion of the Maine Press Association into Aroostook County; covered bridge lost in a freshet; 1872, some 4,000 bushels of potatoes shipped out of the County via the European & North American railroad; 1873, James Cullen lynched by enraged citizens after he had 'murdered two men at Swanback Camp in Chapman Woods'; 1881, arrival of recently completed Canadian Pacific railroad's first train; 1884, the 'Big Fire' so-called, one of many, nearly destroyed the town; 1887, electric lights; 1895, Bangor & Aroostook railroad continued to Presque Isle and Caribou; 1903, Aroostook State Normal School established; 1908,

Carnegie Library; 1910, Aroostook Valley railroad; 1917, Ex-president Taft visits; 1930, airport; 1932, Northeastland Hotel; 1940, Presque Isle becomes a city; 1953, Flying Tigers activated at airbase; 1960, Presidential Candidate John F. Kennedy visits; 1964, former Vice-president Richard M. Nixon visits; 1966, Mark F. and Emily Turner Memorial Library.

At Presque Isle, junction with State 163.

L on State 163 to ASHLAND (alt. 75, Ashland Town, pop. 1980), lumber and potato center, 20 *m*. At Mapleton, 8 *m*., road S to Squapan Mt. (1460 ft.) (*Lookout; campsite*). Soon Haystack Mt. (1341 ft.) and road L to Squapan Lake (*fishing*).

At Ashland, *Lumber and Logging Museum (daily)*.

At 129.5 *m*., the scenic route crosses the Aroostook River and continues through high open country to the outskirts of Caribou. Imposing farmhouses of the prosperous years before 1920, many with a cluster of small neat 'hired man's houses' nearby, and several older-type potato houses built into hillsides are seen on the large potato farms.

CARIBOU (alt. 495, pop. 13,500), 141.1 *m*. On New Year's Day, 1968, Caribou in the heart of Aroostook's agricultural and manufacturing empire, became a city in appropriate ceremonies. Alexander Cochran came here in 1793 looking for a mill site, but settlement did not begin until 1843. First came a scattering of pioneers from Canada via the St. John and Aroostook Rivers. After the Webster-Ashburton Treaty of 1842, settlers began arriving from Southern Maine. Nearly named Lyndon during a controversy that went to the Legislature three times in ten years, Caribou in 1877 received its official name, said to have derived from the animal no longer native to the area. Surrounded by large and fertile farms, and headquarters of the Aroostook Federation of Farmers, rapidly expanding Caribou also has a plant of the Birdseye Division of General Foods Corp., the Maine Bag Co., a fertilizer factory, diesel and steam generating plant, and 175 firms in the potato shipping business. In 1966, cash farm income from potatoes was nearly $80½ million, about 30 percent of Maine's total farm income. The city maintains a large recreation center and is headquarters for many one-day tours. Caribou has its own municipal airport handling executive and charter flights, as well as nearby scheduled airlines and bus service. Also here is a U. S. Weather Station. Caribou's bi-weekly newspaper has won National and Regional awards and the city has many active civic organizations.

Nylander Museum, Main St., (*Mon. through Fri., 2-5 p. m.*) has extensive geology and conchology collections; more than 6,000 specimens include artifacts, shells, mollusks and sea plants; seasonal art exhibits relating to Maine flora and fauna.

Right from Caribou on US 1A to FORT FAIRFIELD (alt. 390, pop. 5,876), 11 *m*., popular Canadian port of entry. Home of Gov. John H. Reed, the town was settled c. 1820 by people from the Canadian provinces and at first considered itself a colony of the provinces. However, during the boundary troubles in 1840, the State of Maine established here a fort named for Gov. John Fairfield and thus the town was named.

Eastern apex of the Potato Triangle with Caribou NW and Presque Isle SW, Fort Fairfield claims to grow more potatoes on its rolling farmlands than any other town in the world. Scores of warehouses line the railroad tracks and business and industrial life revolves around potato growing and processing in which fortunes can be made and lost. A & P has a $3 million freezing plant and there are several starch companies. Thousands participate in the annual three-day *Potato Blossom Festival* in July. Fort Fairfield has exceptional recreational facilities. There is a sporty 18-hole golf course 2½ miles from town at the Aroostook Valley Country Club where players park their cars in the U. S. and cross into Canada to go into the clubhouse and onto the course — no customs or immigration reporting. Near town are facilities for fishing, swimming, boating, picnicking, and the Frontier Fish and Game Clubhouse is open to all comers. A 60-acre winter sports area is maintained by the White Bunny Ski Club — no relative of the national bunny clubs — with a 1,750' T-bar lift on the slope, and skating and tobogganning.

Right from Caribou on State 89 to *Loring Air Force Base* at LIMESTONE, 6 *m.* Based here are SAC bombardment wings, interceptor squadrons and stratotankers in a self-sufficient community of over 11,000. The base was built westerly of Limestone on 12,000 acres that have a solid substrata of limestone but extensive marshes and bogs that were converted through engineering ingenuity. The base was named for Maj. Charles J. Loring, World War II and Korean War hero.

Limestone has many trailer parks for base personnel and does some potato processing and shipping. Gen. Mark Trafton and B. D. Cushman built a dam and sawmill here in 1847, followed later by builders of grist and clapboard mills c. 1869.

Left from Caribou on State 164 to WASHBURN (alt. 390, pop. 2,083), 10 *m.*, home of Taterstate Frozen Foods where frozen french fried potatoes originated. Its year-round municipal swimming pool is a converted mill pond. Named for Civil War Governor Israel Washburn, the community was first settled in 1829 by Nathaniel Churchill.

Left from Caribou on State 161 the so-called Lake Road to Fort Kent gives access to the chain of lakes that are a prime source of recreation and sports (*picnic areas; no overnight accommodations*). At 8 *m.* on this road is NEW SWEDEN (alt. 865, pop. 713), settled in 1870 as a successful immigration ex-experiment. The legislature that year had appointed as Commissioner of Immigration William Widgery Thomas Jr., former Consul General at Gothenburg, Sweden, and was offering free farmlands. Thomas proceeded to Sweden, recruited a colony of 51 men, women and children and returned with them to this Aroostook township which had been set aside for their occupancy. Other people from Sweden soon followed and today's population consists largely of their descendants. Right from State 161 to STOCKHOLM (alt. 865, pop. 649), 2 *m.*, nestling in the hills like a Swiss village and populated by Swedish and French descendants. Their community house was called 'the Capital.'

At 17.3 *m.* on State 161, *Madawaska Lake* (L), family type resort.

At 23.4 *m.* (L), entrance to public picnic area, boat landing maintained by International Paper Co.

At 26.8 *m.* State 162 (R) goes to *Long Lake (see below)*.

At 29.8 *m.,* road (L) to *Square Lake (trout, salmon fishing)*

FORT KENT, 44 *m. (see below).*

VAN BUREN (alt. 495, pop. 4679), 162 *m.,* named for President Martin Van Buren, is another border gateway town on US 1 travelling westerly along the St. John River in Maine. Across the International Bridge is St. Leonard's, N. B., starting point for Restigouche and Gaspe Peninsula trips. Small sawmills, potato and beet industries and manufacture of starch and tennis racquets are economic mainstays. Its public services include a Community Hospital staffed by sisters of St. Martha.

In 1791, Acadian rivermen and farmers settled in this area and carried on lumber operations that grew and prospered in the next century. When extensive operations were being carried on in the vast tracts of land at the head of the St. John River and its tributaries, the river was used to float the huge logs to sawmills and markets. At intervals, booms, or floating chains of logs, were attached to piers and other structures on the banks to hold back the flow of logs. The five small islands in the river near Van Buren formed a barrier that could be utilized as a temporary dam and the place was the scene of great activity during the spring log drives.

The air would be filled with the rumble of cracking ice and the thunder of crashing logs hurtling against each other. Frequent jams occurred. These had to be broken with considerable risk to the drivers who, here as elsewhere, reputedly were a wild, hard-drinking, daredevil crew. Their feats, appetites and vocabularies became matters of legend still preserved in song and story.

KEEGAN (alt. 495, pop. 900), 164.9 *m.,* is part of Van Buren, though it has its own post office.

At 173.9 *m.* a large white Catholic church with two spires nearly a century old dominates the community of LILLE.

GRAND ISLE, (alt. 510, pop. 978), named for the large island in the river, also has its ornate church as do many of the small area villages.

At 181.6 *m.,* road (L) to *Birch Point Golf Club* near Long Lake.

ST. DAVID (alt. 510, Madawaska Town), 183.4 *m.,* is a little parish settlement with much historic significance relating to the Acadians who have made a strong imprint on the region from Van Buren to Fort Kent. After their expulsion from Nova Scotia in 1759, some of the refugees found temporary shelter in the Fredericton, N. B. neighborhood, but, as loyalists from the American Colonies came in great numbers to the St. John Valley after the Revolution, again the Acadians were resented and harassed. They petitioned the governor of Quebec for permission to settle on the upper St. John. The Governor 'in order that they might practise their religion with more freedom and less difficulty,' granted 200 acres per family at a point one and a half miles below the mouth of the Madawaska River. One simple memorial to these gentle people is the *Wooden Cross* on the river bank behind St. David's church, marking the spot where the first Acadians landed in June 1785. This little band was a pure strain of French and each generation to the present has handed down a singular purity in the speech of their native language, not found elsewhere in the region and devoid of the familiar Maritime patois.

MADAWASKA (alt. 595, pop. 5507), 186.2 *m.* Maine's northernmost town, unlike others in the St. John Valley, is predominantly large-scale industrial. Two big mills of Fraser Co., Ltd., stretch along the river bank, while on the Canadian side in Edmundston, are even larger plants and administrative quarters. Liquid pulp crosses the river 24 hours a day in seven huge pipes connecting the mills. Pulp from Canadian timber is converted into printing, groundwood and converting papers in the U. S. by seven modern high speed paper machines. Fraser, with extensive timberland holdings, uses over 250 million cords of various woods annually in production of groundwood and sulphite pulp.

Northern Maine, too, has its sophistication. Mingled with the aromas of pulp, paper and potatoes, is the scent of Jade East, the masculine cologne manufactured in Madawaska.

International Bridge connects US 1 with Canadian Route 2 to Riviere du Loup and Quebec City.

Chief summer recreation is at the north end of Long Lake. In winter there is skiing on Mt. Carmel and curling on Edmundston rinks.

FRENCHVILLE (alt. 501, pop. 1421), beautifully located at a bend of the St. John River, is named for the nationality of its settlers. It was the Valley's largest town in earlier lumbering days, now depends mostly on potato crops.

> Left from Frenchville on State 162 to ST. AGATHA (san tagat') (alt. 615, St. Agatha Town, pop. 1137), 4.5 *m.* on the northwest shore of Long Lake of the Fish River chain. Besides farming and lumbering, St. Agatha is a major year-round recreation area. Rendezvous for fishermen (landlocked salmon), with well-known sporting camps, it also draws snowmobilers, skiers, bobsledders and skaters.

> SINCLAIR (alt. 615, St. Agatha Town), 17 *m.* on the thoroughfare between Long and Mud Lakes has many public accommodations and the Maple Grove Club winter program.

FORT KENT (alt. 530, Fort Kent Town, pop. 4761), 205.8 *m.*, marked by the Catholic church spire with its aluminum tracery, is a Canadian port of entry and the northern terminus of Interstate US 1 (southern terminus,

Highways and Byways

298

Key West, Florida). Across *International Bridge* is Clair, N. B. On the threshold of the vast forested wilderness to the west, it also is a terminus for the famous Allagash Canoe Trip and State Reserve (*see RECREATION*).

In 1829, Jose Nadeau, first Acadian settler, founded what he called 'Le Grand Decharge' at the mouth of Fish River. Rich timberlands soon enticed many enterprising Englishmen to the region.

The friendly gregarious people here are mostly of French Acadian descent and lead active civic and social lives. They are proud of their exceptional educational opportunities that include University of Maine's Fort Kent State College and the John F. Kennedy Institute of Liberal Arts and Sciences, as well as the Hope School for retarded children.

The town is a shopping and service center for citizens from both sides of the St. John River. Potatoes and lumber are principal industries; three plants turn out cedar products. The automated sawmill of the Pinkham Lumber Co. in nearby Nashville Plantation is the only one of its kind east of the Mississippi. Also made here are Princess Kent quality baby clothes trimmed with handmade lace.

Fort Kent's proximity to the 'big woods' offers endless recreational opportunities. Sporting camps, tenting sites, boats, guides for fishing (landlocked salmon) and hunting (deer and bear), are available. Nearby lakes are Eagle, Square, Cross and Long. There are also winter sports.

Fort Kent Blockhouse (1839) State Memorial (*visitors*), maintained by Boy Scouts stands on a slight eminence overlooking St. John and Fish Rivers. In 1839 during intense boundary disputes, the State of Maine sent troops who completed the Blockhouse in 1840 and named it for the newly elected governor, Edward Kent. As the disputes worsened, 10,000 troops were stationed here four years. The Blockhouse shows the painstaking workmanship of another era in its sturdy timbers and the handwrought ironware of doors and windows.

At Fort Kent, junctions with State 161 and State 11 for two side trips.

Left on State 161, a continuation of Main St. W, a beautiful drive along the St. John River. In his *History of Aroostook* (c. 1890), Edward Wiggin says Aroostook is full of grand views and beautiful landscape pictures, but nowhere are they more beautiful than upon the Upper St. John.

ST. FRANCIS (alt. 597, pop. 1058), 17 *m.* is opposite the place where the St. Francis River empties into the St. John. At this point, the St. John ceases to be the Maine-Canada boundary line which goes up the St. Francis to its northernmost point, Estcourt. Folklore claims that the Americans plied Webster and Ashburton of the 1842 Treaty with too much whiskey and took them up the St. Francis River, while the gentlemen thought they were still on the St. John. Be that as it may, the St. John from this point is entirely within the State of Maine.

This region originally was settled by men mostly from southern Maine by way of New Brunswick who came to lumber and settled on big estates that often included a mill, large barns and outbuildings as well as commodious homes where lavish hospitality was extended. Some of the early names were Hunnewell, Savage and Wheeler. These families passed along with the heyday of lumbering and have been supplanted by a predominately French population. En route to St. Francis are seen prosperous seed potato farms operated by French businessmen.

ALLAGASH PLANTATION (alt. 595, pop. 557) 29 *m.* at the mouth of the Allagash River remains a lonely enclave of English-born, English-speaking people in a predominately French area. In the 1820s, their forebears came from the Baie of Chaleur — the Gardners, the Kellys, the McBriartys and the Jacksons, and bloodlines have been preserved. Rivermen here are expert, as might be expected of those living beside the strong-flowing Allagash.

DICKEY, 32 *m.* is the site of a proposed Dickey-Lincoln hydro-electric development on the St. John River.

From Fort Kent S on State 11.

Travelling along Fish River with Bossy Mt. (1480 ft.) W, at 7.3 *m.* (*picnic area*), road L to *Soldier Pond*, 1 *m.*, named during the Aroostook War. At 10 *m.* WALLAGRASS PLANTATION (alt. 820, pop. 818), an Acadian French settlement.

EAGLE LAKE (alt. 602, Eagle Lake Town, pop. 1138) a hunting and fishing area (*guides*) settled ca. 1840 by Acadian-French and Irish immigrants. Major Strickland and his men, heading north from Bangor during the Aroostook War, named the place for the many eagles they saw around the lake, one of the deepest of the Fish River Chain. NE is Square Lake (*campsites*) and S is Three Brooks Mt. (1578 ft.) (*Forest Lookout; campsites*).

At 16.5 *m.,* road R to Deboulie Mt. (1981 ft.) (*Forest Lookout; campsites*), 15 *m.*

At 20.5 *m.* WINTERVILLE PLANTATION (alt. 1012, pop. 215) (*guides*). Road R leads to St. Froid Lake. There are numerous trout ponds and brooks in this area.

At 23.7 *m.* Hedgehog Mt. (1594 ft.) (*Forest Lookout; picnic area*).

PORTAGE (alt. 641, Portage Lake Town, pop. 458) 36.6 *m.* is surrounded by dense forest growth. Portage Lake is 60 *m.* from St. Agatha, terminus of the Fish River Chain of Lakes Canoe Trip (*see RECREATION*). W of Lake is Moose Mt. (1020 ft.). Guides often show visitors the dams and homes of the busy beavers in this area. The animals cut timber for building and repairs and gather poplar, birch and maple bark for their winter food supply.

COMMEMORATIVE

From the painting "Lighthouse at Two Lights," Portland 1929, by Edward Hopper (1883-1967), at the Metropolitan Museum of Art.

TOUR 1A: *From* KITTERY *to* OGUNQUIT, Shore Route
20 *m.*, State 103, State 1A and Shore Road.

Via Kittery, Kittery Point, York, York Harbor, York Beach, Cape Neddick.
Coastal route alternate to US 1.

NORTH of Kittery-Portsmouth Memorial Bridge, State 103 branches E
from US 1, following the Piscataqua River to its mouth, then turning N to
York Harbor where it joins State 1A to Cape Neddick. Part of the State's
oldest road, the route through several southern Maine summer resorts
spans the area of Maine's first plantations (1626 et sequi) where the
State's industry began and where many homes of the early settlers are
occupied today by their descendants.

From Junction US 1 (*see Tour 1, sec. a*), R on State 103 to

KITTERY (alt. 50, Kittery Town, pop. 10,689). Shipbuilding and fishing
have been important here from the time the first ships of the Republic
were built in the Eighteenth century. On several islands geographically
a part of Kittery, the Federal government in 1806 established the Navy
Yard that since has been industrially predominant. Incorporated in 1647,
Kittery has several small boatyards for pleasure craft, craftwood and
related industries, seafood centers, motels, business and service establishments, several picnic areas and two municipal beaches. For cultural
events and much of their shopping, generations of residents have travelled
to nearby Portsmouth, N. H. where the *Strawberry Banke Restoration*
is a major visitors' attraction.

The Kittery Historical Society has placed markers identifying a score of
Seventeenth and Eighteenth century houses, many facing the water which
was the main highway before roads were built. Despite changes made by
succeeding owners, these old buildings may be recognized by such
architectural details as granite or rock instead of brick foundations, or the
single large brick chimney centering the roof of a Cape Cod cottage.

Offshore lie the *Isles of Shoals* (*by boat from Portsmouth; no accommodations*),
called Smyths Iles by Capt. John Smith of Virginia in his report of his
explorations in 1616. The Maine-New Hampshire boundary runs through this
group of islands, inhabited some time before the mainland was settled. In the
late Nineteenth century the larger islands became popular summer resorts
attracting artists, musicians and writers from Boston and other cultural centers.
Celia Thaxter (*One little sandpiper and I*) who spent her girlhood and much
of her adult life on Appledore Island, was the hostess as well as the poet of
the Islands.

Following the shore from Kittery's business center on Government Street,
the *Navy Yard (no visitors)* is seen from several vantage points. First

traffic light marks the first entrance.

The 74-gun ship of the line, the *WASHINGTON*, launched 1815, was the first vessel constructed at the Yard. In 1848, the *SARANAC*, the first side-wheeler, was launched. During the Civil War, 26 vessels were built, including the *KEARSAGE* which fought and sank the Confederate raider *ALABAMA*. The Treaty of Portsmouth ending the Russo-Japanese War in 1905 was signed in what is now the Yard's Administration Building. Since 1914, submarines have been built here, the first being the *L'8*, launched 1917. Half the submarines participating in World War II were designed here; 75 were built between 1942-45, employment reaching an all-time high of 20,446. The Yard built its first atomic submarine, the *USS SWORDFISH* (1956). Its first Polaris missile sub, the *USS ABRAHAM LINCOLN* was completed in 1961.

The fine old red house beyond the Yard's second entrance is known as the *Whipple Garrison*, one of the Colonists' several centers of protection against Indian raids. Gen. William Whipple, a signer of the Declaration of Independence, was born here.

With interesting views of the river, harbor and Navy Yard, the road proceeds 1 *m.* to a bridge over Spruce Creek on either side of which the early settlers established their homes. Occasional cellar holes and old cemeteries in the overgrowth are mute reminders that Spruce Creek was the main highway into the farmlands, pastures and woods now traversed by US 1 and I-95.

KITTERY POINT, across the bridge, is the oldest part of town and is named for an English estate in Kingsweare, Devon.

At the top of an S-curve is the *Lady Pepperrell House* (1760, NHL) (*summer weekdays*). Built for the widow of Sir William Pepperrell, one of the first Americans knighted by the British Crown, it is now owned by the Society for the Preservation of New England Antiquities. Born Mary Hirst of Boston, Lady Pepperrell lived here until her death in 1789, always using her title although it had been made obsolete by the Revolution, and demanding the deference to which she felt it and her former position as wife of the 'richest man in the Massachusetts Bay Colony' entitled her. The elaborate two-story Georgian structure with hip roof and four large chimneys has an ell and a porte cochere of later construction. The heavy main facade lacks refinement despite the corner quoins and pedimanted central pavilion flanked by two pedestaled Ionic pilasters with richly carved caps carrying a bellied fringe and cornice uniting them with the modillioned main cornice.

Perhaps the most interesting room in the house, said to be the work of Peletiah Fernald, a local carpenter, is the small one behind the parlor, with its charming fireplace paneled and finished flush with closets on either side. The collections of fans, dishes and portraits are notable.

The *First Congregational Church,* opposite, was built in 1730, remodeled in 1874 and turned a 90-degree angle to the south. Two original box pews remain, one housing an electric organ. The pulpit with delicate paneling and graceful lines bears the date 1730. Behind the church the Old Parish House (1729) has been much enlarged and serves as the parish community center.

Among the engaging inscriptions on the tombstones in the *Old Burial Ground* between the church and the river, is this one:

> 'A powerful God doth as he please.
> I lost my wife in the raging seas.
> The Kittery friends, they did appear
> And my remains they buried here.'

Near the western wall is the grave of Levi Lincoln Thaxter, husband of Celia, poet of the Shoals. A bronze plaque makes legible his epitaph originally cut into native stone, the only epitaph written for a real person by British Poet Robert Browning.

Private homes beyond the cemetery include those of the descendants of Stephen Decatur, famed for his exploits against the Barbary pirates in the War of 1812, and of William Dean Howells, novelist and essayist.

At the next bend in the road are the grounds of hexagonal *Fort McClary State Memorial* (1812), (*picnicking, playgrounds*). Originally named Fort Williams as a private fort of the Pepperrell family, it was renamed for Andrew McClary who died in the battle of Bunker Hill. The old blockhouse with overhang was built when British ships threatened the harbor and a battle was fought off Cape Ann; it was also garrisoned during the Civil War. The granite blocks forming the seawall are excellent seats for viewing water skiing or Sunday yacht races.

Coleman Avenue, first road L beyond the Park leads to headquarters of the *Kittery Art Association (shows, classes, lectures)*.

Entrance to next road L, a *Memorial Tablet* details the accomplishments of William Pepperrell the younger, the town's most famous son whose services to the British Crown earned him a baronetcy.

Opposite the post office, from a grocery store operated by the same family since 1828, a lane leads to a public landing and launching ramps. Nearby is the original grocery building, now occupied by the Pepperrell Cove Water Ski Club. This area provided George Wasson, marine artist and local color author, with material for his short stories entitled *Capt. Simeon's Store*.

East of the grocery is the *Sir William Pepperrell House* (1682), built for the elder William Pepperrell on his marriage to Marjorie Bray, and now occupied by a descendant. The door and window casings still show the marks of hand cutting, and the windows have the original lights, twelve in the upper sashes, eight in the lower. This house also was the home of John Haley Bellamy, noted for his carvings of ships' figureheads and eagles.

Old houses line both sides of the road. The third beyond the Pepperrell House is *Bray House*, the oldest. Built in 1662 by the shipwright father-in-law of the first William Pepperrell, it is now joined to the second house, once a store and tavern. Beyond Bray House, the fourth house was the home of Carpenter Peletiah Fernald. A long, low red house with three chimneys, it bears the date 1738 but probably is much older.

At the junction of State 103 and Chauncey Creek Road, near a small family cemetery, the Creek Road following the old Atlantic Shore Railway leads to a lobster pound.

Across the first bridge is the road R on Gerrish Island to *Fort Foster*, a town park (*picnic tables, fireplaces; swimming*), affording a view of the New Hampshire coastline and an opportunity to explore the fortifications.

Retrace to mainland and continue along the creek E about a mile to *Sea Point Beach (public; swimming).* The enormous tree visible N across the fields is the famous *Champernowne Elm,* said to have been brought from England by an early Colonist. It is on the site of the dwelling of the first settler, Capt. Francis Champernowne (1614-87), whose grave is in a small cemetery nearby.

Retrace from Sea Point Beach on same road to rejoin State 103, known locally as Braboat Harbor Road. Braveboat Harbor, site of the first ferry, serves as the boundary between Kittery and York. Meandering northward about 2 *m.* along the path of old railroad and trolley lines, the route leads into the historic York area where early explorers discovered the Indian settlement of Agamenticus (*see Tour 1 sec. a*). By 1623 it had been deserted after a plague had decimated Indian ranks. In 1630 English settlers arrived from Bristol and organized Agamenticus Plantation under King James' charter to Sir Ferdinando Gorges who dreamed, albeit futilely, of a great city rising in the wilderness. Through his influence, in 1640 the settlement was named Gorgeana for him and became the first chartered English city in the New World, with Sir Ferdinando's nephew Thomas as mayor. But in 1652 when Massachusetts obtained control of the Province of Maine, Gorgeana was reduced to township status and renamed York.

After the battle of Dunbar, Scotland in 1650, Oliver Cromwell found himself with many prisoners on his hands. More than 1000 were sent to the Colonies, 150 being apportioned to New England to be sold at £ 20 and £ 30 each for service to last six, seven and eight years; proceeds of sales went to the captain of the ship. A year later, after the battle of Worcester, England, more bondsmen were sent over, 275 of them to Boston. Many were brought to Maine. After completing their terms of servitude, the prisoners were free to settle where they chose; twelve remained in York. The first Scot to settle in York (1657) was Alexander Maxwell who had been sold to George Leader of Berwick.

With the increasing friction between the Colonies and the mother country, the people of York took sides, mostly favoring the Colonial cause. They had their own 'tea party' when the sloop *CYNTHIA*, James Donnell, master, anchored at Keating's wharf with a cargo of 150 pounds of tea for his uncle, Deacon Jonathan Sayward. Much incensed, the Sons of Liberty seized the tea and transported it to Capt. Edward Grow's store for safekeeping. The next night a roving band of 'Pequawket Indians' broke in and carried off the tea.

Shipbuilding was an important industry of the early settlement from 1670. Small ships of about 50 tons cargo included shallops, pynnaces, ketches, brigantines and sloops. Coastwise vessels were in trade with the West Indies and the Provinces. Warehouses and wharves lined the shores of York River. The first tannery was at York Corner (1686). Between 1850-60 there were nine mills of various kinds between the ocean and Chase's Pond where the area's first cotton mill was built with the incorporation of the York Cotton Company in 1811. Brickyards flourished until 1902, with a peak of 80,000 daily.

By 1865 summer visitors began to flock to this seaside township. Tourism, now a major industry involving hundreds of hotels, motels and so forth, began in private homes until the first Marshall House was built in 1870. Visitors today choose the liveliness of York Beach or the serenity of York Harbor and Cape Neddick.

On the streets and roads of the area are houses dating from the 1700s, many occupied by descendants of the original builders. The York Society for Preservation of Historic Landmarks has listed 52 buildings which they are identifying with suitable markers. The earliest houses of record were simple story-and-a-half structures of which two remain: the Stephen Preble House on Long Sands Road and the Richard Wood-Joseph Preble House, now private homes, both built in the 1670s. A distinctive type of roof evolved on York houses, with one gable end like a farmhouse and one sloping end. Several houses (six open to the public) have a 'good morning' stairway, most have 'borning rooms' and some have stenciled walls and ceilings. Many have Indian shutters, handhewn beams, handwrought nails and hinges. Flashing was of birch bark; clapboards were hand bevelled.

Continuing on State 103 to Seabury Road.

> Left on this road to the *Elizabeth Perkins House* (L) 1.5 *m.*, (*daily, June-Sept.*). This Colonial house was left to the Landmarks Society by its founder, Elizabeth Perkins. The dining room dates from 1668; the front part of the house was built in 1732.

> Directly across York River here is the house where Mark Twain spent the summer when he spoke at York's 250th anniversary in 1902. Composer Edward MacDowell lived for a time in a house on the river.

Sewall's Bridge, America's first pile drawbridge, was engineered by Maj. Samuel Sewall, opened in 1761, and has been continually in use. Formerly a toll bridge, its draw provided 'a sufficient way for sloops to pass and repass.'

> Right from Sewall's Bridge on Lindsay Road to the *Marshall Country Store* (1867) and *John Hancock Warehouse and Wharf*, 1.8 *m.*, (*daily, May-Oct.*). The Warehouse and Wharf have exhibits of early tools and ship models.

> At 2.2 *m.* is Indian Trail Road. Although now lined with modern houses, there is one early house with hoof-prints on its stairs. Maj. Alexander McIntire long ago rode his horse right up to his bedroom.

At 2.5 *m*. Lindsay Road joins State 1A at York's business center.

Beyond Sewall's Bridge 2 *m*. State 103 crosses New Bridge.

Right on road to Harris Island, York Marina, Town Wharf and their facilities. Many Indian artifacts have been found on Harris Island.

A short distance farther on State 103 is *Sayward House* (1719) (R), birthplace (1759) of Sally Sayward Barrell Keating Wood (Madam Wood), Maine's first novelist. This was the home of her grandfather, 'second wealthiest man in the Province of Maine.' In this area, Sir Ferdinando Gorges ordered a Market Day to be held annually 'forever.' It is commemorated in alternate summers.

State 103 soon joins State 1A on which the tour continues. State 1A was called 'Scituate Men's Row' for Massachusetts settlers who received land grants in 1640 'on condition that a lane be kept through their lots.'

Left on State 1A to

YORK (alt. 50, pop. 4463). In every war, Yorkmen have mustered for battle on the Village Green here in the shade of the tall elms set out in 1753. On the hard-surfaced road in front of the Meetinghouse, it is hard to imagine York's first road in 1642 — two rows of cart-wheel ruts with a horse path in the middle. This was the King's Highway in York for several generations. The first bridge mentioned in Town records is the 'little highway bridge,' probably a crude affair of logs across a ravine. Two and four-wheeled vehicles later replaced carts for transportation and in 1787, the first passenger stagecoach between Portsmouth and Falmouth arrived in York. Between 1887-1925, a railroad served from Kittery to Long Beach and Union Bluffs. Trolley lines operated from 1898 to 1920 between Badger's Island in Kittery to York Corner.

On a knoll overlooking this Colonial village stands the *Old Gaol Museum* (*daily, summer*) built in 1653 as a King's prison, and thought to be the oldest English stone public building still in use in America. Stocks in the stone dungeon show early methods of punishment. Cells, and debtor cells made of heavy timbers studded with iron now contain collections of prison implements and workmen's tools. The gambrel frame portion of the building is appropriately furnished as living quarters for the gaoler and his wife. On display are Seventeenth and Eighteenth century prized decorative arts and documents of old York families. Notable are the 1745 Mary Bulman crewel bedhangings, among the finest examples of this work extant.

Among other places of interest:

In a corner of the Old Burying Ground across from the village stores, the *Wilcox House* (1740) (*daily, summer*), is a museum furnished with Eighteenth century York treasures. In 1766 Edward Emerson secured a 999-year lease on the Parish land which in the Eighteenth century housed a tailor shop, general store and tavern, with a tiny room added in 1821 as the town's post office. This became the home of David Wilcox, the postmaster, remaining in his family until 1954 when it was opened to the public.

Many of the lichen-covered slate headstones in the Old Burying Ground bear somber and conventional designs — the weeping willow, Grecian urn, scythe and Death's head with wings over inscriptions in old English spelling.

Nearby are the *Old School* (1775) and *Jefferd's Tavern* (1750) (*both open daily, May-Oct.*). The School is an authentic example of those of Colonial times, with the 'pupils' and 'schoolmaster' in costume of the period. The Tavern originally stood on the King's Highway in Wells. In 1942 it was removed to York, beam by beam and board by board, and completely rebuilt. Features are the paneled taproom, a replica of a bar of the period, and a long common-room or kitchen with huge fireplace and old utensils. Pewter, china and period furniture are on display.

The *First Parish Church* (1747) on the Village Green is an outstanding example of Colonial architecture.

The *Town House*, originally built in 1734, rebuilt in 1811 and modernized in 1967, houses town offices and an auditorium for public events. *War Memorials* on a boulder between the church and the Town House commemorate men of World Wars I and II as well as the first Maine men to volunteer after the Battle of Lexington.

Near Town House is the *Alexander Bulman House,* home of a doctor who died of fever at the Battle of Louisburg. It was his grieving widow who embroidered in crewel work the beautiful bedhangings displayed at the Old Gaol Museum.

Near the Public Library (1922) is the *Preble House* (*private*), a garrison that survived the 1692 Massacre and later became Green Dragon Inn, home of William Pitt Preble.

Also in the York area are the Nicholas Sewall House (1719) and the Hugh Holman House (1727).

Left from the Civil War monument in the triangle, on Long Sands Road to *Coventry Hall* (1794), a fine example of post-Revolutionary architecture built by Judge David Sewall during Washington's administration and called by a diarist of the day 'one of the grandest (mansions) built in the County.' Judge Sewall who served 12 years as Justice of the Supreme Judicial Court of Massachusetts and for more than 30 years as Judge of the U. S. District Court of Maine, was a Harvard classmate (1775) and life-long friend of John Adams, second president of the United States. One may envision Mr. Adams driving up to Coventry Hall in the finest coach York had ever seen. In 1770 he was a guest at Woodbridge Tavern (1719) where Paul Dudley Woodbridge provided 'Entertainment for the Sons of Liberty.' Judge Sewall is buried in York's second cemetery along with Rev. Samuel Moody of Louisburg, Jeremiah Moulton, famous Indian fighter, and men who served with John Paul Jones. A boulder marks the common grave of those who died in the 1692 Candlemas Day Massacre.

Retrace on State 1A from York to Foster's Clambakes (L) and junction with State 103. Proceed on State 1A to *Gilman Moulton Park* (R), especially for children. *Shoals House* (L) was floated on a raft from Isles of Shoals during an evacuation (1752) before the Revolution.

YORK HARBOR on a headland at the mouth of York River long has been a resort of summer estates and residences. Finley Peter Dunn, Nelson Eddy, Thomas Nelson Page and A. J. Cronin have been among occupants of estates on the oceanside. In the area are the *First Anglican Church* (1636), *Alcock Garrison*, and Varrell Lane to the waterfront (*marine facilities, fishing parties*).

Over the hill on State 1A, the York Harbor Reading Club (1897).

> On Norwood Farm Road (R) is the Rev. Shubael Dummer House, 2.5 *m.* home of York's first minister who was killed in the Candlemas Day Massacre.

State 1A soon reaches *Long Beach (lifeguards, campgrounds).* A two-mile stretch of sand and rocky coast bordering the highway affords one of the few remaining ocean-front drives. From here may be seen Boon Island (*see Tour 1B*) far at sea and Nubble Lighthouse.

> Left on Juniper Lane halfway across the oceanfront Beach Road is York's oldest house (1676) built by Richard Wood.

> Right on Nubble Road at the end of Beach Road, to *Nubble Lighthouse.* The road curves past coastal scenery to rejoin State 1A, on which continue to

YORK BEACH, summer playground (*bathing, surfing, lifeguards*). Here are Short Sands and Animal Forest Parks with amusement rides, shops, restaurants, movies, bowling and the like.

North of York Beach, State 1A meets Shore Road.

> Left on State 1A to rejoin US 1.

Continue on Shore Road 4 *m.* through wooded countryside to Ogunquit.

> En route are Cape Neddick picnic grove (R); Passaconnaway Beach, site of Sylvester Ferry (1652). On Lower Cliff Road, Dr. Elizabeth Blackwell, first U. S. woman doctor, had her summer home.

> Agamenticus Road (R) leads to York Cliffs, a promontory of many views. Next road (R) to Bald Head Cliff, spectacular rock formation (*parking fee*). The bark *ISADORE*, Leander Foss, master, bound for New Orleans, foundered here Nov. 30, 1842 during a severe gale and snowstorm. All hands perished.

> Next left before reaching Ogunquit, entrance to *Cliff Country Club (visitors).*

OGUNQUIT, 20 *m.* (*see Tour 1 sec. a*)

TOUR 1B: *From* WELLS *to* BIDDEFORD, 19.1 *m.*, State 9.

Via Kennebunkport, Cape Porpoise and Fortune Rocks.

THIS coastal loop over a broad peninsula rejoining US 1 at Biddeford runs through wooded areas, often close to rocky shores and sandy beaches (*bathing, boating, fishing*).

State 9 branches E from US 1 at 8 *m.* N of Wells Corner (*see Tour 1, sec. a*), 0 *m.*

At 2.9 *m.*, junction with Kennebunk Beach Road.

Right on this road past Webhannet Golf Club to *Kennebunk Beach*. Rocky spurs cut the mile and a half white sand beach fronted by summer hotels, cottages and homes.

At 2.6 *m.* is the *Monastery of the Franciscan Fathers*. In 1947 Lithuanian Franciscans purchased a handsome estate on the banks of the Kennebunk River on the site of the 1740 Mitchell Garrison. The house, built in 1900, has much of the original paneling, carving and wall coverings. A modern chapel designed by V. K. Vonynas was added in 1957. On the grounds are the Vonynas sculptures that were shown in the Vatican Pavilion at the New York World's Fair, as well as grottoes and shrines and the St. Anthony School for Boys.

The road rejoins State 9 at 4.2 m.

KENNEBUNKPORT (alt. 20, Kennebunkport Town, pop. 1851), 4.4 *m.* State 9 crosses the Kennebunk River and enters *Dock Square*, business center with its many specialty and art shops. Only remnants remain of the shipyards that once flourished when the 'Port was the shipbuilding center of York County. However, many of the stately Eighteenth century homes of the early shipbuilders and sea captains continue to be occupied. Fishing is now the major industry, the farmers of the sea operating year-round.

SE off the mainland is BOON ISLAND, point for mainland boat races and an island of many legends. One story is that Aspinquid's great funeral ceremony (*see Tour 1 sec. a*) also was a blessing that resulted in the naming of the island where the trader *INCREASE* was wrecked. The only survivors, three white men and one Indian, were about to give up hope of rescue from their rocky isolation when they saw rising from Mt. Agamenticus the smoke from the burnt offerings of the hundreds of Indians at the rites for the departed Aspinquid. Heartened at this indication of human habitation, the castaways built a huge driftwood fire that attracted rescuers from the mainland. In gratitude they named the island Boon. The lighthouse here was erected in 1811.

Less than 20 years later, the tale of another shipwreck, this one including cannibalism, that occurred on Boon Island is recounted in a rare Eighteenth century pamphlet. Commander John Deane tells the harrowing tale of his ship, the *NOTTINGHAM GALLEY*, three months out of London with a cargo of cordage, 1000 firkins of Irish butter and 300 cheeses, wallowing down the Maine coast in a howling nor'easter, to pile up on the ledges off Boon Island on the night of Dec. 11, 1710. Little was recovered from the wreck, but twelve of the crew of fourteen survived 24 days without fire or shelter. According to the account: A small amount of water-soaked cheese, some seaweed and one captured seagull provided a common diet for over two weeks until the ship's carpenter died. A vote was taken and against some opposition, the carpenter's bones were stripped, the flesh being designated as 'beef' and other parts carefully categorized and put to use. Fat from the kidneys was used as mutton tallow and applied to the crew's frozen feet. Capt. Deane's narrative later was published in defense of his conduct which apparently was not altogether without reproach, the first edition being London, 1711.

Kennebunkport had its Engagement Cake House of the same period as Kennebunk's Wedding Cake House (*see Tour 1 sec. a*). The lacy gingerbread work was thought to have been added later to the original home built in the 1830s. In the 1960s, it was 'defrosted' and restored to its original appearance. A companionable culinary note: the ancestor of a local family, one David Robinson, an ice dealer, is credited with the invention of ice cream. He 'concocted His famous Dish for Lafayette on the occasion of his Visit to the City of Portland, Maine.' Seeking some special delicacy to tempt the great General, Robinson stirred up a mixture of custard and froze it — Voila, mon General - ice cream.

Right from Dock Square on Ocean Avenue, a five-mile scenic drive returning to the Square, follows the Kennebunk River to the sea, passing the Arundel Yacht Club (*Boon Island races*); the Floats, a riverside building where Booth Tarkington's studio-ship, the *REGINA* was once tied up; the *River Club*, scene of summer social activities; summer hotels; a King's Highway sign; St. Ann's Episcopal rock-built Chapel (1892); and turn-of-the-century summer cottages.

At the rock formations of *Spouting Rock* and *Blowing Cave* magnificent displays of surf are frequent. There are many views of the islands, including Goat Island Lighthouse and Bumpkins Island, seabirds' nesting place.

Leaving the shore, the road turns inland passing Wildwood Chapel (L) where Singspirations are held in summer, then bearing L to return to the village. Mission Art Gallery (L) near Maine St.

Left from Dock Square on Temple St. to South Congregational Church (1824), beautiful example of New England church architecture. On Mill Lane, the Old Perkins Grist Mill (1749) (L) is a summer restaurant.

Left on North St., then L at a fork to *Kennebunkport Playhouse (current and favorite plays, summer)*. Farther along, the Kennebunkport Historical Society *Museum* is the old Burbank schoolhouse (*two days weekly and by appointment, summer*). On a knoll beyond stands the First Parish Church (Congregational c. 1842).

Continue on State 9 past the Baptist Church (1838) and the Graves Memorial Public Library, an 1813 building that served more than 100 years as the Customs House for the busy port.

CAPE PORPOISE (alt. 20, Kennebunkport Town) 6.7 *m.* Not a true cape, but a group of islands in cape-like formation in the coastal contour, Cape Porpoise was the area's first settlement early in the Seventeenth century and was organized as a Massachusetts town in 1653. The original settlement's name, Cape Porpus, was changed c. 1720 to Arundel in honor of the English Earl and the town did not become Kennebunkport until 1821. North Kennebunkport separated early in the Twentieth century and took the name of Arundel after Kenneth Roberts' book of that title was published.

During the Indian uprisings, the town was nearly deserted, resettled in 1714. All the islands are privately owned except Federally owned Goat Island with its Lighthouse and Coast Guard residence. Goat Island was the scene of the only local engagement with enemy forces during the Revolution. At Cape Porpoise pier, a plaque set in stone, overlooking the island, commemorates August 8, 1782 when a British ship of 18 tons was driven off by a party of musket-bearing settlers.

> Straight ahead from the village square is the Pier, fishermen's center popular also with Sunday fishermen.

At 9.6 *m.* a junction with Dyke Road.

> Right on this road to *Goose Rocks Beach*, a cottage colony fronting on a sand beach. A two-mile loop along the beach rejoins State 9 at 10.5 *m.*

At 11.3 *m.* State 9 crosses Kennebunkport-Biddeford line and runs about a mile through scrub woods growth now healing the scars of a disastrous fire (1947).

At 12.4 *m.*, Old Road branches R to beaches and rock-bound coast.

> At 1.6 *m.*, on Old Road, State 208 goes to Biddeford Pool, named for the saucer-shaped cove entered through a gut. Along Fletcher's Neck on the peninsula between cove and sea are many large estates and the Coast Guard Station facing the sea. Pleasure craft dot the cove and dories and lobster traps are scattered around the wharves at the gut.

> Returning on State 208 to Old Road, R to Fortune Rocks. A bronze Marker (L) commemorates the Site of Richard Vines Settlement (1616) where Capt. Vines and a crew of 16 men spent the winter testing the climate for Sir Ferdinando Gorges. Calling the place Winter Harbor, Vines explored the Saco River and environs and found the spot 'healthy.'

> At 1.3 *m.* a side road (R) leads to Hills Beach 1 *m.*, another colony of summer cottages and fishermen's homes stretching to the Biddeford Pool gut. A tall white Monument on Basket's Island (L) is a seamen's landmark. At road's end, a bronze tablet set in stone identifies Fort Mary built in 1710 on Fort Hill and thought to be the site of an earlier fort c. 1688.

> At 1.4 *m.* on Old Road is *St. Francis College* (1953), a Catholic co-educational four-year undergraduate college of liberal arts, its programs planned to serve 1000 students.

Old Road rejoins State 9 for the four miles on to Biddeford, passing Ferry Lane on the Saco River where, some say, Maine's first hotel was built. In any case, Saco court records state that one Henry Waddock was granted the right 'to keep an ordinary to entertain strangers for their money.' The court made some sharp rulings as to the conduct of drinkers: 'Whoever is drunk pays 3s. 4d.; for drinking too much, 2s. 6d.; for sitting after nine at night, 5s., to be imprisoned until he pays, or sit in the stocks for three hours.'

BIDDEFORD (*see Tour 1 sec. a*) 19.1 *m.* at Alfred Street. Left on Maine Street to US 1.

T O U R   1 C : *From* BRUNSWICK *to* HARPSWELL
a. *to* BAILEY ISLAND, 16.4 *m.*, State 24.
b. *to* SOUTH HARPSWELL, 13.7 *m.*, State 123.

Two routes into the Town of Harpswell are given because there is no Town cross-over from one route to the other.

THE Town of Harpswell (alt. 30-40, pop. 2032) is unique in that it is composed of a peninsula and more than 45 islands (*see ISLAND TRIPS*). Bridges join the three largest islands to the mainland and to each other. Covering some 24.6 square miles, the town was incorporated in 1758 and originally was called Merriconeag. Its eight major settlements are strung along 34.8 *m.* of road affording broad vistas and unparalleled seascapes. The coastal terrain, combining rocky ledges, marshes and woodland, is ideal for marsh and seabirds as well as a summer resort for many inland species.

Harpswell's name is said to have been derived from that of a small parish in Lincolnshire, England. Fishing and wood-cutting have been major activities on Harpswell Neck and the islands. Great trees went into the wooden vessels built in many Harpswell shipyards; wood of lesser quality was corded and shipped to Boston for firewood. Today, the extraordinary beauty of the area attracts artists and writers.

BAILEY ISLAND TOUR

Via Great (Sebascodegan) and Orr's Islands.

State 24 leaves Brunswick (*see Tour 1 sec. a*) S at Cook's Corner traffic light, 0 *m.*

At 3.6 *m.*, across a bridge over the Gurnet to GREAT ISLAND, known locally as East Harpswell, the 'Lost Paradise' of Pulitzer-prize-winning Poet Robert Peter Tristram Coffin. Indian Rest is a small summer colony here.

At 4.3 *m.*, junction with an unnumbered road.

> Left on this road is *Cranberry Horn Cemetery*, 1.2 *m.* Poet Coffin and his wife are buried here; he composed both epitaphs. In an iron-fenced plot, the oldest gravestone is dated Sept. 24, 1774.

At 1.4 *m.* is the East Harpswell Baptist Church (1817) (R). For many years the only church on Great Island, it was first known as the First Free Will Baptist Church, with Rev. George Lamb the first minister. The church is of unusual construction, the seating arrangement reversing the usual. The high raised box pulpit is at the rear and rows of pews face the main doors. The raised choir loft is at the front. The old-fashioned pews are of English design with straight backs, narrow seats and doors at either end. Some have foot rests or hymnal racks. The *Old Peabody Pew* is sometimes presented here.

Next is CUNDY'S HARBOR (*deep sea fishing*) where U. S. Senator Margaret Chase Smith has a summer home. A World War II Memorial is near the end of the Town road, 4.7 *m.*

Among the island stories is that of Judith Howard, an early settler on Great Island, who lived alone and made curative medicines and salves of herbs and roots. Her reclusive life soon inspired neighbors to whisper that she was a witch — especially when Judith warned that she would haunt them if, when she died, they buried her near Old Lambo, an Indian who was buried in a field (S of a Cundy's Harbor store). When Judith died in 1768, neighbors, heedless of her warnings, buried her by Old Lambo's side. Whereupon they were plagued night after night by strange sights and disturbances. At last they decided Judith's body must be moved. Her remains were disinterred and taken by ox and sled two miles up the island and reburied on the W side of the main road. Thereafter, Judith's neighbors slept in peace.

At 7.6 *m.* is Card Cove (L) where sea gulls feed; ahead, a fine seascape.

At 8.7 *m.* is *The Gurnet* where furiously rushing tides separate Great Island from Orr's Island. At the S tip of Great Island the highway cuts through a high cliff of gray stratified rock known as The Rock Cut and leads to Orr's Island Bridge joining Great and Orr's Islands. There is a small area for sightseers at the end of Orr's.

At 9.4 *m.* along the Devil's Back, a picnic area (L) affords a breath-taking view of open ocean. The highway follows the ridge of the island its entire length, 4.5 *m.* Originally the island was called Little Sebascode-gan, until the brothers Orr, Joseph and Clement, arrived from Scotland, bought the island and settled here. There is ample anchorage for power and sailboats. A local club sponsors summer sailing competition.

At 11.3 *m.* is the Union Church (L), built in 1855 through the joint efforts of Free Will Baptists, Methodists, Congregationalists and Calvinist Baptists. Nearby is the Orr's Island Cemetery where many interesting old graves and epitaphs in verse may be found.

World Wars I and II Memorials are in front of the Library, 12.3 *m.* An-other church, the Methodist (1875) (L) and parsonage (R) are a short distance on.

At 13.1 *m.* a narrow road (R) leads to a white house near the shore known as the Pearl of Orr's Island House (*private*). This house is said to have been the home of the heroine of the novel of that name by Harriet

Beecher Stowe who was the guest of Samuel Smullen, local grocer and his
wife while she was writing the book.

A girls' summer camp is next (R).

> Orr's old-timers tell the story of Capt. John Wilson and the Thanksgiving Day
> hunt in the mid-1800s that paid off handsomely in Spanish silver — $16,000
> worth. On Cedar Ledges SE of Orr's Island are said to be three holes, two above
> high water and one below, where Capt. Wilson is supposed to have come upon
> the caches of Spanish coins while hunting. Although the Captain is said to have
> bought much land, woodlots, two vessels and a house with his find, skeptics
> say Capt. John made his money 'through hard work.' He had nine children,
> six sons and three daughters. The family lived frugally and worked hard, at
> fishing and farming.

At 13.8 *m.* at S. tip of Orr's, State 24 crosses Will's Strait or Gut on the
Bailey Island Bridge.

> This famous cob-work span completed in 1928 is said to be the only one of its
> kind in the world. Because of the swift tides and battering ice in extreme
> weather, the honey-comb construction on out-cropping ledges was the only
> feasible foundation across the 1200 feet of Will's Gut. Granite blocks, without
> cement or mortar, were laid in cellular or open construction, first lengthwise,
> then cross-wise, crib style. At the center over the deep channel, a single
> 52-foot iron span rests on concrete pillars and the roadway across the bridge
> is reinforced concrete, with a sidewalk for pedestrians.

BAILEY ISLAND is the third island and southernmost settlement on this
tour. (*Sailing, scuba diving, deep sea fishing*).

At 14.7 *m.* a private home (1763) (L) is the oldest house on the island,
and one of the oldest in town. A fine example of pre-Revolutionary
architecture, it was built by Thomas Merryman for his bride, Sarah
Bailey, for whose father, Deacon Timothy Bailey, the island is named.

At 15.1 *m.*, after passing Bailey Island Cemetery (R), is the Chapel of
the Precious Blood (1949) (R), (*Catholic, year-round services*), memorial to a summer resident.

Next is the Island Community Church (L), built in 1866 by a sewing circle
composed of both men and women.

At 15.3 *m.* a road (R) skirts picturesque Mackerel Cove, a large sheltered
anchorage, and leads to the wharf where giant tuna are weighed during
the annual Tuna Tournament sponsored by a local club.

At 15.6 *m.* is the wharf where Casco Bay steamers stop.

At 16.4 *m.* State 24 stops at Land's End. Ledges at the tip of Bailey's
Island afford a magnificent view of the ocean, Merriconeag Sound and

numerous small islands in Casco Bay. Five miles out is *Halfway Rock Light* so called because it is midway between Portland Head Light and Seguin Light at the mouth of the Kennebec. The 76-foot white granite tower (1871) appears to rise abruptly from the water, the Rock itself barely showing above high tide.

SOUTH HARPSWELL TOUR

Via the Harpswells, North, Center and West.

State 123 leaves Brunswick S from US 1 — Sills Drive traffic light, 0 *m.* Here at the N boundary of Bowdoin College campus begins a scenic drive down Harpswell Neck peninsula, not more than 1.5 *m.* wide at any point.

At 6.5 *m.* NORTH HARPSWELL. The Union Church (1841), (L) has been restored and redecorated.

HARPSWELL CENTER, 8.5 *m.* The First Meetinghouse (1757, NHL), good example of early church architecture, has an interesting pulpit with sounding board, and square box pews. Rev. Elisha Eaton was the first settled pastor and 'praying Indians' were part of his congregation. The building is presently also the Town House, Selectmen maintaining offices on the second floor. The Harpswell Center area is known as The Common; Harpswell Day is held here annually in July.

Many of the Neck's first settlers' graves are in the large old cemetery next to the Meetinghouse, including those of the Rev. Mr. Eaton (1702-64) and his son Samuel, also a minister.

The Elijah Kellogg Congregational Church (1843, NHL), opposite the cemetery was built for the Rev. Mr. Kellogg (1813-1901), well-known pastor and author. Although basically a New England style church, it has Gothic trim on the over-size steeple and ogee arch over the entrance door.

Hearse House (L), south, has a well-preserved early funeral vehicle.

It may be appropriately noted here that, like Sleepy Hollow, Harpswell has its Headless Horseman legend. Hoof beats have been heard and the apparition seen at South Harpswell, Gun Point Road, Bailey Island Cemetery and Orr's Island Bridge. Just at midnight when the moon is riding high, a horseman appears to materialize from the picturesque fishhouse standing on The Nubble, a small jetty at Bailey Island. The rider's white robe billows out behind him as his all-white steed scrambles up the hill and gallops toward Orr's Island to keep some mysterious rendezvous. The rider is carrying his head under his arm.

Maine seafaring men who visited the Orient undoubtedly brought back the ancient Chinese legend of the white-garbed traveller on a great white horse

who was bearing an important message through the dangerous Himalaya
Mountains when he was set upon and beheaded by brigands. As he died, he
prayed that even in death he might be permitted to complete his journey and
deliver his message at his destination as promised. As soon as the brigands had
fled, the messenger picked up his head, tucked it under his arm, mounted his
steed and sped on his way. Arriving at his destination, he placed his head
before the person to whom the message was to be delivered and completed
his mission. The headless horseman was then buried with great honor because
he had allowed nothing, not even death, to interfere with his duty. If
Harpswell's Headless Horseman is on a similar mission, he seems not to
have reached his destination.

WEST HARPSWELL, 10.6 *m.* Flower and Art shows are held annually
in this small community with excellent sea views. A local club sponsors
summer sailing competition.

At 10.9 *m.* U. S. Navy Fuel Oil Depot (R).

At 11.3 *m.* West Harpswell Baptist Church (R) (*year-round services*).

SOUTH HARPSWELL 13.7 *m.* (*boating, fishing*). State 123 ends here.

Two poets have used effectively the legend of the *Dead Ship of Harpswell.*
John Greenleaf Whitter in 1886 immortalized the legend in his poem of that
name. According to Whittier, the ship would appear on the horizon as out
of a mist, approach a dock head on, and then would drift out to sea again, stern-
first, against wind and tide. This gives the legend its 'Flying Dutchman'
flavor, for, according to the poem, the ship was doomed to roam on 'baffled
quest' and 'never come to port.'

Robert P. T. Coffin used the story in *John Dawn.* The *HARPSWELL,* her
name in faded letters, her sails gray and old like the color of clouds, was sighted
twice by Capt. James Dawn and twice by Capt. John Dawn. Easter Toothaker
saw the phantom before he leaped overboard to his own death. The ship's
final appearance was to Polly Toothaker at Capt. John's passing and brings
the four-generation Dawn saga to a fitting close. Dr. Coffin had heard the legend
from his Uncle Robert and had talked with oldsters at Harpswell who said
they had seen the phantom. The ship was sighted both to the eastward and
westward of Bailey and Orr's Islands, the residents reported. It was also seen
several times off the Lookout at Harpswell Center. The Dead Ship's last
chronicled appearance was in the 1800s when a guest at South Harpswell
declared he had seen a full-rigged ship sailing into the Sound in full daylight.
When he called others to view the sight, the ship had vanished. The coming
of the phantom ship was believed to be an omen of death, visible only to those
directly concerned. An innocent bystander might not see the ghost ship at all.

T O U R   1 D : *From* BATH *to* PHIPPSBURG, Peninsula Loop,
32 *m.,* State 209, 216, 217.

Via Winnegance, Phippsburg Center, Parker Head, Popham Beach, Small Point,
West Point, Sebasco.

Tour may be taken in reverse or in any portion since all villages are within an 8-mile radius of Phippsburg Center.

THE tip of the Phippsburg peninsula at the mouth of the Kennebec River is the site of the first attempted English settlement in New England where Popham Colonists in 1607-08 built America's first transatlantic trader. Nearby is Fort Popham State Memorial and S on the long beach near Fox Island is one of the State's most beautiful parks.

Roads that once were Indian trails wind through wooded areas scented with pine and bayberry, along rocky shores and sandy beaches. The ten communities around the forested peninsula's perimeter are diverse — seaside fishing settlements nestled on steep ledges, resorts along broad beaches, river and countryside villages. Wrested from the wilderness by the white man more than 350 years ago and evolving through the years of shipbuilding, sawmilling and ice cutting, the large township (18,400 acres, pop. 1121) today is mostly a vacation retreat with fishing the remaining industry, carried on here since the time of the red man.

Attracting many artists, historic and scenic Phippsburg is variously interpreted in the works of John Marin, Ernest Haskell, Stephen Etnier, William Zorach, Lawrence Sisson, William Kienbusch and others.

State 209 SE from Bath (*see Tour 1, Sec. a*) soon bears L across a causeway at Winnegance (Ind.: wind against), once an Indian campground. Ten tidemills formerly operated here and the Morse lumber mill (1801) still is managed by the same family. At Morse Homestead (L), a cannon from the *RICHARD MORSE* (1851). About 1.5 *m.* farther a dead-end road (L) leads to *Sites* of Fort Noble (1734) and Pleasant Cove Meetinghouse (1736). Facing down-river to the wide waters at S end of Fiddlers Reach, the Fort was important in the defense of the Kennebec. State 209 passes the *Sportsmen's Club* (L) (*turkey shoots, civic improvements*).

Another mile to *Dromore*; Burying Ground (R) with graves dating to 1743. Soon, Butler's Hill gives a view of the Kennebec River, Phippsburg Center marked by its white church, and Dromore Bay formed by Lee's Island where in 1717, eight chiefs and 200 Indians planned peace talks. Schooners were built in the Nineteenth century at Stonybrook, foot of Butler's Hill; *Manor House* (c. 1770) (R) and road to W side of town.

PHIPPSBURG CENTER (alt. 20). Wooden shipbuilding commenced here in Colonial days, ended in 1921. Across from the post office the row of fine old sea captains' homes was known as Quality Ridge. A War Memorial marks the Center. The Albert F. Totman Library (R) (*Sat. afternoon and by appointment*) has local reference material, a large art book collection and holds summer art exhibits.

Tour proceeds on unmarked road (L).

Phippsburg Historical Society *Museum* (L) (*weekday afternoons, summer*) is a former one-room school (1859). Changing exhibits include area Indian and Colonial artifacts, documents, shipbuilding memorabilia, paintings and furnishings.

James McCobb House (1774) (L) (*private*), built by Shipbuilder and Trader McCobb has a beautifully paneled interior, original bull's eye glass over the entrance door. A Haskell etching shows the great black walnut tree in the yard. Nearby stood a similar house, the well-known Thomas McCobb Spite House moved by barge in 1925 to Rockport (*see Tour 1, sec. b*).

Congregational Church (1802), first lane (L) (*Sun. morning services, summer*). An outstanding example of early meetinghouses, it has been the subject of several paintings by Stephen Etnier. In front of the church is the family tomb of Maine's first congressman from this district, Mark L. Hill (1734-1842), one of the most prominent men in the early history of the lower Kennebec. Following a career of renowned public service, Hill lost political popularity when he favored the controversial Missouri Compromise with Maine's entrance into the Union as a 'free' state along with Missouri as a 'slave' state. Inscription on the tomb's granite shaft:

> For many years in public life
> Either by executive appointment
> Or popular election; he discharged
> His various duties with official
> Exactness & Christian fidelity.
> The memory of the just is blessed.

From the lane to Center Pond (R) and *Shipyard Sites* (L). The Minott yard here launched in 1893 the last wooden full-rigged ship to be built in America, the ARYAN, 248 feet, 2123 tons. Last new construction at the yard was in 1904, the five masted 251-foot schooner *MARCUS L. URANN* of 1899 tons. Alongside were the Bowker Yards which launched the *LAURA ANNIE BARNES* in 1921, last four-master built in Phippsburg.

Molasses, rum and sugar were cargoes of many of these vessels in the West Indies trade. Recollection of a coastal schooner unloading molasses at the Minott wharf: 'The sail was removed and the boom was used as a derrick. The crew was hoisting hogsheads of molasses and singing

> Up with handses
> Down with asses.
> That's the way to
> H'ist Molasses!'

The road winds past interesting old family cemeteries to

PARKER'S HEAD. Many famous sea captains and marine engineers were born in this craggy village. On his way to Quebec, Benedict Arnold is said to have come ashore here for a rum toddy with the minister.

Until the 1820s, quantities of big Atlantic salmon were caught here and sold for a penny apiece. The village was busy first with its sawmills until these burned in 1867, and then with its ice business, as many as 37 vessels waiting at one time to load ice for the West Indies and South America. Also found here in a large boulder is a deep hole thought by some to have been made by Indians in grinding their corn.

Half a mile on, a narrow road (L) leads to *Cox's Head* (remains of 1812 military earthworks) commanding a broad view upriver and of the mouth of the Kennebec and Fort Popham, the Colony Site on Sabino Head across Atkins Bay, and the islands out to sea. In the river is State-owned Perkins Island with its automated warning signal guiding navigators at the busy river mouth where fishing vessels, industry barges and destroyers as well as pleasure craft ply back and forth.

From Cox's Head one summer's day in 1814, Maine's 'Paul Revere' galloped a dozen miles to spread the alarm in Bath when the British warship *BULWARK* stood off Seguin Island with armed barges poised for attack, and firing cannon. American forces were under command of Gen. William King, later Maine's first governor.

Two miles farther the unmarked road rejoins State 209. Left on State 209 through woods and across salt marshes to *Popham Beach State Park* (R) (*swimming, picnicking, surf-casting, no camping*). Beyond are cottage developments, Ocean View Park (*rentals, restaurant, beach, parking fee*), and Silver Lake (R). Next road (L) curls around Sabino Head to Hossketch Point and the *1607 Popham Colony Site (marker)*.

Although no traces remain, one may imagine the arrival in late August 1607 of the two English vessels bearing approximately 100 male settlers, three months after a similar expedition had arrived at Jamestown, Virginia. Fair indeed was this northern coastal land at this season, but in the dead of winter the wilderness proved far less hospitable than the milder climes of Virginia.

Thanking God for their safe arrival, in the first Episcopal service in America, the northern Colonists, with Sir George Popham as president, started building their settlement in what was to be a "palisaded entrenched fort" named St. George. They built the 30-ton pynnace *VIRGINIA*, the first American-built English vessel to later engage in transatlantic trade and the forerunner of the area industry that became famous around the world. A model of the *VIRGINIA* executed by Carl H. Langbehn is at the Marine Museum in Bath.

Sickness and misfortune beset the Colonists in the bitter winter of 1607-08. Disheartened at the death of Sir George and the waning interest of their English sponsors, the survivors returned to England, their elaborate building plans for the settlement never realized.

In a nearby field is a stone (now covered and seen only by landowner's permission) bearing what runologists have identified as *Runic Markings* attributed to Norsemen, early 11th century, and translated: "year 19 (1018) A. D. is an ill (famine) year." The bucolic explanation is that these marks were made by somebody's grandfather's plow.

Today's Popham Colony is a summer one. Only a handful of rugged individuals remain year-round to brave the stormy ramparts that daunted Vikings and Colonists.

From the Colony Site an old footpath (L) leads uphill to *Fort Baldwin* (1912) manned in two World Wars and affording panoramic views of the Kennebec and out to sea.

State 209 proceeds across a marsh past Popham Chapel (1896) (R) (*Sun. services, summer*) to end on Hunniwell's Point at *Fort Popham*

State Memorial (1865) (*picnicking*). Large historic interpretations depict area scenes including the Popham Colony and the start of Arnold's march in Maine.

Manned seven times, this unfinished semi-lunette is principally known as a Civil War fort. Granite blocks are strewn about as if by a giant hand. Of particular architectural interest are the handsome circular granite staircases which, unlike other sections, have withstood the ravages of time and weather. Sections unsafe for the public have been sealed off.

Coast Guard docks and a local boatowners' landing ramp are within this area.

From the Fort, looking (L) across Atkins Bay is Cox's Head. Easterly across the mouth of the Kennebec is Long Island and Bay Point. Right are islands in open sea (several manned in the War of 1812) — the Sugar Loaves, Stage, Salter's, Pond, Wood, and *Seguin* bearing one of America's earliest lighthouses (1795) which stands 188 feet above sea level, highest on the Maine coast.

In the gay nineties era of Cleveland Amory's *The Last Resorts* POPHAM BEACH (*lunches, cabins*) was the scene of lively social activity — Popham Days, regattas, moonlight sails and excursions, square dancing and church socials. Hotels and boarding houses now long gone were thronged. There were boardwalks lighted with kerosene lamps at night, horse-drawn carriages on the dirt roads, and ladies with parasols and pompadours on the beaches. Folks arrived with their trunks for the season; passengers, merchandise and mail came from Bath by steamer. Everyone flocked for the docking of Eastern Steamships from Boston at the State or Federal piers where now solitary sea gulls perch on the rotting pilings.

Despite rosy plans, Popham never became a Bar Harbor, its heyday fading into history along with the Colonists and the Revolutionists — and the rum-running '20s of less nostalgic memory. Popham settled into somnolence in the summer sun, a vacation sanctuary of dolce far niente, changing under the pressures of the 1960s.

From the Point, a road (L), past a Civil War cannon pointing out to sea, leads to the U. S. Coast Guard's Kennebec River Station (*visitors*). Beyond is a cottage colony (private).

Retrace State 209 four *m.* to junction with State 216.

Left on State 216 to SMALL POINT. A secluded summer colony here is separate from Hermit Island campgrounds (*recreation facilities*).

Enroute, road (R) to *Ailiquippa*, site of Ancient Augusta, 1716 fishing settlement, abandoned in 1721 because of Indian wars. Grist and saw mills later were built and the sloop *PEJEPSCOT* carried lumber and fish to Boston. Phippsburg's first road was cut from here through the wilderness easterly to the Kennebec River. On the Small Point road is the *Sylvester Homestead* (1767), where Phippsburg's first school room was in an upper chamber.

From Popham to Small Point is a region of sandy salt marshes traversed by Morse's and Sprague's narrow salt water rivers and divided to the sea by Morse's Mountain, once known as Mt. Ararat which commands one of the most spectacular views on the coast. The beautiful Popham and Small Point beaches extend outside this region, skirted by fantastic sand dunes, wind-blown and wave-washed, in whose bosoms are buried the drifting wreckage of unknown ages.

In a now nearly inaccessible spot near the Point of Rocks forming the W side of Sprague's River, settlers in 1750 discovered an *Old Burial Place* with over 80 unmarked rough fieldstones, arranged in regular rows, which remains a mystery to this day. The graves, large and small, were laid out Saxon fashion, stones at head and foot of each; some of these markers are not yet obliterated by time and tide. Whether these might be graves of people from Ancient Augusta or even from the Popham Colony has never been established.

Retrace State 216 past junction with State 209 (R), past Small Point Community Church (1828) (R) (*winter services*) to Saw Mill Corner, junction State 216-209 with State 217.

Left on State 217 to road (L) for WEST POINT, 2 *m.*, picturesque fishing village where skilled fishermen have established world tuna fishing records.

This has always been a fishing place, white men through several generations succeeding Indians in taking the bounty of the sea. Visitors learn the source of the neatly plastic-packaged fish of the marketplace and enjoy watching boats come in with their huge slithering catches of cod, hake, mackerel, whiting, etc., for the city markets. Many artists, too, find inspiration in this ruggedly beautiful setting where Artist Ernest Haskell once lived.

On the West Point road, on a high ridge overlooking Casco Bay, a signal station was located in the War of 1812. When suspicious ships were sighted, two huge boards painted black (now at Phippsburg Museum) were manipulated to signal the Munjoy Hill Observatory in Portland 14 *m.* away.

State 217 continues to SEBASCO ESTATES. This resort area includes Rock Gardens Inn and Sebasco Lodge (*golf, tennis, sailing, swimming*). Watah Lake behind the main lodge was Cornelius Ice Pond which suppied great vessels anchored in the deep harbor loading ice for all parts of the world. About 2 *m.* beyond the Lodge Road, a road (L) to *Fish Processing Plants* (*visitors*). From this road, proceed through W side of town back to starting point at Winnegance Causeway. This is on the scenic old Meadowbrook Road meandering through a once populous area of farming, shipbuilding sawmilling and feldspar mining. At times the road skirts *The Basin*, favored by yachtsmen for its excellent harbor.

Alternatively, from Sebasco Lodge Road, retrace State 217 to junction with State 216-209. Left 3 *m.* to Phippsburg Center.

En route, less than a mile is the *Marrying Tree* (R), an ancient oak beneath which an eloping couple were wed on horseback in 1763. The tree also is known as the Sprague Oak for the family that settled here in 1762, and as the Tavern Oak for the tavern located where the nearest house now stands. Mostly rum was served to travellers in early days, the Barbados rum and molasses arriving in dried oak kegs on sailing vessels.

Modern buildings before passing Center Pond (R) to re-enter Phippsburg Center are the Fire Station (R) manned by 33 volunteers; and the Central Elementary School (1958) (L) for 232 pupils (1969). The School, housing gymnasium and Town offices, is the hub of community activities.

TOUR 1 E: *From* BATH *to* GEORGETOWN, 15.3 *m,* State 127.

Via Woolwich and Arrowsic.

CROSSING the Carleton Bridge from Bath to Woolwich (*see Tour 1, sec. a*), this tour takes State 127 (R) at 0 *m.*, swinging S over a series of heavily wooded hills overlooking Sheepscot Bay and its islands.

The *Drawbridge* 0.6 *m.*, over Sasanoa River to Arrowsic Island once had a tollgate tender whose kerosene lantern unfailingly swung out to halt the nighttime traveller.

Left of the bridge, 1.5 *m.* out in Sheepscot Bay is Hell's Gate where reefs and shoals and the roiling tides of the swift-running Kennebec and slower Sasanoa Rivers demand great navigational skill.

ARROWSIC (alt. 25, Arrowsic Town, pop. 177), 6.3 *m.*, site of New Town (1679-89) was one of the earliest settled areas on the lower Kennebec.

Slate markers in the old Denny Cemetery date to 1729. The first meeting-house (1762) overlooked the Kennebec (opposite Phippsburg Center). The Clark and Lake settlement at Hockamock Point, established in 1650 by Maj. Thomas Clarke and Capt. Thomas Lake, Boston merchant-traders who acted as entrepreneurs between settlers and Indians bought Arrowsic Island in 1654 and built dwellings, barracks, a warehouse and a fortified trading post. Sir William Phips as a youth worked as apprentice in their shipyard. Many of the buildings of the struggling first settlers necessarily were fortified. *Phippsburg, Fair to the Wind*, town history, lists the following forts on Arrowsic Island:

> 1658 — Lake's Fort at Spring Cove on the Sasanoa.
> 1680 — New Town Fort at Butler's Cove, N of Green Point.
> 1714 — Watt's Fort at Green Point.
> c. 1714-16 — Denny's Fort at Green Point below Watt's.
> c. 1716 — Preble's Fort at Preble Point, N end of Arrowsic.

The Watt's Garrison was built by John Watts of Boston and the town of Georgetown was incorporated in 1716 with this nucleus.

Denny's Fort was a blockhouse built by Samuel Denny, an educated Englishman who acted as judge and bailiff.

Green Point became Squirrel Point after *H. M. S. SQUIRREL*, bearing Royal Governor Shute of Massachusetts, ran aground there in 1717.

At 8 *m.* State 127 crosses a bridge over Back River to the island of Georgetown on the E side of the Kennebec, early known as Parker's Island for John Parker the First who owned it in the Seventeenth century. Three John Parkers of the historically well-known New England Parker family were prominent in the settlement of the lower Kennebec. The Second and Third John Parkers settled on the W side of the Kennebec in what is now Phippsburg (*see Tour 1D*). The old Town of Georgetown comprised Arrowsic, Woolwich, Bath, and Phippsburg.

GEORGETOWN (alt. 60, Georgetown Town, pop. 790), 11.9 *m.* Sculptor Gaston Lachaise summered in this town which lies on hilly islands. The gradual settling of the continental terrain is very noticeable here. Stretches of marshland, formerly flooded only at high tide, now are waterways, navigable by small craft, even at low tide. Patches of land at intervals are cut off, creating more islands.

Dulse, an edible seaweed, grows on the very rugged shoreline. Doubtless it was from such rocks as these that Moncacht-Ape, a Yazoo Indian, nearly three centuries ago gazed for the first time upon the great waters, fascinated and terrified by their expanse and their roaring as they lashed against the ledges only to fall back each time in huge billows of spent foam. An account in French relates how this red man had traveled from the lower Mississippi Valley to the east coast seeking the place of origin of the North American Indians. The story is told of his first sight of the 'Big Water.'

When I saw it I was so glad I could not speak. My eyes seemed too little to see it all. But the night came — The water was close to us, but below. The wind was big and I think it made the Big Water angry. It made so much noise I could not sleep. I was afraid the blows made by the Big Water on our high place would break it, though it was made of rocks . . . I was a long time without speaking to my friend. To see me always looking and never speaking he thought I had lost my mind. I could not understand where all this could come from. The wind went away before the sun came up and the Big Water was not as angry as it had been. I was surprised to see it coming back to us. That made me afraid. I got up and ran as fast as I could. My friend called to me that I had nothing to fear . . . He said Red Men had seen the Big Water and that it was always traveling, sometimes going away, sometimes coming back. But he said it never came nearer the land at one time than another . . . We went away so we could sleep far away from this noise which followed me everywhere. Until evening I did not speak of anything else to my friend.

At 14 *m.*, L to *Reid State Park (1.5 m. beach and pool swimming, picnic facilities, snack bar, no camping).*

Beyond the Park is *Robinhood Cove* (marina), a summer settlement where Sculptor William Zorach and his artist wife Marguerite spent many summers. Here Zorach created his famous Figure of the Dance now seen at Radio City, New York, and many other works. First known as a painter, he became world renowned for his strong, earthy works in stone and other media. At their Robinhood farm, the Zorachs lived and created in the Maine environment they loved, and brought up their family. A daughter, Dahlov Ipcar, is a well-known artist. Works of the family are familiar to museum-goers in Maine as well as nationally.

FIVE ISLANDS (alt. 40, Georgetown Town) 15.3 *m.* having a beach and good harbor at the mouth of the Sasanoa River, is principally a summer settlement with many boating enthusiasts. State 127 ends here.

TOUR 1 F: *From* WISCASSET *to* BOOTHBAY REGION, 13.8 *m.,* State 27.

Via Edgecomb, Boothbay Harbor and Southport.

SKIRTING coves and inlets, the route runs down the peninsula to one of Maine's largest resort areas.

At 0 *m.* the Fort Edgecomb road (R) branches S from east end of Wiscasset Bridge (*see Tour 1, sec. b*).

FORT EDGECOMB, State Memorial (*summer; picnicking, interpretive displays*), 1.7 *m.*

> Overlooking the Sheepscot River and the Narrows at the entrance of Wiscasset Harbor, the Old Blockhouse and Fortifications were built in 1808-09 for Harbor defense and garrisoned during the War of 1812. It has been extensively restored along with the stockade and parade grounds. Constructed of heavy pine timbers, the first story, 27 ft. wide and pierced for musketry, is overhung by a second story with square portholes heavily shuttered like those on warships of the day. Overall is a watch tower where lookouts got a full-circle view of the river, harbor and surrounding countryside.

NORTH EDGECOMB (alt. 50, Edgecomb Town), 1.9 *m.*, is a small settlement of white houses with lawns running down to the banks of the Sheepscot.

> *Marie Antoinette House* (L) (*seen by owner's permission*) is so called because it was prepared, though never used, as a refuge for the French queen during the Revolution. It was built on Westport Island in 1791 by Capt. Joseph Decker and moved across the river by gundalow to its present location nearly half a century later. Shortly after it was built it came into possession of Capt. Decker's daughter Sarah, wife of Capt. Stephen Clough, master of the "square-starned" ship *SALLY*. He was in the salt and spar trade and made frequent voyages to Le Havre. Legend says he was engaged in a scheme to rescue Marie Antoinette and bring her to America. His great granddaughter wrote in 1918: "Stephen Clough certainly was in France during the Revolution . . . he brought to the United States furniture belonging to Marie Antoinette and the Queen was to have come too, but for the discovery of the plot to save her life. This furniture was divided among the owners of the *SALLY*, the Swans of Boston and the Lees of Wiscasset. The 'thrifty Madam Clough' did make over and wear a black satin dress . . . the robe worn by Louis XVI when he presided

'au Lit de Justice'." Whether the Frenchman of high rank who came to the Clough house might have been Talleyrand or the Queen's son, the Dauphin of France, Capt. Clough never revealed.

Capt. Clough is also one of many sailors credited with introducing coon cats to Maine. Of delicate frame, with long fluffy coats, they are rarely found elsewhere. Seamen like Capt. Clough are said to have taken Persian cats aboard the sailing vessels to catch rats and today's coon cats are supposed to be their descendants.

At 1.9 *m*. junction US 1 and State 27. Right on State 27 to Edgecomb (alt. 50, Edgecomb Town, pop. 450) 5.3 *m*., once the home of the Wawenock Indians who fished along the shores with bone hooks and bone-tipped spears. The early settlers who called the place Freetown, held their first town meeting in 1789. Tales of Capt. Kidd's booty buried here by early settler Samuel Trask have not been proven by treasure-hunters. Perhaps because the fact is that Kidd was hanged in England in 1701 and Trask was born in Salem, Mass. in 1703.

BOOTHBAY (alt. 80, Boothbay Town), 11.8 *m*. The English were fishing at Damariscove, one of Boothbay's outlying islands, as early as 1605 and by 1623 had established a year-round fishing station at Cape Newagen where a few families settled in the 1630s. When King Philip's War spread in 1675, the inhabitants were forced to flee from the Indians. When peace came the following year they returned only to be driven out again in 1689. This ended the first settlement.

In 1730, Col. David Dunbar who had rebuilt the fort at Pemaquid in 1729, laid out the town of Townsend and induced about 40 families of Scotch-Irish Presbyterians then in New England to settle the new town. Despite severe hardships and Indian attacks, the settlement survived and in 1764 Townsend was incorporated as Boothbay. Southport separated from Boothbay in 1842 and Boothbay Harbor became a separate town in 1889. The three towns now comprise the Boothbay Region.

During the Revolution and the War of 1812 British men-of-war harassed the inhabitants and disrupted fishing and trade. In 1775 Lt. Henry Mowatt, Royal Navy, anchored his ships off Boothbay and replenished his provisions with sheep from Damariscove before proceeding to bombard and burn Falmouth (*see PORTLAND*). The Continental Expedition consisting of naval forces and troop-laden transports assembled in Boothbay Harbor in 1779 for their ill-fated attempt to dislodge the British from Major Bagaduce (Castine). A Yankee victory took place within sight of Boothbay in 1813 when the U. S. brig *ENTERPRISE* captured His Majesty's brig *BOXER* in a lively action off Damariscove.

Following the War of 1812, fishing, shipbuilding and shipping prospered. In the 1880s the shipment of ice from local ponds became an important new industry. Large schooners carried thousands of tons of Boothbay ice to American and foreign ports. This trade and the salt fish industry ended in the early 1900s with the introduction of mechanical refrigeration.

Lying between the Damariscotta and Sheepscot Rivers, the Boothbay
Region became a summer resort in the early 1870s when scheduled
steamer service began with Bath which had direct rail and steamer connection with Boston. It has become one of the State's most popular mid-
coast resort areas; all types of accommodations including campsites, as
well as a variety of diversions such as sailing, golf, riding, yacht club
races, clambakes, flower shows, auctions, garden tours, band concerts
and church suppers. There are numerous shipyards in the area for building, storing and repairing steel, wood and fiber glass boats.

Boothbay Playhouse and Theatre Museum (summer), established 1937. A
New York professional resident company presents classical and modern drama.
The Museum has one of the country's outstanding collections of theatre
memorabilia including sculpture, portraits, documents and personal mementoes
of world-famous players.

Nicholas Knight House (1784) (*summer*), opp. post office, a restored two-
story house with attached barn, houses the collections of the Boothbay Region
Historical Society.

Boothbay Railway Museum on 30 acres of land off State 27, has 2¼ miles of
2-ft. narrow gauge railroad (*rides*). The Museum, housed in two restored railroad stations has large collections of railroad memorabilia. On the grounds are
an antique auto museum, country store, barber shop, bank, Depot lunch and
'Boothbay Junction post office.' At the Harbor the museum maintains the
Grand Banks schooner, *SHERMAN ZWICKER* (*guided tours*) with mementoes of the cod-fishing industry.

At 13.1 *m.*, junction with State 96.

Left on State 96 to EAST BOOTHBAY, 2.5 *m.*, boat building center since
1818. Shipyards (visitors) here built the world's largest molded fiber glass
sailing yacht, the ketch *SOLIMAR*, 58 ft., Challenger Class and in 1967, a
replica of the *AMERICA*. En route is the *John Leishman House* (1775),
Boothbay Harbor's oldest house, a Cape Cod with central chimney and two-
story L-shaped wing.

English settlers in the 1600s called East Boothbay *Winnegance* (Ind.: carry-
ing-place). Indians carried their canoes across the narrow neck between the
mill pond and Linekin Bay.

About 6 *m.* farther is *Ocean Point*, early cottage colony, with views of the
sea and outlying islands and Ram Island Light opposite.

BOOTHBAY HARBOR (alt. 40, Boothbay Harbor Town, pop. 5,000),
13.8 *m.* In this busy center of the regional resort, some 50,000 visitors
in summer throng the narrow streets, shops, art galleries, marinas, restaurants and other facilities, considerably obscuring the 'quaintness' of the
former trading and shipbuilding center. Lawrence Sisson and Tom Kavanaugh are among artists who have studios here. Besides tourism,
lobstering, shrimping and ground-fishing are now the local industries. All
types of craft dot the harbor and a summer highlight is the mid-July
Windjammer Days when coastal schooners arrive under full sail. A passenger excursion boat fleet offers 45 scenic sailings daily to Indian, Squirrel,

Monhegan and other offshore islands and to Christmas Cove, Pemaquid, Bath, Linekin Bay and up the Damariscotta and Sheepscot Rivers (*see ISLAND TRIPS*).

In contrast to the teeming mainland, *Squirrel Island* is an unusual and genuine survival of the turn-of-the-century way of life at genteel resorts — large shingle Victorian cottages, no cars, tennis and serenity. Although shaped somewhat like a squirrel, the island is thought to have been named for a 1583 disaster when Sir Humphrey Gilbert's ten-ton bark *LITTLE SQUIRREL* loaded with furs and salt fish for England, broke up and sank in a storm off the island. Indians used the island as a summer fishing spot until the early 1800s, when a few settlers cleared land for lumber and farming. Prosperous gentlemen from Lewiston discovered the island's possibilities as an exclusive vacation retreat and bought it for $2200. The Squirrel Island Village Corporation maintains traditions of selectivity; there are about 108 cottages, 400 inhabitants.

On Sawyer's Island is *Merrill House* (c. 1760), thought to be Boothbay's oldest house. It served as a tavern prior to the Revolution, during which it was plundered and fired by a British landing party. Benjamin Sawyer, its owner and occupant, managed to save it. Sawyer's was formerly known as Ship Island where mast ships were loaded with huge white pine for the British Navy.

At McKown Point on the mainland is the *Marine Biology Laboratory* of the U. S. Bureau of Commerical Fisheries and the Maine Sea and Shore Fisheries *Live Fish Display.*

A scenic loop drive around SOUTHPORT Island may be taken from Boothbay Harbor on State 27 and unnumbered road, 11.5 *m.*

About 2 *m*. on State 27 to Southport Bridge, a drawbridge over Townsend Gut. Three lighthouses, the Cuckolds, Burnt Island and abandoned Hendricks Head Light stand within the limits of Southport which has many picturesque harbors and coves. Another five miles to Cape Newagen where an unnumbered road runs 4 *m*. to complete the loop. Cape Newagen Harbor is the site of an English fishing station c. 1623. The *LITTLE JAMES* was wrecked there in 1624 while fishing for the Plymouth Colony; it cost the Pilgrims many beaver skins to salvage and rebuild the vessel.

TOUR 1G: *From* DAMARISCOTTA *to* PEMAQUID POINT, 14.8 *m.*, State 129 and State 130.

Via Walpole, Christmas Cove, Bristol, Pemaquid and New Harbor.

State 129 branches S from Damariscotta (*see Tour 1, sec. b*), 0 *m.*

At 1.6 *m.* is the so-called 'scalping rock' where in 1747 Indians are said to have killed two women while they were milking their cows.

At 2.9 *m.*, junction with State 130 which the main route follows.

Right on State 129 is WALPOLE (alt. 40, South Bristol Town), 2 *m.*, on the E bank of the Damariscotta River. On the hill (L) is the *Old Walpole Meetinghouse* (1772) (*summer services 3 p. m. Sundays*). A good example of church architecture of the period, it has the original box pews, high pulpit and gallery on three sides.

At 8.1 *m.*, a four-corners. Road R to Clark's Cove and University of Maine's Ira C. Darling scientific center. Road L to the old *Harrington Meetinghouse* (1771) (*museum; summer Mon., Wed. and Fri., 2-5*). Bristol is said to be the only New England town to have built three meetinghouses the same year; the third no longer exists.

SOUTH BRISTOL (alt. 80, pop. 630), 13.2 *m.* The Harvey Gamage Shipyard (R) has been building fine wooden vessels since 1910. It built the sloop *CLEARWATER* that sailed the Hudson River with Pete Seeger campaigning for river clean-up. In 1969 the Yard built the *EXPLORER II*, second of a fleet of research vessels with highly sophisticated equipment for VAST, Inc. (Vocaline Air-Sea Technology), subsidiary of Vocaline Company of America, an oceanographic research organization that services government agencies and other institutions.

The route crosses to Rutherford's Island and CHRISTMAS COVE (alt. 25, South Bristol Town), 14.7 *m.* Boothbay and Pemaquid excursion boats visit the Cove which has a large summer colony.

John Smith is said to have brought his ship to anchor here on Christmas Day in 1614. It is one of '25 excellent good harbors; In many whereof there is ancorage for 500 sayle of ships of any burthen: in some of them for 5000: And more then 200 Iles overgrowne with good timber, of divers sorts of wood, which do make so many harbors as requireth a longer time than I had, to be well discovered,' on which he reported after the voyage. It was Smith's report that helped keep up Gorges' faith in the possibilities of the land; Smith had announced that he would rather live in Maine than anywhere else, adding that if a colony could not maintain itself, even if indifferently equipped, it ought to be allowed to starve.

The main route follows State 130.

At 5 *m.* from Damariscotta, an attractive State Campsite.

BRISTOL (alt. 100, Bristol Town, pop. 1450), 5.7 *m.* Past the Town Hall (1800) (L), on a rise is the Congregational Church. Two roads (L) lead to Round Pond (*see below*).

PEMAQUID alt. 60, Bristol Town), 9.3 *m.*

Right from main highway to the village and continue to PEMAQUID HARBOR with its Fishermen's Co-op and a beautiful view of the Harbor.

At 11.5 *m.* on State 130, junction with Huddle Road.

Right on this road to PEMAQUID BEACH (alt. 20, Bristol Town) and *Fort William Henry State Memorial* (*museum; summer*), 1.3 *m.* The Town maintains the beach and Boothbay and Christmas Cove excursion boats stop here. The Fort tower has a fine view; a stone wall encloses the parade ground. The old *Fort House* (R) was built about 1731. Between it and the Fort Cemetery, an archaeological dig has uncovered many Colonial and Indian artifacts, displayed in a nearby *Museum (summer)*.. The earliest recorded burial in the Cemetery, oldest in Bristol, is said to be that of Hugh March, killed by Indian arrows in 1695. In 1970 the Pemaquid Peninsula was acquired by the State for preservation and development.

The earliest history of Pemaquid is found in occasional references of early explorers. It was visited by David Ingram (*see below*) in 1569, by Captain Bartholomew Gosnold in 1602, by Raleigh Gilbert (*see Tour 1D*) in May, 1607, and by Captain Thomas Dermer in 1619, and others. Captain John Smith of Virginia, in describing his visit to Monhegan in 1614, said that opposite Monhegan 'in the Maine' in a port called Pemaquid, was a ship of Sir Francis Popham whose people had used the port for 'many years.' The Sieur de Monts, who, with Champlain, explored this coast in 1605, mentioned that settlements then existed in this vicinity. It seems probable that a group of Bristol (England) merchants maintained a fishing and trading center with a resident agent here as early as 1600 or before. The history of the cellar holes and paved streets is not satisfactorily explained even now.

The first fort at Pemaquid, then called Jamestown, was a stockade named Shurte's Fort, built about 1630. Pemaquid was granted to Aldworth and Elbridge in 1631 by the Plymouth Council. 'The Angel Gabriel, 1631' became the seal of the Pemaquid Proprietors in memory of the ship that broke up off Pemaquid in the great storm of that date. Fort Shurte and the settlement were destroyed in 1676 by the Indians. Fort Charles was built in 1677 by order of Governor Edmund Andros. In 1689 Pemaquid was again wiped out by the Indians under French direction. The extensive, well-equipped Fort William Henry, built in 1692, was destroyed in 1696 by the French under Baron de Castin.

Fort Frederick, built in 1729 by Col. David Dunbar under royal commission, was destroyed by the residents of the Town of Bristol during the Revolution to prevent its occupation by the British. Between 1745-48 the settlement suffered many depredations by the Indians.

Next to Captain Kidd of another period, probably no pirate in Maine waters has been the subject of so many tales as Dixey Bull. In 1632 a band of French seized the Plymouth Company's trading post at Castine, and captured the sloop, goods and provisions belonging to Bull, who happened to be there at the time as a trader. Fired by a desire for revenge, Bull assembled a crew of twenty-odd men to prey upon shipping. When in 1632 Bull sailed into Pemaquid, sacked the trading post and nearby dwellings, he carried away much booty. Bull's lieutenant was killed during the raid. Although the government at Boston dispatched five sloops to capture the pirate, they failed to find him and returned to Boston. One version has it that Dixey Bull was finally caught and executed at Tyburn, England.

NEW HARBOR (alt. 30, Bristol Town), 12.1 *m.*, a fishing and resort settlement. This was the home of Samoset, the Indian who in March 1621 startled the Pilgrims of Plymouth by appearing among them with the words, 'Much welcome, Englishmen.' He explained that he was a sachem and had learned the language from Englishmen engaged in fishing off Monhegan, and named many of the boat captains. He was apparently accustomed to English fare, eating without comment the food offered. On his next visit he brought Squando. The advice of these Indians enabled the Pilgrims to replenish their dwindling stores, a friendly act that was later repaid with treachery. Samoset was entertained, with other Indian leaders, in 1624 in Portland Harbor by Captain Christopher Levett.

The road L from the hill goes to picturesque Back Cove.

PEMAQUID POINT (alt. 60, Bristol Town) 14.8 *m* at the extreme tip of
the peninsula is marked by *Pemaquid Light* (1827), (*parking*), automated
in 1934. Nearby are the Pemaquid Art Gallery, gift shops and eating
places. A beautiful and awesome sight after a storm, the Point is one of
the most frequently pictured on the Maine coast.

> David Ingram, Richard Browne and Richard Twide are said to have visited
> Bashaba Bessabez here in 1569 on their long overland journey from the Gulf of
> Mexico to Nova Scotia, but Ingram's tales were highly imaginative so that fact
> is not established.

State 130 may be retraced to Damariscotta, or as far as New Harbor for
State 32 to rejoin US 1 at Waldoboro.

> Right on State 32 along the shore, past fish and lobster wharves through Chamber-
> lain village to **ROUND POND** on Muscongus Bay, long ago the home port of
> Atlantic coast fishing fleets. Its granite quarry was well-known. Small boat-
> building, fishing and lobstering are today's occupations.

> Loud's Island, formerly called Muscongus, lies 1.5 *m*. offshore.

> Continuing N on State 32 through BREMEN, then R on Keene's Neck Road
> for the *Audubon Camp* on Hog Island (*access by boat*).

> En route into Waldoboro, the route passes the Old German Meetinghouse (*see
> Tour 1, sec. b*).

T O U R   1 H : *From* THOMASTON *to* PORT CLYDE,
    14.5 *m*., State 131.

Via St. George, Tenant's Harbor and Martinsville.

At the E end of Thomaston (*see Tour 1, sec. b*) near Knox Mansion on the
hill, State 131 bears S into a special tract of land granted to Samuel Waldo
for successfully defending the claim of Thomas Leverett's descendants, the
Proprietors and Associates of the Plymouth Council against the claim of the
British Crown.

At 5 *m*. is Wiley's Corner (St. George), site of Fort St. George (1809),
captured by *HMS BULWARK* in 1814. The Fort, reached only by water,
is under the State Parks system. It was once defended by one old man,
Ephraim Wiley, a Revolutionary war veteran. At the corner is an early
church (1789).

At 7 *m*., a road (L) leads to a great granite quarry, now abandoned, and a small Episcopal chapel of rare grace and beauty.

Farther along the route at Willardham (Wildcat) are lobster pounds and excellent view near more old granite quarries.

TENANT'S HARBOR (alt. 30, St. George Town), 9.8 *m.* is a fishing and boating center with public landing. The Baptist Church here is known for its exceptional stained glass windows. The next road (L) leads to Hart's Neck (Elmore), summer home of the late Thomas Bailey Aldrich. *Spouting Horn* here is a waterspout hurling the sea 40 feet into the air.

MARTINSVILLE (alt. 20, St. George Town), 12.1 *m.* is where Sarah Orne Jewett (*see Tour 8*) wrote *The Country of the Pointed Firs* and is the birthplace of Albert Bickmore, a founder of the Museum of Natural History in New York. Views here overlook Mosquito Harbor.

PORT CLYDE (alt. 30, St. George Town), 14.5 *m.*, (*ferry to Monhegan, public landing*). Artists who have found inspiration here include William Thon who makes his home here, the late N. C. Wyeth and the late Russell Porter, Arctic explorer, architect and astronomer who was associated with the Palomar Observatory. The Lighthouse Point Road offers splendid views of the ocean and islands, including Monhegan and the St. Georges group where Capt. George Waymouth in the *ARCHANGEL* visited in 1605.

> He found 'where fire had been made: and about the place were very great egge-shelles bigger than goose egges, fish bones, and as we judged, the bones of some beast.' The party lingered on this pleasant spot, repairing their ship, catching lobsters and fish, and gathering berries which grew in abundance. Establishing friendly relations with the Indians, the party traded knives and baubles for valuable furs and tobacco. They sailed off with five Indians, Tahanedo, Amoret, Skicoworos, Maneddo and Saffacomoit, who attracted much attention in England. Sir Ferdinando Gorges held three and presented two to Sir John Popham; these gentlemen were the chief backers of Waymouth's expedition. Two of the Indians were sent out on a ship that was captured by the Spanish. A third, Skicoworos, returned to Maine in 1607 on one of the ships of the Popham expedition acting as an interpreter for a time.

The return up St. Georges peninsula may be made via the Old Town Road through Turkey (Glenmere), rejoining State 131 at Tenant's Harbor. Near Wiley's Corner, State 73 (R) goes along the coast to Rockland (*see Tour 1, sec. b*).

> Right on State 73 to a road (R) leading to Clark's Island and one of the few granite quarries in operation in Maine. State 73 leads to SPRUCE HEAD, lobster pound and fine views.

TOUR 1 J : *From* WHITING *to* LUBEC-CAMPOBELLO, 11 *m.*, State 189.

Via West and North Lubec and Quoddy Head State Park.

LANDSMEN and seamen alike are enchanted by the rugged beauty of the most northeasterly area of the United States, reached on this route (*see also Tour 1 K*). The high cliffs of the mainland, the offshore islands, the great fishing fleets, the distinctive character of the villages and their people contribute to a region like no other along the Maine seaboard. Around this northeast end of Washington County are Cobscook Bay, Passamaquoddy Bay, New Brunswick's Deer Island, Campobello Island, and farther out, Grand Manan in the Bay of Fundy. Boatmen know this as a great sailing area, St. Andrews to the north at the mouth of the St. Croix River, Yarmouth, N. S. to the east for Halifax and the Maritimes.

State 189 leaves (R) from Whiting (*see Tour 1, sec. d*), 0 *m.*, crossing Orange River. At 1.5 *m.* a campsite.

At 5.7 *m.* WEST LUBEC. A road N along Cobscook Bay.

> Left on this road to NORTH LUBEC (alt. 80, Lubec Town), 3 *m.* Copper was discovered here in 1836 but attempts at profitable mining failed. Here also are quartz and specular hematite iron veins. The area became known in 1896-98 for the hoax perpetrated by the Electrolytic Marine Salts Company — the Jernagan gold swindle. A gentleman named Jernagan, pastor of a local church and with an unassailable reputation for honesty, promoted a scheme for taking gold from sea water by means of 'accumulators.' Divers planted gold in the water as fast as it was taken out. After a few months of these operations, the promoter, who had sold stock all over the country, disappeared with unknown quantities of gold.
>
> The grave of Hopley Yeaton, called the 'father of the U. S. Coast Guard' is located here.
>
> At the Farnsworth Museum in Rockland (*see Tour 1, sec. b*) are postal reproductions of a painting of Eastport and Passamaquoddy c. 1840 as seen from North Lubec. It depicts Fort Sullivan among high hills, sailing craft in the Bay and well-dressed ladies and gentlemen relaxing in the foreground.

LUBEC (alt. 80, Lubec Town, pop. 2684) (*motel, campsites, marina, island boat service*) originally was a part of Eastport. Incorporated in 1811 and named for Lubeck, Germany, it is known for West Quoddy Head Light and State Park. The sprawling town is shaped like a left hand, West Quoddy the thumb, Lubec village the index finger, followed by the peninsulas of North Lubec, Denbow and Coffins Points. As in Eastport, industry here is allied with fishing. The waterfront, sardine factories and smoked herring sheds (*visitors*) are of interest. Monument and Commercial Streets go to the marina at the north end. From the hilltop can be seen Eastport, Campobello and other islands. Points of interest also include Raven's Gulch at Boot Cove and the Life Saving Station.

Directional signs lead to *Quoddy Head State Park (picnicking, nature trails, no camping)*, 4 *m*., on the easternmost point of land in the United States. The 400-acre Park is adjacent to the famous candy-striped West Quoddy Head Lighthouse (1807) maintained by the U. S. Coast Guard. Rock ledges rise 50 feet or more from the ocean to 190 feet above the sea over rolling land with thick stands of spruce and fir trees. Tides here range from 20 to 28 feet, greatest in the nation.

Seaward views include the high cliffs of *Grand Manan*, 16 *m*. out *(ferry service from Campobello, St. John and St. Andrews)*. Grand Manan is the legendary source of fog, confined like the bottled genie of Aladdin's lamp, except for occasions when it rises, a wisp of mist expanding to cover all things softly in quiet, moist, impenetrable gray. To watch a fog bank roll in and be enveloped in it is another-world experience. The island has a Marine Museum and the Moses Memorial Bird Collection.

Left from the Light a road leads 1 *m*. to the *Flying Place*, a bog area, unique example of Arctic tundra that supports the growth of rare plant species *(protected by law, no picking)* such as the insectivorous pitcher and sundew plants. This flatland once was a lake bed left when the icefield retreated. Clay and peat strata are seen where the sea's wave action has exposed the shores.

At Lubec the route crosses the Roosevelt International Bridge (1962).

CAMPOBELLO ISLAND and *Roosevelt Campobello International Park (daily 9-5, May 15-Sept. 30, free)*, 1.5 *m*. The Park was dedicated in 1964 as an international memorial to President Franklin D. Roosevelt and as a symbol of international peace and good will between the United States and Canada. Maine's Senator Edmund S. Muskie has been chairman of the six-man international Commission that administers the 10.4-acre Park overlooking Friar's Bay. It includes the late President's summer home and grounds. The study and other rooms and furnishings reveal his character and interests. He spent the summers of his youth at Campobello from 1883 when he was a year old until he was stricken with polio in 1921.

A group of New York and Boston entrepreneurs purchased the island in 1879 from heirs of the Eighteenth century settler, Capt. William Owen, as a summer resort for wealthy Americans. FDR's father, James, bought four acres and built a house (1885), no longer standing, which was north of the President's cottage, a wedding present five years after his marriage to Eleanor in 1905.

While his visits after the polio attack were few and brief — the last in 1939 on the *TUSCALOOSA* — Roosevelt's love of the island which he regarded as his second home, and his long association with its people whom he called 'my old friends,' were well known.

Near the Roosevelt home is *Old Friar*, a promontory used as a target by the British fleet when it occupied Eastport in 1814.

Beyond is WELSHPOOL, so named by early settlers from Wales. On a crest at the west end is the home (1835) *(private)* of Admiral William FitzWilliam Owen, a son of early settler, Capt. Owen.

In 1946, Canada's National Historic Sites Committee erected the first memorial to Roosevelt outside the U. S., at the Library in Welshpool. His pew at St. Anne's Anglican Church also is marked.

Across the island E is *Herring Cove* where, in a beautiful grove with one-mile beach, the New Brunswick government maintains a free picnic and camping area.

The road continues around Harbour de Loutre to WILSON'S BEACH (*annual Campobello Fish Fair, August*). In 1765 Ensign Robert Wilson had built a log cabin and fish flakes, and cleared land near the beach. Five years later, Capt. William Owen of the Royal Navy, with a Royal grant, established his settlement near the beach. In his journal he noted that he called the island Campo Bello 'partly complimentary and punning on the name of the Governor (Lord William Campbell), and partly as applicable to the nature of the soil and fine appearance of the Island, Campo Bello in Spanish and Italian being . . . synonymous to the French Beauchamp.' Indians had called the island Abahquict, meaning along or parallel with the mainland; early French settlers had called it Port aux Coquilles.

Farther along to the northernmost point of the island and East Quoddy Head Light. Fascinating stones may be found on the island beaches. Canadian cheese at the country stores is like no other and dulse is 5-10 cents a bag.

TREAT'S ISLAND (alt. 40, Lubec Town) in Cobscook Bay (*by boat*) saw considerable construction during initiation of the Passamaquoddy Tidal Project (*see Tour 1K*); the Dam was to have run directly across the island.

Breastworks and powder magazine are remains of a Civil War fort manned to repel Confederate raiders such as the *ALABAMA*. A down-east historian says, 'In this age of manly interest in highway skimming at 60 mph more or less, it may be difficult to appreciate the enterprise and patriotic pioneer spirit of the Revolutionary War veterans who came to the Passamaquoddy region and dedicated themselves to building its prosperity. The Indian Superintendent for the Eastern District during the Revolution, Col. John Allan (1746-1805), was one of those. His military assignment was to win the loyalty of the Indians to the American cause. This he did most successfully despite discord between military officials at the Halifax, N. S. headquarters and the Boston authorities.' His home was on Treat's Island which he owned and where he ran his store and shipping business. He is buried on the island; a monument and small cemetery is maintained by the Federal government.

Others contributing to the area's history were the United Empire Loyalists who maintained control of part of the Passamaquoddy area for the British and engaged in the development of Canada in the early days. As were the Acadians from Nova Scotia, the Loyalists were expelled from the United States after the Revolution. The Charlotte County, N. B. Historical Society has marked the site of the first Loyalists' landing in 1795.

From the efforts of patriots and pioneers grew the Passamaquoddy trading and shipping that became worldwide, its ships known from the China Sea to New Orleans and San Francisco.

One who tried and failed to redeem himself and his fortunes in this region was Benedict Arnold of the famous Quebec March. Roundly hated by both nations, he found his buildings in St. John burned. He is said to have lived for a time on Treat's Island or Campobello. Col. Allan's books show business records of Arnold's transactions. Both men served under General Washington.

OF
ARCHITECTURAL INTEREST

PAST and present commingle as contemporary architectural expression is adapted to Maine's scenic environment — in public buildings of urban areas and in vacation homes by the sea and in the lakes regions. Compatibility of traditional and contemporary forms is perhaps most strikingly evident on the Mayflower Hill campus of Colby College in Waterville, at Bowdoin College in Brunswick and at the University of Maine which now encompasses five former State teachers' colleges. In such cities as Portland and Rockland, new bank buildings in counterpoint to older structures, often enhance both. While it cannot be said that all new construction — shopping centers, retirees' homes and other public buildings — meet the criteria of aesthetics, it will be noted in the fine examples that can be seen, how well contemporary expression suits the Maine scene.

MAINE STATE CAPITOL DOME AT NIGHT

THE GATCHELL HOUSE (GREEK REVIVAL) AT HALLOWELL

THE MCLEER HOUSE
(FEDERAL) AT
HALLOWELL

CHURCH STEEPLE AT CORNISH

THE RUGGLES HOUSE AT
COLUMBIA FALLS

VICTORIA MANSION AT PORTLAND

THE FARNSWORTH HOMESTEAD VICTORIAN PARLOR AT ROCKLAND

THE BLACK HOUSE STAIRWELL AT ELLSWORTH AND
ALDEN HOUSE CORNICE AT UNION

THE HAMILTON HOUSE AT SOUTH BERWICK

OGUNQUIT MUSEUM

GRACE EPISCOPAL
CHURCH AT BATH

DOUBLE DOORWAYS OF THE GOVERNOR KENT HOUSE AT BANGOR

A WINTER VACATION HOME

LORIMER CHAPEL AND CONTEMPORARY DORMITORY AT COLBY COLLEGE

PROPOSED UNITED NATIONS RESEARCH CENTER AT PEAKS ISLAND

FORESTRY BUILDING
VAULTED ARCH, UNIVERSITY
OF MAINE, ORONO

SENIOR CENTER AT
BOWDOIN COLLEGE

MAINE STATE CULTURAL BUILDING MODEL

A FRENCH EMPIRE BUSINESS BLOCK IN PORTLAND

MODERN BANK IN HISTORIC
MONUMENT SQUARE, PORTLAND

SHAKER MUSEUM, ORIGINAL MEETINGHOUSE, SABBATHDAY LAKE

KENNEBEC HOMESTEAD

TOUR 1K: *From* PERRY *to* EASTPORT, 7 *m.*, State 190.

Via Pleasant Point and Quoddy Village.

State 190 (R) runs SE from Perry, soon sighting the hillside homes of the Pleasant Point Passamaquoddy Indians (*see DAWN PEOPLE*), occupying 400 acres overlooking the Bay. St. Anne's church and the school are near the water. Standing out on the hill is the white wooden cross of the cemetery where there are monuments to Moses Neptune, killed at the Argonne in 1918, and Charles Nola, posthumously awarded the Croix de Guerre for his defense of an advance post until he was killed in World War II.

At 4.2 *m.* the route crosses Carlows Island Dam to Moose Island and Eastport. On the approach the white clustered buildings (R) are Quoddy Village.

The Village was built with relief labor when the Passamaquoddy Tidal Project was begun in 1935-36. After the Project was abandoned in 1937, the Village was occupied by the National Youth Administration, and during World War II by the Seabees. After a three-year feasibility study of the power project begun in 1957 by the U. S. Army Corps of Engineers, Federal holdings were sold to private interests; in 1968 some acreage and buildings were sold for a proposed year-round recreational development.

While small tidal gristmills were operated in Colonial days, the Quoddy Project was the first large-scale attempt to manufacture power from the changes of the sea. Passamaquoddy Bay is said to be one of the few known possible sites for such an undertaking; unusually high ocean tides (average range 13-23 ft.) ebb and flow with great force through the narrow channels connecting two large natural basins adjacent to each other and almost entirely landlocked. Advocates of the tide-harnessing project said great quantities of cheap power could supply farms and industries and the hoped-for development of the State's mineral deposits.

Originated by the late Dexter P. Cooper, the first concept was an International or Two-Pool plan embracing Passamaquoddy and Cobscook Bays. It was limited to a one-pool plan when the Canadian government withdrew. Three small dams were built before the controversial project was abandoned.

EASTPORT (alt. 80, pop. 2537) (*ferry; island and fishing trips*), 7 *m.* This easternmost U. S. city is on Moose Island, prominent in early American and Canadian history. (Quoddy Head at Lubec is the eastern-most mainland point.) Eastport was incorporated as a town in 1748, and included mainland Lubec and Treat's Island. It became an independent city on Moose Island in 1893.

While there is no record of Moose Island's first white settler, it is known that traders and fishermen followed the voyageurs into the area in the 1600s. Ship logs and navy records refer to early landings and encounters with other ships in the harbor. The governors of Nova Scotia and Massachusetts had earmarked it with surveys and land grants in the 1770s. A 1785 map shows 'The Grand Bay of Passamaquoddy' in largest letters.

Eastport saw a colorful period while the Embargo Act was law 1807-09, when it became the center for extensive two-way smuggling. During the War of 1812 it was seized and held 1814-18 by the British and returned to the United States under the Treaty of Ghent. The Webster-Ashburton Treaty of 1842 finally settled the boundary dispute and Moose and Treat's Islands were firmly part of the United States, while Grand Manan, Campobello and other islands went to Great Britain.

Fishing and allied pursuits are the main activities along the waterfront facing the harbor, said to be one of the three best on the Atlantic coast. Bowl-shaped, three by five miles with depths ranging from 90 to 385 feet, it always has been a haven for oceangoing vessels and in severe winters shelters small craft from other ice-bound harbors. The Breakwater, municipal pier, has an outside depth of 25 feet at mean low water. Industries include sardine canning, shrimp and tuna packing, manufacture of fish meal, oil and pearl essence, lobstering, periwinkle gathering and small boat construction; Bay of Fundy boats are in demand for rough waters anywhere. Inquire at waterfront for trips on mail boats operating between Eastport and St. Andrews and Canadian islands (*6 hours*).

The first sardines were packed here after the Civil War when shipbuilding declined. Julius Wolfe built the first factory in 1875 and as the industry grew, Eastport became a national sardine center. In this era the Washington County Railroad did more business than any other of its size. At the old Frontier National Bank on a Saturday morning, hip rubber boots covered with herring scales gave odor and greasy money to the coffers of the city. Herring are herring until packed; then they become sardines. Packing methods have changed since copper sealing was done manually. Now 'raw-pack' methods are favored. Visitors are welcome at the plants.

POINTS OF INTEREST

Fort Sullivan (1808). The Border Historical Society is undertaking restoration of the powder magazine and creation of a park at this site. The Society's Museum is in a portion of the Fort's officers' quarters at 74 Washington St. On July 11, 1814, a British fleet of a dozen warships of 200 guns with troop transports hove to in the harbor. Fort Sullivan with six officers, 80 men and 9 guns, surrendered on demand. No attempt at defense could be made against such odds, but there was satisfaction in knowing that England had sent her best against them, for the British fleet was commanded by Sir Thomas Hardy who took command at Trafalgar when Lord Nelson was mortally wounded. Sir Thomas made Buckman House his residence. The Treaty of Ghent was delayed six months when councillors from Great Britain and the United States parlaying peace in Holland, learned that the British had seized Moose Island.

A spectacular view rewards the climb up the Battery. In clear weather the 26 towers of the Cutler radio transmitters 40 *m*. SW may be seen. N is the St. Croix River; E and SE are islands of Passamaquoddy Bay and the Canadian shores and in the near foreground Old Sow (*see below*). The Vikings' description of strong tides, sea birds, vegetation and fish fits this area well.

A U. S. flag with 15 stars flies at the site of the first meetinghouse at Smith's Corner, High and Clark Sts. where there is another panoramic view.

Peavey Memorial Library (2-5:30 weekdays except Thurs.) has paintings, maps and special exhibits.

Carrying Place Cove, off State 190 near airport, 1 *m.*, public tenting (*June 1-Sept. 30*).

Harris Cove, boat shop (*charters, island and deep sea fishing trips*).

Old Sow, on Dog Island end of Water St., is one of the world's largest whirlpools and has been compared with Norway's Maelstrom. It is seen where the tide and river dispute passage. Average tide is 18.1 ft. with a variation from a maximum of 27 to a minimum of 12 ft. Tides have been recorded as high as 40 ft. with seas pounding through wharf planks and flooding waterfront buildings.

Todd's Head, E end of Capen's Ave. A geodetic triangle here marks the easternmost end of mainland, USA. The Deer Island car ferry leaves here every hour daily in summer, a 20-minute trip. From Deer Island, the Canadian's government's *ABNAKI* free car ferry takes 20 minutes to Letete, N. B. for routes in the Maritime Provinces.

Deer Island, N. B. (pop. 1000), (*ferry*) 17 *m.* long, one of a group known as the West Isles in Passamaquoddy Bay, is on the 45th parallel halfway between the Equator and the North Pole, a scenic island popular with artists and fishermen. Highways and footpaths over the wooded terrain offer beautiful views. Six of the island's seven villages have public wharves. Chocolate Cove has great charm and at Fairhaven is the *Marine Museum and Library.* Boatbuilding, fishing and sardine packing are the industries. Lobster pounds with a combined capacity of more than 1000 tons are among the world's largest.

In 1770, Deer Island, once the habitat of the Passamaquoddy Indians, was under jurisdiction of Nova Scotia when the government made large land grants to army and navy officers. Col. Joseph W. Gorham received the Deer Island grant. Parents of noted American patriot, William Lloyd Garrison, were among the early settlers.

An Indian legend of the island concerns the great Chief Glooscap, venerated for his wisdom and magic powers. He could turn his enemies into a piece of wood or a lump of clay with the wave of his hand — and the sun, wind and rain did his bidding. As Glooscap was paddling his canoe along the shores of the Bay one morning, he saw a pack of wolves chasing a deer and a moose out of the forest into the water. When he saw the bloodthirsty wolves about to make their kill of the tired animals, Glooscap lifted his hand and changed them all into islands. So today, Deer Island and Moose Island (Eastport) are still side by side in Passamaquoddy Bay with the Wolves Islands still in pursuit a few miles offshore.

TOUR 2 MOUNT DESERT ISLAND - ACADIA NATIONAL PARK: *From* ELLSWORTH, Circle Tour 69.2 *m.* State 3, State 198, State 102A.

Via Trenton, Salisbury Cove, Hull's Cove, Bar Harbor, Seal Harbor, Northeast Harbor, Somesville, Southwest Harbor, Bass Harbor, West Tremont.

KNOWN as one of the most dramatically beautiful regions in the world, Mount Desert Island and Acadia National Park dominated by Cadillac Mountain naturally lure visitors to linger in one or another delightful and interesting spot. Rocky and wooded, the island, lying between Blue Hill and Frenchman Bays and nearly cut in half by a fjord, has 18 hills, locally called mountains, and 26 lakes and ponds. There are numerous scenic drives to colorful villages and other points of interest, sails around Frenchman Bay and all manner of recreational activities.

On the island are the Jackson Memorial Laboratory, a school of the dance and in 1969, there were plans for a new liberal arts college stressing ecology, to be called the College of the Atlantic.

Mount Desert Island, as well as the rest of Maine and what is now the United States as far south as the Mason and Dixon Line, was included in the grant called Acadia that was made by Henry IV of France in 1603 to the Sieur de Monts. In 1604, Samuel de Champlain, making his second voyage to the New World, this time with de Monts as his patron, came down the coast after a temporary colony had been established at the mouth of the St. Croix River, exploring the waters as far as Cape Cod. He is credited with the discovery of this island, which he named L'Ile des Monts Deserts, possibly with a punning reference to his patron. A few years later a French missionary colony established here was speedily wiped out by the English who had no intention of permitting France to gain a foothold in a country so rich in furs and forests. In 1688, Louis XIV granted the island as a feudal fief to the Sieur de la Mothe Cadillac — later founder of Detroit — who came to live on his domain. In 1713, Louis XIV was forced to cede the island, as part of a large slice of Maine, to the English. It was granted to Sir Francis Bernard, Royal Governor of Massachusetts, for 'distinguished services.' Bernard visited the place in 1762 and was enchanted by its beauty. At the time of the Revolution Bernard's property in America was confiscated, but later his son succeeded in having half the island returned to the family; a granddaughter of Cadillac managed to gain control of the other half. Several small settlements were made on the land at various times, but it was not until after the advent of the steamboat that the real development began. As more visitors were attracted, from the middle of the Nineteenth century the history of Mount Desert Island, although more rustic, somewhat paralleled that of wealthy and more fashionable Newport. In 1901 the State of Maine moved to preserve the beautiful area by setting aside some of it as a public reservation. In 1916 state control was transferred to the Federal government; it has been extended and the 32,000 acres of the public lands are now Acadia National Park.

The route on this tour circles the island.

ELLSWORTH (alt. 100, pop. 4872) 0 *m.*, is at a junction of US 1 (*see Tour 1, sec. c*) and State 172 (*see Tour 3*).

State 3 branches south (R) from US 1 at 1 *m.*

At 1.3 *m.* is *Stanwood Homestead Museum and Birdsacre Sanctuary* (R) (*visitors*).

> This is the birthplace-homestead of one of Maine's pioneer ornithologists. The Homestead's worn floorboards, small-paned windows, family portraits, heavy bedsteads and patchwork quilts, marble-topped tables and softly faded carpets evoke the quiet dignity of another age. There is an outstanding egg collection, some excellent bird mounts and an unusual assortment of nest structures.
>
> Behind the Homestead lies nearly 50 acres of hillside woodland and swale traversed by many nature trails. No guide is needed along the way, for the trails are clearly blazed, and name tags everywhere identify trees, shrubs, flowers, mosses and lichens. At the base of the north slope a spring-fed pond is the home site for a variety of birds including a pair of wood ducks. Many visitors return season after season to enjoy nature on their own terms in this tract of undisturbed forest that for half a century was the woodland workshop of Cordelia J. Stanwood, the Lady of Birdsacre.

At 4.5 *m.* a road (L) .3 *m.* to Jordan River Country Club (*public golf course and curling rink*).

At 7.3 *m.*, Bar Harbor Airport (L) built and formerly used by the U. S. Navy.

TRENTON (alt. 30, pop. 324) 8.1 *m.* with its miles of shoreline is a summer home area. The town received national attention in 1969 when its voters turned down an industrial proposal involving an aluminum smelting plant and atomic energey electric power facility, the central issue being control of pollution. Promoters failed to persuade the voters there would not be serious air and water pollution.

> *Aqualand*, 1 *m.* from Trenton Bridge entrance to Mount Desert Island, is a seaside animal park, educational and entertaining. School and organization groups annually enjoy the study of native wildlife here. (*Boat rentals and tugboat rides*).

At 9 *m.*, a National Park Information Building (R) and Thompson Island Picnic Area (L). On a short distance, tent and trailer grounds.

At 13.6 *m.*, a turn-off (L) to SALISBURY COVE (alt. 20, Bar Harbor Town). Mt. Desert Island Biology Laboratory (marine) is in this village overlooking the Bay.

At HULL'S COVE (alt. 80, Bar Harbor Town), 16.6 *m.*, a boulder in the cemetery (R) marks the grave of Madame Marie Therese de Gregoire, granddaughter of Cadillac who once owned the island.

ACADIA NATIONAL PARK, *Visitors Orientation Center*, 17 *m*. To fully enjoy the attractions of the great Park, visitors should stop for information at the Center, a Deer Isle granite and shingle building overlooking the Bay and Paradise Hill. Acadia is a special kind of place with a special kind of appeal that Park officials seek to preserve so that future generations will have 'places to walk along a peaceful natural seashore, to hike a mountain trail; places to sail a boat around an uninhabited island, to hear the sound of wind and wave, to re-establish kinship with the nature that molded us for thousands of years.'

> Mountains rise out of the sea in Acadia. Most spectacular view is from Mt. Cadillac (alt. 1530), highest on the U. S. Atlantic coast. The magnificent panorama encompasses seashore, islands, bays and inlets and open ocean. In clear weather, tiny Mt. Desert Rock is visible 26 *m*. out to sea, and Mt. Katahdin more than 100 *m*. in the opposite direction. *Ocean Drive* follows the rock-bound coast for several miles. This and other roads lead to 82-ft. deep Anemone Cave; the Sand Beach; Thunder Hole where the sea roars through a wave-cut granite chasm at certain tides; Otter Cliffs where dense spruce forest gives way to 100-ft. high granite cliffs plunging into the sea. There are islands where seals play, others where gulls and cormorants congregate. There are hiking trials and carriage roads for equestrians.

> From the Nature Center, a path (L) leads to *Robert Abbe Museum of Stone Age Antiquities* (*daily 9-5, May 30-Oct. 15*) near Sieur de Monts Spring. The Museum was dedicated in 1928 to Dr. Abbe, surgeon and archaeologist, who gave the nucleus of the collections. Featured are dioramas depicting seasonal occupations of the coastal Algonquian Indians. Exhibits include birch bark utensils, basketry, bead work, stone and bone artifacts and interpretive displays.

> Visitors may see, understand and enjoy the natural and human history of this area through the Park's Naturalist Program. Park naturalists conduct tours and campfire programs throughout the summer, with leisurely non-strenuous nature walks to observe the distinctive varieties of plant, bird and marine life and geological formations. Illustrated lectures are held in campground amphitheatres at Black Woods and Seawall.

At 18.1 *m*. (L) is *Sonagee* (1903) (*visitors*), overlooking Frenchman Bay.

> A summer estate that was owned by Frederick W. Vanderbilt and later in changing times by Atwater Kent, the lavishly furnished house with landscaped grounds is one of the few that escaped a conflagration in 1947 when forest fires swept Maine. It remains a reminder of Bar Harbor's Belle Epoch as a great watering place for Society's "400" early in the Twentieth century, an era whose manners and mores were supplanted by cafe society and the later jet set and "beautiful people" of the 1960s.

Next (L) is the Bluenose Ferry Terminal for Yarmouth, Nova Scotia and the Maritimes (*summer daily; see ISLAND TRIPS*).

At 19.4 *m*., junction with State 233.

> R on State 233 to Cadillac Mt. Enroute, the Kebo Valley Golf Club (public), a course played since 1892 by many notables including President William H. Taft,

Rockefellers, Fords and Vanderbilts. During exhibition matches in 1920, Walter Hagen set a record that still stands.

BAR HARBOR (alt. 70, Bar Harbor Town, pop. 3634) 19.9 *m.*, is the commercial and recreation center of Mount Desert. Formerly the playground of the wealthy, it now attracts thousands of tourists. Its day as an exclusive resort was drawing to a close in the 1940s when fire, raging several days in 1947, destroyed virtually the whole town except the business district and some year-round homes. Most of the great summer homes and hotels were burned, never to be restored or rebuilt. Motels, motor inns, shops and restaurants have burgeoned to cater to the throngs of restless tourists. Entertainment includes concerts, art galleries, shows and festivals, theatre, lectures, historic museums and the like. There are narrated 2½ hour bus trips to Mt. Cadillac and other scenic points in the Park, boat trips around Frenchman Bay and deep-sea fishing excursions.

In 1970, a teaching and research center in bi-cultural education for Indian youth was established at a former Job Corps Center here.

At 21.5 *m.* (L) is world-famous *Roscoe B. Jackson Memorial Laboratory* (*tours*) where biological research is carried on, notably in heredity and cancer. From here the road goes through a pass between the mountains.

OTTER CREEK village (Mount Desert Town), 24.8 *m.*

SEAL HARBOR (alt. 80, Mt. Desert Town), 27.7 *m.*, summer homes of several Rockefellers.

Thuya Lodge is a natural history museum and reading room.

At 28.2 *m.* (R) an entrance to the Park, the road leading to Jordan Pond and Cadillac Mt., and to Ocean Drive; a bathing beach (L), parking area (R). The route continues along the shore, overlooking the Cranberry Isles, Sutton Island and other smaller islands.

At 31 *m.* State 3 joins State 198.

NORTHEAST HARBOR (alt. 60, Mt. Desert Town), 31.8 *m.*, a beautiful resort of summer homes and hotels (no motels) is the most popular harbor for yachts and pleasure boats east of Camden. The town wharf (*passenger boats to Cranberry Isles*) is extensive, with facilities for all types of craft. *Neighborhood House* presents theatricals.

ISLESFORD (alt. 40, Cranberry Isles Town, pop. 167) is on Little Cranberry Island, 4 *m.* SE by boat. In the little village is Acadia National Park Historical Museum containing Prof. William Otis Sawtelle's collection of maps, documents, pictures, books, furniture, Indian artifacts and other memorabilia on the history of the Mt. Desert area.

The Cranberry Isles, named for great cranberry marshes, are a haven for creative artists (*see THE ARTS*). Rare birds such as Leach's petrel nest here. Cranberries are said to have been called 'craneberries' for the birds who favored them. On nearby Sutton Island was the summer home of Author Rachel Field.

At 33.5 *m*. (R) a public golf course.

The road now follows Sargent Drive 2.7 *m*. along the clifftop beside Somes Sound, a natural fjord and sailing area cleaving the island. The narrow inlet extends 5 *m*. between 150-ft. cliffs.

At 36.2 *m*. the route follows State 198. On about a mile the tour may be shortened by taking State 233 (R) into Bar Harbor.

At 38.8 *m*. the route takes State 102.

SOMESVILLE (alt. 40, Mount Desert Town) 39 *m*., a neat and attractive village, has a mill pond (L) dammed on a stream flowing into the Sound, and lovely church (Congregational 1852).

At 41 *m*. the road skirts Echo Lake lying long and placid 90 feet above salt water. Looming left is Acadia Mt. (alt. 680).

At 44.3 *m*. a road junction.

Left on this road to *Fernald's Point .7 m.,* site of St. Sauveur, first Jesuit settlement in New England.

In 1613 Antoinette de Pons, Marquise de Guercheville acquired the de Monts patent which roughly extended from Philadelphia to Montreal, and later encompassed the whole of North America to the Gulf of Mexico. She dispatched a Jesuit Mission to 'Norumbega' a fabled city thought to exist near the present site of Bangor. Father Pierre Biard, a theology professor at University of Lyon, was placed in charge of the mission with Father Enemond Masse and lay brother, Gilbert du Thet. Sailing on the ship *JONAS*, the party included about 50 sailors and colonists, along with horses and goats, under command of Capt. Charles Fleury.

After crossing the Bay of Fundy, under command of Capt. Charles Fleury, fog and gales drove the ship into Frenchman Bay where it anchored. The company landed, a mass was celebrated and the place was named St. Sauveur.

Indians appeared and told Father Biard that Chief Asticou was ill unto death and desired to be baptized. The priest left in a canoe to administer the rites, but found the Chief to be suffering only from a bad cold. The Chief's encampment was at Manchester Point at the entrance to Somes Sound, an ideal spot with open grassy field and plenty of fresh water. He invited the mission to settle there. The mission accepted; the men set to work and the name of Sauveur was transferred to the place.

After some three or four weeks, Capt. Samuel Argall, patrolling the coast under orders of the Virginia Colony to drive out any French settlers, attacked the mission in his ship *TREASURER* of 14 guns. A few broadsides and some musket fire soon overcame the mission. Du Thet was killed and

15 Frenchmen including Father Masse were sent off in a longboat. Capt. Argall took Father Biard and the remaining men to Jamestown.

And so, says Francis Parkman, 'In an obscure stroke of violence began the strife of France and England, Protestantism and Rome, which for a century and a half shook the struggling communities of North America, and closed at last in the memorable Triumph on the Plains of Abraham.'

SOUTHWEST HARBOR (alt. 40, Southwest Harbor Town, pop. 1372) 45 *m.*, a resort and fishing village in a lovely location, has a sardine plant, boatyard and U. S. Coast Guard Station. Mail and passenger boat to Cranberry Isles.

At 45.9 *m.*, the route follows State 102A (L).

MANSET, another resort village, 46.9 *m.*

At 48.5 *m.* is the community of SEAWALL where there is a long natural wall of large smooth sea-worn rocks cast upon the shore. Within the next mile or so are two campgrounds (R).

SHIP HARBOR, 50.3 *m.* is a tiny natural harbor extending to the edge of the road. Legend says the ship *GRAND DESIGN* of 300 tons, loaded with passengers from the North of Ireland, found haven here after striking on Long Ledge outside the harbor. Following a night of terror, they found that the ship had floated off the ledge and drifted through the narrow inlet into refuge.

BASS HARBOR (alt. 40, Tremont Town, pop. 1008), 51.6 *m.*, a busy fishing and boat-building community.

Left to the *Bass Harbor Country Store* .2 *m.*, authentic restoration of a Nineteenth century general store, pickle keg, cracker barrel and all.

The street continues to the Swan's Island Ferry Terminal .4 *m.* The State ferry *WILLIAM S. SILSBY (frequent scheduled trips daily)* carries cars and passengers to Swan's Island (*see ISLAND TRIPS*), 8 *m.* for a visit to fishing villages, beaches and lighthouse.

At 52.6 *m.* State 102A rejoins State 102 (L) on which continue through Tremont Town. About a mile on, local road (L) to Bernard Village. The route continues through the villages of West Tremont and Seal Cove looking upon the islands of Blue Hill Bay.

At 61 *m.* road (L) .2 *m.* to Pretty Marsh picnic area where Bartlett's Island, largest of those surrounding Mt. Desert, stands out in the Bay.

State 102 bears L to rejoin State 198 at 67.4 *m.* Continue L to rejoin State 3 at 69.2 *m.* Here return either to Ellsworth (L) or Bar Harbor (R).

TOUR 3: *From* ELLSWORTH *to* US 1 ORLAND, 59.3 *m.*, State 172 and State 175.

Via Blue Hill, Sedgwick, Sargentville (to Deer Isle) and Penobscot (to Castine).

LOOPING around the shores of one of the most beautiful and interesting of Maine's many jagged peninsulas, this drive follows the winding Union River south of Ellsworth, skirts lovely Blue Hill Bay viewing Mt. Desert, meanders along Eggemoggin Reach to Deer Isle and swings over to Castine at the mouth of the Penobscot River before moving up the E side of Penobscot Bay. Creative artists, musicians and vacationists have summer homes in the area, particularly around Blue Hill and Deer Isle. Year-round inhabitants include fishermen, retirees and commuters who work in Bangor, Ellsworth, Bucksport and Castine, home of the Maine Maritime Academy.

The peninsula between Penobscot and Union Rivers was granted to David Marsh and others in 1762, the first Massachusetts grant east of the Penobscot. The charter of William and Mary required that Massachusetts grants in Eastern Maine be approved by the King, which he did not do prior to the Revolution.

After the war Massachusetts confirmed the David Marsh grant. The peninsula was surveyed into six townships during 1762-63 and later named Surry, Blue Hill, Sedgwick, Penobscot, Orland, and Bucksport. Still later the boundaries of the towns were changed, and the towns of Castine and Brooksville established from parts of the original townships.

The David Marsh grant also included six townships east of the Union River, then called the Mount Desert River. According to the Rev. Jonathan Fisher, Samuel Livermore, the head surveyor of the grant, upon discovery that the Mount Desert River was the boundary dividing the 12 townships into two divisions, named the river 'Union River' and broke a bottle of rum to commemorate the occasion.

On his trip south from the French Colony at the mouth of the St. Croix River. Champlain inspected the peninsula when he was hunting a less rigorous home for de Monts settlers; Father Biard considered it in 1611 when exploring to find a site for the mission the Marquise de Guercheville proposed to establish; and it was one of the points selected by the Pilgrims as a valuable site for a trading post to obtain the furs that would make them rich. The French and English governments fought for its possession for nearly 200 years.

State 172 branches S from U. S. 1 at Ellsworth, 0 *m.* (*see Tour 1, sec. c.*), which is also at a junction with State 3 (*see Tour 2*).

At 3.8 *m.* is the Gatherings Camp Ground (L) overlooking Union River Bay, (*trailers and tents*).

SURRY (alt. 40, Surry Town, pop. 553), 6 *m.*, after its incorporation in 1803, became a busy fishing, farming, and lumbering village. Some fishing still goes on but many inhabitants work in nearby Ellsworth. Gaily painted summer cottages line the shores of Patten Bay. In winter when this body of water is frozen over it is dotted with the small tent-like houses of smelt fishermen. In spring, alewives rushing up Patten Stream to spawn are caught by the townspeople and smoked.

At 6.3 *m.* is a junction with State 176, to U. S. 1 (R) and to East Blue Hill and Newberry Neck (L) looping back to State 176.

Between Surry and Blue Hill, the route cuts across a subsidiary peninsula, at 9 *m.* (R) a Picnic Area.

At 10.9 *m.* (L) are the Blue Hill Fair grounds and race track.

BLUE HILL Village (alt. 50, Blue Hill Town, pop. 1176), 13.2 *m.* is at the head of a pointed cove near Blue Hill (alt. 940), for which it was named. The Hill provides a particularly impressive view of rugged Mt. Desert Island. Although the village is now chiefly known for its summer residential colony, and craft work, it was a thriving seaport in the middle of the Nineteenth century and before that had had industrial development. Within 40 years of its settlement in 1762, there were several small mills, including one that spun cotton yarn, and the lanes and harbor were echoing all day long with the steady pounding of hammers and sledges in the shipyards. Another source of early prosperity was the mining of minerals in Blue Hill, chiefly copper, though occasional small deposits of gold were discovered and some chalk. Copper (strip) mining has been carried on in recent years.

Author Mary Ellen Chase, born here in 1887, preserved the memories of her childhood in this old seaport in *A Goodly Heritage*; the stories she heard in her youth inspired her novel *Mary Peters*, a tale of life and adventure on this coast.

Jonathan Fisher House (1814) (*2-5 Tues.-Fri., July-mid-Sept.*), Main St., is a memorial to the unusually gifted man who became Blue Hill's first pastor and one of early Maine's most colorful figures. The house contains memorabilia and handiwork of the remarkably versatile and energetic Parson Fisher, scholar, artist, craftsman and farmer who brought culture and dignity to a frontier village in the wilderness. His story is told in Mary Ellen Chase's biography, *Jonathan Fisher: Maine Parson (1768-1847)*.

Planned and constructed by the Parson, the house shows his lively imagination. The two-story rectangular structure with shallow hipped roof appears in Federal style, but the fenestration creates a square impression, and the wide fascia of severely matched boards is hardly Federal at all. Remindful of characteristic Greek Revival entablature, the appearance of the house foreshadows the Greek classical style that flourished in the second quarter of the Nineteenth century.

Parson Fisher made the paint for the house from yellow ocher he discovered nearby and constructed almost all the furnishings, including a clock that ran perfectly for 50 years. Nearby is his Windmill that provided power for machines he devised to saw wood, remove stones from the ground and split straws for hat-making.

So that all parishioners might understand his weekly texts — and perhaps for sheer joy in intellectual exercise — Parson Fisher read them in Hebrew, Latin, French, Greek and Aramaic. The peninsula's rugged hills failed to impede discharge of his clerical duties; it was not unusual for him to walk 35 miles to perform a baptism or to comfort a parishioner in distress. It is not surprising that a town for 40 years under the guidance of this intellectual man should in later years become congenial to artists, writers and musicians.

Holt House (1815) (*visitors*) is the *Museum* and headquarters of the Blue Hill Historical Society.

Kneisel Hall (weekly concerts, summer), Pleasant St., was formerly the studio of Dr. Franz Kneisel (1865-1926), the Roumanian violinist, Boston Symphony Orchestra concert-master (1895-1903) and founder of the Kneisel Quartet, chamber musicians.

At 16.4 *m.* (L) the route follows State 175 S across another small inlet of Blue Hill Bay, soon viewing Blue Hill Falls and the Salt Pond (R). S of the Falls for about 8 miles, the road runs close to the W shore of the Bay where Shell Heaps are relics of the days when Indians came from inland to lay in a winter supply of fish.

SOUTH BLUE HILL (alt. 60, Blue Hill Town) 18 *m.* was the home of Otis M. Candage, retired sea captain, who carved and built more than 100 miniature square-riggers and 200 miniature sloops and schooners.

State 175 runs across the head of the narrow peninsula to BROOKLIN (alt. 100, Brooklin Town, pop. 469), 25.6 *m.* Road junction.

Left on this road to *Naskeag Point* 3 *m.*, the far outer tip of the neck included in the township of Brooklin. In July 1778, William Reed, working in a field near the shore here, saw the British sloop *GAGE* coming to anchor in a cove, preparing to land men in small boats. Hastily procuring his musket and alerting neighbors, he crept near the approaching landing party of 60 men who fired, killing two before they reached shore. Reed's fellow townsmen arrived dragging an old swivel gun; they filled it with nails, filings and pebbles, and fired. At a disadvantage, the landing force returned to the sloop after two men had been captured and five badly wounded; before leaving, however, they fired six houses and three barns, and seized some calves and hogs. Disconcerted by the irregular fighting methods of the inhabitants who seemed more numerous and better armed than they were, the invaders came ashore the following day under a flag of truce and obtained release of their captured men by returning the livestock.

For the next 8 *m.* State 175, known as Eggemoggin Reach Drive, has fine views of the Reach and Deer Isle.

HAVEN (alt. 50, Brooklin Town), 26.5 *m.*, is part of the chain of resort villages along the Reach.

SEDGWICK (alt. 50, Sedgwick Town, pop. 504), 30.4 *m.* In this neat village the white Town Hall (R) was built as a church in 1837, replacing the first church (1794). Four columns ornament the front entrance and a weather vane surmounts the domed cupola. Daniel Merrill, first pastor of the early church, received an annual salary of £50. That the town was not prosperous in those days is seen in official records revealing that all unattached and unmarried females who could not find anyone to support them were warned to leave town.

SARGENTVILLE (alt. 110, Sedgwick Town), 33.6 *m.*, another village of neat white houses, overlooks Deer Isle across the Reach.

At 34.1 *m.* (L) junction with State 15 to Deer Isle Bridge (1938) across Eggemoggin Reach. State 15 bisects the island, running about 10 *m.* from Deer Isle on a wide cove of Penobscot Bay to Stonington.

State 15 swings S over the graceful suspension bridge at 1.4 *m.*, crossing Eggemoggin Reach to Little Deer Isle. Thence it winds E across a causeway to the island of Deer Isle, and S the length of the island to Stonington.

The island of Deer Isle was settled in 1762 by hardy families, largely from eastern Massachusetts. Earlier, Indians visited the islands for clams, indicated by the shell heaps and artifacts that have been discovered. By 1775 there were some 68 heads of families here. In 1789 the Town of Deer Isle was incorporated, the enabling act being signed by John Hancock as Governor of Massachusetts. The original town included three principal islands, Little Deer Isle, Deer Isle and Isle au Haut (*see ISLAND TRIPS*) the latter S of Deer Isle and separated by five miles of water. By 1868 Isle au Haut had grown, and was incorporated as a separate town. In 1897 the southern third of the island of Deer Isle was incorporated as the Town of Stonington. Thus, the present Town of Deer Isle comprises the northern two thirds of the island of Deer Isle, and all of Little Deer Isle.

The economy of the islands has always centered around the sea. In the cemeteries are tombstones in memory of seafaring men who perished on the coast of Africa or lost their lives at sea in the East Indies trade. In the late 1890s, the entire crews of two America's Cup Defenders were Deer Isle mariners, and today many islanders serve in the merchant marine or 'go yachting,' commanding and manning boats and yachts of all sizes for wealthy owners. This is one of the prime lobstering areas on the coast, and there is extensive scalloping and sardine fishing.

For at least three generations, these islands have been a delightful vacation spot, free from the commercialization of the more populous resorts. Old houses and new cottages become summer residences in increasing numbers, and a growing group of people make this their retirement home.

LITTLE DEER ISLE (alt. 80, Deer Isle Town). Near the Chamber of Commerce Information booth a bronze and local granite monument commemorates the Rev. Peter Powers, the first regular minister of the Congregational Church in Deer Isle (1785-1800), a notable divine and fervent Revolutionary patriot. R off State 15, a 2.6 *m.* drive to Eggemoggin at the W tip of the island, a long established summer colony with a magnificent view across Penobscot Bay. Just offshore is small, rocky Pumpkin Island, with a lighthouse used in the days of the steamboat lines.

State 15 bears L across the eastern tip of Little Deer Isle and crosses a winding causeway to the island of Deer Isle. At 3.5 *m.*, a local road L .5 *m.* to the old ferry landing on Eggemoggin Reach. Before the bridge was built, an open skow ferry carrying 3 or 4 cars was towed by a motorboat. Winter ice often made the trip impossible. From this site, a fine view of the broad Reach, the mainland shore and the suspension bridge.

DEER ISLE (alt. 30, Deer Isle Town, pop. 1105) 7 *m.* The village's shopping and service center is on Northwest Harbor, a cove of Penobscot Bay. In early years, the harbor was deep enough to serve as port of call for both sail and steam. Numerous coastwise sailing vessels were registered from here. A sail loft and ship chandlery were active, and there was a U. S. Custom House. Extensive silting of the harbor has since taken place. From the late 1700s to about the Civil War a tidal saw and grist mill, one of several on the island, operated here.

At 7.5 *m.* on State 15, the island is nearly cut in half by coves from E and W. The 200-foot strip between is called the *Haulover*, where Indians and settlers used to portage their canoes. Here was the first meeting and town house. Remains of a stone cattle pound still can be seen. Here also is the first cemetery. Prior to the 1790s graves were marked only by uncut boulders. The Rev. Peter Powers' grave is marked by a well preserved stone.

Left alongside the Houlover a good road leads 5.3 *m.* to SUNSHINE (Deer Isle Town), the eastern tip of the island. At .1 *m.* a marked lane goes to Mariners' Memorial Park, (*visitors, picnicking*). At 1.9 *m.*, the entrance to Les Chalets Francais, a 30-year old French-speaking camp for girls, specializing in riding, ballet, sailing, art and tennis. At Sunshine a left fork goes to a lobster wharf, from which there is a fine view across Jericho Bay to Mount Desert Island and Mount Cadillac. Another marked road at Sunshine leads to the well-known *Haystack Mountain School of Crafts*. In a beautiful setting of woodland and rocky shore, the school offers college-accredited summer courses in arts and crafts with a distinguished faculty. The school also operates *The Centennial House* in Deer Isle village as an exhibit center for the works of students and faculty.

At 9.9 *m.* on State 15 is the hamlet of South Deer Isle (Deer Isle Town), a residential neighborhood. In the 1870s and 80s this was a booming mackerel fishing port of some 200 vessels and a custom house. At 10.9 *m.*, a road junction.

Left on this road 2.4 *m.* to OCEANVILLE (Stonington Town), formerly a fishing community with a clam canning factory, now residential. At .8 *m.* (R) is the quarry of the Deer Island Granite Corp., which also operates large quarries on Crotch Island in Stonington Harbor. The gray and pink granite is known for its superior quality. Many well-known buildings throughout the country are faced with it. A recent notable job was the furnishing of nearly $1,000,000 worth of granite for the John F. Kennedy Memorial in Arlington National Cemetery.

State 15 has its southern terminus in the village of STONINGTON (alt. 50, Stonington Town, pop. 1412) 12.5 *m.* A small deep-water port, it preserves the aspect of a working town of quarrymen and seafaring men. The island-dotted harbor is alive with the boats of lobstermen and fishermen. Here is the large sardine canning plant of the Stonington Packing Co., Inc. Good boats are available in Stonington for conducted tours among the numerous small islands and for deep sea fishing. From here, ferry to Isle au Haut.

Return to Deer Isle village via a local road up the W side of the island. Following along the main waterfront street, the road passes the plant of the Stonington & Deer Isle Yacht Basin Corp., 13.4 *m.* where fishing and pleasure boats are built and repaired. Turning north, at 13.8 *m.* is an excellent view of Mark Island with its working lighthouse and across Penobscot Bay to Vinalhaven. At 14.9 *m.* (R) a cross-island road leads to the Stonington Airport, an accredited airstrip (1750 ft. runway).

At 17.5 *m.* (R) the Island Country Club (*golf, tennis*). Just beyond (R) is the headquarters and *Museum* of the Deer Isle-Stonington Historical Society (*2-5 Wed., Sat., Sun., July 1-mid-Sept.*). A typical farmhouse of the early 1800s, it is furnished in the period and features frequently changed exhibits of island history. Its archives include genealogies, old diaries, old town and custom house records, and the John Richardson collection of steamboat pictures, some 2000 photographs of 300 vessels formerly plying Penobscot Bay waters.

At 18.0 *m.* is the village of SUNSET (Deer Isle Town), named for its spectacular panorama across Penobscot Bay to the Camden Hills in the distance. In Sunset at 18.2 *m.* a side road (L) goes to the *Deer Isle Yacht Club,* (*dock and guest moorings*). At 20 *m.* Deer Isle village, from which proceed N on State 15, returning across the suspension bridge to Sargentville at 27 *m.*

From Sargentville, State 175 veers due N across the head of the peninsula covered by Brooksville. At the crest of Caterpillar Hill 35.8 *m.*, a Picnic Area. Here a spectacular view of Penobscot Bay, Blue Hill Bay and Walkers Pond with Camden Hills in the distance beyond numerous islands.

At 37 *m.*, State 15 (R) goes to Blue Hill.
At 37.6 *m.* (L), State 176 leads to Bucks Harbor and Cape Rosier (alt. 30, Brooksville Town, pop. 477), summer colonies on Penobscot Bay.

State 175 now follows Bagaduce River, a salt water river, about 4 *m.*, crossing it at 41.9 *m.* Picnic area (L).

PENOBSCOT (alt. 25, Penobscot Town, pop. 639), 47.5 *m.*, is a ship-shape hospitable village in a township that is one of the few where stories of buried treasure are true. In 1840 a fortunate resident found about 2000 coins in a hillside near Bagaduce River. Because most of them were French, although there were some Spanish pieces of eight and 25 pine tree shillings and a sixpence dated 1652, it was thought the money might have been buried by the de Castin family when they left for Canada in 1704; or possibly it was pirate loot. The coins are now at the Maine Historical Society in Portland.

At 51.4, a junction with State 166.

Left on State 166 to CASTINE (alt. 80, Castine Town, pop. 824), 7.6 *m.* The route follows along the E shore of the Penobscot River to its mouth. Local residents take great pride in this historic area and have marked more than 100 sites and buildings.

Castine was for nearly 200 years the center of a struggle by three nations for control of the peninsula. In 1629, the King's Council for New England granted the Pilgrims permission to send Edward Ashley to establish a trading post at this point, then called Pentagoet. The post was destroyed in 1631 by the same vigilant la Tour who wiped out the Vines-Allerton post at Machias. As Governor Bradford told the story: ' . . . their house at Penobscot was robbed by the French, and all their goods of any worth were carried away.' Ashley remained, however, and brought in new goods to exchange for furs. Meanwhile, Richelieu in France had sent out a new governor for Acadia with specific orders to keep the English out of the country east of Pemaquid and in 1635 Sieur d'Aulney de Charnisay arrived to destroy the Pentagoet post. He forced the agent to give him a bill of sale for the goods and left the members of the post with 'their shalop and some victualls to bring them home.' When the outraged Plymouth colonists appealed for help to the Massachusetts Bay colonists, the Bay leaders merely gave them their blessing, permitting them to hire a 300-ton ship and its crew. Miles Standish and 20 men in a bark accompanied the little ship, advising the captain how to proceed; but the captain persisted in using up his ammunition by firing from a distance and after inflicting little damage, the ship and bark left Pentagoet.

The Pilgrims in vain warned the Bay Colony of the menacing encroachments of the French. Bay leaders not only declined to act, but later established friendly relations with the French on the coast. Bradford says that bay traders even furnished the French here with 'poweder and shott' because it was 'to their profite.'

Meanwhile a Capuchin mission had been established here; Jesuit Father Druil- lettes visited it in 1646. In 1648, the Capuchins built a Chapel of Our Lady of Hope where the present village church of that name now stands. In 1863 a copper sheet was found in the ground near the place with this inscription: '1648, 8 Junii, Frater Leon Parisiensis in Capuciorum Missione, posui hoc fundamentum in honorem nostrate Dominae Sanctae Spei.'

A few years later, under Cromwell's orders, the English took the place and held it briefly, the French regaining possession in 1670. In 1673 Flemish pirates assailed the fort and kidnaped the governor.

Also appearing on the scene was Jean-Vincent d'Abbadie, Baron de St. Castin (1652-1717), who had been in Quebec. Apparently neglected and deprived of the use of his wealth, the youngster at 15 started out in a canoe with three Abnaki Indians to inspect a royal grant that stood in his name at the mouth of the Penobscot River. Pentagoet pleased him and he determined to stay there. When the fort's governor was kidnaped, Castin, then 21, stepped into his place. He had adopted many of the Indian ways of life and married a chief's daughter. By this time the French had begun to use the Indians to fight the English. They approved of friendly relations with the Indians, but rebuked de Castin for overdoing it.

In 1675 de Castin drove Dutch attackers away and in 1687 ignored English orders to leave. The next year, while de Castin was off on a fishing trip, Sir Edmund Andros arrived and started pillaging. By 1693, when it seemed that the French were giving up their claim to this territory, de Castin made some arrangement with the English to accept the situation; but three years later when Iberville went down to attack Pemaquid, de Castin led a band of Indians in a rear action. He was ordered back to France in 1701.

The little town had a period of peace until the Revolutionary War; in 1779 the British took it, remaining until 1783. The colonists made one attempt to take it back in an ill-starred expedition in 1779 that blighted Paul Revere's hopes of a military career. There was a second British occupation, this time of eight months during the War of 1812.

More than 100 historic sites and buildings have markers and interpretations.

Fort George in Witherle Park where archaeological work was being carried on in the 1960s, was built by the British in 1779 and was the last post surrendered by them at the close of the War of Independence. *Fort Madison,* Perkins St., is another relic of the repeated military occupation of the old town.

The *Maine Maritime Academy* (1941), opposite the park, is the second largest of the nation's five such academies, enrolling 500 young men (1969) in a four-year program, and awarding Bachelor of Science degrees, its curriculum advancing with rapid technological developments. It was the first college in New England to acquire in 1962 a complete nuclear power installation with uranium on loan from the U. S. Atomic Energy Commission. The Academy training ship, the *STATE OF MAINE,* is the former *SS ANCON,* famous World War II command and communications ship that served in virtually every major campaign in Atlantic and Pacific waters and was press ship at the Japanese surrender in Tokyo Bay in 1945.

Wilson Museum (1921) (*2-5 daily except Mon., June-Sept.*) has marine and mineral exhibits, stone age artifacts, local historic material, reconstructions and special events. It is administered by the Castine Scientific Society which also has been restoring as a museum the *John Perkins House* (1783), one of the oldest in Castine. Other early buildings and houses include the Old Meetinghouse (1830), the Abbott, Bartlett, Dyer, Johnston, Wheeler, Whitney and Whiting Houses, all built in the early 1800s, with handsome traditional architectural detail. The *Cate House* at Court and Pleasant Sts., named to the National Register, was the home of Anna Cates who became the wife of Sanford Dole, only president and first governor of Hawaii.

Among Nineteenth century artists who depicted Castine were Fitzhugh Lane and Alice McLaughlin.

Castine's post office (1815) is believed to be the oldest in continuous use in Maine.

Leaving Castine, the route follows N along the eastern shore of the mouth of the Penobscot River.

At 59.3 *m.*, ORLAND and US 1 (*see Tour 1, sec. c*).

─────────────────────────────

TOUR 4: *From* HOULTON *to* NEW HAMPSHIRE LINE (*Shelburne*), 271.5 *m.*, US 2.

─────────────────────────────

Via Island Falls, Lincoln, West Enfield, Milford, Old Town, Orono, Bangor, Hermon, Newport, Skowhegan, Norridgewock, Farmington, Wilton, Dixfield, Mexico, Rumford, Bethel and Gilead. (I-95 express route by-passes towns Houlton to Newport. Side Tours 4A through 4G inland W and NW accessible from I-95).

CROSSING between New Brunswick and New Hampshire, US 2 gives a wide spectrum of inland Maine as it passes through five counties. Side trips lead to the vast mountain and lake country favored by sportsmen (*see RECREATION*). The northern section traverses the rolling potato fields of central Aroostook County. Westerly, great stands of beech, birch and maple are full of wild game. A network of lakes, rivers and streams (salmon, trout and other gamefish) attracts fishermen. Between Island Falls and Mattawamkeag lie 40 miles of wild country from the wooded land of Golden Ridge Plantation to the wide stretches of the Mattawamkeag Swamp. Moving S the road parallels the Penobscot River, through farming and lumbering country, with glimpses of Mt. Katahdin, thence westerly from Bangor. Mountains of the Rangeley group rise N in the forested lake region between Skowhegan and Rumford. The route then winds along the Androscoggin River to Gilead in the White Mountain National Forest.

At Houlton (*see HOULTON*), junction U S 1 and I-95 (*see Tour 1, sec. e*).

Leaving Houlton at 0 *m.*, US 2 passes through Ludlow, a farming township whose single village lies on N shore of Cochran Lake; Smyrna Mills, a potato-raising center in the valley on the banks of the Mattawamkeag River's E branch; and Dyer Brook with its potato warehouses. I-95 access at these points.

> Barns in farming townships recall the early custom of 'barn-raising' when friends and neighbors came from miles around to help a man raise and build the framework of his barn while the womenfolk prepared a hearty meal. At sundown, the men and their families gathered around rough board tables beneath the trees for the feast. After supper, there was dancing in the new barn to the fiddling of square dances, jigs and reels.

ISLAND FALLS (alt. 450, Island Falls Town, pop. 1018), 27.5 *m.* (*Forest Lookout Station; hunting, fishing*). A trading place for farmers and sportsmen, the town has a cedar mill and a starch factory. Mattawamkeag and Pleasant Lakes and numerous streams are in the townships' wooded wildland. A junction here with State 159 for Patten and Baxter State Park (*see Tour 4A;*) I-95 access.

US 2 passes through 20 *m.* of the Macwahoc woods to enter Township 1 Range 5 where the route parallels Molunkus Stream, from Monarda to Macwahoc at 56.5 *m.*, southernmost Aroostook County settlement; enroute two highway picnic areas; another at 61.5 *m.*

At 63.6 *m.*, the highway glides over the site known as 'Sunken Bridge' on the Old Military Road (1830-31); five bridges are said to have sunk along here into Mattawamkeag Swamp.

MATTAWAMKEAG (alt. 212, Mattawamkeag Town, pop. 945), 65.7 *m.*, where the Mattawamkeag River flows into the Penobscot, is a rail junction with extensive train yards and a clothespin mill. Near the village a junction with State 157 for Millinocket and Baxter State Park (*see Tour 4B*); I-95 access at 20 *m.*

WINN (alt. 240, Winn Town, pop. 526), 68.6 *m.*, clinging to the E bank of the Penobscot, was head of river navigation in the days when travel into this area was chiefly by boat.

LINCOLN (alt. 174, Lincoln Town, pop. 4541), 79.6 *m.*, a pulp and paper manufacturing community in the center of Penobscot County, was named for Maine's sixth governor. Other industries include a worsted fabric mill, a shoe factory and lumber manufacturing. Thirteen lakes and ponds in the countryside offer water sports, fishing and hunting. Mattanawcook Pond is one of a chain of lakes and ponds running diagonally across the state. At Lincoln, a junction with State 6.

Left on State 6 to LEE (pop. 555), 10 *m.*, home of Lee Academy, a leading secondary school on land that once was involved in a summer resort development. The former Mt. Jefferson Hotel now is a boys' dormitory. When it was in operation as a hotel in the early 1900s, the Jaehnes brothers created an estate on land that included Mt. Jefferson, now a ski area, and in the village with a long allee of poplars. Dr. George Averill acquired the property and gave it to the Academy which was incorporated in 1845. Averill and WPA funds built Averill gymnasium which houses the Lee Historical *Museum*, seven rooms of local memorabilia on the first floor (*seen by appointment*).

Jeremiah Fifield and his wife were the first settlers of Lee, incorporated in 1832. Mrs. Fifield was given 100 acres of land for being the first woman to settle in this wilderness.

State 6 continues E 31 *m.* to join US 1 at Topsfield (*see Tour 1, sec. e*).

WEST ENFIELD (alt. 130, Enfield Town, pop. 1138), 91.6 *m.* Industry here is pulpwood cutting. I-95 access and junctions with State 6 for Katahdin Iron Works (*see Tour 4C*) and with State 188.

L on State 188 to Enfield (*Cobb Fish Hatchery*) and Cold Stream Pond (*fishing*), 4 *m.* and *Stewart M. Lord Memorial* at Burlington, 15 *m.* Route continues to Saponic and unmarked road to West and Nicatous Lakes at 30 *m.*

PASSADUMKEAG (Ind.: quick water) (alt. 140, Passadumkeag Town, pop. 355), 96.6 *m.* The ancient *Cemetery* used by prehistoric Indians at the Hathaway site appears to be about 3000 years old, according to University of Maine anthropologists researching the area in the 1960s. Several distinct modes of burial were found. Many were cremations; the ashes were placed on top of red ochre (hematite iron ore) which was used to color the graves, giving rise to the now-disproved theory of the 'Red Paint People' as a distinct race.

OLAMON (Ind.: red paint) (alt. 128, Greenbush Town, pop. 565), 101.7 *m.* is at the mouth of Olamon Stream as it joins the Penobscot River.

MILFORD (alt. 115, Milford Town, pop. 1572), 114.6 *m.* The Penobscot River here separating Milford and Old Town, was a lively scene in the heyday of lumbering. Millions of logs driven down the West Branch in spring were handled in the huge sawmills of the two communities. Booms were located two miles upstream. When the logs guided downstream

by the river drivers reached the booms, some 200 men waiting in 'driving'
boats, raced down the Penobscot to Milford and Old Town with the news.
As the winners approached, a cannon on Indian Island was fired and a
general celebration followed.

The Penobscot is Maine's most extensive river with an 8500 square mile basin.
For decades it was famous for Atlantic salmon (Salmo salar) that went upriver
to spawn. As many as 15,000 a year were being taken in the 1860s. But years
of increasing river pollution and dam construction stopped the migration of the
fish. Only 40 fish were taken in 1947, the last year commercial fishing for Atlantic
salmon was allowed on the Penobscot. The last rod and reel fish was caught in
Bangor's famous salmon pool in 1958.

The Atlantic Sea-Run Salmon Commission was organized in 1947 for the
restoration and management of Atlantic salmon in the State of Maine. In the late
1960s industry had moved toward river clean-up and there were some fishways
at some dams. In the fall of 1969, the Commission had tagged 70 salmon at
the Bangor pool and some of the fish had spawned in the clear, gravel-bottomed
streams of Penobscot headwaters.

The highway here swings right, crossing the Penobscot. I-95 access at Old
Town and Orono.

OLD TOWN (alt. 115, pop. 8626), 115.3 *m.* long known for the superior quality of its canoes, now also builds other pleasure boats. The
first English settlers arrived after the Revolution, attracted by the river's
water power potential. Besides boatbuilding, today's industries include two
shoe factories, two lumber mills, a pulp mill, a pulp products plant, a
foundry and a woolen mill.

At the *Old Town Canoe Company Factory,* visitors may watch the process of
canoe construction from steaming and binding the bows and ribs to the varnish-
ing of the finished product. The presence of Indians working with modern
equipment at their traditional craft recalls the silvery birch so skillfully fashioned by their forefathers and Longfellow's romantic lines in *Hiawatha:*

> I a light canoe will build me,
> That will float upon the water,
> Like a yellow leaf in autumn,
> Like a yellow water lily.

Over the bridge on *Indian Island* the Penobscot Indians make their home. Visitors
are welcome at the tribal ceremonies held at various times during the year and
their skillfully woven baskets are for sale.

There are many Indian stories and legends, and an old favorite Penobscot
winter game is called 'snowsnake,' requiring great skill in hurling a special kind
of stick.

Wooden crosses mark most of the graves in the *Two Cemeteries* on the island.
The Catholic cemetery (1688) contains the remains of John Attean (1778-
1858), governor of the tribe for over 40 years; John Neptune (1767-1865),
lieutenant-governor for half a century; and other dignitaries of the tribe. Among
those buried in the other cemetery are Andrew Sockalexis, runner and member of the American team in the Fifth Olympiad at Stockholm, Sweden, (1912),
and ·his brother Louis, Holy Cross graduate and baseball player in the
Cleveland American League Club.

In a small, tree-shaded grassy plot stands a *Monument to the Penobscot Indians Killed in the Revolution.* A bronze tablet lists the names of the men who fought with the Continental forces.

A Catholic mission was established on the island in the 17th century and in the church here the Baron Jean-Vincent de Castin (*see Tour 3*), took the daughter of Chief Madockawando for his bride. About 110 years ago the old church was replaced by a frame building in which was hung a *Picture of the Crucifixion* painted many years ago by Paul Orson, an Indian artist who used the juice of berries for his colors and the tail of an animal for a brush.

ORONO (alt. 80, Orono Town, pop. 8341), 119.6 *m.* The population of this hometown of the State University has nearly tripled with the phenomenal growth of the University. Its industries include the manufacture of paper and pulp, canvas products, oars and paddles.

University of Maine main campus (*Information and guide service, Lord Hall; summer guide service, Wingate Hall*).

The University of Maine includes this 1100-acre main campus, an 18-acre campus at Portland, a new one in 1970 at Augusta, as well as Maine's five former State colleges, Aroostook, Fort Kent, Washington, Farmington and Gorham. The university was established as the Maine State College of Agriculture and the Mechanic Arts in 1862 under the Morrill Act approved by President Lincoln. It opened in 1868 with 12 students and two faculty members. It became the University of Maine in 1897. Today's student body is approaching 9,000 with 600 faculty members.

The Georgian and Gothic features of earlier campus buildings blend with the contemporary architecture of the many new buildings on the main campus overlooking the Stillwater River. The commuter campus at Portland, established in 1957, encompassed the former Peabody Law School four years later. UM-Augusta was established in 1967.

The University has five undergraduate colleges, a Graduate School offering Masters and Ph.D.'s in many areas, summer sessions, and a Continuing Education Division with an enrollment of 11,000.

At Winslow Hall is the *Cooperative Extension Service* which carries information on farming, forestry, home economics, recreation and community development to local communities through 16 county offices. The University's *Audio-Visual Service*, one of the most complete and functional in the country, in the Education Building, serves Maine and New England.

The Dept. of Industrial Cooperation, Boardman Hall, coordinates the University's academic and research facilities to conduct basic and applied research sponsored by business and industry. Also here is the Maine Technology Experiment Station which carries on practical research and testing for state and municipal departments and for industry.

At Holmes Hall is the *Maine Agricultural Experiment Station* for research in agriculture on campus and at three farms. The *Ira C. Darling* oceanographic research center is at Walpole (*see Tour 1G*).

The Maine ETV network and closed circuit television studios are in Alumni Hall.

While the University of Maine was first identified with agriculture and forestry, it has become well known for its work in cultural fields, art, music, theatre, as well as conferences and seminars with national leaders. The Art Department's collections are shown in *Carnegie Hall* and there also are exhibits at the Folger Library, Memorial Union, Alumni Hall and Common West. The Hauck auditorium is the home of the Maine Masque Players; concerts, lectures and the like take place here.

A planetarium is located in Wingate Hall and in South Stevens, is the Anthropological *Museum (11-4, Tues. - Fri.)*, American Indian, Arctic, African and Pacific Micronesian collections. There also is an extensive Folklore Archives.

VEAZIE (alt. 70, Veazie Town, pop. 1354), 123.7 *m.* Gen. Samuel Veazie, a pioneer railroad operator, gave this community not only its name but also its claim to fame. In 1854 the General purchased the narrow gauge Bangor, Milford, and Old Town R.R., which ran through here, and it became known as the Veazie R.R. Completed in 1836 it was Maine's first railroad and one of the oldest in the country. The first rails were made of wood.

In 1834 the General had established the Veazie Bank. Just after the passage of the Federal Act (1866) taxing currency issued by State banks, officials of the Veazie banks refused to pay the tax. This led to the U. S. Supreme Court case, *Veazie Banks vs. Fenno*, in which the Supreme Court upheld the power of Congress to levy such tax. As a result the power to issue State currency was virtually taken from the States.

It is believed that Indians occupied and cultivated their cornlands here where an Indian town known as the Negas was located in the Seventeenth century. Soon after 1657, William Crowne established a fur trading house 'far up ye Penobscot at a place called Negue to which he gave his own name, Crowne's Point.' Veazie, originally called The Plains, was part of Bangor until its incorporation in 1853.

BANGOR (alt. 100, pop. 38,912) *(see BANGOR)*, 128.6 *m.* Junction with US 1A *(see Tour 1, sec. c)*; and State 9 *(see Tour 5)*; I-95 access.

HERMON (alt. 190, Hermon Town, pop. 2087), 136.3 *m.* is near railroad yards of the Northern Maine Junction rail terminus.

The Millerites, disciples of William Miller who preached that the second Coming of the Lord was imminent, won many followers here in the early 1800s. Contemporary newspaper accounts say his followers eventually numbered 50,000 souls, but this is doubtless exaggeration. A day in 1843 was set as the date of the Coming, and the anointed were exhorted to prepare themselves. To be ready for heaven all the believers gave away everything they possessed and disposed of all their property. On the appointed day they donned ascension robes and climbed to hilltops so as to be as near heaven as possible. Some of them mounted the roofs of their houses. All day they stood looking into the sky. Nothing happened. After having been, so they thought, at heaven's very gate, they had to return to an earthly status made more difficult by the loss of their property. Miller attributed the denouement to a miscalculation — whether on his part or the Lord's is not clear. Many of his followers, especially those in the town of Hermon, faithfully rallied around him once more, remaining loyal until his death in 1847. For many years small colonies of Millerites survived throughout the State.

CARMEL (alt. 170, Carmel Town, pop. 1206), 143.3 *m.*, one of the oldest farming towns in Penobscot County, was purchased from Massachusetts in 1795 by Martin Kingsley. Its first settlers were Abel and the Rev. Paul Ruggles; the latter named the place in honor of Elijah's experience on Mount Carmel.

Not surprisingly, Carmel was the birthplace of a religious sect, known as the Higginsites for its founder, Rev. George Higgins, a Methodist pastor; there is still a Higginsville in neighboring Levant. The Higginsites did not eat pork and believed in their ability to heal by faith. Tales of their religious activities were widely circulated and one, concerning the whipping of children in efforts to drive out the Devil, aroused the indignation of the townspeople, who determined to rid the town of Mr. Higgins. Calling him from his home late one night, a group tarred and feathered and drove him away.

ETNA (alt. 305, Etna Town, pop. 486), 146.6 *m. Camp Etna* here has been the site of annual summer meetings of spiritualists since 1876 when Daniel Buswell, Jr. held the first meeting in a tent. Today there is a temple (1880), a clubhouse and numerous cottages on 80 acres of enclosed land amid beautiful groves. A monument marks the grave of benefactor Mary S. Vanderbilt.

NEWPORT (alt. 205, Newport Town, pop. 2322), 155.3 *m.* (*water sports, golf; landing field*), owes much of its beauty to 6000-acre Lake Sebasticook near the center of town and surrounded by summer cottages. Incorporated in 1804, Newport earlier was on the direct route of Indian travel and communication among the French missions. It has large wood-turning and woolen mills and a milk processing plant.

I-95 access. Junctions with State 7 for Greenville and Moosehead (*see Tour 4D*) and with State 11.

L on State 11 to PITTSFIELD (alt. 210, Pittsfield Town, pop. 4010), 7.5 *m.*, a trading center for the surrounding agricultural region, having wool and shoddy mills and a shoe factory. Maine Central Institute (1869) S. Main St., is a college preparatory school. Llewellyn Powers, Maine Governor (1897-1901), Carl E. Milliken, Governor (1917-21) and poet-novelist Hugh Pendexter were born here. Long gone is the Lancey House (1868), famous well into the Twentieth century for its cuisine; salmon was a gourmet favorite. The town has an airport, several parks, a ski slope and a golf course.

The route goes through Palmyra, small agricultural township and Canaan, part of the Plymouth Patent, named for the 'land of milk and honey.'

SKOWHEGAN (alt. 190, Skowhegan Town, pop. 7661), 179.7 *m.* (*picnic areas, golf, park, landing field*), is a historical and cultural community on the Kennebec River. Long before the first white man came to the region in 1771, Indians knew the Kennebec island they called Skowhegan (place to wait and watch) and had taken fighting salmon from the waters below the falls. The original white settlement of the town was made on the island which today is somewhat the physical center although business and industry have spread along the river banks. A 65-foot Abnaki Indian carved by Bernard Langlais became a landmark in 1969. A large granite boulder in the Central Maine Power Company grounds is on the Site of an Arnold campsite (Sept. 29, 1775).

Among distinguished citizens who were born or have lived here is U. S. Senator Margaret Chase Smith who in 1970 had served 30 years in Congress and was Maine's senior senator. Mrs. Smith was elected to the House of Representatives in 1940 to fill the vacancy left by the death of her husband Clyde H. Smith. She served eight years in the House and was elected to the Senate three times. In 1964 she announced as a Presidential candidate. Others: Abner Coburn (1803-85), one of Maine's Civil War governors, for whom Skowhegan's park is named; Daniel Dole, a missionary to the Hawaiian Islands who helped establish and became president of Oahu College; George Otis Smith, a former director of the U. S. Geological Survey; Charles A. Coffin (1844-1926), first president of the General Electric Company; Artemus Ward (Charles Farrar Browne), humorist, who in his boyhood worked a few months in a local printing office.

History House (1839) (*1-5, Tues. - Sat.; June through Sept.*) is a home and museum combined, reflecting the history of the town and the upper Kennebec.

The *State Reformatory for Women*, Norridgewock Ave., opened in 1916.

A popular fair is held annually at the *Fairgrounds*, Madison Ave.

Lakewood Theatre (1901), now called the State Theatre, is less than 5 *m.* N on US 201 which continues to Bingham and the Canadian Line (*see Tour 4E*). In a resort on the shore of Lake Wesserunsett, the theatre presents popular summer fare, often with stars. The resort was an amusement park in the days when patrons arrived by trolley or buckboard and theatre admissions were five and ten cents.

In the vicinity is the *South Solon Meetinghouse*, a restored Colonial church embellished in the 1950s with contemporary frescoes, and the *Skowhegan School of Painting and Sculpture*. The renowned school was founded in 1946 on a 60-acre poultry farm by Portraitist Willard W. Cummings, Artist Henry V. Poor and Sculptor Sydney Simon. An official Army portraitist in World War II, Cummings was known as the Private who Painted Generals; he also has painted such disparate celebrities as Bette Davis and Pablo Casals. Many students on scholarships come from noted art schools in the U. S. and abroad. Among teachers and instructors have been Ben Shahn, Jack Levine, Elmer Bischoff, Xavier Gonzales, Alex Katz and Marguerite Zorach.

At Skowhegan, junction with US 201 N to Bingham and Jackman (*see Tour 4E*).

US 201 SW is identical with US 2 to Norridgewock.

NORRIDGEWOCK (alt. 180, Norridgewock Town, pop. 1634), 184.8 *m.*, derived its name from an Abnaki village called Nanrantsouak (smooth water between falls) located at Old Point here. Jesuit missionaries arrived in mid-Seventeenth century and became friendly with the Indians. In 1809, Norridgewock became the shire town of Somerset County.

The *Sophie May House* (1845), an attractive red brick house with white columns, was the home here of Rebecca Clarke (Sophie May) and Sarah Clarke (Penn Shirley), Nineteenth century writers of juvenile stories. The hall has a graceful staircase with hand-carved ornmentation and the attic has an unusual false floor with a five-foot air space.

The *Danforth Tavern* (1807) is a well-preserved large frame structure with 30 rooms and 12 fireplaces. Its hewn timbers are fastened with hand-wrought nails. Also in the town is an 18-foot granite obelisk erected in 1833 in memory of Father Sebastian Rasle (*see below*).

Directional signs lead to *Old Point* picnic grounds in a beautiful and historic pine grove. This is the site of Nanrantsouak, the Indian village. It lies on the Kennebec-Chaudiere River route, long used by the Indians traveling between Maine and the Quebec region. As early as 1633, when the English were struggling to settle along the coast, Capuchin missionaries from Chaleur Bay were coming up the Kennebec River. After their visits to this section, the Norridgewock Indians asked the Jesuit mission in Canada for missionaries. By the middle of the Seventeenth century the Jesuits had made numerous friends among their converts in the Quebec area, and the help they gave the Indians in various ways had gained them a wide reputation as desirable friends; as a result of reports of Abnakis who had come in contact with them at Quebec, they were invited to establish a mission at Nanrantsouak. Father Gabriel Druillettes undertook the task in 1646, leaving Quebec with some Abnakis, who led him up the Chaudiere and down the Kennebec to the village, where he remained a few months and built a chapel. Later he went down the Kennebec to visit the Capuchin mission at Castine, stopping at the present Augusta, where he met John Winslow, the Pilgrim trader; Winslow, often alone with the Indians and in need of friendly relations with them, had gradually developed a friendly interest in them, and he and Father Druillettes had earnest discussions on the possibilities of converting them all to Christianity and civilization. The Jesuit returned to Canada in 1647.

At this time the leaders of the Massachusetts Bay Colony, determined to ignore the quarrels between Great Britian and France, which were harmful to business, were making overtures to the authorities at Quebec for a free-trade agreement. The French-Canadians, also bored by European quarrels, were prepared to make the agreement and hoped to form an alliance with the Massachusetts colonists against the militant Iroquois. Because the Abnakis surrounding the Pilgrim post on the Kennebec were the spiritual charges of Father Druillettes, he was selected to conduct the negotiations; he set out over his former route in September, 1650. After visiting Nanrantsouak he continued to Winslow's post, where he arranged to have Winslow accompany him to Plymouth and Boston. His negotiations there were not successful, in part, perhaps because the tight-fisted colonists did not see any particular reason for spending hard-earned money to help protect the Canadians from a menace that did not at the time worry them. He returned to take up his work among the Abnakis with whom he lived until 1657.

Several well-known Jesuits were stationed here at one time or another, including Father Joseph Aubry and Father Sebastian Rasle; the latter was in charge from 1691 until 1724. Father Rasle brought ornaments and vessels from Quebec for the Indian chapel, made candles for it from bayberries, and trained a choir of 40 young Indians, whom he dressed in garments of the type used in French Catholic churches.

In 1701, the English authorities ordered the French missionaries to leave.

Colonel Winthrop Hilton's expedition went to Norridgewock in 1704-05, and burned all the church property. Father Rasle used a temporary bark chapel during the construction of a new church, which was not completed until 1718. During this period he broke both legs and was taken by canoe to Canada. On his return he learned a price had been set on his head. In 1722, Captain John Harmon and 200 men swooped down on the village while the warriors were hunting. The partly crippled priest and the old men of the camp hid while the party pillaged the church and the priest's dwelling, carrying off the dictionary of the Abnaki language on which Father Rasle had been working for years. Two years later Father Rasle met his death at the hands of a force under Captain Jeremiah Moulton who pillaged and burned the village. Finding themselves continually attacked, the Norridgewocks left, part of them going to Canada, many joining the Penobscots at Old Town.

Benedict Arnold on his Quebec expedition of 1775 followed in reverse the route down which came Father Druillettes in 1646. He and his men spent nearly a week at Old Point, preparing for the carry around Norridgewock Falls, about a mile north of Old Point. At the time of his visit all that remained of the settlement were ruins of an old Indian fort, a chapel, an old grave surmounted by a cross, and a covered passageway to the river.

According to a legend, Waban (the morning), son of a great chief and the first Norridgewock, was born at Old Point. Waban taught his people much, gave them food in abundance, cleared their streams and paths, and was kind to all creatures of the forest and stream. Although fierce and brave, he spared the birds, talked the language of all wild things of the woods, and became the greatest chieftain of them all. So great was his power that he did not die, but walked through the forest to the Great Spirit, and continued to clear the paths of his people for many generations.

Spanning the Kennebec, the *Norridgewock Bridge* is a four-span structure of the bowstring arch type.

At Norridgewock, junction with State 8 (*see Tour 4E*).

MERCER (alt. 280, Mercer Town, pop. 272), 194.4 *m*., a little settlement sheltered between two hills, is the birthplace of Publisher Frank R. Munsey. On the lawn of a small church (R) is a bronze tablet set in a large millstone commemorating what is believed to have been the *Largest Tree in New England*, an elm of 32-foot circumference, which surely would have made today's American Forestry Association 'Social Register of Big Trees.' At 198.6 *m*., junction with State 27 (L) to Belgrade Lakes, 10 *m*.

At 198.6 *m*., junction with State 27 L to Belgrade Lakes 9 *m*. and Augusta 28 *m*. (*see AUGUSTA*).

NEW SHARON (alt. 340, New Sharon Town, pop. 712), 197.7 *m*. The highway with the village homes alongside slopes about a mile to the bridge over well-named Sandy River. Acres of sweet corn have been grown for canning in the broad rolling fields around here.

FARMINGTON FALLS (alt. 335, Farmington Town), 202.1 *m*., once known as Tuft's Mills, was the site of the launching of the Sandy River's only seagoing vessel, the *LARK* built by Jacob Eaton in 1794. The Topsham party that first explored the area for settlement found two Indian villages, Pierpole's and Phillip's. Pierpole lived in the vicinity until about 1800, often aiding the white people who began settlement in 1781.

Numerous picnic areas, motels and cabins and restaurants are along US 2 from here to the New Hampshire Line.

At 204.3 *m*. at the top of a small steep hill in the Gower Cemetery enclosed by a stone wall, a finely engraved stone notes the death in 1806 of Robert Gower who brought his family to settle in a log cabin in 1782. A year earlier, Stephen Titcomb had built the first log cabin here. A picnic area is in a grove of pines near the site half a mile from the cemetery.

FARMINGTON (alt. 420, Farmington Town, pop. 5001), 207.5 *m*. is the gateway to the popular winter sports and summer vacation regions of the Rangeley Lakes, Sugarloaf and Saddleback Mts. (*see RECREATION*). In the fertile valley on the Sandy River, Farmington was incorporated in 1794 and became the shire town when Franklin County was formed in 1838. It has always been an educational as well as an agricultural center. The early settlers were well-educated for the time; no illiteracy was known. Lemuel Perham, Jr. taught the first school in a log cabin in 1788. Little Blue, the Willows and the May were some of the schools in the 1800s. Farmington Academy, founded in 1807, became a State Normal School in 1864 and is now Farmington State College of University of Maine, its buildings occupying much of the center of town.

Once known for its corn, bean and apple production and its corn shops, Farmington now has but one cannery. Excellent maple syrup has been produced here since 1781. Sugar beets are being grown experimentally. The Franklin County Agricultural Society (1839), one of Maine's oldest agricultural groups, is known for its annual fair at the Fairgrounds in September. Manufacturing enterprises are three wood-turning mills and a shoe factory. Farmington is the terminus of the Androscoggin RR. From 1879 to 1935 a narrow gauge line ran between here and Rangeley.

Nordica Homestead and Museum (1849) (*daily except Mon., summer*) Holly St., is the birthplace of Lillian Norton who became Mme. Giglia Nordica and made her operatic debut in Milan in 1879. The house has many mementoes of the great American singer's career.

The Farmington Historical Society sponsors local Pilgrimage trips and the publication of historical booklets. Other active cultural groups are the Porter Hill Art Association and the Sandy River Players.

Fewacres (private), W side of Main St. A bronze memorial plaque designates this as the home of Jacob Abbott (1803-79), noted author and educator. Also in Farmington is the home of Supply Belcher (1751-1836) who wrote *The Harmony of Maine*, a tune book in 1794.

At Farmington, junctions with State 27 for the Bigelow-Sugarloaf region and Coburn Gore on the Canadian border (*see Tour 4F*) and with State 4 for the Rangeleys and Saddleback (*see Tour 4G*).

At 208.3 *m.* is Farmington's oldest frame house (1789) built by Samuel Butterfield.

At 214.7 *m.*, L 3 *m.* on State 15 to *Wilson Lake Country Club (golf)* on Wilson Lake, summer recreation area.

WILTON (alt. 690, Wilton Town, pop. 3274), 216.1 *m.* Flowing from the Lake, Wilson Stream runs parallel with the main street of Wilton, home of the famous Bass boots. First named Harrytown for a dangerous Indian who lived in the area, it was renamed Tyngstown for the young captain who led an expedition when Warrior Harry was killed. In 1803, Abraham Butterfield who had come from Wilton, N. H., paid the expenses of incorporation for the privilege of having the place named for his former home.

Solomon Adams built Wilton's first cotton mill in 1810. After the Civil War, a large textile mill went into production, continuing until 1961 when it was converted into a wooden-ware assembly plant. This, a tannery and the Bass Company are Wilton's industries (1969).

Maine pulpwood and lumber used to be moved to the sawmills by teams of oxen. A few oxen team-loggers still operate from Wilton and other Franklin County towns. About 4000 cords of roundwood and 300,000 board feet of lumber are twitched from the County's woods by these teams. While most lumbermen these days use high-powered skidders capable of pulling tremendous loads for long distances, the oxen team-loggers find the traditional way works best for them. Oxen can go where trucks and tractors can't and there is not the financial burden of a $15,000 to $20,000 investment in modern machinery. And the oxen are 'company.' Instead of the roar of machinery shattering the stillness of the woods, there is the crunch of snow on a clear cold winter morning, the frost crackling the hardwoods, and the steamy breath of the laboring oxen as they are coaxed along by their drivers.

G. H. Bass and Company (visitors by permission). Now in its second century of producing many types of outdoor footwear, the company's hallmarks continue to be quality and integrity, principles that had noticeably declined in many fields of manufacture in the 1960s. George Henry Bass, a tanner, started to make special knee-high boots for farmers in 1876. Next he made a special caulked boot for the river-drivers. Still later, his moccasins, based upon those worn by Indians, became popular with woodsmen and sportsmen. Various other types of footgear were developed, such as the combat boots that G.I.s wore on all fighting fronts in World War II. Charles A. Lindbergh was wearing Bass boots on his lonely flight over the Atlantic in 1927. Admiral

Richard E. Byrd equipped his men with Bass footgear for his second Antarctic expedition in 1934. The Rangeley moccasin, the Sportocasin for golf and Weejuns, tradenamed in a derivation from 'Norwegian' and 'Injun,' and a molded fiber-glass ski boot that opens like a clamshell are among well-known designs.

At Wilton, junction with State 156 to Weld and Mt. Blue State Park, 20 *m*, (*see RECREATION*).

At 217.9 *m.*, a half-mile of highway was called the Magic Road; it is said a mysterious force pulls a car uphill.

DIXFIELD (alt. 420, Dixfield Town, pop. 2323), 232.8 *m.* was named on a broken promise. When the township, first granted to Jonathan Holman and others, became the property of Dr. Elijah Dix of Boston, he promised to donate a library if the place were named for him. It was, when the town was incorporated in 1803. The townspeople received a box of second-hand medical books and two German dictionaries.

In 1834 Leonard Norcross invented and patented a type of 'diving armor' that utilized Goodyear's invention of India rubber cloth. Old newspaper articles say the Norcross diving outfits were used in raising the Russian fleet sunk off Sebastopol in the Crimean War and in cleaning gunboats in Civil War times.

Located at the confluence of the Webb and Androscoggin Rivers, Dixfield's wood-turning and lumber mills are its chief industries. Charles Forster and son Morris once ran a mill on the N side of Webb Stream, where 'World's Fair' round toothpicks were first made.

At Dixfield, junction with State 142 to Carthage and a camping area on Lake Webb, 10 *m.* The route may be continued to Weld and Mt. Blue State Park, 10 *m.*

At 233.3 *m.*, *Old Meetinghouse on the Hill* (ca 1830) is used today, having served several denominations.

MEXICO (alt. 460, Mexico Town, pop. 5043), 237.2 *m.*, named when incorporated in 1818 to compliment the Mexicans in their struggle for liberty against Spain, is occupied principally by employees of the Rumford paper mills across the Androscoggin. Swift River passes through the W end of the village with a fall of 50 feet.

RUMFORD (alt. 610, Rumford Town, pop. 10,005), 238.5 *m.* Pennacook Falls plunging 180 feet over a bed of solid granite into the Androscoggin River, are seen from the business district on a canal-created island connected to the mainland by three bridges. The Falls supply power for the *Oxford Paper Company*, subdivision of Ethyl Corporation (*permit at office*), one of the largest book paper mills in the country, as well as electricity carried throughout SW Maine. The mills consume more than 1200 cords of wood daily (1968). First called Pennacook, the town, situated where the Ellis, Swift and Concord Rivers flow into the Androscoggin, was named for Count Rumford, one of its proprietors, and incorporated in 1800.

Many Olympic stars first learned jumping at the Chisholm Ski Club whose annual Winter Carnival with competitive sports is held at Chisholm Winter Park.

Left from Rumford on State 120 to the Mt. Zircon Spring Water Company (L) 4.5 *m.*, owners of *Moontide Spring*, as the Indians called it. A 2-mile trail from the bottling works leads to the spring whose normal flow of 42 gallons per minute is said to increase to 60 gallons per minute on the full moon, even as that space-conquered orb affects the tides of the sea.

At Rumford Point, junction with State 5.

Right on State 5 to South Arm 25.6 *m.* via Andover and the Notch. As the route branches NW along the Ellis River Valley, at 1.4 *m.* (L) is a long, bare high ledge on the side of Mt. Dimmock. At 4.1 *m.*, is the trail to *Newry Mine*, a 900-foot climb up Plumbago Mt. The mine is worked periodically for feldspar and other minerals; 107 varieties have been reported. The Bureau of Mines calls it a beryllium ore body. It is known for its watermelon tourmalines and as an early source of pollucite, a rare cesium ore.

At 7.7 *m.*, a road R .2 *m.* to *Lovejoy Covered Bridge* (1867) (*campground adjacent*). At 10.2 *m.* in the N end of Andover's Woodlawn Cemetery (R), the Grave of Molly Ocket, a Pequawket Indian woman who lived in the area and made countless friends by helping as a midwife and doctoring with herbs. Although her gravestone states that she was the last of her tribe, legend says that two of her daughters were married to white settlers. The Ladies Aid Society of Andover first raised money for her stone in 1861. The inscription reads:

> Mollocket
> baptized
> Mary Agatha
> died in the Christian faith
> Aug. 2, A.D. 1816
> The last of the Pequakets.

ANDOVER (alt. 610, Andover Town, pop. 762), 11.7 *m.*, formerly a lumbering town incorporated in 1804, caters to summer campers and tourists. Through the entire township can be seen the heavily wooded Aziscohos Mountains lying N of the Rangeley Lakes on the Canadian border. Ezekiel Merrill, the first settler, came from Fryeburg in 1789 with his wife and children. Friendly Indians paddled the family with their worldly goods down the Androscoggin and up the Ellis River to Andover.

At 12.7 *m.* the road forks. Off State 5 on the road (R) is the *Ezekiel Merrill Homestead* (L), with 'E. M. 1791' on its huge chimney. Continuing another 2 *m.* on this road to Andover Falls (picnic area). A mile beyond the Falls is the *Andover Earth Station (guided tours)*. Built by AT&T, it is now part of Comsat complex and since 1965 has served as a major East coast terminus for commerical space communications via satellites, with Atlantic area nations. It was part of the communications system for the historic

CREATIVE ARTS

INCREASING recognition of the arts as a human imperative, and more creativity in many art forms have been apparent in Maine in recent years. The State's Commission for the Arts and Humanities and private organizations broaden opportunities for people to enjoy music and the performing arts as well as painting, sculpture and other media. Handcrafts, born of necessity in earlier times, have become a highly developed art form in modern times. Generations of painters have 'discovered' many facets of the State's majesty and magic. The history of art in Maine is revealed in the work of artists and craftsmen, past and present, whose interpretations are found in museums, galleries and studios. Only a few examples of course can be included in the picture sections of this book.

VIGOROUS 19TH CENTURY FOLK CARVING AT PENOBSCOT MARINE MUSEUM, SEARSPORT

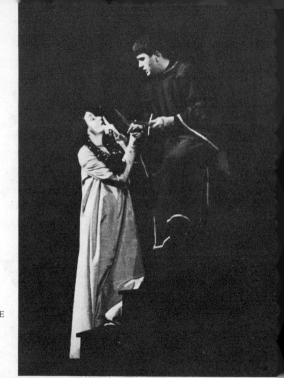

MACBETH AT BOWDOIN COLLEGE

MONMOUTH'S CUMSTON HALL, HOME OF CLASSIC REPERTORY

BACKSTAGE — IN THE DRESSING ROOM

EDWIN BOOTH AS KING LEAR,
A ROGERS GROUP   AT THE
BOOTHBAY THEATRE MUSEUM

OSPREY FROM ELIOT PORTER'S SUMMER ISLAND

HAYSTACK MOUNTAIN SCHOOL OF CRAFTS OVERLOOKS THE ATLANTIC

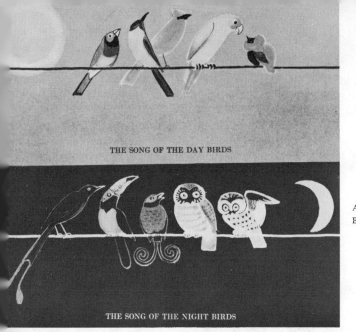

THE SONG OF THE DAY BIRDS

THE SONG OF THE NIGHT BIRDS

A DAHLOV IPCAR
BOOK ILLUSTRATION

WILLIAM ZORACH'S SPIRIT OF THE SEA, BATH CITY PARK

BULMAN 18TH CENTURY
CREWEL EMBROIDERIES
AT YORK GAOL MUSEUM

THE **BELLE MORSE**. 19TH CENTURY EMBROIDERY ON FINE SILK.
BATH MARINE MUSEUM

MARGUERITE ZORACH EMBROIDERY, 20TH CENTURY

SHAKER CRAFTS AT THE SABBATHDAY
MEETINGHOUSE MUSEUM

THE COUNTRY DOCTOR, 19TH CENTURY WEATHERVANE

SOUTH SOLON CHURCH 20TH CENTURY MURAL

ALDER SETTEE MADE BY MICMAC
INDIANS AT WHITNEYVILLE   AND
HEAD OF 65-FOOT INDIAN SCULPTURE
AT SKOWHEGAN

RUFUS PORTER MURAL, 19TH CENTURY, AT MAINE STATE MUSEUM

LADY OF FASHION, 19th CENTURY
CIGAR STORE FIGURE

GILDED EAGLE, 1861, AT THE MAINE HISTORICAL SOCIETY, PORTLAND

YORK COUNTY
GRAVESTONE CARVING,
SECOND OLDEST IN NEW ENGLAND

CLARK FITZGERALD'S SCULPTURE, THE WHOLE MAN, AT COLBY COLLEGE

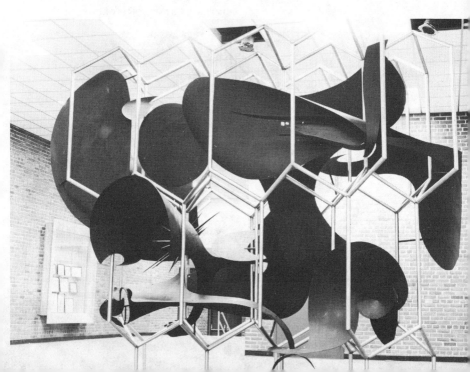

REPERTORY THEATRE, 1970

PORTLAND SYMPHONY ORCHESTRA

moon landing of 1969. Comsat which brought dial telephones to a community that was still using hand-cranked sets, was first called Telstar, a name given to a new District high school at Bethel.

Back at the fork, continuing R on State 5 to The Notch (Township C) 20.7 *m.*, formed by Parkhurst Mt. (alt. 2670) (L) and Old Blue Mt. (alt. 3735) (R) rising steeply above the road. At 22.9 *m.* the Appalachian Trail crosses State 5.

SOUTH ARM (alt. 1480, Township C, pop. 6), 25.6 *m.*, a tiny settlement on Lower Richardson Lake, with its few houses, wharves and long rows of connected storage sheds, is the 'jumping off' place for visitors on their way to the motels and camps scattered through the Rangeley Lakes Region (*see Tour 4G*).

At 248.5 *m.*, the Rumford Wild Animal Park (R), zoo, children's playground and village (*tenting and trailer park*).

NEWRY (alt. 630, Newry Town, pop. 260), 256.6 *m.* was settled in 1781 as Sunday River Plantation, later named by settlers from Newry, Ireland.

A junction here with State 26.

R on State 26 to NORTH NEWRY (alt. 675, Newry Town) (*fishing, hunting*), 4.9 *m.* where feldspar has been mined. Poplar Tavern and Diana Pool in the woods nearby were popular vacation spots in the gay nineties.

Grafton Notch State Park (picnicking, fishing, hiking) 10 *m.*, is one of the most interesting of the State's parks. The Notch is formed by *Old Spec Mt.* (4150 ft.), with the highest Forest Lookout in the State, and *Bald Mt.* (3996 ft.). In the Notch are *Screw Auger Falls* where the swirling waters of Bear River, acting like an auger, have worn holes from 6 in. to 25 ft. deep in the solid rock of the riverbed. Some of the holes have small waterfall showers of their own. Picnicking is pleasant on the nearby ledges. Also here is the *Old Jail*, a chasm 75 ft. deep and 25 ft. across; hikers crawl down and climb up to 'escape jail.' A path into the woods leads to a deep gorge on Bear River; this is *Moose Cave*, cold on the hottest days. It was formed by rocks that broke from Bald Mt. and fell into the river.

Mahoosuc Trail (campgrounds), part of the Appalachian Trail crosses the Park.

UPTON (alt. 1722, Upton Town, pop. 166), (*sporting camps, guides, boats, canoeing*), 27.5 *m.* overlooks Umbagog Lake, source of the Androscoggin River, which drains the Rangeley Lakes region.

At 28.8 *m.* State 26 crosses the New Hampshire Line, 8.7 *m.* SE of Errol, N. H.

At 259.3 *m.* (L) a picnic area overlooks the Androscoggin River.

At 260. *m.*, road R to ski area 3 *m.* and the *Sunday River* or *Artists' Covered Bridge (1870)*, 4 *m.*

At 261.9 *m.*, road R to the once famous *Chalybrate Spring*, 4 *m.* NW side of highway. Icy cold mineral waters bubble here, and before the Civil War, John Chapman built a large hotel, stable, outbuildings, store, bowling alley and bathhouses. The resort declined after the war, however.

BETHEL (alt. 700, Bethel Town, pop. 2408), 262.9 *m.* is the center of a beautiful township in the Oxford Hills. Its name, suggested when it was incorporated in 1796, probably by the Rev. Eliphaz Chapman, an early settler, signifies 'the House of God.' It is situated on both sides of the Androscoggin River whose numerous falls furnish power for several mills downstream. Aware of the importance of a Planning Board and zoning, Bethel citizens maintain and preserve the best of the past. A Historical Society was organized in 1963.

The last foray of Indians into Maine was made in August. 1781 when a party from St. Francis, Quebec, attacked Bethel, plundering and holding two settlers captive until after the end of the Revolution.

A native of Bethel is Margaret Joy Tibbetts, former Ambassador to Norway, who was appointed Deputy Assistant Secretary of State for European Affairs in 1969 and received the Federal Woman's Award that year.

> *Gould Academy* on the brow of the hill, was established in 1836 and is now a private co-educational preparatory school of high standing. Telstar, the new high school, was completed in 1968.

> The *Chapman House* (*private*) W side of Church St., was the home of the late Dr. William R. Chapman, conductor of the former annual Maine Music Festivals.

> *Bethel Inn* (L), one of Maine's best-known hostelries, was built by Dr. John G. Gehring (1857-1932), distinguished neurologist, who built his own home beyond the Inn and late in life converted it into a sanitorium for his patients. Since 1947, the house has been headquarters for the *National Training Laboratories Institute for Applied Behavioral Science*, attracting about 1000 people for research each summer. Results of intergroup relationship studies here have proven useful to American business and education.

> SE on State 26 at Locke Mills is the Mt. Abram Ski Slope, 8 *m.*

At 272.5 *m.*, the old *Peabody Tavern* (ca. 1800) (*private*), in Gilead, once a stopping point on the stage route from Lancaster, N. H. to Portland, Maine.

GILEAD (alt. 710, Gilead Town, pop. 136), 274.7 *m.* Six miles long and three miles wide, this little settlement is on the N line of the White Mountain National Forest. Incorporated in 1804, Gilead was named for the large number of balm of Gilead trees in the center of the town. The highway, with beautiful views of mountains and rivers, is lined with graceful birches. Here Wild River and Bog Brook flow into the Androscoggin as it enters Maine from New Hampshire. In the center of town, an attractive National Forest picnic area (*tent and trailer facilities adjacent*).

> Left from Gilead on State 113, through White Mountain National Forest is Evans Notch, 6 *m.*, with spectacular view of the Presidential Range.

At 277.2 *m.* US 2 crosses the New Hampshire Line, 3.8 *m.* E of Shelburne, N. H.

TOUR 4A: *From* ISLAND FALLS *to* PATTEN and
BAXTER STATE PARK, State 159 and Grand Lake Road, 35 *m.*

Via Shin Pond.

State 159 branches W from Island Falls (*see Tour 4*) at 0 *m.*

CRYSTAL village, 6 *m.*

PATTEN (alt. 541, Patten Town, pop. 1312), 10 *m.*, a busy lumbering
and commercial community (*fishing, woods trails*).

The *Patten Lumberman's Museum* is one of the most fascinating in the
State, with some 5,000 items connected with Maine's early lumbering
days. Curator Lore A. Rogers who devoted many years to assembling
this outstanding collection, was honored with a State award in 1968. The
Museum was built in 1962 with lumber from two log houses (1860) on
Mt. Chase. The interior is of seven varieties of native hardwoods.

Besides the incredible number of tools, there are models of early lumber
camps, blacksmith shop, horses hovel, tote teams and lean-to camp of the
early pine days with open fire under a smoke hole and sleeping berth on
one side and 'deacon seat' in front. In the cook's camp is the wangan box
where the men bought tobacco, clothing and medicine. Staple food was
bread with molasses, beans, salt pork, codfish and split peas, sometimes
supplemented with moose and caribou. The sourdough bread was baked
in Dutch ovens buried in the hot ashes of the open fire and beans were
baked in a 'bean-hole.' On the drive, when the men lived in tents and the
wangan moved frequently, the noon lunch of beans, bread and molasses
and tea was carried in wooden buckets hung on a yoke, or on a handsled.
Made on the farms, the tallow candles that furnished light were followed by
kerosene lanterns.

The extensive tool collection includes woods, driving, blacksmith, wheelwright and carpenters' tools, showing the ingenuity of early lumbermen.
There is also a model of the bateau used in getting supplies upriver and
in driving logs down. In the boats the men carried their cantdogs, an
axe and a pickeroon used to float logs away from the shore. In driving
the big pine logs, early lumbermen used an 8-foot hand spike to keep
logs afloat. Some were fitted with dogs, but for rolling they depended on
the 'swing dingle' or 'swinging bitch,' a short stalk from which the dog
swung freely and was hooked onto the log with one hand.

A modern peavey, used for rolling wherever logs are cut, was donated to

the Museum by the Peavey Tool Co. of Bangor, founded by Joseph Peavey, who in 1861 invented but never patented the original peavey.

Whittlers among the crews occupied their leisure time in woodcarving,.
some showing real skill and artistic taste. Favorite objects were the gum
book, a box in book form with operose binding, and elaborate handles
for their crooked knives, a tool inherited from the Indians.

SHIN POND, 20 *m.* From here on is magnificent, little inhabited country
of great natural beauty, mountains, lakes and streams beckoning hunters,
fishermen, climbers and campers. Genial Forest Rangers supply information and stories of the area. There are several campgrounds but none
of the appurtenances of population centers.

Among artists who have interpreted on canvas the 'big woods' and the
lives of the lumberjacks is Carl Sprinchorn who came to Shin Pond in the
1930s. Artists Marsden Hartley and the earlier Frederick E. Church were
inspired by the splendor of Mt. Katahdin (*see THE ARTS*).

From Shin Pond on unmarked road that soon forks.

> R on unmarked road N to Snowshoe and White Horse Lakes (*campgrounds*),
> 10 *m.*

Continuing from the fork, on Grand Lake Road about 5 *m.* to campgrounds and an unmarked road.

> R on this road to Scraggly Lake (*campgrounds*), about 10 *m.*

At 35 *m.* on Grand Lake Road, Horse Mt. (alt. 1589) (*campgrounds*) at
NE entrance of *Baxter State Park* (*see RECREATION*).

TOUR 4 B : *From* MATTAWAMKEAG *to* MILLINOCKET
and BAXTER STATE PARK, State 157 and Park Road, 67.5 *m.*

Via Medway and East Millinocket.

State 157 moves W from Mattawamkeag (*see Tour 4*) at 0 *m.*, to big industry and thence to the forests and Park region.

MEDWAY (alt. 280, Medway Town, pop. 1266), 20 *m.*, at the confluence
of the Penobscot River and its East Branch that enters the main stream
through a rocky gorge, was important in early lumbering days when logs
were sorted and sent to Bangor in a segregated drive. Inhabitants now

are employed in the nearby paper mills.

EAST MILLINOCKET (alt. 340, East Millinocket Town, pop. 2392), 25 m. With the forest at its back door, this settlement grew rapidly in 1907 when the Great Northern Paper Company's dam and mill were completed. Most of the population is employed in the mills, a large portion being French-Canadian.

MILLINOCKET (alt. 350, Millinocket Town, pop. 7453), 35 m., gateway to Baxter State Park and home of one of Maine's largest paper companies, is also reached from Bangor via express I-95, 78 m.

The Great Northern Paper Company's mills here and at East Millinocket are giants of the nation's paper industry, producing one fifth of all the newsprint manufactured in the U. S., as well as significant quantities of other papers. The huge plants produce 2000 tons of paper daily (1968). Expansion plans were announced in 1969.

The town differs from others in Maine in that it sprang up in response to labor needs. Because of the advantages of manufacturing near the source of raw material, Great Northern built its plant on the Penobscot River near a 141-ft. head of water that furnishes abundant power. The company financed homes for the workers and their families, constructed roads and initiated local government and schools, and stores for goods and services. During a labor shortage in 1969, a colony of Tibetans came to work in the woods for Great Northern.

The State Park Road leaves NE from Millinocket, travelling through unorganized townships of forested mountain and lake country to the SE entrance of Baxter State Park (see RECREATION), 67.5 m. where in red letters on a large white sign are these words: THIS IS GOD'S COUNTRY. DON'T SET IT ON FIRE AND MAKE IT LOOK LIKE HELL. Roaring Brook Road (R) leads a short distance to a Park campsite. The State Park Road continues around the Park to Ripogenus Dam and other Park entrance routes (see Tour 1D).

In the Park is great Mt. Katahdin (Ind.: highest land). Naturalist Henry D. Thoreau, friend of Millinocket's first settler, Thomas Fowler, in 1846 described the mountain as a 'vast aggregation of loose rocks, as if at some time it had rained rocks, and they lay as they fell on the mountains, nowhere fairly at rest, but leaning on each other, all rocking-stones, with cavities between, but scarely any soil or smoother shelf.' Of the view from the summit (5267 ft.), he wrote that the surrounding world looked 'as if a huge mirror had been shattered, and glittering bits thrown on the grass.'

Among many Indian legends woven about the mountain is one that the home of the Mountain King and his lovely but dangerous daughter Lightning was within it; they were served by the Thunders, fierce giant warriors.

Kinaldo, the hero, fell in love with the Mountain King's daughter, after having seen her beautiful face on the storm clouds, and left his tribe to seek her. At last he found her in the terrible depths, and she, returning his love, prevailed on her father to hold a great feast for him in his hall; during the feast she gave Kinaldo a potion that made him forget his former life. For a time they lived happily together, but one night he was wakened from his sleep by the tears of his favorite sister Winona, who had not ceased to pray for his return. Both the king and the mountain princess tried to prevent his leaving, but he persisted. At last the king gave him permission to go, but angrily warned him that those who had tasted the wine of Katahdin could no longer live long among men. Lightning bade her lover farewell, saying 'Go, but tomorrow at sunset I come and thou wilt not forsake me.' Kinaldo made his way down over the rocks and at length reached his home village; he thought he had been away only a short time, but he found many changes had taken place and Winona was already a woman. In spite of his joy over seeing his friends and kinsfolk again, he was restless and uneasy. As evening came a storm began to gather over Katahdin and he heard the mutter of the Thunders, which did not add to his peace of mind. The Thunders came closer and a terror seized him; but suddenly he saw his loved one among the thunderheads. A blinding streak of lightning seemed to reach out and seize Kinaldo. When the storm cleared, Katahdin was bathed in glittering light and the dead warrior lay as asleep at the foot of the mountain.

Another favorite is about a girl who loved the mountain, imagining that it was a strong, handsome young man whom she prayed would one day come to her. After absenting herself from the camp for three years, she returned one day with a beautiful baby boy with eyebrows of stone. Growing in beauty and stature, he performed miracles of hunting that saved the tribe during the terrible winters. But the women's tongues wagged and at last, angered by their cruelty and ingratitude, the mother burst forth: 'Fools, your folly kills you! You must have known from his eyebrows that this was Katahdin's son, sent to save you.' And she took her god-child and departed forever; from that time on the Abnakis were a doomed race, the white men stealing the hunting grounds of the red men and in time exterminating them.

TOUR 4C: *From WEST ENFIELD to* MILO *and* KATAHDIN IRON WORKS, State 6 and State 11, 41.3 *m.*

Via Howland, La Grange and Boyd Lake.

THROUGH woods and fields following the winding course of the Piscataquis River, the route passes broad tranquil ponds and large prosperous farms extending to the outskirts of trim little towns. The area economy is relatively stable. Lumbering was begun here after the reckless boom period that left depleted forests and dead mill towns in its wake; production now on a scientific basis is constant, providing regular employment.

State 11 leaves West Enfield (*see Tour 4*) 0 *m.*

HOWLAND (alt. 150, Howland Town, pop. 1326), 1.6 *m.*, entered from the E over a bridge spanning the Penobscot River, is an industrial and agricultural village at the confluence of the Penobscot and Piscataquis Rivers. Settled in 1818, it has grown up around large paper mills. In spring when the rivers rise suddenly, log jams sometimes make a spectacular display as the swirling waters toss logs and pulpwood high into the air. An access here to I-95.

LA GRANGE (alt. 310, La Grange Town, pop. 424), 12.3 *m*. lies in fertile farming country well-adapted to cultivation. Since it was first settled, c. 1823, the inhabitants have depended upon the soil for their livelihood, farm properties being handed down from one generation to another.

BOYD LAKE (alt. 287, Orneville Town, pop. 176), 15.5 *m*. This obscure town was once the home of the Maxim family whose two sons played a significant role in the destiny of mankind before the atomic age.

Hudson Maxim, brother of Sir Hiram Maxim, machine-gun inventor, (*see Tour 4D*) was born here in 1853. He was an inventor in his own right. Smokeless cannon powder, a shock-proof high explosive for guns of large caliber, gun cartridges, and a new system for discharging high explosives from ordnance were among his contributions. He was paid $50,000 by the U. S. Government for his production of 'Maximite,' an explosive fifty percent more powerful than dynamite, that could propel a projectile through heavy armor plate.

He also was deeply interested in the technique and scope of poetry. He published a weighty volume, 'The Science of Poetry and the Philosophy of Language.' Although, like his brother, he resided in England for many years, he was a frequent visitor to the United States. On one visit he was guest of honor of the Poetry Society of America; his remarks on that occasion are recalled for their scientific erudition.

For the first 18 years of his life he was known as Isaac, having been named for his father, also an inventor. Disliking the name, he had himself called Hudson.

MILO (alt. 295, Milo Town, pop. 2756), 22.3 *m*., an industrial, commercial and farming community, stands at a junction of the Sebec and Piscataquis Rivers that furnish power for several manufactories. The *American Thread Company (permit at office)* manufactures spools and box shooks of white birch.

Notwithstanding modern fire-fighting equipment and warning systems, the populace of towns like Milo are constantly alert to the dangers of that menace of the timberlands, the forest fire. Knowing that entire townships as well as thousands of acres of valuable timber may be laid waste, every able-bodied man, woman, and child springs into action when the first shrill scream of the fire siren pierces the hum of the mills. A moment's delay and the flames, leaping from undergrowth to treetops, may be caught by the wind and fanned quickly into a blistering, roaring inferno, hurtling through the resinous upper branches of the evergreens. Flames sometimes leap 30 feet into the black pall of smoke hanging above the crackling treetops.

As the trees crash to earth in a shower of flames and flying sparks, blazing embers are caught up on a current of acrid smoke and borne far in advance of the fire. Where each spark falls, a new blaze springs up, and in an incredibly short time the fire has reached conflagration proportions. Every means, from bucket brigades to backfiring, is employed to prevent such disasters.

Left from Milo on a tarred road is DERBY (alt. 280, Milo Town), 1.6 *m*. The Bangor & Aroostook RR. *Car Shops* center this well landscaped village with its small parks, playground, swimming pool and tennis courts.

State 6 may be continued from Milo to Greenville and Moosehead, 47.7 *m.* *(see Tour 4D).*

At Milo, N on State 11 to

BROWNVILLE (alt. 350, Brownville Town, pop. 1641), 26.8 *m.* lying on both sides of Pleasant River near a dam. Visible from the highway, on the far bank of the river N of the village are long slate heaps where quarrying was done until 1917. Brownville slate won first prize at the 1876 Centennial Exposition in Philadelphia as the finest roofing slate in the country when it was much used for this purpose.

An unmarked road (L) leads to a campsite and to Sebec and Lake, 8 *m.*

At 27.8 *m.* is Forest Ranger Headquarters of the Pleasant River District.

BROWNVILLE JUNCTION (alt. 390, Brownville Town), 30 *m.* (last gas station on the road). Soon a road R to Schoodic Lake.

At The Prairie, 34.8 *m.*, a dirt road (L) to

KATAHDIN IRON WORKS (alt. 580, Unorganized Township of Katahdin Iron Works, pop. 2) which derives its name from a deposit of iron ore (limonite) discovered in 1843 by Moses Greenleaf on so-called Ore Mt. 'K I,' as it became known, for half a century produced about 2000 tons of 40 to 150 pound ingots. It required 10,000 cords of wood to keep the blast furnace fires going with charcoal made in the 15 charcoal kilns or beehives. The blast furnace and the remaining beehive have been restored to prime condition as a State Historic Site.

In the days of Iron Works operation the community numbered some 100 persons; now only two. The iron first was transported by ox cart, then by horses and finally the railroad was laid from Bangor. During these exciting times, K I boasted a hotel, accommodating 100 people, a photo salon and printed its own scrip that was accepted as legal tender as far as Bangor.

The *Hermitage*, 7 *m.* as the crow flies, nearer 10 on foot or by car over rough terrain, is on the West Branch of Pleasant River. This 'solitude' is a huge grove of exceptionally large white pines. Just off the Appalachian Trail, the site is being preserved by the Nature Conservancy.

Gulf Hagas, a three-mile water-eroded canyon is a spectacular sight, starting 1.5 *m.* up the West Branch of Pleasant River above the Hermitage. Cutting through the slate, the waters have carved many interesting forms to create 'the Grand Canyon of the East.' A side trip off the Appalachian Trail, the round-trip from the Hermitage is about an 8-mile hike.

From the K I road State 11 continues NE 30 *m.* to Millinocket and the Baxter State Park Road *(see Tour 4B)*. Enroute, is Ebeemee Lake, one of several on a direct water course W to Moosehead. Many Indian artifacts have been found in this beautiful territory.

TOUR 4D: *From* NEWPORT *to* GREENVILLE and MOOSEHEAD LAKE, State 7 and State 6, 60.5 *m.*

Via Corinna, Dover-Foxcroft, Guilford and Monson.

HEADING for the big woods and lake country around famous Moosehead, this route goes to the sporting center of Greenville where seasonal sightseers have a choice of spectacular trips by seaplane, boat and car. This primitive country of inland Maine draws poets and artists as well as sportsmen (*see THE ARTS and RECREATION*). Greatest of all New England lakes, Moosehead, 1028 ft. above sea level, is from one to 20 *m.* wide with a 350-*m.* shoreline. Surrounded by rugged mountains and flanked by virgin forest, Moosehead cuts through 35 *m.* of nearly trackless wilderness, a thrilling sight from the air. Abrupt flinty Mt. Kineo rises from the deep water in mid-lake. A densely wooded plateau borders the lake N of Kineo. Lily Bay, Baker, Big and Little Squaw Mts. dominate the S shores.

State 7 leaves Newport (*see Tour 4*) 0 *m.*

CORINNA (alt. 350, Corinna Town, pop. 3951), 6.3 *m.* A woolen mill and a food processing plant provide employment in this community, birthplace of Gilbert Patten (1866), who as Bert L. Standish wrote the Frank Merriwell series of boys' books.

DEXTER (alt. 480, Dexter Town, pop. 4100), 14.2 *m.*, agricultural, industrial and recreational community, lies on a hillside sloping to the S shore of Lake Wassookeag. First settler Ebenezer Small hauled his wife here on a sled from Harmony in 1801.

Samuel Dexter, lawyer and politician who served in three Cabinet posts, never saw the Maine town named for him; he died of scarlet fever in Athens, N. Y. in 1816, the year Dexter was incorporated in his name. He had served as Secretary of War, Secretary of the Treasury and as Secretary of State, administered the oath of office to John Marshall, first Chief Justice of the U. S. His son, Samuel William, later settled in Dexter — Michigan.

In the age of candlelight and homespun the settlers accomplished much with little; they surveyed land titles, cleared farms, erected homes, built mills and schools, cleared roads. Dexter thrived in the latter half of the Nineteenth century, with four large woolen mills, iron foundry, machine and woodmachine shops and a tannery. When population of other Maine communities dwindled after the Civil War, Dexter continued to grow with the influx of French-Canadian families. Its weekly paper, the *Eastern Argus* began publishing shortly before the War; Novelist Holman Day was editor for a time.

Birthplace of Ralph Owen Brewster, U. S. Representative and Senator (1935-62) and Maine's 51st Governor (1925-28), Dexter has two woolen mills, a shoe factory and shoe machinery plant.

Amos Abbott Company Mill (*visitors*) has been managed by the same family for four generations. Amos and Jeremiah Abbott came from Andover, Mass., to establish a carding and fulling mill in the wilderness in 1820 when machinery and supplies were brought from Boston to Bangor in sailing vessels and then hauled by ox teams over rough logging roads to this place. By 1830 the mill had become a complete unit, weaving and finishing cloth. Its 'Abbott grays,' said to 'wear like iron,' were known throughout New England.

At *Abbott Hill*, now a ski area, Sir Hiram Maxim (*see below*) fired the first automatic machine gun in 1890.

Old Grist Mill (1818) (*1-5 daily, except Sun., summer*) is the Dexter Historical Society's Museum. A few grains of oats sprinkle down occasionally from the grain chutes and bins throughout the building which retains the original wood flooring, hand-split plank wall lathes and machinery.

Lake Wassookeag (*boating, fishing, swimming*). An innovative Summer School begun here in 1926 combines scholastic and outdoor activities, with students from all over the U. S. and several foreign countries.

Other points of interest are the Universalist Church (1829) and Abbott Memorial Library.

DOVER-FOXCROFT (alt. 330, Dover-Foxcroft Town, pop. 4173), 27.3 *m.* Foxcroft on the N side of the Piscataquis River and Dover on the south, were settled and developed separately, became one town in 1922. It manufactures King's Arrow pine and hardwood specialties, Moosehead furniture, leather goods and Hathaway shirts. Down East Sled Dog Racing Club events are held here.

Dover-Foxcroft was the home of John Francis Sprague (1848-1926) whose historical writings are among the collections of the Maine Historical Society in Portland. Born in Dover was Mrs. Lillian M. N. Stevens (1844-1914), president of the Women's Christian Temperance Union from 1898 to the time of her death. She was a founder of the national and State organizations. John Colby Weston, first Maine man to enlist in the Civil War, was a native of Foxcroft.

Blacksmith Shop Museum (1863) (*daily, summer*), Park St. This old smithy shop, one of the few remaining, with much of the original equipment, was built by Nicholas A. Chandler who bred and trained horses. It was enlarged in 1883 and continued operations until 1905. In the museum are forge, bellows, anvil and many tools pertaining to rural life in the 1800s. An ox-lifter on display was made in the shop. An 1858 newspaper advertisement called attention to 'Joseph M. Bachelor's patented invention of an Ox-Lifter, by the use of which any ox, however stubborn, can be shod, without any of the hard labor usually attending the raising of the feet, as the worst cases can be handled by the shoer with perfect ease and without injury to the ox.' Names of neighboring farmers chalked about the rafters show where sample horseshoes were kept on hand as individual patterns to guide the blacksmith.

Old Metal Shop and Museum (daily, summer), Park St., has working steam engines dating from 1840.

Lime Kiln Works (c. 1875). From Center Road at Foxcroft golf course, a 10-minute walk to an early lime-burning kiln.

Bird-banding Station and Nature Center (visitors), Garland Road. Scenic lakeside trail with identified trees and flowers; Kettle Hole surrounded by eskers.

Low's Covered Bridge (1830), picnic site, on State 6 and 15 (L).

This tour now travels W and N on State 6 (L). Easterly (R), State 6 goes 13 *m.* to Milo, (*see Tour 4C*).

At 29.3 *m.*, junction with State 153.

R on State 153 to *Peaks-Kinney State Park* and Sebec Lake (*picnicking, swimming, fishing*), 4.5 *m.*

At 34 *m.*, junction with State 23.

L on State 23 to SANGERVILLE (alt. 440, Sangerville Town, pop. 1157), .5 *m.* where bronze plaques mark the birthplaces of Sir Hiram Maxim, knighted by Queen Victoria in 1901 for his inventive genius, and Sir Harry Oakes, mining tycoon, knighted by George V for charitable works.

Hiram Maxim (1840-1916), inventor of the machine gun that bears his name, was 14 years old when he started out to make his fortune, first at a lathe shop in Dexter, later as an apprentice in a Boston shop that made 'philosophical instruments.' When he turned his attention to applied science, he invented a smokeless powder, a gas generating apparatus, a gas headlight for locomotives, automatic steam and vacuum pumps, feed-valve heaters, engine governors and many other devices.

In 1881 certain of his electric patents were put into 'interference' with Edison's, and in four trials, decisions were in Maxim's favor. The Maxim gun was completed only after he had acquired a fortune from other inventions following the establishment of his own factory in England. In time the Prince of Wales (Edward VII) and other members of the nobility became convinced that the device was practicable. After a demonstration in Switzerland, the government of that country gave him an order, with Italy, Austria, and then England following suit. The gun with which he gave his demonstration in England is now in South Kensington Museum.

In the United States the gun was not accepted until the war with Spain (1898). It was used by many nations during World War I. Factories in Spain, Portugal, Sweden, England, and the United States were owned by Maxim for the manufacture of a torpedo boat which he also designed. For his contributions to effective warfare, the inventor received honors and decorations from nearly every sovereign of Europe.

GUILFORD (alt. 430, Guilford Town, pop. 1880), 35.4 *m.*, is an industrial town spreading on both sides of the Piscataquis River. In 1803,
a handful of men settled here with 'a determination to admit on their part
no person as a settler who was not industrious, orderly, moral, and well-
disposed.' In 1806, the men living so harmoniously in the township were
called 'the seven wise men of Guilford.' Historic landmark between Guilford and Sangerville is Low's covered bridge.

ABBOTT (alt. 450, Abbot Town, pop. 404), 39.2 *m.* Junction here with
State 16.

> L on State 16 to KINGSBURY (alt. 520, Kingsbury Plantation, pop. 8). 12.5
> *m.* (*picnic area*). Where the highway passes over a section of *Johnson Mt.*
> (1620 ft.), there is a fine panoramic view of the Bigelow Range with the Ken-
> nebec River in the foreground. State 16 continues to Bingham (*see Tour 4E*)
> at 28 *m.*

MONSON (Monson Town, pop. 852), 46.3 *m.* Moosehorns showing the
way to Monson were erected in 1817. Encircled by dense woods, the
town is perched on a slate ridge that runs many miles N. Deep slate-walled
quarries cut the hillsides where for many years the pit method of quarrying
was used. The Portland Monson Slate Company now mines the slate
which is of exceptional quality and is shipped all over the world. Its uses
include manufacture of electrical goods because of its small mineral
content; it is also used in handcrafts.

The first church north of Bangor was built here in 1831. The town's first
school session was held in Monson Academy in 1848.

> *Monson Slate Museum* (*daily, summer*) displays slate in various forms including
> craftwork.

> *Moosehead Manufacturing Company* (*visitors*) makes high quality Colonial
> furniture.

At 52.9 *m.*, road junction.

> L on this road to SHIRLEY MILLS (alt. 1100, Shirley Town, pop. 214),
> 2 *m.* Humorist Bill Nye, christened Edgar Wilson Nye was born here in 1850,
> a descendant of early settler Benjamin Nye who came to America from Eng-
> land in 1635. When he was two, the family moved to Wisconsin.

> Nye was the first American humorist to express himself in the good spelling
> and grammar of the English language. His wit was pure, uncorrupted by the
> glib gag and wisecrack; his gentle satire delighted world-wide audiences in the
> latter half of the Nineteenth century. He travelled all over as a lecturer, often
> with Poet James Whitcomb Riley and Naturalist Luther Burbank, and gained a
> wide reputation with his amusing letters and whimsical comment on the social
> and political life of the times. Of his birthplace which he visited in later years,
> he wrote:

> > 'There in Shirley, Maine, amid the barren and inhospitable waste of rocks
> > and cold — the last place in the world that a great man would select to be
> > born — began the life of one who in after years rose to the proud height

of postmaster at Laramie City, Wyoming Territory. There on the banks of the raging Piscataquis, where winter lingers in the lap of spring till it occasions a good deal of talk, there began a career which has been the wonder and admiration of every vigilance committee west of the turbulent Missouri.'

When he became postmaster of Laramie (pop. 3000) Nye helped found the *Boomerang*, named for his mule; the paper through his writings soon had subscribers from every state and many foreign countries, and was the beginning of his national fame. Cerebrospinal meningitis ended his career in 1896. Among his many books was '*Comic History of the United States* (1894) in which he said:

Maine is noted for being the easternmost state in the Union, and has been utilized by a number of eminent men as a birthplace. White-birch spools for thread, Christmas trees and tamarack and spruce gum are found in great abundance. It is the home of an industrious and peace-loving people. Bar Harbor is a cool place to go in the summer to violate the liquor law of the State.'

GREENVILLE (alt. 1040, Greenville Town, pop. 2025), 60 *m.*, sporting center for the southern antler of the Moosehead Region (*guides, supplies, boat ramp, seaplanes*), famous for fishing, hunting, canoeing, camping, mountain climbing and winter sports (*see RECREATION*). Down East Sled Dog Racing events are staged here. Accommodations include hotels, motels, sporting camps, public and private campgrounds. Besides the airport on East Road, there are two flying services on the lake shore available for sightseers, hunting and fishing parties. Greenville is a headquarters for the Great Northern and Scott Paper Companies for woods operations, and the West Division of the Maine Forestry Service which has 75 campsites on Moosehead shores. In 1970 the Huber Corporation had begun a recreation development on 200 acres at Beaver Cove, with openspace, cluster type homes on a ridge 300 ft. above Moosehead Lake. There are two boys' camps whose summer trips include Mt. Katahdin and the Allagash River; stores for general services, antique shops and an Indian novelty shop. The *Shaw Library* displays collections of the Moosehead Historical Society.

Moosehead Lake is the breeding ground for salmon, square-tail-trout and togue. Pulp and power interests cooperate with the State Fish and Game Department in the conservation and propagation of game fish and wild game. Flowage and level of the Kennebec River are maintained to help the spawning of game fish. Moosehead Lake is the largest storage basin where water is drawn before spawning time and the level is held from spawning to hatching time. Scott Paper removed a dam on Tomhegan Stream, an important Moosehead tributary, cleared a spawning area at the mouth of 'Roach River, another major tributary, and established several deer yards.

Greenville is a gateway to the last unspoiled wildland in the East. Outdoorsmen who know the great North Country — the Allagash Wilderness Waterway, the great forests, the beautiful mountains and lakes — have wondrous tales to tell. Many areas can be reached only by plane. Lakes and mountains have such Indian names as Chemquassabamticook, Umsaskis, Umbazookas, Cuxabexis, Abacotmetic, Caucomgomac, Musquacook; and descriptive names like Desolation Pond, Ugh Lake, Echo, Bluffer, Brandy, Beanpot, Otter,

Spider, Beetle and Snake.

Time was when hermits dwelt in the wilderness, their supplies brought in occasionally by Forest Rangers and others. Most famous hermit was Jim Clarkson, a powerful man with a flaming red beard, sole resident of Township 9, Range 14, who never shot a deer, but kept many as pets, calling each by name. He later tended Locke Dam. Plane loads of wardens flew in and others came by canoe along the Allagash for his 80th birthday. When he died two years later, Bangor-Hydro-Electric Company established a fund in his memory.

Joe Klimchook was a Cavalry officer in the Imperial Russian Army before becoming the hermit of Russell Stream near Pittston. Hiram Johnson, who once kept two baby pigs in bed with him, floated scrap iron on a raft 22 miles downstream for sale one day. He didn't like the price offered, so poled the iron all the way back upstream and sank it. Hiram burned to death in his camp at Chesuncook Lake after shooting a man. Angus McLean and his nameless partner, on Indian Pond, never spoke to each other, nor would acknowledge one another's presence before a visiting warden. Another Ernest Hemingway was a first rank musician travelling the world with John Philip Sousa's famous band until he was crossed in love and took to the woods. He — with his dogs — was a food faddist, using only raw unrefined sugar, grain and flour. Bill Gordon holed up at Knowles Brook on the St. John River. When given a $15 license, he refused to trap beaver in his pond because he liked the family.

Two trips may be taken from Greenville: (1) Continuing on State 6 NW along W shore of Moosehead Lake to Dole, 63.2 *m*; (2) On the State Park Road (R) travelling NE to Baxter State Park, 46.2 *m*.

TRIP 1

On State 6 NW to GREENVILLE JUNCTION, 1.3 *m*., a Canadian Pacific RR stop, that has a hospital and several service establishments.

UNORGANIZED TOWNSHIP NO. 2, RANGE 6 (alt. 1600), called Big Squaw township (*hotel, sporting camps*), 4.7 *m*. Big Squaw Mt. (3267 ft.), township landmark rising above the S antler of Moosehead, has become a popular ski area (900 acres). The mountain is said to have acquired its name through an Indian legend of the great but quarrelsome warrior, Kineo, who left his tribe to dwell on the mountain that bears his name. Resentment against his fellow tribesmen grew as he became more lonely. Looking down over the black waters of the lake one evening, he saw a bright blade of flame on what is now called Squaw Mt. Next day he investigated. Arriving at dusk at the summit, he found the embers of a fire and beside it his exhausted old mother who had come to bring him back to his kinsmen; as she died, she begged him to return. Kineo buried her by the fire, and overcome with remorse, obeyed her request. And so, the site came to be known as Squaw Mt.

UNORGANIZED TOWNSHIP NO. 1, RANGE 7 (alt. 1050, pop. 5), 16.6 *m*., called Sapling. Numerous small streams mirroring the delicate tracery of white and yellow birch and affording fine fishing, cut through this heavily wooded township on the W shore of Moosehead Lake and the banks of the Kennebec River.

MISERY GORE (alt. 1500), 19.2 *m*., an unpopulated area 25 *m*. long and less than half a mile wide at its widest point, is a sliver of land in no township, having been left by corrections of early township boundary surveys.

The route enters the SE boundary of the UNORGANIZED TOWNSHIP OF ASKWITH (alt. 1400, pop. 56), popular hunting and fishing area known as West Outlet, and also as Taunton and Raynham. Here the W outlet of Moosehead Lake forms the N boundary of a *State Game Preserve* (*no hunting*) which extends through two townships to Squaw Brook.

ROCKWOOD (alt. 1050, Unorganized Township of Rockwood, pop. 137), 19.8 *m.*, sometimes known as Kineo Station (*hotels, camps, cottages; steamer service*), on the W shore of Moosehead Lake. Across the lake, only a mile wide at this point, *Mt. Kineo* (1806 ft.) thrusts above the waters and· far-flung forests of the E shore. This mountain, a round peninsula connected to the mainland by a narrow neck is composed of flint. At the foot, stone implements from early Indian workshops have been found. Many New England tribes came here for flint and it is believed their forebears found here the iron pyrites used for firestones. The *Kineo House* has been a long-time favorite of sportsmen and lovers of primitive lake and mountain scenery.

UNORGANIZED TOWNSHIP OF TOMHEGAN, 27.4 *m.* lying between Moosehead and Brassua (*bras'-a-wa*) Lakes, is another excellent hunting and fishing area.

At 38.7 *m.*, road junction.

R on this road along the S shore of Seboomook Lake (*campsite*) 4 *m.*, to SEBOOMOOK (Unorganized Township of Seboomook, pop. 24) 10 *m.*, a tiny settlement of guides and woodsmen on the extreme N shore of Moosehead Lake (*campsite*). From Seboomook, a road swings R around to Northeast Carry at NE end of Moosehead. Extending from Seboomook is the three-mile Northwest Carry of the West Branch of the Penobscot River, a terminal of the Allagash Canoe Trip (*see RECREA-TION*). A road N from Seboomook runs several miles through the wilderness to *Round Pond (campsite)*.

Pittston Farm, 42.2 *m.*, one of several maintained by the Great Northern Paper Company, is surrounded by broad fertile fields at a junction of the northern and southern branches of the Penobscot River.

At 42.8 *m.*, road junction.

L on this road to the deep-cut 40 ft. *Canada Falls* 2 *m.* A trail one mile N leads to Grand Pitch, another waterfall.

At 49.8 *m.* (*campsite*) a private road (*permit required*) goes N into St. John Ponds area ending at Big Bog.

At 51.9 *m.* (*campsite on Long Pond (L)*) a trail (R) goes 6 *m.* to *Green Mt. Fire Station* for a spectacular view of vast forestlands and deadwater.

At 61.6 *m.*, the Great Northern *Log Storehouse* and *Stables*.

DOLE (Township 3, Range 5), 63.2 *m.* Great Northern has a residence and supply base here. Great stretches of swampland cover much of the township. Around Penobscot Lake and Dole and Long Ponds, the forest struggles with the deadwater overflow.

Boundary Cottage, 68.1 *m.*, is a customs office 5 *m.* SE of St. Zacharie, Quebec. Great Northern woods crews have winter headquarters here for regional lumbering operations. Tote roads are slashed through the forest for transportation of logs by tractor, formerly by horses and oxen, to nearest points of shipment.

TRIP 2

On State Park Road NE at 4 *m.* entering Gore A, No. 2, forest-garbed *Baker Mt.* (3589 ft.) rises above E part of township and *Prong Pond* forms a blue patch on the S boundary.

At 4.5 *m.* LILY BAY (alt. 1040, Unorganized Township of Lily Bay, pop. 2), *Lily Bay State Park (camping, boat rentals and launching, picnicking, swimming and fishing).*

KOKADJO (Ind.: Kettle Mt.) (Unorganized Township of Frenchtown), 11 *m.* has a 6-*m.* lake.

The route passes S end of *Ragged Lake (Campsite),* with views W of Spencer Mt. (3035 ft.).

After a long stretch of woods, past S end of Caribou Lake *(campsite),* at 29.6 *m.* the SE boundary of Unorganized Township No. 3, Range 12, near the deadwater of *Chesuncook Lake* where densely packed weathered driki rises in masses above the surface; fine views up the lake that extends N 18 *m.*

At 34.2 *m.* the road forks *(campsite on Ripogenus Lake).*

R to *Ripogenus Dam* .5 *m.,* storing 20-30 million cu. ft. of water that is released in the West Branch of the Penobscot. Rising 92 ft. across the head of Ripogenus Gorge, the dam was considered a great engineering feat when it was built in 1915-17. This road continues around Baxter State Park to its SE entrance *(see Tour 4B).*

From the fork, State Park Road goes N to Harrington Lake *(campsite)* at 39.2 *m.,* then swings sharp right E with Soubunge Mt. (2104 ft) (L) *(Forest Lookout Station)* to *Nesowadnehunk* campsites in Baxter State Park *(see RECREAtion)* 46.2 *m.* From here, road SE in the Park to Mt. Katahdin and SE Park entrance *(see Tour 4B);* road N joins Grand Lake Road to NE Park entrance *(see Tour 4A);* W and N from the Park, a private road *(permit required)* goes to Chamberlain Lake *(campsite),* Soper Mt. (1410 ft.), through the wilderness swinging E to Ashland *(see Tour 1 sec. e).* Information should be obtained from Rangers regarding Park regulations, facilities and routes.

T O U R   4 E : *From* NORRIDGEWOCK *to* JACKMAN, 78.4 *m.,* State 8 and US 201.

Via Madison, North Anson, Solon, Bingham, Caratunk, The Forks and Moose River.

US 201 and State 8 NW leave Norridgewock *(see Tour 4)* 0 *m.* for historic and scenic mountain and lake country, along the Kennebec River.

MADISON (alt. 290, Madison Town, pop. 3935), 8.7 *m.* named for President James Madison, is a manufacturing town, chiefly of wood products.

The route crosses the Kennebec to the W side to ANSON (alt. 295, Anson Town, pop. 2252), 9.2 *m.*, a residential district of mill employes.

NORTH ANSON (alt. 295, Anson Town), 14 *m.* On the bridge over the Carrabassett River, views of the Falls (L) and the rocky river bed. The slate schist rocks have been strangely carved by the water's action. Junction here with State 16.

> L on State 16 at 1 *m.* road R to Embden Pond (*fishing, Eda Feeding Station*), 5 *m.* Continuing on State 16 to *New Portland Wire Bridge*, an unusual suspension bridge with English steel cables, 8 *m.* State 16 continues to Kingfield (*see Tour 4F*) at 16 *m.*

SOLON (alt. 395, Solon Town, pop. 669), 21.8 *m.* Artifacts from what may have been a permanent campsite of woodland Indians as they travelled up and down the Kennebec were uncovered here in 1969 during a State Museum Apprentice program. Among the findings were reddish-brown pottery with scratched line designs, scrapers used for removing hair and flesh from animals, knife blades, projectile points, rock flakes, charcoal and cooking stones and numerous fire pits used in communal cooking.

The site, a likely spot for spring fishing, is opposite jutting ledges that have rare Indian carvings. Although most of the ledges were blasted away early in the Twentieth century to facilitate log drives, still to be seen on the remaining rocks are low-relief carvings of animals, human figures and talley marks. It is conjectured the area also may have been used as a campsite by Benedict Arnold and his men on their Quebec march. Diaries mention camping above Skowhegan, and a small powder horn with a carved A has been found here.

> Left from Solon a road leads .4 *m.* to an old railroad station and beyond 200 yards S, *Caratunk Falls*, best viewed from the railroad bridge spanning the Kennebec. Extending V-shaped for 30-40 yards on either side of a point of land under the bridge, the falls drop 36 ft., sending up a cloud of spray and mist as the waters strike the jagged rocks below.
>
> On the E bank of the river below the Falls, an old road runs a few hundred yards to *Arnold's Landing* on a ledge near the waters of a quiet little cove. On the roadside, an *Arnold Trail Marker* with flagstaff and tablet, commemorates the overnight stay Oct. 7, 1775 of Arnold's army before the carry around Caratunk Falls.

At Solon the tour follows US 201 NW. On US 201 SE, a short cut to Skowhegan 16 *m.*

BINGHAM (alt. 355, Bingham Town, pop. 1308), 29.7 *m.*, generally identified with Wyman Dam (*see below*), was first settled in 1785 and named for William Bingham.

> Important in the founding of the Republic and richest man of his time, William

Bingham (1752-1804) who founded the nation's first bank in 1781, was a speculator, financier and politician not universally admired. He once owned two million acres of land in Maine (the Bingham Purchase) through complicated arrangements growing out of the financial distress of Gen. Henry Knox (*see Tour 1, sec. c*) and his partner Col. William Duer who had bought by lottery from the Commonwealth of Massachusetts two million acres of Maine land at 10 cents an acre, and another million acres at 20 cents an acre.

The Maine land was 'remote, rugged, uncleared, with its cold climate and short growing season, not well suited for farming. It had little development or organization, and money was so scarce in most of the communities that business, including that of the prostitutes, was done by barter, pins being the most common medium of exchange.' In two years, Bingham's European agent got no takers.

When Bingham's financial situation began to deteriorate, London bankers finally became partners in ownership of a million acres. In his 1969 biography of Bingham, *The Golden Voyage*, Robert C. Alberts suggests that Bingham's relative historical obscurity may have been due to 'Jeffersonian bias' and 'the prevailing degree of liberalism.'

Philadelphia-born and a graduate of Pennsylvania University, Bingham became British consul at St. Pierre, Martinique and later, Continental agent of the West Indies. During the period when many fortunes were made in piracy, the foundation of Bingham's great wealth was laid through his joint ownership of privateers, and active trading. During his later career as a Federalist politician and banker, this evidence of self-interest was not overlooked by Jeffersonians who noted his 'extravagance, ostentation and dissipation.'

At 28, Bingham married 16-year-old Anne Willing who became a great beauty and social leader, 'Queen of the Republican Court.' They lived lavishly in Europe for a time, returning with elegant decorations for a fine new house in Philadelphia where for 20 years Federalist strategy was planned. In 1813, President Adams charged that the Presidency, the Capital and the Country had really been governed by Bingham and his family connections. In the economic panic of 1797, Bingham was the only large capitalist and speculator not ruined, remaining a powerful financial and political figure. He died in England in 1804.

At Bingham, junction with State 16 (R) to Guilford (*see Tour 4D*), 25 *m.*

At Moscow, 31.7 *m.* the *Wyman Dam*, 155 ft. high, 2250 ft. long, was built by the Central Maine Power Company and named for its then president, Walter Scott Wyman. The combination earth-fill and concrete dam with hydro-electric plant raises the river level 135 ft. and has a total storage of 8 billion cu. ft. of water. It created an artificial lake that provides water storage for the headwaters of the Kennebec, including Moosehead and Brassua Lakes, Indian Pond and various other small bodies of water.

In the 1960s recreational interests were pressing for greater participation along with pulp and power in the multiple use of the historic Kennebec River as public interest in pollution control increased. Flowage is utilized by power and pulp companies on a 'family' basis for best use of the resource. The first charter on the river was granted in 1832. At one time 32 concerns depended on its flowage to carry logs and pulp. Today only Scott and Hudson drive pulp on it. Some of the 230,000 cords of Scott pulp is towed over miles of Moosehead Lake and sluiced at the head of the Kennebec at East Outlet.

Flowage also is utilized by the Central Maine Power Company whose dams constructed at Indian Pond, above The Forks and at Bingham, created towing problems. When Wyman Dam's storage lake eliminated one of the best 'downhill' driving stretches on the Kennebec, the power company subsidized costs of original towing equipment needed by the pulp interests and in 1928 agreed to pay $4000 a year toward towing costs. Pollution problems increase as the Kennebec winds its way toward the sea through Solon, Madison, Norridgewock, Skowhegan, Waterville, Augusta and Gardiner.

At 36.7 *m.* Wyman Lake, (*picnic area*).

At 41.4 *m.* the northernmost *Arnold Trail Marker* in the Kennebec section. It was moved here when waters of artificial Wyman Lake flooded the lower slopes of the Kennebec where Arnold left the river in October 1775.

CARATUNK (Ind.: rough and broken) (alt. 560, Caratunk Plantation, pop. 90), 46.4 *m.* lies near the river with *Moxie Mt.* (2925 ft.) (R) to the SE. Near Caratunk the road runs close to the Kennebec. Steep slopes covered with large boulders rise (R) above. (*Beware of falling rocks.*)

The *Appalachian* Trail crosses US 201 here, R to Pleasant Pond and L to Pierce Pond (*campsites*).

THE FORKS (alt. 576, The Forks Plantation, pop. 52), 54.2 *m.* (*picnic area*), is at a confluence of the Kennebec and Dead Rivers. During road construction in 1935, great quantities of red ocher were found in this vicinity in a pit revealed by blasting. A Kennebec canoe trip touches at The Forks (*see RECREATION*).

A road (R) leads to Lake Moxie, Moxie Falls and Mosquito Mt. (2230 ft.), 5 *m.*

At 57.2 *m.* an old tote road (L) (*unfit for cars*) goes to the popular hunting and fishing area of Spencer Stream, Spencer Lake and the Dead River region, 15.*m.*

At 66.1 *m.*, a foot trail Entrance Marker.

L on this trail to Fire Warden's house, 2.5 *m.* A steep trail from here leads to the *Fire Lookout Station (visitors)* on *Coburn Mt.* (3718 ft.). From the tower a great view of lakes and mountains N and W. Enchanted Pond and Stream are SW.

At 70 *m. Parlin Pond Camps*, largest in this area on the main route where accommodations are widely scattered. There is a roadside picnic area and across Parlin Pond E is William Mt. (2395 ft.).

At 76.8 *m.*, junction with State 6 and 15.

R on State 6-15 to Long Pond, 10 *m.* This route continues to Rockwood (*see Tour 4D*), at 31 *m.*

At 77.3 *m.*, US 201 passes over *Owl's Head Mt.* (2380 ft.).

JACKMAN (alt. 1170, Jackman Plantation, pop. 984), 78.4 *m.*, on the shore of Wood Pond is a supply center for hunters and for the lumber industry, and has a popular ski area 12 *m.* S at *Enchanted Mt.* Also a canoe trip terminal, Jackman has an airfield, hotels, motels, cabins, restaurants and other services. SW is Attean Lake and Mt. (2442 ft.).

The U.S. *Immigration Station here must be visited by every person entering from Canada.*

Continuing on US 201 toward the Boundary, MOOSE RIVER (alt. 1170, Moose River Plantation, pop. 205), 81.7 *m.* The Holden House here, built in 1842 has been for many years operated by descendants of first settler Capt. Samuel Holden who arrived in 1820. The inn was a stop for cattle drivers enroute from Boston to Quebec. Lumber operations some distance from the highway are less extensive than formerly.

Once operating in these regions were the rugged, lusty lumberjacks who were supposed to 'sleep in trees and even eat hay if sprinkled with whiskey.' These were the woodsmen who never took off their red flannels from the time they hit camp in the fall until they came out in spring; who never shaved; who chewed great hunks of tobacco, could spit 15 feet into a head wind and hit the mark, and roll off a hair-raising stream of profanity.

Horse-play, stunts, story-telling and singing of such chanteys as 'Little Brown Bull' constituted the social life of the old boys who sometimes worked in the snow to their armpits and who could stand upright on a rolling log in midstream as few can today.

Each spring the lumberjacks left camp and swaggered into the quiet villages to show the outside world what he-men were. They yelled for strong liquor and swore they'd leave no maid along the Kennebec. There were fights a-plenty, gory and bloody; when a man wore the imprints of a lumberjack's calked shoes, he was marked for life as a fighter.

Real 'bean-hole beans' were important in the 'feed' of lumber camps. Pots full of pork and beans were kept all night over rocks placed in the ground and brought to white heat. These were eaten with biscuits made by the camp cook or cookee who rose or fell on the quality of his output.

The days of pioneer adventure are long gone in the lumber industry, today highly organized and mechanized. Most of the great log drives have ended and with them the keen spirit of competition among river-drivers who once prided themselves on their strength, speed and agility in following the drives down the rivers and untangling the jams. Crawling across the logs in their calked boots until the key log was found and loosened and then making their way back to shore as the logs started again was no feat for the timid.

Lumberjacks now live with the amenities of the times. The camps, formerly as barren of femininity as a man-of-war, now furnish homes suitable for women and children and family life. But the challenge is gone and many no longer want to work in the woods.

At 85.9 *m.*, *U. S. Customs Office (all cars entering from Canada must stop for inspection*). From here is the northernmost view of the chain of lakes stretching through Jackman to Moosehead Lake.

Sandy Stream Mt. (2869 ft.) (L) enroute to the border at 95.9 *m.* where US 201 crosses the International Boundary, 93 *m.* SE of Quebec, Canada. In U.S. prohibition days, Line Houses here were popular resorts, liquor being served in the Canadian half of the buildings.

T O U R   4 F : *From* FARMINGTON *to* SUGARLOAF MT. *and* CANADIAN LINE, State 27, 75.6 *m.*

Via Kingfield, Carrabassett, Bigelow, Stratton, Eustis, Chain of Ponds and Coburn Gore.

TOUCHING Sugarloaf Mt. and environs, major inland recreation area, this tour along the historic Arnold Trail travels amid forests, mountains and streams of unsurpassed natural beauty to Chain of Ponds and Coburn Gore at the Canadian border. Portions of Tour 4F and Tour 4G may be combined for a loop tour by taking State 16 at Stratton S 19 *m.* to Rangeley (*see Tour 1G*) for return to Farmington on State 4.

State 27 leaves Farmington (*see Tour 4*) N at 0 *m.*

NEW VINEYARD (alt. 610, New Vineyard Town, pop. 357), 10.8 *m.*, a woodworking town that has four ponds in the lowlands of the NW section. Good fishing in the numerous small streams cutting through the surrounding wooded hills. Roads are shaded by the luxuriant foliage of towering trees whose bases are buried in deep masses of tall lacy ferns.

Many early settlers from the Kennebec River Valley came to this and other Franklin County towns when they were unable to meet sizable levies imposed by lawless land agents.

NEW PORTLAND (alt. 507, New Portland Town, pop. 620), 17 *m.*, is the center of a township given to the people of Falmouth (now Portland), by the General Court of Massachusetts to indemnify them in part for their loss through the destruction of Falmouth by the British fleet in 1775.

> *Wire Bridge* (1812), cable suspension thought to be the last of its kind in New England, was known as Colonel Morse's Fool Bridge. Col. F. B. Morse proposed the bridge when it was agreed that no conventional wooden bridge would withstand the freshets or average high water from the Carrabassett. Plans were made in 1838. The cable from Sheffield, England, was brought up the Kennebec River by schooner, then hauled here by 16 yoke of oxen.

KINGFIELD (alt. 565, Kingfield Town, pop. 864), 23 *m*., S on a narrow intervale in the valley of the Carrabassett River, rapid at this point, that created water power for several mills when lumbering was an important industry here. A boulder, opposite Universalist Church, marks the *Site of the Residence of Governor William King*, proprietor of this region and Maine's first governor. Kingfield is the birthplace of F. E. and F. O. Stanley (1849), twins who developed the Stanley Steamer. Chansonetta Emmons, their sister, became one of the first documentary photographers.

In the 1960s the ever-increasing air-pollution and noise from gas-engined vehicles on the nation's highways had not been remedied. In 1968, the Williams twins of Ambler, Pennsylvania had developed a steam-powered 100 mph roadster. But it was the Stanley twins of Kingfield, Maine, who in the 1890s first developed the steam automobile that on Jan. 28, 1906 clocked an official speed of 127.66 mph at Ormand Beach, Florida. No car weighing only 1800 lbs. ever has equalled this performance. A later trial clocked an unofficial speed of 190 mph — until the car hit a bump in the sand and rolled over into the sea.

The Stanley twins taught school briefly, were great whittlers, even to fashioning violins, and their inventive talents were soon evident. They invented and successfully manufactured a home generator for illuminating gas and the dry photographic plate which they manufactured themselves until Kodak brought out this Maine-born patent. One twin had a photographic studio in Lewiston for several years. The Stanleys also perfected early models of X-ray equipment.

In 1896 they built the first Stanley Steamer, a car faster, lighter and more dependable than any other, that gave a dazzling performance on hills. By 1899 they had produced their first 200 cars. It was headline news around the world when F. O. Stanley and his wife zoomed to the summit of Mt. Washington over dirt trails. The twins had a little racing blood, too, sometimes confounding the constabulary. When a local officer pulled one Stanley in for burning the road at 70 mph in his Steamer, he did a double take when he saw a duplicate whizzing by. The end came in 1918 when F. E. Stanley was killed. He drove into a pile of cordwood to avoid hitting two farm wagons travelling abreast on the highway. F. O. Stanley sold the business which closed in 1925.

At Kingfield, junction with State 16 (R) SE to North Anson (*see Tour 4E*), and with State 142 SW to Phillips (*see Tour 4G*). State 27 and State 16 are identical N.

CARRABASSETT (alt. 842, Unorganized Township of Jerusalem, pop. 11), 33.2 *m*., is no longer a lonely little timberland settlement by the river with a narrow-gauge railway passing through. Carrabassett Valley, with nearby Sugarloaf Mt., the State's largest ski resort, and abundant hunting and fishing, has become an important recreation center with the creation of vacation villages using new building techniques. In 1968 the Dead River Company was engaged in a long-range development of 5000 acres in the heartland of scenic Maine, similar to developments underway in other Maine wildland and coastal areas. The new housing involves a central core with varied modules attached, for comfortable and gracious vacation living in such 'villages' as Poplar Stream, Spring Farm and Redington

North. Along the highways are ski village homes — A-frames, chalets, cabins and camps. Wry comment on the development slogan, 'From here on — your life will never be the same,' was 'neither will Carrabassett Valley.'

At 38.5 *m.* entrance (L) to Sugarloaf Mt. Ski area (*see RECREATION*). The Appalachian Trail crosses here, going L to Sugarloaf Mt. (4237 ft.) and R to Bigelow Mt. (4150 ft.).

BIGELOW (alt. 1305, Unorganized Township of Crockertown, pop. 3), 38.7 *m.*, formerly Bigelow Station, was a terminus of the Sandy River and Rangeley Lakes narrow gauge RR. Crocker Mt. (4168 ft.) (L).

STRATTON (alt. 1170, pop. 666), 46.3 *m.* where Tall Timber Day is an annual summer event. Junction with State 16 along S branch of Dead River for Rangeley Lakes (*see Tour 4G*).

At 50.3 *m. Cathedral Pines* camping area (*May 15-Oct. 15; 100 campsites, trailer sites, boat ramp*), operated by the towns of Eustis and Stratton.

This 300-acre plot of red pines on Flagstaff Lake amid spectacular scenery is part of a tract known as Cathedral Pines, a beautiful stand of Norway pine covering several square miles on both sides of the road; N end of the grove is the site of one of Benedict Arnold's camps during his ill-fated Quebec expedition in 1775. *Flagstaff Lake*, 1150 ft. above sea level covers the site of a town that was flooded out when Long Falls dam was constructed. Bigelow Mt., named for Maj. Timothy Bigelow of Arnold's Army, is seen directly across the lake. The campsites are spaced for privacy with beach and playground for children. There is a beach and picnic area separate from the camping area; special area for groups campers such as Boy Scouts; and a recreation building.

The State has erected interpretive panels depicting Arnold's trials in this area. The expedition led by Arnold was a quixotic project of the early days of the Revolutionary War. A few of the Colonial leaders believed that the French of Quebec, who had been under English rule since 1763, would be eager to join the revolt against the Crown; it was decided that Arnold should take 1100 men up through Maine and meet a force of equal size led by General Richard Montgomery, who would go north by way of Lake Champlain. Arnold and his men, who were poorly equipped and hastily assembled with little training, left Cambridge on September 13, 1775, and six days later had entered the Kennebec, Arnold planning to follow a route that had been explored and reported on by English officials. Progress up the river was slow, because of the time required to construct the boats necessary for the shallower waters, and the autumn rains had begun; many of the men became ill and had to be left behind. On October 19, the diminishing band finally reached Eustis. From there they went up the northern branch of Dead River; on the 23d they lost several scowloads of provisions, which sank in the river. The weather increased in severity and many of the undisciplined Revolutionary heroes decided that they would go no farther. Arnold crossed the present international boundary line on October 25, and after the stragglers caught up with him, went down the Chaudiere River. When Montgomery and Arnold met near Quebec, the former had 500 men left, the latter 510. The attack took place during a December snowstorm, and, though the troops entered the town, they were driven out with heavy losses; Montgomery was killed and Arnold was wounded.

At 51.7 *m.*, road junction.

> L on this road to *Eustis Ridge* (2040 ft.), 2 *m.* for a splendid view of the
> mountains, including Sugarloaf.

EUSTIS (alt. 1185, Eustis Town, pop. 666), 54.1 *m.*, a wooded village;
beyond, campsites (L).

At 58.1 *m.* is *Alder Stream Site* (R) where Arnold lost supplies.

At 62.8 *m.*, *Sarampas Falls Site* (R) is the most northerly of a series of
State sites with Arnold interpretive panels. It is in a birch grove near a
pebbly beach on Sarampas Stream about 200 yards above the small falls
mentioned in Arnold's letters.

The route now crosses the S boundary of CHAIN OF PONDS TOWN-
SHIP. Silvery birch and glossy green maple stand out among the dense
evergreens here, and occasional ponds, traversed by Arnold, gleam through
the silent darkly green wilderness.

> Campers, canoeists and fishermen who annually use the mountain-ringed lakes
> here have a group of sportsmen and conservationists to thank for restoration of
> conditions that had deteriorated around Chain of Ponds. Before State 27 was
> rebuilt in the 1940s, a dam was part of the bridge spanning the outlet of
> Chain of Ponds and marking the beginning of the N branch of Dead River.
> Once abandoned as part of the bridge, the old dam deteriorated and in 1957
> washed away, leaving behind an unsightly shoreline and a mere trickle at low
> water periods.
>
> In 1968 the dam was rebuilt with funds, labor and material donated by
> Canadians as well as Americans to the group undertaking the project, to which
> teenagers gave a boost on weekends. The Central Maine Power Company,
> owners of riparian rights on Dead River, approved the project and the Brown
> Company gave gravel and lumber. The dam's main spillway measures 104 ft.
> and assures constant water level for sportsmen. The water level at the dam
> was raised 4 ft. and nearly 2 ft. at Round and Natanis Ponds, most northerly
> of the chain. The Eustis-Stratton Chamber of Commerce undertook main-
> tenance costs.

At 63 *m.*, deposits of broken slate (L) on the side of Bag Pond Mt. resemble great piles of bituminous coal.

At 63.5 *m.*, a watershed ridge (1360 ft.) where the road widens through a
beautiful growth of white birch. The highway now cuts into the ledge (R)
of Mt. Pisgah and Mt. Sisk about 5 *m.* limiting the outlook to forest and
rough ledges with an occasional magnificent view (L) across deep gorges
to Chain of Ponds shimmering against the wild rugged background of Round,
Snow, Indian Stream and Bag Pond Mountains.

At 68.8 *m.* looking back through the highway aisle, a view of towering
Mt. Pisgah (3325 ft.).

COBURN GORE (alt. 1400, Unorganized Township, pop. 50), 75.6 *m.*, an apparent extension of Arnold Pond and known to many outdoorsmen as Moosehorn, is a sub-station of the Holeb-Jackman port of entry on the boundary that follows the watershed of a low range of mountains whose green-mantled slopes stretch mile upon mile in either direction. Near Arnold Pond, Arnold's expedition crossed the height of land. In 1968 the State of Maine erected interpretive panels welcoming its Canadian neighbors and depicting scenes of the march.

State 4 here crosses the Canadian Boundary, 137 *m.* S of Quebec.

T O U R   4 G : *From* FARMINGTON *to* RANGELEY LAKES and N. H. LINE, State 4 and State 16, 79 *m.*

Via Strong, Phillips, Madrid, Rangeley, Oquossoc, Wilson's Mills.

THIS route, delighting camera enthusiasts, encompasses the well-known Rangeley Lakes Region, long famous for its fishing and hunting and now a popular recreation area for skiers, mountain climbers, rock hunters and boatmen.

State 4 leaves Farmington (*see Tour 4*) 0 *m.*

At 8.6 *m.*, *Birthplace of Elizabeth Akers Allen*, identifiable by a gazebo. In the Victorian summer house Mrs. Allen (1832-1911), newspaper woman and author, did much of her writing in later years. She was thrice married, her second husband being Sculptor Benjamin Paul Akers (*see THE ARTS*).

STRONG (alt. 505, Strong Town, pop. 976), 11.8 *m.*, village (R). Maine's Republican party was founded in this town Aug. 7, 1854 with temperance and opposition to slavery the two specific planks in its platform. Outside Strong, a picnic area (R).

Continuing along the Sandy River W through Avon to

PHILLIPS (alt. 550, Phillips Town, pop. 1050), 19 *m.*, on the river bank, surrounded by wooded hills and many streams in the heart of hunting and fishing country. Shoes, pulp and lumber are the industries here where settlers cleared and farmed the land as big lumbering gradually moved northward. Phillips was headquarters for the narrow-gauge Sandy River-Rangeley Lakes RR that transported people and forest products to and from the North Country. The Sandy River Historical Society and Library has exhibits of railroad relics in the *Ella Vose House.*

Phillips has a three-day Old Home celebration in summer and a town fair with horse shows and horse-pulling events in the fall. Beautiful blankets and yarns are made in a one-man woolen mill. There is a large Fish Hatchery here and rock-hunters favor the hills with their silica deposits throughout the township.

Another area point of interest is *Daggett's Rock*, one of the world's great transported boulders, a 100-ft. granite mass in a cathedral-like setting of trees *(picnicking)*.

Just beyond Phillips, junction with State 142.

L on State 142 to *Mt. Blue State Park (camping, swimming, fishing)*, 10 *m.* Conservation programs are held here. A drive up Center Hill offers a fine view and there are hiking trails for climbers of Mt. Blue (3185 ft.) and Mt. Tumbledown.

State 142 continues S to join US 2 at Dixfield *(see Tour 4)*, at 20 *m.*

MADRID (alt. 845, Madrid Town, pop. 108), 25.6 *m.*, small village on the fast-flowing W branch of Sandy River, is pronounced *Ma* -drid.

R from village center in Chandler Mill stream is lovely *Small's Falls (picnic area)*. A few hundred feet away in Sandy River just before its junction with the Mill stream is another series of cataracts.

At 31.5 *m.* the Appalachian Trail crosses R into the Saddleback Mt. ski area *(see RECREATION);* 4 *m.* to *Forest Lookout* at the summit (4116 ft.).

At 33.5 *m.*, road L to Rangeley Lakes State Park *(see below)*.

RANGELEY (alt. 1545, Rangeley Town, pop. 1087), 39.1 *m.* *(hotels, lodges, camps, guides, boats, golf, water skiing, seaplane base)*, center of the Rangeley Region summer and winter sports area, lies deep in the heart of a forest region that reaches across the Canadian border. Within a radius of 10 *m.*, 40 sparkling lakes and ponds (trout and salmon) lie between rugged evergreen-clad hills and mountains, natural habitat of wild game.

Rangeley Township, the village, the broad lake, and even the adjacent countryside, the Rangeley Region, received their name from Squire James Rangeley, an Englishman from Yorkshire. Soon after his arrival here in 1825, he began the establishment of a great estate patterned after those of his homeland. He asked no price for his land, giving extensively of his acres to new settlers. He built a sawmill and a gristmill and constructed a ten-mile stretch of road through the wilderness to connect the settlement (and its great product, lumber) with the outside world. While developing his holdings, he made his home at Portland, where he had built a mansion on State Street, the city's 'Gold Coast' *(see PORTLAND)*.

A local road from the village leads N to Loon and Kennebago Lakes; East Kennebago Mt. (3825 ft.) (R).

At Rangeley, Junction with State 16.

R on State 16 NE along S branch of Dead River to DALLAS (Dallas Plantation, pop. 211), 4 *m.* (*Cold Spring campgrounds*). Road to Saddleback ski area
runs through this plantation in the NE corner of Franklin County. From *Dallas
Hill,* a view of Rangeley and Mooselucmeguntic Lakes, Haley and Gull Ponds,
Saddleback, Spotted, Bald, Aziscohos, Big and Little Bigelow Mts. Saddleback
Lake is a headwater of the Dead River. One of a network of narrow
gauge railroads once ran through here; trains hauled by miniature locomotives
stopped at every cowpath and could pull 100 cars of lumber.

State 16 continues NE to Stratton (*see Tour 4F*), at 19 *m.*

From Rangeley, State 4 and State 16 W are identical. At 41.6 *m.*, road
L to *Country Club* and nearby *Riding Academy.* At 42.6 *m., Mingo
Springs Golf Course.* The 13-*m.* route skirts four of the six Rangeley
Lakes — Mooselucmeguntic, 7 *m.*, Rangeley, Molechunkamunk and Cup-
suptic.

OQUOSSOC (alt. 1510, Rangeley Town), 46.1 *m.*, was the headquarters
of the dog-sled postal service maintained in winter when many roads
were otherwise impassable. Thrice weekly the team of Baffin Land
huskies mushed through the woods carrying mail to Kennebago and Grant's.
Only 100 people were served but average cargoes weighed 400-500
lbs. because of parcel post merchandise.

At Oquossoc, junction with State 17.

S on State 17 to *Rangeley Lakes State Park (camping, boating, fishing, swimming, water skiing),* amid beautiful scenery.

State 4 bears L and ends 1.2 *m.* at HAINE'S LANDING (alt. 1490,
Rangeley Town). Inquire at marina for boat service to other lake settlements.

State 16 continues NW to road junction, 51 *m.*

R on this road to Cupsuptic River and West Kennebago Mt. (3705 ft.).
L on this road to Pleasant Island campsites.

State 16 soons bends sharply, (*campsite*) travelling SSW past Upper Richardson Lake then winding NW to

WILSON'S MILLS, 72 *m. Campsite* N on Aziscohos Lake; Aziscohos Mt.
(3215) stands S. The *Bennet Covered Bridge* (1901) over Magalloway
River is 1.5 *m.* S in Lincoln Plantation.

From Wilson's Mills, State 16 goes SSW crossing the New Hampshire
border at 79 *m.*, to Errol, N. H., another 8 *m.*

TOUR 5: *From* BANGOR *to* CALAIS, 87.5 *m.*, State 9, The Airline.

Via Eddington, Clifton, Amherst, Aurora, Beddington, Wesley, Crawford and Alexander.

THE Airline, so-called because it cuts cross-county, Penobscot, Hancock and Washington, perhaps has the most colorful history of all the main arteries of Nineteenth century Maine travel. Most direct route between Bangor and Calais, it passes through a sparsely settled agricultural region, blueberry plains and the hunting and fishing territory of the forest and winding streams. Originally planned in 1838-39 as a military road during the Aroostook War (*see HISTORY*) to speed soldiers to the border through the wilderness, it remained unfinished for more than 20 years after the boundary dispute was settled. Little more than a dirt lane, it was opened as a mail route in 1857 when Calais citizens became dissatisfied with the mail service over the highway along the shore. It was improved for use of stages and from the beginning was a likely subject for romantic tales and legends.

George Sprott opened a stage route in competition with the already established Shore Stages. He apportioned 36 horses, the stages to travel between Bangor and Calais six times a week, leaving Bangor daily except Sunday, 9:30 p. m., arrive Calais next day at 3:30 p. m.; leave Calais daily except Sunday, at 12 noon, arrive Bangor next day at 6 a. m. The first trip was made with one passenger and 15 pounds of mail.

The obvious hardships of all-night travel through great distances of wild unsettled territory seemed prime arguments made to order for the competing Shore Line stage proprietors. The competition was keen. The new stage route was nearly 60 miles shorter and one day quicker.

The Shore Line proprietors designed a woodcut in 1860 showing an Airline stage being attacked by wolves, hoping to persuade timid travelers to take *their* stage. The woodcut occupied nearly half the front page of *Gleason's Pictorial,* leading New York illustrated newspaper of the day. The Shore Line's plan boomeranged. The picture aroused so much interest that the Airline Stage became well known and adventurous travellers took it just for the chance to shoot wolves. George Sprott bought the woodcut for $20 and used it in all his advertising and for a time the Airline was known as the 'Wolf Route.'

The Airline was discontinued in 1887 after 30 years of operation, when steamboat service came in. The latter could carry the mail cheaper and was more comfortable for passengers.

State 9 leaves Brewer, across the Penobscot from Bangor (*see BANGOR*) 0 *m.*

BREWER (alt. 40, pop. 9009) was named for Col. John Brewer, first postmaster. Wooden ships were built here, the economy later depending upon the pulp and paper industry.

> *Joshua Chamberlain House (private)*, 80 Chamberlain St. was the home of the General who served his state as Governor (1867-71) and Bowdoin College as president (1871-83). He was noted for his gallantry during the Civil War, received the Congressional Medal of Honor for his part in the defense of Little Round Top at Gettysburg and reviewed and received the arms and colors of the Confederate Army. Chamberlain memorabilia may be seen at the Brewer Library and at the Pejepscot Historical Society Museum in Brunswick.

S of Brewer 5 *m.* on State 15 is a *Cattle Pound* at Orrington.

EDDINGTON (alt. 50, Eddington Town, pop. 958), 4 *m.*, a small farming community on the E bank of the Penobscot, has tourist accommodations. The granite shaft facing the river is a *Memorial to Jonathan Eddy* for whom the town was named. He was a captain in the French and Indian Wars, a colonel during the Revolutionary War, and the first magistrate appointed along the Penobscot River. The river banks in this vicinity have yielded ocher deposits.

> In the days before modern refrigeration, inhabitants of inland villages like Eddington made several trips to the coast for barrels of sand and quantities of clams. A hole was dug in the dirt cellar, then filled with sand in which the clams were buried. The sand was kept wet so the clams would stay alive for use in the cold months. One old sea captain is said to have used the clams as rat-catchers; he said he often went to the cellar and found a rat struggling against a clam that had closed its shell in a tenacious grip on the rat's tail.

State 9 swings E at Eddington.

CLIFTON (alt. 155, Clifton Town, pop. 227), 12.3 *m.* The town's hills are composed of 'puddle rocks' or pudding stone, in which stones of many colors and shapes are held together as a conglomerate. In the town is one of the State's largest modern sawmills. Road L to *Chemo Lake (canoeing, fishing)* .7 *m.*

At 16.3 *m.* picnic site (R) and at 18.3 *m.* Peaked Mt. (1200 ft.) (*Forest Lookout*) (L).

AMHERST (alt. 30, Amherst Town, pop. 168), 23.5 *m.*, a small farming community.

AURORA (alt. 315, Aurora Town, pop. 75), 25.6 *m.* Hunters and fishermen now use the *Village Inn*, former stagecoach stop.

> Increasing the popularity of the Airline Stage in the Nineteenth century were tales of robbers bold. Wesley and Hardwood Hills are said to have been the scene of many attacks by highwaymen because the hills were so steep the horses could not outrun the robbers. One passenger who had been relieved of his watch and chain is said to have retrieved them months later in Boston where he came upon the miscreant and hit him over the head with his cane. Most of the lumber sawed in Ellsworth was cut north of the Airline but lumbering

declined and railroads never reached Aurora. In 1878 Samuel Wasson wrote that Amherst and Aurora 'have reached the cycle of years when farming is to be a paying pursuit.'

At 26.6 *m.*, a road L goes 6 *m.* to *Great Pond* (*sporting camps, hunting, fishing*).

Between 28 *m.* and 30.3 *m.* State 9 passes over the *Whale Back*, an alluvial ridge with 250-ft. elevation. Vast tracts of woodland stretch along either side and in fine weather, Mt. Katahdin 80 *m.* NW, may be seen. In this area, the white flags of startled deer are often seen as they hurdle mossy logs to disappear into the dim forest. Occasionally, especially on crisp evenings, the long bellow of a bull moose echoes over the timberlands and the staccato barking of the fox breaks the stillness.

At 40.4 *m.*, junction with State 193

> R on State 193 about 3 *m.* to *Beaver Colonies* and *Dams* on the W branch of the Narraguagus River. The broad-tailed, silky-furred workers are rarely seen now in this region, but the large dam and several sub-dams they constructed still hold back the river waters over a considerable area, while cleverly built mounds appear like miniature brown igloos projecting from the water.

> State 193 continues S through Deblois (*airfield*) to Cherryfield (*see Tour 1, sec. d*) at 3 *m.*

At 41 *m.*, a well-marked trail.

> Left on this trail about 1 *m.* to Lead Mt. (1475 ft.) (*Forest Lookout Station*). An old story tells of veins of gold believed to run through the mountain. It is said that an Indian often visited nearby settlements offering nuggets of gold in exchange for a drink of rum. Rumor spread that he got it from a hole in the mountain. Finally, a settler plied the Indian with enough rum to extract the story of a huge cave filled with the nuggets, and the promise to lead him there. It is said the two men left the settlement, but the white man never returned.

At 41.2 *m.* the route crosses a bridge over the Narraguagus River, scene of many spring log drives.

BEDDINGTON (alt. 530, Beddington, Town, pop. 19), 42 *m.* A famous passenger on the Airline Stagecoach was Jefferson Davis. In 1858, three years before he became President of the Confederate States, he took the stage from Bangor to Beddington, staying at the Old Schoppe House, now the post office, while visiting with Alexander Bache, great grandson of Benjamin Franklin and then a U. S. Senator. Bache had been at West Point with Davis and was with the U. S. Coast Survey Service, running a base line between Deblois and Columbia. His surveying station was on Lead Mt. from which the coast was triangulated. There is a legend that Davis left a small chest at the Schoppe House, instructing that it be delivered to a man who would give a certain sign. In the fall a stranger came and was given the chest when he made the requisite sign. It was believed the chest contained Civil War documents.

VACATIONLAND

MAINE, the state for all seasons.

THE SWIMMER

LOWER TOGUE POND,
BAXTER PARK

SHOOTING THE RAPIDS, SAGUENAY RIVER

BRADBURY MOUNTAIN STATE PARK, YARMOUTH

PRINCE OF FUNDY FERRY, PORTLAND

CONCENTRATION

THE **BLUENOSE** FERRY, BAR HARBOR

MONHEGAN YACHT RACES

CAMDEN WINDJAMMER

GRAND PRIX

GOLF AT RANGELEY

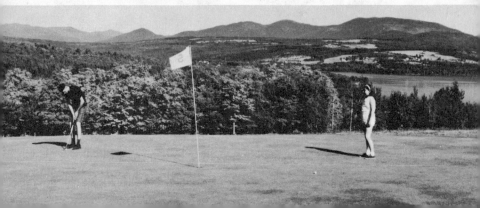

HUNTSMAN'S PRIZE?

MALLARD DUCKS AT MERRYMEETING BAY

PLAYFUL CUBS,
NOT TEDDY BEARS

COW MOOSE AND YOUNG

THE RASCALLY
RACCOON

SWAN ISLAND GAME SANCTUARY

SLED-DOG RACING

PLEASANT MT. SKI CHALET

SKI TRAILS

THE FOX HUNT

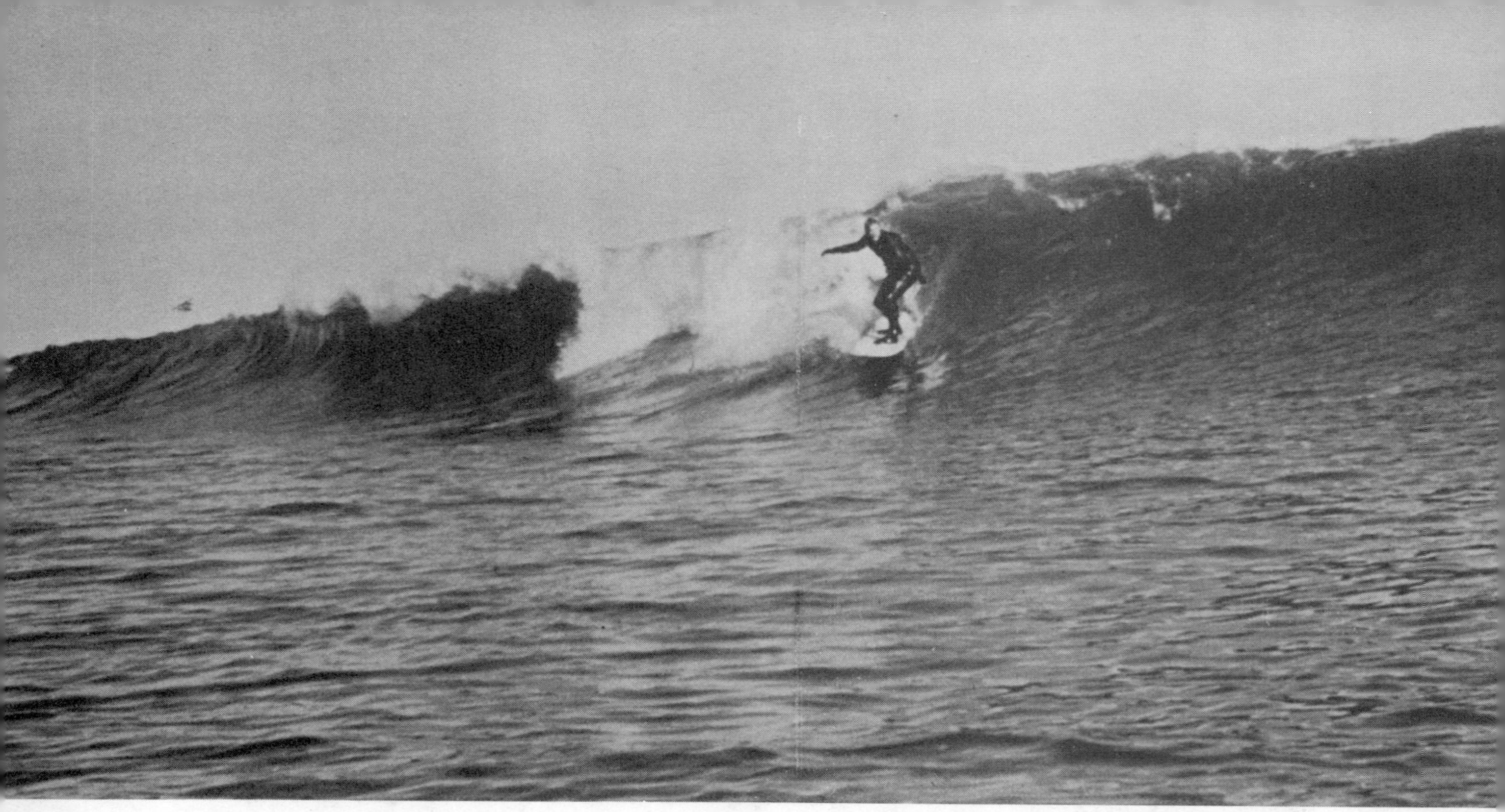

THE SURFER

At 50 *m.*, entrance to a foot trail.

> Left, the trail provides a stiff climb of about a mile to the top of another *Peaked Mt.* (938 ft.) to the *Forest Lookout Station* for a view over the vast blueberry barrens (*see Tour 1, sec. d*).

At 54.3 *m.* a bridge crosses the Machias River, once famous for its log drives (*campsite, picnic area*). The State Fish and Game Department has quarters here.

WESLEY (Wesley Town, pop. 145), 65 *m.* is on a high hill amid extensive blueberry barrens. The *Forest Lookout Station* on nearby Wesley Mt. (540 Ft.), overlooks great wooded areas with Eastport, 32 *m.* away, visible on a clear day.

> There are other stories of Wesley Hill besides those of stagecoach robberies. One is that during the Civil War three Federal recruiting officers were murdered here while trying to enforce draft requirements. Other stories are of prohibition days when rum-runners in high-powered trucks brought contraband liquors from the Canadian border; clashes with revenue officers were frequent.

At Wesley, junction R with State 192 past Bag Lake and Northfield to Machias, about 20 *m.*

At 69.8 *m.*, picnic site and road L to Clifford Lake (*campsite*), Pocomoonshine Lake and Mt. (605 ft.), Big Lake, then at 25 *m.*, joining US 1 at Princeton (*see Tour 1, sec. e*).

At 72.4 *m.*, local road junction.

> Right on this road to *Love Lake* .7 *m.* surrounded by birch-clad hills. Water lilies grow in profusion here, many of the coves being likened to scenes portrayed by Monet. There are several small waterfalls in the streams that empty into the lake; Seavey Brook W tumbles over a series of rocks, forming rapids. Scenery and occasional wild game offer unusual opportunities to photographers.

CRAWFORD (Crawford Town, pop. 80), 75.4 *m.* is a former center of extensive lumber operations. The Airline Stage got its widely advertised name as the Wolf Route from tales told of these towns along the route. It was said that when deep snow impeded the progress of the coach, packs of wolves charged along the wheel tracks and were warded off only by the alertness of the drivers and the quick cocking and firing of hand-loaded and primed guns.

> At *Crawford Lake* (L) (*fishing and swimming*), is *Cedar Cove* on the E shore where perpendicular cliffs rise high above the waters. Says a local guide: 'The cliffs out there are a high eyeful and only the Devil knows how deep.'

ALEXANDER (alt. 420,. Alexander Town, pop. 312), 79.7 *m.* overlooks Meddybemps Lake (R) which is 7 *m.* long, 3 *m.* wide and has 52 islands dotting its surface (*sporting camps*). Stagecoach drivers were glad to

reach this last stop for a change of horses before reaching Calais on the run
from Bangor. Drivers necessarily were a hardy lot. It was a difficult and
dangerous job driving the 93 miles in 18 hours; horses were changed
six times. Drivers were highly esteemed and had absolute authority over
the stagecoach on the road. It is said that once when a passenger demanded a stop for sustenance before the appointed way station, the
driver retorted, 'Don't tell me what to do; when I drive this coach I'm
the whole United States of America.'

A road S from Alexander goes 12 *m.* to Cooper Hill (720 ft.) (*Forest
Lookout Station*) and Cathance Lake (*campsite*).

At 88.6 *m.* State 9 joins US 1 (*see Tour 1 sec. e*) 6.9 *m.* SW of Calais.
R on US 1 to Baring and Moosehorn Wildlife Refuge, 2 *m.*

T O U R   6 : *From* LEWISTON or PORTLAND *to* MT.
WASHINGTON NATIONAL FOREST (Loop), 130.9 *m.*, Maine
Turnpike, State 26-118-35-5 and US 302 (The Roosevelt Trail).

Via Gray, Sabbathday Lake, Poland Spring, Norway-Paris, Waterford, Lovell, Kezar
Lake, Fryeburg, Bridgton, Naples, Sebago Lake, N. Windham.

FROM Portland or Lewiston, 17 *m.* on the Maine Turnpike to Gray, Exit
11. Closely following trails blazed by trappers and Indians between
Canada and southern Maine, this inland route swings through the beautiful mountain and lake counties of Androscoggin and Oxford, westerly to
the foothills of the White Mts., then southeasterly along an almost un-
broken chain of lakes to Cumberland county. In summer the dark
forests form a deep border around rich green fertile farmlands and historic
villages. In the crisp days of autumn, the flaming reds and golds of the
hardwoods in spectacular display bring many Fall Foliage tours. Several
popular resort areas prolong their seasons for this, and there also are
winter sports centers.

GRAY (alt. 310, Gray Town, pop. 2184), 17 *m.* Gladioli and other
flower farms are among agricultural pursuits here where Samuel Mayhall
erected one of the country's first woolen mills ca. 1770. The high school
(R) on Main St. was formerly Pennell Institute (1879).

At 4.1 *m.* N on US 202 a road (R) leads to 260-acre *Opportunity Farm* (1912),
1 *m.*, a boys' school supported by public subscription.

At Gray, L on State 26.

DRY MILLS (alt. 300, Gray Town), 20.1 *m.*

Road R 1 *m.* to *State Fish Hatchery and Game Farm (visitors).* In a long building with parallel troughs of 50-degree running water, millions of inland water fish are hatched to replenish Maine's fishing grounds. This is the largest of the Department of Inland Fish and Game's hatcheries which raise native landlocked salmon, brook and lake trout (togue), brown trout from Europe and rainbows from Washington and Montana eggs. Some varieties grow to good size — up to 30 lbs., for lake trout. The hatchery does its own fertilizing. Trays holding 4000-6000 eggs each are placed in the artificial streams to hatch — in about 50 days. Healthy young fish are taken to feeding stations to grow to stocking size. Lakes and streams are stocked in early spring and summer by truck and by aircraft.

At the adjoining 1300-acre Game Farm, thousands of ring-necked pheasants are bred from state-owned stock for release throughout the State as game birds at designated seasons (*see RECREATION*). Native to Asia, pheasants were once hunted with falcons and goshawks. The cocks are resplendent in colorful plumage. Other native animals may be seen at the Farm including an 800 lb., 6-ft. moose (1970).

SABBATHDAY LAKE (alt. 300, New Gloucester Town), 24.9 *m. Shaker Village and Museum (daily except Sun.).* The Shakers came to Maine in the 1700s, establishing communities here, at Alfred and Gorham. As their numbers declined in the latter half of the Nineteenth century, remaining members joined the Sabbathday Lake colony, established in 1793. Although only 12 Sisters remain, the Village pursues a serene way of life unique in modern times.

The Museum, containing fine examples of their furniture, agricultural and other inventions that became world-renowned, is in the Meetinghouse (1794), built in the classically simple style of an old Dutch home. The 10,300 bricks in the chimney were made in the Shaker brickyard; nails were handmade; woodwork is painted indigo blue. Formula for the paint, never retouched in more than 170 years and with no indication of flaking, has defied modern manufacturers who are unable to analyze it.

Shaker craftsmanship is distinguished for its ingenuity, simplicity and perfection of execution. Delmar Wilson, the Shakers' last great craftsman, died in 1961. In the Museum also are samples of the first waterproof cloth ever made; an iridescent linen and worsted material whose formula modern textile manufacturers have been unable to fathom; and spirit paintings, a spontaneous art form rarely to be seen. Their many inventions were patented by and made others famous. Among them, one of the first horse-drawn mowing-machines, the first circular saw, a vacuum pan for milk that made Mr. Borden famous, a plant press, and a tin distilling unit. In early times the Shakers treated the Indians honestly and cared for their sick and little ones. In return, the Indians taught them the lore of herb-healing and basketry. Shaker baskets used for measures were so accurate they were accepted in all commercial transactions. Their library contains the largest collection of Shaker material in the world.

The Shaker religion — 'hearts to God and hands to work' — based on principles of celibacy, united inheritance and confession of sin, originated among the Comisards of France ca. 1689, and was brought to America by Ann Lee in 1774. Believing in the separation from the 'spirit and element of the world' they do not vote, participate in civic matters or serve in the armed forces.

POLAND SPRING, 28.2 *m.*, still known around the world for its spring waters, was one of Maine's great resorts early in the Twentieth century. The complex included a large hotel commanding sweeping views of the countryside, the Mansion House and Riccar Inn, golf course, bridle paths, carriages and limousine service to and from the 'depot.' Many gala events were held at Poland Spring where national notables often fore-gathered.

The main House with its vast expanses of glass and encircling verandah, tower suites and ballrooms, was furnished with oriental rugs, paintings, fine furniture — and antique plumbing. Dining service had the ordered precision of the Rockettes, even to the white-gloved busboys. When changing times brought this gracious era to a close, the Mansion House closed after more than a century and a half and the main house became the nation's second largest Women's Job Corps (phased out 1969). A stone building on the property, once the Hotel Library, was the State of Maine building at the 1893 Chicago World Fair. Its historical and art works were disposed of at auction.

In 1794 Jabez Ricker of Alfred bought land here from the Shakers of Sab-bathday Lake and established a home; two days after the Ricker family arrived two travellers stopped at their door asking for breakfast. This was the be-ginning of Jabez Ricker's career as an innkeeper. So many travellers con-tinued to stop, asking for accommodations that in 1796 Jabez and Went-worth Ricker opened the Mansion House. The fine water of a nearby spring had no more than local fame until 1844 when Jabez Ricker's grandson, Hiram, drank copiously of the water while haying and was convinced that it had cured him of a chronic dyspepsia. The hotel had become quite a resort and guests began praising the drinking water. This being the period when the fashionable world of Europe and America were 'taking the waters' for all ail-ments of the flesh, the Rickers were soon successful in bottling Poland Water, still used in many parts of the world.

A modern inn nearby now maintains the scenic golf course and ski area.

Riccar Inn houses a television studio owned for a time by Jack Paar.

At 29 *m. Middle Range Pond* (pronounced *'rang'*), center of a group of five ponds (*boating, bathing, fishing*).

POLAND (alt. 310, Poland Town, pop. 1537), 30.8 *m.* spreads over 7 hills.

At 32.3 *m.* junction with State 11.

L on State 11 to *Tripp Pond* (*boating, bathing, fishing*), 1.6 *m.* Road R at 3.6 *m.* goes to West Poland boys and girls camps, and sharp L to *Agassiz Village* at S end of Thompson Lake, 2.3 *m.*, boys camp named for Dr. Louis Agassiz, scientist (1807-73).

R on State 11 to Mechanic Falls and Minot where William Ladd founded the American Peace Society (1828), continuing to Auburn (*see LEWISTON-AUBURN*), 13 *m.*

At 38.4 *m.*, Welchville, *Center Meetinghouse*, junction with State 121.

L on State 121 over the Little Androscoggin River to OXFORD (alt. 248, Oxford Town, pop. 1658), 1.5 *m.* on the N shore of Thompson Lake (*swimming, boating*). First settled in 1794, it soon had a woolen mill and Craigie's Tavern, popular in stagecoach days for its fine bar.

Oxford Plains stockcar racing here, began in the 1950s.

NORWAY (alt. 387, Norway Town, pop. 3733), 44.6 *m.*, on S end of Lake Pennesseewassee has a lively summer colony including artists and writers. A manufacturing town, it is known for its snowshoes. Oxford County's first regimental muster was held here and Norway has sent companies to every war, 3 to the War of 1812, 8 to the Civil War. Humorist Artemus Ward learned the printer's trade at the *Norway Advertiser-Democrat* in the village center, and Statesman Hannibal Hamlin as a lad was a chore-boy in the same office. Popular gathering place for cracker-barrel philosophers for many years was the Weary Club, founded by the paper's editor, Fred W. Sanborn. Artist Vivian Akers, Charles Asbury Stephens, writer of juvenile fiction, Novelist Hugh Pendexter and Don C. Seitz, a *New York World* editor, had homes in Norway. For his trip to the North Pole, Explorer Robert E. Peary had snowshoes made by Mellie Dunham of Norway, once chosen by Henry Ford as champion old-time fiddler.

The *Snocraft Factory* (1900) (*visitors*), one of only two such factories in New England, supplies various types of snow gear to dealers here and abroad. It makes 7 basic snowshoe models for sportsmen, trackers and woodsmen. Lumbermen prefer the chubby bear-paw model; Alaskans are for speed across snowy plains, and the Yukon for uphill climbing. The factory also makes ski-skates, folding sleds and children's side-walk skis. After decades of being regarded as 'old hat,' snowshoeing again is popular with outdoorsmen. The factory turned out all the high-grade skis, snowshoes and dog sleds for the Byrd and Peary Arctic expeditions and produced 70 percent of all the snowshoes required by the government in World War II.

The crafters cut 12-ft. boards of white ash into the various shaped models. In 24 hours, rough boards are cut, planed, formed, sanded, laced, lacquered and readied for wear. The cattle hide or neoprene lacings are knotted by hand.

Adjoining Norway is PARIS (alt. 385, Paris Town, pop. 3601) where in the residential section of *Paris Hill* are some of Maine's most architecturally interesting old homes. South Paris is the industrial center where skis, leather and textile goods are made and the former Burnham and Morrill Company, canners, have been sponsors of the annual Bean-hole Bean Festival. From 1895 to 1918, the Norway-Paris Street Railway connected the two towns, with Electra Park midway in a grove of pines; fare 5 cents, package deal including admission to the Park, 10 cents. Two open-air vehicles for summer and two closed ones for winter operated on 45-lb. T-rails and side brackets with overhead span-wire suspension. A raging blizzard in 1918 and the growing popularity of automobiles ended the trolley line.

Paris Hill Country Club (*tennis, golf; visitors*) usually is the starting place for the annual open house tour of old homes and gardens sponsored by Stephens Memorial Hospital.

In Courthouse Square, the Hamlin Memorial Library is the *Old Stone Jail* (1828), used as Oxford County jail until 1895. The ivy-covered thick-walled stone building is in its original form except for changes in the monitor roof and removal of cells. It has a heavy iron entrance door, grated windows and a 'solitary' cell with large iron key. Beyond the Library is the *Birthplace of Hannibal Hamlin* (1809-91), Maine's 23d governor, a U. S. Senator and vice president under Abraham Lincoln. The *Baptist Church* (1803) has a Revere bell.

The *Olde Academy* (1856) is headquarters for the Paris Hill Community Club (*art exhibits*). Now private dwellings are the *Old Court House*, the *Registry* with slate roof and iron doors, and the *Jailer's House* with Victorian parlor. The *Carter House* (1787), first frame house erected here, now has a Greek Revival entrance. *Old Brick*, a flat-roofed, three-story brick house with fanlighted door, once was occupied by Gen. William Kimball who commanded the first torpedo boat flotilla in the Spanish-American War. John P. Holland, inventor of the submarine, assured Kimball that the submarine was 'A subject that you must have credit for putting into practical shape and introducing.' The *Hubbard House* (1806), with flat roof and cupola, was for many years a well-known inn, now a private residence. *Lyonsden* (1808) was the home of Rear Admiral Henry W. Lyon, commander of the dispatch boat *DOLPHIO* in the Spanish-American War, and of his son, Capt. Harry Lyon, navigation officer of the *SOUTHERN CROSS* on the first transpacific flight in 1929. The lion's head over the door is the figurehead of the *NIPSIC*, first vessel commanded by the Admiral. *Stagecoach House* and *Cotswold* are among other interesting houses at Paris Hill.

Of interest to rock hunters are several mines in this vicinity where a wide variety of minerals may be found (*see RECREATION*).

R from Main St., S. Paris, about 3.5 *m.* to the Tamminen and Harvard quarries on Mt. Mica. NE on State 117 to the Bennet quarry; SE on State 119 to the Foster and Mt. Marie mines. State 26 continues N to *Snow Falls*, 6.2 *m.*, a 40-ft. gorge in the Little Androscoggin; to the *Maine Mineral Store* at West Paris, 8.4 *m.*, a museum of Maine gems on display and for sale; and NW through Bryant Pond to Bethel (*see Tour 4*), 25 *m.*

The New Pennacook Trail from Rumford down through these towns to Gray and Portland was the route used by early settlers in the 1700s. The Trail became a County road in 1795 and was among stagecoach routes in the area. Old maps show roads in what is now forest; some of the early homes built along these roads now are found back in the woods.

At Norway, this tour takes State 118 W.

WATERFORD (alt. 400, Waterford Town, pop. 874). Numerous boys and girls camps are located in this area; public camping grounds at Keoka Beach and Bear Mt. Village, S. Waterford. Orcharding, wood-turning and small business are the occupations.

Artemus Ward House, next to post office. In the *Public Library* are the Waterford Historical Society's collections of memorabilia pertaining to Artemus Ward, best remembered of Maine's Nineteenth century humorists who was born

Charles Farrar Brown here in 1834. He learned the printing trade, became a wandering printer and did some writing, later becoming known for his wit and humor in debating. Browne — the 'e' was added as he became famous — in 1858 created the character of Artemus Ward, an illiterate old showman who delighted newspaper readers with letters about his 'moral wax works, snaix and wild beests of pray.' He became editor of *Vanity Fair* and after it failed, turned to lecturing. Ward was a favorite of President Lincoln who often read excerpts of the humorist's works to soothe members of his Cabinet. On one of his trips to the West Coast, Ward met and greatly influenced Mark Twain who followed many of Ward's comic mannerisms in his own rise to fame. He was enthusiastically received in England where he died at 33 in 1867. He is buried at Elm Vale Cemetery in S. Waterford. A plaque honoring his memory was erected in Southampton on the 100th anniversary of his birth.

Pinehenge School is an ungraded school here based on the philosophy of A. S. Neill of England's Summerhill School and using much of the Leicestershire method of free or unstructured education.

From Waterford, NW on State 35 to N. Waterford (*picnic site; camping at Papoose Pond*), 60.4 *m.*, a station on the 238-*m.* Portland-Montreal oil pipeline.

LYNCHVILLE (alt. 555, Albany Town), 62.4 *m.* is at the SE corner of White Mt. National Forest. The *Bumpus Mine* nearby (feldspar) produced the world's largest beryl crystal (1930). Berylium, a white metal lighter and stronger than aluminum, is extracted from beryl.

From Lynchville, State 35 and State 5 N skirt White Mt. National Forest and proceed to Bethel (*see Tour 4*), 20 *m.*

This tour continues from Lynchville W on State 5.

EAST STONEHAM (Stoneham Town, pop. 180), 67.7 *m.* Most of this township is in the beautiful White Mt. National Forest and attracts many mountain climbers. Old Spec Mt. (2877 ft.) (*Forest Lookout Station*), Rattlesnake and Square Dock Mts. are seen W.

At Stoneham is the gravestone of native son William W. Durgin with these words: 'One of Abraham Lincoln's bearers and escort to Springfield, Illinois. Helped Place Remains in Tomb.' Durgin died in N. Lovell in 1929.

NORTH LOVELL (alt. 441, Lovell Town), 71.5 *m.* is a resort village at the head of Kezar Lake which parallels the highway S for 10 *m.* Road R around the N end of the lake and into the Forest.

CENTER LOVELL (alt. 530, Lovell Town), 75.7 *m.*

Road R 3 *m.* to a trail up E slope of *Sabattus Mt.* (1280 ft.), that appears to be one huge ledge of micaceous rock. The rough 1.5 *m.* trail is largely over the dried bed of a mountain brook. A perpendicular cliff on the W side may be scaled by way of the *Devil's Staircase*, a formation of 250 natural steps embedded in the mountainside.

Near S end of Kezar Lake, Country Club (*visitors*).

LOVELL village (alt. 439, Lovell Town, pop. 558), 81.1 *m.*, on an inter-vale amid forest-covered hills, is the trading center for this western Maine resort area. Among summer homes secluded around Kezar Lake is a lodge owned by Rudy Vallee, stage and screen star.

FRYEBURG (alt. 429, Fryeburg Town, pop. 1874), 91.8 *m.* (*summer and winter sports*), a beautiful old town on a plain in the Saco River Valley, was once the Indian settlement of Pequawket, home of Nescambious, only Indian knighted by the French. Nescambious became identified with the French Colonial Army under Gen. Iberville during the seige of Fort St. John in 1695. His leadership and fighting qualities and the desire of the French for an alliance with the Indians gained him an invitation to France in 1705. He was knighted by Louis XIV and returned to America a year later.

The Saco River rises in Crawford Notch and enters Maine at Fryeburg, travelling 84 *m.* to the sea.

A *Soldiers Monument* in Bradley Memorial Park is on the site of the first Fryeburg Academy (1791) where Daniel Webster was preceptor in 1802. The single building later burned. Today's Academy with several modern buildings is administered by a board of trustees and has a college preparatory summer school.

At the *Registry of Deeds* are Daniel Webster's carefully copied deeds which he did for 25 cents each to supplement his teacher's salary of $29 a month. Of his life in Fryeburg, the future statesman and orator wrote, 'Nothing here is unpleasant; there is a pretty little society; people treat me with kindness and I have the fortune to find myself in a very good family. I see little female company, but that is an item with which I can conveniently enough dispense.'

Webster resumed the study of law after leaving the Academy and his first case, the defense of a widow, was before his own father, Judge Ebenezer Webster. Becoming completely confused, he closed his case by addressing the court:

'Your Honor, I never should have taken this case. Only a good lawyer could have won it. My client owes the $15 but I shall pay the $15 myself be-cause I've failed the poor woman. The poor woman has toiled as no man in our hard working community has toiled. I'll pay it because it is unendurable that any woman should struggle as Mrs. Amhead has struggled and go down defeated by a mean man's cupidity.'

Defendant Moss shouted, 'Dang it! I don't want the money. All I want is an admission it was owed me. I'm satisfied, but you're the worst lawyer I ever heard, Dan Webster. All you have is a voice.'

Fryeburg Library, a stone building that once was a one-room school, has paintings, Lincoln memorabilia and mementoes of Clarence E. Mulford (1883-1956), author of the Hopalong Cassidy series.

First Congregational Church (1850) has a closed belfry and an entrance portico with fluted columns. Opp. the church, a boulder indicates where Arctic Explorer Robert E. Peary, once a Fryeburg resident, placed two Meridian Stones in 1883. The stones indicate true N, enabling surveyors to obtain the magnetic variation.

At the W. Fryeburg *Circus Farm* rare circus memorabilia may be seen.

Fryeburg's agricultural fair is held early in October when the fall foliage is at its best, enhancing the mountain scenery. Genre painter, J. Eastman Johnson (1804-1906), painted Fryeburg country scenes, including the maple sugar farms.

At Fryeburg, junction with US 302 and State 5. W on US 302 to Center Conway, N. H.; 6 *m*. S on State 5 to Cornish (*see Tour 7*), 21 *m*.

This tour continues E on US 302. Soon, road L to *Hemlock Covered Bridge* (1857), over an old channel of the Saco River. It is of Paddleford truss construction with supporting laminated wooden arches.

At 92.4 *m. Jockey Cap* (L), a 200-ft. boulder; trail to the top ends at a monument commemorating Admiral Peary's expedition to the North Pole.

At 93.8 *m.*, road L leads .3 *m*. to a boulder on N end of Lovewell Pond marking the site of Lovewell's Fight May 8, 1725 when a company of 25 Massachusetts Rangers under Capt. John Lovewell battled from dawn to dusk with 80 Pequawket Indians led by Chief Paugus. The Chief and Capt. Lovewell were killed and afterwards the Indians abandoned their seat at Pequawket and fled to Canada. Many camps are on the shores of Lovewell Pond. Brownfield Bog is a State Wildlife Management Area (waterfowl).

At 98.4 *m*. a road R leads to Pleasant Mt. (*Forest Lookout Station; skiing*).

The Fire Tower (*visitors*) on the summit, manned by a fire warden, has a glass-enclosed room permitting an unobstructed view for 30 *m*. with the naked eye, 75 *m*. with field glasses. It is difficult to count the numerous mountain peaks broken only by Kezar Lake N and six other lakes. SE the silver ribbon of Casco Bay unwinds. Temperature at the summit is 20 degrees below that at the base and the wind sweeps across the summit with a velocity close to 50 mph and sings as it strikes the steel framework of the tower rising 50 ft. into the air.

At 102.1 *m*. a long causeway crosses *Moose Pond* which extends as far as the eye can see on either side of the highway, with Pleasant Mt. looming high above the water.

BRIDGTON (alt. 360, Bridgton Town, pop. 2707), 107.8 *m*. is a trading center for this inland all-year resort region, with lovely old houses gracing the main street. The shopping center is on the site of the Pondicherry woolen mills that were named for a French province in India. Bridgton is musically inclined, has published its town history and has sponsored an historic pageant to commemorate its 200th anniversary (1968). Prima Donna Olivia Fremstad was among musicians of note who have summered at Bridgton.

The S tip of Highland Lake is within the village limits; a golf course here and a fine view after a short climb by car. The *Walter Hawkins House* (ca. 1770) (*private*) is at the foot of the lake.

L from Bridgton on State 117 to *Bridgton Academy* (1808), 3.6 *m.*, a co-ed college preparatory school of high standing. The *Spratt Museum (visitors)* on campus displays Indian artifacts, early American farm and home implements and other historical memorabilia and butterfly and mineral collections.

The Academy is in North Bridgton, a summer resort at the edge of Long Lake. At 5.8 *m.* in a neat little cemetery beside the road is the grave of Capt. John Haywood, hero of Bunker Hill, who as a private, seized the sword from the hand of his fallen captain, sprang upon the parapet and led his men in battle.

State 117 continues to HARRISON (*campsites; summer theatre*), 6.2 *m.* at the N end of Long Lake where boatmen may start a 30-*m.* trip through Songo Lock (*see below*). Snowmobile races are held here on 40 *m.* of trails.

At 114.8 *m.*, *Serenity Hill* (R) where dancing goes on in the barn of the old *Hayloft*, a house destroyed by fire on land given as a Revolutionary War bonus to a Private Hill, one of whose sons, Capt. Charles Hill, engaged in clipper ship trade in the Orient.

The story is told that the Captain and his men, on one of their trips to China, liberated several large idols from a Chinese temple and brought them home to Maine. When the heavy idols were found to contain gold, Capt. Hill's share amounted to about $300,000. With part of the money he added a fine house to the old homestead, using the old house as an ell. Chandeliers hung from decorative ceiling rosettes and a lovely balustrade and broad staircase decorated the front hall. Capt. Hill grew restless and once again set sail for the Far East. He was never seen again. It was conjectured that he returned to the temple where the priests recognized him and took their revenge.

NAPLES (alt. 280, Naples Town, pop. 735), 116.6 *m.* (*daily mailboat, seaplanes, water sports, golf*), early was a Maine resort town extolled by Longfellow, Hawthorne and Akers. Water skiing, skin-diving, power cruising, sailing and a country club have replaced the river steamers, canal boats, the famous Bay of Naples Inn and the King's Pines. Naples is identified with Sebago Lake and Songo Lock constructed ca. 1830 for passage of boats from Harrison down through the Oxford-Cumberland Canal to Portland Harbor. Via the original 28 locks, boats could pass through the rivers connecting Sebago and Long Lakes. In summer there are trips through the last remaining wooden lock in Maine (State-owned). Boat-owners can follow the old canal boat route from the headwaters of Long Lake at Harrison and 'lock through' for a unique 30-*m.* trip ending at White's Bridge on Sebago Lake. The Canal was built to replace arduous horse and oxen transportation. Hundreds of 65-ft. flat-bottomed vessels regularly plied the waters between 1830-50. The railroads then caused a steady decline; the last commercial vessel passed through in 1872 and only ditches remain of the canal below Sebago.

In earlier times, Naples people took their politics so seriously that the town was openly divided. Even the one-room school had two doors, one for children of Republicans, one for children of Democrats. The climax came when rabid parental feelings could only be satisfied by hiring two teachers. When Republicans erected a flagpole on the village green, Democrats erected another with fitting ceremonies. Today's voters are not quite evenly divided.

The Naples Historical Society maintains memorials and conducts historical tours. Preserved on the Lamb's Mill Road are *Millstones* used by the early millers. Also on this road, the *Barker Memorial Fountain,* once a watering trough for horses. A marker identifies *Edes Falls,* site of the first settlement. There are numerous local collections of Indian artifacts.

The *Manor* (1799) (*private*) built by first settler, George Pierce, was a hostelry in stagecoach days. It has brick ends, 24-paned windows, a sunrise door and four chimneys.

Perley Pines Park (*picnic area*) is part of a white pine forest that stretched to Bridgton. Some of these were marked in pre-Revolutionary Days with the King's broad arrow for masts for the Royal Navy. The logs were hauled down Skid Hill and rolled across the road through the field to Mast Cove on the shores of Long Lake to be loaded on freighters and carried to the coast. When the last of the King's Pines were cut off in the 1960s they were found to be hollow-hearted.

Seba Smith, Maine's most important contributor to American humor, recounted the exploits of the rough and ready men who made a festive occasion of cutting and loading the pine in this region. Born in 1792 in a log cabin in Buckfield, some 45 *m.* N of here, he later attended Bridgton Academy and Bowdoin College. He was an excellent student, mild in nature and inclined to oppose radical changes in the established order. He became assistant editor of the Portland *Argus* and married Elizabeth Oakes Prince of North Yarmouth, who became an author and America's first woman lyceum speaker. In 1829 Smith started the *Courier,* first daily newspaper north of Boston. Writing under the pseudonym of Major Jack Downing, he pioneered American political satire and became the forerunner of such homespun philosophers as Hosea Bigelow, Petroleum Naseby, Artemus Ward, Mr. Dooley and Will Rogers. The Downing letters became a hit country-wide and the 'Major' soon was on the national scene with advice on how to run the country. Plays and songbooks about Major Downing flourished. In the 1840s Smith produced a book, *My Thirty Years Out of the Senate* which included a collection of the Major's letters during his three decades on the national scene.

The Major's Washington sounds not unlike today's: 'Everybody seems to be running mad and jest ready to eat each other up. Here's Russia snappin her teeth like a great bear, and is jest agoing to eat up the Poles . . . And there's five great Powers trying to pour a healing dose down the throat of the King of Netherlands. In fact, all the Kings of Europe are trying to eat up the people, and the people are trying to eat up the Kings. These are dreadful times, Uncle; I don't know what will become of the world if I don't get an office pretty soon.'

At Naples, junction with State 11 which travels R down W side of Sebago Lake.

US 302 leaves Naples E over a hydraulic bridge spanning Chute River connecting Long Lake (L) and Brandy Pond (R) with a fine view of Mt. Washington and surrounding hills. Seaplanes and boats are wharfed along the causeway. Brandy Pond was so named when a keg of spirits fell overboard from a canal boat.

At 120.8 *m.*, road R into *Sebago Lake State Park* (*camping, fishing, boat launching and rentals*). Between the Park (*day use, swimming*) and the' Park Campgrounds is *Songo Lock* between Crooked and Songo Rivers. Just upriver is the hand-wound, manually-lowered turntable drawbridge.

SOUTH CASCO (alt. 310, Casco Town, pop. 947), 123.2 *m.* lies on a narrow strip of land between Thomas Pond E and Sebago Lake W.

R from S. Casco on Raymond Cape Road to a tall rock and shell formation W near the shores of Dingley Bay with its 14 islands. The various shaped shelves terminate in a large flat hood-like top shelf forming a cave where it is said a young girl was held prisoner by the Indians for three years until her family led an attack and rescued her.

At .4 *m* R is the *Manning House* (1810) (*private*) built by Richard Manning, an uncle of Nathaniel Hawthorne. A large two-story structure, it has eight massive fireplaces and a Christian or Witch door; the interior wallpaper is over 150 years old. The original window glass was imported from Belgium. Nathaniel visited here before the Hawthorne House (*see below*) was built, and Uncle Richard taught the budding genius the rudiments of mathematics, grammar and geography.

The road soon crosses a bridge over Dingley Brook separating the townships of Raymond and Casco. Road L continues along a 4 *m.* strip of wooded land to Raymond Cape at whose tip flint such as used by Indians in making their arrow and spearheads, skinning knives and tomahawks, has been found.

The *Hawthorne House* (1812) (*open for special events, summer*), a 2½ story barn-like structure controlled by a community association, was built by Richard Manning for his sister, Mrs. Hathorne, Nathaniel's mother, who lived here in seclusion after the death of her husband. As a boy, Nathaniel roamed the nearby hills, fished the streams and sat on the rocks in sunny spots engaged in his favorite pastime, reading. A close companion of these early days was William Symmes, a Negro boy about his age. They would listen together to the tales of the men who congregated in Manning's store.

Excerpts in Nathaniel's diary show his deep interest in all he heard: Captain Britton from Otisfield was in Uncle Richard's store today. Not long ago, Uncle brought here from Salem a new kind of potatoes called 'Long Reds.' Captain Britton had some for seed and Uncle asked how he liked them. He answered, 'They yield well, grow very long; one end is very poor, the other is good for nothing.' I laughed about it after he was gone, but Uncle looked sour, and said there was no wit in his answer and that the saying was stale. It was new to me and his way of saying it was very funny. Perhaps Uncle did not like to hear his favorite potato spoken of in that way, and if the Captain had praised it, he would have been called witty.

Another entry concerned a peddler named Dominicus Jordan who told ghost stories. Jordan became Dominicus Pike in Hawthorne's story, *Mr. Higginbotham's Catastrophe*. Nathaniel Hathorne added the 'w' to his surname the year he graduated from Bowdoin, 1825. He spent many vacations at this Raymond home and in later years wrote, 'I have visited many places called beautiful in Europe and the United States but have never seen the place that enchanted me like that flat rock from which I used to fish.'

At 2.2 *m.* in a wooded section of the Cape, two camps, Sebago Wohelo and Little Wohelo, are said to be among the first girls' camps to be opened in this country. The camps are operated by descendants of Luther Gulick and his wife, the founders. Mr. Gulick (1865-1918), pioneer in physical education, founded the child hygiene department of the Russell Sage Foundation and contributed much to the Young Men's Christian Association and the Boy Scouts of America; with James Naismith, he devised the game of basketball, and with Mrs. Gulick, founded the Campfire Girls organization.

At 4.6 *m.*, Camp Wawenock (*private*). Near the lakeshore, *Pulpit Rock*, a 7-ft. pentagonal boulder. Two natural steps lead to its smooth top from which Chief Polin is said to have addressed his tribe, the Rockameecooks. Nearby is *Frye's Leap*, a cliff high above Sebago Lake. Indian hunter Capt. Frye is said to have plunged from this cliff to escape pursuing Indians. Remaining in a cave beneath the cliff until nightfall, he then swam to the large island that today bears his name. Frye's Island is reached by auto ferry from Cape Raymond. The cave is the same in which the first chapter of *The Scarlet Letter* was penned by Hawthorne. On the steep face of these rocks are faint remains of paintings said by some to be the work of Indians. Others say they were part of an advertising stunt of this century to promote trips on a lake steamer (no longer in operation) and were in line with the 'Indian' who regularly emerged from the rocks to thrill passengers. Construction of a 'leisure living' development was halted in 1970 on Frye's Island when pollution threatened Sebago Lake, Portland's water supply.

RAYMOND (alt. 295, Raymond Town, pop. 732), 126.1 *m.* is on Jordan Bay of Sebago Lake with Panther Pond and Crescent Lake on its N boundaries. Little Sebago Lake E is reached from State 85. Industries are in electronics.

Neat homes line the village street off US 302. The *Coughlin House* (1765) (*private*) (R) has its original 6-panel doors, pumpkin pine floors and a wainscot made of a single board 27 in. wide and 13½ ft. long. A State Hatchery here hatches landlocked salmon. Television towers on Brown's Hill are the second highest in the U.S.

Sebago Lake (Ind.: stretch of water) is 14 *m.* long with maximum width of 11 *m.*, and is studded with several small islands. It is well known as the original home of landlocked salmon, salmo-sebago (*see RECREATION*), splendid fighters often weighing 8 lbs. Trout, bass, white perch, pickerel and cusk also are caught here; ice-fishing in winter. Many camps surround the Lake which provides Portland and surrounding towns with drinking water. Marinas for boatmen are found throughout the area.

At 130.8 *m.*, road junction.

> L on this road to *White's Bridge*, 1 *m.*, spanning the mouth of the Sebago Lake outlet. Here Chief Polin of the Rockameecook Tribe assembled his warriors for an attack on Old Province Fort (*see Tour 7*). Below the bridge (L) at the mouth of the Presumpscot River and below the present dam, the Indians had a dam. The Oxford-Cumberland Canal also was in this area.

> Indian artifacts in a large private collection here were discovered about .3 *m.* N on the shores of Lake Sebago in what is said to be one of the largest Indian burial grounds in the United States.

NORTH WINDHAM (alt. 300, Windham Town) 131.8 *m.* L here 8 *m.* on State 115 joining State 4 to Maine Turnpike, Gray Exit, 139.8 *m.* US 302 may be followed through Foster's Corner into Portland at Forest Avenue, 10 *m.*

T O U R   7 :   *From*   PORTLAND   *to*   PORTER   (N. H.   Line),
State 25, 42.8 *m.*

Via Westbrook, Gorham, Standish, Cornish and Kezar Falls.

LEAVING large industrial areas behind, the route runs W through well-wooded farming country, with stands of pine and birch and broad fields colorful with wildflowers in spring and summer.

State 25 leaves Portland at Maine Turnpike Exit 8. At Portland (*see PORTLAND*) are junctions with US 1 (*see Tour 1, sec. a*), US 302 and State 26 (*see Tour 6*).

WESTBROOK (city, alt. 85, pop. 13,820), 4.5 *m.*, has a large French-Canadian population mostly employed in the S. D. Warren Paper Company (1852) (*visitors*), one of the State's largest paper mills whose plant extends along a dam and on both sides of the Presumpscot River in the Cumberland Mills section. In 1969 efforts were under way to eliminate sulphurous odors emanating from the millstacks and permeating the countryside for many miles. Halidon on the N bank of the Presumpscot, was one of several single tax communities founded by paper manufacturer, Fiske Warren.

Once called Saccarappa, Westbrook Town was incorporated in 1814 when Westbrook and Deering were taken from the Town of Falmouth. Sculptor Benjamin Paul Akers was born here and orchestra leader Rudy Vallee lived here as a child when his father was local druggist.

GORHAM (alt. 220, Gorham Town, pop. 5767) (*golf, trotting races, horse show, skiing*), 10.5 *m.*, is the home of University of Maine-Gorham on Old Fort Hill, founded in 1805 as Gorham Academy and later becoming Western State Normal School. Its modified Tudor-style Russell Hall (1934) resembles an old fortress; modern architecture of new buildings blends with earlier styles. *Old Brick House* (1773), now a women's dormitory, was built of locally made brick by Hugh McLellan and his sons; wooden pegs and hand-wrought nails were used in the framework. Author Kate Douglas Wiggin (*see Tour 8*) was a student here. Offering liberal arts and teachers' courses, Gorham displays art in its campus buildings and is known for its music department.

First called Narragansett No. 7, Gorham was granted in 1728 to men who had fought in the Narragansett War in 1675, and their heirs. Capt. John Phinney and his son paddled up the Presumpscot River to make the first clearings on Fort Hill. Gorham's modern industries include a brick kiln and plating and anodizing plants. The Gorham Fair is held annually at Narragansett Park in August.

Baxter Museum (1808) (*summer, Wed.-Sat. afternoon and by appointment*) South St., was the home of Percival P. Baxter, Maine governor and philanthropist. It has Indian artifacts, a rare coin collection and mementoes of all U. S. wars. artifacts, a rare coin collection and mementoes of all U. S. wars.

At Gorham, junction with State 4 South (*see Tour 8*).

R on State 4 and US 202 N to SOUTH WINDHAM (alt. 155, Windham Town), 4.5 *m.*, which lies in two townships, the business and residential section in Gorham. The section in Windham Town (pop. 4498) was formerly an industrial center. The first mill was erected at Mallinson (Horseshoe) Falls soon after the Proprietors obtained rights in 1738. Scenic parts of the Cumberland-Oxford Canal tow path that once cut across Main St. still are discernible.

R on River Road, property of State Correction Center for Men (1919). At 2.6 *m.* (L), the *Parson Smith House* (1764) (*summer*), auspices of the Society for the Preservation of New England Antiquities. The 2½ story structure with fireplace in each room was built by Rev. Peter T. Smith whose fascinating diary was published after his death. His library and some furnishings are in the house. This property also is the Site of *Old Province Fort*. Settlers lived in its stockade almost constantly between 1744-51 due to Indian raids. On one occasion, Ezra Brown and Ephraim Winship, working with others at some distance from the fort, were fired on and scalped by Indians led by Chief Polin who in the ensuing skirmish was killed by Stephen Manchester.

Across from the Parson's House, the mausoleum in the Smith-Anderson Cemetery is said to closely resemble George Washington's tomb at Mt. Vernon.

L on River Road is Newhall .5 *m.* where at Gambo Falls a powder mill (1818) once stood. Traces of the Cumberland-Oxford Canal are seen along the Presumpscot River above the Falls. Upriver, near Leavitt's Falls, is *Babb's Covered Bridge* (1840), oldest of the 10 surviving in the State. Timbers of the old Kemp Locks of the canal are still standing a short distance S of the bridge.

At 7.7 *m.* on US 202 is *Friends Meetinghouse* (1849) (L). Preserved in the attic is a wooden windlass that once raised and lowered a wall partition to separate men from women during business sessions. Quakers began settling this area ca. 1774. At Windham Center, 8.5 *m.* US 202 crosses an old stage-coach road from Portland to Windham Hill and Great Falls. On the Hill, the frequently photographed *Congregational Church* (1835). US 202 continues to Foster's Corner rotary traffic circle at 9.6 *m.*, junction with US 302 (Roosevelt Trail) (*see Tour 6*).

STANDISH (alt. 415, Cumberland County, pop. 2095), 17.7 *m.* A pretty village among apple orchards, Standish was settled in 1750 and has electronics, wood products and clothing industries.

David Marrett House (1789) (*Sun.-Mon. afternoons, summer and by appointment*). In this large 2½ story house, coin from Portland banks was stored during the War of 1812 when it was feared the British would take Portland. Six oxen hauled the money to Parson Marrett's house for safekeeping.

Unitarian Church (1806) is a fine example of early church architecture, with square-towered belfry and box pews.

R from Standish on State 35 is Sebago Lake, 3 *m.* (*boating, picnicking*) (*see Tour 6*).

At 19.7 *m.*, State 118 (R) through Steep Falls and NW along the Saco River, was the Indians' Pequawket Trail, a short cut from the lower Saco to their village of Pequawket (Fryeburg). State 25 was the Ossipee Trail between Maine and New Hampshire.

At 23.2 *m.*, a bridge spans the Saco River, wide and turbulent here which once saw drives of 60 million logs.

EAST LIMINGTON (alt. 240, Limington Town) (*picnic area*), 23.6 *m.*

L a road leads to the *Site of an Indian Village* on N bank of the Little Ossipee River .3 *m.* Nearby in 1773 Deacon Amos Chase built the area's first saw-mill. A later generation built an octagonal house here in 1810 from plans drawn on an 8-sided collar box.

At 24.9 *m.*, junction with State 11. R on State 11 to Sebago Lake and Naples (*see Tour 6*).

L on State 11 to Limington village (alt. 462, Limington Town, pop. 839), 2.1 *m.* overlooking the orchards of a narrow valley amid high wooded hills. On Main St., the *McArthur House* (1797) (*private*), a 2-story weathered structure with gambrel roof. The first floor of the interior is furnished in black walnut. After the Civil War for which he organized the 8th Maine Regiment, Gen. William McArthur returned to his home here to practise law and cultivate extensive apple orchards. Among family possessions are a tomahawk given by Sitting Bull to Malcolm McArthur, an 1865 graduate of West Point, who wrote to his mother of expeditions with Gen. Custer.

CORNISH (alt. 347, Cornish Town, pop. 816), 32.7 *m.* (*York County Campsite 2 m. S of village*).

The *Clifford House* here is on the site of Indian Trader Francis Small's trading post, destroyed by Indian Sagamore Capt. Sunday, a Newichawannock chief. In 1668 Small bought from Capt. Sunday land including Cornish between the Great and Little Ossipee Rivers for such considerations as rum, blankets and beads.

Indians had a village at the confluence of the Ossipee and Saco Rivers where fire pits and artifacts embedded in kitchen middens have been found. There are Indian mounds at the Morrell Farm. At the Indian village site, English carpenters from Biddeford between 1650-60 built a fort that was destroyed in 1676 by British soldiers during King Philip's War.

At Cornish, junction with State 113.

R on State 113 N. On this road in the Richard Fitch Tavern, the militia under Capt. Edward Small assembled to train and later marched to general muster in Raymond during the War of 1812.

At 3.5 *m.* WEST BALDWIN (alt. 377, Baldwin Town, pop. 733). At 5.3 *m Hiram Falls (picnic area).* HIRAM (alt. 382, Hiram Town, pop. 699), 7.8 *m.*, named for the King of Tyre, was settled in 1774 by Gen. Peleg Wadsworth, grandfather of Poet Henry W. Longfellow. He bought 15,000 acres of farmland at 23 cents an acre and built *Wadsworth Hall* (1797) (*visitors*) which later was Longfellow's summer home; a room has been preserved as he used it. The 2½ story frame building has a long ell. The second floor rooms are paneled in white pine with bead and beveled joints. Militia drilled in the Hall during the War of 1812 and it was used as the first school and meeting house in Hiram.

State 113 continues to Fryeburg (*see Tour 6*) at 22.5 *m.*

At 33.7 *m.*, junction with State 5

L on State 5 S to LIMERICK (alt. 535, Limerick Town, pop. 907), 10.3 *m.*, settled in 1775 on the old Pequawket Trail. First town meeting was in 1787 in McDonald's Inn. State 5 continues SW through Newfield, a farming community, and Shapleigh on the E shore of Mousam Lake, into Sanford (*see Tour 8*) at 32 *m.*

KEZAR FALLS (*picnic areas*), 36.5 *m.*, divided by the Ossipee River is in the Town of Parsonsfield, York County (alt. 381, pop. 869) and the Town of Porter, Oxford County (alt. 407, pop. 975). It has a woolen mill and an electric company.

In Parsonsfield on Middle Road, is an *Animal Pound* (1785). This and 137 cemeteries in the town have been restored by the Parsonsfield-Porter Historical Society. Parsonsfield Seminary (1830) is in North Parsonsfield.

In Porter is another Animal Pound (1825) and the *Old Porter Meetinghouse* (1819-24).

The Bullockites, dissenters from the Baptists in the early 1800s, built a church here in 1828. They were fundamentalists led by Elder Jeremiah Bullock and Elder John Buzzell who emulated the Disciples in the rite of washing one another's feet as a mark of humility. When the church was built, no provision was made for heat in the old-time belief that the love of God shown in the fervor of the congregation should be sufficient to create a comfortable temperature.

At 42.8 *m.*, State 25 crosses the New Hampshire Line, to Effingham Falls and Center Ossipee, N. H.

T O U R   8 : *From* PORTLAND *to* OLD BERWICK, 57.3 *m.*, State 25 and State 4.

Via Gorham, Bar Mills, Hollis Center, Waterboro, Alfred, Sanford and the Berwicks.

TRAVELLING SW through historic towns and villages in the earliest settled section of Maine, State 4 (identical with US 202 to Sanford) is readily reached from US 1 and from four Maine Turnpike accesses. Running approximately parallel to State 4 between Gorham and Alfred and several times crossing it is the Old Roadbed of the Portland-Rochester, N. H. Railroad (1870), the Maine Central Railroad's Worcester-Nashua-Portland Line (1900) and the Sanford-Easton Railroad (1949-61). Remains are seen from several points along the scenic route.

The tour leaves Portland from Maine Turnpike Exit 8 on State 25 at 0 *m.*

GORHAM (*see Tour 7*), 10.5 *m.* S from Gorham on State 4.

At 19 *m.*, junction with State 112.

> L on State 112 to Tory Hill Meetinghouse (1822), .6 *m.*, a fine old white church of simple Georgian-Colonial design on the site of the first frame church (1761). The section became known as Tory Hill because the first pastor, Rev. Paul Coffin, and many of his parishioners were Loyalists. This church and neighborhood provided the locale for *The Old Peabody Pew*, a drama presented annually in August in the church ever since it was written by Kate Douglas Wiggin. The author's family burial lot in the churchyard is marked by an imposing Celtic Cross bearing the words 'The song is never ended.'

BAR MILLS (alt. 156, Hollis and Buxton Towns, pop. 2339), 19.5 *m.*, lies on both sides of the Saco River. There is a leatherboard factory in Buxton, birthplace of two midwestern Congressmen, Mark H. Dunnell, Minnesota (1871-83 and 1889-91), and Alanson M. Kimball, Wisconsin (1875-77).

> R from Bar Mills, a road following the E bank of the Saco River and crossing a bridge, leads to SALMON FALLS (alt. 144), 1.3 *m.*, also on both sides of the river. R from bridge on Hollis side is Quillcote (*visitors*), third house (L), for many years the summer home of Kate Douglas Wiggin (1859-1923) whose *Rebecca of Sunnybrook Farm*, *The Birds' Christmas Carol* and other

books were popular with little girls early in this century. Kate Smith, born in Philadelphia, was brought to Hollis as a child. Later the family moved to California where she became a pioneer in kindergarten work. In 1881 she married Samuel B. Wiggin, and after his death, George C. Riggs. Having acquired a literary reputation as Mrs. Wiggin, she continued to use that name. Quillcote, a large 2½ story clapboarded structure, stands well back on a tree-shaded lawn, its gable end to the road. The wide pine boards are from trees cut on the banks of the Saco. One of the five bedrooms was known as the 'painted room,' the walls having been decorated by an itinerant young French artist who early in the Nineteenth century did such work in several Salmon Falls homes.

S of bridge, the beautiful *Gorge of the Saco*, formed by high steep ledges that were its banks, now is nearly flooded by waters backed upstream from the Central Maine Power Company's Union Falls dam 2 *m.* below.

HOLLIS CENTER (alt. 180, Hollis Town, pop. 1195), 22.1 *m.*, was the home of Inventors Freeman Hanson (locomotive turntable) and Silas G. Smith (locomotive snowplow). The Free Will Baptist movement in Maine was initiated here in 1780. It had had less success a century earlier when the Rev. William Screven was jailed at York for his 'blasphemous speeches about baptism.'

At Hollis Center, State 112-117 (L) go SE to Maine Turnpike Access 5 at Saco (*see Tour 1 sec. a*), 11 *m.*

EAST WATERBORO (alt. 295, Waterboro Town), 27.3 *m.*, junction with State 5.

> R on State 5 NW to Waterboro Center, 2 *m.*, (*lakeside picnic area*); *Ossipee Hill* (1058 ft.) (L) (*Forest Lookout Station*). The route continues to Cornish (*see Tour 7*), 20 *m.*

> L on State 5 SE to Maine Turnpike Access at Saco, 12 *m.*

WATERBORO (alt. 270, Waterboro Town, pop. 1059), 30.7 *m.*, formerly South Waterboro, with a patent leather manufactory and electronics plant, was a major victim of the 1947 forest fires that devastated York County. Nearly every building on State 109 for half a mile south was destroyed and villages in outlying areas suffered greatly.

At 33.2 *m.* (L) on a hill overlooking Shaker Pond is *Notre Dame Institute,* a Catholic school for boys housed in the buildings of a former prosperous Shaker Colony. From 1793 the Shaker men tilled the 1500-acre farm and cared for its herd of dairy cattle and the highly respected, primly bonneted Shaker ladies built a profitable business selling baskets, knitted goods and other wares. By 1931 the colony had dwindled and the few remaining members sold their holdings and joined the Shaker Colony at Sabbathday Lake (*see Tour 6*).

ALFRED (alt. 226, Alfred Town, pop. 1201), 35.4 *m.* (*picnic areas*), a village of quiet streets and dignified houses, was a part of land purchased from the Indian Chief Fluellin in 1661 by Major William Phillips. First settled in 1764, Alfred was the North Parish of Sanford until it was incorporated in 1794 and named in honor of Alfred the Great. Waterboro and much of Alfred had been referred to by the Indian name of Massabesec. With the town of York, the original county seat, Alfred became a half-shire town in 1802. In 1832 it became the shire town of York County. It developed as a farming and lumbering community. Now small industries are being established, the central village remaining residential.

The *Courthouse* (R) an architectural gem, holds the oldest continuous county records of any county in the country, dating from 1636.

Congregational Meetinghouse (R) on the village green has a Revere bell (1822), made when Paul's son Joseph Warren Revere was head of the company.

Holmes House (*private*), opp. village green (L) was built in 1802 for John Holmes, one of Maine's first two U. S. Senators and chairman of the committee that drafted the new State of Maine's constitution in 1819. The exterior's most interesting feature is an iron balustrade with a design of bows and arrows that rises from the eaves.

At Alfred, State 111 (L) goes E to Maine Turnpike Access 4 at Biddeford (*see Tour 1 sec. a*), 18 *m.*

From Alfred R on State 4 A to

SANFORD (alt. 300, Sanford Town, pop. 14,962), 39.9 *m.*, part of Major William Phillips' land purchase in 1661 as was Alfred, and called Phillipstown in his honor. There were early mills at the various water power sites on the Mousam and Great Works Rivers but the town was largely agricultural until shortly after Thomas Goodall arrived in 1867 and began the manufacture of carriage robes. His business expanded rapidly. Eventually his three sons, Ernest M., Louis B., and George B., joined him in developing the large and well-known Goodall Industries which manufactured all manner of textiles, including Palm Beach cloth, Seamloc carpets, upholsteries, plush, draperies and dress goods. The recession in textiles in the early 1950s coupled with low labor costs in the Southern mills, was a severe blow to the Goodall Industries and the economy of Sanford. The Burlington Mills, the country's largest textile firm, gained controlling interest in the Goodall Industries by buying its stock at prices far above market value. Burlington operated the mills briefly but in 1954 closed them for good, moving the best of the machinery to its other mills and selling the local buildings. The continuing local industries, chiefly two shops which manufacture American Girl shoes and the Jagger Brothers yarn mill, could not absorb the considerable labor force idled by the collapse of the town's greatest industry.

The town recovered through a national campaign by the Chamber of

Commerce featuring Sanford as *The Town That Refused to Die.* This and efforts of the town's Industrial Development Corporation brought Sanford a diversity of small and medium-sized industries including aircraft, carpets, plastics, shoes, dresses, woven labels, small electrical components, wooden heels and woolens. Sanford is the only Maine town where aircraft are manufactured commercially. The first airplane was made in 1956 by Colonial Aircraft Corporation, now inactive. Aerofab, Inc., has been manufacturing planes since 1963 and Thurston Aircraft Corp., since 1968.

In Willard Park, Central Square, the heroic bronze statue of Thomas Goodall was purchased by popular subscription and erected in 1917.

N on State 109 is *Gowen Park*, 3.6 *m.* a large and attractive municipal park next to an Educational Complex that includes a new high school, vocational school, junior high, Memorial Gymnasium, Dr. Stephen A. Cobb Stadium.

At 4.8 *m.* is SPRINGVALE (alt. 348, pop. 2379), the smaller of the two villages of Sanford town. *Nasson College* here, founded in 1912 as Nasson Institute, a two-year vocational school for girls, was chartered as Nasson College in 1935, became co-educational in 1951. It is a liberal arts college with an enrollment of about 900.

L of highway is Ridley Hill (760 ft.); R, picnic site.

At 6.1 *m.*, on the Mousam River, a short trail leads to *Indian's Last Leap*, a chasm formed by two large boulders 20 ft. apart. Legend says that an early settler fleeing from Indians cleared the chasm in one bound. Chief Nahanda leaped short, struck his head against the cliff, fell into the river and drowned.

L from Springvale on State 11A at 2.4 *m.* is a blazed but rough trail of half a mile or so to the *Harvey E. Butler Memorial Sanctuary* owned by the New England Wildflower Preservation Society. Here is perhaps the finest stand of great laurel (rhododendron maximum) in northern New England.

At Sanford, junctions with State 11 and State 109.

State 11 goes N to Limington and State 25 (*see Tour 7*) and SW with US 202 to East Lebanon (*picnic area*), to cross the Salmon Falls River at South Lebanon, to Rochester, N. H., 16 *m.*

State 109, running between Wells on the Maine coast and the Lake Winnipesaukee Region in New Hampshire, from Sanford goes SE to Maine Turnpike Access 2 at Wells (*see Tour 1 sec. a*), 14 *m.*

From Sanford this tour continues on State 4A to junction with State 4 at 42.7 *m.*

E of junction at .4 *m.* (L) a boulder on the *Site of Old Emery Tavern.* A plaque states that in 1797 Louis Philippe, later King of France, with his two brothers and Talleyrand stopped at the tavern, and that Lafayette was a visitor in 1825. The future king and his brothers may have stopped there but Talleyrand was not in this country at the time and there is lack of corroborative evidence regarding Lafayette's visit.

Sanford Municipal Airport, 1.9 *m.*, services private and business planes, has a flying service, an aircraft manufacturing company and another manufacturing aircraft parts. From 1943 until after the end of World War II the Navy operated the field as Naval Air Facility-Sanford, a satellite of the Brunswick Naval Air Station, and trained fighter pilots. Across from the airport is Sanford Industrial Estates, an area purchased in 1959 by a group of local citizens organized as the Industrial Development Corporation. Plants there include American Cyanamid Company, Sprague Electric and Adams Trucking.

At the junction, R on State 4.

At 45.5 *m.*, *Sanford Golf Club* (*visitors*). The 9-hole course lies on E side of Bauneg Beg Pond, a beautiful small body of water surrounded by stands of second growth pine.

NORTH BERWICK (alt. 230, North Berwick Town, pop. 1833), 50.6 *m.* The Berwicks originally were part of the town of Kittery and known as the Parish of Unity. Not until 1713 did Berwick become a separate town. A century later, South Berwick was incorporated (1814), and North Berwick, in 1831. In 1894, Sarah Orne Jewett, famous for her portraits of New England life, wrote:

'I find myself always speaking of my native town as Berwick, though the original town was long since divided and divided again. South Berwick is really the oldest of the three, to which most of the earliest history and tradition belongs; and the newer settlements and townships are its children; but the old people never seemed to make any difference in their own minds . . . It is all one Berwick to me . . . The courage of the Plaisteds, and the nameless heroine who saved all her neighbors in the Tozier garrison, are as much my inheritance as if an imaginery line had never been struck across the land in 1814. I am proud to have been made of Berwick dust; and a little of it is apt to fly in my eyes and make them blur whenever I tell the old stories of bravery, of fine ambition, of good manners, and the love of friend for friend and the kindness of neighbor to neighbor in this beloved town.'

North Berwick, though a small village, has many handsome old homes and long has been the site of small but important and successful industries. Reuben Neal gained fame by building a church organ in his farmhouse. Paul Rogers became a famous clockmaker; his grandfather clocks still are keeping time in the town. In 1855 William Taber built a sawmill for the manufacture of wooden boxes. William Hill and John Lang established a woolen mill on the bank of the Great Works River in 1862; their first big order was a government contract for blue woolen blankets for the Union Navy. One of the most ingenious manufacturers was John E. Hobbs who designed the Hobbs Hub-Runner that permitted travelers in the horse and buggy era to remove carriage wheels and slip hub runners on wheel axles when an early snowstorm hit. Longest lived of all North Berwick industries is the Hussey Manufacturing Company, founded in 1835 and still flourishing. Its first product was the Hussey plow, soon followed by other farm implements. As demand for these declined, steel products were produced — ladders, fire escapes, latticed flagpoles, portable bleacher seats and grandstands. Newest local industry is the Simplex Wire and Cable Company.

Like all Maine towns, North Berwick has its legends, one of the most charming concerning Charles Dickens and the famous Berwick sponge cake which was formulated and baked in a small restaurant near the railroad station. The story goes that on one of his American tours Dickens passed through North Berwick with Kate Douglas Wiggin, then a girl of twelve, and stepped off the train to buy some North Berwick sponge cake for his young friend.

At North Berwick, junction with State 9 which goes SW to Berwick, 9 *m.* and E to Maine Turnpike Entrance in Kittery, 9 *m.*

SOUTH BERWICK (alt. 110, South Berwick Town, pop. 3112), 57.3 *m.*, site of the first permanent settlement in Maine (1631, at the mouth of the Asbenbedick or Great Works River), is renowned for its many handsome historic homes and its academy, oldest secondary school in Maine. The oldest frame schoolhouse, the oldest dwelling and the site of Maine's first water power development also are in Berwick. Annually in August, the Old Berwick Historical Society sponsors a tour of several houses including the Sarah Orne Jewett Memorial, birthplace of Miss Jewett whose *Country of the Pointed Firs* has been called the 'best piece of regional fiction to have come out of Nineteenth century America,' and Hamilton House, the favorite American dwelling of many connoisseurs.

Ambrose Gibbons, Roger Knight and Thomas Spencer, with servants of patent holder, Capt. John Mason, arriving here from England in May 1630 to plant a colony, cast anchor at the foot of Little John's Falls on the Newichawannock River. In 1634, English carpenters and millwrights built the first saw and grist mills at the Upper Falls, and the first cows were landed at Cow's Cove. Not many wives came over and Gibbons, Capt. Mason's factor, asked him to send a good husband and wife to tend the cattle and to make butter and cheese, adding that 'maides are soon gone in this country.' Along the declivity sloping to the water may be seen the artificial terraces of the 'Vineyard' where the first attempts were made to grow grapes commercially in America.

Between 1638-51, records show that three families and two bachelors were living at Great Works and a new mill was begun at Lower Falls. Bachelors Basil Parker and Peter Weare both later served as York Recorder of Deeds. In 1651 the town of Kittery granted to Richard Leader 400 acres lying ½ mile each side of Little Newichawannock River including the now abandoned mills of Capt. Mason's heirs. The grant included from near Lower Falls to Faggoty Bridge over Slut's Corner Brook, E of which 150 acres were laid out for ministry land in 1669. Earliest meeting-houses dating from 1663 were destroyed by fire or otherwise demolished.

Leader had been in charge of the Lynn Iron Works which employed many

Scotchmen who had been captured by Cromwell in the battle of Dunbar, 3 September 1650. He revived the decaying Mason mills and is said to have set up a gang of 15 saws; the area and Newichawannock River have been called Great Works ever since. The ship *GOODFELLOW* brought over more refugees and wanderers as the result of Cromwell's invasion of Ireland. Other mills were built at Quamphegan and Salmon Falls. When Leader left Great Works, Scotchmen got land grants. One Alexander Maxwell in 1654 was flogged in court 'for his grosse offence in his exorbitant and abusive carages towards his master, Mr. George Leader.' In 1684 the selectmen of the Parish of Berwick voted to maintain John Emerson 'or some other' in the ministry for ten years. From 1693 to 1699 James Stacpole was licensed to sell 'beere, Cyder, rum, provisions, victuals, horsmeate and lodging,' and in 1696, 'to keep a public house of Entertainment in his now dwelling house.' Long before the Revolution, ships were being built at Pipe Stave Landing.

AROUND OLD BERWICK

Beginning on State 103 at Shorey's Brook, to *Vaughn Woods Memorial (mid-May to mid-Oct.)* 2.5 *m.*, a 200-acre tract originally part of the Col. Jonathan Hamilton House estate. This unspoiled stretch of forest winding a mile along E branch of the Piscataquis River 'shall forever be left in the natural wild state, and forever be kept as a sanctuary for wild beasts and birds', according to the will of the donor, Mrs. Henry G. Vaughn. The main Park trail along the river passes Cow Cove where the ship *PIED COW* landed cattle from Denmark in 1634, then winds back through stands of pine and hemlock, beech and maple, red and white oak and white and black birch, the latter uncommon in the Maine woods. The High School Science Club has marked several species of indigenous trees.

At 2.6 *m.* is the handsome country mansion called *Old Fields*. This is the only portion of the land originally acquired by Maine's first permanent settler, Thomas Spencer (ca. 1632) that continues in possession of his descendants. The present 1797 house was erected by his great-great-grandson, General Ichabod Goodwin, on the site of the Spencer garrison — the largest in the country at the time of the Second Indian War. The house appears earlier than its 1797 date, partially because of the incorporation of many of the features of an earlier dwelling, which was almost completely destroyed by fire. The chimney, front entrance, some windows, and certain of the woodwork appear to have survived. There is a stenciled room of particular interest and paintings by Edwin Lord Weeks.

Across the road is Vaughn's Lane leading to Lower or Pipe Stave Landing. First low house (R) belonged to Miss Olive Grant, the village dressmaker who appeared in Miss Jewett's stories. Beyond the Hamilton House gate is the site of the Jewett shipyard from whose wharves the family carried on extensive trade with the West Indies.

Hamilton House (1787) *(mid-June to mid-Sept.)*, owned by the Society for the Preservation of New England Antiquities, was built by the merchant and West Indies trader, Col. Jonathan Hamilton. It is a remarkable late Georgian mansion in a superb riverside setting and was the primary setting for Sarah Orne Jewett's novel *The Tory Lover*; it held 'a certain grand air . . . hard to match in any house . . . ' With its broad sweep of lawns and magnificent formal gardens, Hamilton House is one of the most satisfactory restorations in America, and is handsomely furnished with Chippendale, Hepplewhite and Sheraton pieces, Sandwich glass and Leeds pottery.

L at the head of Vaughn's Lane and the junction with Vine St., is the oldest house in Maine, that of Thomas Spencer, built for him by his father-in-law, William Chadbourne, and now incorporated in a plain two-story structure.

At 2.7 *m.* on Vine St., the *Old Fields Burying Ground* (R), dating from the Seventeenth century, with many inscriptions of interest. Somewhere in the oldest section is the little headstone marking the grave of Hetty Goodwin, captured by the Indians in 1690 and taken to Canada where she remained until rescued by her husband.

Next R, the *Major Thomas Leigh House* (1726), a charming dwelling overlooking Leigh's Mill Pond on the Great Works River. Nearby stood New England's first water-powered gristmill. Across the bridge the road follows one of the vineyard terraces built by the Mason colonists in the first recorded attempt at commercial grape growing in America.

At 3.5 *m.*, Old Mill Road (R) leads to the site of the first water power mill in the new world (ca. 1623). Here also was the first blanket manufactory in this country. The Burleigh Mills (1854) in operation for almost a century, were nationally known for their fine woolen blankets and auto robes.

L at junction of Vine and Liberty Sts., the *Chadbourne House* on part of a great tract of land Humphrey Chadbourne purchased from the Newichawannock Indians. His great-grandson Judge Benjamin Chadbourne gave ten acres as the site for Maine's earliest secondary school. The House, probably built in 1670 and extensively altered in 1770, has especially fine woodcarving in its front rooms, entrance hall and stairway.

At end of Liberty St. L at Quamphegan Falls and the Upper Landing is the site of Deacon Foote's Mill, at one time the only producer of custom cloth in this country. The *Counting House of the Portsmouth Company* (ca. 1830), brick classic revival, sole surviving building of the Nineteenth century cotton mills here, is the home and museum of the Old Berwick Historical Society. In the second story hall, candlelight balls were held for mill employes.

From junction of Liberty and Vine Sts., L on Vine and across State 236 to Academy St. Crowning the hill (L) is *Hayes House*, Berwick Academy dormitory, a house built in 1815 overlooking the village and the river. On the hill, dominating the village is the Academy's *Fogg Memorial*, granite library and auditorium with stained glass windows by Sarah Whitman. Berwick Academy was founded in 1791 when Maine was still part of the Commonwealth of Massachusetts; its original building, now the administrative center, is the oldest frame building still in use as a school in the U. S. Its charter bears the signature of Gov. John Hancock. Buildings on the 150-acre campus include several historic homes. The Fogg Memorial and the Sarah Orne Jewett Creative Arts Center, once part of the home of Artist Marcia Oakes Woodbury, are open to visitors.

On Academy St. at its junction with Main St., the *First Parish Church* (Parish of Unity), has six pieces of Colonial silver presented to the church during the long ministry of its second pastor, Rev. Jeremiah Wise (1707-56).

On Main St., the principal building of the Academy of St. Joseph once was *Frost's Tavern*, its parlors restored and the hand-painted French wallpaper, that must have pleased General Lafayette on his visit here, still in good order.

In the heart of the village, cor. Main and Portland Sts., stands the *Sarah Orne Jewett Memorial* (1774) (*visitors*), owned by the Society for the Preservation of New England Antiquities. The 2½ story clapboarded house with dormer windows is notable for its well-proportioned Doric portico; the woodcarving in the entrance hall, which three ship's carpenters worked on for 100 days; its fine staircase and paneling; and the French flock wallpaper in its master bedroom. Miss Jewett once wrote: 'I was born here and I hope to die here (she did), leaving the lilac bushes still green and growing, and all the chairs in their places.' Miss Jewett's bedroom-study remains much as she left it — her desk, her books, her pen undisturbed. And in recent years the garden she tended and enjoyed has been restored.

Miss Jewett's first biographer, Harvard Professor F. O. Matthiessen, wrote of her: ' . . . she takes her place next Emily Dickinson — the two principal women writers America has had.' A serious writer, seeking, usually successfully, to describe a portion of New England life truthfully and with understanding, Miss Jewett revealed her purpose in an autobiographical fragment:

> When I was perhaps fifteen the first city boarders began to make their appearance near Berwick, and the way they misconstrued the country people and made game of their peculiarities fired me with indignation. I determined to teach the world that country people were not the awkward, ignorant set those people seemed to think. I wanted the world to know their grand simple lives; and, so far as I had a mission, when I first began to write, I think that was it.

Her writings reveal that she achieved her purpose. In *The Country of the Pointed Firs, A Native of Winby, A White Heron, The King of Folly Island* she pictures the rural and coastal New England she saw as she accompanied her doctor father on his round of sick calls at country and shore homes. Her stories show the resourcefulness, the wry humor, the simple goodness of Maine people in what is frequently spoken of as the period of New England decline, when the day of the shipbuilder and merchantman was over, when manufacturing began to invade the rural villages, and when hundreds of ambitious New Englanders abandoned their stony farms and idle harbors for places where sheer existence did not seem so difficult. So honestly and sensitively did Miss Jewett interpret her New England that Henry James called her . . . mistress of an art of fiction all her own . . . surpassed only by Hawthorne as producer of the most finished and penetrating of the numerous short stories that have the domestic life of New England for their . . . subject.'

Along Main St. in various stages of repair are several fine Victorian structures, some with French mansard roofs; these were erected following a fire in 1870 that destroyed most of the business section.

N on Portland St. are several well-preserved Colonial and Federal houses including that of Dr. Low, noted astronomer and publisher of *Low's Almanac.* Highway construction destroyed a magnificent cloister of elms here. About 5 *m.* out on Portland St., the *Quaker Burying Ground* dating with the first Friends Meetinghouse built here ca. 1750. In 1881 William Hill, a founder of the North Berwick Woolen Mill, gave the beautiful stone walls surrounding the tree-shaded cemetery.

R from Jewett Park on Agamenticus Road, is another cemetery, where Miss Jewett is buried. Where the road turns sharp R, Knight's Pond road continues to *Spring Hill,* recreation area. Beyond on a short road L is the site of the first Baptist Church in Maine (1768).

On Agamenticus Road past the junction with Knight's Pond Road, the mid-Eighteenth century Warren Schoolhouse, now a dwelling, is across the road from Gladys Hasty Carroll's Nineteenth century farmhouse. Mrs. Carroll became famous for her *As the Earth Turns* (1933), printed in every major foreign language.

The story of these and other houses in this historic locale is told in *Dunnybrook* (rev. ed. 1952).

ISLAND TRIPS

SEA islands have held a fascination for mankind since history began. Who has not dreamed of his romantic isle, remote and beautiful — perhaps in the Mediterranean's 'wine-dark seas' of Homer's ancient Greece, in the South Seas of Gauguin, or the Indies? As sea islands become the last bastion of undefiled nature in the 1970s, more and more seekers after the dream would make it a reality.

Discovered in the Seventeenth century, Maine's myriad islands lacing her 2500-mile coastline are among the most beautiful and diverse in the world, jewels on the bosom of the Atlantic. In the Nineteenth century, another Homer expressed on canvas the great power of the Atlantic whose American northeast continues to inspire poets and painters, lured by the mystique of islands in the sea.

Several islands have the same name, even in the same area. Many are named for animals whose shapes they resemble, or for topographical, geographical or historical features. Single islands often were named after early settlers who dwelt thereon or retain their Indian designation. The mid-coast *Swan's Island*, not to be confused with Merrymeeting Bay's *Swan Island*, is said to be the only one with an 'official' apostrophe s. Whether or not named for a person or thing, many island names have acquired an s, without which when spoken would sound strange to the native ear. And of course, the islands abound in pirate lore, Indian legends and tales of the early struggles of the Colonists and man against the sea, the fisherman, the sailor, and the lighthousekeeper, all adding their bright color to the tapestry of American literature.

Twentieth century travel makes more attainable the exhilaration of sailing and the island experience. Maine ports are reviving the summer boat services that languished after the decline of the steamboat era. All types of transport are available along the coast, from ferries, steamers and windjammers to fishing schooners, yachts and motor launches — and some small planes for a breathtaking overview.

There are two international ferries traversing the Bay of Fundy and four State of Maine coastal ferries that carry cars and passengers, a fifth carrying passengers only. The *Bluenose* (Canadian National Railways) (346 ft., 6000 tons, six 2,000 hp diesels, 18½ knots) travels between Bar Harbor and Yarmouth, Nova Scotia (*100 m.; 7 hrs., daily June 22-Sept. 23; tri-weekly otherwise*). It carries 600 passengers, 150 cars, has a limited number of day cabins, 2 lounges, cafeteria, newsstand and bar.

The *Prince of Fundy* (June 1970) (387 ft., 12,000 bhp diesels, 22 knots; stabilized, air-conditioned, drive-through landing), is operated by Sweden's Lion Ferry, Canadian American Line, between Portland and Yarmouth, N. S. (*187 m., daily, two-hour stopover*). For this 22-hour mini-cruise, the first class *Prince*, built in West Germany in 1969, carries a crew of 110 and is designed for 1000 passengers (cabin space for 525) and 200 vehicles including trailers and buses. Carribean-style cruising comes to Maine, with Swedish-American cuisine, two dining-rooms, deck lounge and sun decks, teenage room, casino, several bars, entertainment, dancing and international tax-free gift shop. Conventions of up to 400 persons can be accommodated, with special land tour arrangements.

The Maine State Ferry Service fleet of modern, steel-hulled, oceangoing vessels, carry up to 175 passengers and from 11 to 24 vehicles (*advance reservations*). They are the Governor Curtis, the Governor Muskie, the Everett Libby, the William S. Silsby and the North Haven, all Coast Guard inspected, equipped with the latest navigational aids and operated by qualified personnel.

Ship ports, all accessible from the Maine Turnpike and US 1 are on the mainland of these principal bays: Casco, Boothbay Harbor, Muscongus, Blue Hill, Penobscot, Frenchman, Pleasant, Englishman, Machias, Cobscook and Passamaquoddy (*see TOUR 1 and RECREATION: Coastal Cruising*). For an hour or a day, or overnight, at modest cost, there are sightseeing and fishing trips and visits to mainland and island resorts as well as secluded islands, a thrilling way to see and enjoy the beautiful coast of Maine.

In summer, there are scenic, sunset, moonlight, early risers, picnic, clambake, and supper sails, deep-sea fishing and charter service. Salty skippers season the voyage with narrated commentary, sometimes historical, sometimes humorous, often informative for those interested in navigation, oceanography and marine life. Many boats provide snacks and blankets against the sea breezes; equipment is supplied on fishing trips. Below are some sample trips. Boat schedules vary and should be checked, along with other information on the type of trip selected, at the point of departure. Cameras and wraps are recommended. For near-coastal islands and those reached by road from the mainland, see land Tours 1C through 1K.

CASCO BAY ISLANDS

From Portland, Custom House Wharf: Lion Ferry *Prince of Fundy* overnight to Yarmouth, Nova Scotia; State Ferry to Peaks, Long and Chebeague Islands; Casco Bay Lines, one to 4-hr. trips, 10 to 60 *m*; the *Abenaki*, the *Island Adventure* and the *Island Holiday*, capacity 900; group charter cruises, parties.

Cruises encompass islands offshore Portland, Yarmouth, Falmouth, Freeport, and Harpswell.

Halfway Rock Light marks the center of the outer border of 200-sq.-*m.* Casco Bay whose shoreline winds many miles from Cape Elizabeth (Portland) to Cape Small Point (Phippsburg), 20 miles apart by water. Geologists say this once was the mouth of the Androscoggin River, the sandy inner islands formed from sediment carried downstream and deposited upon jutting reefs. Its mouth finally blocked, the river deviated to its present channel, joining with the Kennebec at Merrymeeting Bay. Of the several hundred islands, most of the sizeable ones are heavily wooded with great cliffs and crescents of smooth beach. Some were fortified for early protection of Portland Harbor. There are many uninhabited islands and innumerable ledges, shoals and knobs, with colorful names — Irony, Uncle Zeke, Rogue, Scrag, Pound of Tea, Junk of Pork, Diamond, Jewell, Stepping Stones, Brown Cow, Big Hen, Great Whaleboat. There are four Rams, two Cushings, two Crow Islands and several Pumpkin Knobs.

On *Hog Island* is forbidding Fort Gorges (c. 1865), briefly commissioned, commanding Portland Harbor's main ship channel. *House Island* had Fort Scammell and an earlier blockhouse.

Cushing Island, year-round home of many Portlanders and a summer colony, has a history dating from 1623 when Capt. Christopher Levett built a strongly fortified house on its northern extremity.

PEAKS ISLAND (alt. 45, Portland ward) (*hotels, inns*), most heavily populated of the Casco Bay Islands and a popular summer resort early in the century, is the site of a proposed UN International Conference Center and staff retreat. Architectural plans call for a building atop 2 concrete Naval gun emplacements (World War II), to house some 238 delegates, with dining facilities, library, outdoor theatre and heliport. Many nationally known figures have summered here; in recent years, UN correspondents have been visitors.

When Portland was Falmouth (*see PORTLAND*), the island was owned in early days by Michael Mitton, son-in-law of George Cleeve, Portland's first settler. Renowned as a huntsman and fowler, Mitton's amazing tales of his adventures included one involving an encounter with a triton who grasped the side of his boat. When Mitton severed the merman's finny hands with one blow of his hatchet, they clung to the boat for some time before he could pry them loose.

Longfellow's poem *The Wreck of the Hesperus* is based upon one of the major tragedies in Peaks annals. Caught in the great gale of 1869, the schooner *HELEN ELIZA* was driven ashore in the night and was ground to pieces on the jutting rocks. All hands were lost except one lad who had previously been the sole survivor of a vessel that foundered in a West Indies hurricane. Deciding to tempt fate no more, he retired from the sea to a farm in New Hampshire, where he slipped off a log in a small stream and was drowned.

GREAT DIAMOND ISLAND (alt. 39, Portland ward) (*golf course, cottage colony*), its precipitous seawalls fringed about with golden seaweed evoking tales of mermaids, has a greatly diversified surface — deep ravines, ragged elevations and green slopes extending to the shores. On the E side, commanding Hussey's Sound, Fort McKinley was a sub-post of Harbor defenses. *Little*

LANDSCAPE AND SEASCAPE

THE natural beauties of the State of Maine, coastal and inland, are widely known and speak for themselves.

CATHEDRAL BOWL, MOUNT KATAHDIN

CHIMNEY POND, BAXTER PARK

MT. KATAHDIN

MUNNA OLAMMON UNGUN -- GULF HAGAS GORGE

ISLAND SUNSET

HANCOCK POINT

POPHAM BEACH STATE PARK

MT. KINEO, MOOSEHEAD LAKE

ALONG OCEAN DRIVE, BAR HARBOR

'LION OF THE BAY' — PASSAMAQUODDY

SURF

TRANQUIL LITY

WOODLAND FALLS

THE OLD APPLE TREE BY THE STONE WALL

BY THE OLD MILL STREAM

INDIAN SUMMER — HARVEST TIME

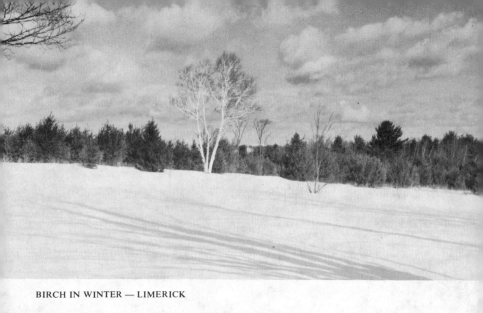

BIRCH IN WINTER — LIMERICK

CROOKED RIVER AT EDES FALLS, NAPLES

WINTER ARTISTRY

SNOW-ON-THE-MOUNTAIN

Diamond (alt. 27, Portland Ward), one of the prettiest islands in the Bay, is connected with Great Diamond by a sandspit.

LONG ISLAND. Once occupied by Indians, this 1,000-acre island with beaches, groves and fields, became industrialized when King Resources Associates acquired the U. S. Navy fuel oil depot established here in World War II. Whether the company would drill 100 *m.* off the coast by agreement with the State of Maine depended upon the outcome of a Federal suit contending that Maine does not have jurisdiction.

Cliff Island in the outer Harbor, a summer resort, is marked by sawtooth reefs, great coves, low sandbars, beautiful pine groves — and pirate legends. Here, it's said, was the lair of notorious pirate and smuggler, Capt. Kieff, who salvaged the cargoes of vessels he caused to be wrecked on the reefs. On stormy nights, he patroled the shore with a horse, lantern swinging from its neck, to decoy passing vessels into the narrow channel to pile up on the reefs. Sailors whose bodies washed ashore from the wrecks are said to be buried in *Kieff's Garden*, a grassy mound rising above the island road near a ravine. *Jewell Island* is nearby.

GREAT CHEBEAGUE (alt. 70, Cumberland Town) (*see Tour 1, sec. a*), is mainly a summer resort. From the eminences of this second largest of the Casco Bay Islands, its pine groves interspersed with broad fields and sandy beaches, are striking views of the mainland and other islands.

Mackworth, at the mouth of the Presumpscot River, has been owned since 1888 by the family of the late Percival P. Baxter, Maine governor and philanthropist. A training camp occupied it during the Civil War. It had been a gift in 1631 of Sir Ferdinando Gorges to Arthur Mackworth, deputy of the Bay.

Cousins Island (alt. 29, Yarmouth Town), called Susquescon by the Indians, was settled by John Cousins in 1645. First crops were sown at Cornfield Point on the N end. Across a bridge is *Littlejohn*, long an Indian campground identified by many shell heaps and artifacts.

Great Moshier is little changed since adventurer Hugh Moshier left London city life in the 1640s to settle here. On *Little Moshier* (W) is the site of an Indian burying ground.

Bustin's Island (alt. 28, Freeport Town) has the tale of one 'Swindler' Ransom, early perpetrator of a silver fraud who disappeared from here as suddenly and mysteriously as he came when his hoax was exposed. For a time he duped Portland silversmiths by producing a small ball of silver when he stirred molten lead with a little black rod. The hollow end of the rod was found to contain a thin silver coin.

At Harpswell, bridges connect BAILEY'S ISLAND on Mericoneag Sound and ORR'S ISLAND on Harpswell Sound to the mainland (*see Tour 1C*).
Among islands off Harpswell are the *Whaleboats* and *Goose Islands* and their *Goslings*.

Ragged Island was the summer home of Poet Edna St. Vincent Millay, and earlier, a favorite haunt of Rev. Elijah Kellogg who used this setting as the locale for his Elm Island stories. Devil's Well and Ghost Cliff are on the W shore.

EAGLE ISLAND, also known as Sawungun. Admiral Robert E. Peary's former summer home here is under State restoration (1970) for public visitation. Round fortress-like structures at the base of the house overlooking the sea were Peary's library and workshop. Three fireplaces incorporated in a triangular form are of fieldstone and white quartz. Construction of the house was begun in 1904, five years before Peary's discovery of the North Pole.

Haskell's Island. Tales of rat-infested ghetto tenements in the Twentieth century are matched by a horrifying rat and cat tale involving this island nearly a century ago when the solitary inhabitant, a lobsterman, was devoured by swarms of squealing rats that had overrun the island. A dozen husky cats were brought in. They cleared out the rats and grew so strong and fierce they frightened off prospective city buyers. One day an army of dead felines was found stiffly stretched upon the shore. They had been poisoned in the night. No cats, no rats on Haskell's Island to this day.

Birch Island. Walter Merriman of Ireland was the first settler here among the silver birches. Like many another, he was kidnaped and sold for his passage money, coming here after serving his indenture. A flourishing colony of farmers developed, but 50 years later they abandoned their fields and orchards to join the California gold rush.

Bombazeen was the home of the Indian Sagamore of that name. Bitter foe of the English, he was killed in 1724 on the Kennebec River by men of Capt. Moulton's expedition enroute to Norridgewock.

Capt Mowatt's fleet, on the way to destroy Falmouth (*see PORTLAND*), is said to have anchored off *Flag Island*, named for its cattails.

Great Mark Island is a nesting place for seabirds. *Little Mark* was named for the 50-ft. U. S. Government marker (now with beacon) placed in 1827. The 20-ft. room at the base of the obelisk, designed as a shelter for shipwrecked mariners, later was used as a sheepfold. *Eastern* or *Woody Mark* was the scene of counterfeit operations at the turn of the century.

Shelter Island was a refuge for Mere Point settlers during Indian raids, and later a smugglers' hideout.

BOOTHBAY HARBOR and MONHEGAN

From Boothbay Harbor, Fisherman's Wharf: 45 summer cruises from an hour to a day, around the Harbor, along the coast among the islands and up the rivers.

A major Maine boating center, Boothbay Harbor is dotted with all types of pleasure craft, lobster and fishing boats. Seasoned skippers operating Coast Guard inspected boats of varying capacities, reassure landlubbers who feel queasy about being water-borne — 'inner waters are as smooth and sparkling as champagne, without the dizzying aftermath.' Larger craft are used in outside waters such as trips to historic Monhegan 10 *m.* out. Typical trips:

SQUIRREL ISLAND (*see Tour 1F*), 3 *m.* has been a popular trip on the *Nellie G's* since 1902. Threading through the busy Harbor and along the wooded shores for an hour, points of interest en route include Harbor Island, the Carrousel movie site. Tumbler Island, U. S. Fish Hatchery and Aquarium, Mouse Island, Burnt Island Light, Capital Island. Seven trips daily, so time to stop over at Squirrel. There is a twilight sail nightly and a Church boat Sunday mornings for All-Saints-by-the-Sea.

Capt. Dave and Capt. Marian Dash run the *Holiday*, 2-3 hour morning and afternoon sailings; sunset cruises. Itineraries include Pemaquid Point, Lighthouse and Beach, Thread of Life, Inner Heron Island, Ovensmouth up the Sheepscot, Five Islands, Southport, Reid State Park, outer islands, the Whites, Heron, Fisherman and Damariscove. Capt. Dash originated Boothbay's Windjammer Days.

A combination ocean and inland excursion is the 41 *m.* trip of 3¼ hrs. up the Kennebec River via Fort Popham to Bath, returning via turbulent Hell's Gate, on the *ARGO* with Capt. Eliot Winslow, master mariner and first officer of the Bath Iron Works Naval destroyer trial runs (*see Tour 1 sec. a*). Capt. Winslow was commander of the *USS ARGO*, Coast Guard cutter, during World War II and named his own boat after her. Seabirds nesting in the outer islands, seals, an occasional eagle, seven lighthouses, colorful harbors and beautiful scenery are among the sights. A 2¼ hr. cruise around Southport includes Love's Cove where Capt. Winslow's *USS ARGO* anchored the day after the last of four Nazi submarines surrendered to her off Portland May 19, 1945. On specified days there are sunset cruises with a chicken bake afloat.

The Magnum Boat Line features daily deep-sea fishing trips as well as sightseeing cruises. The *Magnum II* carrying 100 passengers takes a 3-hr. coastal cruise with stopovers at Christmas Cove and Pemaquid Beach. The *Magnum River Queen* (165 passengers, snack bar), modern reproduction of a Mississippi River packet, stern-wheel and all, travels between Boothbay Harbor and Bath through Townsend Gut, Sheepscot River, Robinhood Cove. Embarking at Bath allows a 1½ lunch stopover at Boothbay.

Capt. Charles H. Wade, skipper of the 60-ft. *Balmy Days*, has been making the all-day trip to fabled MONHEGAN for 30 years. The ruggedly beautiful island is the historic home of seafarers, fishermen and artists. Monhegan also may be reached from Port Clyde (*see Tour 1H*) on the *Laura B* with Capt. Earl S. Field. Monhegan, named Island in the Sea by the Indians, is about a mile long and half a mile wide, with the highest cliffs on the New England coast. It is known for its Cathedral Woods and trails, its art colony and as the site of the earliest fishing settlements. Actually there are two Monhegans: Monhegan proper with its shops, artists' studios, fishing shacks and hotels and the other Monhegan named Manana lying parallel and forming one side of the harbor. On the bleak Manana side there are only the Coast Guard Station and the home of a solitary shepherd of whom Yolla Niclas has written in *The Island Shepherd*, the story of the young man who left a big city corporation for the primitive life. Boys usually can be hired to take visitors over in a rowboat for a short visit. Whether Jack Frost and King Neptune, or the Norsemen left the carvings on the rocks of Manana, makes for interesting speculation on a summer's day.

John Cabot touched Monhegan in 1497, followed by Bartholomew Gosnold, George Waymouth and Champlain. The island became a base for explorers including Capt. John Smith, the first to mention it by name in his log book. While he was exploring elsewhere his crew remained to cultivate the land, trade with Indians and enjoy the bountiful fish supply. Because of the abundance of fish and the level lands for flakeyards (drying racks), Monhegan's reputation grew in Europe and gradually became headquarters for Portuguese, Norse, Basque, Breton and English fishermen. It became a trading and shipbuilding center and during the days of sail was a chief port of call for vessels bound overseas, the last landfall before sighting Europe.

Artists discovered Monhegan in 1878 and many of the nation's foremost artists have painted here — Robert Henri, Eric Hudson, George Bellows, Rockwell Kent, Sears Gallagher, Jacqueline Hudson, Andrew Winter, Jay Conway, Alfred Fuller and many others. Early artists gathered to talk over coffee in the lighthouse kitchen; Marie Stephens, the little French wife of the keeper, acquired a valuable collection of paintings.

Picturesque weathered houses surrounded by picket fences and bright flowers are set on the rough winding roads that lead to the great cliffs and *Cathedral Woods* with its towering pines, hushed, mysterious and beautiful. In spring the meadows are carpeted with wild flowers; in fall warm red sumac blends with bright yellow bracken and white birch, a foil for the dark green pines. In early spring, perfume of the sweet grass in the swamp mingles with the scent of the pines and the clean salty sea air. Many birds make their home on the island, their sweet music accented by the wild call of sea gulls, accompanied by the haunting boom of the surf — singing of far-off times and places.

Monhegan is a spellbinding, fearsome, magical and lonely place in winter. A mail boat calls three times a week. A dramatic sight is White Head Cliff; water from a nearby spring is frozen gold as it spills over to the rocks below. New Year's Day is Trap Day on Monhegan which has the best fishing grounds in the world. There's a special short six-months season for the catch here; one year 17 Monhegan lobstermen caught more than 170,000 pounds of lobsters in that period. By common agreement among the 100 or so families, since 1909 no lobsters are trapped from sunset June 25 to the dawn of January 1 — Trap Day — when lobster boats piled with traps and gear purr out of the harbor on the Atlantic, so cold it smokes sea vapor. Soon bright painted buoys are bobbing on the icy deep. The season is on.

PENOBSCOT BAY ISLANDS

From Rockland, Camden and Lincolnville (*see Tour 1 sec. c*): State ferries; cruisers and schooners, daily; windjammer cruises, 1-2 weeks.

Stretching away into the Gulf of Maine and the Atlantic, the magnificent islands of Penobscot Bay adorn one of the world's most beautiful sailing areas. From mainland ports against their backdrop of lovely Camden Hills, any one of the numerous scenic sails among these beguiling islands finds visitors prone to linger, loathe to leave. There are more than 60 islands in the Fox Islands Archipelago, so-called for the silver foxes that once roamed the woods.

VINALHAVEN (alt. 40, Vinalhaven Town, pop. 1273) (*from Rockland: State Ferry the Gov. Curtis, year-round, 1 hr. 25 min., 13 m.; the Victory Chimes, cruises*).

Leaving Rockland Harbor, breakwater (L) with lighthouse on Jameson's Point; Owl's Head Light tipping the rocky wooded peninsula (R). Settled in 1765 by the Carver family of Massachusetts, Vinalhaven was named for a forebear of Poet Harold Vinal. Nearby Hurricane Island was the subject of his poem of that name.

Quarrying became a flourishing industry, the fine granite used in many well-known structures such as New York's Church of St. John the Divine and Brooklyn Bridge. Something like the war machines of ancient Rome was the galamander, a special vehicle devised to lift and transport the huge blocks of granite. Galamanders with their huge high wheels were almost all handmade except for a power trip-hammer used to fashion the ironwork, and were painted 'Elder Littlefield' blue. Jumbo, the largest one, was made here and was drawn by an 8-horse hitch. A restored galamander and examples of the granite industry which had a limited revival in 1969, are seen in the Historical Society's outdoor exhibition.

Vinalhaven has a large colony of musicians, artists, teachers and writers, and many summer visitors. There are inns and shops, boating, fishing, rock-hunting in the old granite quarries, concerts and like events, and many interesting coves and bays for picnicking.

The Community Medical Center is known for Dr. Ralph P. Earle's diabetic research project and an unusual health care program. Behind the Center on a hillside in Ambrust Park is an attractive miniature lake graced by wooden sculptures. From here a path leads to the top of a massive granite outcropping and a splendid view of village, harbor and sea. Brown's Head Light overlooks Fox Islands Thoroughfare; Lane's Island, connected by causeway, is a Nature Conservancy preservation; a camping area is planned for Arey's Cove.

NORTH HAVEN (alt. 50, North Haven Town, pop. 384) (*from Rockland: State Ferry the North Haven, 1 hr. 10 min., 11 m., across Fox Islands Thoroughfare*), has opulent summer homes and a yacht club. Anne Morrow Lindbergh wrote of the island in her *North to the Orient*.

MATINICUS (Matinicus Plantation pop. 100) (*from Rockland: the MV Mary B with Capt. Norris Young, 2 hrs. 40 min., 23 m.*). The Maine Audubon Society's summer program schedules a trip here to the nesting grounds of sea-birds. This beautiful 800-acre 'unspoiled' island out in the Atlantic engenders romanticism. Dirt roads, few cars and but one set of tourist cabins. A few small sailboats among the lobster boats; fishhouses perched on high pilings. A maze of paths leading to magnificent views of the coast and smaller barren islands. Lonely sand beaches and coves of brightly colored rocks. There are many great story-tellers on the island, theirs not the patronizing parodies of commerce with synthetic down-east accents, but the true and native art, fast disappearing. The islanders' college-educated offspring are unlikely to choose the tough strong life of their forebears. Summer people are buying land at disturbing prices. How long Matinicus?

Among islands being preserved by Nature Conservancy in this area are *Big Jordan*, given by Charles and Anne Lindbergh, and *Mark Island* given by Garrison Norton, assistant Secretary of State under President Truman and assistant Secretary of the Navy under President Eisenhower.

Camden, too, is a great sailing area, with several one and two-hour trips among the islands.

The *Cynthia J* (38 ft., 34 passengers), Captains Gil Hall and Rusty Robinson; 7 daily trips, hauling lobster traps demonstrated.

The *Betselma*, Capt. Ralph Wooster; 5 daily, several evening cruises.

The *Sea Lark*, Capt. George Roundy, sails around Islesboro and Dark Harbor; clambake on Warren's Island.

And the *Mattie, Mercantile, Mistress, Sea Otter, Mary Day* and *Adventurer*.

ISLESBORO (alt. 40, Islesboro Town) *from Lincolnville: State Ferry the Gov. Muskie, 25 min., 3 m. (inns, boat landing ramps, picnic areas, airport),* center of a charming resort region. The township includes North and South Islesboro, Seven Hundred Acre and Job Islands and several islets. It was part of the Waldo Patent, was settled in 1769, and was visited earlier by the Church Expedition of 1692 in a campaign against the Indians. During the British occupation of nearby Castine (*see Tour 3*) in the War of 1812, Islesboro inhabitants found neutrality forced upon them. In the severe winters that froze Penobscot Bay as far out as Isle au Haut, ox-drawn sleighs often crossed the ice to the mainland.

At the ferry terminal (*picnic area*), the tower of Sailors' Memorial Lighthouse affords fine views. Sunset services are held on summer Sundays at the stone pulpit on the grounds.

A 42-passenger excursion boat plies between here, Camden and Lincolnville. Boat landing ramps are at the ferry terminal and the Town landing at Dark Harbor. There are public picnic areas at each end of the island, camping and boat rentals at East Shore and access to Warren's Island, 76 acres of wildland and ledges which the State is preparing as a yachtsmen's park for cruising families. In October and November, there is bow and arrow deer hunting in 9000 acres. Islesboro has a 'Day on the Island' Fourth of July celebration.

ISLE AU HAUT (alt. 35, Isle au Haut Town, pop. 45) *from Stonington* (*see Tour 3*): *toll ferry-mail boat; the Palmer Day II, Capt. Reginald Greenlaw; 6 m.*

The shimmering haze hovering over Isle au Haut may evoke thoughts of a northern Bali H'ai, but not for the down-east Yankee:

> Says the summer man, when the fog hangs low,
> 'There's a bridal wreath over Isle au Haut';
> But the fisherman says, when he launches his boat,
> 'It's gosh darn foggy off Isle au Haut.'

No mirage, the island is said to have been discovered in 1604 by Samuel de Champlain and given the name Ille Haute in the French Seventeenth century spelling. Through its vicissitudes, 13 spellings of the name have been recorded, in Latin, English and French, from Haute, Haulte and Holt and finally the present. The Holt corruption is thought to have been the influence of land surveyor, Joseph Holt, in the mid-1700s.

The township comprises three large and several small islands. A fishing community and summer retreat for wealthy men of the cloth, business and government, about half the island is now part of Acadia National Park. The first major land gift to the Park was Isle au Haut Mountain, given by the Bowditch family of international nautical renown. Near the East shore, cedars, maples and silver birches fringe the steep banks of a mile-long lake whose amber-hued waters fed by subterannean springs are of interest to geologists.

The 50-passenger *Palmer Day II* has 7-hr. deep-sea fishing trips and 2-hr. sightseeing excursions from the Stonington landing. Often seen are eider ducks, fish hawks, porpoises, seals, sharks, tuna, an occasional whale and other marine wildlife.

BLUE HILL BAY

SWAN'S ISLAND (alt. 50, Swan's Island Town, pop. 402) from Bass Harbor (*see Tour 2*): State Ferry the Everett Libby or the William S. Silsby, 40 min.,

5 m.; also servicing Frenchboro, Long Island Plantation, 8 m.

Champlain visited this 5875-acre island, one of the Burntcoat group, a century and a half before it was purchased by Col. James Swan of Fifeshire, Scotland, who succeeded in colonizing the Burntcoats. Arrested by the French government for a debt for which he was not responsible, Swan remained in St. Pelagie debtors' prison 22 years rather than securing his liberty by accepting the charge and paying the debt, despite the urging of his friend Lafayette. Not until Louis Philippe ascended the throne of France were Swan and others released. An old and broken man, he died three days later.

Swan's Island, Minturn and Atlantic are the three island villages, offering picnic areas and beaches, hiking and woods roads and scenic gems for artists and photographers. There's a beautiful lighthouse on Hockamock Head. Other places around the island: Goose Pond, Mackerel and Toothacher Coves and Irish Point.

ACADIA AND WAY DOWN EAST

In the famous Mount Desert region between Frenchman and Blue Hill Bays there are numerous scenic sails that make a pleasant adjunct to a visit to *Acadia National Park* and its many attractions (*see Tour 2*).

From Bar Harbor wharf: 1-2 hr. sails around Frenchman Bay for a waterborne view of the 'Ile des Monts-Desert,' sighting the various resorts and other islands in the Harbor. Ferry *Bluenose* to Yarmouth, N. S., 7 hrs. From Southwest or Northeast Harbor: the *Vagabond* to Islesford and the Cranberry Islands (*see Tour 2*).

On up the coast there are boats for hire at communities on Gouldsboro, Pleasant, Chandler, Englishman and Machias Bays.

At EASTPORT there are interesting trips to Deer Island and around Passamaquoddy Bay (*see Tour 1K*) where great fishing fleets are in operation.

From Eastport wharf: ferry to Deer Island, New Brunswick, passengers, trucks and trailers, 30 min. The *Friendship,* Capt. George Harris deep-sea fishing and excursions, St. Croix Island, St. Andrews and other Canadian points, 6 hrs.

From Deer Island, N. B.: Fredericton free government ferry to Letete, N. B., passengers and vehicles, 30 min.

IV. RECREATION

RECREATION

AMONG world-famous vacation regions, Maine is one of the few that offers year-round, the recreation and relaxation so highly prized in the Twentieth century. Since the discovery of this immense richly endowed land in the New World of the 1600s, many generations have rediscovered and extolled Maine's scenic beauties and diverse charms in all seasons — the great coastline, the romantic islands, the vast primeval forests and the magnificent mountains, lakes and waterways. Travel brochures do not exaggerate when they say that every form of outdoor enjoyment is here in lavish abundance and invigorating climate for the sportsman and nature lover — fishing, hunting, canoeing, swimming, surfing, sailing, nature and saddle trails, hiking, mountain climbing, camping, picnicking, foliage and island trips, photography, competitive sports and spectacles (*see RECREATION MAP and TOURS for orientation*). To each his own: helpful to vacationists of all persuasions are 30 Vacation Planners available from the State Department of Economic Development.

A few statistics may indicate the scope of 'vacationing' in Maine. Recreation, dating from Colonial days, has become an economic factor second only to the great woodlands. In 1654 the Court of Saco granted one Henry Waddock the right 'to keep an ordinary to entertain strangers for their money.' In the Eighteenth century, hunters, fishermen and nature lovers began coming in increasing numbers. By the mid-Nineteenth century, numerous hotels and boarding houses were devoted to their entertainment. Old Orchard's four-mile beach was officially dedicated to the resort business in 1840; other sections of Maine's 3,000-mile coastline became popular and the economic impact of 'recreation' began to be felt by the late 1800s. Cleveland Amory, describing the era in *The Last Resorts*, mentions Bar Harbor which at the turn of the century had become an exclusive playground for the wealthy. By 1920, the State's tourist income was estimated at $20 million; in 1930, about $85 million. With the mid-century increase in population and leisure, in 1970 the anticipated figure was half a billion as Maine's year-round population of just under a million swelled in summer to four million — not to mention the influx of spring, fall and winter sportsmen. The State is so large and diverse that so far its sense of spaciousness remains unaffected. Newcomers soon find it would take a lifetime to explore it all.

Every sixth home in Maine is a vacation or second home. Of the 70,000 of these, 40 percent belong to out-of-staters. They are valued at approximately $700 million, 15 percent of the State's tax base. From Kittery to

Calais, demand for waterfront property far exceeds supply. Prices for ocean frontage in the 1960s soared from $10 to $100 a foot. Inland, recreation homes and ski huts are a-building.

Additional thousands are trending into Maine to camp out at State and private sites, either in tents or more elaborate vehicles, even 24-foot trailers. While much Maine vacationing is family style and may involve several activities, some 12,000 youngsters are harbored in 220 summer camps where activities range from the hardy life at Outward Bound 'downeast' to studies in natural environment and cultural pursuits.

Besides the extensive private recreation developments in Maine, the State has an expanding Recreation program involving several State Departments with headquarters at Augusta, Maine 04330 (*see also GENERAL INFORMATION*). These should be consulted for brochures and essential information including laws, regulations, licensing, conditions, fees, etc. which are subject to change.

State Highway Commission maintains some 200 rest areas in picturesque roadside spots. Some have outdoor grilles, running water and sanitary facilities; all have benches and tables — and rubbish disposal containers. The Commission's official Highway Map locates ports of entry, airports, State parks, campsites and highway picnic areas, Forest Ranger headquarters and lookout stations.

Bureau of Watercraft Registration and Safety supplies a guide and laws for coastal and inland boating, marinas.

For snowmobiling there is the *Maine Snowmobile Association*, Box 186, Winthrop, Maine 04364 and the *Paper Industries Office*, 133 State St., Augusta, Maine 04330.

State Sea and Shore Fisheries and *Inland Fisheries and Game Departments* supply information on fishing and hunting laws, licensing and resources pertaining to their respective areas, coastal and inland. They maintain laboratories, experiment stations and game farms, and stock waters.

State Forestry Department. The Maine Forestry Service maintains 230 campsites, some deep in the woods where rangers and wardens are helpful. The Service's Authorized Campsite Program in the 10½ million-acre Maine Forestry District is administered in cooperation with private landowners to provide safe and sanitary camping and picnicking in a natural environment and as a forest fire prevention measure. These areas are equipped with safe fireplaces, picnic table and pit toilet. Drinking water usually is available but constant purity cannot be guaranteed; boiling or chlorinating is recommended. In the Forests:

It is legal to kindle fires only at State Forestry-designated campsites and lunch-grounds. It is *unlawful* to camp and kindle fires in the State's unorganized territory except at Forestry campsites without obtaining a permit from the nearest State Forest Fire warden or landowner. *Extreme care* is urged at all times with camp or lunch fires, matches and smokers materials while travelling in the woods. Campers are expected to leave a clean site for those who come after and to respect the rights of landowners.

Access to Forest campsites may be over road, trail or water. Most road access routes are privately owned, open to the public under a 'multiple use' policy. Some have nominal toll charges; others may be closed for reasons of fire protection and public safety. Recreationists should note and respect the regulations. Many privately owned forest roads not shown on the official State Highway map are located on Sportsmen's Maps distributed by the following landowners: Brown Company, Berlin, New Hampshire; Dead River Company, Bangor, Maine 04401; Georgia Pacific Corp., Woodland, Maine 04694; Great Northern Paper Company, 6 State St., Bangor; International Paper Company, Chisholm, Maine 04222; Oxford Paper Company, Rumford, Maine 04276; Penobscot Development Company, Great Works, Maine 04468; Scott Paper Company, Winslow, Maine 04901; Standard Packaging Corp., Brewer, Maine 04412.

Park and Recreation Commission. New State parks (1.5 million visitors in 1969) are opening every year. Always scenic, often historic, the current 22 parks offer various combinations of activities from swimming, fishing, and boating to hiking and mountain climbing. All have picnic areas and facilities, many have campsites, some are open to snowmobiling. The Commission also administers the 100-mile *Allagash Wilderness Waterway*, famed for canoe journeys, which is part of a projected 200,000-acre Wilderness Park. Great Northern Paper Company has donated 770 acres to the project. The Commission keeps an updated inventory of all Maine trails — hiking, biking, saddle, snowmobile, etc.

Shoreside and lakeside, parks are found in sightly locales from Cape Elizabeth to Quoddy Head, from Sebago, Rangeley and Moosehead to the Aroostook. The Table on the following page gives locations, facilities and dates (*see TOURS for environmental description; Tour 2 for ACADIA NATIONAL PARK*).

PARK	LOCATION	Picnic	Bathing	Snack Bar	Fishing	Camping	Hiking	Boat Launching	Boat Rental	Scenic Road	OPEN DATES
Aroostook	Presque Isle	X	X			X	X	X			May 15-Oct. 15
Bradbury Mt.	Pownal	X				X	X				May 1-Nov. 1
Camden Hills	Camden	X			X	X	X	X		X	May 15-Nov. 1
Cobscook Bay	Dennysville	X			X	X		X			May 15-Oct. 15
Crescent Beach	Cape Elizabeth	X	X	X							May 30-Sept. 30
Grafton Notch	Grafton	X					X			X	May 30-Oct. 15
Lake St. George	Liberty	X	X		X	X		X			May 1-Nov. 1
Lamoine	Lamoine	X			X	X		X	X		May 30-Oct. 15
Lily Bay	Greenville	X			X	X		X	X		Ice out-Oct. 15
Moose Point	Searsport	X									May 30-Labor Day
Mt. Blue	Weld	X	X		X	X	X	X	X	X	May 30-Oct. 15
Peaks-Kenny	Dover-Foxcroft	X	X		X	X					May 30-Labor Day
Popham	Phippsburg	X	X		X						May 30-Labor Day
Quoddy Head	Lubec	X			X			X			May 30-Labor Day
Rangeley	Rangeley	X	X		X	X		X	X		Ice out-Oct. 15
Reid	Georgetown	X	X	X	X	X	X	X	X		April 15-Dec. 15
Sebago Lake	Naples	X	X	X	X	X	X	X	X		May 1-Oct. 15
Two Lights	Cape Elizabeth	X									April 15-Dec. 15
Warren Island	Islesboro	X			X	X					May 15-Sept. 30
Allagash Wilderness Waterway											
Baxter Park	Millinocket	X	X		X	X	X			X	May 15-Oct. 15
Pemaquid Restoration		X	X				X				

BAXTER STATE PARK

Baxter State Park, a magnificent 200,000-acre wilderness area in north central Maine, is the gift of philanthropist and former governor, Percival P. Baxter, to be perpetuated in its natural state. The Park is administered for public use by a three-man Authority: the State's Attorney General and Commissioners of Forestry and Inland Fisheries and Game. Within the Park, Mt. Katahdin (5,267 ft.), highest point in Maine and most outstanding east of the Rockies, rises majestically to dominate a vast area of lesser peaks, lakes, streams and forest. Katahdin has stimulated man's imagination since the first red men called the region their home.

Indian legend says that Mt. Katahdin was created by the Council of Gods as their sacred meeting place. Pamola, one of the lesser Gods, became angry when refused a place at the Council and retreated to Pamola Peak where he has since made his home. The Indians believed that those who ventured on the mountain would incur Pamola's wrath and be seen no more. Today, when storm clouds swirl around the summit and the wind whistles across the Knife Edge, Pamola is stirring.

Charles Turner and a party of surveyors in 1804 made the first recorded ascent of Katahdin. As lumbering operations moved to the mountain's vicinity, access became easier and ascent more frequent. Philosopher-naturalist Henry David Thoreau in 1846 reached the Tableland by way of Abol slide. In the late 1800s, sporting camp owners began advertising Katahdin climbs as attractions. Thus several trails to the peak were first established.

Geologically, Mt. Katahdin is the result of an intrusion of granite rock that has been sculptured to its present form by 300 million years of erosion and glacial action (*see Dabney Caldwell's 'The Geology of Baxter State Park and Mt. Katahdin.'*) Katahdin's summit, Baxter Peak, specifically is the northern terminus of the famous 2,000-mile Appalachian Trail. There are 45 other peaks and ridges, 18 of them more than 3500 ft. high. Principal land features are: Pamola Peak, the Knife Edge, Baxter Peak, the Tableland, the Saddle, Hamlin Peak, the Northwest Plateau, and the North Peaks. Lying below are the Great Basin, the North Basin, the Northwest Basin and the Klondike Plateau.

Information: Baxter State Park Authority, Augusta, Maine 04330; Appalachian Mountain Club, 5 Joy St., Boston, Mass.

Season: May 15-Oct. 15.

Roads: dirt, narrow and winding. Drive with extreme caution within or below posted speed limits. Travel permits for those not stopping in the Park.

Campgrounds: fee; Ranger-supervised.

Regulations: camping restricted to designated areas assigned by Rangers. Reservations (recommended) must be paid in advance for bunkhouse, lean-to shelter, trailer or tent space. Write Reservation Clerk, Baxter State Park, Millinocket, Maine 04430; tel. Millinocket 723-5201. Camping or use of fire along trails, on table land or summit of Mt. Katahdin are prohibited. No pets, no snowmobiles allowed in Park.

Approaches: From the west, from Greenville over Greenville-Millinocket Road *(private, open to public use),* to Ripogenus Dam, 40 *m.* Northern fork here is shortest route to western and northern campgrounds, Nesowadnehunk and South Branch Pond. *From the south,* from Millinocket, branching R at 16.2 *m.,* dirt road leads to Togue Pond and Gatehouse, thence to Roaring Brook campground, 26 *m.* Left fork at Gatehouse leads to Abol, Katahdin and Nesowadnehunk Streams campgrounds. *From northeast,* from Patten via Grand Lake Road which branches toward the Millinocket-Greenville Road at Nesowadnehunk campground or continues toward Millinocket via the Nesowadnehunk Tote road. South from Grand Lake Road at 30 *m.,* road to South Branch Pond campgrounds. Other popular campgrounds are at Basin and Russell Ponds.

Trails: 20, about 83 *m.*:

    Hunt Trail, Katahdin Stream to Baxter Peak, 5.20 *m.*
    Abol Trail, Nesowadnehunk Road to Thoreau Spring, 2.76 *m.*
    Marston Trail, Nesowadnehunk Road to North Brother, 3.74 *m.*
    Chimney Pond Trail, Roaring Brook to Chimney Pond, 3.30 *m.*
    South Turner Trail, Roaring Brook to South Turner, 2 *m.*
    Russell Pond Trail, Roaring Brook to Russell Pond, 7 *m.*
    Saddle Trail, Chimney Pond to Baxter Peak, 2.17 *m.*
    Cathedral Trail, Chimney Pond to Baxter Peak, 1.70 *m.*
    Knife-Edge Trail, Pamola to Baxter Peak, 1.10 *m.*
    Dudley Trail, Chimney Pond to Pamola, 1.25 *m.*
    Hamlin Ridge Trail, Chimney Pond to Hamlin Peak, 1.96 *m.*
    Northwest Basin Trail, The Saddle to Russell Pond, 7.96 *m.*
    North Peaks Trail, Hamlin Peak to Russell Pond, 6.85 *m.*
    Old Pogy Road, Russell Pond to McCarthy Field, 10.45 *m.*
    Pogy Notch Trail, Russell Pond to South Branch Pond, 9.65 *m.*
    North Traveler Trail, South Branch Pond to North Traveler, 2.55 *m.*
    Helon Taylor Trail, Roaring Brook to Pamola Peak, 3.17 *m.*
    Owl Trail, Katahdin Stream to the Owl, 2 *m.*
    Rum Mountain Trail, Abol to South Peak, 4.50 *m.*
    South Branch Mt. Trail, South Branch Pond to South Branch Mt., 4 *m.*

M O U N T A I N E E R I N G

Information: Maine Forest Service; Appalachian Mountain Club.

BECAUSE it is there is the mountain climber's reason why. More and more people are discovering that mountain climbing, symbol of man's aspiration to reach upward and to surmount all obstacles in his path, offers unique spiritual rewards as well as physical well-being. Novice, intermediate and expert find conditions to their liking in Maine, from easy slopes to the sheer and formidable. And always the magnificent view from the summit — vibrant living beauty of the seemingly limitless greenclad forests embracing hundreds of glistening lakes, miniature villages nestling in the valleys, far-reaching farmlands sweeping to the horizon. Not the least of the pleasures en route are the botanical, geological and wildlife revelations.

Maine has ten mountains over 4000 feet, a hundred more than 3000 feet, countless others. Some of the better known: Katahdin, Old Spec, Bigelow, Sugarloaf, Haystack, Kineo, Cadillac (*see GEOGRAPHY, TOPO-GRAPHY*). Obviously the more difficult ones are only for experts, who have called Mt. Katahdin, sentinel of the last great wilderness of the east, one of the most desirable in the world. For this and other such challenges, extensive preparations are necessary.

Intermediate climbs are for the physically fit, but not for the elderly or the very young. Extended trips are possible from mountain to mountain, following old lumber roads and telephone lines. Camping out during mountain climbing and hiking expeditions is practical because of limited accommodations in wilderness areas. Besides the Maine Forestry Service campsites, fishing and hunting lodges when open have eating and sleeping facilities, but hiking the Appalachian Trail, for instance, means longer walks between camps nowadays than heretofore.

Families can safely and comfortably enjoy the lesser slopes, often located near resorts and camping areas and taking from a few hours to a day. Usually there are well-defined trails and in wooded areas, often a fire tower to climb for the view and a friendly warden to describe points of interest.

While experts presumably are well informed about preparations and equipment for serious mountain climbing expeditions, a few basic tips are given here for the uninitiate.

Never travel alone. Avoid travelling unfamiliar terrain after nightfall. Know what you are undertaking; don't over-estimate your capacity. Allow ample time. Travel time with stops to enjoy surroundings averages a maximum of 2 *m.* per hour, about 1 *m.* per hour climbing, double that for rough, steep terrain. Carry pack with extra lunch, compass, map, fire-making material, rain garment and sweater. Wear well-broken-in shoes at least a half size larger than normal, silk or lisle socks under woolen hose. Feet subject to blisters may be previously hardened by soaking several times for 15 minutes in tannic acid solution (1 oz. powder to 2 qts. water). Poisonous snakes are unknown in Maine. Take mosquito and black fly deterrents July-August. Water canteens needed only on highest peaks. Observe fire-building laws and private landowners' regulations.

FISHING

INLAND: fly fishing, casting, trolling; lakes, ponds, rivers, streams.
Catch: salmon, trout, togue, bass, perch, pickerel, whitefish, smelts.
Regions: Sebago, Rangeley, Moosehead, Belgrade, Katahdin, Allagash, Fish River, Narraguagus, Grand Lakes.

COASTAL: rod and reel, handline, spear; offshore, deep sea.
Catch: striped bass, flounder, pollock, mackerel, bluefin tuna, tautog, cod haddock, halibut, swordfish.
Regions: Kittery to Eastport. Charter and/or head boats at York Harbor, Ogunquit, Kennebunkport, Cape Porpoise, Pine Point, Portland, Small Point, Bailey Island, Boothbay Harbor, Monhegan, Spruce Head, Vinalhaven, Sunshine, Stonington, Bar Harbor, Seal Harbor, Cranberry Island, Bass and Winter Harbors, Sorrento, Prospect Harbor, Jonesport, Cutler, Eastport.

Regulations: seasons, licenses, limits; State Departments of Inland Fisheries and Game and Sea and Shore Fisheries; Bureau of Watercraft Registration and Safety; local officials.

THE fighting gamefish of Maine's cold inland and coastal waters have attracted anglers from far and near ever since Colonial days when salmon sold for a penny apiece. Every angler has his favorite, from the kingly trout, famous landlocked salmon and bass to saltwater Atlantic salmon, striped bass and giant tuna. While spring, summer and fall are the usual fishing seasons winter has its ice fishing devotees.

In the big lake and river fishing regions there are fishing camps and guides. Planked or smoked salmon and trout are epicurean delights — you may learn how to do it. Easily accessible lakes, ponds and brooks offer enjoyment for the less serious fisherman.

For coastal fishing cruises, experienced crews man Coast Guard inspected and licensed charter and head boats (*advance reservations recommended*), equipped with safety and communications devices and often with electronic systems for depth recording and fish finding. *Charter* boats carry up to six persons at a fixed price per boat per day, *head* boats average 30 persons at a fixed price per head per day or may be chartered for private groups. Ask the boat captain about the Maine Tackle-Busters Club, an honorary association of saltwater sports fishermen who have landed the big ones.

The ocean is no place for the inexperienced and uninformed. Private boat owners should be capable and knowledgeable, familiar with the Maine Boating Guide and Laws. Local officials will advise on tackle, bait and equipment. They should be consulted for regulations on taking softshell clams, scallops and marine worms and regarding closed areas.

INLAND WATERS

Atlantic salmon: Maine has the only sea runs of Atlantic salmon in the United States. Fishing above tidewater (*license required*) is done with English salmon and dry flies, Maine streamers and locally originated patterns. The fish are found in the Machias, East Machias, Narraguagus, Dennys, Sheepscot, Pleasant and Penobscot Rivers. 'Black salmon,' those that have wintered over, are caught in spring; 'bright' or fresh-run season is May through mid-September.

Landlocked salmon: the famous salmo sebago is hardly distinguishable from its sea-run forebear. They are found in some 200 lakes and rivers, are marvelous gamefish on flies, trolled or cast on a wide variety of lures.

Brook trout: some of the most famous flies originated in Maine, long known for its fly-fishing for brook trout, to some the most flavorful fish of all. Except for black bass, trout once was the most widely distributed of all gamefish in the country. Today it is limited pretty well to Maine and a few other states and Canadian provinces. The Eastern brook trout, sometimes called squaretail or speckled, is found in stocked waters and in many wilderness ponds and streams, reached by car, sometimes by boat, canoe or small plane. Caught with 2- or 3-ounce wand and dry fly, the fish run from half a pound to six or seven pounds.

Brown trout: these are increasing in Maine where hundreds are caught. Wherever stocked, the brown has done well and is a fighter.

Rainbow trout: Wyman Dam Pool in the Kennebec River at Bingham is the scene of exciting fishing every season when heavy rainbows come to the lures (flies and spinners) and fight in the fast waters. The 'bow is not widely stocked.

Black bass: The smallmouth is widespread in all coastal counties and inland to central Maine; largemouths are found in fewer waters. The bass, a worthy antagonist, often has been called the national gamefish, as it exists in most of the 50 states. Because landlocked salmon and trout are more popular species with resident sportsmen, black bass have flourished nearly unmolested in many Maine rivers. They hit savagely in the special fly fishing season, and continue to strike all summer and early fall.

Togue: or lake trout are found in most waters containing salmon and Eastern brook trout. Many northern wilderness ponds contain only trout and togue. A heavy, solidly built fish, the biggest togue are taken on deep trolling gear.

White Perch: Closely resembling black bass in shape and habits, perch is a popular food fish, its flesh white, sweet and delicious. From boats and bridges, fishermen angle for this fish with worms and spinners in spring; later, with small streamer flies. Sizes run from 6 inches to 2 pounds. The world's record white perch, (4 lbs., 2 oz.) was caught in Maine in 1949.

Pickerel: These are so numerous in Washington County that they may be caught and offered for sale. Elsewhere in central and southern Maine, pickerel fishing is excellent. These sweet-meated but bony fish run from two to four pounds, sometimes slightly heavier.

Other sporting fish in inland waters include whitefish, yellow perch, blueback, golden and smelts.

COASTAL WATERS

Tuna: Largest quarry sought by marine sports fishermen is the bluefin tuna or horse mackerel which can mean a four or five-hour battle with a giant of the sea weighing up to 1000 pounds. Heavy and expensive gear is required and neophytes do best to go out with experienced captains in properly equipped charter boats. Although experienced local fishermen take the species from small boats or dories, by handline or harpoon, this is not recommended for the novice. Giant tuna are those weighing over 300 pounds; school tuna weigh up to 300 pounds. They range the entire coast of Maine, usually well offshore, but they are curious and intrigued by commotion and will chase bait close to the coast. They frequent offshore rips where clashing currents confuse and tumble bait. School tuna often will take Japanese feathers, nylon eels or plugs trolled at fairly high speed close to the wake of the boat. Giants seldom take an artificial lure. Chumming — fresh herring or mackerel tossed overside — coaxes tuna to surface. Bailey Island, Casco Bay and Ogunquit have Tuna Clubs and tournaments. Bailey Island tournaments were begun in 1939 by native fishermen who took pride in 'ironing' the largest or the most horse mackerel. Only in recent years were the rod and reel sportsmen accepted. In 1968 Al Jolson brought in a giant bluefin weighing 835 lbs., record for the last ten years since official records were filed.

Tautog: Less well known is this coastal ranger that runs inshore during spring and fall, into deep water summer and winter. Always frequenting rocky, shelly areas or wrecks and pilings, tautogs have been caught in Casco and Penobscot Bays and along Boothbay Harbor ledges. Fishfinder rigs with sinkers heavy enough to resist tidal currents are advised.

Cod: The major species landed by charter and head boats, cod run from two to five pounds, though 20-pounders are not uncommon. They are found in estuaries or near rocky ledges in spring, otherwise offshore and will take most any edible bait. The codfish drail or sinker is best to present the bait right on the bottom.

Halibut: Good eating, these may run several hundred pounds, are now becoming a popular gamefish.

Mackerel: All along the coast, inshore in summer, mackerel chase bait to the mouth of inlets but never move into fresh water. Chumming keeps school mackerel in a feeding mood close to the boat so they will hit jigs and flies. Head boats take out special evening trips. Mackerel also are caught with light tackle from shore.

Pollock: Small harbor pollock swarm close to shorelines. Larger ones are offshore but in spring and fall chase schools of bait inshore. They are hard and active in spring, may even jump like salmon.

Haddock: These frequent hard bottom but not ledge or rock areas or heavy marine growth.

Flounder: This small-mouthed fish ranges inshore in spring and fall, in deeper waters in summer. Here is your filet of sole. Spreader rigs are used in winter. A gamey flatfish, the sand flounder chases bait into the surf in summer.

Hake and cunners also are plentiful; not so the swordfish.

HUNTING

Game: deer, bear, bobcat, fox, raccoon, rabbit, fisher, mink, otter, skunk, squirrel.

Birds: ruffed grouse, woodcock, pheasant, ducks, Canada geese, seabirds.

Regulations: seasons, licenses, limits; Department of Inland Fisheries and Game. Firebuilding restrictions; Maine Forestry Service. No Sunday hunting. No night hunting except raccoon and skunk. No dogs used to hunt deer. No open season on moose, caribou, lynx or sable. Game and birds in preserves and sanctuaries protected. Special deer season for bow and arrow hunters. *Hunting with firearms requires particular precautions.* Wear hunter orange. Know what you are shooting at. Be careful of fire in the woods.

HUNTING and fishing are a $55 million business in Maine. Rifle and shotgun hunters bag some 35,000 deer annually during open season which varies in different areas. While white-tail deer are the most sought trophy because Maine bucks are much heavier than those in other states, there are many other opportunities to seek game animals, birds and waterfowl.

The Department of Inland Fisheries and Game carries on game management in cooperation with Fish and Game organizations. A longer hunting season is allowed in northern Maine to help balance the level of deer. If the deer harvest is too small, many die in other ways; there is not enough food for an unchecked deer population and many would starve. In deer yard areas where food supply is poor, game managers clear and plant areas with trees whose young shoots provide food for the animals.

As famous as the White Hunter of the African safari is the Maine Guide, respected and praised by thousands who have hunted in Maine since Thoreau, the great naturalist visited these vast wilderness areas more than a century ago and paid tribute to the knowledge and ability of his guides. By tradition they are experienced, careful and trustworthy; they want to make a Maine hunting trip a memorable experience. They know their territory and where the game is likely to be. Like the ship's captain on the high seas, the Maine guide is master in the woods; he expects his rules of safety to be followed, otherwise he terminates the relationship. If by rare chance a hunter is lost, he knows his guide will find him before sundown.

The guide will meet the hunter at the sporting camp and accompany him into the woods each day, or he will take the hunter by canoe deep into the wilderness, camping each night in the open. Hunting camp proprietors follow a century's tradition of their ancestors and know their business. Camps in deep woods country offer 'luxury' in the rough for those who want a contrast to everyday comforts. Others are gracious little inns with all the comforts of home amid hunting territory. Common to all is good food in astonishing quantities. Those who live off the woods and work hard have enormous appetites and expect everyone to 'eat hearty.' This is surprisingly easy after a day in the crisp air of the aromatic woodlands. And there are those who do not hunt, neither do they fish, but simply enjoy the rest and relaxation of the camps.

GAME

Deer: Theodore Roosevelt once called Maine deer the outstanding specimens of their kind in the world. Here, under ideal conditions, they attain their greatest growth. Known as the Virginia or White-tailed Deer, these graceful animals are found in virtually every Maine township. Deer have increased near the centers of population and there is superb shooting on old deserted farms as well as in the wild lands. The Department of Economic Development sponsors The Biggest Bucks in Maine Club for those who shoot a buck weighing at least 200 lbs. woods dressed. Nearly 500 such deer are bagged annually, an appreciable number weighing 300 lbs.

Bear: The large population of bears, which also may be trapped, attracts many hunters. Closed season Jan. 1-May 31. The Maine Black Bear Club issues a card and shoulder patch to those who have legally shot a bear weighing 100 lbs. or more. All bear killed must be reported within seven days to the Fisheries and Game Commissioner.

Bobcat: No closed season on these wily animals, often accused of deer killing. Ferocious in appearance, bobcats are extremely shy, are taken chiefly by running them with dogs.

Fox: Hardy and shifty, red fox also are abundant state-wide. Unlike in the South, horses are not used to any extent in Maine fox-hunting. The hunter does his own legwork, unleashing his hounds for swift and certain action.

Raccoon: Foxier than the fox, the 'coon will 'tree' before going far. Tracking is done mostly at night when the hunters follow the baying hounds either on the dark or the light of the moon. A new note in the song of the hounds indicates when the quarry is treed. Then comes the fun of getting him down. 'Coons also make great pets — not favored by farmers who know how smart they are in the cornpatch. De-scented skunks may be pets, too; but few would recommend the porcupine.

Rabbit: Rabbit hunting is a favorite sport particularly in farm areas where rabbit dogs abound. Distributed widely in large numbers through the State, the big Maine rabbits are also excellent eating. Except for coastal cottontails, Maine rabbits are mostly "snowshoe" hares, so-called because of their hind feet.

BIRDS

Ruffed grouse or partridge: King of upland game birds, the partridge, a comparatively big bird, is wary, fast on the get-away and presents a difficult shot. A good bird dog adds much to the sport, although many gunners 'walk' the birds up.

Woodcock: Maine is one of the country's greatest breeding grounds for this lively little migratory bird known as the 'timberdoodle.' Hunters get two cracks at the woodcock. Early in the season native birds are hunted. When these head south, flights from the north continue to alight in Maine covers, furnishing good gunning throughout the season. Because woodcock 'lie close,' dogs are needed. Once flushed their erratic flight is a challenge to the wing shot.

Ducks: Maine's hundreds of miles of coast and thousands of inland waters offer the best in duck hunting. Many ducks breed in Maine; in the fall, thousands in migration tarry here on their way South. Merrymeeting Bay at the mouth of the Kennebec River is one of the most famous duck-hunting regions in the east. Other salt water bays and inlets, as well as inland lakes and streams attract thousands of duck hunters each fall. The popular ducks are the black, scaup, goldeneye, ringneck, a few mallards and other species. Some Canada geese are shot. Offshore shooting is for sea ducks — eiders, scoters, etc.

Pheasant: At the State Game Farm in Gray, many thousands of pheasants are hatched annually under scientific conditions. The Department of Inland Fisheries and Game stocks hundreds of covers directly and also supervises stocking under a cooperative plan with Maine sportsmen who raise birds from eggs or chicks produced at the Farm. Most productive covers usually are found in coastal counties and inland to central Maine.

ARCHERY AND CAMERA

During the special archery season on deer, bow and arrow hunters take their share of the big ones to qualify for the Biggest Bucks in Maine Club. Archery hunters also have a club of their own, the Maine Bow and Arrow Club, whose members qualify by taking any of the larger game animals. The skilled bowman finds a fair target not only in deep woods but around the fields and orchards of Maine farms. And proud and lonely bucks prance along the trails of old logging roads in the forests.

Stalking game with a camera has many rewards and no closed season. Trophies may be pictures of a magnificent buck poised for flight, a bear indulging in one of his antics or a moose feeding on lily pads or swimming a stream.

CANOEING

CANOEISTS get to know and love the heart of Maine in ways experienced perhaps by no other outdoorsmen. Some of the many thrilling courses of the great maze of inland waterways penetrating the forests of the State are for the highly experienced and require a guide; others are less arduous and demanding. Dams, stirring rapids, waterfalls tumbling into deep pools, shoal, rocky water and portages challenge the skilled canoeist whose journey may be at once exciting and leisurely. There is unforgettable primeval beauty as the canoe glides to the silent dip of the paddle in the stillness of the woodland. Camping and fishing are added pleasures. Many boys' and girls' camps include camping-canoe trips in their programs. For novices and those unfamiliar with Maine waters, information and advice from the Maine Forestry Service or Department of Inland Fisheries and Game are essential.

Allagash Wilderness Waterway: Perhaps best known of Maine's canoeing areas, the hundred miles to be explored here may be taken in portions as desired. The longest trip through the Waterway: Telos Lake to West Twin Brook, 92 *m.* A five-mile paddle across Telos Lake through Round Pond into Chamberlain Lake; 10 *m.* from the foot of Chamberlain to Lock Dam. A side trip here: 3 *m.* W of Lock Dam to the mouth of Allagash Stream. An experienced canoeist can make a six-mile trip with pole and paddle up this Stream to the matchless solitude of Allagash Lake in the shadow of Allagash Mountain. Canoes only are permitted on the Lake and Stream which are closed to aircraft, motors and mechanized equipment.

A short portage from Lock Dam continues the main course with a 12-mile paddle across Eagle Lake, a two-mile run through the thoroughfare, and 5 *m.* more of lake to Churchill Dam. Below the Dam, the nine-mile trip through Chase's Rapids requires poling. Famed for its white water canoeing, Chase's Rapids needs an experienced man in the stern, able to guide the canoe through the rocks when the water is running high.

The trip across Umsaskis Lake is 5 *m.* to the Long Lake thoroughfare where the private Ashland-Daquam Road crosses the Waterway. Another 5 *m.* through Long Lake into the ten-mile river run to Round Pond. From the N end of the Pond an 18-mile paddle to Allagash Falls, a third of a mile portage and an eight-mile run to West Twin Falls, end of the Allagash Wilderness Waterway. Many continue another 5 *m.* to Allagash Village, a frontier town settled by the English but now occupied by Acadian descendants, at the confluence of the St. John and Allagash Rivers. From here it is about 15 *m.* down river to St. Francis, 15 more to Fort Kent.

St. John River Trip: Northeast Carry to Fort Kent, 201 *m.* (*three weeks, guide recommended*). The full trip down the St. John is the longest in the State. Starting at Northeast Carry at the upper end of Moosehead Lake, part of the trip is through the heart of Maine's wilderness. Fast white water in sections of the river call for utmost skill. Along the way, stops of several days may be made. There is excellent fishing and an abundance of game to be observed. Visit beaver 'works' on many side streams.

Fish River Chain of Lakes Trip: St. Agatha to Fort Kent, 52 to 93 *m.* (*three days to two weeks, guide recommended*). One of the most interesting, varied canoe trips, with worthwhile side trips, this one is flexible to suit the canoeist's available time. The main course takes in Long, Mud (Salmon), Cross, Square and Eagle Lakes. At Eagle, the traveller has two choices: 1) to Portage 27 *m.* S through St. Froid and Portage Lakes; 2) N to Fort Kent 21 *m.* from the town of Eagle Lake via Wallagrass. It is 6 *m.* from the thoroughfare leading into Eagle Lake, to the town, 4 *m.* to Wallagrass. There is much rough water, several bad rapids and a few carries between Wallagrass and Fort Kent. Fish River Falls 2 *m.* above Fort Kent must be carried. From St. Agatha it is approximately 65 *m.* to Fort Kent, 60 *m.* to Portage and 81 *m.* to Fish River Lake.

East Branch (Penobscot) Trip: Northeast Carry or Chesuncook Dam to Grindstone, 118 *m.* (*two weeks*). The East and West Branches of the Penobscot River have long been known to canoeists. (The St. John trip starts in West Branch waters). This East Branch trip may start from Northeast Carry, Moosehead Lake, paddling 20 *m.* NE on the West Branch into the N end of Chesuncook Lake; or from Chesuncook Dam at the foot of the Lake N to upper end of Lake. The trip goes NE to Chamberlain Lake, SE on Chamberlain Lake to Telos Lake, Webster Lake, Matagamon or Grand Lake, then enters the East Branch of the Penobscot, travelling S to Grindstone, through indescibably beautiful scenery. From Stair Falls, a lovely cataract, the course goes through the four pitches of Pond, Grand, Hulling Machine and Bowling Falls and along the 15-mile run to the mouth of Wassataquoik Stream. The mouth of this Stream marks the beginning of white water variously named Whetstone, Burnt and Grindstone Falls and best not run in rush water.

East Grand Lake - St. Croix River Trip: Orient to Calais, 95 *m.* (*one week, guide recommended*). Putting in at Orient at the head of East Grand Lake, paddle through chain of lakes to Forest City, good place to restock food. Cross Spednic Lake to Vanceboro, continue down St. Croix River to Woodland, paper mill site. Continue down the St. Croix bordering Canada to Calais. Red Beach with its granite out-cropping is here and historic Dochet's Island.

Attean Lake Trip: Wood Pond, Attean Pond, 30-40 *m.*, (*three days, guide recommended*). This trip may be taken either of two ways. Leave Jackman on the Canadian-Pacific and get off at Boston Ranch on Holeb Pond. Go to outlet of Holeb Pond into Moose Pond, to Attean Pond and into Wood Pond. A quarter mile carry at Holeb Falls. Entire trip, approximately 30 *m.* Or start at Jackman, go across Wood Pond to Attean Pond where there is a carry of 1¼ *m.* to Holeb Pond. The entire trip, 40 *m.*

Moose River Trip: Moose River Post Office to Rockwood, 29 *m.* (*two days, guide necessary*). Only very expert canoeists should attempt this trip without a guide. It is through wild country, — fine fishing, fast water, easy portages. Put in Moose River N of Jackman near post office, paddle downstream to Long Pond, through to Moose River and continue to Brassua Lake. A private road and bridge (open to public) downstream from Long Pond. Paddle down Brassua, carry around dam, continue on Moose River into Moosehead Lake and Rockwood. May be continued down Moosehead 20 *m.* to Greenville.

Penobscot River Trip: Wytopitlock to Rockland, 82 *m.* to Bangor, (*five days*). Some of the best canoemen do not care to run the river between Wytopitlock and Mattawamkeag; white water can be dangerous at high water. One may put in on the Mattawamkeag River however, paddle to the Penobscot then continue S to tidewater at Bangor and even proceed farther in the protected reaches of the lower river to Bucksport, Searsport, Belfast or Rockland.

Kennebec River Trip: The Forks to Bath, 125 *m.* (*one week*). This is a fine all-river trip beginning at The Forks at the confluence of the Kennebec and Dead Rivers, reversing the course of Arnold's men in their bateaux on the fatal march to Quebec in 1775. It passes Bingham, Solon, Norridgewock, Anson, Madison, Skowhegan, Hinckley, Shawmut, Fairfield, Waterville, Winslow, Augusta, Hallowell, Gardiner, Randolph and Richmond, into Merrymeeting Bay where the Androscoggin joins the Kennebec. Shoal water, sunken logs and rocks between Shawmut and Fairfield. Bingham Dam holding back Wyman Lake is the largest of ten dams on the course which ends at Bath.

Shorter trips, one to three days:

Fish Stream, Patten to Island Falls, 12 *m.,* (*one day*); and *Molunkus Stream,* Sherman Mills to Macwahoc, 28 *m.,* (*two days*). Both of these are short and easy through wooded areas; trout waters, no carries. Return for round trip. Good trout fishing also on *Union River - Great Pond Trip,* Amherst to Brandy Pond, 36 *m.,* (*two days*). Paddle L past mouth of Alligator Stream, up Main Stream 1 *m.* to Buffalo Stream, NE another mile into Brandy Stream, upstream 1½ *m.* to Brandy Pond. For another *Union River Trip,* Amherst to Blue Hill, 35 *m.* (*two days*), put in at West Branch Union River, paddle S to Graham Lake, SW to Union River outlet, to Ellsworth, continuing to Union River Bay, thence to Blue Hill Bay. Here the trip may be continued to any of the harbors on Mt. Desert Island, or W to Blue Hill. Longer and more difficult is the Baskahegan Stream-Mattawamkeag River Trip, Danforth to Mattawamkeag, 40-46 *m.* (*three days*), four carries; bass and pickerel water; spring trout fishing.

Among many other trips: Chain of Ponds, Flagstaff Lake Flowage and Dead River, Rangeley Lakes, Androscoggin River, Belgrade Lakes, Moosehead Lake, Ossipee River, Crooked River and Sebago Lake, Penobscot West Branch, Cobbosseecontee Stream and Lake Maranacook, Damariscotta River and Lake, Kezar Lake and Saco River, Grand Lake and Machias River.

COASTAL CRUISING

Information: All boatowners should be familiar with *Maine Boating Guide and Laws* and essential navigational information available from the Bureau of Watercraft Registration and Safety, with basic knowledge of harbors and anchorages.

Free Boating Courses: U. S. Power Squadron, 27 Town Landing Road, Falmouth Foreside, Maine; U. S. Coast Guard, 1400 Custom House, Boston, Mass.; American Red Cross, 97 State St., Portland, Maine; Pine Tree State Boat Owners Council, 186 Lisbon St., Lewiston, Maine.

Principal Bays and Boat Centers: Capes and beaches, Kittery to Cape Elizabeth; Casco Bay, Boothbay Harbor, Muscongus, Penobscot, Blue Hill, Frenchman, Englishman, Machias, Cobscook and Passamaquoddy Bays.

Landfalls: For orientation, description of shoreside points and attractions, see MAP, TOUR 1 and side tours, and ISLAND TRIPS.

PLEASURE craft, from million dollar yachts to dories, in summer share the blue waters along Maine's 2500-mile coastline with commercial vessels. The magnificent coastline is so vast — equal to half the Atlantic seaboard — that all can enjoy the freedom of the seas which like all freedoms implies certain responsibilities (*see Maine Boating Laws*). From Kittery to Eastport, safe harbors and innumerable protective islands make this one of the world's best boating areas, power or sail. U. S. Coast Guard stations operate along the coast and the small boatman seldom is more than a short run from a safe haven when the weather freshens. He also can explore coves and inlets and tidal rivers far inland. Shoreside in the historic coastal towns long experienced in meeting seamen's needs, there are marinas, landing ramps and supply depots. There are boatyards to repair, fit or build boats to specifications and handle winter storage. There are boatels, inns, restaurants, shops and varied entertainment and coastal parks, forts, historic sites and art galleries and museums for a change of pace.

Coming up the Atlantic coast under sail or power, it is 'sailing down to Maine' or 'down-east,' not 'up to Maine' as landlubbers might think. This is because prevailing winds, especially in summer, are such that one is sailing downwind, as did the giant clippers, schooners and down-easters in the great days of sail.

Passenger steamers and large pleasure yachts began coming to Maine in the Nineteenth century when Bar Harbor and the Penobscot Bay area became popular among wealthy cottage and yacht owners, with a big social season ashore and afloat. In the 1970s all manner of craft dot the bays and harbors of Maine's seaboard as more and more landsmen discover the exhilaration of sea cruising. Some summer boatmen like the rivers and streams and the 'inland seas' of Maine's big lakes. Owners of small boats transport them overland to inland or coastal marinas. Non-boat owners too can enjoy sea-going experiences — windjammer cruises, fishing, island-hopping and sightseeing via State ferry and private boatlines operating from many points (*see TOUR 1; ISLAND TRIPS*). Local and longtime summer residents do their sailing and boating in their own areas with occasional trips up and down the coast, cruising from a day to two weeks. Water skiing, sailing and power boat races enliven the summer scene.

Newcomers to Maine's vast coastal area with its myriad islands soon realize it would take the better part of a lifetime to explore in all its variations from the capes and beaches of the south to the great bays and long inlets mid-coast and the bold promontories down-east. Many take a new segment each season to become familiar with its special attractions.

SAILING DOWNEAST

Kittery to Cape Elizabeth: The southern part of the Maine coast is a well-sheltered area of capes and beaches with many resorts and much of historical interest ashore. Along here are the Yorks, Cape Neddick, Bald Head Cliff, Ogunquit, Wells, the Kennebunks, Biddeford Pool, with many other communities in between, and offshore, Boon Island Light and Isles of Shoals.

Casco Bay: Approximately 300 islands, some mere dots, others largely populated, are scattered over the Bay known for its safe anchorages since the Seventeenth century. Several islands were fortified to protect the harbor in early days. The mainland shore stretches many miles from Cape Elizabeth (S) to Cape Small Point (NE), only 20 *m.* apart in direct line. On Casco Bay is Maine's largest city, the port of Portland (shopping, points of interest, sailing races). Portland Headlight, Maine's oldest lighthouse (1791) is at South Portland and Two Lights State Park is at Cape Elizabeth, another park at Crescent Beach. Peak's is the largest island; among others, Great and Little Diamonds, separated from Long Island by Hussey's Sound, Cushing's, Cliff and Jewell. Great and Little Chebeague are off Falmouth and northerly on the mainland are Yarmouth, South Freeport and Mere Point. Shoreside S of Brunswick are South Harpswell and Gurnet. Through Mericoneg and Harpswell Sounds are Bailey, Eagle, Orr's, Sebascodegan, Ragged and Birch Islands; Quohog Bay and New Meadows.

Near Cape Small Point on the Phippsburg peninsula are Sebasco yacht basin on W side, mouth of the Kennebec River on E side, site of the first attempted English settlement in New England (1607), with Seguin Light offshore and Bay Point opposite. There are launching ramps a short distance up-river at Phippsburg Center and at the ship-building city of Bath 12 *m.* Merrymeeting Bay, famous game bird preserve is in this area (boat facilities).

Boothbay Harbor Region: From the mouth of the Kennebec to Muscongus Bay, the jagged coast is characterized by long peninsulas reaching out to sea and long inlets cutting far inland. En route to Boothbay from the Kennebec, there are the Sheepscot and Sasanoa Rivers to be explored — Five Islands, MacMahan's, Robinhood Cove, Wiscasset, Southport. Newagen is on the point entering Boothbay Harbor with Ocean Point on the NE point opposite. In the embrasure, the Harbor is a humming boating center, with yacht clubs, races, cruises, boatels, inns, seafood restaurants and shops. Summer theatre, museums and the like are diversions. Squirrel Island is here, Damariscove Island farther out, and still farther, famous Monhegan 10 *m.* out, equidistant from Port Clyde. Rounding Ocean Point, a trip up Damariscotta River leads to a pleasant resort area. Just N of Ocean Point is Christmas Cove and South Bristol.

Muscongus Bay: Pemaquid Point Light E of Christmas Cove marks the entrance of Muscongus Bay. At Pemaquid is a fort and an archaeological museum of artifacts from excavations at an early settlement site here. Northerly are Round Pond and Medomak. On the next large peninsula is Friendship, known for its sloops, and up through Long Cove are St. George and Thomaston. SE of Friendship is Port Clyde; on around the point to Tenant's Harbor, Ash Point and Owl's Head.

Penobscot Bay: Long known as one of the most beautiful sailing areas on the Atlantic coast, Penobscot Bay embraces some of the largest of Maine's islands populated by one to six towns and villages. Plenty of time should be allowed here for sightseeing. Entering the Bay from the S, Rockland is the principal mainland port. Offshore are North Haven 11 *m.*, Vinalhaven 16 *m.*; SE 23 *m.* is Matinicus with Criehaven Harbor and another Ragged Island. Along the coast above Rockland are Rockport and Camden. Opposite Lincolnville is the island of Islesboro and Gilkey's Light. N is Belfast and Searsport; up Penobscot River to Bucksport and Bangor. On the E side of the river mouth is historic Castine where the Maine Maritime Academy is located. SE is Deer Isle and beyond S is Isle au Haut; Swan's, NE on Jericho Bay. There also are harbors at South Brooksville, Sargentville, Sedgwick, Brooklin and Eggemoggin Reach.

Blue Hill Bay: Around the point at Naskeag past Long Island to Blue Hill Falls. Time should be planned for visiting great Mt. Desert Island lying between Blue Hill Bay W and Frenchman Bay E. Here are Acadia National Park and Mt. Cadillac, Bar Harbor yachting center and numerous resort communities. Acadia with its combination of mountains, lakes, forest and seashore is one of the world's beauty spots. On the W side of Mt. Desert are Somesville, Seal Cove, West Tremont and Bernard; Bass Harbor at the southern tip is 5 *m.* from Swan's Island.

Frenchman Bay: Blue Hill and Frenchman Bay and Somes Sound (fjord) constitute some of the best sailing grounds on the coast. Sailing up the E side of Mt. Desert: Southwest Harbor, Cranberry Isles and Islesford, Manset, Northeast Harbor, Seal Harbor, Otter Creek, Bar Harbor, Hull's Cove, Salisbury Cove. N on the mainland, Lamoine State Park, Hancock Point, Sorrento and SE to Winter Harbor and Schoodic Point. From the point, again NE to Prospect Harbor, Corea, a bay to Gouldsboro, another to Steuben. Crossing E from Corea to Petit Manan Point, soon enter Pleasant Bay, area of untrammelled beauty. Off South Addison at NE end of the bay are Great Wass and Beal's Islands. Next large port is Jonesport.

Englishman Bay: Beginning with Pleasant Bay the rugged beauty down-east in this Washington County region is unmatched. Leaving resort life astern, the boatman feels the thrill of the explorer in a new land. Although it is approximately 70 *m.* from Northeast Harbor (Mt. Desert) to Passamaquoddy Bay, there are a score of harbors to put in; a safe anchorage is never more than a short run. From Jonesport, proceed through Chandler Bay into Englishman Bay and around to Roque Bluff where a recreation development is planned.

Machias Bay: ENE into Machias Bay, past Starboard, Cross Island (R) to Buck's Harbor and Machiasport. From Cross Island NE to Cutler: the world's largest radio transmitters are here. From here to Sail Rock and Quoddy Head Light, the nation's easternmost point.

Passamaquoddy Bay: Fine sailing here to Lubec and Eastport, westerly into Cobscook Bay (State Park). Unusual tide and current conditions at the entrances of Passamaquoddy Bay. Off Eastport and Lubec is Campobello Island, Roosevelt International Memorial. North is Perry and the Pleasant Point Indian Reservation and New Brunswick's Deer Island. At the mouth of the St. Croix River is Dochet's Island, National Historic Monument to the first French settlers (1603), and St. Andrews, New Brunswick; upriver to Red Beach and Calais.

WINTER SPORTS

Information: Department of Economic Development.

Snowmobiles: registration and regulations, Department of Inland Fisheries and Game; Park and Recreation Commission; wilderness permits, Paper Industry Office, 133 State St., Augusta, Maine 04330.

MAINE'S vast expanse and long, dependable snow season has made the State increasingly popular with winter sportsmen, particularly snowmobilers and skiers whose numbers have multiplied a thousand-fold since 'ski-trains' used to operate out of Boston. Their interests are represented by the Maine Ski and the Maine Snowmobile Associations. All kinds of winter sports are found in all counties, from York to Aroostook. A network of superhighways and access roads open year-round speed the metropolitan sportsman to remote areas blossoming with inns, restaurants and apres ski life along with all the outdoor facilities. Besides skiers and snowmobilers, others come for ice fishing, ice boating, skating, curling, sled dog racing, fox, rabbit and bobcat hunting and snowshoeing, one of the oldest winter sports. Many kinds of snowshoes are made in Maine. International snowshoe meets, with races and other spectacles are held in Lewiston.

Mountainous Maine has 54 ski areas (1969); one is among the top four in the country. There are slopes and facilities for novice, intermediate and expert, night skiing, cross-country trails, ski patrols, schools, shops, supplies and snow-makers — just in case. Several developments are expanding and new ones are opening each year. Snow conditions are broadcast daily in season.

Snowmobiling became so popular in the 1960s that ten State parks (*see State Park Table*) and portions of Acadia National Park, were opened to the sport along with numerous private areas. Several hundred miles of the Allagash Wilderness is a winter wonderland. Communities hold safaris, rallies, races and interclub competitions. The Maine Snomobile Association and local clubs urge all operators to observe the Maine Snowmobile Law respecting property, safety and protection of agricultural and other lands and wildlife. Snowmobilers should be familiar with regulations not only in urban areas but in wilderness and agricultural regions and near waterways where permission from owners for use of land and roads must be obtained.

Collegiate and community winter carnivals, ice hockey and sled dog racing have thousands of followers. The Down East Sled Dog Racing Association heads the Maine circuit of the New England Association, staging events

MAINE PORTRAITS

THE character of Maine people is frequently portrayed in art and history. Here are a few 'portraits.'

THE EMERY FAMILY OF NORTH BERWICK, 1834

SIR WILLIAM PEPPERRELL

GENERAL HENRY KNOX

GENERAL SAMUEL WALDO

MR. AND MRS. ROBERT HALLOWELL GARDINER

COLONEL AND MRS. THOMAS CUTTS

HENRY WADSWORTH
LONGFELLOW PORTRAIT

JAMES BOWDOIN, III AND SISTER ELIZABETH

MAINE LOBSTERMAN

FISHERMAN'S FAMILY

YOUNG FISHERMAN AND DORY

MAINE COAST

ABRAHAM HANSON
OF BANGOR

THE ROCKING CHAIR

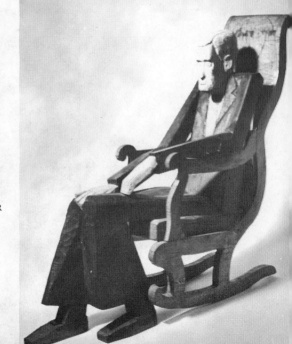

ACADIAN WOMAN OF MADAWASKA

MARK LANGDON HILL,
MAINE'S FIRST SOUTHERN
DISTRICT CONGRESSMAN,
1813-1823

LUMBERMAN JOHN ROSS,
MASTER RIVER DRIVER
OF THE PENOBSCOT

STATESMAN
JAMES G. BLAINE

MADAME GIGLIA NORDICA
OF FARMINGTON, OPERA STAR

ARTEMUS WARD, HUMORIST

SIR HIRAM MAXIM, INVENTOR

JOHN STEVENS, PASSAMAQUODDY INDIAN GOVERNOR

at Augusta, Greenville, Glenburn, Milo, Dover-Foxcroft, and champion-ships at Ellsworth. Open races usually are 12-15 miles cross-country, mostly with huskies, although hounds, setters, pointers and mongrels are entered in some races. Sometimes as many as 60 teams are entered in one race. There is prize money and the Governor's trophy.

SOME SKI AREAS

Bald Mountain: From Bangor SE on State 1A to Holden, 13 *m*. Facilities: 2200 ft. double chair lift; 1100 ft. T-bar; 900 ft. rope tow; novice to expert trails; night skiing; lower and summit lodges.

Camden Snow Bowl: From Maine Turnpike Exit 8 (Falmouth) NE on I-95 and US 1 to Camden, 75 *m*. Ragged Mt. overlooks Camden Hills and Penobscot Bay. Facilities: 4088 ft. T-bar and 800 ft. rope tow service; 6 trails and lighted open slope, novice to expert; 900 ft. vertical rise; ski rentals; skating. Accommodations: lodge, lunch bar.

Chisholm Winter Park: From Maine Turnpike Exit 12 (Auburn) NW on State 4 and 108 to Rumford, 40 *m*. Black Mountain. Facilities: 2200 ft. T-bar; 20- and 40-meter jumps; 4 mile-long trails; night skiing; shop. Accommodations: lodge, snack bar, sundeck.

Colby College Area: From I-95 off North St. (Waterville) to Area, 1 *m*. Facilities: 70 acres; 1200 ft. T-bar; bunny, intermediate slopes, expert trail; 32-meter jump (intercollegiate); night skiing; snow-making. Accommodations: lodge, fireplace, snack bar.

Eaton Mountain: From I-95 at Fairfield NW on US 201 to Mountain 12 *m*. S of Jackman, 79 *m*. Facilities: 4200 ft. double chair lift, 1200 ft. T-bar; 900 ft. beginners lift; five trails novice to expert; two open slopes; Natur-Teknik school, shop, rentals. Accommodations: base lodge, snack bar; overnight, Jackman and The Forks.

Hermon Mountain: From Bangor W on US 2 to area, 10 *m*. Facilities: 2000 ft. T-bar, 2 rop tows; 2000 ft. slope, two 1600 ft. slopes; 2500 ft. trail, ¾ mile trail. Accommodations: lodge, lunch counter, fireplace.

John Abbot Titcomb Slope: From Maine Turnpike Exit 12 (Auburn) N on State 4 to Farmington, 46 *m*. Family area. Facilities: Poma lift and rope tow servicing two novice, one intermediate trails and two open slopes; two cross-country courses; two 35-meter jumps; junior, adult instruction; night skiing. Accommodations: warming hut, snack bar.

Lost Valley: From Maine Turnpike Exit 12 (Auburn) to Valley, 4 *m*. Facilities: 1000 ft. double chair lift; 900 ft. T-bar and rope tow servicing novice and intermediate trails and an 8-acre slope; 30 meter jump; cross-country trails; night-skiing, school, shop, snow-making. Accommodations: lodge, snack bar.

Mars Hill: From Bangor N on I-95 and US 1 to Mars Hill, 133 *m*. Poma-lift, four unloading areas; 2 long winding trails, expert, intermediate; beginners slope; night skiing; shop. Accommodations: ski and patrol lodges.

Mt. Abram: From Maine Turnpike Exit 11 (Gray) NW on State 26 to Locke

Mills near Bethel. 48 *m.* Facilities: T-bars 1000-1650 and 3350 ft.; ¾ mile expert, two longer intermediate trails; sport shop, repairs, rentals, sales. Accommodations: lunch area; nearby inns, motels.

Mt. Agamenticus: From US 1 and 1A at York, 4 *m.* W. Facilities: chair lift, T-bar and rope tow servicing 4 trails and open slope; night skiing, school, shop, rentals; snow-making. Accommodations: lodge, lunch bar.

Mt. Jefferson: From Bangor N on US 2 and State 6 to Lee, 52 *m.* Family area. Facilities: 2000 ft. T-bar, 600 ft. rope tow; 5 trails and beginners slope. Accommodations: lodge, snack bar, area lodgings.

Northmen Ski Area: On US 1 S of Caribou, 1 *m.* Facilities: 1000 ft. T-bar, trail and open slope; registered patrol; night skiing; snack bar.

Pleasant Mountain: From Maine Turnpike Exit 8 (Portland-Westbrook) NW on US 302 to Bridgton, 35 *m.* Facilities: 11 slopes and trails, novice to expert; 4200 ft. double chair lift, 3000 ft. and 2000 ft. T-bars; 700 ft. novice area and T-bars; school, shop, rentals. Accommodations: two-story lodge with balcony, snack bar, cafeteria; Area motels and restaurants.

Poland Spring: From Maine Turnpike Exit 11 (Gray) N on State 26 to Poland Spring, 10 *m.* Facilities: 2000 ft. T-bar, open slope; two trails, cross-country trails; night skiing; shop; skating and pung parties. Accommodations: hut, snack bar, cafeteria; area motels and restaurants.

Saddleback Area: From Maine Turnpike Exit 12 (Auburn) NW on State 4 to Rangeley, 87 *m.* Facilities: 4600 ft. and 1400 ft. chair lifts; 1400 ft. and 3000 ft. T-bars; 13 intermediate to expert trails with 1400 ft. vertical descent; 4 novice trails; a 10-acre open slope; school, shop, rentals, patrol, snow-making; warming shelter and snack bar at mountain top. Accommodations: base lodge (800 people), carpeted cafeteria, nursery, sundeck; motels, churches, stores in Rangeley area.

Sky-Hy Park: From Maine Turnpike Exit 9 (Falmouth) NE on I-95 to Brunswick and Topsham, 25.6 *m.* Family area. Facilities: 700 ft. T-bar, 10 trails, beginners slope; night skiing on 5 trails; school, shop, snow-making. Accommodations: lodge, snack bar.

Squaw Mountain: From Maine Turnpike end, Augusta, N on I-95 to Newport, N on State 7 to Dover-Foxcroft, WNW on State 6 to Greenville, 103 *m.* Facilities: 6,000 ft. double chair lift; 3000 ft. and 2000 ft. T-bars servicing 7½ miles of trails, novice to expert; school, sport shop, rentals, full-time patrol. Accommodations: large base lodge and cafeteria; inns, motels.

Sugarloaf Mountain: From Maine Turnpike Exit 12 (Auburn) N on State 4 and State 27 to Sugarloaf between Stratton and Kingfield, 60 *m.* Facilities: more than 30 miles of trails; 9000 ft. 4-passenger gondola rising 2600 vertical ft. to summit cafeteria; 5 T-bars spanning 15,000 ft.; vertical rise 2200 ft.; school. Accommodations: two lodges, two base cafeterias, hexagonal glass summit lodge and cafeteria, huge sun deck. Numerous area hotels, motels and chalet apartments.

Sunday River: From Maine Turnpike Exit 11 (Gray) NW on State 26 to Bethel, 53 *m.* Facilities: 3000 ft. and 220 ft. T-bars in tandem one mile to summit; novice area with 2600 ft. T-bar; 6½ miles of trails; 85-acre open slope, 1450 ft. vertical rise; school, shop, rentals, repairs, patrol. Accommodations: lodge, cafeteria, sundeck; excellent inns at Bethel.

White Bunny Area: US 1 Aroostook County at Fort Fairfield, on Currier Rd., 2 *m.* Facilities: 1750 ft. T-bar, open slope, two trails; night skiing. Accommodations: lodge, snack bar; motels in town.

OTHER GOINGS-ON

Golf, tennis, bowling, boxing, wrestling, interscholastic games, stockcar and horse racing, skeet shooting, dog trials, jazz and folk music, square dancing, community sings, church suppers, auctions, shows, festivals, excursions and sight-seeing tours are on the Recreation calendar. Visitors can learn locally where the action is.

An increasingly popular family pastime is Treasure Hunting — 'prospecting' with pick and hammer in Maine's old mines and quarries for gemstones and metal specimens (*see MINERALS*). Chalcopyrite, galena, pyrite and sphalerite are the principal metal ore minerals, found mostly in eastern Maine in the Hancock County Blue Hill area and around Lubec and Eastport in Washington County. Fresh sulphide ore minerals of copper, lead and zinc are shiny, the colors varying from bright brassy yellow to dark steely gray after their rusty cover is removed.

Beautiful blue and green colored stones are the carbonates formed when metallic copper minerals are dissolved by rain and ground water. Specimens of red rhyolite are collected at Jasper Beach and other red beaches in Washington County. Gold many be panned along Swift River tributaries in western Maine.

Mica minerals (isinglass) — muscovite, biotite and lepidolite; quartz — glassy, rose and smoky; and vesuvianite are found in southwest central areas as are most gemstones, beryl, topaz, tourmaline and garnet which are most often found in waste dumps containing quartz and feldspar. Because good gemstones are brittle, care must be taken in breaking them from their pegmatite pods. Some of New England's richest gem finds have been uncovered in geodes or pockets of Maine quarry walls.

Some of the popular gemstone and mineral areas:

Topsham-Brunswick: Consolidated, Fisher and Staples quarries, 4 *m.* N of Topsham on State 24; garnets, green tourmaline, smoky quartz.

Rumford: Black Mountain, 12 *m.* N of Rumford on State 120 and dirt roads;

pink tourmaline, lepidolite, spodumene and a rare variety of white beryl.

Rubellite Mine, gem beryl, vari-colored tourmaline, rutile, pollucite, fluorescent pegmatites actively being quarried.

Paris-Hebron: Foster and Mt. Marie mines, Haverinen and Mills quarries, NW of Hebron; beryl, garnet, tourmaline, quartz crystals, sometimes columbite, tantalite and pollucite.

South Paris: Mount Mica, popular for its great variety of minerals.
Tamminen and Harvard quarries; amethyst, citrine, smoky quartz, tourmaline, beryl.

Bennett quarry; South Paris-Rumford Road; beryl, topaz, tourmaline, lepidolite, apatite, amblygonite, manganese minerals.

Newry: N of Bethel; rose quartz, apatite, tourmaline, beryl.

For further information see *Maine Mineral Collecting*, Robert G. Doyle, State Geologist, Augusta, Maine 04330.

CHRONOLOGY

1000-10   (*ca.*) The Norsemen, first Europeans known to have visited North America, probably explore coast of Maine.

1492   Era of active exploration in western hemisphere begins with Columbus' voyage.

1497-99   Explorations of John and Sebastian Cabot along entire coast of New England, forming basis for all future English claims to this region.

1524   Giovanni da Verrazzano, in service of France, explores to 35 degrees N. Lat. First to give Aranbega (Norumbega) as a definite locality.

1525   Estevan Gomez, a Portuguese exploring for Spain, names the Penobscot *Rio de los Gamos* or 'river of stags,' because of many deer there.

1569   David Ingram and two other English sailors, marooned by Sir John Hawkins, make overland journey from Gulf of Mexico to Nova Scotia. Ingram later wrote account of their adventures, telling of splendors of mythical city of Norumbega on Penobscot River.

1600   Fishermen and explorers are in Passamaquoddy Bay region.

1602   Bartholomew Gosnold, in bark *CONCORD* out of Falmouth, England, takes back furs, sassafras, and cedar from Maine coast, his voyage causing renewed interest in New World.

1603   Martin Pring, sent by merchants of Bristol to trade with Indians, makes careful survey of Maine coast from the Piscataqua to the Penobscot, naming islands in Penobscot Bay 'Fox Islands.'

Henry IV of France appoints Sieur de Monts Lieutenant-General of La Cadie, giving him seignorial rights to territory between 40 degrees and 56 degrees N. Lat.

1604-05   Sieur de Monts with company of gentlemen-adventurers establishes colony on St. Croix Island (Dochet's Island, near Calais);

Samuel de Champlain makes extensive explorations and detailed maps of islands and coastline of Maine; colony disbands after hard winter and removes to Nova Scotia.

1605   Captain George Waymouth, in the *ARCHANGEL*, lands at Monhegan Island; he trades with Indians, finally kidnaping five of them, whom he takes back to England, after examining environs of St. George River.

1606   James I of England grants two charters 'to colonize Virginia'; one company, known as the London Company, being granted right to colonize 'Southern Virginia' (34 degrees to 38 degrees N.); the other, known as West of England Company (or Plymouth Company), given right to colonize 'Northern Virginia' (41 degrees to 45 degrees N.); the intermediate territory being open to either colony after having settled its original area.

1607   Sunday, August 9, the GIFT OF GOD and the *MARY AND JOHN* bearing English colonists, rendezvous at Allen's Island between Monhegan and St. George's Point.

        Popham Colony, called St. George, planted August 13 on Sabino Head at the end of Sagadahoc (Phippsburg) Peninsula, by the mouth of Kennebec.

1608   Popham Colonists build 30-ton pynnace *VIRGINIA OF SAGADAHOCK*, first English vessel constructed in New England, to become America's first transatlantic trader. They give up their settlement and return to England.

1609   Henry Hudson, in the *HALF MOON*, during his search for a Northwest Passage, puts into Casco Bay to repair his storm-battered vessel after a tempestuous voyage.

1611   Father Pierre Biard, Jesuit priest, accompanies French traders into Maine and establishes first Indian mission at Indian Island on the Penobscot, beginning spread of Christianity among Maine Indians and friendly relations between them and the French.

1613   St. Sauveur, a mission and settlement, established by French Jesuits at entrance to Somes Sound on Mt. Desert Island; its colonists are shortly expelled as trespassers on English soil by Captain Samuel Argall of Virginia, who sets them adrift in open boats.

1614   Captain John Smith visits Monhegan Island and deserted Sagadahoc colony, sounds 'about 25 excellent harbors' on Maine coast, and makes map of region from Cape Cod to Nova Scotia, which he calls New England.

1616-17 Captain Richard Vines and crew of 16 men spend winter at mouth of Saco River to prove Maine climate not too severe for Europeans; names site Winter Harbor.

1620 Pilgrims land at Plymouth from the *MAYFLOWER*. Great Patent of New England, covering territory from Philadelphia to Gulf of St. Lawrence, issued by King James. Territory placed under a council at Plymouth, England.

Permanent settlement established on Monhegan Island.

1622 Land between Merrimac and Sagadahoc (Kennebec) Rivers granted to Sir Ferdinando Gorges and Captain John Mason by Great Council of New England.

1623 First successful settlement on the mainland in Maine begun at Saco by Richard Vines and others; marks beginning of active settlement along coast west of Penobscot Bay.

First sawmill in America in operation on the Piscataqua.

Gorges attempts to establish general government for New England, sending Robert Gorges to Maine for this purpose, but is unsuccessful.

Christopher Levett builds home on Hog or House Island in Portland Harbor; here he plans to erect city with funds from collection in churches throughout England on proclamation issued by the King. Although Levett fails, proclamation calls wide attention to possibilities for colonization in Maine.

1626-29 Trading posts established at Pentagoet (later Castine), Cushnoc (Augusta), Richmond and Machias.

Contention begins between British and French over Acadia-in-Maine, region between Penobscot and St. Croix Rivers.

1629 Plymouth Colony of Massachusetts granted territorial and trading rights to 'all that tracte of lande . . . adionethe to the River of Kenebeke . . . the space of 15 English miles on each side of the river.'

Trading post established at Machias by Pilgrims; soon captured by the French.

Pilgrims are able to pay most of debts incurred by '*MAYFLOW-ER* expedition with furs from Kennebec region.

Mason and Gorges divide their province: Mason takes land west of the Piscataqua and names it New Hampshire; Gorges takes land east of the Piscataqua and names it New Somersetshire.

1630-31   Plymouth Council (England), perceiving that its own authority may soon pass, grants eight patents to New England lands, including Kennebec, Lygonia, Waldo (or Muscongus), and Pemaquid grants.

1632   French raid English trading house at Pentagoet. Fort at Pemaquid attacked and demolished by notorious English pirate, Dixey Bull.

English cede Acadia to France by Treaty of St. Germain-en-Laye.

1635   John Winter establishes first shipyard on Richmond Island.

First gristmill recorded at Berwick.

Pilgrims remaining at Pentagoet trading post driven out by French under De Charnisay.

Council of New England surrenders its charter to the King, who has become suspicious of liberties allowed colonists.

Sir Ferdinando Gorges made Governor-General of all New England; sends his nephew, William Gorges, to colonies as deputy-governor.

1639   William Gorges organizes government of New Somersetshire, with first legally organized court in Maine held at Saco under his jurisdiction; returns home in same year.

Gorges obtains charter from Charles I for region incorporated as 'The Province and County of Maine.'

Thomas Purchase, first settler of Pejepscot on the Androscoggin (now Brunswick), assigns to Governor Winthrop of Massachusetts 'all the tract at Pejepscot.'

1640   Thomas Gorges appointed Deputy-Governor of Province of Maine. 'First general court' (legislative assembly) under Maine charter established at Saco.

1641   Gorgeana (York) chartered as first English city in America under feudal tenure of Gorges.

1646   Father Gabriel Druillettes establishes Indian mission in the Norridgewock territory.

Court of law upholds grant of Province of Lygonia as separate from Province of Maine.

1647   Sir Ferdinando Gorges dies. Parliament declares his grant invalid. Thomas Gorges nevertheless appoints Edward Godfrey deputy-governor.

Piscataqua Plantation formed, including present towns of Kittery, North and South Berwick, and Eliot.

Kittery, settled 1623, as Piscataqua Plantation, first in Maine, incorporated as town.

1650   (ca.) Maine in great confusion as result of contradictory grants, Indian raids, pirates on coast, and lack of organized government.

1651   Massachusetts claims all Maine land south of lat. 43 degrees 43' 12" with eastern point on Upper Clapboard Island in Casco Bay.

Sir William Phips born at Woolwich.

1652   Province of Maine comes under jurisdiction of Massachusetts Bay Colony in spite of inhabitants' protest; Massachusetts General Court appoints commissioners to settle northern boundary of colony.

York (formerly Gorgeana) incorporated as town.

1653   John Wincoll of Kittery and Edward Rishworth of York, representatives from Maine, seated in Massachusetts General Court.

Wells, Saco, and Cape Porpoise (Kennebunkport) made towns.

1654   French lose control of all territory in Maine.

1655   Acadian Province confirmed to English, who hold it 13 years.

1658   Scarborough (settled 1630) and Casco (settled 1632) incorporated as towns.

Isles of Shoals and all territory north of the Piscataqua to the Penobscot (belonging to Massachusetts) made County of Yorkshire.

1660   Re-establishment of monarchy in England under Charles II results in tightening of Colonial government.

1662   First Quaker meeting in Maine held at Newichawannock.

1663   Strong feeling manifested between people of Maine and those of Massachusetts; Robert Jordan of York County is fined by Massachusetts General Court for saying, 'John Cotton (of Boston) is a liar and has gone to hell.'

1664   Ferdinando Gorges, grandson of original proprietor, obtains royal order restoring his Province of Maine; Massachusetts judges expelled from province.

Charles II, planning an American empire, grants royal province to his brother, Duke of York, including region between the St. Croix and Pemaquid, to be called County of Cornwall.

Royal commissioners set up independent government in Maine.

1667-70   Treaty of Breda and supplementary articles give France disputed area east of the Penobscot, with Nova Scotia.

Baron de St. Castin, French fur trader, comes to New England.

1668   Four commissioners from Massachusetts convene at York, commanding people of Province of Maine to yield obedience to Massachusetts Colony. Royal agents forcibly ejected from Maine.

1672   Massachusetts formally extends its jurisdiction to Penobscot Bay.

1673   Dutch seize French fortifications at Pentagoet.

1674   Region between Kennebec and Penobscot Rivers organized as County of Devonshire.

New royal patent issued to Duke of York; Sir Edmund Andros becomes Governor of New York and Sagadahoc (County of Cornwall).

1675   King Philip's War begins in Maine; emboldened by conflict in Massachusetts, Maine Indians attack English settlements; Scarborough and Casco completely destroyed.

1676 Charles II decrees that Massachusetts does not have 'right of soil' in Maine and New Hampshire.

Dutch again capture fort at Pentagoet, but English drive them out.

Indian warfare continues; many settlements attacked and burned.

1677 Province of Maine purchased from Gorges' heirs by Massachusetts for £1250 sterling (about $6000).

Indian hostilities continue. Governor Andros, fearing French aggression in Duke of York's Sagadahoc Province, dispatches a force from New York to Pemaquid.

1678 Commissioners from Massachusetts negotiate peace with Indians at Casco.

1680 Provincial government established by Massachusetts; Thomas Danforth appointed 'President of Maine.'

1685 James II replaces Charles II on English throne; Massachusetts Charter annulled.

1686 Sir Edmund Andros appointed Royal Governor of New England Colonies, and immediately starts aggression on Maine frontier.

1688 Baron de Castin, enraged by English attacks, organizes Maine Indians; many settlements along the coast destroyed. James II dethroned and replaced by William of Orange.

Andros attacks Penobscot and sacks stronghold of Baron de Castin, thus precipitating King William's War.

1689 People of Massachusetts imprison Governor Andros, and Danforth is restored as provincial president of Maine.

1690 French and Indians from Canada sweep Maine until only four settlements remain inhabited.

Sir William Phips takes Port Royal in Nova Scotia.

1691 Massachusetts obtains its second charter; Province of Maine now becomes District of Maine, including Colony of Sagadahoc between the Kennebec and the St. Croix.

Sir William Phips appointed Royal Governor of Massachusetts Bay Colony, helped by Cotton Mather and his faction.

1692   Great funeral ceremony on Mt. Agamenticus for revered Indian Sachem Aspinquid.

1696   Father Sebastian Rasle Mission established on the Kennebec; John Eliot is Protestant contemporary in southern Maine.

French capture Fort William Henry at Pemaquid, vantage point of eastern coast.

1697   Treaty of Ryswick establishes peace between France and England; Acadian boundary remains undetermined, France claiming all land to the Penobscot.

1699   Mere Point (Brunswick) Treaty with Indians marks end of King William's War.

1700   Unknown limner paints first known portraits in Maine, Sir William Pepperrell family.

1703-13   Queen Anne's War (third Indian war). Only remaining settlements in Maine are Kittery, Wells, and York.

1719   First schoolhouse built, at Berwick.

1722   Lovewell's War (fourth Indian war) begins with sudden raids on towns of southwestern Maine.

1724   English sack Norridgewock Indian village at Old Point, killing Father Sebastian Rasle, missionary-teacher.

1725   Colonial soldiers from Massachusetts defeat Pequawket Indians at battle of Lovewell's Pond, Fryeburg.

1726   Dummer's Treaty at Falmouth with 40 Maine chiefs brings better feeling and establishment of government truck houses for Indian trading.

1732   John Winter establishes Maine's first shipyard on Richmond Island near Portland.

1732-33   Massachusetts offers Maine land to settlers free to increase immigration into Maine. Resettlement definitely under way.

1739   Boundary with New Hampshire fixed by King George II and Council.

1740   German settlers begin arriving to establish Waldoboro.

1743   Population about 12,000.

1744-48 King George's War (fifth Indian war) begins, causing temporary exodus of many settlers to other Colonies.

1745   Louisburg captured by English soldiers and Colonial forces commanded by William Pepperrell of Kittery.

1754   Sixth Indian war; Indians of Maine now struggling against complete extermination.

1755   Acadians dispersed throughout American Colonies; many later settle along St. John River in Maine.

        Fort Halifax built at Winslow.

1759   Quebec falls to the English. Massachusetts takes complete possession of Penobscot region.

        Sally Sayward (Barrell Keating Wood), Maine's first novelist, is born at York.

1760   Peace made with remnants of Maine Indians at Fort Pownall.

        Worst hurricane in the memory of the settlers.

        Cumberland and Lincoln Counties established.

        Definite efforts made by land proprietors to attract settlers from other Colonies, British Isles, and Germany.

1761   First pile bridge in North America built at York (still in use).

1763   Peace of Paris; New France ceded to Great Britian.

1764   Census is taken; population about 24,000.

1770   John Adams, second U. S. President, visits a York tavern.

1774   Show of resistance to Parliamentary taxation in Maine towns, notably Saco, Falmouth, and Machias.

1775   Benedict Arnold leads expedition from Augusta to Quebec by bateau and on foot.

Falmouth burned by British under Captain Henry Mowatt.

British vessel *MARGARETTA* captured by Colonials at Machias — first naval engagement of Revolution.

Maine's first post office established at Falmouth. First Liberty Pole at Machias.

1776   Declaration of Independence; General William Whipple of Kittery a signer for New Hampshire.

First Quaker meetinghouse is built at Eliot.

1777   Ship *RANGER* launched at Kittery under command of John Paul Jones.

1778   John Paul Jones sets sail for England in *RANGER* beginning his great naval career. Receives first foreign salute to Stars and Stripes.

Continental Congress divides Massachusetts into three electoral districts, of which northernmost, including York, Cumberland, and Lincoln Counties, is called District of Maine.

1779   British take Castine and build Fort George there; revolutionists fail to take fort. Other coast towns of eastern Maine occupied or cannonaded by British forces.

1780   Constitution of Massachusetts adopted, giving Maine eight senatorial representatives.

1781   Cornwallis surrenders at Yorktown; end of hostilities.

1783   Treaty of Versailles; England recognizes independence of United States. St. Croix River set as eastern boundary of country. Indians become wards of State.

1784   Canadian Province of New Brunswick established, and long boundary dispute in the Aroostook begun.

1785   Question of separation from Massachusetts arises, causing establishment of Falmouth *Gazette*, first newspaper in Maine, as organ to aid in agitation for separation.

Band of Acadians fleeing Nova Scotia settle at present-day Madawaska.

1786   Portland (formerly Falmouth, once Casco) incorporated as town.

State lands on navigable rivers sold to soldiers and immigrants at $1 an acre.

1787   On adoption of United States Constitution, Maine is made a representative district, having 93 towns and plantations.

Stagecoaches begin operating between Portland and Portsmouth.

1788   Slavery abolished in Maine and Massachusetts.

1789   Hancock and Washington Counties established.

1790   Population 96,540.

William Bingham owns more than 2,000,000 acres of Maine lands.

1791   Portland Head Light, today the oldest lighthouse on Atlantic coast, established at Cape Elizabeth; Joseph Greenleaf, first keeper, appointed by George Washington.

First academies open at Berwick and Hallowell.

1793   French Revolution; much political partisanship in America. The Clough House at Edgecomb (near Wiscasset) prepared as a refuge for Marie Antoinette.

Shakers establish settlements at Alfred and New Gloucester.

Federalist and Democrat-Republican Parties formed in United States.

1794   Bowdoin College receives its charter from Massachusetts General Court; officially opens in 1802.

First theatrical performance in Maine at Portland.

1795   General Henry Knox takes up residence at *Montpelier*, his mansion in Thomaston.

1796   Jonathan Fisher becomes first pastor at Blue Hill.

1788   Slavery abolished in Maine and Massachusetts.

1799   Kennebec County established.

The Portland Bank, first bank in Maine, opened.

1800   Population 151,719.

1801   Maine's first free public library founded at Castine.

1802   Dorothea L. Dix, prison reformer, born at Winterport.

1804   Bangor Theological Seminary first incorporated as Maine Charity School.

1805   Oxford County established.

1806   Portsmouth Navy Yard built at Kittery.

1807   Embargo Act on foreign commerce passed by National Government; causes severe economic depression in New England. Much smuggling in Maine, centering around Eastport.

        Henry Wadsworth Longfellow born at Portland, February 27.

        District votes 9404 to 3370 against separation from Massachusetts.

        Farmington Academy, later first State Normal School, incorporated.

1809   Embargo Act repealed.

        Somerset County established.

        Settlers and landowners in "Malta War' at Windsor.

        Hannibal Hamlin, Vice-President of U.S. 1861-65, born at Paris (Maine), August 27.

        First cotton mill in Maine established in Brunswick at falls of the Androscoggin.

1810   Population 228,705.

        Great internal development in Maine resulting from Embargo Act.

        England increases impressment of American sailors.

1812   War between United States and Great Britain seriously affects shipping on Maine coast. Smuggling between Canada and Maine practiced on large scale.

1813   American brig *ENTERPRISE* captures British brig *BOXER* off Pemaquid Point.

Maine Literary and Theological Institute now Colby College, established.

Harpswell preacher-author Elijah Kellogg born.

Corporal punishment totally abolished in Massachusetts and Maine.

1814   British seize and occupy Maine coast from the St. Croix to the Penobscot; Eastport on Moose Island declared to be part of New Brunswick.

Treaty of Ghent brings peace between United States and Great Britian.

1815   Foreign occupation of Maine soil ended.

Peter Edes founds Bangor's first newspaper, the *Weekly Register.*

Beginning of western migration, known as 'Ohio Fever,' which continued until about 1870, causing alarming decrease in Maine's population.

The *WASHINGTON*, 74-gun ship of the line, first vessel launched at Kittery-Portsmouth Navy Yard.

1816   Penobscot County established.

Year of the great cold, known as 'eighteen-hundred-and froze-to-death.'

Enoch Lincoln, later Governor of Maine, writes Maine's first poem, *The Village.*

1818   Waterville (Colby) College opened; obtained charter in 1820.

1819   Convention for framing State constitution meets at Portland, October 11.

1820   Maine admitted as a State to the Union; capital at Portland; William King elected first governor.

Mid-Nineteenth century lumber boom begins.

Moses Gerrish Farmer, electrical pioneer, is born at Eliot.

Population 298,335.

1822   Steamship *KENNEBEC* begins service between Portland and Portsmouth, forerunner of steamship era.

1825   Lafayette given enthusiastic reception on visit to Maine.

1827   Augusta chosen as site for State capital.

Waldo County established.

1828   William Ladd founds American Peace Society at Minot.

1829   State Capitol cornerstone laid at Augusta.

Seba Smith founds *Courier,* first daily newspaper, at Portland.

1830   Population 399,455.

Cumberland and Oxford Canal opened.

James G. Blaine, famous Maine statesman, born in Pennsylvania, January 31.

1831   Maine refuses compromise boundary solution offered by King of Netherlands.

1832   State capital removed from Portland to Augusta.

Steamboat travel inaugurated between Bath and Boston.

1834   Charles Farrar Browne (Artemus Ward), noted humorist, born at Waterford, April 26.

State Anti-Slavery Society formed.

State Prohibition Convention held at Portland.

1835   First shoes, manufactured at Auburn (West Minot).

Financial panic engendered by timberland speculation.

1836   Bangor, Old Town, and Milford Railroad completed, first in State and one of earliest in country.

1838   Franklin and Piscataquis Counties established.

Earthquake felt throughout New England, vibrations lasting for 20 days after; chimneys and lighthouses thrown down.

'Aroostock War' begins. Serious hostilities between Maine and New Brunswick citizens avoided by mediation of General Winfield Scott.

1839   'Aroostock War' ends, and Aroostock County established.

John Knowles Paine, America's earliest noted composer, and Thomas Brackett Reed, eminent statesman, born in Portland.

1840   Population 501,793.

Granite quarrying begins at Vinalhaven and Franklin.

Hiram Maxim, inventor of modern machine gun, born at Sangerville, February 5.

Two of the nation's seven millionaires are Thomaston sea captains.

1842   Webster-Ashburton Treaty fixes northeastern boundary at last.

1845   The BANGOR, one of earliest iron steamships, is built for service to Boston.

1846   Four-mile ice jam on the Penobscot floods Bangor and terrifies its inhabitants.

Sale of spirits forbidden in Maine except for medical or mechanical purposes.

1847   Maine's first child labor law enacted.

1848   Maine supplies more than half total American ship tonnage.

The *SARANAC*, first steam side-wheeler launched at Kittery-Portsmouth Navy Yard.

1849   Bangor afflicted by cholera, causing 151 deaths; Mayor William Abbott dies in office.

Sarah Orne Jewett, author of *The Country of the Pointed Firs*, born at South Berwick, September 3.

Maine adventurers sail in Maine ships around the Horn to California gold fields.

1850   Population 583,169.

        Edgar Wilson (Bill) Nye, humorist, born at Shirley, August 25.

        In this decade Bangor is world's leading lumber port.

1851   Prohibition enactment, known as 'the Maine law,' framed by
        Neal Dow, prohibits manufacture and sale of intoxicating
        liquors in any part of State.

1853   Clipper *RED JACKET* launched at Rockland; unbeaten record
        New York-Liverpool, 13 days, 1 hr. 25 min.

        Roman Catholic See of Maine and New Hampshire established
        during 'Know-Nothing' Party's anti-Catholic anti-foreign agita-
        tion. Hostile mobs burn Bath and Lewiston churches. Rev.
        John Bapst tarred and feathered, run out of Ellsworth on a rail.

1854   Androscoggin and Sagadahoc Counties established.

        Anti-slavery Whigs and Free-Soilers unite throughout country
        to form the Republican Party, which at once becomes very strong
        in Maine.

1855   Maine State Seminary, now Bates College, incorporated.

1856   A State Board of Agriculture is established.

1857   Lillian Norton (Madame Giglia Nordica), noted prima donna,
        born at Farmington, December 12.

1858   Robert Browne Hall, band music composer, born at Richmond.

1860   Population 628,279.

        Knox County established.

1861-65 Civil War, to which Maine contributed 72,945 men and
        $18,000,000.

1862   Maine State College of Agriculture and Industrial Arts (now
        University of Maine) established.

        Appearance of first horse-cars precede extensive electric trolley
        system.

1863   Confederates seize the *CALEB CUSHING* from Portland Harbor and put to sea, pursued by other Portland vessels; having no ammunition, they burn the boat and are taken prisoners.

1864 Bates College receives charter.

William Pitt Fessenden (b. Portland 1806) is appointed U. S. Secretary of Treasury.

1865 Civil War ends.

Author Holman Day is born at Augusta.

1866 Great Portland fire of July 4 and 5 destroys 1800 buildings, with loss of over $6,000,000; aid rushed from all parts of country.

First National Soldiers' Home established at Togus.

Gen. Joshua Chamberlain becomes governor of Maine.

1867 National Grange becomes active in Maine.

1869 Influx of Scotch, English and Canadian labor to Maine mills begins.

Edwin Arlington Robinson, poet, born at Head Tide in Alna, December 22.

1870 Population 626,915.

First carload of potatoes shipped from Aroostook to Boston.

State colonization venture brings about establishment of New Sweden, with importation of Swedish colonists.

Maine's popularity as summer resort region begins to be felt.

Railroad transportation by this time well established.

1872 First Federal Fish Hatchery established at Bucksport to propagate Atlantic salmon.

1873 State legislature passes law providing State aid for free high schools.

1875 Compulsory education bill passed by legislature.

1876 Death penalty abolished in Maine; restored 1883; finally abolished 1887.

1877   Artist Marsden Hartley born in Lewiston.

1878   Greenbackers and Democrats win State election.

1879   Freak snowstorm in Portland, July 4.

1880   Population 648,936.

        Economic decline in rural areas begins to be marked.

        Mass production phase of Maine's largest industry, lumbering,
        begins.

        Harvested on the Kennebec: 640,000 tons of ice.

1881   Maine statesman James G. Blaine, U. S. Secretary of State; pres-
        idential candidate 1884.

1884   Bath Iron Works organized.

        Artist Winslow Homer settles at Prout's Neck.

        Artist Waldo Peirce born at Bangor.

1885   The last person to be hanged in Maine is a British sailor accused
        of murder in Bath.

1888   Melville W. Fuller (b. Augusta 1833) becomes Chief Justice of
        the U. S. Supreme Court.

        The GOVERNOR AMES, first five-masted schooner built on
        the Atlantic coast, is launched at Waldoboro.

1890   Population 661, 086.

1892   New constitutional amendment requires education qualifications
        for voting.

        Pulitizer prize-winning poets Edna St. Vincent Millay born at
        Rockland and Robert P. T. Coffin born at Brunswick.

1893   Severe economic depression, continuing to 1895, widely felt in
        Maine.

        The ARYAN, last full-rigged wooden vessel built in America is
        launched at Phippsburg.

1894 Composer Walter Piston, three times winner of Pulitzer prize in music, is born at Rockland.

      Dr. Henry H. Best, co-discoverer of insulin, is born at West Pembroke.

1895 Bangor & Aroostook Railroad reaches Presque Isle and Caribou.

1897 Maine Music Festivals inaugurated by William R. Chapman; opera stars come to Maine.

1898 Battleship *MAINE* blown up in Havana Harbor; followed by Spanish-American War to which Maine furnishes one volunteer regiment of 1717 men.

1899 The *KAUILANI* (now the last surviving American square-rigged vessel) is built at Bath Iron Works.

1900 Population 694,466.

      (ca.) The famous Bangor House, host to four U. S. presidents and other notables, evades the hatchet of anti-saloon agitator, Carrie Nation.

1902 Lakewood, first summer theatre established at Skowhegan.

1903 University of Maine establishes a School of Forestry.

1905 First Forest Fire Lookout in U. S. established on Squaw Mountain.

1907 Widespread economic depression.

      Largest dam of its time in New England built at Ellsworth.

1909 Export of hydro electric power prohibited.

1910 Population 742,371.

      Resettlement of northeastern boundary controversy with Great Britian.

      Democratic State victory for first time in 30 years; Frederick W. Plaisted of Augusta, elected Governor.

1911 Bangor fire causes more than $3,000,000 damage.

      Direct primary adopted; initiative and referendum law passed.

1914   Outbreak of World War I. *KRONPRINZESSIN CECILIE*
        North German Lloyd liner with cargo of gold, interned at Bar
        Harbor.

        Maine Public Utilities Commission created.

1915   Workmen's compensation law adopted.

        The Maine-built *WILLIAM P. FRYE* is sunk by German
        cruiser, first American sacrifice to Prussian militarism.

1917   United States enters World War I; Maine legislature passes
        emergency act providing for $1,000,000 in State bonds for war
        purposes.

        First Navy constructed sub *L-8* launched at Kittery-Portsmouth
        Yard.

        Ripogenus Dam completed, great engineering feat in wilderness.

        First Farm Bureau is organized at Ellsworth.

1918   End of World War I, to which Maine contributed more than
        35,000 men and more than $116,000,000.

1919   Lafayette National Park (renamed Acadia National Park in 1928)
        created by act of Congress.

1920   Centennial year. Maine receives new impetus toward forest
        conservation, permanent roads, publicity for its vocational
        facilities.

        Women permitted to vote. Maine women first to exercise
        franchise.

        Population 768,014

1921   Consolidation of leading Maine newspapers.

        Maine names first Forestry entomologist in U. S.

1923   City Manager-Council form of government established in
        Portland, resulting in adoption of plan by many other towns
        and cities of State.

1924   Winter port of English steamers changed from Portland to Hali-
        fax, N. S., because of tax on imported goods.

1925   Old Orchard Pier dance Casino is mecca of Maine's 'flaming youth' of the Jazz Age depicted by Artist John Held, Jr. and *College Humor.*

1926   First radio parish in America founded at Portland.

1927   First State Highway snow removal program.

Opening of the Carleton Bridge over the Kennebec at Bath ends 150 years of ferry service by the *GOVERNOR KING.*

1928   Maine sees first 'talking' motion pictures.

Only known cobwork bridge is built at Bailey's Island, Harpswell.

1929   Stock market collapse marks beginning of depression years; effects not felt immediately in Maine.

Popular vote on power question makes Maine last state to prohibit exportation of hydro-electric power from State.

1930   Population 797,423.

Air transport inaugurated.

Cargo ship *JACONA* converted in first U. S. attempt to furnish portable power begins operation at Bucksport. Later supplies power to Portsmouth, N. H.

Wyman Dam at Bingham completed.

Eastern Music Camps founded at Sydney.

Admiral William Veazie Pratt, Belfast native, becomes President of U. S. War College and Chairman of Naval operations.

1931   State Administrative Code consolidates departments and agencies of Maine's government under five commissions.

Mt. Katahdin State Park given to State by ex-Governor Percival P. Baxter of Portland, 'to be preserved in its natural state forever.'

1932   Waldo-Hancock suspension bridge dedicated.

Portland and Boston steamer service discontinued.

Pari-mutuel betting on horse racing legalized.

1932   Louis J. Brann of Lewiston becomes Maine's first Democratic
        governor in 18 years.

        Closing of Jefferson Theatre at Portland ends several decades of
        professional theatre that brought Maine the nation's leading
        actors.

1933   Nation-wide bank failures cause general suffering in Maine's
        rural areas. Ninety-eight of Maine's 109 banks eventually
        reopen after moratorium.

        Federal projects instituted during depression of the 1930s.

        Ellsworth fire causes $1,250,000 damage.

        Maine ratifies repeal of 18th amendment.

1934   State prohibition amendment repealed. State Liquor Commis-
        sion created. State stores open Dec. 22.

        Indians enfranchised by Federal legislation.

        State Game Farm established at Gray.

1935   Construction begun on Passamaquoddy Tidal Power Project.

        Eastern Steamship Lines, Inc., discontinue service between
        Boston and Bangor and Penobscot River ports.

1936   Maine suffers most disastrous floods in its history; $25,000,000
        loss.

        Eastern Steamship Lines, Inc., discontinue service between
        Portland and Bar Harbor and New York.

        Construction on Passamaquoddy Tidal Power Project abandoned.

1937   Bath Iron Works builds America's Cup defender *RANGER;*
        never lost a race.

        Moosehorn Wildlife Refuge established at Baring.

1939   Broiler industry begins to become significant factor in Maine
        agriculture.

1940   Population 847,226.

        Selective Service Act produces first compulsory peacetime

military conscription in U. S. history.

Maine begins offshore aquacultural studies.

Presque Isle becomes a city.

1941   Legislature creates Maine Turnpike Authority.

Maine Maritime Academy opens at Castine.

At South Portland yards, New England Shipbuilding Corporation lays the keel for the first of 30 British cargo ships authorized
by Lend Lease before our entry into World War II; 266
Liberty ships will follow.

Japanese attack on Pearl Harbor, 7 December. United States
declares war on Germany, Japan and Italy.

President Franklin D. Roosevelt comes ashore at Rockland
after signing the Atlantic Charter with Prime Minister Winston
Churchill aboard the *PRINCE OF WALES* off Newfoundland.

1942   Portland becomes port of call for U. S. Navy which acquires
Long Island in Casco Bay for installations.

1943   Brunswick selected as site for Naval Air Station.

1944   Mechanization begins increase in size and operation of Maine
farms; fewer small ones.

1945   Formal end of World War II in Germany, 8 May. VJ Day 15
August. Maine contributed 95,000 personnel in all service
branches.

1946   Rural electrification begins.

Skowhegan School of Painting and Sculpture founded.

1947   Kittery-Portland segment of Maine Turnpike completed.

U. S. Bureau of Commercial Fisheries establishes West Boothbay laboratories for study of marine biology.

Disastrous forest fires sweep the state.

Herschel Bricker inaugurates Shakespearean productions at
Camden.

1948   Margaret Chase Smith *elected* first woman Senator in history.

1950   Population 913,774.

Rail passenger service curtailed.

25 June. North Korean Communists invade South Korea starting Korean War.

Haystack Mountain School of Crafts founded at Deer Isle.

1952   Colby College completes transfer to 40 buildings on new Mayflower campus at Waterville.

1953   Limestone Air Base dedicated 3 August.

1954   Edmund S. Muskie elected first Democratic governor since
1934 and fifth since 1854. Fernald law prohibiting export of
power repealed during his administration.

Hurricanes devastate trees and fishing gear, with extensive flood
damage.

Indians become eligible to vote in Federal, State and County
elections; Maine the last State to enfranchise Indians.

1955   Legislature creates Department of Economic Development.

Maine Turnpike extended to Augusta.

1956   *USS SWORDFISH*, first U. S. authorized atomic submarine,
launched at Kittery-Portsmouth Navy Yard.

1957   Legislature's School Administration District Act consolidates
public schools for greater efficiency.

Maine abandons its September election and adopts November
dateline of other states.

Tenure of governor changed from two to four years. John H.
Reed first to serve full four-year term.

1958   Edmund S. Muskie elected to U. S. Senate.

1960   Population 969,265.

Maine Central Railroad discontinues passenger service.

1961   Kittery-Portsmouth Navy Yard launches its first Polaris missile
submarine, *USS ABRAHAM LINCOLN*.

Radar station, sector of air circumferential continental network, established at Brunswick Naval Air Station.

District courts established to replace municipal and trial justice courts.

State begins historic sites and archaeological program.

1962 'Early Bird' communications satellite constructed at Andover; North American link since 1965.

Oceanographic and ecological studies intensified at university and colleges in this decade.

1963 President John F. Kennedy addresses University of Maine at Orono three weeks before his assassination in Dallas, Texas.

Vocational-technical Institute system created.

Colby College establishes place of early Maine artists in American Art history.

1964 Bath Iron Works delivers its 142d destroyer to U. S. Navy; builds first guided missile destroyer leader, *USS DEWEY*.

Democrats win legislative branch for the first time since 1910 and cast their electoral vote for a Democratic president for the first time since 1912 and the second time since 1852.

World's most powerful radio transmitters in operation at Cutler.

1965 Interstate 95 completed to Howland.

Boston & Maine Railroad drops remaining passenger service.

Maine first state to establish Department of Indian Affairs.

All-time high farm income $282,680,000.

This decade marked by effects of social legislation; industrial and agricultural diversification; growth of electronics; urban renewal.

1966 Yankee Atomic Corporation begins construction of New England's largest nuclear steam electric generating station at Wiscasset.

Coastal Maine National Wildlife Refuge begun.

Samuel S. Silsby becomes Maine's first State Archivist.

Franklin D. Roosevelt's Campobello estate dedicated as International Park.

State Commission for Arts and Humanities created.

Referendum vote authorizes $4,800,000 for State Cultural Building to house Archives, Library and Museum.

1967   Maine's total manufactures valued at $2.2 billion.

Interstate 95 completed to Houlton.

State Museum Authority and Commission created.

Enabling legislation enacted for creation of historic districts.

Donald B. MacMillan's Arctic expedition schooner *BOWDOIN* becomes museum at Camden.

1968   Increasing controversy over public versus private power as engineering studies made of Dickey-Lincoln Dam public power proposal.

Dow Air Base at Bangor phased out to become international airfield and industrial complex.

Bowdoin College establishes Peary-MacMillan Arctic Museum.

Maine Times, weekly newspaper, established at Topsham.

U. S. Senator Edmund S. Muskie, Democratic candidate for vice president, identified with environmental improvement.

Maine's five state colleges become part of University of Maine.

State Housing Authority created.

Border 'incident' over industrial pollution at Easton.

International Paper Company installs world's largest drum at Jay.

Portland and Bangor airports designated as international jetports.

Caribou becomes a city.

Fishing industry landings: 218.7 million lbs.

1969   Maine's first State income tax levied as government struggles with budgetary problems.

Oil and gas explorations in Gulf of Maine.

Oil companies seek Maine sites (Portland, Machiasport) for refineries and depots.

Maine seeks establishment of a free port.

Conservationists organize to support measures of safe-guarding natural resources, and abatement of land, water and air pollution.
Legislature enacts some environmental protective and improvement measures. Environment Improvement Commission, Wetlands Control Board created.

Allagash Wilderness Waterway and Damariscotta Shell Heaps, among world's largest, under State protection.

Sesquicentennial Commission named for 1970 observance of State's 150th anniversary of statehood.

Nation's second largest Women's Job Corps phased out at Poland Spring.

U. S. Weather Bureau takes over operation of Navy radar station at Brunswick.

1970   Projected population 1, 019,400.

Maine's Sesquicentennial year observed state-wide all year opening with special Legislative session 14 January.

The *PRINCE OF FUNDY* scheduled to begin Portland-Nova Scotia ferry service in June. The *BLUENOSE* service already operating Bar Harbor-Nova Scotia.

Plans initiated for International Conference Center at Peaks Island.

Lumber interests continue recreation developments.

State acquires historic Pemaquid Peninsula; has 22 State Parks in developing Recreation program.

Bowdoin College establishes Afro-American Studies Center.

Portland Society of Natural History exhibits rock from Moon Landing.

Maine feels the effects of the Vietnam War, inflation and the disarray of youth.

PROJECTIONS:

1971   Dedication of Cultural Building at State Capital.

1972   Completion of Wiscasset nuclear power generating plant.

1976   Pollution abatement program scheduled for completion.

      U. S. Bicentennial celebration.

SELECTED READING LIST

PRESENTED here is a selected list of books dealing with Maine in its various aspects. Hundreds of titles on Maine are available, some not readily so, others of recent date obtainable at any book store. The selections here are representative of the categories in which they appear. Omitted are poetry and fiction; documentary and rare volumes primarily of interest to the scholar; and local histories and genealogies, too numerous to mention. Readers interested in the latter are urged to visit the local library or the rooms of the local historical society of which there are more than 100 in the State's sixteen counties.

Valuable works necessary as source material in any study of early Maine history frequently were printed in small editions and are available only in the larger libraries. These include such works as James Phinney Baxter's *Sir Ferdinando Gorges and his Province of Maine* (3 vols.), Rosier's *Relation of Waymouth's Voyage to the Coast of Maine*, Henry O. Thayer's *The Sagadahoc Colony*, and *The Jesuit Relations and Allied Documents* edited by Reuben Gold. Researchers will find a wealth of material at the Maine Historical Society Library, the Bangor Public Library and the State Archives and Library.

Available for information and study in special fields are publications of the various departments of State government, the State University and colleges.

GENERAL WORKS

Attwood, Stanley B. *Length and Breadth of Maine.* Augusta, 1946.
Fassett, Frederick G., Jr. *A History of Newspapers in the District of Maine.* Lewiston, 1915.
Hasse, Adelaide R., comp. *Index to Economic Material in Documents of Maine, 1820-1904.* Washington, 1907
Griffin, Joseph. *History of the Press in Maine.* Brunswick, 1872.
Lawton, R. J., comp. *Franco-Americans of the State of Maine.* Lewiston, 1915
Maine Register, State Yearbook and Legislative Manual. Portland, 1969. (Published annually since 1870; currently by Tower Publishing Co.)
Pope, Charles H. *Pioneers of Maine and New Hampshire, 1623 to 1660.* (c. 1908) (reprint, 1965)
Ridlon, Gedeon R. *Saco Valley Settlements and Families.* Portland, 1895. (reprint, Brattleboro, Vt., 1969)
Scales, John, editor. *Piscataqua Pioneers, 1623-1775.* Dover, N. H., 1919.

Spencer, Wilbur D. *Maine Immortals*. Augusta, 1932.

Sylvester, Herbert M. *Maine Coast Romance* (pioneer settlements 1605-1690), 5 vols. Boston, 1904-09.

Varney, George J. *Gazetteer of Maine*. Boston, 1881.

Williamson, Joseph. *A Bibliography of the State of Maine from the Earliest Period to 1891*. 2 vols. Portland, 1896.

TRAVEL AND DESCRIPTION

Appalachian Mountain Club. *The A.M.C. Guide to Paths on Katahdin and in the Adjacent Region*. Boston, 1933. Folding map.

Beston, Henry. *Northern Farm*. New York, 1948. *White Pine and Blue Water*. New York, 1950.

Bradshaw, Marion. *The Maine Land*. Bangor, 1941. *The Maine Scene*. Bangor, 1947. *Nature of Maine*. Bangor, 1944. (Photo albums of Maine)

Chase, Mary Ellen. *A Goodly Heritage*. New York, 1932

Coatsworth, Elizabeth. *Maine Memories*. Vermont, 1968. *Maine Ways*. Boston, 1947. *Country Neighborhood*. New York, 1944

Coffin, Robert P. Tristram. *Kennebec: Cradle of Americans*. New York 1937

Dietz, Lew. *The Allagash*. Rivers of America Series. New York, 1968.

Dole, Nathan H. and Gordon, Irwin L. *Maine of the Sea and Pines*. Boston, 1928

Drake, Samuel Adams. *The Pine-Tree Coast*. Boston, 1891

Elkins, L. Whitney. *The Story of Maine: Coastal Maine*. Bangor, 1924

Field, Rachel. *God's Pocket*. (Life on the Cranberry Isles)

Fuller, Nathan C., editor. *Down East Reader*. Philadelphia, 1962.

Hamlin, Helen. *Pine, Potatoes and People*. New York, 1948

Jewett, Sarah Orne. *The Country of the Pointed Firs*. Boston, 1896. (Paperback: Doubleday Anchor)

Josselyn, John. *New England Rarities*. 1638. (reprint, Portland, 1969)

Loomis, Alfred E. *Ranging the Maine Coast*. New York, 1939

Lunt, Dudley C. *Woods and the Sea*. New York, 1965

McCorrison, A. L. *Letters from Fraternity*. New York, 1931. (Life on a Maine Farm)

Munson, Gorham. *Penobscot; Down East Paradise*. Philadelphia, 1959

Murchie, Guy. *St. Croix, the Sentinel River*. New York, 1947

Moore, Jim. *Maine Coastal Portrait, by Three Maine Photographers; Jim Moore, Kosti Ruohomaa and Carroll Thayer Berry*. New York, 1959

Nutting, Wallace. *Maine Beautiful*. Framingham, Mass. 1924 (Picture album)

Porter, Eliot. *Summer Island*. New York, 1966. (Sierra Club — Ballantine Books, abridged)

Ranlett, Charles, editor. *Maine Mountain Guide*. Boston, 1962 (Appalachian Mountain Club)

Rich, Louise Dickinson. *Coast of Maine*. Philadelphia, 1963. *We Took to the Woods.* New York, 1942.

Roberts, Kenneth. *Trending Into Maine.* Boston, 1938.

Simpson, Dorothy. *The Maine Islands in Story and Legend.* Philadelphia, 1960.

Stanton, Gerret S. *Where the Sportsman Loves to Linger.* New York, 1905. (A narrative of the most popular canoe trips in Maine)

Thoreau, Henry D. *The Maine Woods.* Boston, 1864. Many later editions. (Paperback: Apollo)

Tremblay, Wendall L. *Maine Outdoorsman's Almanac.* 1970

ARCHAEOLOGY AND THE INDIANS

Eckstrom, Fannie Hardy. *Old John Neptune and Other Indian Shamans.* Portland, 1945. *Indian Place Names of the Penobscot Valley and the Maine Coast.* Orono, 1941. (University Studies No. 55). *Handicrafts of the Modern Indians of Maine.* Bar Harbor, 1932.

Maine Historical Society. *The Indians of Maine.* Portland, 1969. An inventory.

Maine Writers Research Club. *Maine Indians in History and Legend.* Portland, 1952.

Smith, W. B. *Indian Remains of the Penobscot Valley and Their Significance.* Orono, 1926. (University Studies, No. 7)

Speck, Frank G. *Penobscot Man.* Philadelphia, 1940.

Starbird, Charles M. *The Indians of the Androscoggin Valley.* Lewiston, 1928.

Willoughby, Charles C. *Prehistoric Burial Places in Maine.* Cambridge, Mass., 1898. (Paperback: Kraus).

HISTORY AND POLITICS

Arber, Edward, editor. *Travels and Works of John Smith.* Edinburgh, 1910.

Ahlin, John Howard. *Maine Rubicon: Downeast Settlers During the American Revolution.* Calais, Maine, 1966.

Alberts, Robert C. *The Golden Voyage: The Life and Times of William Bingham, 1752-1804.* Boston, 1969.

Ames, Blanche A. *Adelbert Ames, 1835-1933.* New York, 1964. (Civil War hero, military governor of Mississippi.)

Banks, Ronald F., editor. *A History of Maine: A Collection of Readings on the History of Maine.* Dubuque, Iowa, 1969.

Burrage, Henry S. *Gorges and the Grant of the Province of Maine, 1622.* Augusta, 1923. *Maine in the Northeastern Boundary Controversy.* Portland, 1919. *Beginnings of Colonial, Maine.* Portland, 1914.

Byrne, Frank L. *Prophet of Prohibition, Neal Dow and His Crusade.* Madison, Wisconsin, 1961.

Callahan, North. *Henry Knox, General Washington's General.* New York, 1958.

Chadbourne, Ava H. *Maine Place Names and the Peopling of Its Towns.* Freeport, 1955. (Also issued by counties.)

Clifford, Harold B. *Maine and Her People*. Freeport, 1957.
Clifford, Philip G. *Nathan Clifford, Democrat (1803-1881)*. New York, 1922.
Collins, Charles W. *The Acadians of Madawaska, Maine*. Boston, 1902 (Publications of the New England Catholic Historical Society)
Connors, Robert V., Kirk, Geneva and Snow, Richard. *A Text on State of Maine Government*. Lewiston, 1966.
Dow, Sterling T. *Maine Postal History and Postmarks*. Portland, 1943.
Dunnack, Henry E. *Maine Forts*. Augusta, 1924.
Fairchild, Byron. *William Pepperrell, Merchant of Piscataqua*. Ithaca, N. Y., 1954.
Griffiths, Thomas Morgan. *Major General Henry Knox and the Lost Heirs to Montpelier*. Monmouth, 1965.
Hatch, Louis Clinton, editor. *Maine: A History* (Centennial Edition). New York, 1919. 5 vols.
Hormell, Orren C. *Maine Towns*. Brunswick, 1932.
Hunt, H. Draper. *Hannibal Hamlin of Maine; Lincoln's First Vice President*. Syracuse, N. Y., 1969.
Jellison, Charles A. *Fessenden of Maine; Civil War Senator*. Syracuse, N. Y., 1962.
King, Willard L. *Melville Weston Fuller, Chief Justice of the United States Supreme Court, 1888-1910*. New York, 1950.
Lucey, William L. *Edward Kavanagh: Catholic Statesman Diplomat from Maine, 1795-1844*. Francistown, N. H., 1947.
Maine Historical Society. *Maine Province and Court Records*. Portland 1928-1964. 5 vols.
Marriner, Ernest *Kennebec Yesterdays*. Waterville, 1954. *Remembered Maine*. Waterville, 1957.
Moody, Robert E. *Proprietary Experiment in Early New England History: Thomas Gorges and the Province of Maine*. Boston, 1963.
Pattangall, William R. *Meddybemps Letters and Maine's Hall of Fame*. Lewiston, 1924.
Pullen, John H. *Shower of Stars: the Medal of Honor and the Twenty-seventh Maine*. Philadelphia, 1966. *Twentieth Maine: A Volunteer Regiment in the Civil War*. Philadelphia, 1957 (Paperback: Fawcett)
Preston, Richard A. *Gorges of Plymouth Fort: A Life of Sir Ferdinando Gorges*. Toronto, Canada, 1953.
Robinson, William A. *Thomas B. Reed, Parliamentarian*. N. Y., 1930.
Spencer, Wilbur D. *Pioneers on Maine Rivers*. Portland, 1930.
Smith, Marion J. *History of Maine From Wilderness to Statehood*. Freeport, 1961.
Staples, Arthur G. *Just Talks*. Lewiston, 1919.
Wallace, Willard M. *Soul of A Lion*. N. Y., 1960 (The life of Joshua Chamberlain)
Williamson, William D. *A History of Maine*. 2 vols. Hallowell, 1832. (Reprint 1967. Bondwheelwright, Freeport).

ECONOMIC HISTORY, GENERAL

Barrows, Harold K. *Water Resources of the Kennebec River Basin, Maine.* Washington, 1907.

Barrows, Harold K. and Babb, Cyrus C. *Water Resources of the Penobscot Basin, Maine.* Washington, 1912.

Boardman, Samuel L., comp. *Agricultural Bibliography of Maine, 1850-1892.* Augusta, 1893.

Chadbourne, Walter W. *A History of Banking in Maine, 1799-1930.* Orono, 1936 (University Studies No. 37)

Chase, Edward E. *Maine Railroads: A History of the Development of the Railroad System.* Portland, 1926.

Clapp, Frederick G. *Underground Waters of Southern Maine.* Washington, 1909.

Day, Clarence A. *Ezekiel Holmes, Father of Maine Agriculture.* Orono, 1968. (University Studies No. 86) *A History of Agriculture in Maine, 1604-1860.* vol. 1, Orono, 1954. *Farming in Maine, 1860-1940.* vol. 2. Orono, 1963. (University Studies, Nos. 68,78)

Halden, Theodore, and Knight, Russell. *The Songo River Steamboats.* New York, 1969.

Moody, Linwood W. *The Maine Two Footers: the Story of the Two Foot Gauge Railroads in Maine.* Berkeley, Cal., 1959.

Pressey, Henry A. *Water Powers of the State of Maine* Washington, 1902.

Scontras, Charles A. *Organized Labor and Labor Politics in Maine, 1880-1890.* Orono, 1966. (University Studies, No. 83)

Smith, Lincoln. *The Power Policy of Maine* Berkeley, Cal., 1951.

THE FOREST

Allis, Frederick S. *William Bingham's Maine Lands, 1790-1820.* Boston, 1954. 2 vols. (Publications, Colonial Society of Massachusetts)

Barker, F. C. *Lake and Forest as I Have Known Them.* Boston, 1903.

Coolidge, Philip T. *History of the Maine Woods.* Bangor, 1963.

Davis, Harold A. *An International Community in the St. Croix, 1604-1930.* Orono, 1954. (University Studies No. 64)

Day, Holman, F. *King Spruce.* New York, 1908. (A pleasant introduction to the Maine woods and lumbering)

Eaton, Louis M. *Pork, Molasses and Timber.* New York, 1954.

Eckstorm, Fannie Hardy. *David Libbey: Penobscot Woodsman and River Driver.* Boston, 1927.

Hempstead, Alfred Geer. *The Penobscot Boom and the Development of the West Branch of the Penobscot River for Log Driving.* Orono, 1931. (University Studies No. 18)

Holbrook, Stewart H. *Yankee Loggers: A Recollection of Woodsmen, Cooks and River Drivers.* New York, 1961.

Jorgensen, Frederick E. *Twenty-five Years A Game Warden.* Brattleboro, Vt., 1937.

Pike, Robert E. *Tall Trees, Tough Men*. New York, 1967.

Springer, John H. *Forest Life and Forest Trees*. New York, 1851.

Tower, Gordon E. *Forest Trees of Maine and How to Know Them*. Augusta, 1908.

Wilkins, Austin H. *Forests of Maine*. Augusta, 1932.

Wood, Richard G. *A History of Lumbering in Maine, 1820-1861*. Orono, 1935. (University Studies, No. 33)

THE SEA

Black, F. F. *Searsport Sea Captains*. Searsport, 1960. (A collection of photographs from the Museum with biographical sketches)

Bonyun, William and Gene. *Full Hold and Splendid Passage*. New York, 1969.

Borden, Norman E. Jr. *Dear Sarah: New England Ice to the Orient and other Incidents from the Journals of Captain Charles Edward Barry and his Wife*. Freeport, 1966.

Brace, Gerald W. *Between Wind and Water*. New York, 1966.

Calderwood, Ivan E. *Days of Uncle Dave's Fishhouse*. Rockland, 1969.

Chase, Mary Ellen. *Silas Crockett*. New York, 1935. (A novel that gives the reader 'the feel' of the Maine seafaring life)

Coffin, Robert P.T. *Captain Abby and Captain John*. New York, 1939.

Day, Clarence P., and Meyer, William E. *The Port of Portland and Its Hinterland*. Portland, 1923.

Eskew, G. L. *Cradle of Ships: A History of the Bath Iron Works*. New York, 1958.

Friendship Sloop Society. *Lasting Friendships*, 1970. (Technical data on this historical sailing craft)

Haggett, Ada M. and Isaacson, Dorris A. *Phippsburg, Fair to the Wind*. Lewiston, 1965. (Popham Colony and early shipbuilding)

Hennessey, Mark W. *Sewall Ships of Steel*. Augusta, 1937.

Jones, Herbert G. *Portland Ships Are Good Ships*. Portland, 1945. (The Liberty ships built in South Portland in World War II)

Leonard, Mary, and Kirstein, Jane. *Family Under Sail*. New York, 1970.

Lubbock, Alfred Basin. *The Down Easters: American Deep-Water Sailing Ships, 1869-1929*. Boston, 1929.

Peck, Henry Austin. *Seaports in Maine: An Economic Study*. Orono, 1955.

Richardson, J. M. *Steamboat Lore of the Penobscot*. Augusta, 1946. (4th edition, 1950)

Rowe, William H. *The Maritime History of Maine*. New York, 1948.

Sterling, Robert T. *Lighthouses of the Maine Coast, and the Men Who Keep Them*. Brattleboro, Vt., 1935.

Thompson, Margaret J. *Captain Nathaniel Lord Thompson and the Ships He Built, 1811-1889*. Boston, 1937.

Wasson, George S. *Sailing Days on the Penobscot; With A Record of Vessels Built There*. Compiled by Lincoln Colcord. Salem, Mass., 1932.

Wheelwright, Thea, and Knowles, Katherine. *Along The Maine Coast*. Boston, 1967.

NATURAL HISTORY

Bastin, Edson S., and Davis, Charles A. *Peat Deposits of Maine*. Washington, 1909.

Bastin, Edson S. *Geology of the Pegmatites and Associated Rocks of Maine*. Washington, 1911.

Dale, Thomas N. *The Granites of Maine*. Washington, 1907.

Darling, Louis. *The Gull's Way*. New York, 1965.

Doyle, Robert G. *Maine Mineral Collecting*. Augusta, 1962.

Everhart, W. Harry. *Fishes of Maine*. Augusta, 1958. (Dep't of Inland Fisheries and Game)

Fernald, Charles H. *Grasses of Maine*. Augusta, 1885.

A Guide to Maine's Natural Resources. Freeport, 1962. (Prepared in cooperation with the Bryant Pond Conservation Education School, Conservation Education Foundation of Maine, and Maine State Department of Education)

Holmes, Ezekiel, and Hitchcock, Charles H. *Second Annual Report Upon the Natural History and Geology of the State of Maine*. Augusta, 1862.

Jackson, Charles T. *First Report on the Geology of the Public Lands in the State of Maine*. (Senate document No. 89.) Boston, 1837. *Second Report . . .* Augusta, 1838. (Plates)

Laycock, George. *The Diligent Destroyers*. New York, 1970.

McKee, John. *As Maine Goes*. (Photographs, despoliation of Maine coast) Brunswick, 1966.

Miller, Olive Thorne. *With the Birds in Maine*. Boston, 1908.

Palmer, Ralph S. *Maine Birds* Cambridge, Mass., 1949. (Based largely on data gathered by Arthur Herbert Norton)

Perham, Frank C. *Geological Field Trips in Southern Maine*. (N. E. Intercoll. Geol. Conf., 1965)

Prudden, Theodore M. *About Lobsters*. Freeport, 1962.

Rand, Edward L., and Redfield, John H. *Flora of Mount Desert Island, Maine*. Cambridge, Mass., 1894.

Ricker, Percy LeRoy. *A Preliminary List of Maine Fungi*. Orono, 1902.

Tebbetts, Leon H. *The Amazing Story of Maine*. Portland, 1935. (Relates to the State's Geological history)

Toppan, Frederick W. *Geology of Maine*. Schenectady, N. Y., 1932.

Williams, Henry S., and Breger, Carpel L. *The Fauna of the Chapman Sandstone of Maine*. Washington, 1916.

ARTS AND HUMANITIES

Arvin, Newton. *Longfellow, His Life and Work*. Boston, 1962.

Barry, Phillips, Eckstorm, Fannie Hardy, and Smyth, Mary W., editors. *British Ballads from Maine*. New Haven, 1929.

Barry, Phillips. *The Maine Woods Songster*. Cambridge, 1939.

Beam, Philip C. *Winslow Homer at Prout's Neck*. Boston, 1966.

Coffin, Robert P. Tristram. *Lost Paradise: A Boyhood on a Maine Coast*

Farm. New York, 1934.

Colby College. *Maine and Its Role in American Art, 1740-1963.* New York, 1963.

Colcord, Joanna C. *Sea Language Comes Ashore.* New York, 1945. *Songs of American Sailormen.* New York, 1938. (Paperback, 1969)

Coxe, Louis O. *Edwin Arlington Robinson: Life of Poetry.* New York, 1969.

Day, Holman F. *Pine Tree Ballads: Rhymed Stories of Unplaned Human Natur' up in Maine.* Boston, 1902.

Eckstorm, Fannie Hardy, editor. *Minstrelsy of Maine: Folk-Songs and Ballads of the Woods and the Coast.* Boston, 1927.

Edwards, George T. *Music and Musicians in Maine.* Portland, 1928.

Eliot, Charles William. *John Gilley, Farmer and Fisherman.* (Biography of a Sutton Island milkman)

Gould, John. *Last One In: Tales of a New England Boyhood.* Boston, 1966.

Gray, Roland P., editor. *Songs and Ballads of the Maine Lumberjacks, with Other Songs from Maine.* Cambridge, 1924.

Gurko, Miriam. *Restless Spirit: the Life of Edna St. Vincent Millay.* New York, 1962.

Howells, John Mead. *The Architectural Heritage of the Piscataqua.* New York, 1937.

Ives, Edward D., editor. *Fleetwood Pride, the Autobiography of a Woodsman, 1864-1960.* (Northeast Folklore, Vol. IX, 1967) *Larry Gorman: the Man Who Made the Songs.* Bloomington, Indiana, 1964. *Folksongs of Maine.* (Northeast Folklore, Vol. VII, 1965)

Lee, W. Storrs. *Maine, A Literary Chronicle.* New York, 1968.

Lipman, Jean. *Rufus Porter, Yankee Pioneer.* New York, 1968.

Loomis, Charles D. *Port Towns of Penobscot Bay.* St. Paul, 1922 (In White Pine Series of Architectural Monographs)

Macdougall, Allen R., editor. *Letters of Edna St. Vincent Millay.* New York, 1952. (Paperback: Grosset and Dunlap)

Matthiessen, Francis Otto. *Sarah Orne Jewett.* Boston, 1929.

Nason, Emma Huntington. *Old Colonial Houses in Maine.* Augusta, 1908.

Roberts, Kenneth. *I Wanted to Write.* New York, 1949.

Sadik, Marvin. *Colonial Portraits at Bowdoin College.* Brunswick, 1966.

Smith, Chard P. *Where the Light Fails; A Portrait of Edwin Arlington Robinson.* New York, 1965.

Sprague, Richard S., editor. *A Handful of Spice.* Orono, 1969.

Walker, C. Howard. *Some Old Houses on the Southern Coast of Maine.* St. Paul, 1918   (In White Pine Series of Architectural Monographs)

Wilson, Forest. *Crusader in Crinoline; Harriet Beecher Stowe.* Philadelphia, 1941.

EDUCATION

Brown, Herbert Ross. *Sills of Bowdoin.* New York, 1964.

Chadbourne, Ava H. *A History of Education in Maine.* Orono, 1936.

Marriner, Ernest C. *The History of Colby College.* Waterville, 1963.

Survey of Higher Education in Maine. Orono, 1931. (Made by the University of Maine, in co-operation with Bates, Bowdoin and Colby Colleges)

Stetson, William W. *Study of the History of Education in Maine and the Evolution of Our Present School System.* Augusta, 1901.

RELIGION

Allen, Stephen, and Pilsbury, William H. *History of Methodism in Maine, 1793-1886.'* Augusta, 1887.

Burrage, Henry S. *History of the Baptists in Maine.* Portland, 1904.

Chase, Mary Ellen. *Jonathan Fisher.* New York, 1940.

Clark, Calvin M. *History of the Congregational Churches in Maine.* Portland, 1926. 2 vols.

Dow, Edward F. *A Portrait of the Millennial Church of Shakers.* Orono, 1931. (University Studies, No. 19).

Hinshaw, David. *Rufus Jones, Master Quaker.* New York, 1951.

Lucey, William L. *The Catholic Church in Maine.* Francistown, N. H., 1957.

Sprague, John F. *Sebastian Rasle: A Maine Tragedy of the Eighteenth Century.* Boston, 1906.

York, Robert M. *George B. Cheever, Religious and Social Reform (1807-1890).* Orono, 1955. (University Studies, No. 69).

SESQUICENTENNIAL 1970

Banks, Ronald F. *Maine Becomes a State: The Movement to Separate Maine from Massachusetts, 1785-1820.* Wesleyan Press, Connecticut.

Coxe, Louis O. *The Birth of a State.* Drama premiered by Portland Players; televised by METV.

Griffiths, Thomas Morgan and Arthur Morgan. *Pictorial History.* Lewiston.

HISTORIC SITES AND MUSEUMS

Inquire locally for museum hours and special events. Unless otherwise noted, the names of historical societies and museums incorporate the names of the communities in which they are located. Historical collections also may be found in many libraries and on house tours.

NATIONAL HISTORIC LANDMARKS

James G. Blaine House, Augusta
Congregational Meetinghouse, Harpswell
Fort Halifax, Winslow
Daniel Coit Gilman House, Northeast Harbor
Winslow Homer Studio, Scarborough
McIntire Garrison, York
Wadsworth Longfellow House, Portland
Old Gaol, York
Lady Pepperrell House, Kittery Point
St. Croix Island National Monument
Stowe House, Brunswick

STATE MEMORIALS

Fort Edgecomb
Fort George, Castine
Fort Halifax, Winslow
Fort Kent
Fort Knox, Prospect
Fort McClary, Kittery Point
Fort O'Brien, Machias

Fort Popham, Phippsburg
Fort Pownall, Stockton Springs
Fort William Henry, Pemaquid
John Paul Jones Memorial, Kittery
Katahdin Iron Works, Milo
Mere Point Memorial
Montpelier, Thomaston

Vaughn Woods, South Berwick

HISTORICAL MUSEUMS

Robert Abbe Museum, Bar Harbor
Androscoggin Society Wagg Museum, Auburn
Aroostook Society, Houlton
Bangor Society, G.A.R. Memorial
Baxter House, Gorham
Black House, Ellsworth
Bath Marine Museum
Boothbay Railway Museum
Boothbay Schooner Museum
Boothbay Region Society, Nicholas-Knight House
Border Society Barracks Museum, Eastport
Bosworth Civil War Museum, Portland
The BOWDOIN, ship museum, Camden
Brick Store Museum, Kennebunk
Bucksport Society Depot Museum
Burnham Tavern, Machiasport

Camden-Rockport Society, Old Conway House
Chapman-Hall House, Damariscotta
Coast Guard Museum, Rockland
Deer Isle-Stonington Society, Salome Sellers House
Dexter Society Grist Mill Museum
Dover-Foxcroft Society, Blacksmith Shop Museum
Dresden Society
Farmington Society
Forest and Logging Museum, Ashland
Franklin Society, Granite Museum
Friendship Marine Museum
Fort Western Museum
Gray Society
Hawthorne House, South Casco
History House, Skowhegan
Islesboro Society
Jabez Knowlton Country Store, Newburgh
Jonathan Fisher Memorial, Blue Hill
Kennebunkport Society
Landmarks Preservation Society, York Old Gaol
Lee Society
Lincoln County Cultural & Historical Association,
    Old Jail Museum, Firehouse and Pownalborough Courthouse
Machiasport Society
Maine Historical Society, Portland
Maine State Museum, Augusta
Madawaska Society
Matthews Farm Museum, Union
Monhegan Associates Lighthouse Museum
Monson Slate Museum
Moosehead Society, Greenville
Mt. Desert Island Society, Somesville
Museum of Childhood Antiquities, Waldoboro
Mussel Ridge Society, Owl's Head
New Sweden Society
Nordica Memorial Homestead, Farmington
Nylander Museum, Caribou
Old Orchard Society
Patten Lumber Museum
Peary-MacMillan Arctic Museum, Bowdoin College
Pejepscot Society, Brunswick
Pemaquid Archaeological Museum
Pemaquid Society, Harrington Meetinghouse
Penobscot Heritage, Bangor
Penobscot Marine Museum, Searsport
Phippsburg Society
Phillips Society
Portland Society of Natural History
Ruggles House, Columbia Falls
St. Croix Society, Calais
Sawtelle Museum, Islesford
Scarborough Society
Searsport Society
Sebec Society, One-room School Museum
Seashore Trolley Museum, Kennebunk
Shaker Museum, Poland Spring
Stewart M. Lord Memorial, Burlington
Tate House, Portland
Thoreau Museum, Milford
University of Maine Anthropology Museum, Orono

Vassalboro Society
Victoria Mansion, Portland
Victorian Museum, Newfield
Vinalhaven Society, Granite Museum
Waldoborough Society
Washburn Memorial, Livermore
Waterford Society, Artemus Ward House
Waterville Society, Redington Museum
Wilson Museum, Castine
Wiscasset Music Museum
Yarmouth Society
York Institute, Saco

INDIAN SNOW PAINTING FROM "LAND OF THE FOUR DIRECTIONS" BY
FREDERICK JOHN PRATSON — CHATHAM PRESS, OLD GREENWICH, CONN.

INDEX

ADDENDA

1. *P. 53,* State Government.
    In 1971, the 105th Maine Legislature was considering measures for State government reorganization that would consolidate agencies and bureaus under eleven major Departments. Many of the State agencies mentioned in this book would then be identified with one or another of these Departments.

2. Between *pp. 242-243,* TOWN AND COUNTRY photographs.
    As the face of Maine's principal cities and towns changes under urban renewal, model cities and other plans, it is becoming more widely recognized that their character is retained through preservation of the historical sites and buildings that have been significant in their development. The natural beauties of picturesque villages and towns are enhanced by their old homes and churches. And seasonal changes in the countryside have their own special attractions.

CREDITS

The Herring Net by Winslow Homer; Art Institute of Chicago.

Dory by Winslow Homer; Boston Museum of Fine Arts.

Drinking Hard Cider by Eastman Johnson; Henry Strater Collection.

A Morning View of Blue Hill Village by Jonathan Fisher; Farnsworth Museum.